Data-Driven Business Decisions

STATISTICS IN PRACTICE

Statistics in Practice is an important international series of texts which provide detailed coverage of statistical concepts, methods and worked case studies in specific fields of investigation and study.

With sound motivation and many worked practical examples, the books show in down-to-earth terms how to select and use an appropriate range of statistical techniques in a particular practical field within each title's special topic area.

The books provide statistical support for professionals and research workers across a range of employment fields and research environments. Subject areas covered include medicine and pharmaceutics; industry, finance and commerce; public services; the earth and environmental sciences, and so on.

The books also provide support to students studying statistical courses applied to the above areas. The demand for graduates to be equipped for the work environment has led to such courses becoming increasingly prevalent at universities and colleges.

It is our aim to present judiciously chosen and well-written workbooks to meet everyday practical needs. Feedback of views from readers will be most valuable to monitor the success of this aim.

A complete list of titles in this series appears at the end of the volume.

Data-Driven Business Decisions

CHRIS J. LLOYD
University of Melbourne
Melbourne Business School
Carlton, Victoria, Australia

WILEY
A JOHN WILEY & SONS, INC., PUBLICATION

Published by John Wiley & Sons, Inc., Hoboken, New Jersey
Published simultaneously in Canada

For general information on our other products and services or for technical support, please contact our Customer Care Department within the United States at (800) 762-2974, outside the United States at (317) 572-3993 or fax (317) 572-4002.

Wiley also publishes its books in a variety of formats. Some content that appears in print may not be available in formats. For more information about Wiley products, visit our web site at www.wiley.com.

Library of Congress Cataloging-in-Publication Data:

Lloyd, Chris J.
Data driven business decisions / Chris J. Lloyd.
p. cm. – (Statistics in practice)
Includes index.
ISBN 978-0-470-61960-5 (cloth)
1. Decision making–Statistical methods. 2. Problem solving–Statistical methods. 3. Statistical decision. 4. Data mining. I. Title.
HD30.23.L593 2011
658.4'033–dc22

2010046373

Printed in Singapore

10 9 8 7 6 5 4 3 2 1

For Lina, Ali, and Oli

Contents

Preface

Quantitative methods are part of the core course for attaining a Master's in Business Administration (MBA) at virtually every reputable business school, and for good reason. Most business decisions involve uncertainty, trade-offs, and ultimately monetary values. These kinds of problems require something more than judgment and qualitative generalities. They require numbers and frameworks for dealing with uncertainty. Otherwise you are just guessing.

There is broad consensus among business academics on what main topics should be covered in an MBA quantitative methods course. Keeping in mind that the MBA aims to produce better managers rather than mathematical technocrats, there are four general areas that managers need to know about.

1. *Data Handling and Excel* There are a lot of data out there and the standard platform is Excel. Excel also has some special features that make it especially suitable for business management.
2. *Uncertainty* There is statistical uncertainty in business data that needs to be acknowledged and measured wherever possible. This is an important mind-set. Maybe if more people had this mind-set there would not have been a global financial crisis.
3. *Relationship between Inputs and Outputs* The relationship between business outputs and the main drivers cannot be discovered only with tables and plots. Most managers let themselves down with primitive and misleading summaries of their data. Even basic data analysis requires the now widely available tool of multiple regression.
4. *Complex Decisions with Trade-Offs and Uncertainty* These need to be handled systematically, and a very general framework for handling complex decisions is decision trees. Complex payoffs can be summarized by a single number, the mean value. In most cases, the mean payoff should be maximized.

What about the course materials that deliver this knowledge? There are several unique features of an MBA that require academics to develop course materials different from what might be appropriate for undergraduates. This is especially the case for technical subjects such as statistics. In practice this means a much greater emphasis on:

- problems that are well grounded in a business context,
- summarizing analyses in simple English,
- translating analyses into business decisions,

and much less emphasis on

- problems that have already been put in mathematical or statistical form,
- detailed theory of the methods used, especially algebra, and
- minor technical details.

Most top business schools are already teaching this way, which makes it surprising that there is currently no text that reflects the unique classroom experience of MBAs. On the contrary, standard business statistics textbooks that are recommended at prestigious business schools seem to follow a traditional and even antiquated pedagogical approach.

This book aims to fill this market gap. It grew from courses taught at two highly ranked business schools over some 12 years. They were delivered entirely electronically (no hard copy of any kind was distributed) and I encourage presenters and student alike to access the electronic version of this book.

Chris J. Lloyd

To the Student

The book is divided into 20 limited but substantial topics. Each topic should not take more than a couple of hours for an intelligent person to digest, even if you have never done quantitative analysis before. Keep in mind, though, that you need to properly understand each topic before you move on. Almost every topic in the book depends critically on, and will refer to, earlier topics in the book.

The material for this book is best viewed electronically. Ideally, you will want to have the data sets open as you read the text so that you can confirm the calculations being presented. For your convenience, the 20 topics on the CDROM correspond to the 20 chapters of the book. Within each topic you will find Excel files that are described and analyzed in the text, short exercises called Check Your Understanding, solutions to these exercises, and one or more cases that illustrate the methods of that chapter (as well as earlier chapters).

There is some software that you will want to install as early in the course as you can. Both are Excel add-ons: StatproGo is for regression, and Treeplan is for decision trees. StatproGo is provided in the CDROM. An academic version of Treeplan is available for very little cost at http://www.treeplan.com/. Since the Mac version of Microsoft Office does not allow add-ins, you will have to run Office in Windows to get much out of this book. Most Mac machines can easily emulate Windows these days, but if you are a Mac lover, keep in mind that you will have to be living some of your life in the Windows environment for this part of your course.

The use of mathematics in this book is low. You will not need to know much algebra. There are not very many formulas, and those formulas that are used are coded into an Excel template after being properly explained. The material could be easily understood by any intelligent person, including someone who does not like math. (Years from now, you will not remember any formulas anyway!)

What I hope is that you will come away from the book with an appreciation of how to think about quantitative business problems, what is possible, and what are the common mistakes. Maybe you can even continue using standard techniques such as regression. This can only raise the standard of the conversations you will have with colleagues and improve the level of your decision making.

To the Teacher: How to Build a Course Around This Book

Course Structure. The order of the topics is quite deliberate. However, the first two chapters cover the basic ideas of performance measurement and data handling. The early introduction to Excel is especially important to the way I teach, because I want students to do all the calculations themselves. Some students wonder why they need to do this, if they will not be analysts themselves. The reason is that you learn more deeply when you do something yourself.

I believe that you need to study probability before you try inference. So, all the probability material comes first, in Chapters 3–8. The remaining 12 chapters are on various aspects of inference and data analysis. There are four chapters on multiple regression.

Class Structure. Each of the 20 topics in the book corresponds to one 90-min class. I expect students to have read most of each chapter prior to the class. They should also have read at least one case, and have done some preparatory calculations for the case, which you may make part of the formal assessment. It is amazing how much better a class goes when 100% of the students have opened the data, thought about the problem, and done some calculations.

The class is best built around a single case. However, statistics cannot be taught entirely in "case mode." There is some lecturing that has to be endured. Some of the basic concepts and theory I explain at the beginning of the class, some throughout the case, and then further ideas and extensions are covered in the wrap-up and epilogue.

Cases. The cases are not cases in the Harvard or Ivey sense. I have found that for a technical core course like statistics, it is counterproductive for students to have to cope with the competing conceptual frameworks of full-blown integrated cases. However, I have written the cases to have two key properties, namely, that there is plenty of context and that the problem is not translated into a required calculation. This is a key skill that I hope the students learn: how to translate a problem into a calculation.

The cases are not limited to particular countries or regions; there are Australian, Asian, European, and American data. The examples cover market surveys, market testing, advertising, customer management, finance, economics, minerals exploration, health care, and business ethics. None of the examples is simple or superficial.

The cases involve extensive and detailed calculations that the student needs to emulate. Students have to have their laptops open in class to get the full learning experience.

Mathematical Level. The mathematical standard of the course is very low. I think it is better to rely on both Excel templates and conceptual templates. An example of a key conceptual template is the idea of adding and subtracting a certain number of variability measures to a target.

Software. Since the book makes use of two Excel add-ons, the student will need to run Windows. StatproGo is entirely free, being a modification of the well-known freeware Statpro. Decision tree calculations are supported by Treeplan, which has also been improved for use with this book. It is not provided on the CDROM but individual or site licenses are cheaply available at http://www.treeplan.com/.

Some Unique Conceptual Features. You should be warned that the book deliberately avoids many features and ideas that you might consider central to statistics. The first is the idea of population and sample. I do not mention it at all and I urge instructors to abandon the sample–population paradigm for teaching business statistics. The alternative is the *data-generating mechanism*. This is a coherent alternative to the population–sample paradigm and is much more appropriate for business.

Neither will you find anything about the *t*-distribution. In practice, this is hardly different from the standard normal distribution, and it is better to simply use the central limit theorem with the caveat that for small samples more sophisticated methods are required. In truth, for small samples we should all be doing bootstrap calculations, not using the *t*-distribution, but this is not appropriate for business students.

You will not find anything about pooled standard deviations. I believe that there is nothing to be gained from assuming equal variances and that it unnecessarily complicates the theory. When it comes down to it, the equal variance and unequal variance *t*-tests give almost identical results in most cases. When they do not, it is because the standard deviations are different and so the pooled standard deviation is wrong!

Apart from these omissions, the rest of the treatment is orthodox.

CHAPTER 1

How Are We Doing? Data-Driven Views of Business Performance

1.0. Introduction: What Is the Issue?

Very few business outcomes are completely predictable. If they were, decision making would be so much easier. But as in life, we have to look at what the world throws at us and try to make sense of it.

If we collect data on a **business variable** then, because of the many factors that are not under our control, we will see a range of values. Here are some examples:

- Weekly **sales figures** over a year. The 52 numbers will vary greatly. Some of the variation we might attribute to calendar events like Christmas. But much of the variation is not predictable or easily explicable.
- **Daily returns** of a stock. In a year there might be 250 trading days, and so there will be 249 daily growth figures. These numbers are almost completely unpredictable. Typically just over half of them are positive and just under half of them are negative. You might think that good trading days occur in runs that can be used to predict tomorrow's result. You would be wrong.
- The **sale prices** of a large number of apartments sold in a particular area. Certainly we can anticipate that some properties will be worth more than others, but it all depends on who attends the auction and the available stock, and we will often be surprised at the price that is actually achieved.
- **Satisfaction ratings** of a surveyed list of customers. Every customer has a different experience with your business. Even if the experience is the same, every customer will respond differently.

Data-Driven Business Decisions, First Edition. Chris J. Lloyd.

When we have data on a business variable that we are interested in, the first thing we need is an idea of the range of likely values. Unless the data set is very small, it is quite impossible to understand the numbers without the aid of graphical or other summary techniques. In this chapter we look at producing a chart that describes the business variable and its so-called **distribution**. These charts are useful for quickly grasping the overall shape of a set of numbers, including what is a typical value, the overall spread of the data, and whether or not there are some unusual data values that are inconsistent with the others.

We also look at two simple numbers that can be used to describe this distribution—the **sample mean** and the **sample standard deviation** (SD). Breaking your data up into different segments and seeing how the mean and SD change is one simple way of getting a basic understanding of what drives the business variable.

M-TEL CALL CENTER: CASE BRIEFING

Esther Ching manages the complaints section of a call center, located in India. The call center is owned and run by M-Tel, a Malaysian telco company. Her section handles all billing complaints and service difficulties. The main products are landlines, mobile telephones, and Internet access.

She has a worksheet in front of her that contains a bewildering array of numbers, describing 1120 calls automatically stored by an automatic monitoring system. Each row describes a call. The variable *hold* records the number of seconds the customer was kept on hold before reaching the operator. The column headed *service* records the duration of the call in seconds. The column headed *rating* gives a satisfaction rating from very dissatisfied (VD) to very satisfied (VS). In addition, the gender of the customer and the consultant is recorded.

Esther has to prepare a report and one of the issues that has been previously raised is the role of gender in handling complaints. She is interested in contrasting the behavior of males. Are male customers less easy to please and less patient than female customers? Do customers respond better or worse to a consultant of the same gender, or doesn't it matter? What kinds of tables and charts might shed light on these questions?

As explained in the full case, there are also data on how long the consultant has been working for the call center. This could also have an effect on customer experience. But before we start, what is the main business outcome that Esther should care about?

1.1. SETTING OUT BUSINESS DATA

Most business data can be thought of this way. You have a large number of individuals or business items or **observational units** that have been included in the database. These might be different customers or different days of the year, or different apartments that we sold through an estate agent. For each of these, we have measured or recorded a set of numbers that we think are relevant to the business. These are the **business variables**. For instance, we might measure customer satisfaction and waiting time of customers; we might measure the day of the week and revenue for the different days of the year; or we might measure the sale price and floor area of the different apartments.

Typical Arrangement of Data

Each row is an observational unit and each column is a variable.

In Excel, it is common to arrange the data so that each row represents a different observational unit, and that each column represents a different variable. The first 10 rows of the call center data are displayed below. The observational units are different calls that were handled through the center. The variables are ID (just a label for the call) and five other variables as described in the case briefing. So for the first call, a male (M) customer called, waited 90 s, was served by a female (F) consultant for 280 s, and delivered a satisfaction rating of 3.

ID	Hold (secs)	Service	Rating	Customer	Consultant
84493	90	280	3	M	F
84496	88	305	4	F	F
84497	77	237	1	M	F
84499	94	261	3	M	M
84500	56	285	5	M	F
84501	59	267	4	M	F
84503	134	340	1	M	M
84504	108	315	4	M	F
84505	203	346	2	M	M
84507	71	213	1	M	M
..	..	..	..	..	..
..	..	..	..	..	..

This is the most convenient form for data to arrive. In practice, real data will often be spread over several sources and will contain wrong or missing data. For instance, you might have four different data sets depending on the gender of the customer and consultant. The spreadsheets FF, FM, MF, and MM contain these different subsets of the full data. For most purposes, it is best to have all the data on a single spreadsheet.

Finding Errors with Sorts

Sorting the data is a quick way of finding errors, because the erroneous values will often be extreme. To sort on a particular column, click on any cell in that column, go to the data menu, and then click either the AtoZ or ZtoA button. This will quickly show you the largest and smallest values in each column (which erroneous values will often be), as well as rogue characters like blanks and stray text.

If you sort on the consultant gender (column F), you will find that call 86428 has the gender recorded as D. This was obviously an error and since D is next to F on the keyboard, we might infer it should have been an F. Change it into an F now and store the file.

Finding Errors with Plots

Erroneous values can often be detected by plotting the data. The idea is that such points will probably stand out from the bulk of the data. For instance, to examine the holding and service times you might start by plotting one against the other. To do this, you select the two columns (including the headings), go to the Insert ribbon, and select the scatter plot chart. The resulting chart is below. Each point represents one of the 1120 calls. The horizontal axis is the holding time and the vertical axis is the service time. Excel always puts the leftmost columns on the horizontal axis and puts the rightmost column/s on the vertical axis.

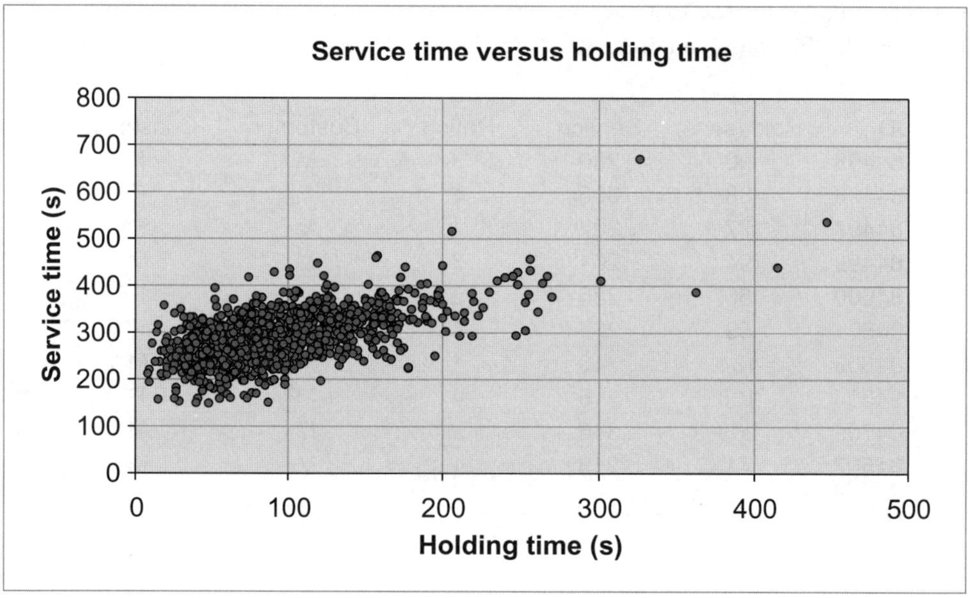

The first thing you notice is that there appears to be some sort of relationship between the holding time and the service time. We might speculate why this would be so but it would only be speculation. Perhaps those who have a more important problem are prepared to hold for longer before hanging up and, when they finally reach the consultant, it takes longer to resolve. Or perhaps those who are forced to wait longer to reach the consultant are determined to get the most that they can out of their call and take the opportunity to resolve other minor problems and questions that may occur to them.

We can also see some unusual points to the right of the plot. These calls involved very long waiting times of the order of 5–8 min. These could possibly be misrecorded—for instance, 420 s might actually have been 42 s.

However, since the times were recorded electronically in this instance, they are unlikely to be wrong. Misrecorded data are probably less of a problem these days with electronic recording, but not all data are recorded electronically. When you have survey data that have been entered into a spreadsheet by hand, it is common to find wrong data values—often 10 times too large or 10 times too small because of a misplaced decimal point! Such errors are often easily spotted with a graph.

1.2. Different Kinds of Variables

Not all data can be taken at face value. A number is sometimes not even a number. Data come in different "flavors." Just as important, variables can be classified by their function in the business. The call center data nicely illustrate the different kinds of measurement scales and functions that arise in practice.

Different Flavors of Data

Ordinal Data The most interesting variable is Rating, which can be any whole number from 1 to 5. It is important to realize that these numbers are nothing more than labels. In particular, a rating of 4 does not mean that the customer was twice as satisfied as a rating of 2. The numbers 1–5 were actually just a numerical translation of the responses VD, dissatisfied (D), neutral (N), satisfied (S), and VS, as described in the case. Data of this kind are called rank or **ordinal** data. You can pretend these numbers are numbers if you like—for instance, you can calculate an average rating across all customers—but you need to bear in mind that the measurement scale is not objective. The practical difference between VS and S might be quite different to that between S and N. A more practically relevant analysis would assign appropriate numbers to the five ratings, perhaps reflecting the costs in terms of future customer retention and profits (which could perhaps be obtained from a follow-up study of these customers).

Categorical Data Gender is a **categorical** or **nominal** variable. It makes no sense at all to talk about average gender. Often, variables like gender are recorded as 0 and 1 instead of as F and M. In this case, you can calculate the average of the 0's and 1's. This will give you the proportion of customers who are male, assuming M was coded as 1. But, generally speaking, you will not calculate averages of categorical data. Rather, such variables are used to break the data up into different business segments.

Interval and Numeric Data The holding and service variables are genuine numbers—measured in seconds. Such data are called **interval** data. Not only are these data interval, but zero does mean zero (even though there were no such calls). Such data are called **numeric**.

There is no ambiguity at all about what these numeric data mean, and you can calculate their average as well as other more complex statistics: you can rescale them, for instance, by dividing them by 60, which would change the units to *minutes*, and you can even do strange things like calculate their square! We will do this in the final chapters when we are trying to detect nonconstant growth in a business.

Different Business Functions of Data

The key variables are the ones that measure the performance of the business. These are the ones you want to influence and manage. The point of collecting and analyzing the data is to understand the range of performance and to see what factors might be driving the performance. To begin building a conceptual model to analyze the data you need to think of what variables you really care about and what factors you think might affect these variables.

Performance Measures What constitutes a **performance measure** is subjective and depends on who is looking at the data. To illustrate, the customer's main performance measure is the Rating. Customers would presumably be happy with any changes that increased their satisfaction rating. Is holding time a performance measure? Certainly, the customer would prefer a shorter holding time, but this may already be accounted for in the rating. In fact, if you look at the case you will see that the rating does implicitly suggest that the customer should include their holding time in their assessment. So holding time is probably not a performance measure in itself, but it does affect the performance measure.

To look at performance from the call center manager's point of view, we would need to know her key performance indicators (KPIs). These would surely include maintaining an acceptable level of service to customers but will also surely involve controlling costs. So Esther would care about rating because it is one way to monitor if she is maintaining customer service. She would also care about service time, because this is a direct cost input. If consultants spend unnecessarily long periods of time on a call then they will not be as productive in terms of calls handled per hour. So from Esther's viewpoint there are two performance measures here. When there are multiple performance measures, then we often need to combine them somehow into a single measure of performance. It is not obvious how to do this in the present case. We talk about combining performance measures in Chapter 2.

Input or Driver Variables A simple metaphor for a business is as an industrial process that takes various inputs and produces outputs. This is a completely inadequate metaphor in many respects! But it is a helpful way to explain what I mean by **input variables**. These are variables that come logically before the performance measures that you care about and which we suspect will influence performance. You will see in the later chapters of this book that we typically use the symbol X for input variables and Y for performance measures.

Looking at Rating as the performance Y variable, the most obvious input variable is *holding time*. We suspect that longer holding times will reduce the Rating. Service time may also affect the Rating but it is not at all clear how. Customers will not want a longer or a shorter call for its own sake. They will want a call that takes precisely as long as is required to solve the problem. So it is not clear that service time will have a simple effect on rating. We will have to look at the data to see what it is. Certainly though, holding time and service time are inputs into the Rating. They come prior to the Rating and influence the Rating.

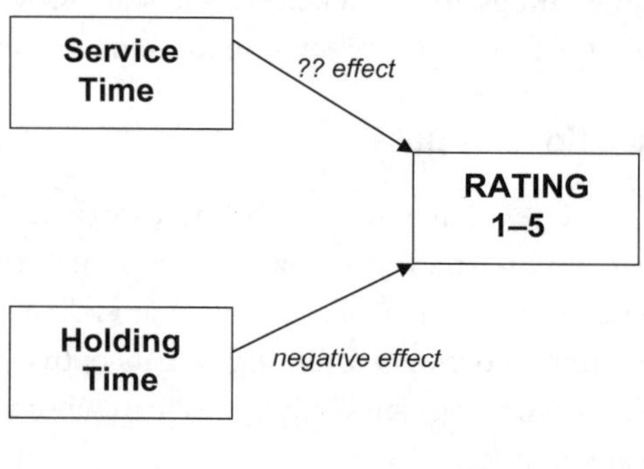

Looking at Service time now as a performance variable (remember it is a cost from Esther's viewpoint), what might influence it? Perhaps the gender of the main actors could have an effect; that is, the gender of the consultant and of the customer. What combinations of gender are associated with the longest and shortest service times? The data will tell us.

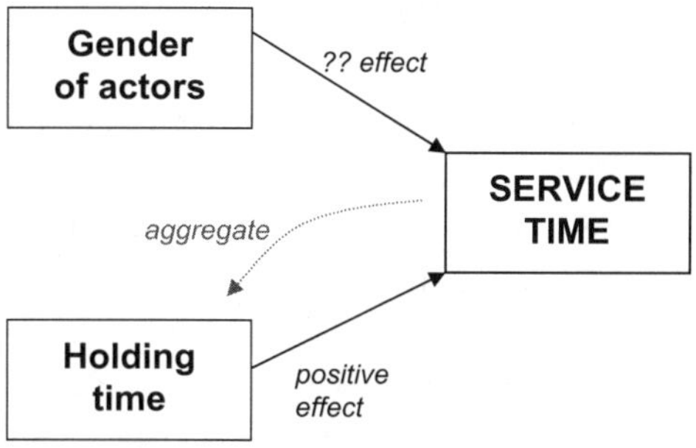

What else might influence service time? We already saw in the plot that longer holding times are associated with longer service times. So holding time is an input into service time. It comes before the service time and, perhaps surprisingly, seems to influence the service time. Looking at a different level though, an excessively long service time will directly affect the holding time—not of the present customer but of the next customer. So service time also affects holding time. We will not be able to see this in the present data because it is on the level of an individual customer. However, we might see it if we had aggregated data, say at the hourly level. We might expect to see longer holding times in those hours when the service times were systematically longer and the queue grew longer.

Modifying or Segmenting Variables Often we want to consider different market segments separately. For many products, gender is a natural segmentation. For segmenting variables like gender, we are often interested in first asking whether the performance measure is different for the different segments/genders. In this case, gender is really just a special kind of input variable—it is something that affects the performance.

More subtly though, we are often interested in seeing how the segmenting variable might itself affect the relationships between other variables. For instance, is the relationship between service time and rating different for the two genders? Segment variables are most commonly handled by simply breaking the data up into the different segments, though there are more sophisticated ways of measuring segment differences. These are explained and illustrated in Chapters 18–20.

Missing Variables It is essential to think whether you have forgotten to measure or collect important variables before you start the analysis. If you do not measure it, you can't account for it. Failure to account for critical factors can completely invalidate your analysis and lead to not only wrong but completely absurd conclusions.

As a simple example, you might look at how your sales vary from week to week as you increase and decrease your price. You could plot your sales against your price and try to see the relationship. But if you did not measure your competitor's price, which may well be moving in response to yours, then you will get completely the wrong impression of how pricing policy affects your sales. There is an example of exactly this nature in Chapter 17.

1.3. THE IDEA OF A DISTRIBUTION

It is very easy to forget that nearly all business variables are uncertain and to mistakenly conceptualize a variable like *next month's sales* as a single figure. Of course next month's sales *will* be a single figure when you finally see it. But from the viewpoint of a month prior, it is an uncertain number and is best conceptualized quite differently. The **data distribution** gives you a tabular or graphical representation of the spread of likely values of the business variable. It is also visually helpful in understanding the sample mean and the sample SD, which will be introduced a little later.

You start with a column of observed values of your business variable—possibly a very long column! Several of the data sets in this book involve thousands of observational units. It is very difficult to understand a long column of numbers. The data distribution is a simple tabular summary. For simple variables, you can look at the table and see exactly what it says. However, most people can only hold half a dozen numbers in their head at a time. So when the variable is more complicated, even the data distribution can usefully be further summarized as a chart. Human minds can hold and process charts much more efficiently than tables of numbers.

What Is the Data Distribution?

Suppose we have a set of repeated observations on an unpredictable business variable, typically sitting in a column of an Excel spreadsheet.

> **DEFINITION**
>
> The **data distribution** or **frequency distribution** of a business variable is a list of *all observed values* of the variable together with the *number of times* these values are observed.

> The relative frequencies will add up to 100%.

The number of times the value occurs is called its *frequency*. For instance, 193 customers might give you a satisfaction rating of 1 out of 5 on a particular survey. You would immediately then ask—193 out of how many? So commonly, we divide the frequency by the number of observational units—which is then called the *relative frequency*. If there were 1120 customers in the survey, the relative frequency would be 193/1120 = 0.171 or 17.1%. The data distribution would be a table of the five relative frequencies for the five possible satisfaction ratings.

The data distribution can be represented as a table with observed values ordered from smallest to largest in one column and frequencies in the adjacent column. When there are too many observed values the table itself starts to become complicated and hard to digest. In this case, it can be represented as a chart.

EXAMPLE 1 *Deepwater Bay real estate*

This data set, which is in the file ex2 (HKRE).xls, is analyzed extensively in later chapters. It lists the characteristics of 108 apartments that were sold in Deepwater Bay, Hong Kong, in 1995. Ultimately, we will be interested in explaining the sale price of these apartments in terms of their characteristics. In other words, the characteristics will be input variables and the performance measure will be sale price. For now, however, we are just interested in getting on overview of the characteristics themselves. The four characteristics listed are the number of bedrooms, the number of bathrooms, the number of dedicated car parking spaces, and the age of the apartment since construction.

Below is a tabular summary of the data distribution of the Beds, Baths, and Cars characteristics. Most of the apartments have two or three bedrooms, one or two bathrooms, and one car parking space. It is easy enough to look at this table and get the main message, so there is probably no reason to display it as a chart.

Number	Beds	Baths	Cars
0	0	0	4
1	0	42	96
2	54	62	8
3	44	4	0
4	9	0	0
5	1	0	0
Total	108	108	108

The age variable is a bit more complicated because there are more distinct ages represented in the data set. The youngest apartment was 1 year old, the oldest was 22 years old, and every age in between is represented by at least one apartment in the data set. This is best displayed as a chart.

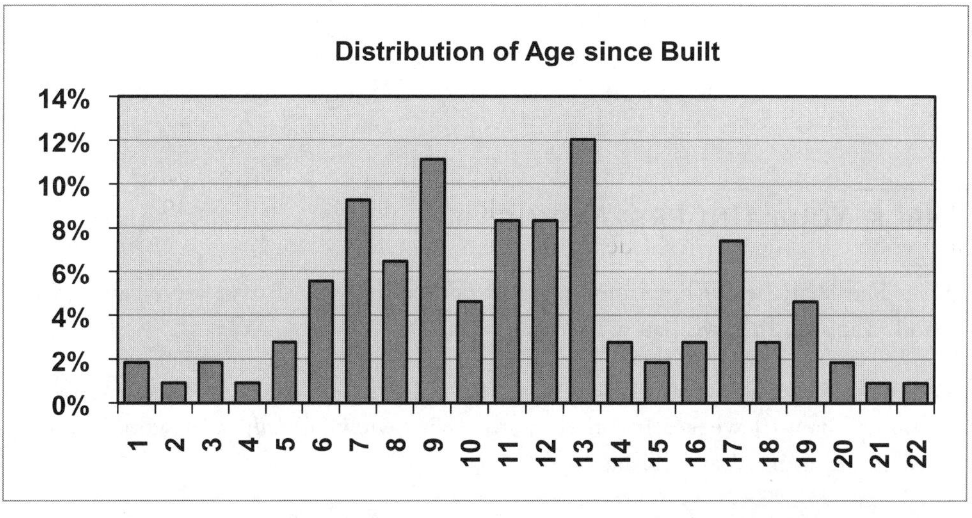

You can very quickly see from this chart what age most apartments are—from about 5 to 15 years. It is much more difficult to see the pattern in the table below, which is what the chart is representing in a visual form. The relative frequencies are just the frequencies divided by 108, and then displayed as a percentage. It is, to some extent, a matter of taste whether you use a table or a chart to summarize the data distribution. Very simple distributions like that of beds, baths, and cars can even be put together into a single table—as I have done above. The larger the number of distinct values in the data set, the more complicated and space taking the table will be, and you will start to think about using a chart instead.

Age	Freq	Rel Freq
1	2	1.9%
2	1	0.9%
3	2	1.9%
4	1	0.9%
5	3	2.8%
6	6	5.6%
7	10	9.3%
8	7	6.5%
9	12	11.1%
10	5	4.6%
11	9	8.3%
12	9	8.3%
13	13	12.0%
14	3	2.8%
15	2	1.9%
16	3	2.8%
17	8	7.4%
18	3	2.8%
19	5	4.6%
20	2	1.9%
21	1	0.9%
22	1	0.9%

Check Your Understanding

Q1. The chart below describes daily car sales at a car yard over a typical 10-week period. Suppose that we had a full year's data.

(a) Roughly, how do you think this chart would change based on 52 weeks of data rather than 10 weeks? In other words, what view of *daily sales* would you get with an entire year of data?

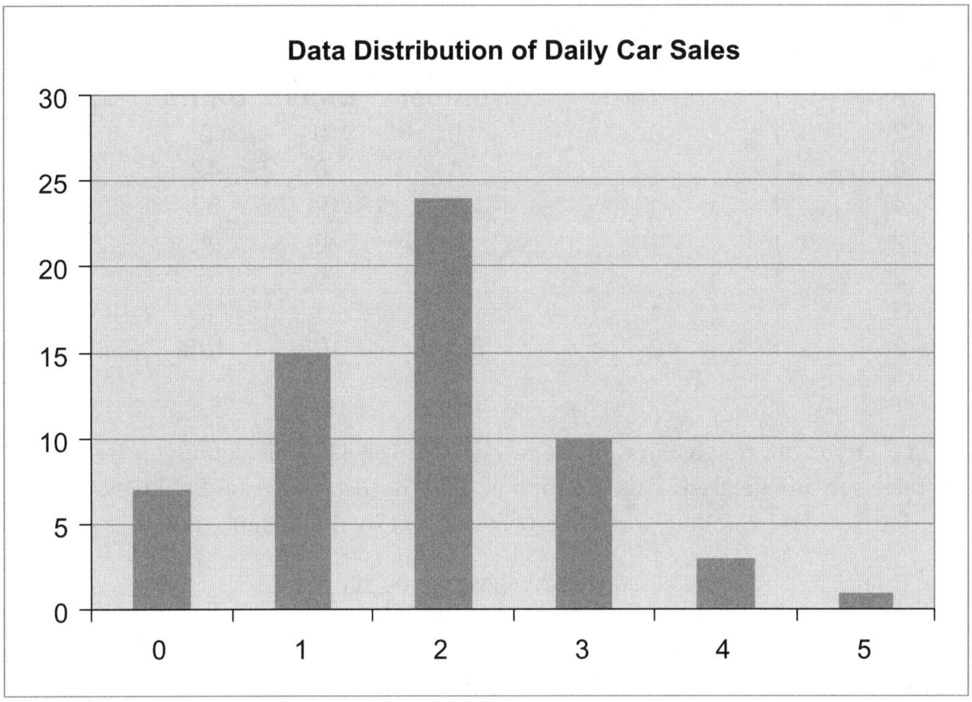

(b) Consider *weekly sales*? This is a different performance measure. To get the data distribution you would look back over the year and see how many cars you sold each week. You would have 52 numbers and then you would convert them into a data distribution and then into a chart. What would this chart look like?

Producing the Table in Excel

The first step is to create the table of frequencies. There are several ways to achieve this using ordinary Excel. The simplest is to use the Excel function **COUNTIF**, which has the Syntax

=COUNTIF(data, criterion).

Here, "data" is the range of the spreadsheet containing the column of data values and "criterion" is the value or text string you are looking for. The function counts up how many of the values match the criterion. For numerical criteria, just enter the number you are looking for. For text strings, for instance if you want to count up how many males are in the data set and these are labeled "M" for males, then the text is entered with the double quotes.

Open the file ex2 (HKRE).xls and click on the tables tab at the bottom. You will see the frequency tables for Beds, Baths, and Cars displayed earlier and also below.

	D	E	F	G	I	J	K	L
row 1	BEDS	BATHS	CARS					
row 2	3	1	1		Number	Beds	Baths	Cars
row 3	2	1	0		0	0	0	4
row 4	2	1	1		1	0	42	96
row 5	4	1	1		2	54	62	8
row 6	2	1	1		3	44	4	0
row 7	2	1	1		4	9	0	0
row 8	3	1	1		5	1	0	0
row 9	2	1	0		Total	108	108	108

To create the frequencies for Beds, click on cell J3. This counts up how many 0's there are in the Beds data in column D. The data range is D2:D109 and the criterion you are searching for is the 0 in cell I3. So the formula is

=COUNTIF(D$2:D$109,$I3).

The reason for the "$" symbols is to fix the data range so that it will not move when the formula is dragged down and to fix the search value in cell I3 so that this will not move when we drag to the right. Your instructor will explain how to drag a formula and the use of the "$" symbol. The total in cell J9 is calculated using the internal Excel function SUM. The formula is

=SUM(J3:J8).

This should equal the number of apartments (here 108) and serves as a check that the frequencies have been calculated correctly. To calculate the frequencies for baths and cars, you simply drag the formulas in column J to the right. The data ranges will automatically move across to columns E and F. Because there is a "$" symbol before the "I" in the criterion field, these cell references will remain in column I, which is what we want because column I contains the numbers that we are searching for in the data.

A template, data_distribution.xls, has been provided, which will give both the tabulated data distribution and a chart when the raw data is copied into column A.

Producing the Chart in Excel

Because there are 22 different ages represented in the data set, the data distribution table for Age is probably too complicated to digest. To create the chart, open the worksheet Age and mark out the data in columns I and K from rows 2 to 24. To mark out disconnected ranges like this you need to mark out the first section, then hold down the control key, and then mark out the next section.

To create a chart you either click on the chart wizard (in XL2003) or go to the Insert ribbon. First, select the Scatter plot chart. This will plot the numbers 1–22 on the horizontal axis and the relative frequencies on the vertical axis. Right click on any part of the chart and select "Change chart type" and change it into a column chart. This will produce the chart displayed earlier. All the cosmetic aspects of the chart can be customized by right clicking on the part of the chart you want to change—for instance, the axes, the external chart area, the internal chart color, the color of the bars, and how separated they are.

1.4. Typical Performance: The Sample Mean

EXAMPLE 2 *Salary data*

The data in ex3 (salaries).xls describe 273 employees in a firm. The background of these data is in the case NTC Pay Equity in Chapter 18, but for the present it is enough to know that these employees were within a single business unit of the company, and that there was interest in relating their annual salaries to their age, experience, and other variables.

Below is a chart of the age distribution, measured to the nearest year. To summarize this distribution, it would be enough to say what a typical or central age was, and how much variation there is around this central value. These two features do not give you the chart exactly, but they give you the broad outline.

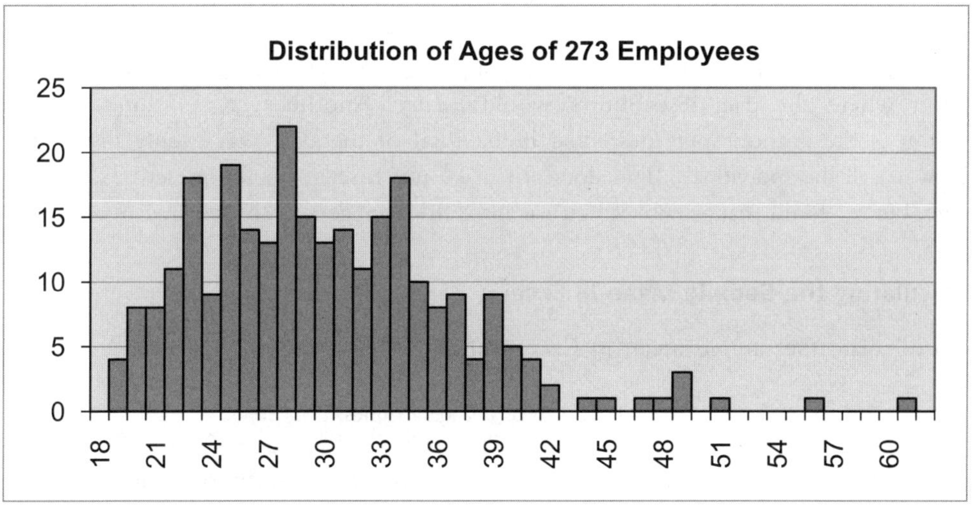

Apart from a few much older employees, the vast majority of the work force is between 20 and 40 years old. A rough central value looks to be around 30 years old and the vast majority of the workforce is within 10 years of this. There is an objective way of calculating the central figure and the typical deviation figure that we have just estimated by eye.

The **sample mean** or **sample average** of a variable is, as almost every one knows, the total of the observations divided by how many there are. It is denoted by the variable symbol with a "bar" above it. A general formula for the sample mean is:

$$\bar{x} = \frac{x_1 + x_2 + \ldots x_n}{n} = \frac{1}{n}\sum_{i=1}^{n} x_i.$$

The Greek Σ sign means the "sum" of whatever is to the right of it. In this case, it means add up the individual observed values of the variable, and then multiply by the reciprocal of the number of observation, which we are calling n.

You can judge the sample average quite accurately when you have the data distribution in front of you as a chart. It is *the point where the chart would balance* if the bars were weights. Looking at the distribution of ages, the balancing point looks close to the earlier quoted central value of 30. When it is calculated, we find that the total of the 273 ages is 8221 so the sample mean is 8221/273 = 30.1.

Interpretation

The role of the sample mean is mainly as a single summary measure of the middle of a distribution. It gives you a typical or central outcome for the unpredictable business variable.

The sample average is not necessarily a value that the variable is likely to take. For instance, nobody in the data set actually had an age of 30.1! Even rounding the mean to the nearest whole year—30 in this case—we find that this is not the most common value in the data set. The sample mean measures the middle by the point where the data distribution would *balance*. Another way to think of it is that it is the amount per individual if the total of the data was evenly distributed between all the individuals. This does not make much sense for the present example of Age, but it would make sense if you calculate the average weekly revenue over a year.

Calculating the Sample Mean in Excel

To calculate the sample mean in Excel from a list of raw data values use

=AVERAGE(raw data values).

When the data come to you already expressed as a data distribution rather than in raw form, the mean is calculated using

=SUMPRODUCT(values, rel frequencies).

A template called frequency_distribution.xls has been provided, which will automatically calculate the average when you enter the values and the frequencies.

One way to see how the input variables affect the performance measure is to break the data up by different values of the input variable and see how the sample mean performance changes. It is quite tedious to break the data set up into different segments and then calculate the average of each segment. There is a simple tool in Excel that does this automatically, which is explained in Section 2.3.

Other Location Measures: Median and Mode

The **median** of a distribution is the point where the data are divided into the bottom 50% and upper 50%. It is the probabilistic middle of the data. In the case of the age data, there were 273 employees, so if we arranged them from youngest to oldest, the middle one would be the 137th. You can find the median by sorting the data and scrolling down to row 137. This person has an age of 29 so this is the median. However, there were several employees aged 29 so it is not quite right to say that 50% of the employees were older and 50% were younger than 29. But that is the rough interpretation of the median.

The **mode** of a distribution is the most commonly observed value. In contrast, the mean is not necessarily even a possible value of the variable! The mode of the age data is 28. There were 22 employees of this age and this is the largest frequency in the data distribution. You can see it clearly in the earlier chart.

You can calculate the median of a large data set by using the Excel function MEDIAN. There is no direct Excel function for the mode.

1.5. UNCERTAINTY IN PERFORMANCE: SD

Below is a chart of the data distribution of the *years of experience* of the same 273 employees mentioned in the previous section. You can see that the mean is around 10 years—it is actually 10.6 if you calculate it. But there is a great deal of variability around this figure.

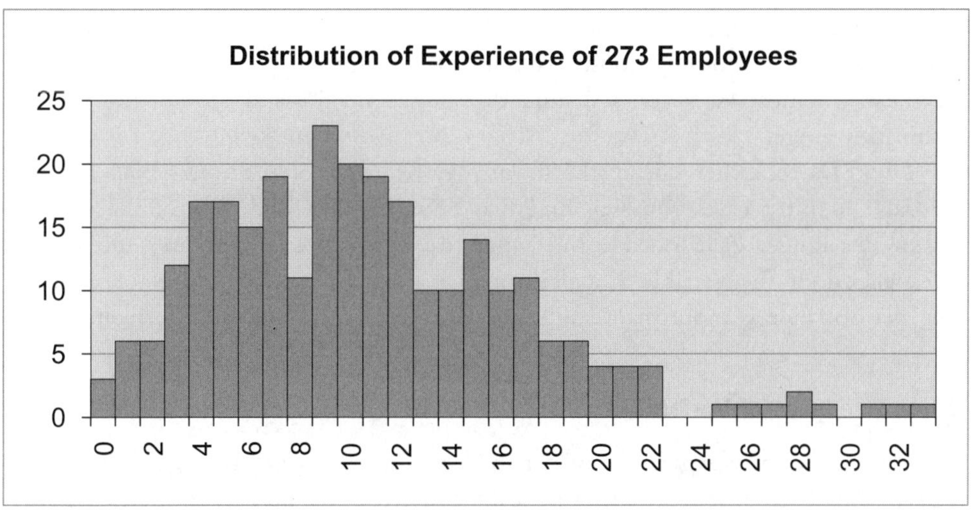

What would be an objective way to measure the level of variability in a set of numbers? How about we look at how far each individual deviated from 10.6 years of experience? Some are very close to 10.6 years. Some are very far. The average of this deviation figure would be a sensible measure of variability. This is roughly what the

> The **sample SD** of a variable is a measure of the spread or variability of numbers in a sample. The square of the SD is computed by
>
> $$s^2 = \left(\frac{n}{n-1}\right)\frac{1}{n}\sum_{i=1}^{n}(x_i - \bar{x})^2.$$
>
> The SD is the square root of this and denoted by s.

sample SD measures. It measures typical variation from the mean. Looking at the chart, you might guess that a typical deviation around the mean of 10.6 years is somewhere around 5 years. The SD is harder to judge from a chart than from a sample mean. This does not make it any less useful or valid.

The factor $n/(n-1)$ is a bit annoying. It makes the answer slightly larger than it would otherwise be. It also means that we will not be able to calculate the SD of a single number—which makes sense. When the number of data points n is large, the factor makes hardly any difference at all.

In Excel the function STDEV(raw data values) gives the sample SD. The SD of the experience data is 6.2. When the data come to you already as a data distribution, you can use the template frequency_distribution.xls as mentioned earlier.

Together, the sample mean and SD give you the main features of the data distribution—the middle and the spread. As soon as I tell you that the mean experience is 10.6 years and the SD is 6.2 years, you can imagine in your head what the data distribution will roughly look like.

Interpretation of SD

One SD on either side of the mean may be considered the *typical* range of the data. There is absolutely nothing unusual about a data point being 1 SD above or below the mean. In most cases you will find that between 65% and 75% of the data are within this range.

Two SDs on either side of the mean may be considered the *reasonable* range of the data. In most cases you will find that between 90% and 98% of the data are within this range. Data outside this range are very unusual and may merit some investigation. If the variable is a performance measure, you would want to know why performance is more than 2 SDs above or below the mean performance level.

Other Measures of Variability

A common alternative measure of variability or spread is the **interquartile range** (IQR). This is based on the idea of breaking the data up into the bottom 25%, the top 25%, and hence the middle 50%. The IQR is the length of the middle 50% of the data. For instance, if the median salary is \$28,500 per annum (pa), if 25% of people earn less than \$16,300 pa and 25% earn more than \$65,700 pa, then the IQR is \$65,700 − \$16,300 = \$49,400.

For the experience data, sort the employees from least experienced to most experienced. Scroll down 25% of the way, which is about the 68th least experienced. This person has 6 years experience. Now look 68 rows from the bottom. The 68th most experienced person has 14 years experience. The difference is 14 − 6 = 8, so the IQR = 8.

In Excel you can calculate IQR by finding the so-called first quartiles, the point where 25% of the data are smaller, and the third quartile, the point where 25% of the data are larger. Then type

=QUARTILE(raw data, 3) − QUARTILE (raw data, 1),

which subtracts one from the other.

Another measure of variability is the **mean absolute deviation** (MAD), which is the average difference between each individual value and the mean—as described in the first paragraph of this section. For subtle mathematical reasons, this is not as popular or useful a measure of variability as SD. For the experience data it equals 4.8. It typically tends to be about 25% smaller than the SD. The Excel function for this is AVEDEV.

All the measures—SD, IQR, and MAD—measure typical variation on an absolute scale. Whether a given deviation is considered large or small depends on the context. But one natural benchmark is to compare the variability to the typical value of the business variable. For instance, a \$32,000 variability in weekly revenue would be very large if a typical weekly revenue is \$100,000, but would be practically negligible if the weekly revenue is \$10,000,000.

Open the file ex3 (salaries).xls with the data for the 273 employees. The column headed *salary* gives the annual salary of these employees in units of US\$1000. The SD is \$13.5K. This should be compared with the typical or mean salary, which is \$74.3K.

DEFINITION

The ratio of the SD to the mean is called the **coefficient of variation** (CV). It measures typical variation as a proportion of a typical value of the variable. It is usual to quote it as a percentage.

$$\begin{aligned} CV &= \text{Sample SD}/\text{Sample Mean} \\ &= \$13.5K/\$74.3K = 0.182 \end{aligned}$$

or 18.2%. We say that there is an 18.2% variability in annual salaries of these 273 employees. This is quite a high level of variability and we expect that we will be able to explain much of these differences by looking at key variables such as age, experience, and other variables. These other variables are given in the NTC Pay equity case in Chapter 18.

CHECK YOUR UNDERSTANDING

Q2. You have 52 weekly percent growth figures for three different high-tech stocks, namely Cisco (CSCO), Microsoft (MSFT), and Hewlett Packard (HPQ) for the calendar years of 1999 and 2000. Below I have listed various summary statistics about the weekly growth of each stock. Each summary number is describing the 104 weekly growth figures over the 2 years. In the fourth column, I have given summaries of the growth performance of a hypothetical portfolio where you put 50% of your money in CSCO, 40% of your money in MSFT, and 10% of your money in HPQ.

	CSCO	MSFT	HPQ	Portfolio
Mean	1.81%	1.37%	0.75%	1.53%
Median	1.69%	0.76%	1.01%	1.59%
Std deviation	5.54%	5.41%	5.84%	4.63%
Minimum	–16.1%	–9.2%	–11.4%	–12.0%
Maximum	15.4%	22.8%	22.1%	11.4%
First quartile	–1.59%	–2.21%	–3.03%	–1.17%
Third quartile	5.65%	5.24%	3.95%	4.73%
IQR	7.24%	7.44%	6.98%	5.56%

(a) Comment on the figures for SD and IQR. What do these numbers indicate?

(b) Calculate the CV of the return on each investment. In simple words, what do these numbers indicate about the volatility of stock returns?

(c) Why might you want your investment to have a low CV? Which has the lowest CV?

1.6. CHANGING UNITS

The mean, median, and mode all measure typical or middle values of a distribution. They measure this in different ways but they are all so-called measures of *location*. Measures of location satisfy the following simple rules:

- If you add a constant K to all the data values then the location measure increases by K.
- If you multiply all the data values by a constant K then the location measure is multiplied by the same factor K.

The SD, IQR, and MAD all measure typical variability. They measure this in different ways but they are all so-called measures of *scale*.

- If you add a constant K to all the data values then the scale measure stays the same. The variable is exactly as variable as it was before.
- If you multiply all the data values by a constant K then the scale measure is multiplied by the same factor K.

The relevance of this to business analysis is illustrated by looking again at the data in ex2 (HKRE).xls, which describes 108 apartments sold in Hong Kong. If you look at the worksheet *final sale price* you will see the prices in the left column, which are expressed in Australian dollars, calculated at the December 1995 exchange rate. The mean is \$979.9 and the SD is \$264.3.

However, the estate agent charged a fixed fee of \$22K per sale. Column C gives the sale price net of these charges. The mean of these numbers is \$22K less than \$979.9, which is \$957.9. The SD is unchanged at \$264.3. The government charged a 12% value-added tax (VAT) on the sale price net of estate agent costs. The numbers in column D are equal to the numbers in column C times 0.88 and represent the money left after VAT is paid. The mean and SD are both multiplied by the factor 0.88. The mean becomes \$843.0 and the SD becomes \$232.6.

Finally, let us convert the figures back into Hong Kong dollars since that is where the sales took place. The exchange rate at the end of 1996 was \$5.16 Hong Kong dollars to the Australian dollar. Column E gives the received payment after commission and taxes in Hong Kong dollars, obtained from column D by multiplying by 5.16. The mean and SD are both multiplied by 5.16. The mean payment is HK\$4.35 million and the SD is HK\$1.2 million.

Price	Less k$22 Commission	Less 12% VAT	in $HK @ $5.16
979.9	957.9	843.0	4349.8
264.3	264.3	232.6	1200.1
27.0%	27.6%	27.6%	27.6%

The CVs are also given in each case. Remember that this is the SD as a proportion of the mean, expressed as a percentage. Notice that when the data are multiplied by 88% and then multiplied by \$5.16, the CV does not change. This is because the mean and SD both change by the same factor, so the ratio is unaffected. When you add a number to the data, as when we subtracted the \$22K commission, the CV does change because the mean changes, while the SD does not.

The main upshot of all this is that when you subtract taxes from business outcomes or convert numbers into different currencies, the mean and SD also change in the same way—and the CV stays the same.

CHECK YOUR UNDERSTANDING

Q3 In 2007 there were 48 middle managers in a firm. Their mean salary was \$100K pa. The SD of their base salary is \$19.7K.

(a) In 2008, they received a salary increment of \$10K each. What was the mean and SD of their salaries?

(b) In 2009, they received a salary increment of 10% each. What was the mean and SD of their salaries?

(c) In 2010, they received a variable percent salary increment, which averaged 10% but which depended on their base salary. What can you say about the mean and SD of their salaries?

(d) How is the CV affected in each case—higher, lower, the same, or not determined?

	2008	2009	2010
Mean			
Stdev			
CV			

Pushing a Bit Further

When you do something more complicated than just change units, it is not so clear what will happen to the mean and SD. For instance, suppose I have a portfolio of stocks and all of them rise. I check the percent growth of each of my stocks and find that the average growth was 10%. You would think then that the total value of my portfolio would increase by 10%. But it may not!

Open the spreadsheet ex4 (investing).xls in the Data and Examples folder. You will see 10 hypothetical stocks with different amounts invested. The total value of my portfolio was initially \$1900, heavily weighted on stock 1. All stocks grew but, luckily for me, stock 1 grew the most. However, the average growth of the 10 stocks is still 10%. The final value of my portfolio is \$2180, fully 14.7% higher than I started! This cannot happen if you have equal investment in each stock. But it is usually not a good idea to have equal exposure to all stocks, as we will see in a future topic.

You might like to play around with this template. What happens if I put more money in stock 10 and less money in stock 1? The moral of this story is to be careful about simplistic statements about means (and also about SD). For instance, if I give an average 10% bonus to my entire workforce, it does *not* follow that my wages bill will go up by 10%!!

1.7. SHAPES OF DISTRIBUTIONS

Gross summary measures of location (such as mean or median) and scale (such as SD or IQR) tell us quite a lot about the data distribution. But there may be other features of interest that are not revealed by these numbers. Thinking visually, the center and spread of a data distribution does not tell you everything about the *shape* of the distribution. Here are three issues to keep in mind when you are trying to understand, describe, and summarize a distribution.

Asymmetry and Skewness

Some data distributions are such that the largest observed values are way larger than the mean, whereas the smallest values are not all that small. Demand and price data are often like this, partly because the lower end of the distribution is constrained to be positive. Such asymmetry may be of some practical importance or interest. The SD would not tell us that variations on the upside are much larger than variations on the downside.

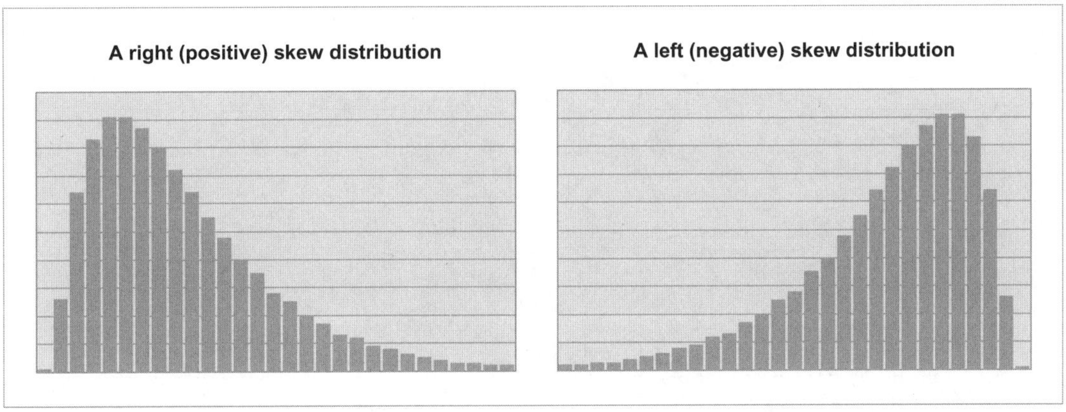

A generic chart displaying this kind of behavior is above left. Such a distribution is called *right or positively skew*. You will often know that a distribution is right skew if the mean is much larger than the median, though a better way to detect skewness is to look at the data distribution.

It is possible for a distribution to be left skew—where variation on the downside is larger than variation on the upside. This is common for human performance data where most people are performing close to some natural limit. The long left tail might be inexperienced employees who have not yet acquired the skills to perform at the highest levels.

Skewness is worth keeping in mind when thinking about SD. It was earlier pointed out that roughly 95% of the data will be within two SDs of the mean. However, if the data is skewed then you would not find the extreme 5% evenly distributed at the top and bottom. With right skewed data you might find 4% in the upper tail and 1% in the lower tail.

There is a numeric measure of **skewness** but it is not easy to interpret and we do not cover it in this book. But the idea of skewness or asymmetry is worth keeping in mind when it comes to describing the more subtle aspects of the distribution. The business issue here is whether overperformance is more or less common than underperformance.

Very Heavy Tails

SD or IQR describe typical variation about the middle. These measures are not good at describing *extreme* variation. The *return* on a stock is its proportional change over a time period. Stock returns are typically subject to extreme outcomes—some trading periods see large proportional increases or decreases in value that are much larger than the typical changes.

The chart below is for weekly returns on the Hong Kong stock market index known as the Hang Seng Index. Notice the occurrence of some very high and also some very low returns. The SD of this data set is 1.7%, which does not tell us much about the extreme returns. There is a numeric measure of *heavy tails* called **kurtosis** but we do not cover it in this book. However, it is worth being aware of this further aspect of a variable's distribution.

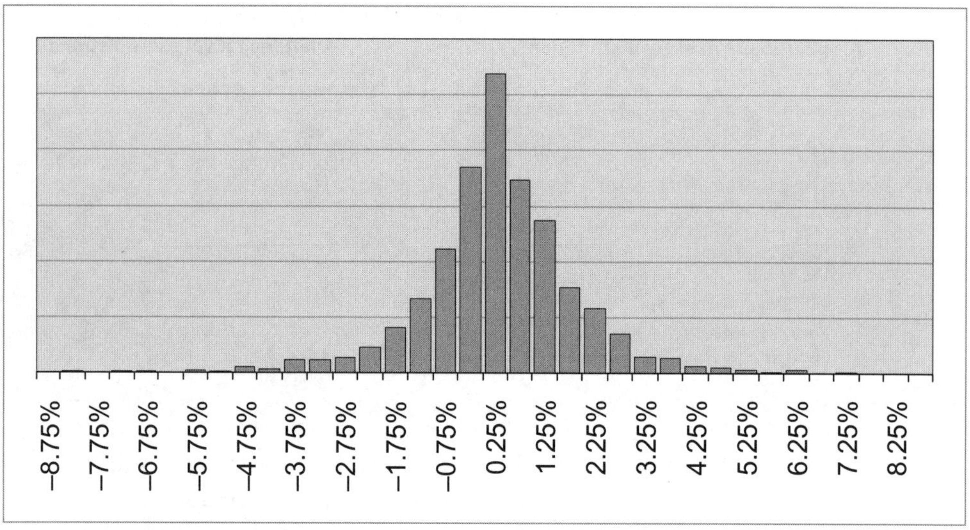

The business issue is whether or not extreme performance ever happens—where by extreme we mean more than 3 or 4 SDs from the mean. This is obviously always going to be rare, but for most regular performance outcomes it virtually never happens. For heavy-tailed distribution, however—such as occur in finance—you do find the occasional but truly exceptional (either good or bad) outcome.

Multimodality/Segmentation

A data distribution like the one below might describe the monthly mobile phone bills across a sample of customers. It is quite obvious that there are two distinct groups of customers—maybe on different call plans, or maybe the right-hand group consists of business customers and the left-hand group consists of domestic customers.

Measures of location and scale cannot alert you to this fact. Indeed, it would be rather meaningless here to quote the mean value of 98.4 and the SD of 11.8. When you have a data distribution like this you will not usefully summarize it with these two numbers. You would be much better off trying to discover what label defines the two market segments.

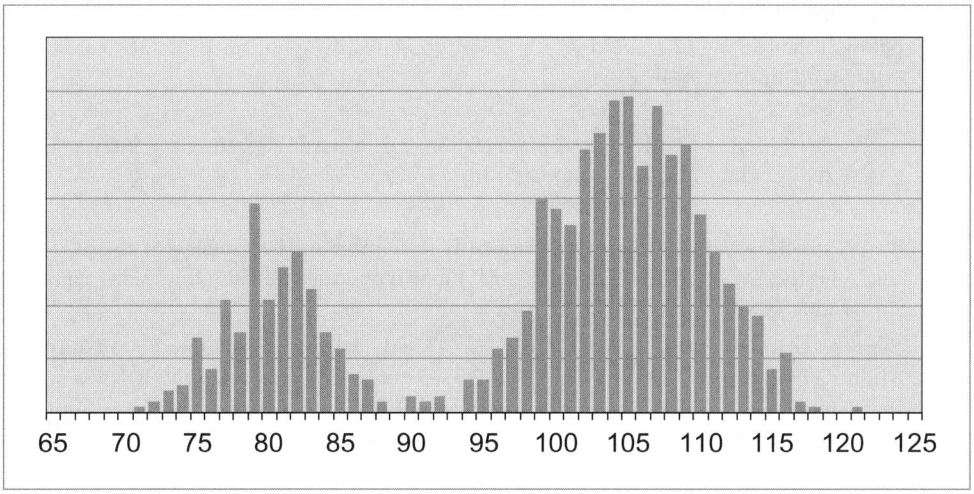

1.8. SUMMARY

Data come in various flavors—categorical, ordinal, and numeric/interval. You should also classify business variable into performance measures (the outcomes you really care about), input variables (the ones you think may affect the performance outcome), and segmenting variables (corresponding to different market segments).

The **sample mean** measures the center of a distribution. In practical terms this means the central or typical value of the variable. The **sample SD** measures the spread of a distribution. In practical terms this means the uncertainty or variability of the variable. There are alternative measures to mean and SD but these are less commonly used.

When you change currencies, mean and SD change in the same way. When you add or subtract a constant to a data set, the mean changes but the SD does not. The **CV** measures variability in proportional terms. It is the SD divided by the mean, expressed as a percentage.

The data distribution can be largely summarized by these three numbers. But there are more subtle aspects of the data distribution that the mean and SD suppress, such as asymmetry, heavy tails, and segmenting.

EXERCISES

E1. You are given the following 15 data values: 0, 3, 1, 0, 1, 1, 1, 3, 4, 3, 2, 0, 2, 0, and 0. Obtain the relative frequency distribution, the mean, and the SD. First use ordinary Excel and COUNTIF to calculate the frequencies and relative frequencies. Then use the Excel template data_distribution.xls to confirm your answers.

E2. Consider the frequency distribution below. What proportion of the data is between 2 and 4 inclusive? What proportion of the data values is odd? What is the mean and SD? Use the Excel template frequency_distribution.xls.

Value	1	2	3	4	5	6	7	8	9	10
Frequency	49	144	244	197	159	97	51	15	6	3

E3. As explained in the class notes, the symbol Σ means "sum" or "add." Using the samples below, calculate Σy_i, Σx_i^2, and $\Sigma\, x_i^2 y_i$. The point of this question is to make sure you understand this notation.

X-sample	1	2	3	4	5	6	7	8	9	10
Y-sample	9	14	24	17	59	7	5	5	2	1

A quick way to do these calculations is to name the data ranges; for instance, call the x sample "x" and the y sample "y." Then you can calculate $\Sigma\, x_i^2 y_i$ by typing = sumproduct(x,x,y).

E4. Suppose that you have 1 year of data on weekly sales at a supermarket in units of $1000. The mean is 27.4 and the SD is 2.5. Describe the typical weekly sales *in* words that could be understood by a nonstatistician. What would happen to these figures if you subtracted the weekly costs of $12,400 from the 52 weekly sales figures?

E5. Below are the lengths of five waiting times in a queue measured in minutes. Calculate the mean and SD. Then convert the five times into seconds and calculate the mean and SD again. What happens to the mean, SD, and CV?

Data in minutes: 21.8, 26.1, 31.4, 15.7, and 20.0.

E6. In the histograms below the gray bars represent sample A and the white bars represent sample B. Estimate by eye the mean and SD of each sample. Why are the gray bars so much taller?

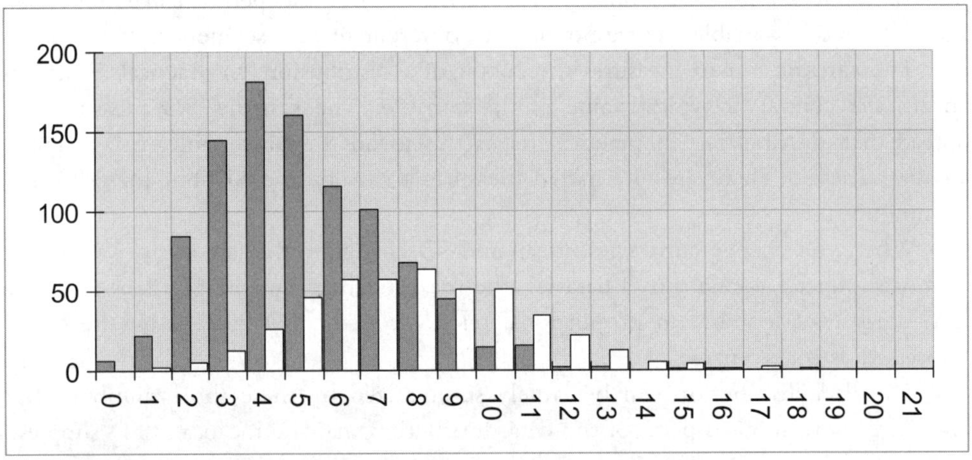

E7. For 1241 apartments sold in a certain area in 2002, the mean price is $459,000 and the SD is $76,000. Consider three apartments that sold for $545,000, $295,000, and $395,000. Which of these is most unusual? Are any of them really unusual statistically?

E8. A sample of 450 consumers was surveyed on their typical weekly consumption coffee in units of *cups*. They were asked how many cups of coffee they purchased over a typical week. There were 296 men in the survey and 154 women. For men, the mean consumption was 19 cups with an SD of 21.0. The median consumption was 13. For women, the mean consumption was 16.6 cups with an SD of 19.7. The median expenditure was 13. There were 73 male consumers and 65 female consumers who did not drink coffee at all.

Describe the distribution for males and females in ordinary words. How much difference is there between males and females?

CHAPTER 2

What Stands Out and Why? Who Wins? Data-Driven Views of Performance Dynamics

2.0. INTRODUCTION: WHAT IS THE ISSUE?

Describing performance data by its distribution, perhaps summarized by the mean and standard deviation, is fine as a first step but is not much use in itself. We want to know what factors drive high and low performance. We want to see how our management interventions affect performance. We want to investigate and quantify performance differences across market segments.

Here are a few more specific examples.

- You have daily sales figures for a supermarket over 10 weeks. How do sales figures compare across the 7 days of the week? Different days are associated with higher and lower sales.
- A telephone company mails advertising brochures to a randomly selected group of customers. How effective is the mail-out? This involves a comparison of the behavior of customers who received the brochure with customers who did not.
- You want to know how the purchasing habits of male and female customers differ. How many products do they typically purchase on a shopping trip? How much do they spend per purchase?

Questions such as these motivate the methods and ideas in the chapter. The key idea is breaking data up into meaningful subgroups and comparing the performance across the groups.

Data-Driven Business Decisions, First Edition. Chris J. Lloyd.

But there is another issue that we have completely ignored up to now. Not all business performance can be summarized in a *single* number. It is part of the complexity of modern work that we have to achieve in several dimensions at once. For example, the call center might care about both customer satisfaction ratings and the number of calls handled per hour. Business academics like me are assessed on their teaching and their research success. A human resource manager might be assessed on her budget targets as well as on the retention levels of the workforce. The value of a share is assessed by its price, its dividend, its volatility, and its growth potential.

Sometimes there is a sensible way to combine different performance measures. For instance, for valuing a share the price is often divided by the company earnings per share to give the so-called *price-to-earnings ratio*. This converts two performance measures into one. Other performance measures cannot be combined in any obvious manner. For instance, how would you combine the teaching and research performance of a business academic?

There is a way to convert different, and apparently incompatible, performance measures onto a standard statistical scale. This scale measures how each number sits within the distribution. The rescaled performances are called ***z*-scores** and are useful in their own right for identifying extreme performance levels (both good and bad). But they also served another purpose. Apparently incompatible variables such as research and teaching, once they are converted to the same *z*-score scale, can be combined by simply adding or averaging. This provides one objective way of combining two (or more) performance measures into a single bottom line.

SYDNEY BUSINESS SCHOOL (SBS) PERFORMANCE APPRAISAL: CASE BRIEFING

Dr. Adam Christopher is Dean of Faculty at the SBS. The SBS is an independently financed school of the publicly owned and funded University of Eastern Australia (UEA). Central to Adam's role is recruiting new faculty as well as managing and developing their careers. Business academics are in very short supply and he is constantly reminded that faculty have other options. This manifests as a rather high turnover rate—much higher than in a conventional academic department,

All academics sign a contract which requires them to be formally appraised in two dimensions of achievement—teaching and research. The contract also states that

"equal weight will be given to teaching and research."

There is a yearly bonus pool depending on the financial success of the school and this bonus pool is divided up among all faculty, but a larger bonus is given to those who receive a higher appraisal. For the present though, Adam has to come up with a way to rank the academics from highest to lowest based on the existing data. The Dean will make the final decision on how to distribute the bonus pool.

Adam opens the data file. How should he proceed? Which academics seem to be the best performers? Who could be advantaged or disadvantaged by the different methods he might use?

2.1. Different Layouts of Business Data

Much of this chapter is about analyzing data that have been broken up into subsets. There are two ways that subsets of data can be laid out. One has the subsets explicitly separated. The other has the subsets indicated by a coded variable. It does not ultimately matter how the data are laid out, but you need to recognize and understand the different layouts in order to use the various tools that Excel and StatproGo provide.

The most common and probably the best layout of business data is exactly as we describe in Chapter 1. Each row is an individual outcome. Each column is a variable. All the data are there in one rectangular area of a worksheet. Different market segments or other groupings of the data are coded into one of the columns. For instance, you might have a column that records the gender of the customer. Data in this standard form are called **stacked**.

You might also find data that have been separated into different subgroups and may even be sitting on different worksheets. For instance, you might have one data area for males and another for females. These data are called **unstacked**. If you wanted to, you could easily stack the male data on top of the female data, and then create a column indicating whether the record was for a male or female, and then the data would be stacked again.

EXAMPLE 1 *U.S. Labor Census*

Each month the Bureau of Labor Statistics in the U.S. Department of Labor conducts the "Current Population Survey" (CPS), which provides data on labor force characteristics of the population, including the level of employment, unemployment, and earnings. Approximately 65,000 randomly selected households are surveyed each month. The sample is chosen by randomly selecting addresses from the most recent decennial census.

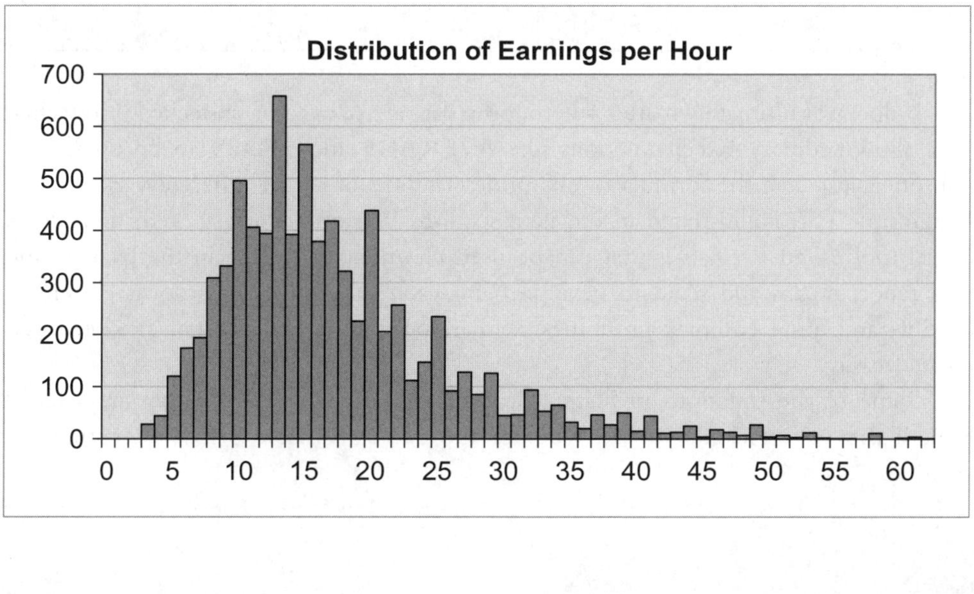

The survey conducted each March is more detailed than the other months and asks questions about the earnings during the previous year. The data in ex1 (census).xls are for full-time workers in 2007, defined as workers employed more than 35 h per week for at least 48 weeks in the previous year. There are almost 8000 records listed in this spreadsheet. The first column gives the average earnings per hour (EPH). The second column gives educational achievement such as high school diploma (HS) or a bachelor's degree (UNI). The next two columns give the age and gender.

The data are stacked. All the data are within a single rectangular field. One might think of the two different genders and two different educational segments as defining four subgroups of the population. The worksheet *by gender* unstacks the data into males and females separately. The worksheet *by gender & education* further unstacks the data by educational segment.

You can use a tool in StatproGo to convert stacked data into unstacked data. Select a cell anywhere in the data area. Next, select the Data_Utilities menu and then Unstack data. The first dialog box asks you about the coding variable. This is the column that contains the labels that define the groups you want to use to unstack the data. We will unstack by gender, so select gender. The next dialog box asks which variables you want to unstack. Select all three variables EPH, Education, and Age. You will find the results of this operation in the worksheet *StatproGo by gender*. Apart from the rather ugly formatting, you should find that the numbers all agree with those on worksheet *by gender*.

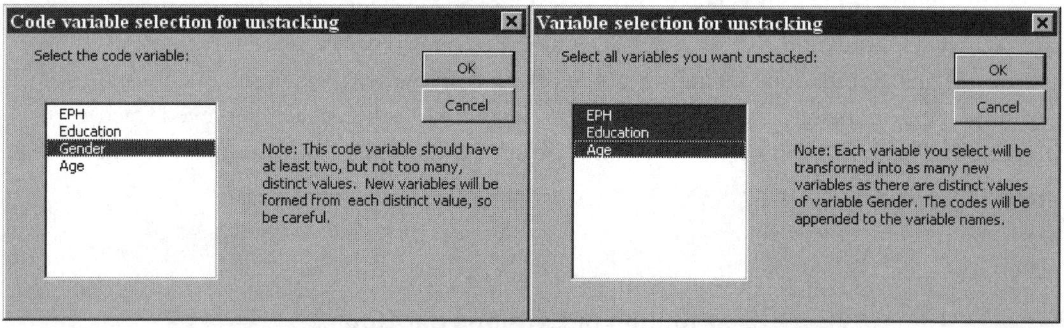

It does not ultimately matter whether the data are stacked or unstacked. Unstacked data allow ordinary Excel functions like AVERAGE and STDEV to be used. You can often just drag the formula to obtain descriptions of all the different variables and subgroups. This is illustrated in the next section. When data are stacked, there is an Excel tool called Pivotables that can be used to unstack the data in the background and report means and standard deviations for each subgroup. This tool is extremely flexible and quite complex groupings, with respect to several criteria, can be investigated easily.

Some of the functions in StatproGo will ask you whether the data are stacked and, if they are stacked, will ask you for the coding variable before executing the routine.

2.2. Comparing Performance across Different Segments

The worksheet *by gender and education* contained the U.S. Labor Census data unstacked with respect to gender and educational attainment. There are four groups of data. An obvious issue of interest is the extent to which educational group and gender affects earnings.

We could give the data distribution of the performance measure EPH for each of these four subgroups. But four different charts would not make comparison very easy. Putting all the data distributions on the one chart is possible, but makes for a very complicated chart. That is why we have means and standard deviations. These summarize the distributions and can be more easily understood and compared across the four groups.

The simplest way to obtain the average of the four groups is to type

=AVERAGE(A8:A2800)

into cell A1. Why A2800? Each group of data has a different number of individuals that determines the number of rows. The largest of the four groups has 2772 individuals. So if we scan down to any row past 2772, we can be sure of including everyone. Remember: blank cells are ignored by Excel functions.

If you now drag the formula across to cell I1, you will find that the mean EPH and mean Age will be calculated for all four groups. (You should delete the result for E1 because you are calculating the average of a blank column.)

To calculate the standard deviations you can repeat this idea by typing

=STDEV(A8:A2800)

into cell A2 and dragging across. You might also be interested in knowing the number of people in the four groups. The Excel function COUNT will count the number of nonblank cells in a data range.

These averages and standard deviations can then be collected into a table like the one below. You can immediately see a clear pattern in EPH. Men earn roughly $4 more per hour, regardless of level of education, while those with a university degree earn around $7 more regardless of gender. The typical standard deviation is around half the mean—in other words, the coefficient of variation in each case is around 50%. So there is a great deal of variation in earnings. This tells us something very important—that we have not measured the most important variables that determined earnings.

One obvious variable that might determine earnings is age and experience. Older people will tend to be on a higher salary because of their extra experience. We can check this possibility by looking at the mean age of the four groups. We see that there is hardly any difference. So any differences in earnings, for instance, between males and females, cannot be explained away by males in the sample possibly having more experience.

		W-HS	W-UNI	M-HS	M-UNI
EPH	mean	$11.9	$18.5	$14.9	$22.0
	Stdev	$5.4	$8.2	$7.2	$10.4
AGE	mean	43.1	41.8	42.6	43.7
	Stdev	12.3	12.1	12.0	11.9
	Count	1574	1739	2772	1901

Of course, there are other factors that could account for the differences, such as the industry sector and the level of the job.

CHECK YOUR UNDERSTANDING

Q1. Open the data in Q1.xls and look at the worksheet called *unstacked data.* This is the call center data from Chapter 1 and has been broken into males and females.

Use ordinary Excel to produce a table describing the differences in hold and service times for males and females as well as satisfaction rating. How many people are in the two gender groups? How might you reorganize the data and what are the key differences that you would highlight?

2.3. COMPLEX COMPARISONS: USING PIVOTABLES

For the U.S. Labor force data, the main outcome variable is EPH. Interest would naturally center on understanding the drivers of EPH. The age, gender, and educational level of the workers have also been recorded and are obvious drivers of salary—though it is of course illegal to pay different rates to males and females for the same work.

In the previous section, we looked at breaking data up into subgroups and calculating the means and standard deviations of each group. The data for the different groups were in different columns; that is, the data were unstacked. To break the data up into age groups as well would be a very tedious task.

Pivotables is a tool that comes standard with Excel. It provides a simple and intuitive interface for breaking data up into subgroups based on other measured characteristics—for instance, age, education, and gender. Pivotables is applied to stacked data and the breaking up into subsets—or unstacking—is done invisibly in the background. For each subgroup, you can display various statistics such as the mean of the performance variable, the standard deviation, and the number of observations within that group.

Blank Pivotable in Excel 2007

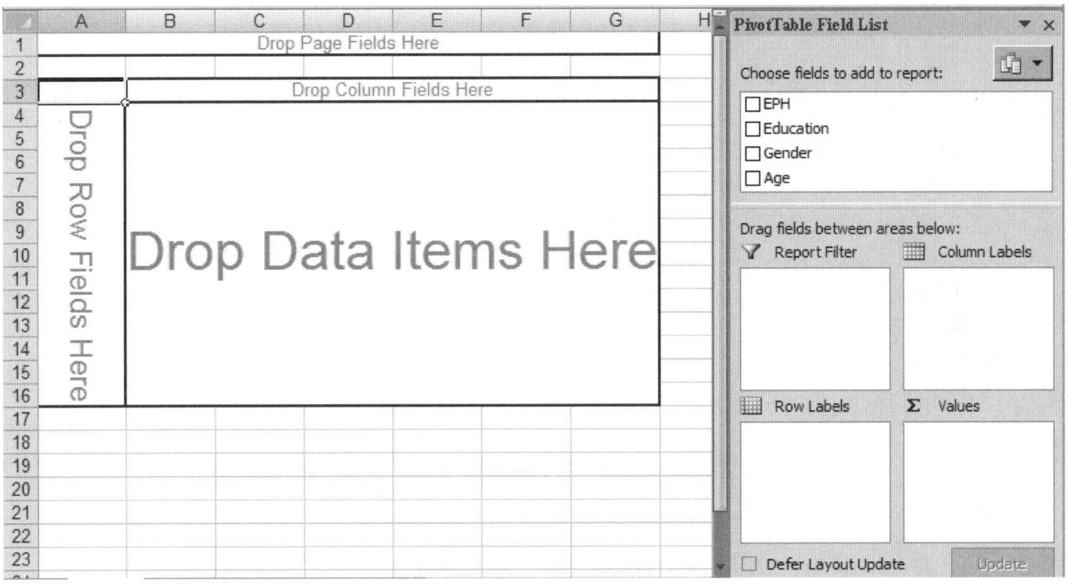

Starting Pivotables

Pivotables can be found in the Data menu in Excel 2003 or the Insert ribbon in Excel 2007. If you click on any cell in the rectangular data area before invoking Pivotables then it should automatically find the data area. Click OK (Excel 2007) or Finish (Excel 2003) and you will immediately find yourself on a fresh sheet with a blank table.

Icons will have been automatically created for all variables in the data area, using whatever labels you used at the top of each column. In our case, there are four variables, and so there are four icons called EPH, Education, Gender, and Age.

Breaking the Data into Segments

Suppose now that we wanted to segment the data into two genders and education levels—four groups in all. Such an "unstacking" of the data is achieved by dragging the relevant icons into the *row* or *column* field. For instance, dragging Gender into the column field will break the data into the two gender groups in the background and the results will be displayed in two columns. We could then drag the Education icon into the row field to complete the unstacking into the four gender–education combinations.

Whether you select the row or column fields only affects the orientation of the table—not its substance—and you can easily change your mind later. For instance, you might later decide to have both gender and education in the row field, which would give a table with four rows corresponding to the four combinations of gender and education, rather than having two rows and two columns.

Choosing Statistics to Display

So far, there is nothing that has been calculated for these four segments and so you will find that the table is empty. To calculate some kind of a statistic for each segment, the simplest technique is to drag the relevant icon into the data field, either directly into the section "Drop data Items here" or (for Excel 2007) into the bottom-right section of the field list.

For instance, if we want the average EPH for each group, drag the EPH icon into the data field. You then have to select what kind of statistic to calculate. By default, Excel will choose the SUM of EPH for each group—which makes little sense here. If we want to change this to the *average* EPH, then right click on the Sum of EPH button that will be visible in the table. Select Field Settings (Excel 2003) or Value Field Settings (Excel 2007) and the Field dialog box appears.

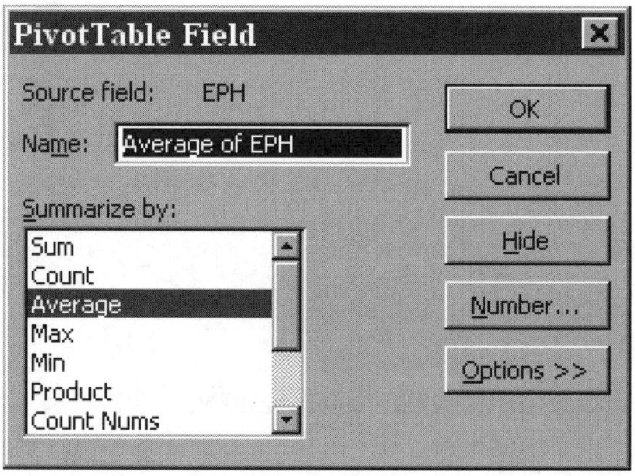

Select Average instead of Sum and then click OK. You should now find that the average EPH for all four groups appears in the table. Excel tends to choose rather bizarre and inappropriate formats for numbers in Pivotables. Below is the table that I obtained and each entry contains eight decimal points! It would be sensible and worthwhile reducing this to one decimal point and even changing the format to currency. The grand totals can be removed, if you prefer simply by right clicking on the Grand Total label and selecting Hide (Excel 2003) or remove Grand total (Excel 2007).

Average of EPH	Gender		
Education	F	M	Grand Total
HS	11.91894075	14.88317881	13.80961445
UNI	18.47183707	21.98595115	20.3070928
Grand Total	15.35856849	17.77262247	16.77114979

The resulting table is below and clearly displays the $3–$4 gender difference and the roughly $7 education difference in the mean EPH. However, we have ignored age, which would be an important factor in pay scales. Older employees have more experience and can expect higher pay rates.

Average of EPH	Gender	
Education	F	M
HS	$11.9	$14.9
UNI	$18.5	$22.0

Segmenting by a Numeric Variable

Both gender and education are categorical variables. Gender has two categories and so produced two segments. But age is a numeric variable. It has been measured to the nearest year and so if we used it to segment the data, we would have 42 different age "groups," from 21 to 62.

Create a Pivotable with age in the row field and gender in the column field. Report the statistics average EPH again by dragging EPH into the data field and selecting the statistic *average*. You get a very large table with 43 rows and 3 columns. One way to see the pattern in this table is to change it into a chart. In Excel 2007, if you select any cell in the Pivotable and insert a line chart you will get a similar graph to the one below. In Excel 2003, if you click on any cell in the Pivotable and insert a chart then you will find a multiple bar chart that opens on a separate chart sheet. You can easily change this to a line chart by right clicking and choosing Chart Type.

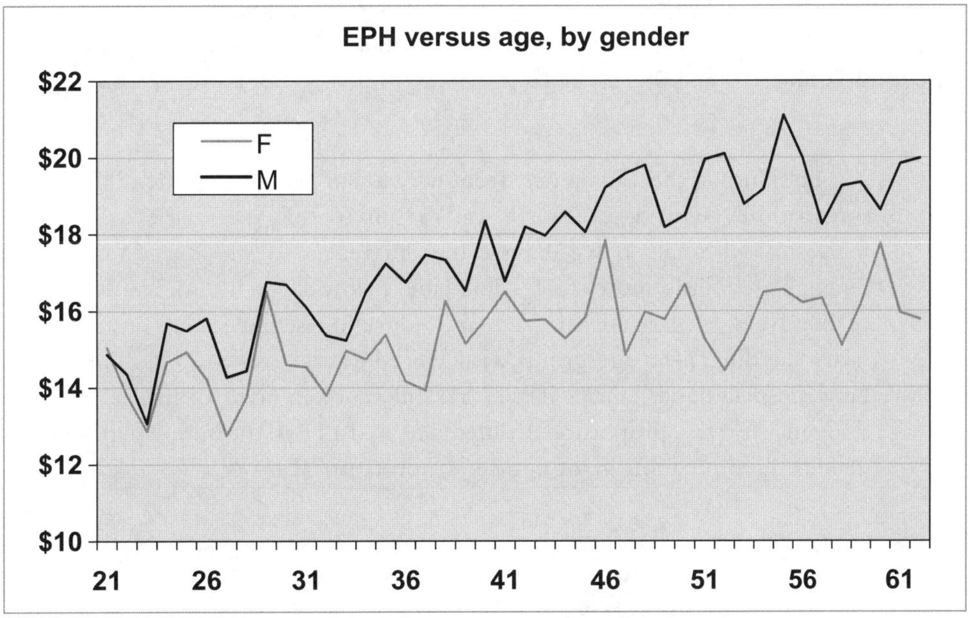

We can see the gender gap very clearly. Moreover, we can see that the gap persists across all ages and widens for higher age groups. Perhaps this is due to older employees having forged their careers in an earlier generation when gender pay differences were tolerated. Of course, the data cannot tell you whether this is the reason or not.

We can see that there is a great deal of erratic up and down movement in the chart. One way to remove this "noise" from the picture is to classify the ages into groups—say from 21 to 30, from 31 to 40, and so on. Pivotables has an automatic way of *grouping* the variables in the row or column field. To group the ages, right click on the Age button in the table and select Group (Excel 2007) or Group and Show Detail and then Group (Excel 2003). You will see a grouping dialog box which asks for a start value, an end value, and a by value. I suggest you let start = 21, end = 70, and by = 10.

To create an even more refined analysis, drag the education icon into the column field. You have now broken up each age group into the four combinations of age and education. The table is displayed below—with all grand totals and subtotals removed to make the patterns clearer. Additionally, I have calculated the difference between the male and female EPH for each combination of age and education using ordinary Excel formulas.

	Females		Males		Difference	
Age	**HS**	**UNI**	**HS**	**UNI**	**HS**	**UNI**
21-30	$11.2	$16.8	$13.4	$18.2	$2.2	$1.4
31-40	$11.4	$17.7	$14.3	$20.4	$2.9	$2.7
41-50	$12.3	$19.2	$15.4	$22.6	$3.2	$3.4
51-60	$12.5	$19.6	$15.7	$24.5	$3.2	$4.9
61-70	$12.0	$20.8	$16.4	$24.6	$4.4	$3.7
Grand Total	$11.9	$18.5	$14.9	$22.0	$3.0	$3.5

Looking at the Difference section, we can see that gender differences increase systematically with age. One reason for this is that the salaries of both groups are increasing with age. If we express the differences in *proportional* terms then the differences are a little more stable. The table below shows the differences as proportions of the average salary for that age and education segment. For instance, the average salary for the 21–30 age group with HS education was $12.6K. The $2.2 difference between males and females is a 17.3% difference in favor of males. Whether the raw difference or the proportional difference in EPH is the more pertinent measure of gender discrimination is, of course, a nonstatistical issue.

Age	HS	UNI
21-30	17.3%	8.1%
31-40	21.7%	14.2%
41-50	22.1%	16.2%
51-60	22.1%	21.8%
61-70	30.0%	16.2%
Overall	21.5%	17.3%

Some Excel Quirks and Tips

The Difference section of the table was not created using Pivotables. It required ordinary Excel. For instance, to get the $2.2 figure for the 21–30 and HS education group, I want to subtract the $11.2 from the $13.4. You can use an Excel formula to do this and then just drag across one cell and then down.

You will find, though, that if you select a cell in the Pivotable then the formula bar contains complex formulas associated with Pivotables and you will not be able to drag the formula. So, when calculating values from Pivotables you are better off either copying the table somewhere else as raw data or alternatively typing explicit cell references for the cells of the table you want to access.

> This is an Excel quirk that can be turned off using an Excel "option."

You may sometimes find that the Pivotables interface disappears and you want to make some additions or changes to the chart. To get the interface back you should

- Right click and select Show Field List in Excel 2007.
- Right click and select the Chart Wizard and then Layout in Excel 2003.

CHECK YOUR UNDERSTANDING

Q2. The data in Q2.xls list the number of defective items detected per week at a plant manufacturing video chips during a 52-week year.

Use Pivotables to produce

- The data distribution of the number of defectives per week.
- A table of the total defectives, average defectives, and standard deviation of defectives for each quarter.
- A chart of the number of defectives per quarter.
- The data distribution of the number of defectives per week, separately for each quarter.

2.4. UNUSUALLY HIGH OR LOW OUTCOMES: *Z*-SCORES

When examining performance data, you can quickly determine what the normal range of performance is. Typical or "par" performance is the sample mean. Most performance is within 1 standard deviation and the vast majority is within 2 standard deviations. Performance outside this range, say 3 standard deviations away, is highly unusual and worth further investigation.

It is very easy to calculate how many standard deviations above or below the mean a particular outcome is. This tells you where the performance outcome sits within the context of the sample of performances that you have at hand.

What Are Standardized Data?

When data are unstandardized, it is *not* possible to say whether a given value is high or low. For example, if sales this week were \$12,400 you cannot say if it is high or low—you need to compare it with data from other weeks.

A set of numbers is **standardized** if the sample mean equals 0 *and* the sample standard deviation equals 1. Standardized values are denoted by *z*.

Once data are standardized, the values mean something very specific in terms of how good or bad the performance was. If $z = 2$, then the corresponding x value is 2 standard deviations larger than the mean. If $z = -3$, then the corresponding x value is 3 standard deviations smaller than the mean. A standardized value of 3 is unusually high and a standardized value of −3 is unusually low. A value between −1.5 and +1.5 is not really unusual at all.

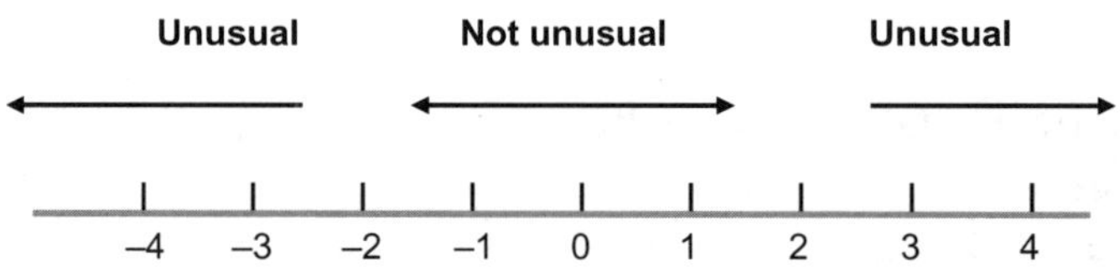

What Is a *z*-Score?

z-Scores are standardized measures of performance. Let's imagine starting with a set of numbers $x_1, x_1, \ldots, x_n$, in an Excel column, each measuring some kind of performance. For the sake of being specific, suppose that high values are good—so we are not measuring something like "number of errors," but something positive like "number of items correctly assembled."

DEFINITION

Calculate the sample mean $\bar{x}$ and the sample standard deviation s. Subtract the sample mean from each value and then divide by the standard deviation. The resulting numbers are called **z-scores** and measure "how many standard deviations above or below the mean" each outcome is.

In terms of a formula the *z*-score is calculated from the *x* outcome as

$$z = \frac{x - \bar{x}}{s}.$$

z-Scores are the same regardless of the original units of the performance measure. Change from euro to U.S. dollar and the z-scores will not change at all. Change from feet to centimeters. It has no effect on the z-scores. The z-scores measure how far each performance *stands out from the crowd.*

You should consider an outcome is quite normal if the standardized value is between −1.5 and 1.5.

There are no formal rules for saying when an outcome becomes unusual. You might start thinking a point is unusual when the standardized value is larger than 2.5 or much smaller than −2.5. But it depends on how much data you have. If you have a really large data set, for instance, thousands of daily returns on a share, then you will expect some "unusual" days and so in a sense they are not really unusual at all, in the sense of requiring any special explanation.

Calculating *z*-Scores in Excel

Beginning with a set of numbers in a column, you can use the Excel functions AVERAGE and STDEV. For instance, if the data comprise 10 numbers and are in the range A2:A11, then type

=(A2–AVERAGE(A$2:A$11))/STDEV(A$2:A$11)

into cell B2 and then double click the bottom right corner of cell B2. If you do not understand why you need the $ sign then this will be explained in class.

X	Z
103	-0.86
108	-0.74
112	-0.64
118	-0.49
238	2.47
135	-0.07
109	-0.71
156	0.45
142	0.10
158	0.50

The sample mean of the original data is 137.9 and the standard deviation is 40.5. The most unusually large value is the fifth value of 238, which is 2.47 standard deviations larger than the mean. None of the other values are particularly unusual, as their standardized values are in the range from −1.5 to 1.5.

CHECK YOUR UNDERSTANDING

Q3.

(a) A real estate agent is about to sell a property. He examines company records and extracts the sale price of 75 properties during the last year that are of a similar size, location, and quality to the one he is about to sell. He calculates the sample mean as 6.4 and the squared sample standard deviation, s^2, as 0.35.

Subsequently, the property is sold for HK$5.5 million. Is this an unusually low price?

(b) At the same real estate company, the agent decides to obtain data from the relevant professional body on all sales in Hong Kong that year. From over 15,000 records of sale, he selects 712 properties that are of similar size, location, and quality to the one he has just sold for HK$5.5 million. The sample mean is 6.2 and the squared sample standard deviation, s^2, of the 712 sales prices is 0.07.

He notes that the average price of HK$6.2 million dollars is lower than the figure of HK$6.4 million from company records, so his sale price of HK$5.5 million does not look so bad. Or does it? How unusual is this price? What important difference is there between the summary data for the company and for the industry as a whole?

(c) For the weekly sales data in Q3c.xls, identify any weeks that were unusually high or low by calculating the z-scores. Plot the z-scores against time. Can you think of a better way of standardizing these sales figures?

EXAMPLE 2 *What is an unusual salary?*

In the previous chapter we looked at data on the salary of 273 managers, as well as their age, experience, and gender. The background of this data is in the case of NTC Pay Equity in Chapter 18. You can examine the data in ex3 (salaries).xls. There is a wide range of salaries from the $30,000 range up to over $100,000. The overall data distribution is on the main worksheet *salary data*, and has a fairly regular unimodal shape apart from a peak in the $50K–$55K category. The mean value is $74.3K and the standard deviation is $13.5K.

To convert the salaries into z-scores, we subtract 74.3 from each of the 273 salaries and then divide by 13.5. In the left plot below, the resulting z-scores are plotted against employee number, which is essentially a random order.

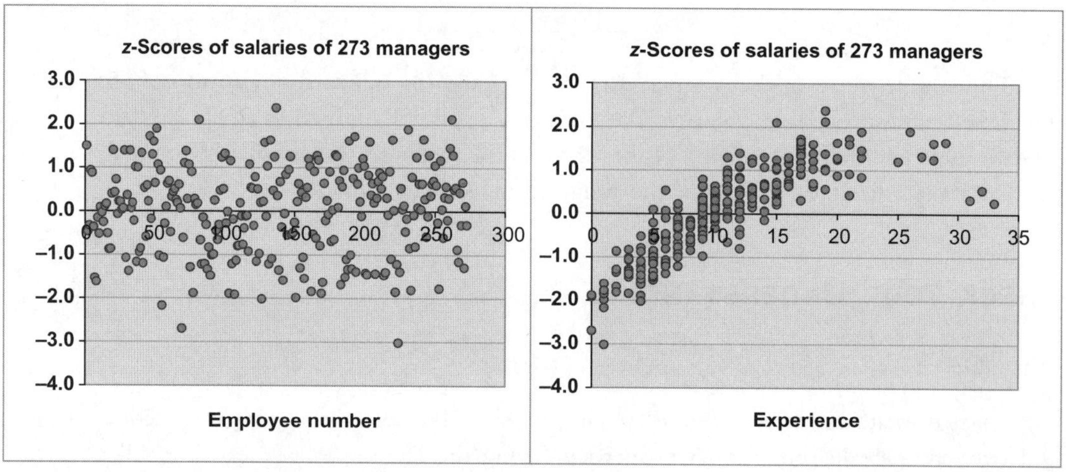

There are very few highly unusual salaries here. The most unusual has a *z*-score of –3.02 and is a male employee with the lowest level of experience (0–5 years) and an actual salary of $33.5K, the lowest in the data set. Why was this person's salary so low? The obvious reason is that he had little experience. We can investigate this further by changing the order of the data to start with the lowest experience group and end with the highest. You can do this by using the sort button on column B, which contains the exact years of experience. The *z*-score plotted against experience are in the right plot above. We see that indeed, the lower/higher *z*-scores are associated with the lower/higher levels of experience.

2.5. HOMOGENEOUS PEER GROUPS

The point of a *z*-score is to compare a data value with a group of data values—in practice, to compare an individual with a peer group. It would make no sense to measure people's heights and to mix up males and females and basketballers and nonbasketballers. You would just find the highest *z*-score would be a male basketballer and the lowest would be a female nonbasketballer. These individuals would indeed be unusual, but in a sense that is readily explained. The point of *z*-scores is to point to unusual individuals after taking account of the drivers that are obvious and have already been measured.

If you are trying to identify "unusual" salaries then you should surely allow for the factors that are *known* to affect salary. The main one is experience. Age and gender should not affect salary at all—at least according to the law!

To do this we need to consider each manager within their own experience group. The mean and standard deviation of each group are found using Pivotables and are in the table below. Notice how the mean salary systematically increases with experience. Notice also that the standard deviation of each group is much smaller (around 6–7) than the overall standard deviation of 13.5. That is because we have broken the data into groups of similar experience and there is consequently less variation of the salary within each experience group.

Salary broken down by Experience grouping		
Exp Group	Mean	Stdev
0-5	56.32	7.26
6-10	71.49	6.72
11-15	81.30	6.81
16-20	89.97	5.85
21-25	90.36	7.35
Overall	74.29	13.52

To calculate *z*-scores within each group is a little tedious. The easiest way is to sort the data in experience order and, for each group, subtract off the correct mean and divide by the correct standard deviation from the above table. When you do this you will find that some of the *z*-scores are very different to what they were before. These experience-adjusted *z*-scores are in the column headed *Z(exp)*.

Employee 3400 with the least experience and the lowest salary is still very unusual, with a *z*-score of −2.54. The average salary of others in his group is $56.3K and the variation around this is $7.2K so his salary of $37.8K is clearly very low. However, look at employee 3625 with a salary of $75.5K. Previously we considered him very much in the middle of the distribution since the overall mean was $74K. His *z*-score was 0.09. But taking account of his low experience, he has a very high salary with a *z*-score of +2.64. Another example is employee 3392, whose salary of $77.7K was previously considered very much in the middle of the distribution ($z = 0.26$), but since she is in the highest experience level where the mean salary is $90.3K, she is now considered rather low with a *z*-score of −1.88.

The moral of this is that in calculating *z*-scores you should compare an individual with their "peers," not with whatever sample that happens to be convenient. It makes little sense to say that the least experienced manager has an "unusually low" salary without first taking account of the fact that low experience managers *should* have lower salaries.

Pushing a Bit Further

A plot of these "experience-adjusted" *z*-scores is below, plotted in order of least to most experienced. I have also used a different plotting shade for each experience group. There was an unusually high salary—employee 3426 who earns $102.6K and is in the 11–15 experience group. The *z*-value is 3.14. You can see him in the middle of the plot. But notice that he was at the highest experience end of the 11–15-year group. Is this the reason his salary was so high?

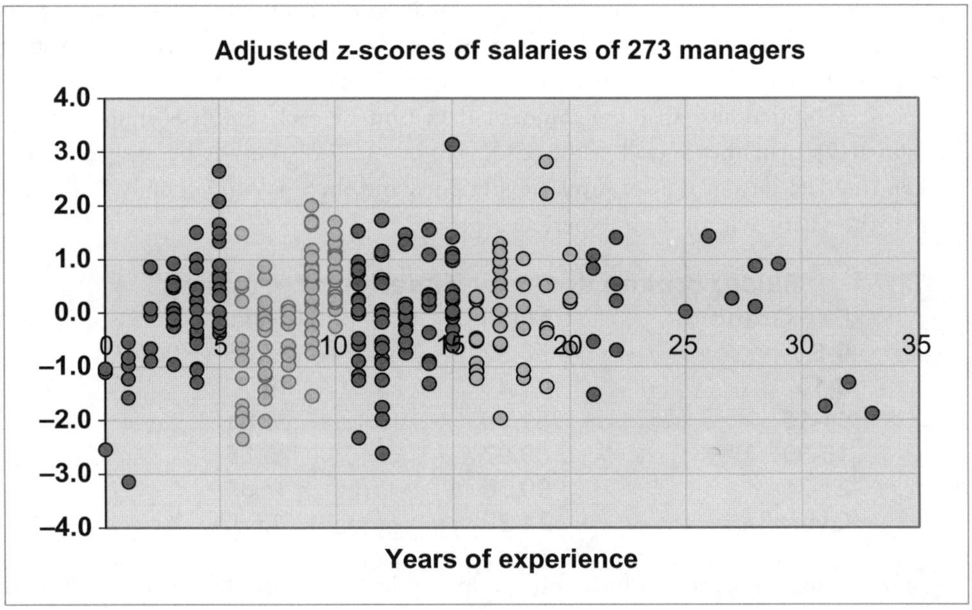

It very much seems that way! Look within each experience group and you can see an increasing trend in the *z*-scores from left to right. This means that, even with the groups of similar experience, there is still a tendency for the more experienced to have higher salaries. The bottom line is that we have not yet completely adjusted for the experience effect and we may falsely identify individuals as having unusually high or low salaries when these are entirely or mainly due to their higher or lower experience within the group.

Is it possible to completely adjust for experience? Yes it is, and you will learn how to do it in Chapters 17–20. Using regression, one can describe the relationship between salary and experience mathematically—without breaking the data up into crude experience groups—and then see how much above or below the trend each individual lies. This measure of a point's unusualness is called a **standardized residual**. It is very similar to a z-score in its conception and use.

2.6. Combining Different Performance Measures

There are rather few business domains where performance is measured by a single number. For example, Master's in Business Administration (MBA) students in a particular course may have their learning assessed by exam mark, group assignment mark, and class participation. The head of a publicly listed company may be assessed on yearly profit as well as share price. An operations manager may be assessed on both the quantity and the quality of the production line. Business schools are assessed according to no less than 20 different metrics by the *Financial Times* (FT) business school ranking.

Two Performance Measures

In the SBS performance appraisal case, Adam Christopher has to assess 36 academics on two quite different performance dimensions, namely research and teaching excellence. He is required to give equal weight to both dimensions. One quick way of gaining an appreciation of how an individual sits within the group is to plot one performance measure against the other. In the plot, the further top and right you are, the better you perform.

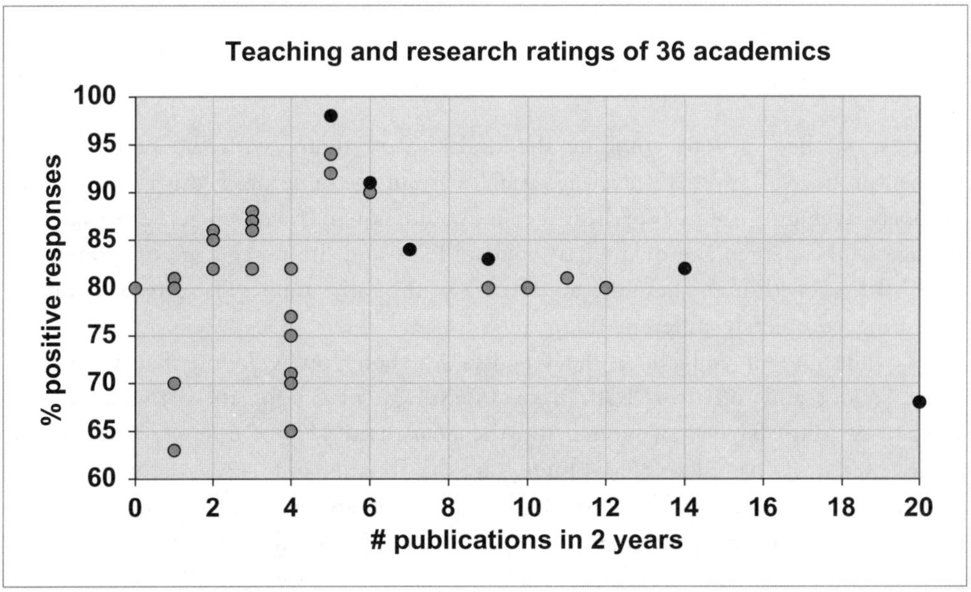

If an individual has both better teaching and research performance dimensions than another then they dominate that other. In the plot, this means being above and to the right. This is called *dominance*. So we can immediately tell you that most of the 36 academics could not possibly be ranked highest. The only individuals that do not have anyone who dominates them are displayed with a darker symbol. There are six such individuals and any reasonable final ranking would need to rank these individuals highly.

It is not clear which of these six are the best. Each is better in one dimension but worse in the other. Who is ranked higher will depend on the *exchange rate* you use for research and teaching. z-Scores are a way of establishing this exchange rate.

Many Performance Measures

To fix our ideas, let's imagine an Excel spreadsheet with a quite large number of competitors (say 100 international business schools) each assessed by a quite small number of performance measures. The performance variables might be: (1) the average salary of students 3 years after graduation, (2) the percentage of students with employment 3 months after graduation, (3) the percentage of faculty members with a Ph.D., (4) the research output of the school, (5) the percentage of women in the senior governance of the school, and (6) the percentage of overseas students in the full-time MBA program. So we would have 100 rows and 6 columns of data. The data for the 2005 FT business school rankings take just this form and are in ex4(FT).xls.

For some purposes, you need to combine the different dimensions of performance into a single overall measure of performance. Certainly, business schools are ultimately ranked by the FT ranking exercise. So somehow the FT combines the six very different scores into a single number. How do you combine the different scores?

If you care equally about all the different measures then your first instinct may be to calculate the average. It is very important to realize that this is not automatically a sensible thing to do. In fact, it is often a silly thing to do. For a start:

> You cannot meaningfully calculate the average of a set of numbers unless they are in the same units.

So it would be crazy to combine the dollar salary figure with the percentage of women on board figure. But even if variables are in the same units, this is not enough to justify averaging them. For instance, it would not make much sense to take the average of the percentage of international students and the percentage of women on the board, even though these are apparently in the same units. These two scores are measuring completely different things.

To illustrate, if you check the FT data set then you will find that William & Mary School and Wharton both have an average of 25 for these two measures. William & Mary has 9% of women on the board and 41% of international students while Wharton has 8% of women on the board and 42% of international students. If we give both a score of 25 then we are necessarily saying that the exchange rate for the percentage of women on the board and the percentage of international students should be 1 for 1. It is not obvious that the exchange rate should be 1 for 1.

	Benchmarking of 6 performance measures across 100 schools					
	Salary	Employed	Women	International	Faculty Ph.D	Research
Min	71	43	0	8	28	72.1
Max	199	99	57	98	100	323.3
Mean	128.9	83.6	16.5	46.4	91.2	151.8
Stdev	25.9	10.3	10.2	22.9	11.0	51.2

In fact, if you look at the overall distribution of the six measures in the table above, you will see that the percentage of women score is far less variable than the percentage of international students score. This suggests that it is "harder" to get an extra 1% of women on the board than it is to get an extra 1% of international students.

It is the variability of the different measures that is the key to combining them in a statistically and practically defensible way. The principle is that if a school is really *outstanding* on a particular score then it should receive larger credit. If it is in the middle of the distribution it should receive little credit. And we already know how to measure how outstanding or normal a performance outcome is. We look at the performance within a pool of competitors and use the *z*-score.

Let's look at London Business School (LBS). They did well in the salary dimension. Their mean salary is $147K compared with $128.9K for the 100 peer schools. The standard deviation is 25.9 so their performance is 0.7 standard deviation above the mean. Their best performance is in the percentage of international students. They have 86% of their student body from outside the U.K. compared with a mean of 46.4% for the peer schools. This is 1.73 standard deviations above the mean.

	Raw Scores and Z-scores for London Business School					
	Salary	Employed	Women	International	Faculty Ph.D	Research
Raw score	147	85	8	86	98	179.3
Z-score	0.70	0.14	-0.83	1.73	0.62	0.54
Mean	128.9	83.6	16.5	46.4	91.2	151.8
Stdev	25.9	10.3	10.2	22.9	11.0	51.2

The six *z*-scores are now on the same statistical scale. A score of +2 means outstandingly good, 0 means average, and −2 means outstandingly bad. So it makes sense to average these—if you really did have to combine them into a single number.

But of course, you do not have to combine them, unless, like the FT, you need to come up with a final ranking of all schools. It is quite useful to look at all of the *z*-scores to see the overall profile of performance for the school.

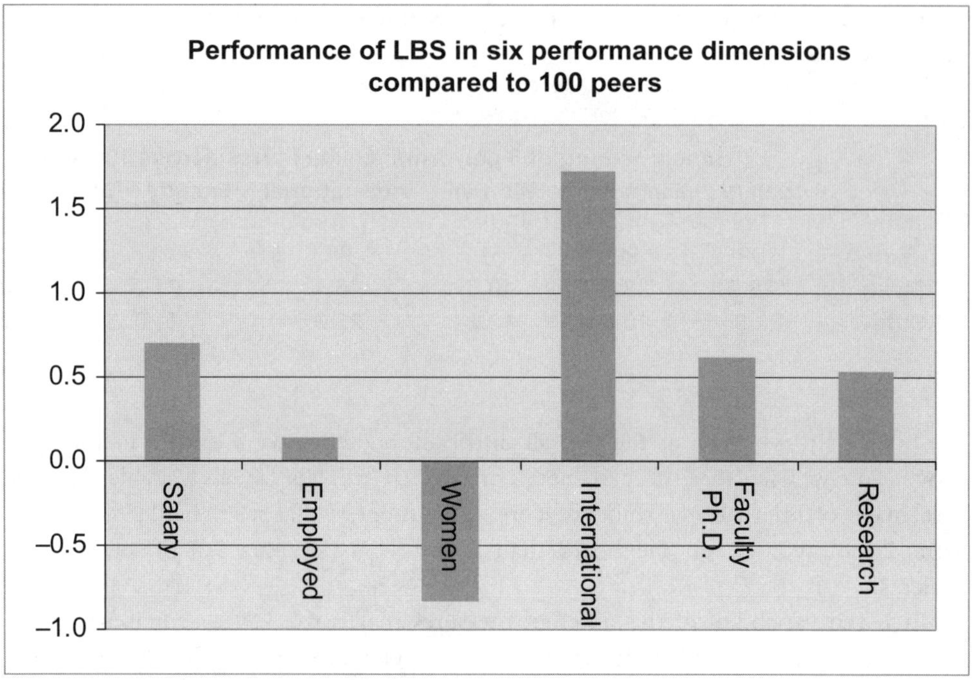

This plot not only shows the dimensions where LBS is above or below average. It measures how far above or below average the performance is on the z-scale. It is clear that only the percentage of international students is at all outside the normal range, at least for the pool of 100 peer business schools that have been used for this exercise.

The peer group obviously matters. You get a quite different profile if you restrict attention to the European schools. Why? Because the mean and standard deviations are different, and these are used to compute the z-scores.

Finally, what about ranking the schools? You could take the simple average of the z-scores for each school. The average z-score for LBS is 0.48. You can make the same calculation for all the other 99 schools and rank them from highest to lowest. This has been done on the *ranking* worksheet in cx4(FT).xls. LBS is ranked 14th and the top-ranked school is Lancaster, which you might consider surprising.

Does the FT actually calculate z-scores and average them? Yes, they certainly do. You can check for yourself on the FT Business website. But they did not rank Lancaster number 1 in 2005. Wharton was ranked first in 2005.

Pushing a Bit Further

One reason for the different results obtained here is that we have ignored 14 other dimensions that the FT used to arrive at their ranking. Probably the most important one is the percentage increase in student salary from starting the course to 3 years after graduation. The second reason for the unusual result is that Lancaster's good results are mainly driven by the percentage of women (z = 3.98) and the percentage of international students ($z = 1.64$). These are not considered the most important performance dimensions by most stakeholders.

Consequently, the FT does not use a simple average of the z-scores. They use what is called a **weighted average**. Much more weight is given to the salary dimensions than the other dimensions. Research is also highly weighted. The weighting for the six dimensions are roughly given below.

Salary	Employed	Women	International	Faculty Ph.D	Research
50%	5%	3%	10%	12%	20%

To calculate a weighted average, you multiply each weight by the z-score and add them up. You can use the function

=SUMPRODUCT(weights, scores)

to do this. When you apply this weighted average of z-scores you find that Lancaster ranks 54th (with a weighted average z-score of almost exactly zero) and LBS ranks 11th (with a weighted average z-score of 0.69). You should check the _ranking_ worksheet in ex4(FT).xls to make sure you understand the calculation.

Final Thought

There is an important principle of computer science called "garbage in, garbage out." If you feed rubbish data into the most sophisticated data analysis you still get rubbish. The relevance to FT rankings of business schools is that we have not thought carefully enough about how the six performance measures are calculated and whether they are "fair." By "fair," I mean that a school that gets a better score on that dimension should, all other things being equal, be ranked higher.

There is a major problem with the Salary variable. Some schools accept students only from the United States, and U.S. students tend to get much higher salaries than schools located, for instance, in Hong Kong. There is another performance measure that is not analyzed here that counts the percentage increase in salary. Again, this measure is not at all fair because schools that accept students with little work experience and from poorer countries will find their students' salaries increase by a much larger percentage and stand to look much better than they really are. The variable I have labeled Research is also measured in an unfair manner. First, larger schools will have more research output. The FT ranking tries to downweight this effect but larger schools are still given a big advantage just for being bigger. Not only that, but only a very restricted set of research outputs is counted at all. The FT has a list of 40 mandated research journals that they count. Everything else is ignored. I might receive the Nobel Prize, but the FT ranking will not use it to assess the research standing of my institution.

In short, the FT index is a terrible and misleading index—not because they use z-scores, which is smart—but because some of the key performance measures have not been properly thought through.

If you are going to use *z*-scores for any kind of performance measurement in a practical business environment, don't rush ahead in the excitement of coding up your Excel spreadsheet. Take the time to go through each of your basic performance measures and ask yourself—are these numbers garbage?

2.7. SUMMARY

Data can come in **stacked** or **unstacked** form—it ultimately makes no difference which. You can use StatproGo to convert from one form to the other.

The Excel tool **Pivotables** is useful for unstacking data in the background and reporting various statistics for the unstacked groups. This is useful for seeing patterns and differences in the data, in order to see what might drive performance.

The unusualness of a number can be measured by its ***z*-score**. In terms of a formula the *z*-score is calculated from the *x* outcome as

$$z = \frac{x - \overline{x}}{s}.$$

The *z*-score measures how many standard deviations above or below the mean a given performance is. This may be used to identify whether a particular performance is within the standard range or is unusually high or low. *z*-Scores outside the range from −2.5 to 2.5 might be considered very unusual. *z*-Scores within the range from −1.5 to 1.5 are fairly normal. To be meaningful, the data should be broken down into homogeneous groups. Otherwise, the high and low performers will be easily explained by the heterogeneity, and will not be "unusual."

Different performance measures should not ordinarily be combined by averaging because they are typically on different scales and often in different units. If they are combined then there must be a special reason, such as price-to-earnings ratio for a stock.

Apart from these special cases, a general alternative is to convert all the performance measures into *z*-scores. They are then on the same absolute scale and can, if required, be averaged or summed. Weighted averages can be used to give more importance to some performance measures if this is appropriate. Choosing homogenous groups to create each of the performance *z*-scores is still essential.

EXERCISES

E1. For 1241 apartments sold in a certain area in 2002, the mean price is \$459,000 and the standard deviation is \$76,000. Consider three apartments that sold for \$545,000, \$295,000, and \$395,000. Which of these is most unusual? Are any of them really unusual statistically?

E2. For 1241 apartments sold in a certain area in 2002, the mean price is \$459,000 and the standard deviation is \$76,000. A particular apartment has a *z*-score of 3.78. What did it sell for?

E3. You have 689 contract employees in an assembly and packaging plant and have measured the number of items completed per hour—over a 3-month period. Across these 689 employees the average number of items completed is 24.2 and the standard deviation 3.1. A particular worker, Bonnie, has a z-score of +0.6. Describe in ordinary language Bonnie's absolute and relative performance.

E4. A sample of $n = 3$ currency traders have their average weekly portfolio growth measured. These three numbers are converted into z-scores. Neville has a z-score of −1.147. Ann has a z-score of 0.459. What can you say about the third trader, Brian?

E5. You are reviewing sales figures and are particularly interested in four salespersons: Fred, Ann, Jim, and Jane. The figures you have are sales figures for 2001–2003 (in units of $1000). In addition, you have the average sales across the whole workforce for each year as well as the standard deviation. Note that the mean and standard deviation are for the whole workforce, not for Fred, Anne, Jim, and Jane. They may be relevant for comparing the performance of each salesperson against the total sales force for each year.

	2001	2002	2003
Fred	$282	$212	$271
Ann	$246	$306	$225
Jim	$335	$315	$227
Jane	$366	$248	$288
Mean	$295	$175	$255
Stdev	$51	$13	$32

On the basis of their historical performance, how would you rank the four salespersons? There is not a single correct answer to this question.

E6. You are reviewing three candidates for possible promotion to management of call center operations. Each has previously managed a call center within your company. The promotion will be made on the basis of who has been the most successful manager of their individual call center. There are four relevant criteria. The first is rate of turnover of staff, which you would like to be low. The second is average customer satisfaction. The third is the average number of calls handled per day. The fourth is the total wages (TW) bill, which you would like to be low.

You have benchmark figures across your company and three other companies. The data cover 26 call centers in total, all comparable to the call centers in your company. However, the call centers differ drastically in size from about 5 to 20 operators. The data are in Q6.xls. The performance of the three candidates is given in the same file.

(a) For each of the three candidates, calculate z-scores for each of the four performance measures.

(b) Which candidates do very well or very poorly in which performance dimensions?

(c) Calculate the average z-score for each candidate. On this basis, who is preferred? Remember: low turnover and wages are preferred, so you should probably switch the sign of the z-score!

(d) Plot the TW against calls per hour (CpH). Why do you think the plots looks like it does?

(e) The plot in (d) suggests combining TW and CpH into a ratio and using Cph/TW as a single performance measure instead of TW and CpH separately. Calculate Cph/TW for the 26 call centers and also for the three candidates.

(f) Calculate z-scores for the performance measure Cph/TW for the three candidates. On the basis of the three performance measures of turnover, satisfaction, and Cph/TW, who is the preferred candidate?

E7. The data in Q7.xls are the salary data examined in this chapter, but with an extra column giving the age of the manager.

(a) Use Pivotables to give a table that describes how salary depends on age. Use 5-year categories for age, starting from 15 and ending at 65.

(b) Use Pivotables to give a table that describes how salary depends on experience. Use 5-year categories for age, starting from 1 and ending at 35.

(c) Use Pivotables to give a table that describes how salary depends on both age and experience together. Does it look like age or experience is the real driver of salary?

E8. The data in Q8.xls list the sale price of 137 motor vehicles—all of the same make—that sold at auction in a particular month. In addition to the sale price, you have information on the age of the vehicle, the number of miles it has recorded, and the presence or absence of three optional features. Use Pivotables to answer the following questions:

(a) How many cars have what optional features? Create a table that allows me to see, for instance, how many of the 134 cars have tinting and leather trim but no extra airbags.

(b) Describe how the sale price depends on the age of the vehicle.

(c) Describe how sale price depends on mileage.

(d) Describe how sale price depends on both age and mileage. Use 0.5-year groups for age and 10,000-mi groups for mileage. Does it look like age or mileage is the real driver of sale price?

E9. In Chapter 1, we considered some data on the satisfaction of customers with their experience with a complaint call center, reproduced in Q9.xls. The gender of the operator and the customer was recorded. It was mentioned that the service time and the customer satisfaction might depend on the combinations of gender. The data are in Q9.xls. This can be investigated by breaking the data down into different gender combinations.

(a) Break the data into the four gender combinations by dragging the customer and consultant icons into the row field.

(b) For each gender combination, give the data distribution of satisfaction. To do this, drag the rating icon into the column field and drag the ID icon into the data field and change to count.

(c) For each gender combination, give the mean satisfaction. You will need to undo some of the steps in (b) and have the rating icon in the data field with *average* as the statistics.

(d) Does the service time depend on the gender combination? How?

(e) We suspect that holding time impacts negatively on rating. Starting from the Pivotable in (c), produce a Pivotable that accounts for holding time by grouping this into 30-s intervals. Within each holding time group, is there a clear effect of gender combination on satisfaction?

E10. The data in Q10.xls give the sale price of 173 houses that sold at auction in the eastern suburbs of a southeastern coastal city of 4 million people. The number of rooms and the area of the block are also listed.

(a) Calculate z-scores for the 173 sales. Which sales were "unusually" high and low? Why do you think this was?

(b) Break the data by number of rooms and give the average and standard deviation of price for each room group. Give a typical price range for each room group—where by typical range we mean within 1 standard deviation of the mean. Record these figures under the headings Low and High in the worksheet *rooms z-scores*.

(c) Double click on cell D3. This uses an Excel function VLOOKUP to recode the number of rooms into the average sale price for homes with that number of rooms. It uses the data in the table over in columns K, L, and M. Double click on cell D4. This uses an Excel function VLOOKUP to recode the number of rooms into the standard deviation sale price for homes with that number of rooms. It should now be very easy for you to calculate the z-scores in column G, where each home is compared only with other homes that have the same number of rooms. What is the most unusually high- and low-priced home now?

(d) Break the data by area. Categorize area to the nearest $100\,\text{m}^2$, that is, groups 300–399 and 400–499. Give the average and standard deviation of the price for each area category. Give a typical price for each area category. Copy the average,

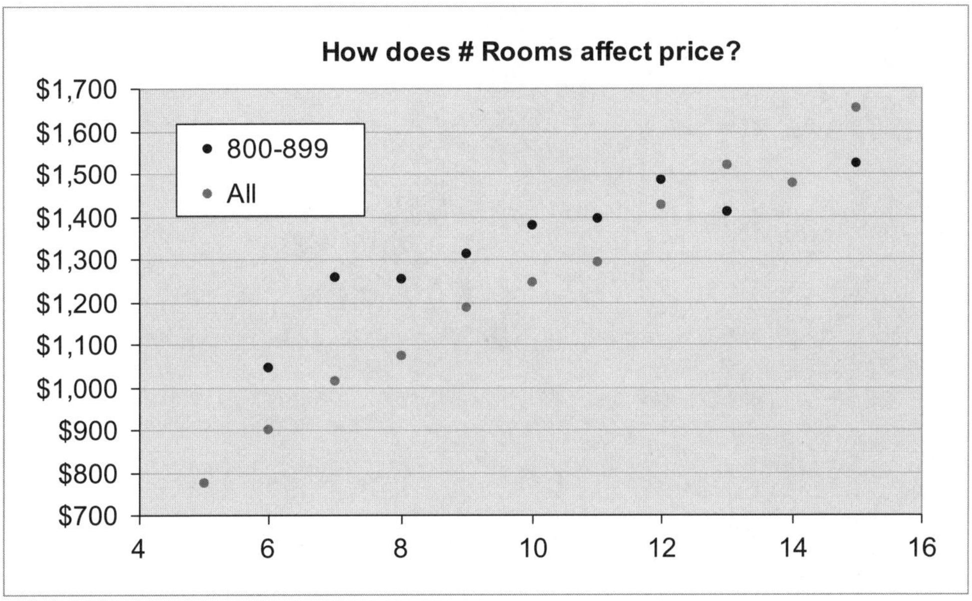

standard deviation, low, and high prices into yellow cells in the empty table in the worksheet <u>*area z-scores*</u>.

(e) As in part (c), double click on cells D3 and D4 and create the z-scores that compare each home with other homes on similar area blocks. Which is the most highly and lowly priced home now?

(f) Use Pivotables to break the data up into homes with different numbers of rooms and also different areas, that is, a two-dimensional table. You can now, with a little effort, produce the plot below. For the number of rooms varying from 5 to 15 it plots the average sale price. It also shows a plot of these average prices but restricted to homes with an area range of 800–899. It is obvious that the rate at which the price increases for 800–899-m^2 homes is slower than for homes in general. Why do you think this is? Which is the "correct" representation of the effect of the number of rooms on the sale price?

CHAPTER 3

Dealing with Uncertainty and Chance

3.0. Introduction: What Is the Issue?

Probability is a set of rules and ideas for dealing with uncertainty. When properly applied, it allows us to understand, predict, manipulate, and account for the unpredictable nature of most business outcomes. Here are four instances where you would need some probability theory to arrive at a rational decision.

Finance Some share analysts claim to be able to pick when the market will rise and when it will fall—not 100% of the time but consistently better than guessing. What really constitutes outstanding performance for the task of predicting stocks? To pin the question down, suppose we asked the analyst to predict the percentage change in tomorrow's market index and we then allocate this into five categories: little change, moderate fall, moderate rise, large fall, and large rise. The definitions of these categories could be adjusted so that each happens with equal probability (20%). Over 1 year (250 trading days), the analyst makes a prediction of what kind of market it will be the next day. So the analyst should get around 20% of 250 or 50 predictions correct (if she is essentially guessing). How much better than 50 would she need to do to distinguish herself as a genuine market seer?

Health Care Suppose you test positive for certain lymphocytes that are indicative of leukemia. The test is not 100% accurate but there are data on the track record of the test applied to a wider population. What sort of calculations would answer the burning question in your mind: "What is the chance that I have leukemia?"

Data-Driven Business Decisions, First Edition. Chris J. Lloyd.

Market Research You are considering market testing of a product prior to full development. You have data on the likely monetary outcomes of the product if you just go ahead. You also have information on the accuracy of the market testing. Is it worth paying for market testing? How much should you pay? If you get a positive test assessment for a particular product then how likely is it that the product will be successful (and is therefore worth launching)?

Market Segmentation How does age and gender relate to customer loyalty? There are different ways to look at such a question. We could look at the different segments and describe the likelihood of different loyalty outcomes within the segments. Or we could look at the different loyalty groups and describe the distribution of the different market segments within the loyalty groups.

These are the kinds of questions that can be answered using the concepts of probability, conditional probability, and mean value—which are the three key ideas in the next two chapters. A key skill in applying the methods is to focus on what could happen and how the outcome of interest relates to what could happen. A key requirement is to then identify the uncertain events and payoffs that are important to the question and to assign *numbers* to all of these. Only then can you get a quantitative answer. You can and should consider the reliability of the key numbers you used. Excel is ideal for this kind of sensitivity analysis.

NET PROMOTER SCORE: CASE BRIEFING

Angela Braut works in the market research unit of the customer relations section at a major bank. The market research group has surveyed over 1000 existing customers on their loyalty and now wants to summarize the data. The main measure they are interested in is the *Net Promoter score*, which is the proportion of customers who would very likely recommend the bank minus the proportion who would very likely not.

The bank Angela works for has around 7 million customers, which is about 15% of the market share. She has data on the age and gender distribution of the general population as well as the 7 million existing customers. A total of 1138 bank customers have been surveyed. They were contacted both through online banking and also through a written survey sent out with a small subset of last month's bills. The data are in NPSdata.xls.

Looking at the survey results, it is clear that the majority of customers would not recommend the bank. How does this differ by gender and age group? How could she present this data in a simple way that will be quickly understood by senior managers?

3.1. Framing What Could Happen: Outcomes and Events

Probability is concerned with uncertain outcomes that can't be perfectly predicted. The first step in a proper analysis of such problems is to identify what the possible outcomes could be. Sometimes there can be only a few possible outcomes or sometimes there can be a very large number of possible outcomes. Conceptually, to even begin to think about how likely it is that something will happen, you need to have considered everything that could happen.

The **sample space** (denoted S) is the set of all possible outcomes. It is not of direct interest in itself. It is part of framing the problem. An **event** is something that we want to calculate the probability of, and will be a subset of the sample space.

EXAMPLE

As a very simple nonbusiness example, if I roll a die twice, then there are 36 possible outcomes (six possible outcomes on each of two throws). So the sample space S contains 36 elements of the form (11), (12), …, (56), (66). In a game of chance we might be interested in knowing the likelihood of "the total being at least 10." This is an event and could be represented as

$$\{(55),(64),(46),(56),(65),(66)\}.$$

There will not be many coin or dice examples in this book, as they have little to do with business or management. But such examples are useful vehicles for establishing the basic concepts.

Set Operations and Relations

There are three basic operations we use to manipulate events or sets. These are *union*, *intersection*, and *complement.*

We often want to talk about the chance that this happens *or* that happens. This is the **union** operation and is represented symbolically by $A \cup B$, which we vocalize as "A or B." Here, A and B are just any two events that we may be interested in.

We often want to talk about the chance that this happens *and* that happens. This is the **intersection** operation and is represented symbolically by $A \cap B$, which we vocalize as "A and B."

Last, we often want to talk about the chance that something *does not* happen. This **complement** operation is represented by $\overline{A}$, which we vocalize as "not A."

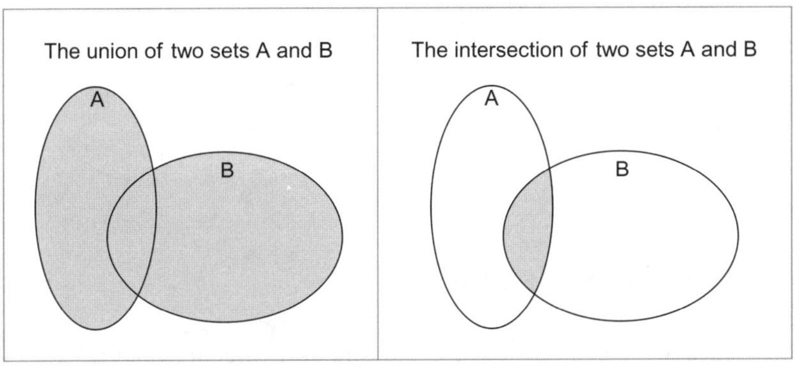

Events are sets, and sets can be very helpfully represented as set (or Venn) diagrams. This is not the only way they can be represented. For instance, toward the end of this chapter we will represent the sample space and various events as a *tree*. It all depends on the example. But for conveying basic concepts in an immediately digestible way, simple set diagrams are very useful. For instance, the left-hand graphic represents the union of two sets, in words "*A* or *B*." The right-hand graphic represents the intersection of two sets, in words "*A* and *B*."

EXAMPLE

If *A* was the event "the total from throwing two dies is at least 10" and if *B* was the event "the two throws are identical," then the sets can be represented as

$$A = \{(55), (64), (46), (56), (65), (66)\}$$

$$B = \{(11), (22), (33), (44), (55), (66)\}.$$

The union of the two sets is

$$A \cup B = \{(11, (22), (33), (44), (55), (66), (64), (46), (56), (65)\}$$

while the intersection is

$$A \cap B = \{(55), (66)\}.$$

The sets $\bar{A}$ and $\bar{B}$ would be quite long to list. Each would contain the 36–6 elements of the sample space that are not in the respective sets *A* and *B*.

There are also logical relationships between events. If one event *A* is contained in another event *B*, then we represent it symbolically by $A \subset B$ and vocalize it as "if *A* then *B*" or even more simply, "*A* implies *B*." If two events have an empty intersection then they are said to be **mutually exclusive**. This can be vocalized as "*A* and *B* cannot both happen." These concepts have been represented in the diagrams below. The left graphic represents "*A* implies *B*" and the right graphic represents "*A* and *B* cannot both happen."

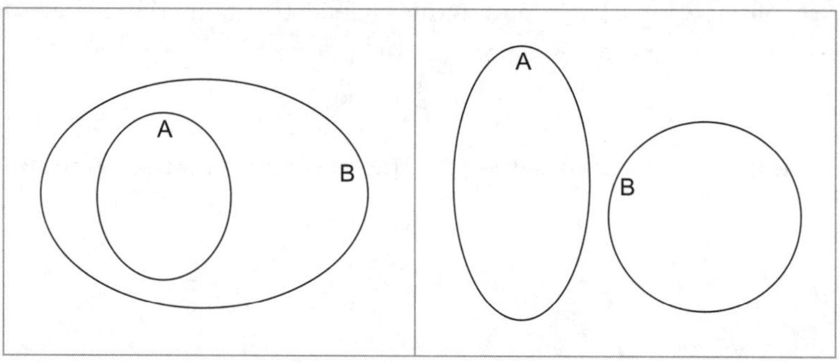

CHECK YOUR UNDERSTANDING

Q1. Three dice are rolled. How many possible outcomes are there? (This may seem like a very easy question but there are actually many possible answers!)

Q2. You are a consultant considering taking a job from a particular client. You are tying to decide whether you will charge \$3000 per day or \$5000 per day. The client has not decided yet whether to hire your services. If she does, then it is not clear whether the job will require extra assistance from expert consultants. Neither do you know whether the client will end up satisfied with your job or whether you will get any return business. What is an appropriate sample space for this scenario?

3.2. How Likely Is It? Probability Basics

Nearly everyone is familiar with the idea of measuring the likelihood of something by a number between 0 and 1, where 0 means it will never happen and 1 means that it definitely will. Many textbooks will have pages of formulas describing how to manipulate these numbers in various situations. There will be few such formulas in this book—because most of the ideas of probability can be conveyed more easily with set diagrams and simply logic.

> In fact, events with probability 0 can actually happen; see Chapter 7!

Probability Is Like Area

The only extra idea we need is that *the probability of an event can be represented by its area*. So larger sets represent events with larger probabilities. The probability of the whole sample space is 1, so we bound all the sets of interest by a sample space, often represented as a rectangle, whose area we imagine is exactly 1.

Thus, for instance, formulas that you might see in a textbook, such as

$$\Pr(A \cup B) = \Pr(A) + \Pr(B) - \Pr(A \cap B)$$

can be immediately understood when you see the diagram below. The area inside "*A* or *B*" could be calculated by adding the area of *A* to the area of *B*, but you would have to subtract off the intersection set UNITED NATIONS New York and Geneva, 2008 $A \cap B$, otherwise it would be double counted.

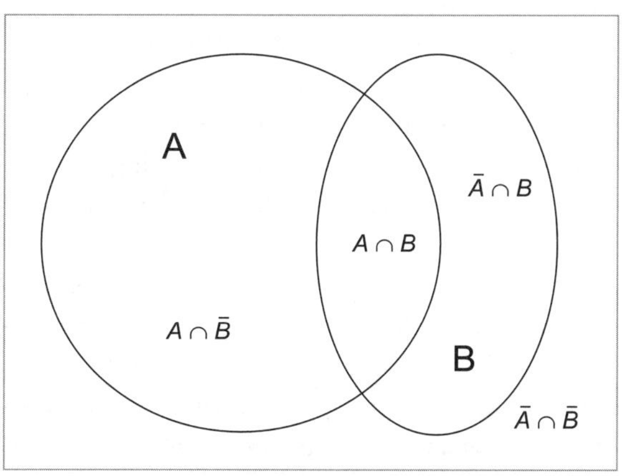

In a similar manner, if we were interested in the chance that *A* happens but *B* does not, then we first must realize that this means "*A* and not *B*," which is represented in the diagram by the region $A \cap \overline{B}$. You would not need to be a mathematical genius to realize that this area can be obtained by starting with the area of A and subtracting the area of $A \cap B$. This is just what is generalized in the formula

$$\Pr(A \cap \overline{B}) = \Pr(A) - \Pr(A \cap B).$$

Another obvious formula is $\Pr(\overline{A}) = 1 - \Pr(A)$. These formulas are obviously true regardless of the size and shapes of the areas A and B. They say something about how areas and probabilities work in general.

Why does the area idea work? Because we can think of a thought experiment where area would indeed be probability. Imagine that the sample space is a target of exactly $1\,\text{m}^2$. Imagine that I throw a dart at the target and that I am such a bad shot that I am equally likely to hit any point on the target. Then the chance that I hit any particular region would be. … the area of that region! What this proves is the areas *can be* probabilities. The implication though is far deeper—that the rules of area are the same as the rules of probability. Area, then, is a metaphor for probability and is made visual with set diagrams. Use them whenever you can!

CHECK YOUR UNDERSTANDING

Q3. Use a set diagram and the rules of probability to explain why $\Pr(\overline{A} \cap \overline{B})$ always equals $1 - \Pr(A \cup B)$. Think of a real-world example to illustrate its use.

Where Do the Probabilities Come From?

The probability rules are simple and follow the rules of area. But these rules do not tell us the actual probabilities of different events. They only tell us how to use these probabilities once they have been assigned. How are probabilities assigned?

In some simple examples probabilities are based on logic or symmetry. For instance, if two dice are rolled then there are 36 possible outcomes and if the dice are fair then each has the same probability, 1/36. There are rather few business contexts where probabilities are assigned on the basis of logic or symmetry.

When probabilities do not follow from logic, they may often be estimated from previous data: if an event has happened $x\%$ of the time over a large sample in the recent past then we estimate the chance of it happening next time to be $x\%$. We need only keep in mind that we are using historical proportions to estimate what the true probabilities might be.

So we have another metaphor. Proportions behave like probabilities. Again, there is a thought experiment linking the two concepts. If I randomly choose someone from your class then what is the probability they are female? It is just the proportion of females in the class. So for this example, probability is proportion. As with area, this single example where probability equals proportion gives us a new metaphor for probability. Probabilities follow all the rules of proportions. Conversely, any question about proportions will be subject to the rules of probability.

When there is neither logic nor data to appeal to, probabilities can be assigned subjectively. For instance, a firm might make one strategic move and be interested in the likely response of its major competitor. You could not assign probabilities to the competitor's response using logic or previous data. But you might give a subjective estimate and a range of reasonable values around this.

CHECK YOUR UNDERSTANDING

Q4. There are five socks in a drawer. Three of them are black and two are gray. You choose two at random. What is the chance that you get a matching pair?

Q5. You have data from the Bureau of Statistics concerning the distribution of males and females among families of different sizes. Among the 1.36 million families with exactly two children, the distribution of genders is as follows:

Both girls	Mixed	Both boys
408,000	570,000	382,000

You meet a woman for the first time and you ask her if she has any children. She says she has two. When you ask her if she has any daughters she replies that she does. What is the probability that she has two daughters?

3.3. MARKET SEGMENTS AND BEHAVIOR; PROBABILITY TABLES

When there are two underlying characteristics of interest then it is often convenient (but not essential) to arrange the sample space as a table. A common application of this to business would be when we are interested in both a customer's market segment and his or her consumer behavior. We would be particularly interested in the relationship between these.

Market segments can sometimes be based on very complex measurements and statistical formulas. However, here I just mean simple things like gender, age group, or occupation. Consumer behavior might include the amount spent on the product, the satisfaction with the product or service, the attitude to the product, or the likelihood of buying the product.

EXAMPLE 1 *Car seat covers*

A market survey involved asking a random sample of 577 customers at a general hardware store the maximum price they would pay for a certain brand and type of car seat cover. They were offered three possible responses: \$99, \$89, or less than \$89. They can only select one of these three categories. Each customer can be either male or female and also can be in one of three possible price categories. So there are six possible outcomes in this sample space. Here is an obvious case where the data are going to be our proxy for probability. There is certainly no symmetry here—it would make no sense to assign an equal probability of 1/6 to the six possible outcomes.

	$99	$89	<$89
Females	61	92	66
Males	154	104	100

Most of the customers in the store were male. This does not invalidate any of the calculations we are about to do. So long as the sample was random—not deliberately or accidentally biased toward one kind of customer—it is fine to take the figures in the table as representative of the customer base as a whole. We can convert these into proportions by dividing by 577.

	$99	$89	<$89
Females	10.6%	16.0%	11.4%
Males	26.7%	18.0%	17.4%

Where is the set diagram here? We are not using one! We instead represent the sample space as a table—here with six cells representing the six outcomes. Rather than using the area of the set to represent the probability, we are putting the probability in the cell. If you wanted a set diagram to represent these six probabilities it is not particularly easy to do. Below is my best attempt.

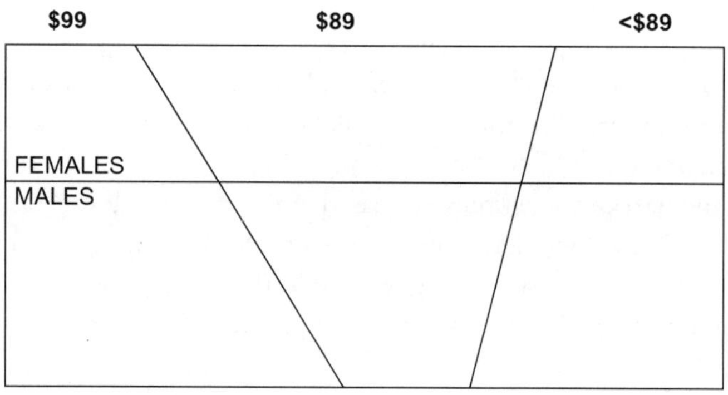

Marginal Probability

When there are two (or even more) variables involved in a problem, we sometimes want to say something about each variable alone—for instance, the distribution of customers across the market segments (ignoring their consumer behavior). Or we might want to say something about the overall distribution of their consumer behavior without worrying about the segments.

When data are set out as a table, this is simply done by adding the rows and the columns. These probabilities are called **marginal probabilities**—because they appear in the margins of the table. They describe the probabilities of one factor or characteristic, ignoring the other.

EXAMPLE 1 (Continued) *Car seat covers*

Adding rows and columns gives the table below:

	$99	$89	<$89	All
Females	10.6%	16.0%	11.4%	38.0%
Males	26.7%	18.0%	17.4%	62.0%
All	37.3%	33.9%	28.8%	100.0%

We can immediately see that 62% of customers are male. We can also see that the three pricing preference categories are very roughly one-third each. The figures 37.3, 33.9%, and 28.8% describe the characteristic of pricing preference overall, ignoring gender.

CHECK YOUR UNDERSTANDING

Q6. A survey of 500 London beer drinkers was undertaken. Each was asked about their favorite kind of beer. The data are below.

	Stout	Lager	Light
Male	82	205	123
Female	9	27	54

(a) Give the table of relative frequencies or proportions.

(b) Give the marginal probabilities. What is the probability that a customer prefers stout?

(c) What is the chance that a customer is a female who does not prefer stout?

3.4. EXAMPLE IN HEALTH CARE: TESTING FOR A DISEASE

Probabilities tables are not only useful for seeing how market segments are related to consumer behavior. They can also be used whenever there are two factors of interest. The example in this section involves testing for a disease. The factors of interest, then, are the true disease status of the patient and the result of the test. Ideally these would be the same, but of course in practice they are not.

Both leukemia and lymph infections lead to elevated levels of certain lymphocytes, which can produce swollen lymph glands. But levels can become elevated for other reasons and lead to swollen glands in otherwise healthy individuals. It is of obvious interest to be able to distinguish between a lymph infection, which responds to antibiotic treatment, and leukemia.

A blood test can reveal the level of lymphocytes. A person's level is said to be "normal" if it is within 2 standard deviations of the mean for healthy individuals. It is said to be high if it is between 2 and 3 standard deviations above the mean and very high if it is more than 3 standard deviations above the mean. In this case, then, there are three levels of lymphocytes in blood (the diagnostic test dimension) and three levels of possible disease status. So there are nine outcomes in the sample space.

Over 10 years, roughly 35,000 people were tested and their true disease status followed up through national medical records. The results are tabulated below.

	Normal	High	Very High	Total
Healthy	33142	507	459	34108
Lymph infection	43	226	255	524
Leukemia	8	77	296	381
Total	33193	810	1010	35013

What is the probability of someone having leukemia? Out of 35,013 people, only 381 had the disease so a sensible estimate of the probability is 381/35,013 = 1.09%. Let's convert all of the counts into proportions so that we can better see what is common and what is rare. Since this is a very large database, we would be pretty confident that these proportions are close to the actual probabilities of the difference outcomes.

	Normal	High	Very High	Total
Healthy	94.7%	1.45%	1.31%	97.4%
Lymph infection	0.12%	0.65%	0.73%	1.50%
Leukemia	0.02%	0.22%	0.85%	1.09%
Total	94.8%	2.31%	2.88%	100%

This is a rare disease. There is an old doctor's saying that "rare diseases should be diagnosed rarely." If we decide that anyone with high or very high lymphocyte levels has leukemia, then we will drastically overdiagnose this disease, since there are 2.31% + 2.88% = 5.19% or 1820 people in this category. Even if we decide that only those with very high lymphocyte levels have leukemia then we still overdiagnose the disease. This might be a good thing if we take account of the fact that it is worse to misdiagnose someone as healthy than to misdiagnose them as sick. However, there is no guarantee that those who are diagnosed sick will actually be the unfortunate patients that have leukemia.

They key question we need to answer is: "If someone has a very high blood level of lymphocytes then what is the chance that they have leukemia?" We are now asking a question about a specific subset, namely the 1,010 people who had a very high reading. This is a conditional probability and is the subject of the next topic.

3.5. Conditional Probability

Probability represents uncertainty. Uncertainty can change when you are given further information. For instance, once I say you have very high lymphocyte levels, your chance of having leukemia is presumably higher than the 1.09% baseline level.

We use the notation $\Pr(A \mid D)$ to represent the conditional probability of an event A of interest when we have been provided with data D. For instance, A could be leukemia and D could be very high lymphocyte levels. How does conditional probability relate to ordinary unconditional probability?

DEFINITION

The probability of an event A given an event D is defined to be

$$\Pr(A \mid D) = \frac{\Pr(A \cap D)}{\Pr(D)}.$$

In words, the conditional probability is the probability of both happening divided by the probability of the conditioning event D.

Why is it defined this way? There are two arguments.

The Set Diagram Visual Argument

One is based on thinking of probability as area. Imagine again that I am throwing a dart randomly at a target and that I have an equal chance of hitting any point. Conditional on the knowledge that I landed inside region D, what is the chance I hit region A? You would surely focus on the area D, which you know has happened, and then look at the shaded region as a proportion of the region D. You have done nothing else than visually estimate $\Pr(A \cap D)$ divided by $\Pr(D)$.

In this case, A is initially quite probable, maybe around 50% or a little higher. But conditional on D, the probability is much smaller. We already know we are in D, and the chance of being in the shaded region is small—perhaps around 2%.

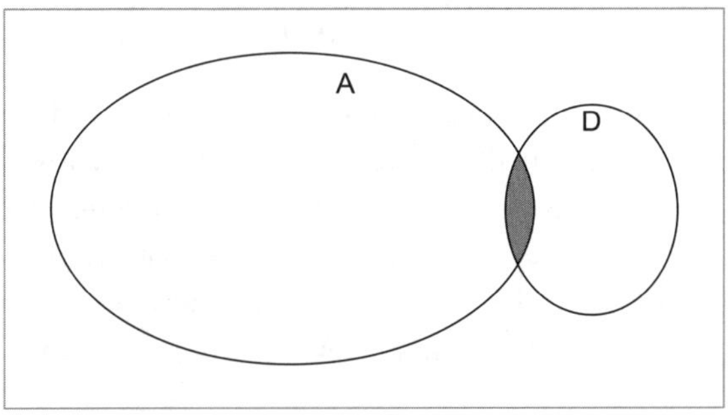

The Logical Argument

A second argument is to imagine first observing the data D and then observing whether or not A happened afterwards. The probability of observing the data D is $\Pr(D)$. The probability of the event A, after having observed D, would have to be $\Pr(A \mid D)$, since once we have actually observed D it is given. So the probability of observing D and A in sequence is

$$\Pr(D \cap A) = \Pr(D) \times \Pr(A|D).$$

Rearranging this equation we again have $\Pr(A \mid D) = \Pr(A \cap D)/\Pr(D)$, which is the formula for conditional probability.

EXAMPLE 2 (Continued) *Leukemia diagnosis*

On the basis of a large database of more than 35,000 patients, we have the table below listing the probabilities of the nine possible outcomes. We will assume from now on that patients with very high lymphocytes are diagnosed with leukemia. They would then be subject to much more expensive and invasive tests to determine their disease status, essentially without error. We will also assume that those who have only high levels are told they have an infection and given antibiotics.

	Normal	High	Very High	Total
Healthy	94.7%	1.45%	1.31%	97.4%
Lymph infection	0.12%	0.65%	0.73%	1.50%
Leukemia	0.02%	0.22%	0.85%	1.09%
Total	94.8%	2.31%	2.88%	100%

The disease of leukemia is rare with prevalence in this population of 1.09%. If we diagnose someone as having the disease when their lymphocyte level is very high then we will diagnose almost three times as many people—2.88%—with the disease. But the critical assessment we want is how likely it is that someone whose lymphocyte level is very high has the disease.

The event $D = VH$ here is testing very high. Focus on the highlighted column above. The event $A = L$ here is having leukemia. Out of the 2.88% who are very high, 0.85% has leukemia. So the conditional probability is

$$\Pr(A \mid D) = \Pr(L \mid VH) = \frac{\Pr(L \cap VH)}{\Pr(VH)} = \frac{0.85\%}{2.88\%} = 29.3\%.$$

So the patient who tests positive probably does not have the disease. This would be picked up when they are given the more invasive and expensive follow-up tests.

The chance that someone who tests positive has leukemia is 29.3%. A quite different question is: "What is the chance that someone with leukemia is picked up by this test?" It might sound similar to the previous question but it is not. This is a question more of interest to health managers, to the government, and to pharmaceutical companies. It concerns the public health issue of what proportion of disease we correctly treat. It has nothing to do with individual patients.

To answer this question, we must focus on patients who have leukemia and ask how many of them we pick up. The conditioning event $D = L$ now is leukemia and the event of interest $A = VH$ is having very high lymphocytes.

	Normal	High	Very High	Total
Healthy	94.7%	1.45%	1.31%	97.4%
Lymph infection	0.12%	0.65%	0.73%	1.50%
Leukemia	0.02%	0.22%	0.85%	1.09%
Total	94.8%	2.31%	2.88%	100%

Focus on the conditioning event—the leukemia row highlighted above. Out of the 1.09% of people with leukemia, 0.85% will be detected through very high lymphocyte levels. So the conditional probability is

$$\Pr(A \mid D) = \Pr(VH \mid L) = \frac{\Pr(VH \cap L)}{\Pr(L)} = \frac{0.85\%}{1.09\%} = 77.7\%.$$

This is a much higher probability and suggests that the test is moderately accurate. It picks up more than three-fourths of those with the disease. Why, then, is there only a 29% chance that someone who has very high lymphocytes has the disease? Largely, this is because the disease is very *rare*. Hardly any of the patients have the disease to start with. So it is not so surprising that, even after diagnostic tests suggest they have the disease, not so many turn out to actually have it.

Don't Confuse Pr(*A*|*B*) with Pr(*B*|*A*)

The probability of A given B is not the same as the probability of B given A. In terms of the formula

$$\Pr(A \mid B) = \frac{\Pr(A \cap B)}{\Pr(B)} \quad \text{while} \quad \Pr(B \mid A) = \frac{\Pr(A \cap B)}{\Pr(A)},$$

the denominator of the calculation is different. These two conditional probabilities need not be close. In extreme cases, one of them can be close to 1 and the other can be close to 0.

If you interpret them in words, there is no reason they should be the same. In words, $\Pr(A \mid B)$ answers the question, "If A happens then what is the chance B happens?" Whereas, $\Pr(B \mid A)$ answers the question, "If B happens then what is the chance A happens?"

EXAMPLE 3 *Stereotyping criminals*

The figures I am about to give you are roughly correct for the United States. The proportion of males in the population is 48.5%. (Actually, if you divide the population by age groups you find that the males are more than 50% in the younger age groups but are less in the higher age groups, as they die younger). The proportion of people who are males and have a criminal record is 1.4%. Finally, the proportion of people who are males with a criminal record is 1.3%.

What is the probability of being male given you have a criminal record? What is the probability of having a criminal record given you are male? Why are these two numbers so different? Which ones are relevant when and to whom?

Let's calculate the numbers first. Call the event of being male M and of having a criminal record C. We are told $\Pr(M) = 48.5\%$, $\Pr(C) = 1.4\%$, and $\Pr(M \cap C) = 1.3\%$. So

$$\Pr(M \mid C) = \frac{\Pr(M \cap C)}{\Pr(C)} = \frac{1.3\%}{1.4\%} = 92.8\%$$

while

$$\Pr(C \mid M) = \frac{\Pr(M \cap C)}{\Pr(M)} = \frac{1.3\%}{48.5\%} = 2.7\%.$$

The first probability tells us that most criminals are male. The second tells us that very few males are criminals. Both statements are correct. It is certainly not the case that 92.8% of males are criminals and you need not start running away from the next male you see on the street.

The figure $\Pr(M \mid C) = 92.8\%$ is relevant to public policy. If we want to reduce crime then we should focus on interventions that impact on males rather than on females. If we are trying to assess the success of such an intervention, then we would look at the crime rate among males, currently $\Pr(C \mid M) = 2.7\%$, and see if it was reducing. Of course, there are other factors that are strongly associated with crime, the most important ones being socioeconomic status and age group. But gender is one of the strongest factors.

We can construct the full probability table from the information given. The numbers that are underlined were given. Those in italics were obtained by subtraction.

	Crim	No Crim	Total
Male	<u>0.013</u>	*0.472*	<u>0.485</u>
Female	*0.001*	*0.514*	*0.515*
Total	<u>0.014</u>	*0.986*	1.000

EXAMPLE 2 (Continued) *Leukemia diagnosis*

Probabilities of disease status after the test are called **diagnostic probabilities**. They are of interest to individual patient cases. They tell us what the test says and how to use it. The probabilities of test outcomes given disease status describe the *intrinsic accuracy* of the test. They are of interest to health professionals. They tell us how well the test will work in general on different subsets of the population. Most importantly, we will be interested in how many diseased individuals we detect (called the *sensitivity* of the test in medical contexts). On the other hand, we also care about how many healthy individuals pass the test (called the *specificity* of the test in medical contexts). Our example is a little more complicated because there are three outcomes for the test and three disease groups.

It is interesting to calculate all the possible conditional probabilities—of both types—and put them in a table. It is very easy to do once the probabilities are organized into a table, and this is the main reason tables are such a convenient way of setting out the sample space. Open the file example 2(leukaemia).xls to see the formulas that are used. In each case, you only need to type the formula into the top left cell and then drag across the whole table, using the $ symbol appropriately.

To calculate the diagnostic probabilities, divide each value in the table by the column total. (You need a dollar sign before the row number in the denominator of the Excel formula).

	Normal	High	Very High	Overall
Healthy	**99.8%**	62.6%	45.4%	97.4%
Lymph infection	0.1%	**27.9%**	25.2%	1.50%
Leukemia	0.0%	9.5%	**29.3%**	1.09%
Total	100%	100%	100%	100%

We can see from this that

- If you have normal lymphocytes then there is a 99.8% chance that you are healthy.
- If you have high lymphocytes then you are still probably healthy. There is a 27.9% chance you have an infection and a 9.5% chance of leukemia.
- If you have very high lymphocytes then you may well be healthy (45.4%). There is a roughly equal chance that your have either an infection or leukemia.

To calculate the probabilities that are of interest to health professionals—those of the test results giving the true disease status—divide each value in the table by the row total. (You need a dollar sign before the column letter in the denominator of Excel formula). The results are below.

	Normal	High	Very High	Total
Healthy	**97.2%**	1.5%	1.3%	100%
Lymph infection	8.2%	**43.1%**	48.7%	100%
Leukemia	2.1%	20.2%	**77.7%**	100%
Overall	94.8%	2.31%	2.88%	100%

It looks like the infection is the most poorly diagnosed—of those with a lymph infection, we only correctly diagnosed 43.1%. However, 43.1% + 48.7% = 91.8%

are diagnosed as having some disease, and those misdiagnosed with leukemia will get corrected later with the more invasive and expensive test.

CHECK YOUR UNDERSTANDING

Q7. Draw a set diagram to demonstrate that $\Pr(A \mid B)$ is not the same as $\Pr(B \mid A)$.

- In your diagram, try to arrange for $\Pr(A \mid B)$ to be a large probability but $\Pr(B \mid A)$ to be a small probability.
- Suggest some real-world examples where this might be the case.

Q8. In the leukemia diagnosis example, suppose that we decide to provisionally diagnose someone with leukemia if their reading is "high or very high." In the previous discussion, we were only diagnosing someone with leukemia if they were very high.

- What is the probability that someone with leukemia will be correctly diagnosed?
- What is the probability that someone who does not have leukemia will be correctly diagnosed?
- You walk into a doctor's surgery and have above-normal lymphocyte levels (i.e., high or very high). You are diagnosed with leukemia. How worried should you be?

Q9. Suppose that a certain company has a work force, 57% of whom are males and that one-third of whom exercise at lunchtime. Overall, 22% of employees exercise during lunchtime.

- What proportion of females exercise at lunchtime?
- What proportion of those who exercise are male?

3.6. HOW STRONG IS THE RELATIONSHIP? MEASURING DEPENDENCE

> If one of these holds, the other will also. There is no need to check both.

In the leukemia example, we saw that the chance of an untested individual having leukemia was 1.09%, but this chance increased to 29.3% if someone returned a very high lymphocyte level. This is an example of a positive relationship between two events. When the event *VH* happens, it increases the chance of *L*. In symbols, $\Pr(L \mid VH)$ is larger than $\Pr(L)$.

DEFINITION

Two events A and B are **positively dependent** or associated if knowing one event occurred increases the chance that the other occurs. You can check whether two events are positively dependent by checking either that $\Pr(A|B) > \Pr(A)$ or that $\Pr(B|A) > \Pr(B)$.

Negative dependence means that knowing one event occurred decreases the chance of the other. You test this by seeing if the conditional probability is *smaller than* the unconditional probability.

With the leukemia example above, L and VH are positively related since $\Pr(L|VH)$ is greater than $\Pr(L)$. It increases from 1.09% to 29.3%. You could also look at the issue of dependence of L and VH by seeing how having leukemia increases the chances of very high lymphocytes. If we did not know a person's disease status then the chance of a very high lymphocyte level is 2.88%. However, if we know that a person has leukemia then this increases to 77.7%. So $\Pr(VH|L) = 77.7\%$ is much larger than $\Pr(VH) = 2.88\%$.

EXAMPLE 1 (Continued) *Car seat covers*

Recall that in this example there was a survey of 577 people who were asked the highest price they would pay for a car seat cover.

	$99	$89	<$89	All
Females	10.6%	16.0%	11.4%	38.0%
Males	26.7%	18.0%	17.4%	62.0%
All	37.3%	33.9%	28.8%	100.0%

To see which events are related to which and how, we can calculate all possible conditional probabilities in a table. Dividing by row totals gives the probabilities of different price segments conditional on gender.

	$99	$89	<$89	All
Females	27.9%	42.0%	30.1%	100.0%
Males	43.0%	29.1%	27.9%	100.0%
All	37.3%	34.0%	28.8%	100.0%

We immediately see that males are more likely than females to be in the highest price group. Formally we can say that the chance of being in the $99 group increases from 37.3% to 43.0% when you are a male. In symbols, $\Pr(\$99 \mid M) = 43.0\%$ is higher than $\Pr(\$99) = 37.3\%$. So these events are positively related.

One would hope that the \$99 event is then negatively related with being female. Indeed, since Pr(\$99 | *F*) = 27.9% is less than Pr(\$99) = 37.3%, this is the case.

We could also look at the reverse conditional probabilities of gender given the price segment. These are obtained by dividing the original table of probabilities by their column totals. The columns below now describe the gender distribution within each pricing group.

	\$99	\$89	<\$89	All
Females	28.4%	46.9%	39.8%	38.0%
Males	71.6%	53.1%	60.2%	62.0%
All	100.0%	100.0%	100.0%	100.0%

We can see that males are a high proportion of the \$99 group. But this does not tell us much by itself because most of the sample were male anyway—62%. It is the fact that Pr(*M*| \$99) = 71.6% is greater than Pr(*M*) = 62%, which tells us that the events *M* and \$99 are positively related—confirming our earlier conclusion. There is a negative relationship between the events \$99 and *F* because Pr(\$99 | *F*) = 29.4% is less than Pr(*F*) = 38.0%.

All these calculations are in the file example 1 (carseats).xls.

A Measure of Dependence

Here is a sensible way to measure how strongly two events are related. Think about the example above where we saw being male, *M*, was positively related to being in the \$99 group. If you told this to your boss he or she would no doubt want to know how strong the effect was. He or she might ask, "How much more likely is it that a \$99 customer will be a male?" We saw that the chance of being male increases from 62% to 71.6%—a factor increase of 1.154. This is the measure of dependence that I recommend—the factor by which the probability of one event increases or decreases when you are told the other event.

In symbols the recommended measure is the ratio

$$r = \frac{\Pr(A \mid B)}{\Pr(A)}.$$

When the ratio is greater than 1, the two events are positively related and ***r*** measures how strong this dependence is. If the ratio is less than 1, the two events are negatively related and r measures how strong this negative dependence is.

You might wonder whether we could get a different answer for the ratio r if we instead look at the ratio of $\Pr(B|A)$ to $\Pr(B)$. In fact, you get exactly the same answer using $r = \Pr(B|A)/\Pr(B)$. For instance, in the car seat cover example, the overall chance of being in the \$99 group was Pr(\$99) = 37.3% and this increases to Pr(\$99 | *M*) = 43.0% when you know someone is male. The ratio is 43.0:37.3, which is 1.154—the same answer we obtained before.

There is a third formula for the dependence measure *r*, which is probably the most simple to use if you have not already calculated all the conditional probabilities. The general formula is

$$r = \frac{\Pr(A \cap B)}{\Pr(A) \times \Pr(B)}.$$

EXAMPLE 1 (Continued) *Car seat covers*

Let's see how this formula works. The original probability table is reproduced again below. The probability of being male *and* in the \$99 group is 26.7%. Divide this by the marginal probability of being male (62%) and by the marginal probability of being in the \$99 group (37.3%). The answer is

$$r = \frac{\Pr(M \cap \$99)}{\Pr(M) \times \Pr(\$99)} = \frac{0.267}{0.62 \times 0.373} = 1.154.$$

	\$99	\$89	<\$89	All
Females	10.6%	16.0%	11.4%	38.0%
Males	26.7%	18.0%	17.4%	62.0%
All	37.3%	33.9%	28.8%	100.0%

This makes the calculation pretty easy—just look at any cell and divide it by its corresponding row and column total. And you do not need to even think about which event is being conditioned on at all. After you have calculated the number 1.154 you can immediately say, "The chance of being male is a factor 1.154 higher if you are a \$99 customer" and also "The chance of being a \$99 customer is a factor 1.154 higher if you are a male."

Independence

If the probability of one event increases or decreases when the other event happens then the events are positively or negatively related, respectively. What if the probability stays the same? In other words, what if the dependence ratio $r = 1$?

In this case we say the events are **independent**. From a probability point of view, events being independent means that if I tell you one event happens, then it does not affect at all the chance of the other event happening.

When two events are independent, then

$$\Pr(A \cap B) = \Pr(A) \times \Pr(B).$$

Many people mistakenly assume that this is true for all events. They assume that the chance of two things both happening is the chance of one thing times the chance of the other. This is certainly not true in general. If the events are independent then it is.

EXAMPLE 1 (Continued) *Car seat covers*

In the table below, I calculated the dependence ratio for each of the six possible pairs of events we might consider. This is quite easy to do if you know how to use the $ sign in Excel. You should check the formula that I used in example 2(leukemia).xls. I have also put the marginal probabilities in the table. The table tells you about both gender and price group as well as how these factors affect each other.

	$99	$89	<$89	All
Females	0.748	1.237	1.048	38.0%
Males	1.154	0.855	0.971	62.0%
All	37.3%	34.0%	28.8%	100%

None of the events are exactly independent because none of the ratios is exactly 1.0. However, the <$89 event is almost independent of gender. It has a very slight positive association with being Female (r = 1.048) and a very slight negative association with being male(r = 0.971). However, the original count in the female <$89 cell was 66. If this had instead been 63 then the ratio would be 1.000. So we might easily argue that the ratio r = 1.048 is close enough to 1 as we could reasonably expect real data to be. Gender and the <$89 event are practically independent.

This means that low-paying customers are no different in their gender split than general customers. They would hardly differ from the 62/38 split of all customers. Conversely, males are no more or less likely than females to be low paying. The proportion in the low-paying group would be close to 28.8% for both genders.

The strongest association is $89 and female. In general, 34% of customers are in this group, but females are 1.237 times as likely to be in this group and males are 0.855 times as likely.

Some Simple Rules of Dependence

In the previous example we saw that the measure of dependence for females and $89 was 1.237, indicating a positive relationship. The dependence of males and $89 was 0.855, indicating a negative relationship. You might expect that if being male is positively associated with something, then being female must be negatively associated with the same thing. This is indeed the case. Using the number r to measure whether two sets are positively or negatively related, one can prove the following common sense properties.

If A is positively related to B, then

1. A is negatively related to $\bar{B}$
2. $\bar{A}$ is negatively related to B
3. $\bar{A}$ is positively related to $\bar{B}$

If A is negatively related to B, then

1. A is positively related to $\bar{B}$
2. $\bar{A}$ is positively related to B
3. $\bar{A}$ is negatively related to $\bar{B}$

3.7. PROBABILITY TREES

Many problems involve sequential or contingent elements. For instance, a medical test on a person may have several different results. These results may indicate any of several possible disease states. Each disease state will have its own prognosis.

It is sometimes helpful to set out all possible outcomes as a so-called **tree**. A table of possible outcomes would not be as convenient because it would not display the connections of events.

How is a tree constructed? You start with a **node** at the left. This represents the first logical step or element in the story. You draw branches from the node for each possible outcome of this step. At the end of these branches you add other nodes and branches if there are further steps in the problem. And you can add further nodes and branches to these as well.

A Generic Tree

For instance, in the tree below there are three possible outcomes at the first step. If outcome A happens there are no further steps. If outcome B happens there is another step with four possible outcomes, labeled D, E, F, and G. If outcome C happens there is another step with two possible outcomes, D or H, one of which was also a possibility from the B node. There is a third step from nodes E to G, and in both cases the same possible outcomes, I or J, can happen.

Probabilities are assigned to each branch, though I have not done so in the diagram. These are conditional probabilities of following that branch, given you get to the previous node. These probabilities necessarily add to 100% across all branches leaving a node. Looking at the tree below, we will finally end up at A, D, F, I, or J. The probabilities on the branches determine how likely these different final outcomes are.

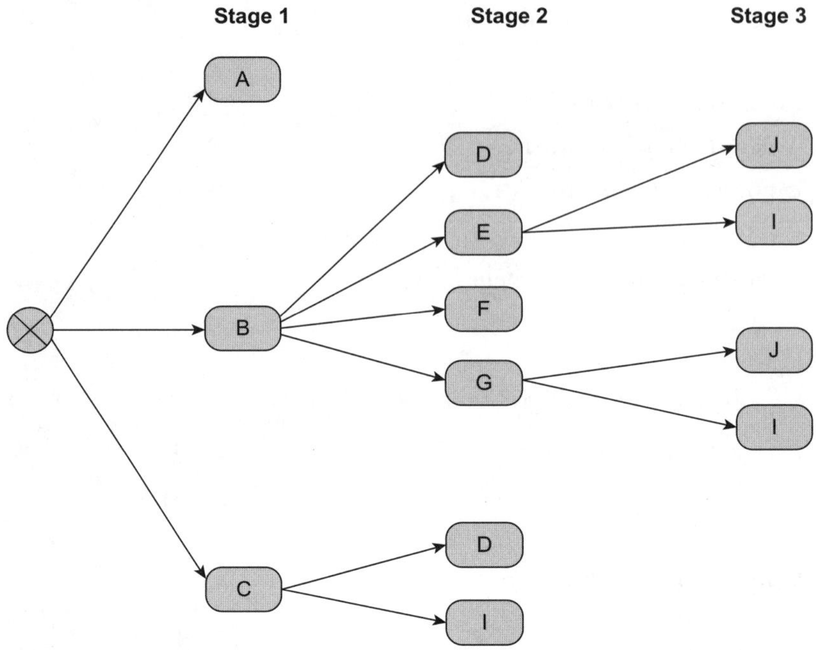

EXAMPLE 2 (Continued) *Leukemia diagnosis*

For the example involving diagnosing leukemia from a test of lymphocyte levels, we imagine three steps of a patient story. At the first step, the lymphocyte levels are tested and there is one of three outcomes. On the basis of the outcome, the patient is said to have leukemia if the test is very high, and declared healthy otherwise. These outcomes are not displayed on the tree. They follow logically from the test so there is no need to show them. If the patient is on the very high branch then they are immediately tested with a definitive test and their disease status established. If the patient is on the normal or high branch then their disease status will not be determined until much later with follow-up studies. A third element has also been added to the story, namely the prognosis of the patient if leukemia is detected.

The tree is displayed below and one of the final nodes has been highlighted. This represents a patient who tested high (and was presumably declared healthy), but subsequently was found to have leukemia, which was untreatable (perhaps because of the delay in diagnosis).

To complete the tree into a probability tree we need to assign numbers to each branch. These numbers should be the probability of the event just to the right, conditional on all the events leading to it (on the left).

The probabilities at the first node are the probabilities of testing normal, high, or very high. These were determined from the data. All other probabilities are conditional on the earlier nodes. For instance, following the high path, the probabilities (62.6%, 27.9%, and 9.5%) of the different disease outcomes conditional on a normal test were calculated earlier. The rest of the figures are also conditional probabilities that were calculated earlier.

Finally, we might suppose that those who test very high are declared to have leukemia and, of those who do have the disease, are detected earlier than they otherwise may have been. So, we might expect that their prognosis is better than those who pass the test (on the normal and high branches) and whose disease progressed further before being diagnosed. We suppose that there is a 70% chance of being treatable on the early-detection-very-high arm and a 50% chance of being treatable on the other arms.

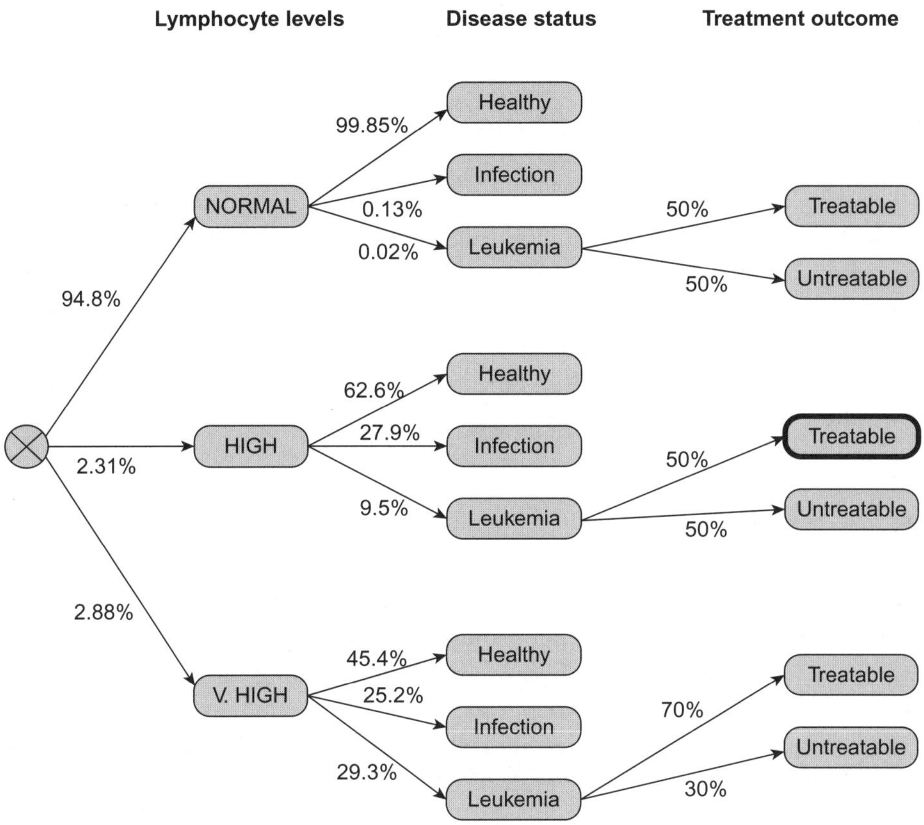

We can now use the tree to make some probability calculations. Each probability in the tree is the chance of progressing to the next node, conditional on the previous boxes. Therefore, to calculate the probability of any node, you simply multiply all the probabilities of the branches leading to it.

What proportion of people end up having *treatable leukemia*? The three nodes labeled "Treatable" correspond to three different patient histories, but all ending in terminal diagnosis. The first one on the normal branch has a path probability of 94.8% × 0.02% × 50%, which is 0.014%. For the next (highlighted) treatable node you get 0.110%, and for the last treatable mode on the very high (V. High) branch you get 0.592%. The total of these three is 0.713%—less than 1% of the population.

What proportion of those who test "Very High" are ultimately untreatable? This is now a question conditional on testing "Very High." So we confine attention to that part of the tree beginning with the node labeled "Very High." The probability of being untreatable is

$$0.293 \times 0.3 = 0.0879.$$

In the same manner the probability of being untreatable conditional on testing "High" is

$$0.095 \times 0.50 = 0.0475.$$

CHECK YOUR UNDERSTANDING

Q10. You have quoted \$3000 per day for a consulting job. There is a 70% chance the client will be satisfied with this and sign the contract. If the job is a simple one then there is a 90% chance you will be able to successfully complete it yourself. In this case there is an 80% chance the client will be satisfied. From the job description there is a 20% chance you may need an outside expert for this job. The expert will be able to solve the problem in 60% of cases. In this case there is again an 80% chance the client will be satisfied.

3.8. SUMMARY

Framework The first step in any problem involving probability is to understand and then represent the sample space—the set of all possible outcomes. An event is any subset of the sample space. Events are combined using set operations of union ($\cup$) and intersection ($\cap$) of sets.

The sample space can be represented in many ways, including set diagrams, tables, or a probability tree.

Probabilities Represent the chance of something happening—on a 0–1 scale. Probabilities must add up to 1 over the sample space. They can be represented as the area in a set diagram. In business applications, the numbers typically come from historical data or from expert judgment about the event in question.

Conditional Probability These describe the chance of an event A when you have available relevant data D. For instance, if I tell you that your product has been favorably assessed by a market research firm, then the chance of it succeeding is presumably higher. They are calculated by confining attention to the conditioning event and by dividing all probabilities by that of the conditioning event. In symbols,

$$\Pr(A \mid D) = \frac{\Pr(A \cap D)}{\Pr(D)}.$$

Probability Tables When there are two characteristics of interest, the sample space is usefully represented as a table. In this case, you just put the probabilities in the cells.

For probability tables, conditional probabilities are calculated by confining attention to the row or column implied by the conditioning and dividing all probabilities in that row or column by their total.

Probability Trees Problems that involve sequential or contingent elements can often be usefully represented as a tree. Each node represents an event. All possible events contingent on an earlier event are connected by branches.

Each branch is labeled with the conditional probability that the right node occurs given that you arrived at the left node. Unconditional probabilities are obtained by multiplying probabilities along the branches leading to a node.

Dependence Events are **positively dependent** if one event happening *increases* the chance of the other event happening. Events are **negatively dependent** if one event happening decreases the chance of the other event happening. The degree of dependence between two events is measured by

$$r = \frac{\Pr(A \cap B)}{\Pr(A) \times \Pr(B)}.$$

If $r > 1$ they are positively related, and if $r < 1$ they are negatively related. If $r = 1$ they are **independent**.

Independence Independent events are events which do not affect each other in terms of probability. If I tell you one event happened, then this does not alter the chance of the other event happening. Usually, but not always, independent events are logically or physically independent.

If A and B are independent then the probability both A and B happening (their intersection) is the probability of one happening *times* the probability of the other happening. This is *not* true for dependent events.

EXERCISES

E1. Suppose that 18% of employees of a given corporation engage in physical exercise during the lunch hour. Moreover, assume that 57% of all employees are male and 12% of all employees are males who engage in physical exercise during the lunch hour.

(a) If we choose an employee at random from this corporation, then what is the probability that this person is a female who engages in physical exercise during the lunch hour?

(b) If we choose an employee at random from this corporation, then what is the probability that this person is a female who does not engage in physical exercise during the lunch hour?

(c) What proportion of female employees engage in physical exercise during the lunch hour?

(d) What proportion of employees who engage in physical exercise during the lunch hour is male?

E2. The data in worksh eet Q2 describe a survey of 1200 randomly chosen potential customers and lists probability distribution (estimated from the survey) of the number of weekly exposures to a TV advertising campaign. The ad is shown several times each weekday but many potential customers do not see the advertisement because it is shown during working hours. The number of exposures to your TV advertisement is inferred from knowing what times they were watching the TV.

Make sure that you understand how to use Excel to count up how many of the 1200 viewed the advertisement 0 times, 1 time, 2 times, and so on. I have converted these into proportions, which may be interpreted as probabilities. To answer the questions below, you can forget about the original source data and just treat the table below representing the probabilities of the different numbers of exposures.

Exposures	0	1	2	3	4	5
Probability	0.47	0.19	0.15	0.11	0.05	0.02

(a) What is the probability of seeing the ad six (or more) times?
(b) Produce a plot displaying the probability distribution with probabilities on the vertical axis and the number of exposures on the horizontal axis.
(c) What is the probability of seeing the ad at all?
(d) Given that a customer sees the ad, what is the probability that they see it more than four times?
(e) Out of the 100 customers, how many total viewings of the ad would you expect? (You may assume that a customer who views the ad more than five times will view it exactly six times). Therefore, *what is the expected number of viewings per customer?*

E3. A local beer producer sells two types of beer, a regular brand and a light brand with 30% fewer calories. The company's marketing department wants to verify that its traditional approach of appealing to white-collar workers with light beer commercials and blue-collar workers with regular beer commercials is indeed a good strategy. A randomly selected group of 400 local workers are questioned about their beer drinking preferences, and the data shown in the table below are obtained.

Preference	Light	None	Regular	Total
Blue Collar	111	17	122	250
White Collar	79	12	59	150
Grand Total	190	29	181	400

(a) From the data in worksheet Q3, use Pivotables to obtain the data in the table.
(b) Given that a worker likes beer at all, what proportion prefers light beer?
(c) What is the probability that a worker prefers regular beer, given that he is a blue-collar worker who likes beer?
(d) What is the probability that a worker prefers light beer, given that he is a white-collar worker who likes beer?
(e) What proportion of workers in the sample are white-collar workers or do not like beer at all?

E4. A manufacturer produces integrated circuit chips. Over the long run the fraction of bad chips produced by the manufacturing process is around 20%. Thorough testing is expensive but there is a cheap test. All good chips pass the cheap test but so do 10% of bad chips.

(a) Given that a chip passes the test, what is the probability that it is a good chip?
(b) If a company sold all chips that passed the test, what fraction of what they sold would be bad?

E5. Imagine you have data on your clients over the past 3 years. It is standard to survey clients at completion of the job and for simplicity this has been reduced to a two-point scale, namely "Satisfied" or "Unsatisfied."

	Further	Pay	Withhold
Satisfied	0.211	0.428	0.041
Unsatisfied	0.042	0.163	0.115

There are three business outcomes you are interested in. First, the client asks for further work and extends the job (and pays more money); second, the client accepts the job and pays; or third, the client withholds payment for the job. We will take the numbers in the table to represent the true probabilities of the events, though they are really proportions extracted from the 3-year database.
(a) What is the probability that a client is satisfied?
(b) Given that a client asks for further work, what is the probability that he or she is satisfied?
(c) Given that a client is unsatisfied, what is the probability *that he or she withholds payment?*

E6. You are trying to assess the effectiveness of an advertising campaign for a product that is bought by 20% of people. A survey shows that 40% of people recognize your advertisement, while 12% of people both recognize your advertisement and buy your product.
(a) Does seeing the advertisement increase the probability of purchasing?
For another advertisement, 30% of people recognize it while 10% both recognize it and buy the product.
(b) Which of the two ads seems to be the most effective?

E7. You conducted a survey of 1000 people and asked them about their attitude to your product. There are three possible responses: negative, neutral, and positive. The data are in the table below. It is important to know that the equal numbers of males and females were chosen by survey design. From background knowledge you know that only 15% of your customers are male.

	Negative	Neutral	Positive	Total
Male	141	247	112	500
Female	168	177	155	500
Total	309	424	267	1000

(a) What proportion of males is positive?
(b) What proportion of customers overall is positive?
(c) Given that a customer is positive, what is the chance they are male?

E8. "Domestic violence is the single most likely cause of death for women under the age of 45." How might this statistic be manipulated? Is this statistic relevant to the question? What is the question anyway? What other statistics might you quote?

E9. You have surveyed a random sample of 1000 drivers and have classified them according to two characteristics: (1) their gender and (2) their self-reported use of the car horn in answer to the question "How many times have you used your car horn in anger over the past week?" You can estimate the probability of each possible outcome by dividing the frequency by 1000.

	0	1	2	3	4	>4
Females	81	89	45	13	3	2
Males	11	55	129	181	178	213

(a) What is the marginal distribution of car horn use? How would you describe overall car horn use in words?
(b) What is the marginal distribution of gender?
(c) Calculate the probability of using your horn 0, 1, 2, 3, 4, or >4 times conditional on being a male and compare this with the set of numbers for females. Try and describe the difference in words.
(d) Given that someone used their horn 0 times, what is the probability they are male? Given that someone used their horn >4 times, what is the probability they are male?
(e) Are any events close to independent?

E10. This is a purely theoretical question for those more comfortable with algebra.

(a) Two events A and B are mutually exclusive. Could they also be independent?
(b) Two events C and D are such that C is contained in D. Are they mutually exclusive or independent?

Consider two events A and D. What can you conclude about $\Pr(A \mid D)$ if

(c) A and D are mutually exclusive?
(d) $D \subset A$?
(e) $A \subset D$?

E11. You meet a woman for the first time and you ask her if she has any children.

"Two," she replies. "Do you have any daughters?" you ask. "Yes," she replies.

(a) What is the probability that she has two daughters?
(b) How might this answer change if she had instead replied, "Yes. My youngest is a daughter."

E12. Refer to the probability tree for leukemia in the text.

(a) What is the probability that someone gets leukemia?
(b) If someone tests high, what is the chance they have treatable leukemia?

CHAPTER 4

Let the Data Change Your Views: The Bayes Method

4.0. Introduction: What Is the Issue?

Most business outcomes are unpredictable and yet we often have to make a decision that depends on that outcome. To do so systematically and objectively, we need to describe the uncertainty of the outcome with probabilities. For instance, we may judge that a new product has a 50% chance of succeeding. But this 50% is not set in stone. It may change if we obtain further information. For instance, if the product receives a positive market test, or if the main competing product is recalled or if the economy hits a sudden boom, then the probability of success should surely be revised to a value higher than 50%.

There is a systematic method for updating a probability to reflect new data of this kind. It is called the Bayes method and is very easy to implement. To apply it, you need some extra probabilities relating the data to the business outcome. These may not always be easily available but if you are going to do anything better than guess the chance of business success, you will need to obtain or estimate these probabilities.

Data-Driven Business Decisions, First Edition. Chris J. Lloyd.

TITAN MINERAL EXPLORATION: CASE BRIEFING

Titan Resources is searching for sites with minable levels of titanium. From rough geological and satellite data they can narrow the field of likely sites greatly but even among these more promising sites it is estimated that no more than 1 in 500 will be minable. To test a site, a core sample is taken and analyzed. It is known from previous data that the core sample analysis is very accurate—it will usually correctly reveal whether or not a site is minable.

Specifically, for minable sites the core sample will be positive with probability 0.95 while for unminable sites the core sample will be negative with probability 0.98. You have just tested a site and found that the core sample indicates that it is minable. Should you bring out the test mining equipment?

As explained in the full case, the figures 1 in 500, 0.95, and 0.98 could all vary from site to site, so it is worthwhile to be able to generalize the calculation.

4.1. The Bayes Method in Pictures

> In this context the data are an event such as "the product had a positive market test." It is not just data in the general sense.

Many problems involve predicting which of several possible states of the world will come to pass. Often there may be just two states—success or failure, for instance—but there can easily be more than two; for instance, a Master's in Business Administration student grade for a particular course might end up being H1, H2A, H2B, H3, or pass. Halfway through the course you will have a better idea than at the beginning but you will not be able to say for sure. Bayes is a method for calculating the chances of the different states after having observed or becoming aware of some relevant data.

Before giving the algorithm, it may be useful to see a graphic representation of the various quantities involved. There is no need to draw a diagram in practice—it is just a visual device for helping you to initially understand what the Bayes method does. It is also a good review of probability and conditional probability.

> The probability of the states must always add up to 100%.

We denote possible states of the world by S1, S2, S3, S4 … In the diagram below we imagine that there are four possible states that might come to pass. The states are typically business or performance outcomes. In the diagram, S1 is the least likely state and S4 is the most likely state. Roughly the probabilities of these states are 5%, 15%, 20%, and 60%. In other words, if you were forced to predict which state of the world will come to pass you would guess S4 and be fairly confident (60%) that you will be correct. You would be very confident that S1 will not come to pass. These are called prior probabilities because they give the chance of the states prior to observing relevant data *D*.

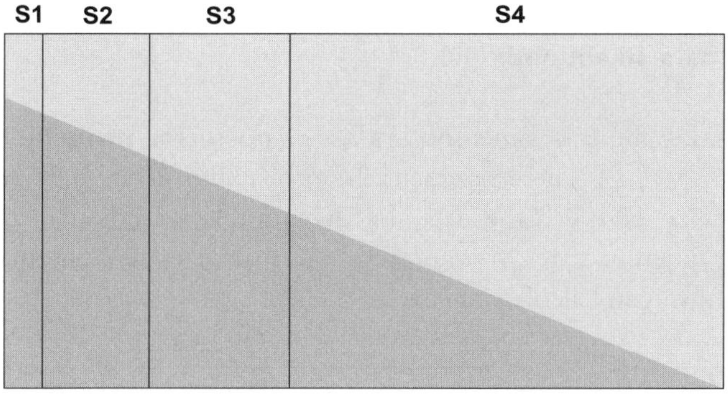

We now observe some relevant data *D*, represented by the darker section. The chance of the four states should now be considered conditional on *D*. To see this visually, just confine your attention to the darker region *D* and judge the areas of the four states as proportions of this dark region. It looks like S2, S3, and S4 are roughly equally likely while S1 is much less likely than these other three. Just by estimating the relative proportions by eye, we might judge that the probabilities of the four states S1, S2, S3, and S4 are roughly 10%, 30%, 30%, and 30%, respectively. The extra information *D* made S4 less likely (it dropped from 60% to 30%) and the other states more likely than they were before.

In order to perform the Bayes calculation you need to know the chance of seeing the data *D* conditional on the different states. In our diagram, these can be estimated visually from looking at each state (i.e., each vertical rectangular region) and judging what proportion of each vertical strip is dark. For instance, if the true state of the world is S1, then it is quite likely we would observe *D*—perhaps around 70%. For S2 and S3 the probabilities are around 65% and 55%, respectively. On the other hand, if the true state of the world is S4, then it is quite unlikely we would observe *D*—perhaps around 15%.

The Bayes method is a way of converting the 70%, 65%, 55%, and 15% figures into the 10%, 30%, 30%, and 30% figures, respectively. It is a general method for reversing conditional probabilities—in this case from the probability of the data given to the probability of the states given the data.

4.2. THE BAYES METHOD AS AN ALGORITHM

To use the Bayes method you need the following ingredients. Not every business problem will be in the right form to use the Bayes method:

Key Ingredient 1 A list of possible states of the world.

Key Ingredient 2 A list of values for Pr(*S*1), Pr(*S*2), Pr(*S*3), ... giving the probability of the different states before seeing the data. These are called **prior probabilities**.

Key Ingredient 3 A list of values for Pr(D | S1), Pr(D | S2), Pr(D | S3), ... These are called **data likelihoods** (DLs).

The result of using the Bayes method is a list of **posterior probabilities** Pr(S1 | D), Pr(S2 | D), Pr(S3 | D), ... These represent the probability of the different states of the world, after having observed the data, and having taken account of the prior probabilities of the different states. The posterior probabilities will automatically add up to 1. Here is how you calculate them.

1. For each state of the world multiply Pr(S) by Pr(D|S).
2. Calculate the total of the values in step 1.
3. Divide the values in step 1 by the value in step 2. These are the posterior probabilities.

For instance in the earlier diagrammatic example we had four states, S1–S4. The prior probabilities were 5%, 15%, 20%, and 60%. The DLs were 70%, 65%, 55%, and 15%. The calculation is set out in a table below. In the left column I list the states. In the second and third columns are the prior probabilities and the DLs. The rest of the table is generated from the algorithm.

The column labeled "Product" is obtained by multiplying each prior probability by each DL—step 1. The product column is then summed to obtain the answer 0.3325—step 2. Then each number in the product column is divided by their total and the answer listed in the fifth column—step 3. We have now calculated that the chances of the four states S1–S4 are 10.5%, 29.3%, 33.1%, and 27.1%, respectively, which is quite close to the 10%, 30%, 30%, and 30% that we earlier estimated by eye.

Don't bother adding up the DLs. Their total does not mean anything. They certainly do not add up to 100%.

State	Prior	DL	Product	Posterior
S1	0.05	0.70	0.035	0.105
S2	0.15	0.65	0.0975	0.293
S3	0.2	0.55	0.11	0.331
S4	0.6	0.15	0.09	0.271
Total	1		0.3325	1

This algorithm is very easy to automate in an Excel template, which is provided for you as the file bayes_template.xls. To use this template you simply type in the names of your states (you can just call them S1, S2, etc. if you like), then the prior probabilities and then the DLs. The posterior will be displayed as soon as you have entered all the information—but not before. This template also allows you to associate monetary payoffs with each state, but we will not think about this much until next chapter.

Does the total of the product column (0.3325) mean anything? Yes. It is equal to the *marginal* probability of the data; in other words, the probability of the data taking into account your not knowing what the state of the world is. Depending on the particular example, this number may or may not be of any interest. Usually, the primary output of the Bayes method is the posterior column, which tells us how likely the states are after having seen the data D.

The example is completely artificial. How do these ideas map to a generic business problem? The states are nearly always business or performance outcomes that you want to predict—for instance, the site is or is not minable, the accused is guilty or innocent, or this insuree will be a low, medium, or high claimer. There should be a small finite number of states.

To set prior probabilities, you must have some idea of how likely the different states are to begin with. These may be subjective or they could be based on historical data or a combination of both. If you really have no idea how likely the states are then you cannot use Bayes (and you are in a fair bit of trouble businesswise). The prior probabilities must add up to 100%.

The DLs are conditional probabilities of the data. They tell us how likely the data would be supposing different states of the world. So we know under which states of the world the observed data are likely and under which states they are unlikely. These numbers are not of any intrinsic interest themselves. Why? Because we actually observe the data D! Why would you want to know the probability of something after it was observed? For its own sake you wouldn't. But the numbers help you to calculate the probabilities of the states given the data—which *are* of intrinsic interest because we don't know which state of the world occurs and we want to deal with the uncertainty probabilistically.

4.3. Example 1: A Simple Gambling Game

You might think gambling has nothing to do with business. You would be wrong on several counts. First, gambling itself is big business, and if you run a casino you had better get the odds right. Second, most business decisions are gambles in the sense that success is not guaranteed and the chance of failure needs to be weighed against the costs of losing and the payoff of winning. This sounds like gambling to me! Third, gambling games are good first examples for students because the probabilities involved are objectively easy to understand and believe. Rather than thinking where the probabilities come from, you can instead focus on the methodology.

Here is a gambling game. There are two fair dice put into an urn and an additional very biased die—three dice in all. The biased die actually has all numbers equal to six. All players have this information. The croupier selects a die at random from the urn. The chosen die cannot be seen by the players and they have no way of knowing if it is a fair or biased die. The croupier throws the selected die and announces the result. She announces the result, "It is a six." The croupier then prepares to throw this same die a second time and you are invited to bet on the result of this second throw. Here are some questions whose answers might help you to place an informed bet: *How likely is it that another 6 will come up on the next throw? How about the numbers 1–5? How likely is it that an even number will come up?*

How does Bayes apply? Think about it this way. Sitting as the bettor considering placing a wager on the second toss, what is the unknown state of the world that you would most like to know but do not? Clearly it is the *type of die* that the croupier selected. So there are *two states* of the world: the selected die is fair (S1) or it is an "all-six" die (S2). From the description of how the die is selected, it is clear that the chance of the die being fair is two-thirds, provided that it really was selected at random from the urn. So our two states, S1 and S2, have *prior probabilities*, two-thirds and one-third, respectively.

What is the data *D*? Ask yourself, what information do you have that is relevant to assessing what kind of die it is? Clearly the (only) data you have is the result of the first toss—a six. And you would think that this makes it more likely to be a biased die, since this is the value that the biased die always gives. The chance of the die being biased is now surely larger than one-third, but we will need to use the Bayes method to find out how much more likely.

Why will the Bayes method help me? Because I want to know the chances of the die being fair or "all six." And Bayes gives me exactly this—the probability of the states given the data, that is, the chances of the die being fair or not, after having seen the result of a 6 on the first throw. Once I know how likely it is that the die is fair or biased, I can work out the chances of different numbers on the second throw and decide whether or not to bet.

To apply the algorithm we need the DL numbers. These are the probability of the data *D* given the different possible states, that is, $\Pr(D|S1)$ and $\Pr(D|S2)$. If there is any step in the Bayes method that you may sometimes get confused about, it will be getting the DL values.

Now $\Pr(D|S1)$ is the probability of getting a 6 if the die is fair. The answer is obviously 1/6. Whereas, $\Pr(D|S2)$ is the probability of getting a 6 if the die is an "all-six" die. The answer is obviously 1. These are the two DL values we need and the overall Bayes table looks like the one below.

State	Prior	DL(6)	Product	Posterior
All-6 die	0.333	1.00	0.333	0.750
Fair die	0.667	0.167	0.111	0.250
			0.444	

You can check the formulas in example1 (gambling).xls. The product and posterior columns are the result of applying the Bayes algorithm. The result is that there is a 75% chance that the die is an "all-six" die. Before we saw the data of a "6" there was only a one-third chance the die was biased. Now there is a three-fourth chance. It makes sense that the chance of the die being biased should go up.

How likely is it that another 6 will come up on the next throw? We are now in a position to work this out. If the die is fair (a 25% chance), then there is a one-sixth chance of a 6, whereas if the die is an "all-six" die (a 75% chance) there is a 100% chance of a 6. So the overall chance of a 6 is

$$0.25 \times (1/6) + 0.75 \times 1 = 0.7917$$

There is an almost 80% chance of a 6.

How about the numbers 1–5? We can work out the chance of getting a 1 in a very similar manner to how we worked out the chance of getting a 6. If the die is fair (a 25% chance) then there is a one-sixth chance of a 1 whereas if the die is an all-six die (a 75% chance) there is no chance of a 1. So the overall chance of a 1 is

$$0.25 \times (1/6) + 0.75 \times 0 = 0.0417$$

and the calculation is exactly the same for 2, 3, 4, and 5. One could get this answer more quickly. Since probabilities must add up to 100% and since the outcomes 1–5 are equal likely, the 79.17% chance of a 6 means that the chance of any other number is (100% – 79.17%)/5, which is 4.17%. However we get there, the overall list of possible outcomes on the second toss and their probabilities are as set out in a table below. This is called a **probability distribution**.

Outcome	1	2	3	4	5	6
Chance	4.17%	4.17%	4.17%	4.17%	4.17%	79.17%

How likely is it that an even number will come up? If we add up the probabilities of 2, 4, and 6 we obtain the answer 0.875. Alternatively, we could have argued that if the die is biased there is a 100% chance of an even number (since 6 is even), while if the die is fair there is a 50% chance of an even number and so the overall probability of an even number is $0.25 \times (1/2) + 0.75 \times 1 = 0.875$.

GAMBLING PAYOFFS

In almost every game of chance you are required to bet money upfront—which you lose if your gamble is unsuccessful. If you win then the house will pay you back some amount more than your stake. A common way of quoting the payoff is to say how much you will get back on a gamble of $1. So all such payoffs are more than $1. For instance, if you are betting on the toss of a fair coin then a fair payoff would be $2 because you end up winning $1 if you win and losing $1 if you lose. In general, if the probability of something happening is p and you bet on it, then a fair payoff is $1/p$.

The probabilities we have calculated can be used to infer the fair payoff. For instance, if you bet $1 on any of the numbers 1–5, then the casino should pay you $24 when you win—because 24 is the reciprocal of 0.0417. Probably the casino will give you less then this, since they need to make a profit. If you bet on the more likely outcome of a 6 then the casino should give you $1.26, which is the reciprocal of 0.7917. Again they would no doubt give you less then this. If I wanted to bet on an even number then a fair payback would be $1.14, which is the reciprocal of 0.875. We talk more about fair payoffs and breaking even in the next chapter. The key point for now is to understand the Bayes calculation.

Here are a couple more questions that might be of interest to the house: *When the initial number that comes up is not a 6, the situation is not very interesting. Why? How often does this uninteresting situation occur?*

If any other number besides a 6 comes up then we learn a lot—the die could not possibly be the all-six die. It is definitely fair!

It is still instructive to go through the Bayes table to see how it gives us this answer. The data are now some other values besides 6. It does not matter which—let's suppose it is a 1. So our hypothetical data D is now 1, not 6. The DL column must always list the probability of the data given the different possible states—here the probability of a 1 given the different possible dice. Obviously Pr(1 | fair die) = 1/6, while Pr(1 | all-six die) = 0. So the Bayes table is:

> The total of the product column is the marginal probability of the data.

State	Prior	DL(1)	Product	Posterior
All-6 die	0.333	0	0	0.0
Fair die	0.667	0.167	0.111	1.00
			0.111	

Bayes correctly tells that we are 100% sure it is a fair die. This is a rather unsatisfactory outcome for the casino because the punter will not be interested to bet on what they (should) know is a fair die. So a sensible question might be

> how often will the first throw of whatever die is chosen be a 6, which puts the casino and the punter in the more interesting situation?

The answer is actually already sitting there in the first Bayes table. It is 0.444, which is the total of the product column. The total of the product column gives you the probability of the data, which in that table was the event of a 6. Exactly four times out of nine in the long run, the croupier will announce a 6. The other numbers 1–5 will arise one time out of nine on average. You can see this value (0.111 in decimal form) at the bottom of the product column in the table just above.

CHECK YOUR UNDERSTANDING

Q1. You want to build a spam filter which automatically flags spam and puts it in a separate folder. There are several key words that indicate when an e-mail is, or is not, spam. For instance "health" is often associated with spam while "sincerely" is associated with nonspam e-mails.

If you wanted to use Bayes to build your spam filter, what would be the states, what would be the data, and what numbers would you need for the DLs?

Where would the prior information come from?

Q2. You are an insurance company and you want to assess the risk associated with a potential car accident insurance customer, based on their driving record and other factors such as age and sex.

If you wanted to use Bayes to build your risk assessment algorithm, what would be the states, what would be the data, and what numbers would you need for the DLs?

Where would the prior information come from?

4.4. Example 2: Bayes in the Courtroom

You are a juror in a court case. At the beginning of the trial the judge quotes the following passage from the *Manual on Human Rights for Judges, Prosecutors and Lawyers: A Trainer's Guide* (New York and Geneva: United Nations, 2008):

> The defendant is presumed to be innocent. He may be convicted only if the prosecution establishes that he is guilty of the offence. For the prosecution to discharge its burden of proving the guilt of the defendant, it is required to prove beyond reasonable doubt that he is guilty.

It occurs to you that this biases the process in favor of the accused in two ways. You are supposed to begin by assuming he is innocent. And then you can only convict if the evidence forces you to the opposite extreme. The evidence has to be so strong that you move from being almost sure he is innocent (at the directive of the judge) to being almost sure he is guilty.

Because you had done a statistics course 5 years earlier, you like to work with numbers, so you decide to operationalize the judge-imposed presumption of innocence by assuming a 95% chance the accused is innocent of the charge of theft. You do not necessarily believe this yourself. You actually think that he is probably guilty or he would not be in court. But you also believe in the justice system so you are going to act as if you were 95% sure he is innocent.

Now comes the evidence. Two independent eyewitnesses have identified the accused as the person who was carrying a $10,000 LCD TV out the front door on the night in question. You do not consider these witnesses particularly reliable and expert evidence is given in court that visual recognition of a stranger from the distance of a neighboring house is not very easy. You argue to yourself:

> if the accused is guilty then there is around a 99% chance that the witness will recognize the accused as the thief. On the other hand, if the accused is innocent then there is some chance that a witness would still claim they recognized him—around 5% according to the expert witness who was called by the prosecution. What is your assessment of the likelihood that the accused is guilty? Would you convict on this evidence?

> States are the unknowns that you want to predict

What are the states of the world that we would like to know? Clearly, the accused is either guilty, G or innocent, I. Let's use these symbols instead of the unenlightening S1 and S2. We decided to assign 5% probability to G and 95% to I, prior to hearing any evidence at all. This may not be what we personally believe—some people might believe that 99% of people who proceed to trial are guilty—but that does not prevent you following with the judge's directive and seeing where it leads.

The data *D* here is the evidence, namely the identification by two eyewitnesses of the accused. We need to write down the DLs, that is, we need to calculate how likely it is that the accused would be identified by two eyewitnesses if he were guilty and also if he were innocent. If he is guilty then there is a 99% of being identified by one eyewitness. If the two eyewitnesses behave independently—which is one of the reasons that witnesses are not permitted to talk to each other, otherwise they might influence each other—then the chance of two identifications is $0.99 \times 0.99 = 0.9801$. On the other hand, if the accused is innocent then there is only a 5% chance of a single (false) identification and the chance of being doubly unlucky is $0.05 \times 0.05 = 0.0025$.

Why do we want to use the Bayes method? Because we want to know the probability of the states (guilt or innocence) after having seen the data (the evidence). Of course, the numbers listed above, which will be used in the calculation, are not precise and a wise juror would vary all of these numbers slightly to see how much difference they make. Excel is a great tool for doing this. The Bayes calculation is set out in example2 (court verdict).xls and below and leads to the conclusion that there is a 95.4% chance of guilt.

State	Prior	DL	Product	Posterior
G	5.0%	0.9801	0.0490	95.4%
I	95.0%	0.0025	0.0024	4.6%
Total	100.0%		0.0514	100.0%

We have moved from a 5% chance of guilt to a 95.4% chance of guilt. We are just about as sure now of his guilt as we were previously sure of his innocence—though our previous assessment of his innocence was forced upon us by the judge.

This may not lead you to conviction by itself—or it may. There is no correct answer. The judge would have directed you to convict "only if you are convinced beyond a reasonable doubt" but will not have told you what "reasonable" means. After hearing the eyewitness evidence there is still a 4.6% chance of innocence, which you might decide is reasonable doubt. To convict you might have already resolved that the posterior probability of guilt must be at least 99%.

Checking Assumptions

What do you think is the most important assumption in this argument? Certainly the prior probability of 95% for innocence is key. Try varying this figure in the spreadsheet and see how the posterior probability of guilt changes. The data are the two eyewitnesses and are not changing. You are changing how you view the accused before the evidence is known and how this would change your view after the evidence. Suppose you say to yourself:

> Well, I think that at least 50% of people who actually appear in court are guilty—otherwise they wouldn't be there. It is probably more than 50% but I will suppose it is 50% just to give them the benefit of the doubt ...

You will find the posterior probability of guilty is now 0.997. This should be enough evidence for anyone you would have thought. So this might be what you really believe. But the beauty of having a clear and objective method like Bayes is that you can follow through the consequences of assuming a different prior probability of guilt—5% instead of 50%—and see where it leads you. You can do more than just say that the accused is less likely to be guilty. You can say exactly how much less likely.

The other key figures in the example are the DL figures, which were the squares of the figures 0.99 and 0.05. If you vary the 0.99 figure you find it has very little effect on the answer, but if you vary the 0.05 figure it has much more effect. I would not be very confident that the 0.05 figure is accurate—just the fact that it is rounded off to 0.05 makes me skeptical. If it were 0.1 instead, then you will find that the posterior probability of guilt is 84%, so there is a 16% chance of innocence—reasonable doubt in the mind of most people.

The most important assumption in our analysis, however, turns out to be that the two eyewitness identifications are independent, which is the whole basis of the $0.9801 = 0.99^2$ and $0.0025 = 0.05^2$ figures. This is quite unlikely to be true. Why? Some people tend to fit the stereotypical image of a thief more than others. If you look like a criminal then *both* eyewitnesses will be more likely to identify you, whereas if you look like a Boy Scout both will be unlikely to identify you. So the testimonies of the two eyewitnesses will be dependent on how the accused appears and, through this common link, will be dependent on each other—without either witness trying to influence the other.

So multiplying 0.05 by 0.05 is probably not valid and the figure $0.05 \times 0.05 = 0.0025$ could actually be much larger. If you play around with the cell 0.0025 in example2 (court verdict).xls, then you will find that it has a large effect on the result. For instance, if you change it to 0.025 then the chance of being guilty is only 67.4%.

Pushing a Bit Further

Here is an extension of this example that you might like to consider in class or in your own time. You are told that the accused actually confessed to police. But later, it is established that the accused was beaten and the confession was forced. You are instructed by the judge to disregard the confession. However, recalling again your statistics course from 5 years ago you know that data should never be disregarded. You argue to yourself:

> If the accused is guilty then he is likely a professional or at least a serial burglar and would be likely to stand up well to police pressure. The chance of a

confession is small—around 10%. If the accused is innocent then it is probably a case of mistaken identity. The person will not be a criminal at all, and would likely succumb to the pressure of a violent police interrogation. You estimate that there is a 50% chance such a person would give a false confession.

What is your assessment of the likelihood that the accused is guilty? You will first have to think about the prior probabilities of guilt or innocence. By prior we mean prior to the evidence of the forced confession, but we did have the eyewitness evidence at this point. Does the justice system's refusal to consider evidence of forced confession help or hinder the accused?

4.5. Some Typical Business Applications

Information Technology Security Is an e-mail spam or not? Each e-mail can be in one of two unknown states. The prior probability is the chance of a random e-mail being spam, which could be estimated from historical records. It could vary with time during spam attacks and also depend on the server. The data are the text in the e-mail, specifically the occurrence of various key words in the text or subject line. You will need values for the DL, which are the likelihoods of the various text strings for the possible two types of e-mail. Bayes will give you a figure for the probability the e-mail is spam. Where you set the critical value for this probability will depend on the costs you associate with spam getting through the filter compared with nonspam being caught in the filter.

Quality Control Is an item defective or not? Each item can be in one of these two unknown states. The prior probability of each state could be estimated from previous records of product returns as well as from engineering principles, depending on the product. The data might be the outcome of some kind of quality test. You will need values for the DL, which are the likelihoods of defective items and nondefective items passing the quality test. Bayes will give you a figure for the probability the item is defective, after the quality test.

Product Launch How successful will my product be? This business outcome could take a continuum of possible values but you could class the outcomes as very bad, bad, neutral, good, or very good—so there are five states of the world in this case. The prior probability would be hard to estimate scientifically. You would probably use subjective probabilities based on your own judgment of how successful the product is likely to be. The data could be some kind of market research assessment that includes expert panels and customer focus groups, resulting in a single prediction of success or failure for the product. You will need values for the DL, which are the likelihoods of products with different outcomes getting a positive or negative market assessment. Bayes will give you a figure for the probability of different product outcomes, taking account of the market assessment result.

Insurance Will this prospective insurance customer be a high-claiming customer or a low-claiming customer over a particular time horizon? Each customer has a hidden risk state that you would like to predict. The prior probability of the different risk class of customer could be estimated from industry records. The data might typically include age, gender, and previous claim history. You will need values for the DL, which are the likelihoods of different classes of customer having the given age, gender, and claim history. Bayes will give you a figure for the probability the customer is low or high risk, taking account of the gender, age, and claim history. This will presumably determine the premium charged, depending on the costs associated with high and low claimers.

Credit Card Fraud A credit card can have its information "skimmed" and unauthorized persons can access the account. At any time, a person's credit card account is either compromised or not—these are the two states. The prior probability of a card being compromised would be very low—most cards are secure at any given time—and could be estimated from the total number of such events as a proportion of all cards in the system. When a card is compromised there will be characteristic patterns of use that contrast with the more typical use of a secure card. So the data will be the pattern of use, say over the past day. This "pattern" might be the total expenditure, the number of transactions, as well as the types of products purchased. The DLs would describe as accurately as possible the likelihood of the observed usage pattern for compromised cards and secure cards. Bayes would tell you the chance the card is compromised. If this chance is sufficiently high, the bank would contact the customer or even freeze the card. Costs would determine this protocol.

Medical Testing You may or may not have a disease. Each patient is in one of these two states (there could also be intermediate states). The data are the results of an imperfect diagnostic test for some kind of marker of the disease, for instance the prostate-specific antigen test of prostate cancer. You will need values for the DL, which are the likelihoods of diseased and nondiseased individuals passing the diagnostic test. Bayes will give you a figure for the probability the patient has the disease after testing for the marker.

4.6. SUMMARY

The Bayes method is used to update our assessment of the chance of an outcome in the light of new relevant data. It is applicable when you

- Have a finite list of **states** of the world that you want to predict
- Are able to put probabilities on the chances of these states of the world, called **prior probabilities**
- Have observed some relevant data D
- Are able to put probabilities for observing the data supposing the different states of the world, called **DLs**

The result of the Bayes method is a list of probabilities of the states of the world given the data, called **posterior probabilities**.

The Bayes method can be used more than once in a given application. The posterior probabilities of the first application become a summary of your beliefs about the likely states of the world and can be used as the prior probabilities for the next application of Bayes.

The Bayes method is equally applicable when the prior probabilities or DL probabilities are objective (such as in the gambling example), are subjective (such as in the courtroom example), or are empirically based on historical relative frequencies. In any of these cases, the correct way to combine the information embodied in these probabilities is the Bayes method.

EXERCISES

E1. You are trying to classify drivers in terms of accident risk. You define the top 25% of drivers to be Good, the bottom 25% to be Bad, and the rest as Medium. From historical data you believe that Good drivers have a 95% chance of no accident in any given year, Medium drivers have a 90% chance, and Bad drivers have a 75% chance. You also believe that the chance of having multiple accidents in a given year is 3% for Good drivers, 5% for Medium drivers, and 15% for Bad drivers.

(a) What is the probability that a driver has exactly one accident in a year (1) given that he is a Good driver, (2) given that he is a Medium driver, and (3) given that he is a Bad driver?

(b) A prospective customer has a record of having had zero accidents last year. What is your assessment? Is he a Good, Bad, or Medium driver?

(c) A prospective customer has a record of having had one accident last year. Would you classify him as a Good, Bad, or Medium driver? How sure are you?

E2. A manufacturing process produces computer chips in large numbers. Over the long run the fraction of bad chips produced by the process is around 20%. Thorough testing is expensive, but there is a cheap test. All good chips pass the cheap test but so do 10% of bad chips.

(a) Given that a chip passes the test, what is the probability that it is a good chip?

(b) If a company sold all chips that passed the test what fraction of those they sold would be bad?

E3. Suppose you are using a lie detector to decide if a person is telling the truth or lying. You are given the following information about the accuracy of the "lie detector" technology. If someone is lying, then there is a 95.25% chance they will get a red light on the test. If someone is telling the truth, then there is a 99.75% chance they will get a green light on the test.

Suppose you have a person about whom you are quite suspicious—you assess the probability that they are lying as 75%. How would you assess their likelihood of lying after a positive test? How about after a negative test?

E4. We are trying to decide whether to release a new TV program, which is at the pilot stage. Our prior distribution for the three possible outcomes is that 9% are monsters, 17% are hits, and 74% are flops. We are going to do some market testing. To give an idea of the accuracy of the market testing, you are told the following set of conditional probabilities:

Pr(+|Monster)	0.889
Pr(+|Hit)	0.706
Pr(+|Flop)	0.419

(a) A program is market tested and received a positive assessment. Use the Bayes method to obtain the posterior distribution.
(b) A program is market tested and received a positive assessment. Use the Bayes method to obtain the posterior distribution.
(c) What is the chance of a program being positively assessed?

E5. Hartnett car company has a 12% market share. They are trying to assess the value of their long-standing advertising campaign. A standard way of doing this is to ask purchasers whether they recall the advertising campaign at the point of purchase. It turns out that 75% can recall the main details of the campaign. They also have general market research data, which indicate that among those people who do not own a Hartnett, only 21% recall the major details of the campaign. On average, Hartnett makes a profit of $12,200K on each customer.
(a) What proportion of people overall recall the major details of the campaign?
(b) Given that someone recalls the major details of the campaign, what is the probability that they will buy a Hartnett?
(c) On average, Hartnett makes a profit of $12,500K on 12% of the car-buying population so their average profit per member of this target population is 12% of $12,500K, which is $1460. Given that someone recalls the major details of the campaign, what is the average profit per member of the target population?

E6. You are in a court case as a juror. Because you are told by the judge that it is up to the prosecution to prove that the accused is guilty, you decide to assign a prior probability of 5% that the accused is guilty of the charge of theft. Two independent eyewitnesses have identified the accused as the person who was carrying a $10,000 TV out the front door on the night in question. You do not consider these witnesses particularly reliable and expert evidence is given in court that visual recognition of a stranger from the distance of a neighboring house is not very easy. You argue to yourself: *if the accused is guilty then there is around a 99% chance that the witness will recognize the accused as the thief. On the other hand, if the accused in innocent then there is some chance that a witness would still claim they recognized him—around 5% according to the expert.*

What is your assessment of the likelihood that the accused is guilty? Would you convict on this evidence? This was solved in the text and we found that the posterior probability of guilt is 95.4% but that there are some critical assumptions in this calculation, mainly the prior probability of guilt and also the 0.0025 figure in the DL.

You are now told *that the accused actually confessed to police.* But later, it is established that the accused was beaten and the confession was forced. You are instructed by the judge to disregard the confession. However, having done a statistics course you know that data should never be disregarded. You argue to yourself: *if the accused is guilty then he is likely a professional or serial burglar and would be likely to stand up well to police pressure. The chance of a confession is small—around 10%. If the accused is innocent then it is probably a case of mistaken identity. The person will not be a criminal at all, and would likely succumb to the pressure of a violent police interrogation. You estimate that there is a 50% chance such a person would give a false confession.* What is your assessment of the likelihood that the accused is guilty?

E7. You are trying to predict whether a student admitted into a business school will finish in the top 25% or bottom 25% of the class. We classify such results as High and Low, respectively, and the 50% in the middle are classified as Medium.

Based on historical data, the following claims can be made about the General Management Aptitude Test (GMAT) as a predictor of a student's performance:

- Looking back at students that finished with a Low performance, 56% had a low GMAT, 40% had a medium GMAT, and 4% a high GMAT.
- Looking back at students that finished with a Medium performance, 8% had a low GMAT, 86% had a medium GMAT, and 6% a high GMAT.

- Looking back at students that finished with a High performance, 8% had a low GMAT, 28% had a medium GMAT, and 64% a high GMAT

(a) Suppose that someone arrives at the school with a low GMAT. What would you say about their likely performance?

(b) What proportion of students being admitted to the school would receive low, medium, and high GMAT scores?

(c) If, on the basis of their GMAT score, you classify students into their most likely outcome group, then what proportion of students would have their performance correctly predicted?

E8. Spam is a serious problem, especially for Web-based e-mail services such as *TepidMail.* You are setting up a spam filter that will be available to all users. It is based on searching for certain text strings in the e-mail that are associated with either spam or nonspam. Specifically, the text string "health" is associated with spam while the keyword "sincerely" is associated with nonspam.

A detailed examination of your e-mail database over the past 6 months reveals that the proportion of spam going through *TepidMail* accounts is 23%. You want to give users the option of turning the spam filter on or off, and to help their choice you want to provide them with information on the probability that deleted mail is nonspam as well as the proportion of mail they will receive that is spam.

The figures in the table below have been extracted from historical records and give the proportion of spam e-mails that contain each text string, as well as the proportion of nonspam e-mails (termed OK) that contain these same text strings.

Keyword	"Health"	"Sincerely"
From SPAM emails	62%	2%
From OK emails	6%	44%

It can also be assumed that the occurrence of these text strings, within each e-mail type, is independent. For instance, the chance of an OK e-mail containing the word *health* but not the word *sincerely* is 6% times 56%, or 3.36%.

(a) Suppose that an e-mail contains the word *sincerely*. What is the probability that it is spam?

(b) Suppose that an e-mail contains the word *health*. What is the probability that it is spam?

(c) Suppose that an e-mail contains the word *health* but not the word *sincerely*. What is the probability that it is spam?You decide to set the spam filter to automatically delete any e-mail that contains the word *health* but not the word *sincerely*. Deleted e-mail is still accessible to the user, but they need to look through a separate spam folder where the mail is held and assess the messages individually. All other e-mail is considered OK and delivered to the user's main account. Obviously, the ideal situation would be to have all e-mails in the spam folder being spam and all e-mails delivered to the user being OK.

(d) What proportion of mail is sent to the spam folder?

(e) What proportion of mail in the spam folder is actually OK?

(f) You might also have considered simply deleting any e-mail that contains the word *health* and not worrying about the word *sincerely*. How much use is the extra word *sincerely* in classifying e-mails? Quantify your answer in terms of the total error rates of the two possible spam rules.

E9. Suppose that in the general population, 1% have leukemia, 4% have infection of the lymphs, and the remaining 95% have healthy lymphatic systems.

You walk into the doctor's surgery and he says you have tested positive for leukemia. This test is known to be highly accurate. It only falsely diagnoses about 1% of healthy patients with leukemia. When it is applied to people who in fact have the disease, it diagnoses 99% of them correctly. For people with a lymphatic infection, which causes similar symptoms, it diagnoses 50% with leukemia.

How worried should you be? Is there a 99% chance that you have the disease?

E10. The gambling game described in this chapter started with two fair dice and one biased die in an urn. Suppose the house changed the game so that there are two biased dice and one fair die. They would also need to tell this to players. How do you think this would change the attractiveness of the game to players? How would you set the payoffs? You will need to not only calculate probabilities but think what kind of events do people like to gamble on.

CHAPTER 5

Valuing an Uncertain Payoff

5.0. Introduction: What Is the Issue?

Business managers need to anticipate the future. The problem is that the future is uncertain. Very few performance measures and also many costs are inherently unpredictable. Next month's *sales*, the *return* on an investment, and the *price* I will receive on an asset—none of these can be predicted exactly in advance. Yet we will have some idea of the most likely value and the level of uncertainty. There are also unpredictable costs such as the *price* I will need to bid to secure an asset, the *fine* or penalty the business might incur, the *cost* of a new housing project, and the *interest rate* in 6 months time.

Quantities that cannot be predicted exactly are called **random variables**. The payout an insurance company faces on a policy is one example. The actuarial section of the company spends a great deal of effort assessing the likelihood that an insuree will make claims of various sizes. Many will probably make no claim in a given year. Some will make modest claims. A small proportion might make a large claim. The probabilities of these outcomes are critical for the insurance company in setting the premium. What they care about is that the total premium of all insurees will more than cover the total claims. So they really care about the *average claim per insuree*. With thousands of contracts, the company "plays the game" thousands of times each year.

Many other decisions faced by managers are "once off." You will not get to play thousands of times. The future profit on your newly launched product is but one example. It might make huge profits or it might fail to break even. This might, in turn, depend on whether competitors launch a similar product and on the state of the economy, but these are also random variables.

Random variables are described by their **probability distribution**. The probability distribution describes everything we know about the likely values of a random variable. It describes the range of possible values and how likely these values are. The

Data-Driven Business Decisions, First Edition. Chris J. Lloyd.

probability distribution can be summarized by its **mean**, which gives a central or trend value for the business outcome, and the **standard deviation**, which measures the uncertainty. These are *not* the same as the sample mean and sample standard deviation.

VALUE OF INFORMATION: CASE BRIEFING

You are facing a situation where one of your senior vice presidents (VPs) is leaking valuable information. You suspect it is someone called Frank Berger but you are only 75% sure. If you terminate his employment it will cost you $150K in the usual termination payments. However, if he is actually innocent it will cost you a total of $1700K, which includes him suing you for wrongful dismissal as well as the continuing losses incurred from the true culprit. Your cost distribution is given in the left-hand column of the table below.

There is a security firm that can reduce your uncertainty about the identity of the leaker. When all is said and done, if you use the security firm then you will end up with a cost distribution described in the right two columns. These numbers require a fair bit of calculation to obtain. But after you have done the work to calculate them, the decision of whether or not to hire the security firm remains. And the decision has been distilled into a comparison of two cost distributions.

Cost	Probability	Cost	Probability
$150	75%	$175	24.53%
$1700	25%	$195	15.93%
		$270	47.78%
		$995	0.80%
		$1,395	2.70%
		$1,725	8.18%
		$1,820	0.10%

Which of these two cost distributions would you prefer? Is the security firm "worth it"? Further details of the background to this problem are available in the full case.

The sum of the probabilities is always equal to 1.0.

5.1. WHAT IS A PROBABILITY DISTRIBUTION?

DEFINITION

The **probability distribution** of an unpredictable business variable is just a list of **all the possible values** that the variable can take together with the **probabilities** of all these possible values.

Often we drop the word "probability" and just talk about the *distribution of the variable*. The probability distribution does not necessarily depend on data—though often we may have used historical data to arrive at our best assessment of the probability distribution. Sometimes it will be based on a few critical numbers that come from the business process. Sometimes it may depend on expert judgment and experience.

There are various ways of displaying a probability distribution. The simplest is as a table. Another very effective method is to present it as a graph. Sometimes a probability distribution is described by a mathematical formula.

EXAMPLE 1 *Daily car sales*

From long experience, a small car yard owner knows how likely it is that he will sell various numbers of cars in a day. These are listed in the table below.

Number	**0**	**1**	**2**	**3**	**4**	**5**	**>5**
Probability	0.15	0.28	0.29	0.17	.08	.03	0.00

The business performance measure here is *the number of cars sold in a day*. It is unpredictable but its likely values can be summarized in terms of probabilities. The table describes everything the owner knows about the number of cars he will sell per day. For instance, there is an 85% chance that he will sell at least one car and no chance that he will sell more than five cars.

Notice that this distribution is very variable. We cannot put a number to how variable at the moment. But in an informal sense you would have to agree that there is a great deal of uncertainty about sales on a given day.

You are possibly thinking to yourself—what day of the week are we talking about here? Wouldn't the distribution be different for different days? Surely, Saturday would be a big day for car sales? The above table describes sales per day in general, not for a specific day but on average over all working days.

Below is a possible distribution for Saturdays. If you compare it with the first distribution, it seems that you are more likely to sell more cars. You might expect that the distribution for a particular day of the week would also be less variable than the general distribution, since you know more about the selling conditions. It is rather difficult, though, to tell whether the Saturday distribution is more or less variable than the general distribution. We will need a measure of variability before we can check this properly.

Number	**0**	**1**	**2**	**3**	**4**	**5**
Probability	0.02	0.18	0.31	0.24	.17	.08

CHECK YOUR UNDERSTANDING

Q1. What is the probability that the car yard owner will sell *more than* two cars on a Saturday? In the text, it was asserted that on Saturdays "you are more likely to sell more cars" than on a general day. This is a statement comparing the two distributions, reproduced for your convenience below:

Number	0	1	2	3	4	5
General day	0.15	0.28	0.29	0.17	.08	.03
Saturday	0.02	0.18	0.31	0.24	.17	.08

Do as many calculations as you can to verify or contradict this assertion.

5.2. Displaying a Probability Distribution

A probability distribution can be displayed graphically by plotting the possible values x_1, x_2, x_3, … of the business measure on the horizontal axis against the corresponding probabilities

$$\Pr(X = x_1), \Pr(X = x_2), \Pr(X = x_3)\ldots.$$

on the vertical axis. In even simpler terms, you plot the probability (vertical y) against the number (horizontal x). Bar charts are best for this. With a little practice, such graphs give you an immediate appreciation of the likely values of the variable, including its most likely range and how variable it is.

EXAMPLE 1 (Continued) *Daily car sales*

The graphic below displays both the general distribution of daily car sales and the distribution for Saturday, allowing easy comparison of the distributions. Each gives a visual display of where sales are likely to be—the higher the bar the more likely that number of car sales is.

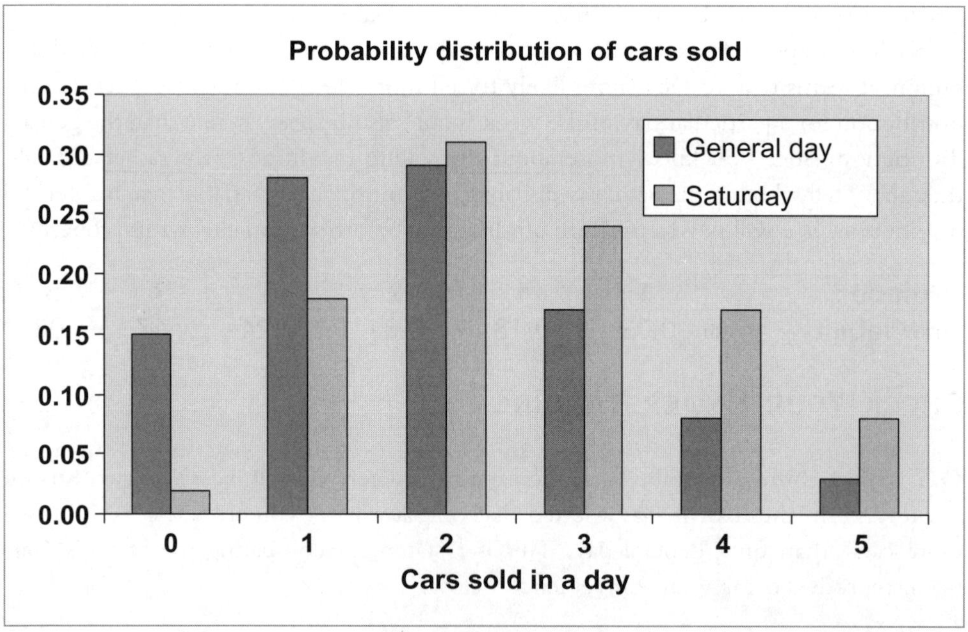

If you examine these two graphs you should be able to see that the Saturday distribution has higher bars in the right of the plot and lower bars in the left of the plot. In other words, on Saturday you are more likely to sell more cars and less likely to sell less cars (than a general day).

The single most important concept to take away from this chapter is the idea of the probability distribution as a single description of a business variable. Whenever you have an uncertain business variable—whether it is a payoff or a cost—you should try and think visually of the range of likely values of that variable—rather than think about a single likely value. A bar chart is a natural way to visualize a range of likely values. Even if you do not know the probability distribution, this is the mental image you should always carry with you for an uncertain business outcome.

Plotting Probability Distributions in Excel

To produce the plot of the probability distributions above you should first right click and select the data with the variable values as the first row followed by the probabilities in the next two rows. To be explicit, the data should be set out as in this table:

Number	0	1	2	3	4	5
General day	0.15	0.28	0.29	0.17	.08	.03
Saturday	0.02	0.18	0.31	0.24	.17	.08

Excel will take the first row to be on the horizontal axis, and the next two rows will be on the vertical axis, which is what we want. If you set it out like this

General day	0.15	0.28	0.29	0.17	.08	.03
Saturday	0.02	0.18	0.31	0.24	.17	.08
Number	0	1	2	3	4	5

then Excel will take the first row of probabilities on the horizontal axis, which is not what we want. The spreadsheet car sales.xls has the data set out in the correct way as well as the final bar chart. You can also set the data out columnwise, with the variable values on the left column and the probabilities to the right. Excel will automatically understand what you mean either way. Make sure that you select the variable labels as well.

The second step is a little unusual. When selecting the type of graph do not select bar chart—select scatter plot instead. If you select bar chart, then Excel will also plot the numbers 0, 1, 2, 3, 4, and 5 as data and will label the bars 1–6. So choose a scatter plot instead. This gives the left plot below. To change it into a bar chart, right click on the plot area, select Chart Type then Column as shown in the screenshot below. This converts the scatter plot into a vertical bar chart but with variable values 0–5 as the labels—which is what we want.

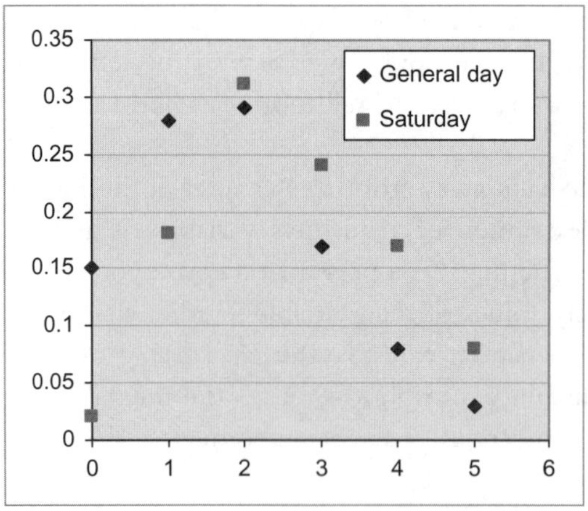

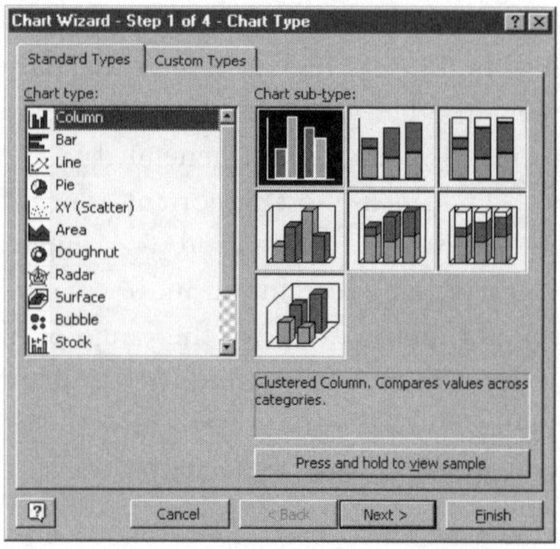

You can make all sorts of cosmetic changes to the chart into the attractive bar chart shown earlier, by right clicking various parts of it. For instance

- The grid lines can be removed by right clicking and choosing *Clear.*
- The background of the central Plot Area can be changed by right clicking this area, choosing **Format Plot Area**, and then selecting a color. The area outside the plot area (called the Chart Area) can be changed in the same way as the Plot Area.
- Title and axis labels can be added by right clicking on the chart and selecting Chart Options (see below).
- The axes can be reformatted by right clicking and choosing *Format Axis.* The axis scale and tick marks can be chosen as well as the size, font, and format of the numbers.

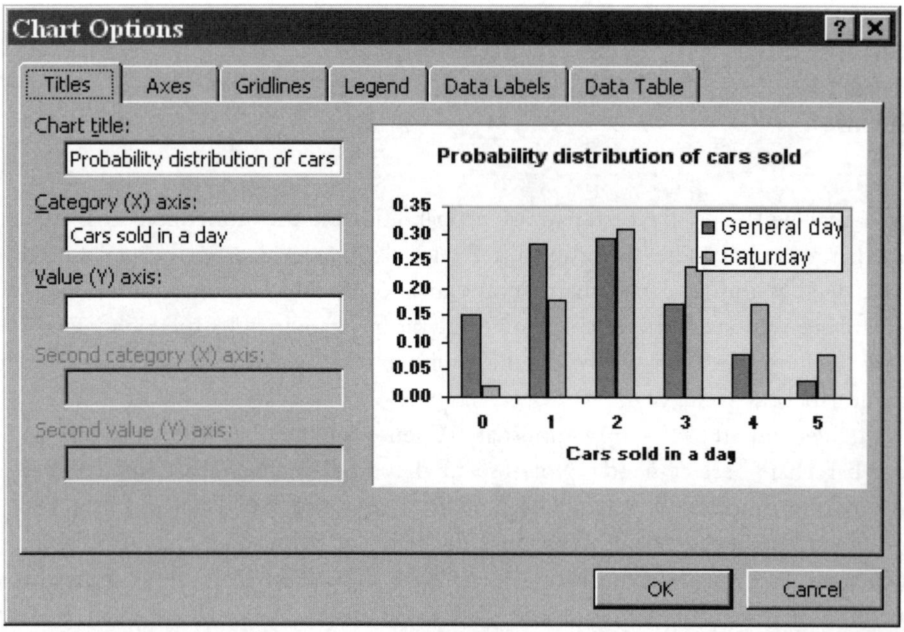

CHECK YOUR UNDERSTANDING

Q2. Try and produce a graph that is as identical as possible to the one shown earlier for car sales.

There are other ways of describing the range of likely values to the probability distribution. The probability function is the most straightforward and common.

5.3. THE MEAN OF A DISTRIBUTION

It is important to appreciate the concept of a probability distribution, giving the whole range of possible and probable values of a business variable. Having said that, the distribution can be largely summarized by two numbers, one telling you a central or typical value for the variable and the other telling you how variable or uncertain the variable is. Thinking visually, if I tell you that next week's sales will probably be around \$150K but there is a \$10K uncertainty in this figure, you can start to visually reconstruct the probability distribution in your mind.

> The notation Σ means *sum all terms of the form* x_ip_i, Note that x_ip_i; means x_i times p_i

DEFINITION

The **mean** of a variable is a single number that describes a *central or typical value* of its probability distribution. It is calculated from the probability distribution of the variable as follows. If we denote the possible values of the variable by $x_1, x_2, x_3, \ldots$ and their corresponding probabilities by $p_1, p_2, p_3, \ldots$ then the mean is

$$\mu = x_1p_1 + x_2p_2 + x_3p_3 + \ldots = \sum_i x_ip_i'$$

We will justify this measure in the next section, but it is worth pointing out at the outset that the mean measures the center of the probability distribution in a special way—as the balancing point of the probability distribution. This is very similar to how the sample mean measures the balancing point of the data distribution.

Second, we can talk about the mean of the variable or the mean of its probability distribution interchangeably. So we can talk about the "mean return on an investment," which is the mean of the probability distribution of the return on that investment.

In more mathematical textbooks the mean is often called **expected value**, though this is not a very good name—because the mean is not necessarily a value you expect to see. As a simple example, if I throw a fair die once then the probability distribution of the result has the probability one-sixth assigned to the outcomes 1–6. You can check that the mean of this distribution is 3.5. This is not a value you can ever observe, but it is certainly the central value. Indeed, if you look at the chart of this distribution, the only sensible measure of the center is 3.5.

EXAMPLE 1 (Continued) *Daily car sales*

For the random variable X = number of cars sold in a day the general probability distribution has been given in the first two columns.

Number x_i	Probability p_i	$x_i p_i$
0	0.150	0.000
1	0.280	0.280
2	0.290	0.580
3	0.170	0.510
4	0.080	0.320
5	0.030	0.150
Totals	1.00	1.84

The calculation for the mean is set out in the third column and gives the answer 1.84. Again, we cannot ever sell 1.84 cars. It is a single central value that takes account of the possible values and how probable they are.

Computing the Mean in Excel

There is no direct function like AVERAGE as there is for sample mean. Remember, the sample average is computed on an observed sample of data. The mean in this chapter is a measure of the typical or central value of a variable, before it has even been observed. It is computed from the probability distribution.

To calculate the mean, supposing the x-values have been named "x" and the probabilities named "p," type

=SUMPRODUCT(x, p).

CHECK YOUR UNDERSTANDING

Q3. Calculate the mean daily car sales for Saturday. Before you do so, we earlier compared the Saturday and general distributions. On the basis of this do you expect the mean to be larger than 1.84 or smaller than 1.84? Looking at the table below, try to guess where the balancing point would be.

Number	**0**	**1**	**2**	**3**	**4**	**5**
Saturday	0.02	0.18	0.31	0.24	.17	.08

5.4. EXAMPLE: FINES AND VIOLATIONS

You face a regulatory regime where you are inspected for compliance with occupational health and safety (OHS) standards three times during the year. You are allowed to fail one of these inspections without being fined, but two failures incur a fine of \$200K and three failures incur a fine of \$500K. You are told the result of each inspection soon after it occurs.

No OHS system is perfectly adhered to and there is a chance that even the most well-managed firm could fail an inspection. Suppose that you believe that there is a 90% chance that you will pass any inspection.

What is the probability distribution of the fine? Therefore, what is the mean fine? Suppose that you are told that you failed the first inspection? How much, if anything, does this cost you?

The fine depends on the number of violations during the year, which can equal any value of 0, 1, 2, or 3. Assuming that each inspection is independent, the probability of zero violations is easy to calculate. This is the chance of passing all three inspections, which is $0.9^3 = 0.729$. Similarly the chance of three violations is $0.1^3 = 0.001$, which is very small. The chance of exactly one failure is a bit tricky. This might happen in various ways. For instance, you might fail the first inspection and pass the next two, and the probability of this is $0.1 \times 0.9 \times 0.9 = 0.081$. But the violation could also occur on the second occasion or the third occasion instead. So there are three ways of having one violation, all with probability 0.081, which gives 0.243. The probability of two violations can be worked out in a similar way or by subtraction.[1] The distribution is displayed below. The fine corresponding to each number of violations is also listed. It is very likely that there will be no fine at all. There is only a $0.027 + 0.001 = 0.028$ chance that you will be fined.

The sum of the probabilities is always equal to 1.0.

Violations	0	1	2	3
Fine	\$0	\$0	k\$200	k\$500
Probability	0.729	0.243	0.027	0.001

The variable of interest here is the fine. The number of violations is what determines the fine, but is not of primary interest in itself. The mean fine is obtained by multiplying the fines by the probabilities and adding up. The result is 5.9 or \$5900 dollars. The uncertain fine described in this table is, in the sense of mean value, equivalent to losing \$5900 every year.

Now, let us suppose that you fail the first inspection. You are not fined, so in an immediate sense this has cost you nothing. But what has happened to your chance of a fine? Surely it has gone up now. To investigate this, we think about the remaining two inspections and how many of these we might fail. The number of failures from the remaining two inspections will be 0, 1, or 2. The chance of 0 failures is $0.9^2 = 0.81$. The chance of two failures will be $0.1^2 = 0.01$ and so the chance of

[1] If you found it difficult to obtain these probabilities, you will find it much easier after the next chapter. It is an example of the **binomial distribution**, which will be studied in detail.

one failure is 1 − 0.81 − 0.01 = 0.18 (since probabilities have to add up to 1.) This is in the table below.

Violations in remaining 2 inspections	0	1	2
Fine	$0	k$200	k$500
Probability	0.81	0.18	0.01

The fines corresponding to these violations are also listed. Notice that one failure (on top of the original one) now gives a fine of $200K. The mean value of this probability distribution is $41K.

So how much did the first violation cost you? Immediately it appears to have cost you nothing. The bailiff does not appear at the door with any letter of demand. However, the mean fine that you face for the remainder of the year suddenly increases from $5900 to $41,000. So in terms of mean value, it has cost you $41,000 − $5900 = $35,100. This cost is an uncertain cost but it is no less real for being uncertain. Looked at another way, your chance of a fine has increased from 2.8% to 20%. Only a very bad manager would fail to account for this deterioration of business risk.

In fact, the figure of $35,100 still *underestimates* the cost. We should really be comparing our mean fine of $41,000 with what it would be if we had *passed* the first inspection. If you think about it, if we pass the first inspection then the probabilities in the payoff table will be identical to the one above since we still need to look at how many violations we will have in the remaining two inspections. But the only way we will get a fine now is if we fail both these remaining inspections, and it will only be the smaller of the two fines. Here is the payoff table and the mean value is $2K.

Violations in remaining 2 inspections	0	1	2
Fine	$0	$0	k$200
Probability	0.81	0.18	0.01

So how much did the violation cost you? Comparing the mean fine when you pass the first test ($2000) and the mean fine when you fail the first test ($41,000) the cost is $39,000. These calculations are all in the spreadsheet fines and violations.xls.

Pushing a Bit Further

If you want to avoid these fines, you might wonder why the firm doesn't simply manage better so that the 10% figure goes down. The answer is obviously that this would cost money. There is a trade-off between the administrative cost of increasing compliance and the costs of the fines.

Suppose that it costs you $1000 to increase the chance of passing an inspection by 1%. So in the current situation, your total OHS costs are $90K for your current 90% chance of passing plus $5900 for the fine, making a total cost of $95,900. You might like to code the previous analysis into an Excel spreadsheet with the 90% figure feeding into the formulas so that it can be varied. You will then be able to see what value minimizes the total cost. If you do this correctly, you should find that the optimum OHS policy is to set compliance effort so as to achieve a 91% chance of passing an inspection—not very different from the current policy setting.

But all this assumes that the policy is kept fixed during the year. We already noted that when you fail the first test your mean fine and risk goes way up. So surely you should increase your compliance effort. At the other extreme, if you pass the first two inspections then you can never get fines, even if you fail the last one. Does this mean you can reduce your compliance effort to zero?

5.5. Why Use the Mean?

The mean is not the only way to measure the central or typical value of an uncertain variable. But in most cases it is the most sensible way and, for business application, it is almost always the best starting point. There are three very different arguments for using the mean.

The Long-Run Argument

If you are facing an uncertain payoff and if you are going to face this uncertain payoff again and again, then you would surely be interested in the average payoff over a large number of occasions. It is a mathematical fact that the long-run average payoff in the future will be close to the mean. The longer you "play" the closer the average will be to the mean.

You can think of the mean then as the theoretical value for the long-run average if you face the uncertain payoff many times. Now in business it is not very common that we will face the same uncertain payoff again and again and again. But it is reassuring that the mean μ has this nice property. Even if we are not going to make the decision thousands of times, a good decision should surely not lead to bad results in the long run, even in the hypothetical long run.

The Conservation of Money Argument

Suppose that you have a business outcome with a payoff table like the one below. All dollar values are in units of $1,000,000. Your mean value is $1.94 so you have a profitable business in terms of mean. However, you are worried about the high chance of a bad outcome where you lose considerable money.

	Chance	Your payoff	Deal with Jane	Jane's Payoff
Bad	5.0%	-$10	$0	-$10
OK	92.0%	$2	$1	$1
GREAT	3.0%	$20	$15	$5

You have an old business partner Jane who offers to cover your $10 loss if it happens. In return, she wants half the profit for the OK outcome and $5 of the $20 for the Great outcome. Your payoffs are in the column Deal with Jane. The mean value is \$1.37. So you are \$0.57M worse off in mean, but you have removed the risk. Jane's payoff is also listed in the column. And her mean payoff is … \$0.57M. So no mean money has been created or destroyed. You essentially have paid Jane a \$0.57M mean value, which you have lost, in exchange for less risk.

Not all measures of overall value of a payoff distribution necessarily satisfy this notion of conservation of money. Mean value necessarily always does.

The Short-Run Logical Argument

Suppose that I have a 10% chance of winning a prize valued at \$$V$. Think of an urn with 10 balls in it, one of them containing a prize symbol. What price P would you pay for a draw from this urn? You probably know the answer but let's try and get there by logic. The key idea is that the value of the game is the total of the value of the balls in the urn. The blank balls are worth nothing. The ball with the prize is worth P, which is why you are willing to pay P.

Suppose now that one of the blank balls is removed from the urn and replaced with another prize ball. There are now *two* balls in the urn with the prize symbol. Each of these has the value P because each gives you a 10% chance of winning \$$V$. You have two chances of winning the prize now. Surely, the value of this game, that is, the value of all the balls in the urn, must be $2P$.

Next suppose that the second prize ball is replaced with a blank ball so that there are again nine blank balls and one prize ball. Except, suppose that the prize was doubled in value to \$$2V$? Surely, it again follows that the value of this game must be twice what it was originally, namely $2P$.

So we have concluded that when you double the prize for a fixed chance of winning the value of the game should double. We also concluded that when you double the chance of winning a fixed prize then the value of the game should double.

Finally, suppose that all 10 balls carry the prize symbol so you are guaranteed to get \$$V$. Obviously the value of this game is then \$$V$.

With these three assumptions it is possible to prove mathematically that the price you should pay for the game is equal to the value of the prize times the probability of winning. We conclude that a chance p of getting value V is worth Vp. This is a mean value. Why? Because the payoff is

Winnings	**\$0**	**\$V**
Probability	1–p	p

and multiplying the winnings by the probabilities gives

$$\mu = 0 \times (1-p) + V \times p = Vp.$$

What about more complicated payoffs like in the payoff "game" below? Again, imagine balls in an urn, this time 100 of them. Fifty of then are blank and are worth nothing. Thirty of then have a \$2000 prize and each ball presents a 1% chance of this prize. So, each of them is worth \$20 for a total of \$600. There are 19 balls with a prize of \$5000 and each of these is worth \$50 for a total of \$950. The last ball has a prize of $100,000 and so is worth $1000. The value of the game is the total value of the balls in the urn—$2550.

Payoff	Chance	Value
$0	0.50	$0
$2000	0.30	$600
$5000	0.19	$950
$100,000	0.01	$1000

There is nothing about the long run in this argument. It applies to a single decision as well as to a repeated decision, though for repeated decisions we have the additional long-run average argument for the mean value.

RISK

Some readers, especially from a financial background, will be wondering about risk. How can I say that the above game is worth $2550 when the payoff is uncertain? In the real world, people are risk averse. Won't they pay more for a guaranteed payoff of $2550 than an uncertain payoff with a mean of $2550? Most will. The variability of the payoff is important and in some business contexts (such as finance) it is just as important as the mean. But the mean is still central to valuing an uncertain payoff. It is sometimes called the *risk-neutral* valuation.

5.6. The Standard Deviation of a Distribution

A probability distribution is largely described by the typical or central value (one measure of which is the mean) together with a measure of how uncertain the variable is. If I tell you that next week's sales will probably be around $150K but there is a $10K uncertainty in this figure, you can start to visually reconstruct the probability distribution in your mind. This section introduces a measure of uncertainty of a business variable.

Variance does not have any meaning.

DEFINITION

The **standard deviation** is a number, usually denoted by σ, which describes the *spread* of a probability distribution and therefore the intrinsic variability or unpredictability of the variable. It is calculated from the probability distribution of the variable as follows. If we denote the possible values of the variable by x_1, x_2, x_3, ... and their corresponding probabilities by p_1, p_2 ,p_3, ... then the square of the standard deviation[1] (which is called variance) is

$$\sigma^2 = \sum_i x_i^2 p_i - \mu^2$$

Again, the notation Σ means *sum all terms to the right,* so the formula directs you to take each possible value of the variable, square it, multiply it by the probability, and sum the results. Finally, subtract off the square of the mean. If this all sounds tedious, it is! And there are quick ways to do it.

Again, as with the mean we can talk about the standard deviation either of the *variable* or of the variable's *probability distribution.* For instance, the "standard deviation of the return on an investment" is the standard deviation of the probability distribution of the return on that investment. In simple words, it measures the typical uncertainty of the variable.

Interpreting Standard Deviation

If you know the standard deviation of a variable then you immediately know quite a lot about the *typical* and *reasonable* variation of the variable. First, there is about a 65–75% chance that the variable will be within 1 standard deviation of the mean, that is, between $\mu - \sigma$ and $\mu + \sigma$. So, 1 standard deviation can be roughly interpreted as *typical* variation. Second, there is roughly a 90–99% chance that the variable will be within 2 standard deviations of the mean, that is, between $\mu - 2\sigma$ and $\mu + 2\sigma$. So, 2 standard deviations can be roughly interpreted as *reasonable* variation. It would be unusual for the variable to be more than 2 standard deviations away from the mean.

For example, if monthly sales have a mean value of $136,000 and a standard deviation of $2000 then we have a good idea of what the sales are likely to be next month. Our best guess trend value is $136,000 and the uncertainty in this prediction is $2000. Specifically, we would expect sales between $134,000 and $138,000 (typical variation) and be very confident of sales between $132,000 and $140,000 (reasonable variation).

EXAMPLE 1 (Continued) *Daily car sales*

For the random variable X = number of cars sold in a day the assumed probability distribution has been given in the first two columns.

Number x_i	Probability p_i	$x_i p_i$	$x_i^2 p_i$
0	0.150	0.000	0.000
1	0.280	0.280	0.280
2	0.290	0.580	1.160
3	0.170	0.510	1.530
4	0.080	0.320	1.280
5	0.030	0.150	0.750
Totals	1.00	1.84	5.00

The calculations for the mean, set out in the third column, gives an answer of 1.84, which was given earlier. The calculation for the mean of the squared values is in the fourth column, with a total of 5.00. The standard deviation is therefore

$$\sigma = \sqrt{5.00 - 1.84^2} = \sqrt{1.614} = 1.271$$

The typical variation of the variable is between $1.84 - 1.27 = 0.57$ and $1.84 + 1.27 = 3.11$. Since this particular business variable can only equal whole numbers, we would judge that the variable is likely to be between 1 and 3. You can see from the probability distribution that this is the case—the probability is actually 0.74. Reasonable variation is between $1.84 - 2 \times 1.27 = -0.7$ and $1.84 + 2 \times 1.27 = 4.38$. Again, rounding this to the nearest non-negative whole number, we would conclude that the variable is highly likely to be between 0 and 4. In fact, there is a 97% chance the variable is in this range.

So unless you wanted to know very specific outcomes for this variable (for instance, what is the probability of 1 or fewer sales?) it is sufficient to know the mean and standard deviation. These two numbers tell you that daily sales will likely be in the range 1–3 and will almost certainly be in the range 0–4.

Computing the Standard Deviation in Excel

There is no direct function like STDEV as there is for sample standard deviation. Remember, the sample standard deviation is computed on an observed sample of data. The standard deviation in this chapter is a measure of the uncertainty of a variable, before it has even been observed, and is computed from the probability distribution.

To calculate standard deviation in Excel, supposing the *x*-values have been named "x" and the probabilities named "p" type

=SUMPRODUCT(x, x, p) – SUMPRODUCT(x, p)^2,

which gives σ^2, and then use SQRT to get the standard deviation σ of the distribution.

Excel Template

In practice, there is not much point doing this calculation yourself and so I have provided a template, probability_distribution.xls, which does the following for you automatically:

- Gives a bar chart of the full probability distribution
- Displays the mean as a vertical line
- Represents variation as horizontal line extending 1 standard deviation either side of the mean

All you have to do is copy or type the values of the variable and their corresponding probabilities into columns B and C. The chart for the car sales data is below. The template also produces another chart called the cumulative distribution, which is described in the next section.

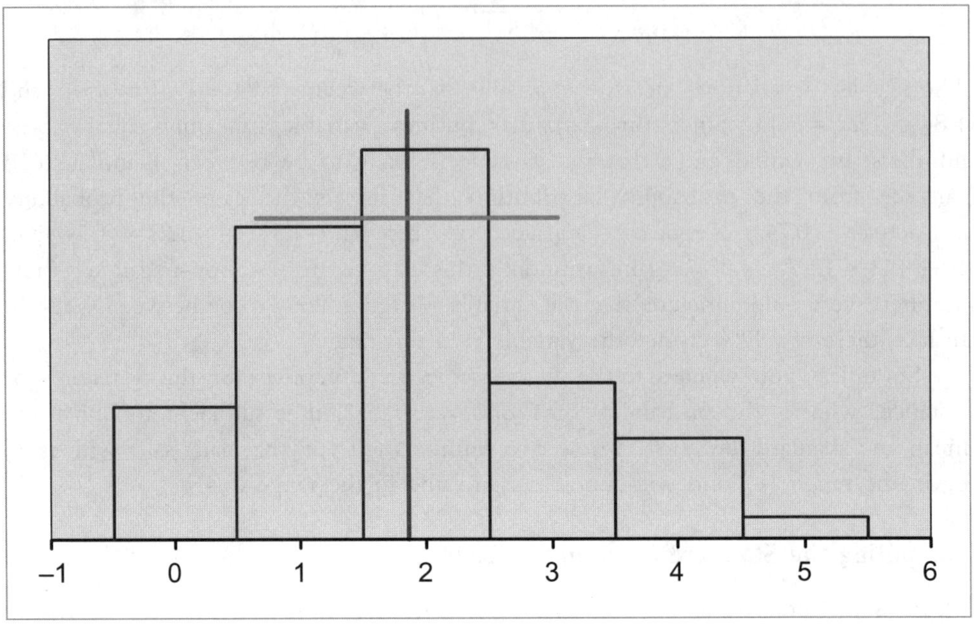

CHECK YOUR UNDERSTANDING

Q4.

(a) A certain investment of $10,000 has a 90% chance of a modest profit of $500. There is also an 8% chance of a $1000 profit. On the downside, there is a 2% chance of losing all your money. What is the mean and standard deviation of the profit? Do you think that the mean is a fair measure of the value of this investment opportunity?
(b) A certain investment has an uncertain profit on $1000 invested according to the following table.What is the mean and standard deviation of this distribution?

Profit	-$250	-$100	$0	$500	$1000
Prob	.12	.23	0.36	0.22	0.07

(c) How do answers in (b) change if the maximum payoff is $10,000 instead of $1000? In each case, calculate the coefficient of variation (which is the standard deviation divided by the mean).

5.7. COMPARING TWO DISTRIBUTIONS

In the briefing for the Value of Information case at the beginning of this chapter, two payoff distributions were tabulated. These are reproduced in the table below. The left one corresponds to acting immediately and firing the suspected employee.

The other corresponds to using a security firm to gain more certainty about who the culprit might be.

The left distribution is very simple. The second is rather complicated. We can use the probability_distribution.xls template to summarize and compare them. The mean of the "act now" option is $537.5 with a standard deviation of $671.2. The mean and standard deviation describe this "act now" payoff distribution, which is a 75% chance of a small cost and a 25% chance of a huge cost. The "act later" option has a mean of $391.5 and a standard deviation of $449.4. So the mean cost is lower and the uncertainty, as measured by the standard deviation, is also lower. High mean payoff with low uncertainty would usually be preferred. So it sounds like you would prefer the "act later" option, which is a reasonable conclusion in this case. However, standard deviation is only one measure of risk. There is a chance of facing an even higher cost with the "act later" strategy, namely $1725. This is unlikely but far from impossible.

Act Now without seeking more information		Get more information and then act on it Later	
Cost	Probability	Cost	Probability
$150	75%	$175	24.53%
$1700	25%	$195	15.93%
		$270	47.78%
		$995	0.80%
		$1,395	2.70%
		$1,725	8.18%
		$1,820	0.10%

The template will produce for you another way of looking at probability. Instead of listing the chances of all the various payoffs we list the chances of all the various payoffs *or lower*. For instance, with the "act later" option, the chance of a cost of $270 or lower is 88.24%. The template also produces a plot of the so-called **cumulative distribution function** (CDF), which is a function with "steps" at each point. This plot tells you the chance of the cost (or payoff in other examples) being less than or equal to any value you want to test. For instance the chance of the cost being less than $500 is 75% for the "act now" option and is 88.24% for the "act later" option.

If you now look at the *worksheet comparison* you will see both distributions displayed on the same sheet. For a cost variable, you want the CDF to be higher rather than lower. Why? Because you would like the chance of the cost being less than any value to be as high as possible. The distributions for "act now" and "act later" are below and it looks like the "act later" option is mainly higher than the "act now" option. This means that for most cost targets you might set—any value between about 250 and 1600 from the graph—you are more likely to fall below that cost using the "act later" option than the "act now" option.

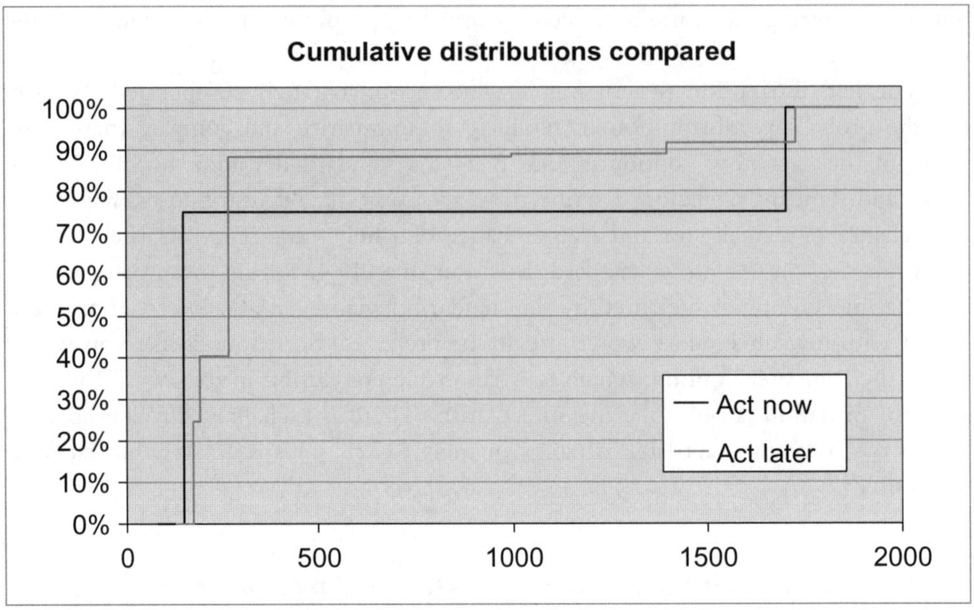

So our original reasoning that we would "act later" because the mean cost was lower and the risk was also lower is largely born out. However, if we were especially concerned with keeping costs below very low values we would not choose the "act later" options. For instance, with a cost target of $250 we see that there is a 75% chance of being under this if we "act now" but only a 40.46% if we "act later."

Warning

For most business problems, the natural performance measure is something that you would like to maximize (like profit) rather than minimize (like cost in the previous example). For these examples you want the CDF to be *lower* rather than higher. This is because you want it to be less likely that your profit will fall below any target value.

5.8. Conditional Distributions and Means

The probability distribution tells you about the likely values of the business variable. If further information becomes available about the variable, then the probability distribution may change.

For instance, it might become known that the business variable will fall within a particular range. The probability distribution should reflect this knowledge. The appropriate way to represent this knowledge is to calculate the conditional probabilities of all the possible outcomes. This is called the conditional probability distribution.

The key idea of conditional probability was to focus attention on the known event and then calculate each probability as a proportion of the probability of the known event. For a probability distribution, this simply means taking the possible values of the business variable consistent with the conditioning event and then rescaling them so that they add up to 1.0.

For instance, in the earlier example on fines, the original fine table was as given below. The mean fine was $5.9K and the standard deviation was $36.0K as you can check for yourself using the template. Relative to the mean value, this very large standard deviation means that the fine is very, very uncertain.

Violations	0	1	2	3
Fine	**$0**	**$0**	**k$200**	**k$500**
Probability	0.729	0.243	0.027	0.001

Now suppose that you wanted to know what the mean fine will be *if there is a fine*. It is quite unlikely that this will happen—the chance is 2.8%. But we want to assume that there is a fine so that we can answer the question. Before calculating, it is good practice to try to anticipate the answer. Since the mean is a typical or central value it is always some value in the middle of the possible values of the variance. Since the fine will either be $200K or $500K we know that the mean fine will be somewhere in this range. Since a $200K is more likely than a $500K, we anticipate that the mean will be closer to $200K than to $500K.

To calculate this, we imagine that we were told that there has been a fine. This becomes the conditioning event and it means that there must be either two or three violations. To calculate the conditional distribution we take the columns consistent with a fine (i.e., two or three violations) and rescale the probabilities, here 0.027 and 0.01, so that they add up to 1. This is done by dividing both of them by their total, 0.028. The result is the table below.

Violations	0	1	2	3
Fine	**$0**	**$0**	**k$200**	**k$500**
Probability	0	0	0.964	0.039

This says that, if there is a fine, then it is overwhelmingly likely to be the smaller $200K fine. The mean fine is now calculated to equal $210.7K. The standard deviation is $55.7K.

It is quite standard to judge the standard deviation by comparing it to the mean. In fact, the standard deviation divided by the mean has a name, it is called CV. Conditional on there being a fine, the CV is 55/7/210.7 = 26.4%.

5.9. SUMMARY

Most business variables are uncertain. If we are going to deal systematically with this uncertainty, we have to resort to probability to describe them. The **probability distribution** is a list of all possible values of the business variable together with the corresponding probabilities. It tells you everything that there is to know about the uncertain business variable. For instance, it tells you how likely it is that the variable will be within any specified range.

The probability distribution is interpreted in much the same way as a data distribution except it describes what is likely to happen rather than what has already happened.

The **mean** of an uncertain business variable is a single number measuring the central or typical value of the variable. It can be justified as a predictor of the long-term average of the business variable, or on more basic logical grounds.

The **standard deviation** of an uncertain business variable is a single number measuring the typical uncertainty of the variable. It measures typical uncertainty of the variable about the mean. The variable will likely fall within 1 standard deviation of the mean and will very likely be within 2 standard deviations of the mean.

The **CV** of an uncertain business variable is a single number measuring the standard deviation as a proportion of the mean.

You can modify a probability distribution if you know, or want to consider the eventuality, that the variable is within a certain range. Set all the probabilities outside the range to zero, and then rescale the remaining probabilities so that they add up to 1.0. This is called a **conditional distribution**.

You can calculate the mean and standard deviation of a conditional distribution just like any other distribution. The mean and standard deviation are then called the conditional mean and conditional standard deviation.

EXERCISES

E1. You are going to invest $1000 in a certain investment. The value of the investment after 1 year is uncertain but your assessment of the chance of various values is summarized in the table below. For instance, you assess a 2% chance that the company will go bankrupt and a 4% chance of a major setback for the company that would halve the share price. On the other hand, you assess a 5% chance of increasing your value of $1500.

Value	Chance
$0	2.00%
$500	4.00%
$1,000	8.50%
$1,020	10.00%
$1,040	14.50%
$1,060	16.50%
$1,080	18.00%
$1,100	12.50%
$1,200	9.00%
$1,500	5.00%

Use the appropriate Excel template to find the mean and standard deviation of the value of the investment after 1 year, as well as the mean and standard deviation of the percentage growth of the investment after 1 year.

E2. As an obstetrics specialist (baby deliverer) you face a small but nonzero chance of being sued for negligence. You estimate that the chance of being sued in any year is 5%. If you are sued you estimate that there is a 30% chance you win the case with costs awarded, a 40% chance you win the case but have to pay legal fees of $100,000 and a 30% chance you lose the case and have to pay a total of $1,000,000, including all legal fees.

(a) How much would a reasonable yearly insurance premium be?

(b) The insurance company is worried about the increasing trend in litigation. They think that the probability of you being sued could be as high as 10%. How much premium will they charge?

(c) The insurance company estimates that payouts when you lose are more likely to be \$5,000,000 than \$1,000,000 and want to insure on this basis. How much will the premium be?

(d) If the insurance company estimates that (1) the chance of being sued is 7%, (2) the chance of winning but without costs awarded is 35%, (3) the chance of losing is 35%, and (4) the amount you will pay out when you lose is \$2,000,000, then what is a fair premium?

E3. You are playing a game based on tossing two coins. If the result is two heads you win \$5. If it is two tails you win \$1, and if it is mixed you win nothing. It costs \$2 to play. Should you play?

E4. Suppose you play a game that costs \$1 to play. You win if a certain event comes to pass (for instance, my horse runs a place), otherwise you lose your stake. Suppose the probability of the event occurring is p.

(a) Supposing that you are paid \$$W$ when you win, what is the mean value of your payoff?

(b) What should the payoff be so that the game is "fair"?

E5. A system contains four components, at least three of which must function in order for the system to function. At a given time the number of components, n, that are not functioning has the probability distribution given below.

n	0	1	2	3	4
Prob	0.55	0.05	0.02	0.15	0.23

(a) What is the mean number of components functioning at any time?

(b) What is the standard deviation of the number of components functioning at any time?

(c) What is the probability that the system functions? Does this contradict the answer to part (a)?

E6. The return on a certain telco share over the next 12 months is uncertain. On the basis of a detailed analysis of historical data and company fundamentals, the probability distribution below is accepted as the best summary of likely returns.

Return(%)	-5	-4	-3	-2	-1	0	1	2	3	4	5	6	7	8
Probability(%)	1	2	3	4	6	8	13	17	15	11	8	6	4	2

(a) What is the mean return?

(b) If the risk-free rate (RFR) is 3.5%, then what is the probability of the share growing faster than the RFR?

(c) What is the probability of a positive return?

(d) What is the standard deviation of the return? (I suggest that you use the template for this). What does this measure?

(e) What is the mean return, conditional on you not making a loss?

(f) Suppose we considered monthly return rather than yearly. What would you expect the probability distribution of monthly returns to look like? Collect some data and check!

E7. On the basis of a large database of driver surveys you have estimated the probabilities in the table below for drivers classified by (1) their gender and (2) their self-reported use of the car horn in answer to the question, "How many times have you used your car horn in anger over the past week?"

(a) What is the mean number of car horn uses per week?

	0	1	2	3	4	5
Females	0.081	0.089	0.045	0.013	0.003	0.002
Males	0.011	0.055	0.129	0.181	0.178	0.213
All	0.092	0.144	0.174	0.194	0.181	0.215

(b) By dividing each row by its total, calculate the probability distribution of car horn use for Males and Females separately.

(c) What is the mean number of car horn uses per week for a male?

(d) What is the mean number of car horn uses per week for a female?

E8. You are facing a situation where one of your senior VPs is leaking valuable information. You suspect it is someone called Frank Berger but you are only 75% sure. If you terminate his employment it will cost you \$150K in the usual termination payments. However, if he is actually innocent it will cost you a total of \$1700K, which includes him suing you for wrongful dismissal as well as the continuing losses incurred from the true culprit. Your cost distribution is given in the left-hand column of the table below.

There is a security firm that can reduce your uncertainty about the identity of the leaker. When all is said and done, if you use the security firm then you will end up with a cost distribution described in the right two columns. These numbers require a fair bit of calculation to obtain. But after you have done the work to calculate them, the decision of whether or not to hire the security firm remains. And the decision has been distilled into a comparison of two cost distributions.

Cost	Probability	Cost	Probability
\$150	75%	\$175	24.53%
\$1700	25%	\$195	15.93%
		\$270	47.78%
		\$995	0.80%
		\$1,395	2.70%
		\$1,725	8.18%
		\$1,820	0.10%

Which of these two cost distributions would you prefer? Is the security firm "worth it"? Try to describe in fairly simple language why you would prefer one to the other.

E9. The table below gives the probability distribution of the number of inconsistencies/errors in a personal tax return, broken down by those taxpayers who prepare their own return and those who use a tax agent.

	NUMBER OF INCONSISTENCIES							
	0	**1**	**2**	**3**	**4**	**5**	**>5**	**Total**
Self	5.5%	5.1%	13.4%	11.7%	5.9%	2.8%	0.0%	44.4%
Agent	16.6%	13.8%	8.0%	10.5%	4.3%	2.4%	0.0%	55.6%
All	22.1%	18.9%	21.4%	22.2%	10.2%	5.2%	0.0%	100.0%

(a) What is the mean number of errors for a taxpayer?

(b) Conditional on being a taxpayer who prepares their own return, what is the mean number of errors?

(c) Given that someone makes no errors, what is the probability they used an agent?

E10. The table below gives the probability distribution of the number of occasions on which a person makes a purchase from a *Rustic Lane* clothes store in a year, as well as their gender. For example, 20.5% of the target population are expected to purchase on three occasions. Of these, 11% will be male and 9.5% will be female.

	Males	Females	Total
0	15.2%	7.7%	22.9%
1	5.1%	6.8%	11.9%
2	11.4%	7.0%	18.4%
3	11.0%	9.5%	20.5%
4	3.4%	10.9%	14.3%
5	1.8%	5.4%	7.2%
6	0.7%	3.1%	3.8%
7	0.4%	0.6%	1.0%
>7	0.0%	0.0%	0.0%

(a) What is the mean number of purchases per year for a customer of unspecified gender?

(b) What is the distribution of the number of purchases per year, conditional on being male? Hence what is the mean number of purchases per year for male customers?

(c) What is the distribution of the number of purchases per year, conditional on being female? Hence what is the mean number of purchases per year for female customers?

(d) Given that someone makes at least one purchase, what is the mean number of purchases in a year?

(e) Given that someone makes six purchases, what is the probability they are male?

(f) Given that someone makes at least one purchase, what is the probability they are male?

E11. *Cost–benefit analysis.* Many problems involve weighing a known cost against an uncertain benefit. Suppose the cost of a project is $\$C$ and that the possible value of the project is $\$V$, however the probability of this payoff is p.

(a) Write down an expression for the mean payoff. This will be an algebraic expression in terms of V, C, and p.

(b) What condition on p will ensure that the mean payoff is positive?

E12. You are offered a place at a gaming table to play the game described by the payoff table below. It costs nothing to play (but money is held in escrow to make sure that you pay your losses).

Payoff	$1000	$500	-$50000
Prob	0.25	0.7	0.05

(a) What is the mean payoff per game played?

(b) Would you play this game even once? Why/why not?

(c) Can you explain a situation where a rational person definitely would play the game?

(d) Would you play this game all night? Why/why not?

(e) Can you relate the payoff table to the horse betting strategy of placing a large amount of money on the favorite to win or place?

CHAPTER 6

Business Problems That Depend on Knowing "How Many"

6.0. Introduction: What Is the Issue?

Many of the business outcomes that managers care about are counts—the number of defectives in a batch, the number of complaints resolved in a day, and the number of respondents who recognize my brand, to name just a few. With just a few plausible assumptions, such variables will follow one of three standard probability distributions. The point of knowing the distribution is that you can predict the likely range of the business variable and even say how likely it is to be larger or smaller than some level of interest. For instance, you could state the probability of there being more than 12 defectives in a shipment of 500.

Suppose that you survey 500 customers on whether or not they recognize your brand. Suppose also that on the basis of historical norms you expect 35% or 175 to recognize your brand. But you have been spending more money than usual on advertising. *How many* more than 175 would convince you that the extra money had been worth the expense? You would not be convinced with 176 brand recognitions. It would need to be higher than this to really convince you. You would need to know what an *improbably high* value is.

This example involves counting up how *many times* something happens out of a fixed number of opportunities (called trials). This kind of count is described by the **binomial distribution**.

Suppose that you have to supply an order for five very expensive computer chips. They must be manufactured individually and sequentially. The chips are easily damaged or contaminated during manufacture and only two-thirds of manufactured chips are functional. Their faulty status is only determined after manufacture. *How*

Data-Driven Business Decisions, First Edition. Chris J. Lloyd.

many will you have to make to get five functioning ones? This will be central in assessing the mean cost of filling this order. In this case, we want to know how many attempts (i.e., trials) it will require to get a certain number of successful outcomes. The uncertainty of such a count is described by the **negative binomial distribution**.

Suppose that the mean number of phone calls arriving per hour is 235. I have enough staff to handle 300 calls. *How many* calls will arrive in the next hour? More to the point, what is the chance of more than 300 calls arriving? Should I increase or decrease my staff? In this case, we are counting up how many times something happens during a fixed period of time. There are no separate trials as such. Rather, the event can happen at any point of time during the fixed period. This kind of count is described by the **Poisson distribution**.

Occupational Safety and Health Administration: Violations of Safety Regulations. Case Briefing

Carol Katz works for the Occupational Safety and Health Administration (OSHA) monitoring the integrity of safety processes at *airports*.

The current system of assuring and monitoring safety standards involves unannounced inspections and audits of airports each month. There is a rolling system of fines applied to airports that violate standards, depending on how many times they violate as set out in the table below.

These are total fines for the year. Notice that no fine is imposed for the first violation during a year. The second incurs a \$100K fine, the third incurs a \$150K fine, the fourth incurs a \$250K fine, and the fifth incurs a \$500K fine. Each further violation is fined a further \$1M but this number of violations is probably unlikely.

Each calendar year the inspection regime begins afresh. The results of safety inspections are not available to the general public but they can be obtained by the carriers.

Fine table of total year fine by # violations						
Violations	0	1	2	3	4	5
Fine (\$1000)	0	0	100	250	500	1000

Airports have the power to improve their safety standards. OSHA has estimated that it would cost around \$2.5 M per annum (for staff and retooling) to reduce violations rates from 100% to 0%. For the sake of simplicity, Carol decides to assume that the relationship between violation rates and expenditure is linear. Thinking a little more about violation rates, she decides that she will measure this by the probability $\boldsymbol{p}$ of a violation in any given month. So the relation between safety cost and violation rate is

$$\text{Safety Cost (\$1000)} = 2500 \times (1 - p).$$

Carol has to assess how well the system is working and identify any strengths or weaknesses. She knows that the system is far from perfect. Violations are still happening. To try to assess the system she decides to put herself in the shoes of the airport. She says to herself:

> If I were running an airport and subject to this safety inspection regime I would worry about the monetary and reputational costs of safety violations. On the other hand, reducing the chance of these violations costs money. … The chance of a fine depends on my violation rate $\boldsymbol{p}$. So does the safety cost. What value of $\boldsymbol{p}$ would minimize my cost?

Further details and background are available in the full case.

6.1. The Binomial Distribution

The binomial distribution arises in the following context.

- We are interested in whether a certain event occurs or not.
- There is a sequence of opportunities (generically called *trials*) for the event to happen.
- We are interested in counting *how many* times the event happens.

To use the binomial distribution several extra assumptions need to hold.

1. The number of trials, often denoted by $\boldsymbol{n}$, is prespecified and fixed. For example, we might count the number of trading days where Westfield shares rose during 2009. The number of trading days $n = 247$ is fixed.
2. If the event occurs on one trial this does not affect the chance of the event on any other trial. The trials are said to be *independent*. Rises and falls of a stock on one day do not have any affect on their chances of rising or falling on another day. So this assumption would hold for the Westfield example.
3. The probability of the event on any trial, often denoted by $\boldsymbol{p}$, is the same for each trial. This may not be exactly true for the event of a rising stock—in bull markets the chance of rising will be higher than in bear markets—but during stable financial periods it would not be far from the truth. It is an empirical fact that stock rises and falls do closely follow the binomial distribution in most cases.

> The symbol "$n!$" means multiply the integer n by all integers less than it. For example, $4! = 4 \times 3 \times 2 \times 1 = 24$.

DEFINITION

A business variable X has the **binomial** distribution if its probability distribution has the following mathematical form:

$$\Pr(x \text{ events from } n \text{ trials}) = \frac{n!}{x!(n-x)!} p^x (1-p)^{n-x}.$$

The possible values of x are 0, 1, 2, ... , n.

The formula above gives the probability of any particular outcome x. You do not have to remember this formula! There is an Excel function that we can use to calculate binomial probabilities. To apply the binomial distribution you need to be confident that the context and assumptions listed above are correct and you also need to know the numbers n and p.

Some Simple Examples

The absolute paradigm example of the binomial distribution is tossing a fair coin 100 times and counting how many heads you get. Tosses are trials and the event of interest is a head, so $n = 100$ trials and the probability of the event occurring is $p = 0.5$. Each toss of the coin (i.e., each trial) is independent, and the probability of the event is fixed and constant, providing you are tossing the coin fairly. This example has nothing to do with business. It is just a useful conceptual metaphor to keep in mind for later examples.

What do you think the *mean value* would be? What would be the typical or central number of heads out of 100? The obvious answer is 50, and this is the correct answer. A picture of the probability distribution is displayed below left. Remember that this shows the probability of various numbers (of heads in this case). In principle, you could have any number between 0 and 100 heads but the chances of such extreme outcomes are almost zero. While the mean value is 50, it looks like the number of heads would likely be in the range from about 40 to 60. So even though this is not a business example, there is something extra you get from the binomial distribution—an idea of the uncertainty in the number of heads. And you can easily calculate the chance of a specific outcome, say of getting "55 heads or more."

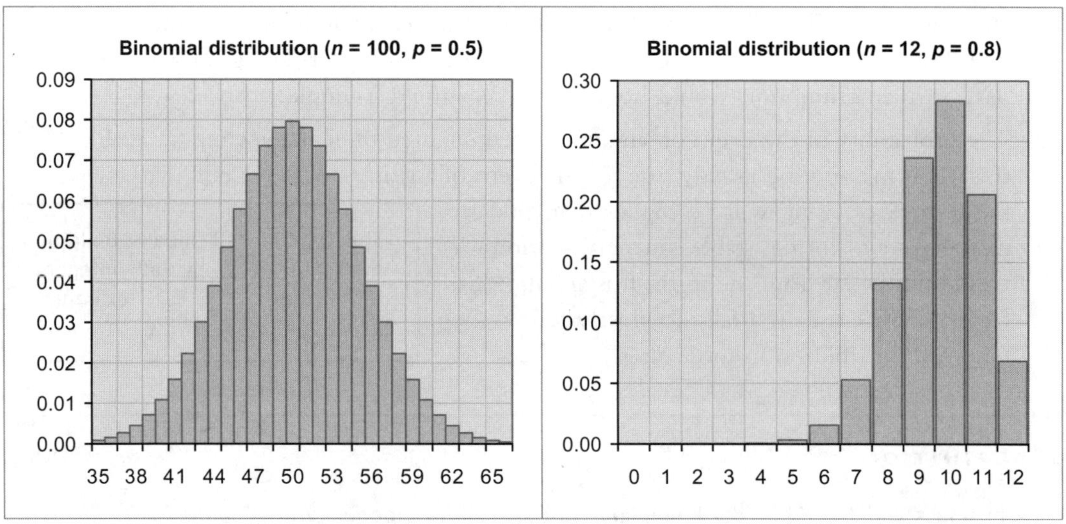

The binomial distribution with $n = 12$ and $p = 0.8$ would arise in a situation where there were 12 independent trials and we were counting how many times a particular event of interest happened, where the event was rather likely (since $p = 0.8$). A simple example would be: "Out of the 12 hotel bookings I accepted this weekend, how many will turn up?", where we had some reason to suppose that the probability of a customer turning up is 0.8—perhaps based on previous records. This probability distribution is displayed in the right plot above. What do you think the mean value would be? You can see from the graph that it is around 10—the exact value is 9.6.

Using Excel

The binomial distribution is calculated using the internal Excel function **BINOMDIST**. You need to supply the value for x then n then p.

To compute the probability of seven successes from 12 trials when the success probability equals 0.8 you type

=BINOMDIST(7,12,0.8,FALSE).

The answer is 0.0532. In the plot of the distribution above right, you can see that the bar labeled "7" is indeed just above 5%. The fourth field FALSE means that you do not want a cumulative probability. You just want an ordinary probability. In fact, the plot itself was produced by applying the function BINOMDIST to the numbers 0,..,12 and plotting a bar chart. If you wanted to compute the probability of seven *or fewer* successes from 12 trials with a success probability of 0.8, then you must realize that this is a cumulative probability. So you type

=BINOMDIST(7,12,0.8,TRUE).

The answer is 0.0726. You cannot see this directly in the plot. It is the total of all the bars from 7 to the left. BINOMDIST will either calculate the probability of an *exact given value* (if you put FALSE in the last field) or the probability of a *given value or less* (if you put TRUE in the last field).

CHECK YOUR UNDERSTANDING

Q1.

(a) You survey 500 customers on whether or not they recognize your brand. On the basis of historical norms you expect 35% or 175 to recognize your brand. How does this relate to the binomial distribution?

(b) You know that the long-run rate of defectives among computer chips is 1 in 750. If you order 1500 per week, and you want to predict how many will be defective, what distribution would be appropriate? Do you think the assumptions of the binomial will approximately hold?

6.2. THE MEAN AND STANDARD DEVIATION

If each of the n trials has the same probability p of the event then you might expect that the mean number of times the event occurs would be n times p. And you would be quite correct. If there is a 20% chance of rain on each day of a week then the mean number of rainy days is 1.4 (7 times 0.2). The formula for the standard deviation is also quite simple, but not so obvious.

For a binomial distribution with parameters n and p the mean of the probability is $\mu = np$ and the variance of the distribution is $\sigma^2 = np(1 - p)$. The standard deviation is the square root of the variance.

EXAMPLE

Below is a table of the binomial distribution with $n = 12$ and $p = 0.8$. The probabilities were obtained in Excel using BINOMDIST(x,12,0,.8,false) with x being the cell reference to the left. The probabilities were plotted against the x-values to produce the earlier plot.

The mean can be obtained in the usual way by multiplying each x-value by its probability and adding up. You get the answer 9.6; however, it is obviously quicker and more convenient just to use the formula $\mu = n \times p = 9.6$. To get the standard deviation, square each x-value, multiply by p, and add up to obtain 94.08. Then subtract the mean squared to get the answer 1.92 for the variance. It is obviously **way** quicker just to use the formula $\sigma^2 = np(1 - p) = 1.92$. The standard deviation is the square root of this, which is 1.386.

Binomial Distribution n=12, p=0.8			
x	Probability	xp	x^2p
0	0.0000	0.000	0.000
1	0.0000	0.000	0.000
2	0.0000	0.000	0.000
3	0.0001	0.000	0.001
4	0.0005	0.002	0.008
5	0.0033	0.017	0.083
6	0.0155	0.093	0.558
7	0.0532	0.372	2.604
8	0.1329	1.063	8.504
9	0.2362	2.126	19.134
10	0.2835	2.835	28.347
11	0.2062	2.268	24.945
12	0.0687	0.825	9.896
Total	1.000	9.60	94.08

CHECK YOUR UNDERSTANDING

Q2.

(a) You survey 500 customers on whether or not they recognize your brand. On the basis of historical norms you expect 35% to recognize your brand. What is the *likely range* of responses from the survey?

(b) You know that the long-run rate of defectives among computer chips is 1 in 750. If you order 1500 per week, then the expected number of computer chips is obviously 2. But what can you say about the uncertainty in this figure (without actually calculating any binomial probabilities)?

(c) On any given day, the probability that a car salesperson sells a car is 0.88. During a 6-day week, on how many days will the salesperson sell a car? Warning: the answer is not a number!

(d) Over a year, the car salesperson has sold 622 new cars. Each of them comes with a 3-year guarantee that commits the manufacturer to full replacement if the car has a "serious fault." It is thought that the probability that a car has a serious fault is 0.004. How many of the cars that the salesperson sold will have to be replaced? Suppose that 3 years later we find that seven have had to be replaced. What do you think about the assumption that the probability of a serious fault is 0.004?

Pushing a Little Further

Why would a "how many" variable *not* be binomial? In the previous chapter we considered the number of cars that were sold at a car yard in a day. The distributions for a general day and for Saturday specifically are in the table below. Could these distributions be binomial? Let's concentrate just on the Saturday distribution.

Number	0	1	2	3	4	5
General day	0.12	0.28	0.35	0.14	.09	.02
Saturday	0.02	0.18	0.31	0.24	.17	.08

Suppose we knew that in any given hour you cannot sell more than one car because of the administration and paperwork involved. The working day comprises say, 8 h. In each hour you will sell a car or you won't. So the total number of cars sold sounds like it might be binomial with $n = 8$ and p equaling the probability that you sell a car in any given hour.

Below is a comparison of the actual car sales distribution with the binomial distribution with $n = 8$ and $p = 0.325$. Why did I use $p = 0.325$? Because the mean of this binomial distribution is $n \times p = 8 \times 0.325 = 2.60$, which is the mean of the actual distribution we are trying to match. Apparently the two distributions are not the same, though they are not drastically different. Is the difference really large enough "to matter"? *How well do the data fit the theory?*

We will look at issues like this in great detail in later chapters. You might like to open the file binomial_cars.xls and play around with different values of p to see how closely you can make the binomial match the actual distribution. You will find that there is no way to make them the same.

Two Possible Distributions		
x	Binomial (n = 8)	Actual
0	0.04310	0.02
1	0.16600	0.18
2	0.27974	0.31
3	0.26937	0.24
4	0.16212	0.17
5	0.06245	0.08
6	0.01503	0.00
7	0.00207	0.00
8	0.00012	0.00
Value of p:	0.325	

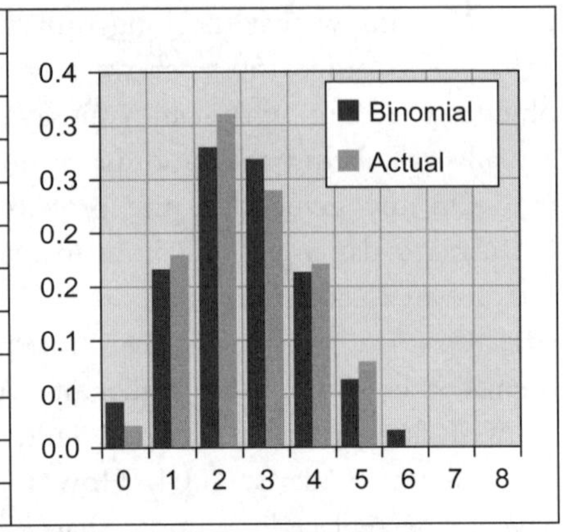

Looking back at the assumptions of the binomial distribution, why might the distribution *not* be binomial? The main assumptions underlying the binomial distribution are first, that there are a fixed number of trails (we assumed $n = 8$ since there are 8 h in the working day), second, that trials are independent, and third, that the probability of success is the same for each trial. All of these assumptions are suspect here.

A trial here is a 1-h period—or any time period you might consider sensible during which the salesperson can start and complete a sale. Why could we not take a trial to be 48 min, in which case $n = 10$? We could have more success in matching the distribution in this case—but you will find that you still cannot get a perfect match. Second, trials may not be independent. A sale at one point of time may reduce the chance of a sale thereafter—the salesperson may be less motivated or the more sellable cars may no longer be available for sale. More obviously, the probability p of a sale in an hour (or some alternative time period defining a trial) would vary over the day. Very few people would buy a car first thing in the morning or during the lunch hour.

But when all is said and done, the distribution is not terribly different to a binomial distribution and we would not go terribly wrong if we used binomial probabilities. It is quite common, and permissible, to use distributions that are only approximately correct, though one should always assess how much effect any errors may have on the final decision.

6.3. THE NEGATIVE BINOMIAL DISTRIBUTION

Recall the basic context of the binomial distribution—there is a sequence of independent trials and an event that may or may not happen on each trial. Let us call the trial a success when the event happens and a failure when it does not. The chance of a success is the chance that the event happens, denoted by p.

If we ask "How many successes X will we have from n trials?" then the distribution is binomial. If we ask a different question—"How many failures Y will occur before we get ***r*** successes?"—then the distribution is a different one—called negative binomial.

DEFINITION

A business variable y has the **negative binomial** distribution if its probability distribution has the following mathematical form:

$$\Pr\left(y \text{ failures before the } r^{\text{th}} \text{ success}\right) = \frac{(y+r-1)!}{y!(r-1)!} p^{y}(1-p)^{r}.$$

There is no natural limit to how large y could be, so the possible values of y are 0, 1, 2, ...

When $r = 1$ the distribution is called the **geometric**.

The formula above gives the probability of any particular outcome y. Again, you do not have to remember this formula! There is an Excel function to calculate it. To apply the negative binomial distribution you need to be confident that the context and assumptions listed above are correct and you also need to know the numbers r and p.

Some Simple Examples

Suppose we were hiring executives to three positions. Suppose that the proportion of candidates that would be suitable for the job is 0.65. How many unsuitable candidates would we expect to interview before we filled the three positions? Here a success is a suitable candidate, $p = 0.65$ and $r = 3$. The distribution is plotted below.

The chance of there being $y = 0$ unsuitable candidates is the chance that the first three *are* suitable, which is obviously $0.65^3 = 0.275$. The other probabilities are not so straightforward to work out, which is why we have the negative binomial formula. It looks like there will be between zero and three unsuccessful interviews before you get the three executives hired, so there will be between three and six interviews in total.

As another example, a worker in a call center has a 2.5% chance of making a successful sale on any call. How many unsuccessful calls will he or she have to make to achieve a daily target of 10 sales? The trials here are calls and since the customers on different calls do not interact, the chances of success would be close to independent. The number of unsuccessful calls would have the negative binomial distribution with $r = 10$ and $p = 0.025$. This is plotted below right. It looks like the number of calls could be anywhere between 200 and 700. This is a very uncertain business outcome.

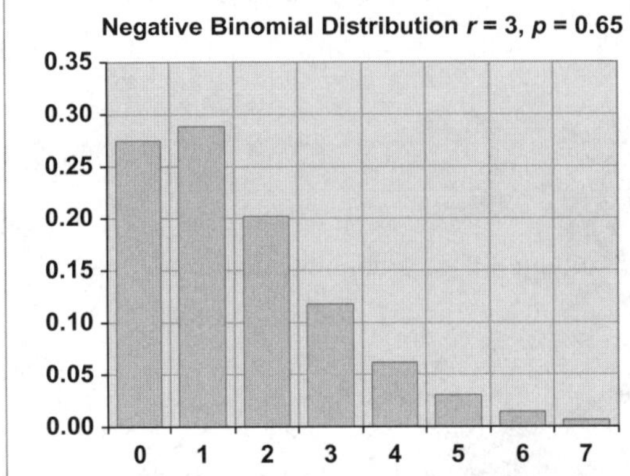

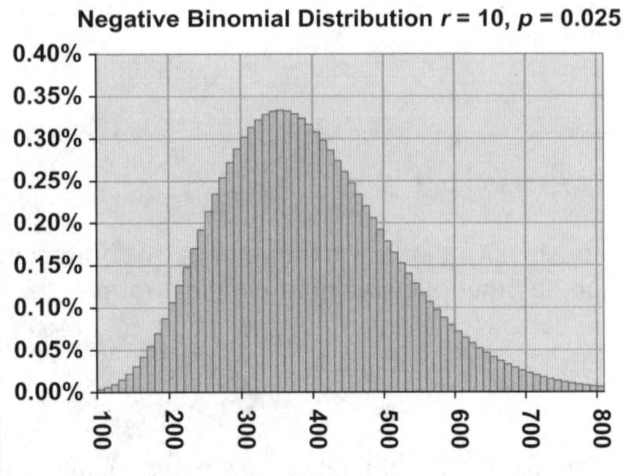

Using Excel

The negative binomial distribution is calculated using the internal Excel function **NEGBINOMDIST**. You need to supply the value for y then r then p.

To compute the probability of three unsuitable candidates before the third suitable executive (remember $r = 3$, $p = 0.65$), you type

=NEGBINOMDIST(3,3,0.65).

The answer is 0.118. In the plot of the distribution above left, you can see that the bar labeled "3" is indeed around 11.8%. For calculating the chance of three or less unsuitable candidates, there is no shortcut as there was with BINOMDIST. You just have to calculate all the probabilities from $y = 3$ down to $y = 0$ and add them up (or you can use the provided template).

The Mean and Standard Deviation

If you know a variable is a negative binomial, and you know the values of r and p, then you can immediately calculate the mean and the standard deviation.

> For a negative binomial distribution with parameters r and p the mean of the distribution is $\mu = r(1 - p)/p$ and the variance of the distribution is $\sigma^2 = r(1 - p)/p^2$. The standard deviation is the square root of the variance.

EXAMPLE

For the example of interviewing executives the number of unsuitable candidates was a negative binomial with $r = 3$ and $p = 0.65$. Using the above formulas, the mean is 1.62 and the standard deviation is 1.58. This suggests a typical range of 0–3 and a reasonable range of 0–5.

For the call center example, $r = 10$ and $p = 0.025$, so the mean is 390 and the standard deviation is 125. This suggests a typical range from 265 to 515 and a reasonable range of 140–640. This is consistent with the plot above.

Check Your Understanding

Q3.

(a) You have to supply an order for five very expensive computer chips. They must be made sequentially. The chips are extremely delicate and only two-thirds of manufactured chips are functional. Describe the distribution of the number of chips you will need to make to satisfy the order.
(b) There is a $14,800 set-up cost for retooling if you are going to take the order at all. In this case, it will cost $2700 to manufacture each chip. If you charge $7500 each then what profit will you expect to make? What price per chip would you consider to be "breakeven"?

Pushing a Bit Further

The negative binomial is sometimes used to describe a business outcome even when the outcome *does not arise from a sequence of binomial trials at all.* In this case, using the distribution is often based on existing empirical evidence that the distribution does indeed describe the outcome's historical pattern of variation.

A case in point is the number of times a person is exposed to an advertisement. Even though there is no obvious way to think of advertisement exposure as arising from counting the number of failures to the rth success, real data usually look very like the negative binomial.

In applications of this kind, one often knows the mean and standard deviation and then needs the values of r and p for the negative binomial distribution. There are simple formulas that can be used for this.

> For a negative binomial distribution with mean μ and variance σ^2, the parameter $p = \mu/\sigma^2$ and the parameter $r = \mu^2/(\sigma^2 - \mu)$.

For example, suppose the number of exposures to an advertisement has a mean of 4.5 and a standard deviation of 3.2. Then, using the above formulas gives the parameters $r = 3.53$ and $p = 0.439$. We can then answer questions such as "What is the probability that the advertisement will not be seen at all?" You might wonder what it means for $r = 3.53$ to not be a whole number. It just means that the distribution is somewhere between $r = 3$ and $r = 4$.

To compute negative binomial probabilities where r is not a whole number, you will have to use the template negbino_calculator.xls. This template also calculates the values of r and p when you know the mean μ and standard deviation σ using the formulas above. If you type 4.5 for the mean and 3.2 for the standard deviation in cells H7:H8, you will see that the values $r = 3.53$ and $p = 0.439$ appear in cells H2:H3. Type these values into the main panels in cells E2:E3 and enter the x-value into cell E4. The probability of 0 exposures is then 0.0547.

6.4. The Poisson Distribution

The Poisson distribution arises when the events we are counting can occur at any point during a fixed time period of length T. So unlike the binomial distribution, there is not a fixed number n of opportunities for the event to occur. As with the binomial distribution, we are interested counting *how many* times the event happens but there is no maximum number for this count.

> If the rate is not constant, just use the average rate over the time period.

To use the Poisson distribution several assumptions need to hold.

1. Events occur *independently*. For instance, a telephone call arriving at an exchange at a certain time does not make it more or less likely that a call will arrive in the very next instant.
2. Events occur at a constant mean rate (denoted by α) per unit of time. For instance, telephone calls might arrive at a mean rate of 1.9 per second.

DEFINITION

A business variable x has the **Poisson** distribution if its probability distribution has the following mathematical form:

$$\Pr(x \text{ events during time period}) = e^{-\lambda}\lambda^{x}/x!$$

The variable x can take any non-negative value. As with the negative binomial distribution, there is no maximum possible value.

> Make sure α and T are in the **same units.** If T is in seconds then α should be a rate *per second*.

There is only one parameter for the Poisson distribution—denoted λ. When events occur at a mean rate α and you want to know how many will occur in a time period T then use the value $\lambda = \alpha T$.

Some Simple Examples

Suppose that calls arrive at a telephone exchange at a mean rate $\alpha = 1.9$ per second. How many calls will arrive during the next $T = 60$ s? The parameter $\lambda = \alpha T = 114$ and the Poisson distribution is displayed in the left plot. The likely number of calls is in the range 100–130. Notice that all the probabilities are rather small here—the largest is about 0.04. This is because there are many possible values for this variable and the probabilities have to add up to 1.0. What do you think the mean value would be? If there are 1.9 calls per second on average for 60 s you would surely expect a mean of 114—and that is the correct answer.

Suppose force 8 summer cyclones in Hong Kong occur randomly in time at a rate of 1.15 per month. How many cyclones will there be in the $T = 3$-month cyclone season? The parameter $\lambda = \alpha T = 3.45$ and the Poisson distribution is displayed in the right plot. It is most likely there will be three cyclones but it could easily be anywhere from one to five cyclones.

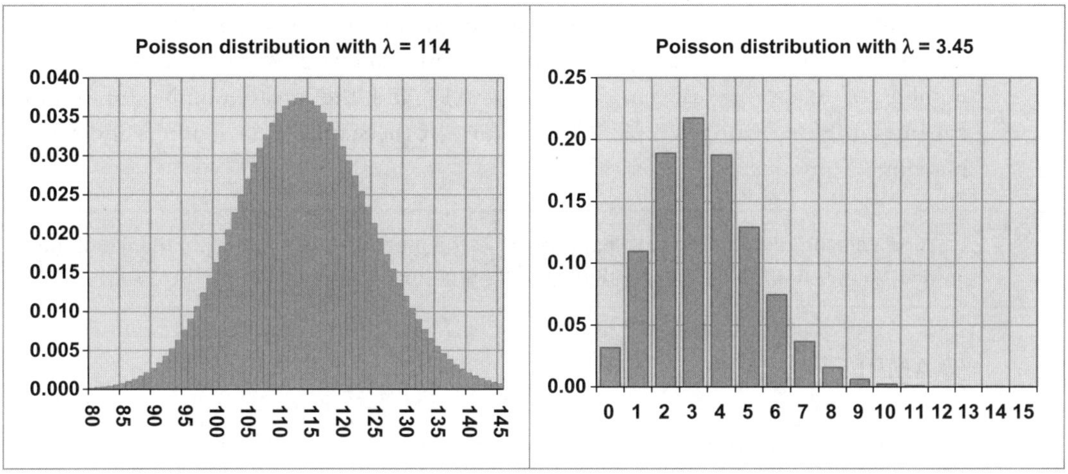

Using Excel

The Poisson distribution is calculated using the internal Excel function **POISSON**. You need to supply the value for x and then λ.

To compute the probability of exactly 125 telephone calls when $\lambda = 114$ type

=POISSON(125,114,FALSE).

The answer is 0.021. The reason this is quite small is that there are rather a lot of possible values that this variable could take. To compute the probability of 125 *or fewer* telephone calls you type

=POISSON(125,114,TRUE),

which gives the answer 0.859. This is the total of all probabilities from 125 to the left. The chance of *six or more* summer cyclones in Hong Kong is computed by calculating the chance of five or fewer and then subtracting from 1. Just type

=1 – POISSON(5,3.45,TRUE)

to obtain 0.136. This is the total of the probabilities to the right of "5" in the above right plot.

Excel Warning

There is a problem with the Excel function POISSON if the value of x is large—say, larger than about 150. For instance, if the mean number of telephone calls per hour is 150 and you want to know the chance of there being 145 or less calls then you would type POISSON(145,150,true). Unfortunately, Excel gives an error in Excel 2003 and will give errors in Excel 2007 for larger values of λ. There is a practical solution to this annoying problem and I have coded it into the file poisson_calculator.xls, which will work for values up to around 2000. Indeed, this template can be used in all cases if you desire.

The Mean and Standard Deviation

If events happen at a mean rate α per unit of time, and you count how many events there are over a time period T, then the mean number of events should surely be $\lambda = \alpha T$. So the mean of a Poisson variable with parameter λ is just λ. So the mean number of telephone calls in an hour is 114 and the mean number of summer cyclones in Hong Kong is 3.45. The formula for the standard deviation is also simple, but not so obvious.

> For a Poisson distribution with parameters λ, the mean is $\mu = \lambda$ and the variance of the distribution is $\sigma^2 = \lambda$. The standard deviation is the square root of the mean λ.

EXAMPLE

Below is a table of the Poisson distribution with $\lambda = 3.45$, which is the distribution of summer cyclones in Hong Kong. The probabilities were obtained in Excel using POISSON(x,3.45,false), with x being the cell reference to the left. The table should in principle continue on downwards indefinitely; however, after $x = 13$ the probabilities are almost zero and can be ignored.

The mean can be obtained in the usual way by multiplying each x-value by its probability and adding up. You get the answer 3.45; however, it is obviously quicker and more convenient just to use the formula $\mu = \lambda = 3.45$. To get the standard deviation, square each x-value, multiply by p, and add up to obtain 15.352. Then subtract the mean squared to get the answer 3.45 for the variance. It is obviously **way** quicker just to use the formula $\sigma^2 = \lambda = 3.45$! The standard deviation is the square root of this, which is 1.86.

Poisson Distribution with λ=3.45

x	Probability	xp	x^2p
0	0.0317	0.000	0.000
1	0.1095	0.110	0.110
2	0.1889	0.378	0.756
3	0.2173	0.652	1.955
4	0.1874	0.750	2.998
5	0.1293	0.646	3.232
6	0.0743	0.446	2.677
7	0.0366	0.256	1.795
8	0.0158	0.126	1.011
9	0.0061	0.055	0.491
10	0.0021	0.021	0.209
11	0.0007	0.007	0.079
12	0.0002	0.002	0.027
13	0.0001	0.001	0.008
...	...	...	...
Total	1.0000	3.450	15.352

As always, the mean and standard deviation tell you a great deal about the probability distribution. The mean is 3.45 and the standard deviation is 1.86, so a 1 standard deviation range is 1.6–5.3. Rounding to the nearest integer, we conclude that there will probably be from two to five cyclones. The 2 standard deviation range is −0.3–7.2. Rounding to the nearest integer, we conclude that there will almost certainly be from zero to seven cyclones. If you check the detailed distribution you will find these statements are born out. The exact chance of from two to five cyclones is 72% and the exact chance of from zero to seven cyclones is 97%.

6.5. Some Typical Business Applications

Picking Stocks Some stockbrokers, perhaps most, claim to be able pick whether a stock will go up or down, not every time but better than guessing. How many predictions should someone get correct in a week, a month, or a year if they are completely guessing? What is the uncertainty in these figures? What sort of an outcome would be truly impressive? What kinds of outcomes can be explained away as good or bad luck?

This involves counting the correct guesses of the stockbroker. We would use the binomial distribution with n equal to the number of stock tips made by the broker and p equal to the probability that the broker is correct by sheer luck—a figure slightly larger than 0.5 in a rising market. You would then look at how many guesses the broker got correct and ask, "How likely is it that someone would get this many correct by guessing?" If the probability were small, you would be impressed because the broker would have achieved something that is unlikely to happen if he or she is just guessing.

Passenger Management Airlines overbook planes because they know some passengers will not turn up. Suppose that the chance of a passenger not turning up is 0.024 so the chance of turning up is 0.976. You book an airbus with 520 seats but you accept 530 bookings. How many passengers will turn up? This will be binomial with $n = 530$ and $p = 0.976$. You would ideally like exactly 520 to turn up but it may well be less than this (in which case you lose some money since you are required to put them on a next plane where there is a free seat) or more than this (in which case you will have to compensate those whose booking is not honored).

Quality Control You know that the long-run rate of defectives among computer chips is 1 in 750. If you order 1500 per week, how many will be defective? This would be binomial with $n = 1500$ and $p = 1/750$. *How many* would you need to order to be practically sure of getting 1500 functioning chips? This would be a negative binomial with $r = 1500$ and $p = 1/750$.

Printing Typos At a particular newspaper, it is known that typos occur at a mean rate of 1 per 3.76 m of text. Thought of another way, they occur at a rate of 0.136 per meter. A typical edition has 78 pages each, each page being 35 cm wide with 110 lines. So the total length of print is 3003 m. Instead of events in time here we can think of events occurring randomly along the 3003 m of print. So the distribution will be Poisson. If a new system was introduced and the next paper has 65 typos then in assessing whether the new system was an improvement you would ask, "How likely is it to get so few errors?"

Market Surveys You survey 500 customers on whether or not they recognize your brand. On the basis of historical norms you expect 35% or 175 to recognize your brand. But you have been spending more money than usual on advertising. *How many* more than 175 would start to convince you that the extra money had been worth the expense? This would involve the binomial distribution with $n = 500$ and $p = 0.35$ and you would want to look at how improbably large the observed outcome is.

Demands on a Telephone System The mean number of phone calls arriving per hour is 265. I have enough staff to handle 300 calls. *How many* calls will arrive in the next hour? What is the chance of more than 300 calls arriving? Should I increase or decrease my staff? In this case, we are counting up how many times something happens during a fixed period of time. This kind of count is described by the Poisson distribution.

6.6. SUMMARY

Many business outcomes depend on counting how many times a particular event happens, either from a sequence of opportunities or *trials* or during a fixed period of time.

The **binomial distribution** is used when counting the number of events that occur from a fixed number n of *independent* trials. You need to know the number of trials (n) and the probability of the event (p). The mean is $\mu = np$; the variance $\sigma^2 = np(1 - p)$, and the standard deviation is the square root of this. Use the Excel function BINOMDIST(x,n,p,false/true) to calculate probabilities.

The **negative binomial distribution** is used when counting how many trials it takes to achieve a certain number of successes, or more precisely how many failures you well see before the rth success. You need to know the number of success (r) you are waiting for and the probability of a success (p). The mean is $\mu = r(1 - p)/p$; the variance is $\sigma^2 = r(1 - p)/p^2$ and the standard deviation is the square root of this. Use the Excel function NEGBINOMDIST(x,n,p) to calculate probabilities.

The **Poisson distribution** is used when counting how many events occur in a fixed amount of time. You need to know the rate α per unit time at which events occur and the time period T. The mean is $\mu = \lambda = \alpha T$; the variance is $\sigma^2 = \lambda = \alpha T$ and the standard deviation is the square root of this. Use the Excel function POISSON(x, λ,false/true) to calculate probabilities.

EXERCISES

E1. An insurance salesman meets with eight prospective customers each week. From historical data, the proportion of these customers who take out a policy is 18%.

(a) What is the probability that the salesman will sell three or more policies in a given week?

(b) What is the probability that the salesman will sell 12 or more policies in a given month (assuming a month is exactly 4 weeks)?

(c) What is the probability that the salesman sells 156 or more policies in a year (assuming a year is exactly 52 weeks)?

(d) What are the mean and standard deviation of the number of policies he sells in a week, a month, a year? What do you notice about these three distributions?

E2. A market survey is given to 1000 people. One of the questions concerns whether the person recognizes the brand name X. It is known that roughly 60% of people respond "yes" though this varies to some extent over time, and one of the purposes of the survey is to monitor this.

(a) How many of the 1000 people would you expect to recognize brand X? Your answer should not be a single number!

(b) Based on your answer to (a), how uncertain and unreliable is the *proportion* of people who recognize brand X?

(c) If a particular survey gave the result of 62% recognition and then a month later the proportion had dropped to 57%, would you be convinced that brand recognition is really decreasing?

E3. You survey 500 customers on whether or not they recognize your brand. On the basis of historical norms you expect 35% or 175 to recognize your brand. But you have been spending more money than usual on advertising. *How many* more than 175 would start to convince you that the extra money had been worth the expense?

E4. The distribution below is the binomial distribution with $n = 4$ and $p = 0.3$. You have formulas that allow you to immediately calculate the mean and standard deviation. The point of this exercise is to convince you that the formulas are correct, and also to check that you know what mean and standard deviation are.

x	Prob
0	0.2401
1	0.4116
2	0.2646
3	0.0756
4	0.0081

(a) What are the mean and standard deviation using the quick formula appropriate for the binomial distribution?

(b) Calculate the mean and standard deviation from first principles and hence confirm that the quick formulas give the right answer.

E5. XYZ mutual fund has outperformed the index in 33 of the past 52 weeks. On this basis they are claiming that they can systematically outperform the market.

(a) What do you think of this claim?

(b) Assuming that XYZ are not outperforming the market, what is the chance they would get to make this claim during a 10-year period?

(c) How many years would XYZ have to wait before they can make such a claim?

E6. Historically, your brand has 68% brand recognition in the market. From a survey of 250 customers describe in words the likely number who will recognize your brand. What is the chance that 182 or more recognize your brand?

E7. You are determined that the underlying proportion of customers who give your products the lowest possible rating for meeting expectations on a 5-point scale is to be no higher than 10%. Suppose it is exactly 10%. From a survey of 100 customers describe in words the likely number who will give your product the lowest possible rating. What is the chance that, by bad luck, 15 or more out of the sample report the lowest level of satisfaction?

E8. You are testing items off a production line and your benchmark proportion of defectives is 3%. Suppose that the true defective rate is 3%.
- **(a)** From a sample of 100, what is the probability that the sample has five or more defectives?
- **(b)** From a sample of 300, what is the probability that the sample has 15 or more defectives?
- **(c)** From a sample of 1000, what is the probability that the sample has 50 or more defectives?

E9. Airlines overbook planes because they know some passengers will not turn up. Suppose that the chance of a passenger not turning up is 0.024 so the chance of turning up is 0.976. You book seats on an airbus with 520 seats but accept 530 bookings for a particular flight. You would ideally like exactly 520 to turn up but it may well be less than this (in which case you lose some money since you are required to put them on an alternative flight) or more than this (in which case you will have to "bump them" off the flight and compensate). The key issue then is how many passengers turn up. Suppose that the revenue on each seat is $450 and the compensation costs you $300. What profits will you be likely to make?

E10. A mining company has, as part of its strategic plan for the year, a goal of establishing at least three new viable sites. Ultimately only 1 in 30 sites are viable. What is the
- **(a)** chance that more than 120 sites will need to be tested?
- **(b)** mean and standard deviation of the number of sites that will need to be tested?
- **(c)** required probability of a site being viable to reduce the chance in (a) to 10%?
- **(d)** first step in assessing a site is a core sample? If the core sample is positive then there is a 72% chance the site is viable. How many positive core samples will you need to achieve the goal?

E11. A market research company needs to have 500 respondents to a phone survey. On past performance, 22% of people called will agree to the survey. The cost of each call is 23 cents for the call plus 32 cents for the interviewer if the person declines and $3.16 for the interviewer if the person accepts. The company has budgeted $1750 for executing the survey.
- **(a)** What is the distribution of the number of people who decline?
- **(b)** If Y is the number of people who decline then give a formula for the cost of the survey in terms of Y.
- **(c)** What are the mean and standard deviation of Y?
- **(d)** What is the probability that the cost of the campaign exceeds the budget?

E12. The board of Metropolis Business School wants to appoint a new dean and director. They retain a headhunting firm to suggest candidates. There is a fixed cost of $100,000 for providing 10 willing candidates who fit your criteria. However, some of these candidates may well be completely unsuitable and you will only find out by interview. The interviews are costly in terms of a return business class airfare (around $11,000), accommodation ($2000), and (uncharged) cost to the board of their time ($1500 for each of the 12 board members). It is estimated that, from the list provided by the headhunter firm, only 70% will actually be suitable. The board wants a list of four suitable candidates for final consideration.

(a) What is the chance that there will get their four candidates from the list of 10?
(b) What is the chance they need to interview nine or more candidates?
(c) How many candidates will they need to interview? Describe the distribution, as well as its mean.
(d) If 10 candidates are not enough for 4 candidates, there is an extra $20,000 cost for providing each extra candidate. What is the mean cost?
(e) Another headhunting company can deliver candidates with a 75% chance of being suitable. How much money would this save you?

E13. Emergency patients arrive at a large hospital at the rate of 0.33 per minute. On average, 22% of emergency patients are triaged into the most serious category.

(a) What is the probability of six or more arrivals during the next 30 min?
(b) What is the probability of six or more arrivals during the next 30 min that are triaged into the most serious category?
(c) If there are 25 patients that arrive in the next hour, what is that chance that more than half of them will be triaged into the most serious category?

E14. At a particular newspaper, it is known that typos occur at a mean rate of 1 per 40.76 m of text. Thought of another way, they occur at a rate of 0.0.0245 per meter. A typical edition has 78 pages, each page being 35 cm wide with 110 lines. So the total length of print is 300,300 cm, which is 3003 m. Instead of events occurring randomly in time here we can think of events occurring randomly along the 3003 m of print. A new system was introduced and the next edition had 65 typos.
(a) How convinced are you that the new system has reduced the rate of typos?
(b) The next edition has 70 errors. On the basis of the first two editions after the new system, how convinced are you now that it has reduced the rate of typos?
(c) Over the next month there are 20 editions with a total of 1182 errors so the average errors per edition are 59.1. Dividing by 3003 m, the mean typos per meter is 0.0197, so we will take this to be our best guess for the new mean rate α.
(d) What is the chance of less than 75 errors in the next edition?
(e) What is the chance that every edition next month will have less than 75 errors?
(f) How many editions next month do you think will have less than 75 errors?

E15. A call center in Delhi operates 16 h per day, 6 days per week. The mean number of phone calls arriving per hour is 265. There are 60 staff, each costing $3.55 per hour, each of whom can handle five calls per hour to the center. So the cost per hour is $213 and this gives the capacity to handle 300 calls. If the number of calls exceeds 300, the excess are diverted to the United States and processed at a cost of $6.40 per call.

(a) How many calls will arrive in the next hour? Give your answer in completely nontechnical terms.
(b) What is the chance of more than 300 calls arriving?
(c) What is the mean cost per hour?
(d) What is the best staffing level?
(e) Give the distribution of the number of hours during the 16-h period where the center will fail to meet capacity. Make any basic assumptions you need.
(f) Give the distribution of the number of days in the week where the center will, at least once, fail to meet capacity. Make any basic assumptions you need.

CHAPTER 7

Business Problems That Depend on Knowing "How Much"

7.0. Introduction: What Is the Issue?

Some uncertain business outcomes can take a truly huge number of possible values. For instance, the demand for grain next month might be any number between 0 and 1000 tons. If you measure this to the nearest kilogram then there are a million possible outcomes—from 1 to 1,000,000 kg. If you wanted the *probability distribution* of this variable you would have to list all these outcomes and the probability of each! This is hardly practical. Not to mention that if we measured the grain demand to the nearest gram rather than kilogram then there would be a billion possible outcomes!

For variables that take an effectively infinite number of values we do not use the probability function to describe their uncertain behavior. Instead we use a curve, and areas beneath the curve represent probabilities. The two most useful distributions of this kind are the **normal** and the **lognormal**. Here are some examples where you could use the methods of this chapter.

Suppose someone sits a management aptitude test and get a score of 123.1. How good is this score? What percentile would the person be in?

Suppose we are filling a bag of product with a target weight of 10 kg. There is a typical 22-g uncertainty in the amount of product delivered. In order to satisfy the packing claim of 10 kg, we set the fill level slightly above 10 kg. How likely is it that the bag will contain at least 10 kg of product?

A manufactured item needs to be within 0.006 mm of the target 1.5 mm to function correctly. The manufacturing process has an inherent error of 0.5%. What diameter should we target and how many items will be defective?

Data-Driven Business Decisions, First Edition. Chris J. Lloyd.

Demand for my product is likely to be about 12,100 per month with a standard deviation of 122. Product left over and not sold is completely spoiled. How should I set my production level to maximize mean profit?

All of these problems involve an uncertain business outcome that can be described by the normal or the lognormal distribution.

SUPERGROW LIME AND REGULATIONS: CASE BRIEFING

SuperGrow Ltd. produces a range of garden fertilizers, one of their largest selling items being lime. It costs 42 cents per kilogram to source, transport, and package, and a 20-kg bag wholesales for $11.95. Bag labels clearly state the 20-kg contents.

The current weekly demand for the product is around 12,500 bags, which is around 650,000 bags per year, giving a yearly revenue of around $7.7M. Subtracting the cost of the lime at 42 cents per kilogram (around $5.5M) and various additional fixed costs (of $350,000) leaves a profit from this particular product line of around $1.85M.

SuperGrow has a problem, though. Lime when mined often already contains moisture and it absorbs moisture easily if stored. Consequently, the lime SuperGrow puts into the bag always contains moisture. The bags breathe to release this moisture, otherwise the lime would set almost like cement. The problem is that if SuperGrow delivers 20 kg of product into the bag at point of packaging then the weight decreases as the lime dries out and by the time it is sold it may be considerably less than 20 kg.

How much less? Typically the lime decreases in weight by around 2.7%. Currently, SuperGrow deals with this problem by deliberately overfilling the bags. Currently, they deliver almost 21 kg of lime into a bag because they know that it will dry out by around 2.7% and end up weighing 20.4 kg. They do this because the amount of moisture in the lime is *variable* and the time until a bag sells, during which it is drying out, also varies. Consequently, the amount of weight reduction in a bag is variable—sometimes more than 2.7% and sometimes less. From historical data, weights will typically vary around their target value by around 300 g.

In addition, there is a complex regime of fines that the company may face from the regulator. The question is—what is the best fill level to set on the bags? How much money would it be worth spending to solve the whole drying problem (supposing that there is a technical solution)?

Further details of the background to this problem are available in the full case.

7.1. THE NORMAL DISTRIBUTION

The **normal distribution** is a special and important probability distribution. It has a central role in the practice of statistics and data analysis.

Unlike the probability distributions such as the binomial or Poisson in the previous chapter, the normal distribution describes the behavior of a random variable that takes a *continuum* of possible values. It is therefore impossible to list all possible values and their corresponding probabilities.

For this reason, the normal distribution is not described by a list of all possible values and their probabilities. Instead, it is described by a *bell-shaped* curve. The curve gives an idea of where the variable is more or less likely to be. More specifically, *areas beneath the curve* give the probability of the random variable being in any particular range.

Total area under the curve is 1.0.

Each normal distribution is specified by two numbers: the parameter μ is at the center of symmetry of the curve and is also the theoretical **mean** of the variable. The parameter σ measures the width of the curve and is also the **standard deviation** of the variable. More practically, it measures how unpredictable the variable is.

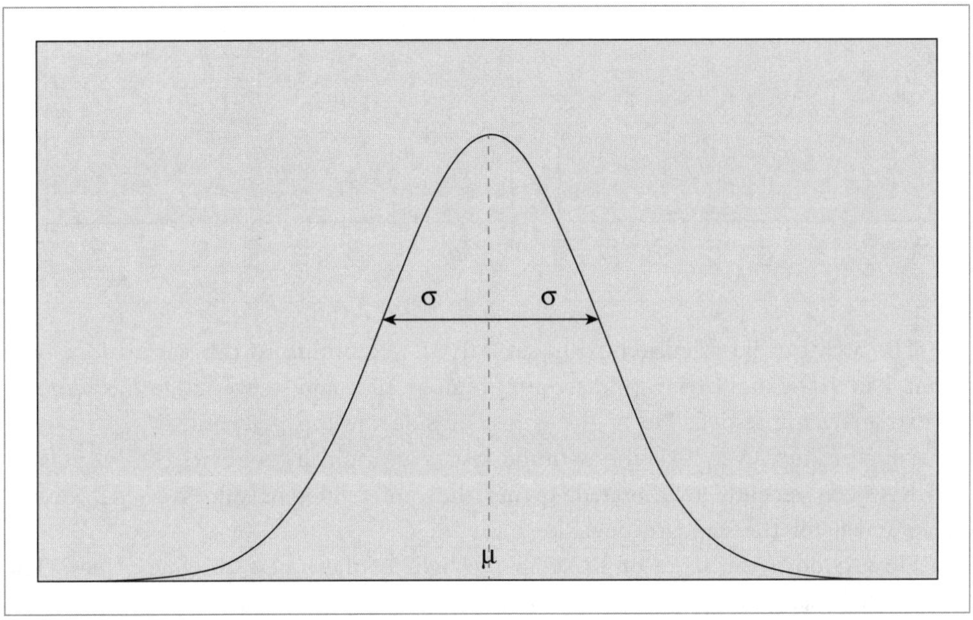

The standard deviation can be interpreted very clearly for a normal variable. The probability that the variable is within 1 standard deviation of the mean is 68%. The probability that it is within 2 standard deviations of the mean is 95%. For instance, if the demand for grain is normal with a mean of 3 tons and a standard deviation of 0.25 tons, then there is a 95% chance that demand will be between 2.5 and 3.5 tons.

Normal variables are hardly ever more than 3 standard deviations from the mean. Thus, there is virtually no chance that the grain demand would be outside the range 2.25–3.75 tons. There is really no realistic chance at all that it would be as low as 2 tons or as high as 4 tons (which is 4 standard deviations from the mean).

EXAMPLE 1 *Management aptitude tests*

A management aptitude test has been calibrated against a reference population of management candidates in such a way that the distribution of test scores is normal with mean $\mu = 100$ and standard deviation $\sigma = 10$.

Q. If a candidate scores 123.1 on the test, then how good a candidate is he or she? What percentile is he or she in?

One way to answer this question would be to ask, "What proportion of candidates in the long run will score as high as 123.1?" This probability can be represented as an area on the normal curve as represented below in the left-hand graphic.

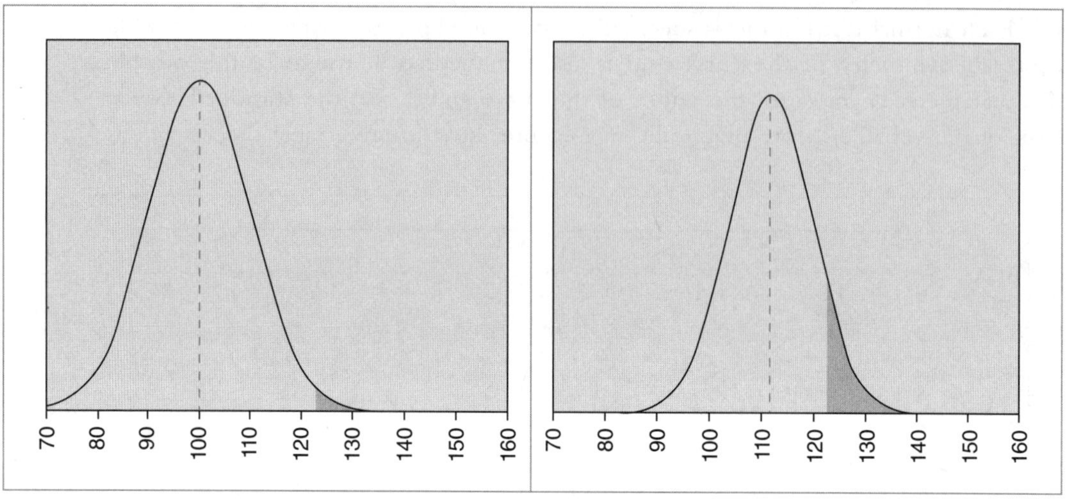

The area can be calculated to equal 0.0104. According to this calculation, only about 1 in 100 candidates would score as high as 123, and so we judge this score to be extremely impressive. He or she is just outside the top percentile.

Suppose, however, that the aptitude test was originally calibrated 20 years ago, and has been recently recalibrated, giving the quite different values of 112 for the mean and 8 for the standard deviation.

How good is the score of 123.1 in the light of these new baseline values? The chance of scoring as high as 123.1 is represented in the right-hand graphic. The area is calculated to equal 0.0826 (see below), so around 1 in 12 people would score this high. The score is still judged to be quite good but not nearly as outstanding as when we used the old baseline values. He or she is in the top decile but is no longer judged to be in the top percentile.

Percentiles of the Normal Distribution

When I tell you that a variable, such as demand, is normal with a certain mean and standard deviation, you can immediately picture the curve in your mind. The variable will probably be within 1 standard deviation of the mean and is highly likely to be within 2 standard deviations. However, we can be more specific than this if desired.

The following statements are true for a normal variable.

- There is a 68% chance it will be within 1 standard deviation of the mean.
- There is a 95% chance it will be within 2 standard deviations of the mean.

In addition, you can find the upper and lower quartiles, deciles, and percentiles by adding and subtracting the appropriate number of standard deviations to and from the mean. This is summarized in the table below:

percentile	Lower	Upper
25% (quartile)	Subtract 0.675 σ	Add 0.675 σ
10% (decile)	Subtract 1.645 σ	Add 1.645 σ
1% (percentile)	Subtract 2.236 σ	Add 2.236 σ

EXAMPLE 1 (Continued) *Management aptitude tests*

A management aptitude test has been calibrated against a recent reference population of management candidates in such a way that the distribution of test scores is normal with mean $\mu = 112$ and standard deviation $\sigma = 8$.

There is a 68% chance that someone will score between 104 and 120 and a 95% chance that someone will score between 96 and 128. The standard percentiles are in the table below, obtained by adding and subtracting the correct number of standard deviations ($\sigma = 8$) to and from the mean ($\mu = 112$). The template normal.xls calculated these for you automatically.

percentile	Lower	Upper
25% (quartile)	106.6	117.4
10% (decile)	101.7	122.3
1% (percentile)	93.4	130.6

A score of 130.6 puts you in the top percentile and a score of 106.6 puts you in the lower quartile.

7.2. Calculating Normal Probabilities in Excel

The internal function NORMDIST is available in Excel for calculating normal probabilities. It calculates the probability that the variable is *less than* any chosen value x, which would be represented on the bell-shaped curve as the *area to the left of* x. The syntax is

$$=\text{NORMDIST}(x, \mu, \sigma, \text{TRUE}).$$

The last field TRUE causes the function to calculate the area to the left of x. If you put FALSE then the function returns the value, that is, the *height* of the curve at x. This option is not useful for data analysis (but it is useful for producing the graphs like the one below!)

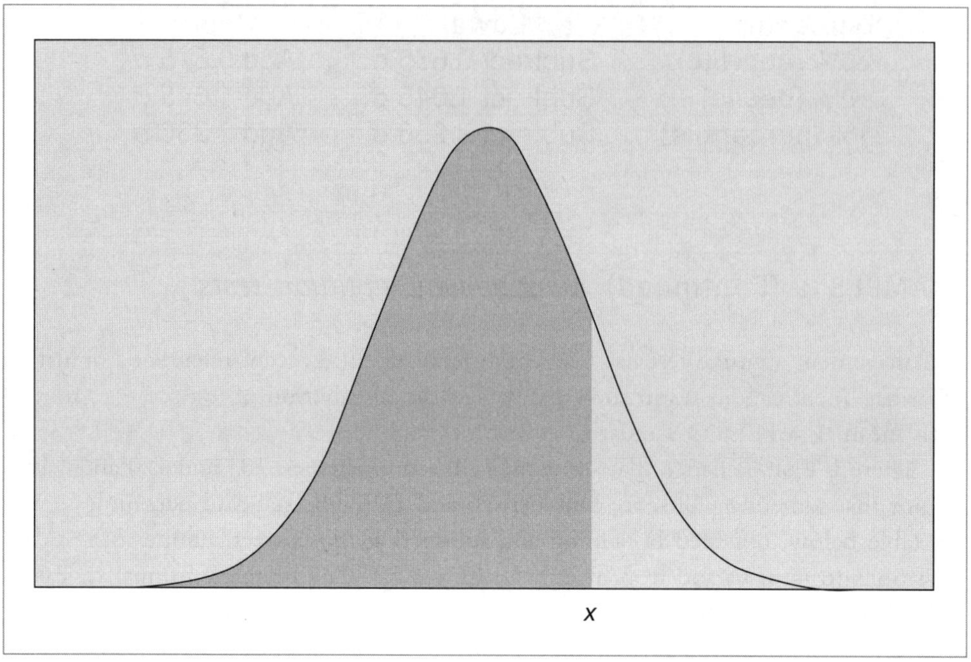

Areas to the **right** of a value x can be calculated by using Excel to find the area to the left and then subtracting the answer from 1 (since the total area under the curve is 1). Areas *between* two values x and y can be calculated by using Excel to find the area to the left of y and then subtracting off the area to the left of x.

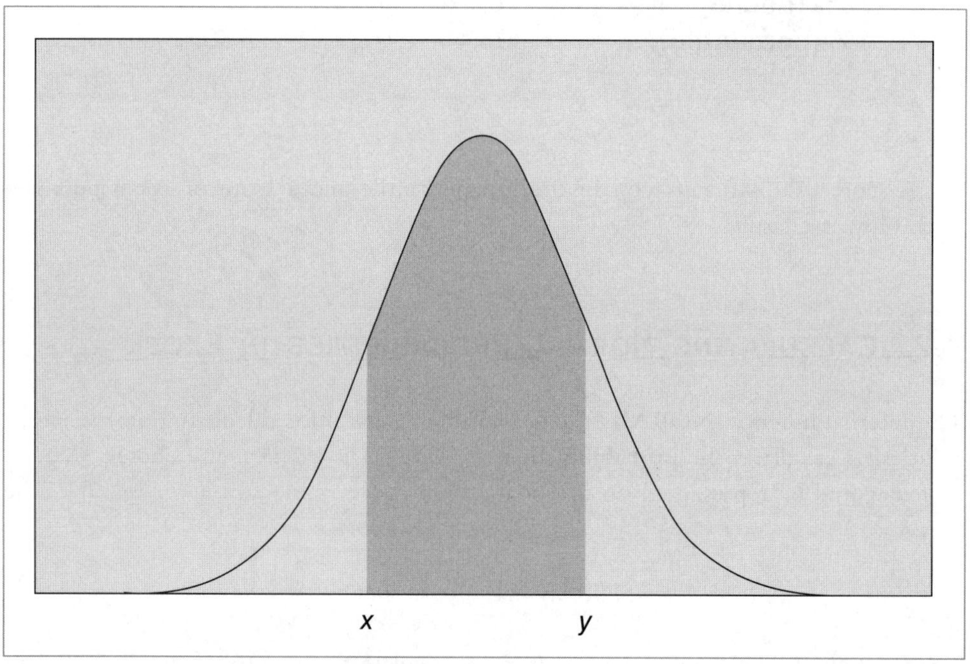

There is also an Excel template called normal.xls to help you with these kinds of calculations. It will give you the area both to the left and right of x, to the left and right of y, and the area between x and y.

EXAMPLE 1 (Continued) *Management aptitude tests*

A management aptitude test has been calibrated against a recent reference population of management candidates in such a way that the distribution of test scores is normal with mean $\mu = 112$ and standard deviation $\sigma = 8$.

Q. Suppose that only those who score at least 100 are offered employment. What proportion of these will score over the general mean level of 112?

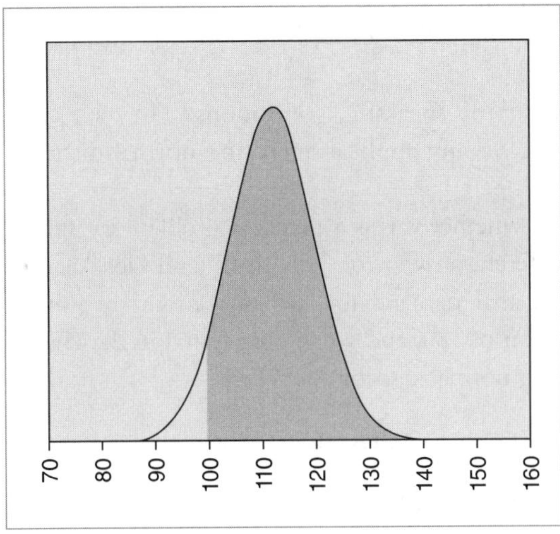

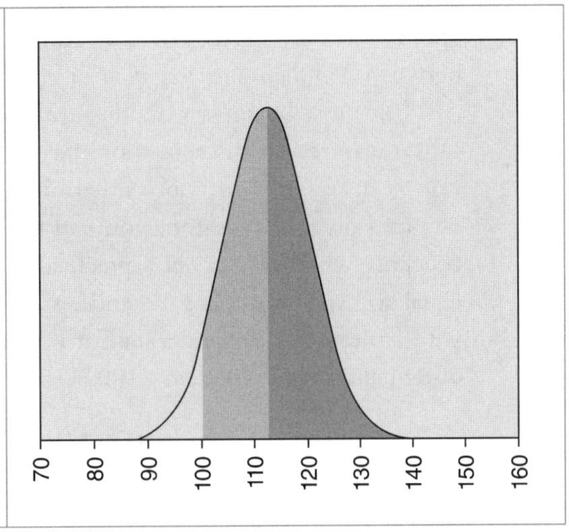

This is actually a *conditional* probability. Given you are offered employment, what is the chance you score over 112? Geometrically, this is asking for the dark gray region as a proportion of the total gray region. We first find out what proportion are offered employment by scoring over 100—shown in the left graphic. The probability of this is the area to the **right** of 100 and is calculated by typing

=1 – NORMDIST(100,112,8,TRUE),

which gives 93.3%. The area to the right of 112 is

=1 – NORMDIST(112,112,8,TRUE),

which gives 50%. The normal distribution is symmetric about the mean so in this case we could have stated the answer without even using Excel. So the proportion of candidates who score over 112 out of those who score over 100 is 0.500/0.933 = 0.536. So by restricting offers to those with a score over 100, we will expect 53.6% of employees to be above the average level (of 112).

The Normal Is Only an Approximation

For the normal distribution to be exactly correct, the variable must first take a continuum of possible values and second, must have the special bell shape. It is a fact of nature and mathematics that many variables will have the special bell shape. Whenever a business variable is subject to a large number of random influences, the sum of these influences will result in variation that is well described by the normal distribution.

The best way to check if the normal is applicable is to have background data on the variable and check to see if the historical data distribution looks symmetric and bell shaped—at least roughly.

What about the first assumption though—of the variable taking a continuum of possible values? Some real-world variables are continuous—like the height or weight of a person. For a continuous variable it makes no difference whether I ask for the chance of the variable being "less than 180" or "less than or equal to 180"—since there are so many possibilities around 180 that the chance of an outcome of exactly 180 is virtually zero. For the continuous variables you can ignore the distinction between *less than* and *less than or equal to.*

But most business variables are not, strictly speaking, continuous. They are typically measured in discrete monetary units. So any application of the normal distribution is necessarily an approximation.

In a given application, you can check whether this is a practical problem by simply checking whether you get a practically different answer for "less than" and "less than or equal to" questions. For instance, suppose that demand for cars in a month is normal with a mean of 1200 and a standard deviation of 180, and we are interested in the chance of demand being less than 1100. Using the normal distribution

=NORMDIST(1100,1200,180,TRUE)

gives the answer 28.9%. If you change the 1100 to 1099 the answer changes to 28.7%, and if you change the 1100 to 1101 it changes to 29.1%—hardly a practically important difference.

In most business applications, the variable can potentially take a truly huge number of possible values and continuity is no a practical issue. For instance, the chance of revenue this month being more than $35,000 will be virtually identical to the chance that it is more than $35,000 and 1 cent.

If the difference is of a magnitude that is more of a practical worry, one rough adjustment you can do is to add or subtract 0.5 to the x-value to make the event *bigger.* For instance, to find the chance of 1100 or smaller you use 1100.5 but to find the chance of 1100 or bigger you use 1099.5. This is called the **continuity correction**.

CHECK YOUR UNDERSTANDING

Q1. From examining the previous year's records, it is determined that the weekly sales from a store are normally distributed with a mean equal to $7200 and a standard deviation equal to $660.

(a) What is the probability that the store will have sales exceeding $8000 next week?

(b) This week's sales are down to $5900. How unusually low were sales this week?

(c) Over the next 26 weeks, describe how many weeks you will expect to see sales exceed $8000?

Q2. Weekly sales are normally distributed with a mean of $1250 and a variance of 450.

(a) Make a statement about next week's sales that you can be 95% sure about.

(b) Make a statement about next week's sales that you can be 98% sure about.

(c) What are the upper and lower quartiles of sales? What do these mean in simple words?

7.3. COMBINING NORMAL VARIABLES

Normal variables have the nice property that when they are added together they are again normal. By normal we mean that the shape of the distribution has the special bell shape and that we can work out exact probabilities using the function NORMDIST. Provided you know the mean and standard deviation of each business variable involved, and they are normal, you can answer questions about the likely value of the typical kinds of combinations of variables that you might encounter in a business environment. The key issue is to find the mean and the standard deviation of the combination. The rules for combining normal variables are easy to remember.

Accumulating Revenue Streams

Rule 1 The sum of several normal variables is still normal.

Rule 2 The mean of the sum is equal to the sum of the means.

Rule 3 Provided the variables are *independent*, the **variance** of the sum is the sum of the variances. The variance is the standard deviation squared.

EXAMPLE 2.1

Suppose that demand each week for your product has a mean of 7000 units with a standard deviation of 350. The coefficient of variation (CV) is 350/7000, which is 5%. This is the typical variability of demand, which will probably be within 10% of 7000, that is, somewhere in the range 6300–7700. The chance of demand being within this range is 95%, because this is within 2 standard deviations of the mean.

Now consider the demand over a 4-week month. Below is the calculation for the mean, variance, and standard deviation of the monthly demand.

	Mean	Stdev	Variance
Week 1	7000	350	122500
Week 2	7000	350	122500
Week 3	7000	350	122500
Week 4	7000	350	122500
Month	28000		490000

The mean demand is 28,000, the variance is 490,000, and so the standard deviation is $\sqrt{490{,}000} = 700$. The CV is 700/28,000, which is 2.5%. So the relative variability of monthly demand is less than that of weekly demand. It is highly likely that demand will be within 5% of the mean, that is, in the range 28,000 ± 1400 or between 26,600 and 29,400.

Combining Revenues in Different Currencies

Rule 4 When you change currencies, a normal variable remains normal and the mean and standard deviation just change currencies.

EXAMPLE 2.2

You have income streams from three arms of your business—located in the United States, Europe, and Hong Kong. The mean and standard deviation in the local currencies (divided by 1 million) are in the table below, as well as the foreign exchange (FX) rates. What is the chance that income will exceed US$40 million?

	Mean	Stdev	FX
US	12.30	1.15	1.00
Europe	4.97	0.62	1.650
HK	125.30	18.20	0.124

We multiply the mean and standard deviation by the FX rate to get the income streams in US$ from each source. From there, we know the mean is the sum of the means and the variance is the sum of the variances. The calculations are in the table below.

	Mean	Stdev	Variance
US	12.30	1.15	1.323
Europe	8.20	1.02	1.047
HK	15.54	2.26	5.093
Total	36.04		7.462

The mean is just over $36M and the variance is 7.462. The standard deviation is $\sqrt{7.462}$, which is $2.73M. So the chance of income exceeding $40M is

$$=1 - \text{NORMDIST}(40, 36.04, 2.73, \text{true}),$$

which gives 7.34%.

Subtracting Costs from Revenues

Profit equals revenue minus costs. Since revenues and costs are uncertain, so is profit.

Rule 5 The mean of a *difference* of two variables is the difference of means.

Rule 6 Provided the variables are *independent*, the **variance** of a difference of variables is the *sum* of the variances.

EXAMPLE 2.3

You have a revenue stream and costs with mean and standard deviation below. There are also fixed costs of \$12.5M. The mean profit is calculated to be \$10.5M. Provided that revenues and costs are independent, the variance of the profit is 61.21. Notice that we *add up* the variances, even though profit is revenue *minus* costs. The standard deviation is $\sqrt{61.21}$, which is \$7.82M. If the revenue and costs are normally distributedthen so is the profit.

	Mean	Stdev	Variance
Revenue	45.200	6.400	40.960
Costs	22.20	4.50	20.250
Fixed	12.50	0.00	0.000
	10.50		61.21

The chance of actually losing money can now be calculated by typing

=1 − NORMDIST(0,10.50,7.82,true),

which gives 0.090. There is about a 91% chance of making money and a 9% chance of losing money. All the calculations for this section are in ex2.xls.

CHECK YOUR UNDERSTANDING

Q3. You have the mean and standard deviation of demand at two stores in New York and Boston, as well as that of total demand across the two stores.

	Mean	Stdev
New York	12000	1600
Boston	16500	2200

(a) What is probability that the New York demand will exceed 14,000?

(b) What is the probability that the Boston demand will exceed 19,000?

(c) What is the probability that the total demand will exceed 33,000?

Q4. Your monthly sales are described in the table below and roughly follow the normal distribution.

	Mean	Stdev
Jan	125	13.1
Feb	102	11.2
Mar	122	13.3
Apr	135	14.7
May	155	15.5
Jun	134	12.3
Jul	131	11.4
Aug	147	12.5
Sep	176	16.7
Oct	187	21.4
Nov	199	23.5
Dec	235	32.7

(a) For each month, what is the probability that sales will be within 10% of the mean?

(b) For the whole year, what is the probability that sales will be within 10% of the mean?

(c) What is the CV for each month and for the yearly total? Why do you think this is?

7.4. Comparing Two Normal Distributions

There are many situations where you will want to compare likely performance measures under two different scenarios. For instance, you might have a decision to either take a product to market now or take it to market later and risk more competition, and want to compare the profit distributions under the two scenarios. We look at a decision problem exactly like this in the next chapter.

If you are prepared to assume that performance has a normal distribution then comparing the two performance distributions is simpler. The normal distribution is specified by its mean and standard deviation. So provided that the performance measure is something positive, like net profit, we would like the mean to be large and the standard deviation to be small. So if one strategy leads to a payoff where the mean is higher and the standard deviation is lower, we would probably prefer it. However, it is not quite as simple as that.

One sensible and systematic way to compare two distributions, normal or otherwise, is to compare their **cumulative distribution functions (CDF)**. This gives the chance of profit being *less than* any value. We would ideally like the CDF of a performance measure to be lower. Why? Because we want the chance of being below any performance level to be as low as possible. So for the CDF of a positive performance measure, low is good.

The left panel below is a plot of two normal distributions with means of 500 and 600 and identical standard deviations of 60. The normal distribution with mean $\mu = 600$ and standard deviation $\sigma = 60$ is always below the normal distribution with mean $\mu = 500$ and standard deviation $\sigma = 60$. What this means is that for any profit level you set at all, I am less likely to fall below it using strategy 1 than strategy 2. This means that strategy 1 dominates strategy 2. In this case, regardless of risk aversion, we would prefer strategy 1. However, often no strategy has this property of **dominance**.

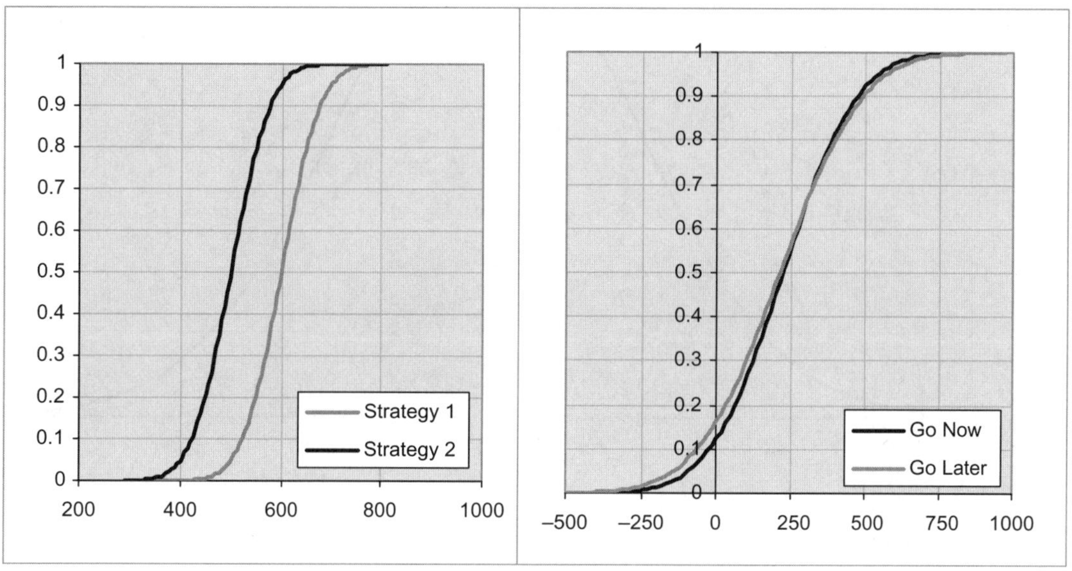

The right plot shows the normal distribution with mean $\mu = 224.5$ and standard deviation $\sigma = 192.4$, which corresponds to a decision to go to market now, and the normal distribution with mean $\mu = 214.5$ and standard deviation $\sigma = 217.0$, which corresponds to a decision to go to market later and risk competition. You might think that going to market now would be a clear winner, since the mean is higher and the risk is lower. As you can see, however, the comparison is not so clear cut. For lower payoff levels, especially losses, you would prefer to Go Now (it is lower), so if you are very risk averse this would be your decision. On the other hand, if you care mainly about pursuing the high profits (for instance, you had some bonus incentive) then Go Later is preferred (it is lower), so this would be your preferred decision.

7.5. The Standard Normal Distribution

The **standard normal distribution** is the special normal distribution with a mean of 0 and a variance of 1. You might wonder what business application this would possibly have. Do any business variables have a mean of 0 and a standard deviation of 1?

The standard normal distribution arises if we think of the previous normal calculations in an alternative way. Let's look at the outcome of a normal business variable and count how many standard deviations above or below the mean it is—kind of like a z-score. For instance, for the aptitude test with a mean of 112 and a standard deviation of 8, a score of 123.1 is 11.1 over the mean, which is 11.1/8 = 1.387 standard deviations above the mean. This immediately gives us a feeling for how high it is in statistical terms, even before we calculate any probabilities.

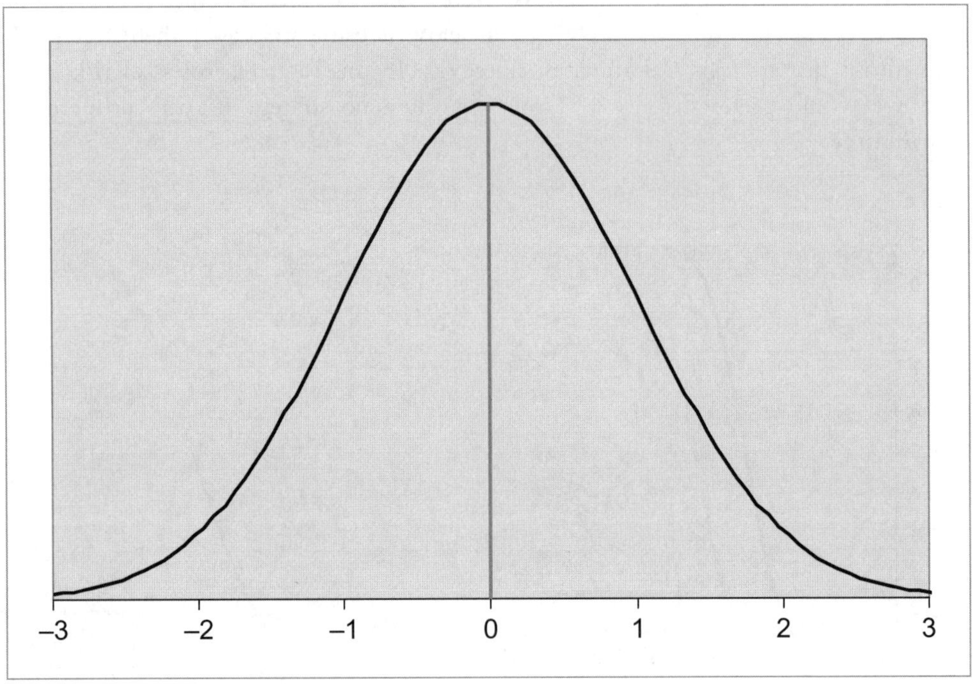

z-Values

This can be expressed in a general formula. If a business variable X is normal with mean μ and standard deviation σ then

$$z = \frac{X - \mu}{\sigma}$$

measures how far above or below the mean the outcome is, in units of standard deviations. A score of +3 is outstandingly high and a score of –3 is outstandingly low.

These ***z*-values** have the standard normal distribution—the distribution is still normal but the mean is 0 and the standard deviation is 1. The curve for this distribution is above. As you can see, standard normal variables are *almost always* within the range of –3–3. It is statistically *impossible* for a normal variable to take a value more than 4 standard deviations away from the mean

Using NORMSDIST

The idea of z-values provides an alternative way to both think about and calculate normal probabilities. For instance, the aptitude score of 123.1 corresponds to z = 1.387

standard deviations above the mean. The chance of getting this high a score is the chance that z, whose distribution is standard normal, is greater than 1.387. So we type

$$=1-\text{NORMDIST}(1.387,0,1,\text{TRUE}),$$

which gives 8.26%, just as we obtained previously.

There is a special function in Excel specifically for the standard normal distribution, which saves you from having to input the mean of 0, the standard deviation of 1, or the TRUE field. It is called NORM**S**DIST. You will get the same answer of 8.26% if you just type

$$=1-\text{NORM}\mathbf{S}\text{DIST}(1.387).$$

Application to Data Analysis

We often use data to estimate some business fundamental—for instance, the average production faults per week is an estimate of the underlying long-run fault rate. We might want to compare weekly fault rates with a particular benchmark fault rate that we want to achieve. To do this properly, we need to take into account that the weekly estimated fault rates are not 100% reliable—they involve their own random variability.

Statistics packages routinely produce a measure of reliability of a data-based estimate, called a **standard error**. This measures the standard deviation of the data-based estimate, in other words its reliability. It is also a mathematical fact that, under most common circumstances, the errors in a data-based estimate can be described by the normal distribution.

Commonly, we will be interested in some target or benchmark value of performance, call it μ_0. If the data-based estimate deviates too much from this benchmark, then we will be inclined to conclude that the target is not met. We measure deviations of the estimate from the target in units of standard errors. In other words, we calculate a kind of z-value:

$$z=\frac{\text{estimate}(X)-\text{benchmark}(\mu_0)}{\text{standard error}(\sigma)}.$$

This has an approximate standard normal distribution. For instance, if the z-value equals +2 then the data-based estimate is 2 standard errors above the benchmark and we would be quite confident that the true mean performance is above the benchmark.

For historical reasons, the z-value just described is called a ***t*-value**. You will learn much more about this in Chapters 9 and 10. Indeed, this is one of the main reasons that the standard normal distribution is mentioned at all.

EXAMPLE

A manufacturing process produces faults at an unknown rate, but a long-run rate of seven faults per day is considered acceptable. During the past 24-working-day month, the average number of production faults per day was 7.65 with a standard deviation of 2.32. The standard error given by the computer program is 0.473.* How likely is it that the rate would be as large as 7.65 if the real underlying rate is seven faults per month?

The z-value or t-value is $(7.65-7.0)/0.473 = 1.374$, so the observed fault rate of 7.65 is 1.374 standard errors above the benchmark of 7.0. The probability of this happening by "bad luck" is

=1 – NORMSDIST(1.374),

which gives 0.084, or 8.4%. It is quite unlikely that such a high fault rate would occur by chance if the real underlying fault rate is 7.0. It is more plausible that the underlying fault rate is higher than 7.0.

CHECK YOUR UNDERSTANDING

Q5. You have collected data on weekly sales over a certain period of time. You want to know whether sales are increasing over time.

A computer program gives you an estimate of the growth rate in sales. It estimates that sales are growing at a rate of 1.5% per year but it also estimates that this estimate is uncertain and itself has a standard error of 0.4%. How sure can you be that sales are really growing?

7.6. EXAMPLE 3: DEALING WITH UNCERTAIN DEMAND

You are in the buying department of a large retailer and need to order the latest season of Versace bags. These cost you \$395 dollars each and you sell them for \$660 at full price. However, if demand is too low you will have to sell some at a large, loss-making discount at the end of the season.

Your best guess is that demand this season will be 1550 but there is an uncertainty in this figure, which you assess at about 220. In other words, demand should be within the range 1550 ± 220 and is very likely to be in the range 1550 ± 440. You have abundant data that suggest that demand, while uncertain, can be described by the normal distribution.

How many should you buy? If you buy too few, you will be missing out on lots of profit—you make a profit of \$265 per bag in the best case. If you buy too many though, you stand to lose money. But the calculation depends on how much money you stand to lose, which depends on the discounts that you will have to offer.

Your store policy has already been set. Stock not sold by the end of the season is sent to your discount store chain and sold for \$249, which represents a loss of \$146. So the upside profit of selling a bag for full price is more than the downside

* The formula for this standard error is given in Chapter 9.

loss of having to discount it. This suggests that you should be pretty aggressive in how many bags you buy. In the extreme case that there was no downside cost (for instance, if Versace allowed you to return any unsold bags and receive a full refund), then you would buy as many bags as you could reasonably sell.

Suppose you decide to buy 1600 bags. You actually expect to have 50 bags left over at the end of the season. However, this may still be a good stocking level since we will have made all that profit on the 1550 bags. And there is still a chance we will sell all 1600.

There is a powerful economic technique for problems of this kind. You should *think at the margin*. Let's look at the very last bag we bought and ask if this was a smart move. This will then give us an idea whether we should have instead bought 1599 or 1601, which should lead us to the best stocking level.

Our last bag will either be sold during the season or not. If it is sold we make \$265 and if it is not we lose \$146. We only need the chance it is sold. This occurs exactly when the demand exceeds 1600. If the demand is more than 1600 we will sell that last bag. If it is less than 1600 we will not sell it. And we can use the normal distribution to find these chances. The chance of not selling this last bag is

=NORMDIST(1600,1550,220,TRUE),

which gives 59.0%. So we have the payoff table below:

	revenue	profit	Chance
Sell	\$660.00	\$265.00	41.0%
Discount	\$249.00	–\$146.00	59.0%
Mean	\$417.6	\$22.6	

How would you react to a 59% chance of losing \$146 but a 41% chance of making \$265? I would take this bet! And this is the bet you take when you buy the 1600th bag. The bet can be summarized as mean value (MV), which is \$22.60.

So in mean, the last bag purchased is profitable. This suggests that we should have purchased even more bags than 1600. But how many more?

Using Solver or Goalseek

The calculations above have been coded into example 3(versace).xls. The key figure that the manager can control is the number of bags that are purchased, currently set at 1600. This determines the 41% probability of sale and 59% chance of forced discount which, in turn, determines the MV of \$22.6. If we change the cell containing 1600 then the cell with the \$22.6 will automatically change, provided we have linked all the calculations.

The optimum stocking level will be when the mean profit of the last bag is *zero*. This means that we are just undecided about whether to purchase the last bag or not. Geometrically, you can think of us just being at the top of the profit hill—one extra bag more or less will not change our profit.

So the task becomes to vary the cell containing 1600 to a different value so that the cell currently containing $22.6 contains zero. This can be done by trial and error but there is a tool for doing this faster. **Goalseek** is a tool that comes standard with Excel. In Excel 2007 you find it on the data ribbon under What If Analysis. In Excel 2003 it is under the Tools menu.

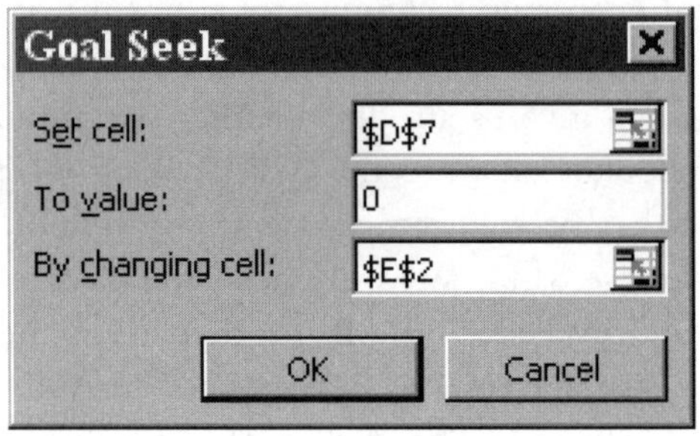

The dialog box requires you to set the cell that you are trying to control. Here we want the value in cell D7 to end up equaling zero. The cell we are allowed to change, which currently holds the value 1600, is cell E2. When you click OK you will find that the required value is 1632. The 1632nd bag is the point where we would not buy any more (because the MV of the next will be negative). The chance of selling this bag is only about 35.5% and there is a 64.5% chance of having to sell it at a discount and lose. But the reward-to-risk ratio of 265:146 means that we can be quite aggressive and accept an almost two-thirds chance of losing money. So our stocking problem is solved. We buy 1632 bags.

An alternative tool in Excel is **Solver** (which may or may not be installed with Office). This works very similarly to Goalseek but it is more powerful. First, it can maximize or minimize a cell, as well as perform the simpler task of setting a particular target. Second, you have the ability to vary more than one cell to achieve this aim. We will use Solver later in Chapter 13 to determine investment allocations in a financial portfolio.

Pushing a Little Further

This analysis does not actually tell you what the total profit will be—it tells you about the profit of the last bag, which tells you the best stocking strategy. This is typically the case with *thinking at the margin*.

The mean total profit can be obtained by finding the total of the mean profit of all the bags you purchase. The first bag has a MV of $165 because it is almost guaranteed you will sell it. The 1632nd bag has a MV of zero and you would stop here. The 1600th bag has a MV of $22.6. The total profit is obtained by adding up all these MVs. This has been done in the *total profit* worksheet of example 3(versace).xls. A plot of the total profit against the number of bags bought, up to 1800 bags, is below. The optimum is at 1632 bags and the mean profit at this point is about $377K.

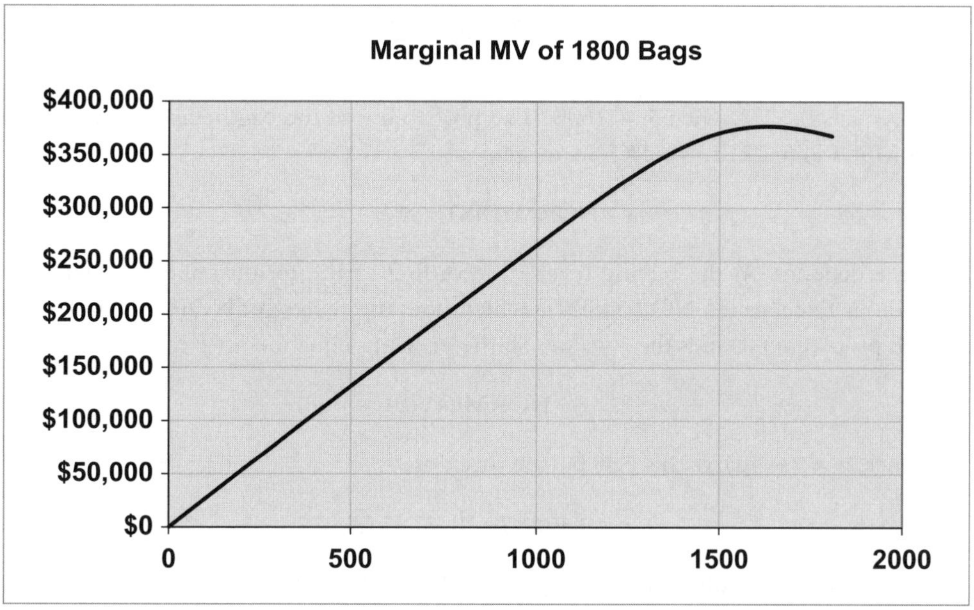

There is a direct formula for finding the optimum stocking level for problems like this, which avoids having to use Goalseek or Solver. We just generalize the previous calculation with symbols.

	payoff	Chance
Reward	R	1-p
Risk/Loss	–L	p
	MV	

The key number is p, the probability of not selling the last bag. If the reward is $\$R$ and the loss is $-\$L$ and if there is a probability p of the loss then the MV will be

$$\mathrm{MV} = (1 - p) \times R - p \times \mathrm{L}$$

For this to equal zero we require

$$\frac{1-p}{p} = \frac{L}{R},$$

and solving this for p we find that

$$p = \frac{R}{L+R}.$$

For instance, in our previous example, this gives $p = 265/(265 + 146) = 64.5\%$. So we should set the buying level so that the chance of selling the last bag being left unsold is 64.5%. The chance of not selling the bag is the chance that demand is less than the stocking level, initially set at $x = 1600$. In our case we used NORMDIST but we could have instead used the standard normal distribution. The z-value is

$$z = \frac{x-\mu}{\sigma} = \frac{x-1550}{220},$$

which equals 0.2273 when x = 1600. The probability of the bag being unsold is then NORMSDIST(0.2273) = 41%. So in general

$$\text{NORMSDIST}(z) = p$$

where z depends on the buying level x, according to the formula above. There is a function in Excel called NORMSINV which does the reverse of NORMSDIST—for a given probability it finds the z-value. So the previous equation for p can be written as

$$z = \text{NORMINV}(p),$$

and since z = (x—μ)/σ this can be rewritten as

$$x = \mu + \sigma \times \text{NORMINV}(p).$$

The final step is to substitute the expression for p that corresponds to the optimum stocking level, which gives the final formula

$$x = \mu + \sigma \times \boldsymbol{NORMSINV}\left(\frac{\boldsymbol{R}}{\boldsymbol{L}+\boldsymbol{R}}\right).$$

In our case we get

$$x = 1550 + 220 \times \boldsymbol{NORMSINV}\left(\frac{265}{146+265}\right).$$

and if you type the formula

=1550 + 220 * NORMSINV(265/[146 + 265])

into Excel it will give you the answer 1631.6. So the target number of bags to buy is 1632.

If you do not understand the algebra above that is okay. The point is that (a) there are often mathematical formulas for solving these kinds of "best business setting" problems and (b) even without these formulas, you can get the solutions from Excel and Goalseek.

7.7. Dealing with Proportional Variation

The normal distribution is fine most of the time, but there are a couple of minor problems. First, most business variables are positive. You are never going to have negative demand. Yet, a normal variable can always be negative. A more practical problem is that many business variables simply do not look like they are normal. When you gather real data on business outputs such as demand or revenue and look at the data distribution it is often not even symmetric around its mean. The normal distribution is symmetric.

Symmetry and Proportional Variation

As an example, below is the distribution of the yearly sales of a suburban newspaper. On the horizontal axis is the circulation in thousands and on the vertical axis is the number of days with that circulation. The mean circulation is 124,000 per day with a standard deviation of 36,000 per day. But this standard deviation conceals the fact that the highest circulation is about 120,000 higher than the mean while the lowest circulation is only about 60,000 less than the mean. The distribution is *not symmetric*. However, the astute reader may have noticed that the highest circulation is about twice the mean while the lowest circulation is half the mean. So there is symmetry in this data but it is a different kind of symmetry.

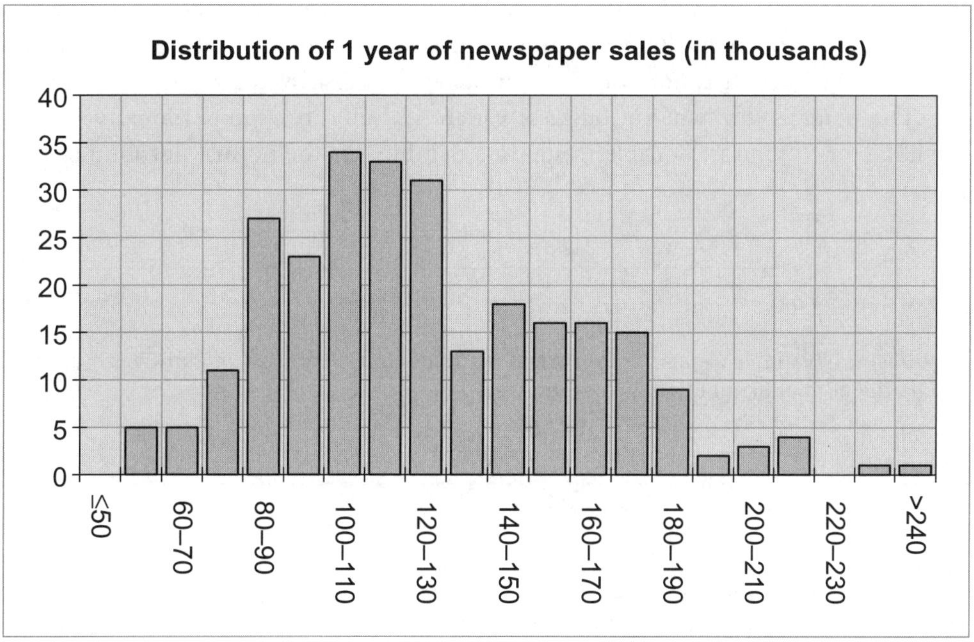

The reason why variables, such as demand, are not symmetric is that they are subject to *proportional variation* rather than absolute variation. To see why this causes asymmetry, imagine that the underlying trend demand is 1000 units but there is a 10% chance that it will be 25% higher and a 10% chance it will be 25% lower. So the probability distribution would be

Low	800	10%
Trend	1000	80%
High	1250	10%

Notice that the high demand is 250 higher than the trend level but the low demand is only 200 lower, because 800 = 1000/1.25 is 25% lower than 1000. The distribution is not symmetric. The mean then turns out to be 1005—greater than the "trend" level of 1000.

A Special Distribution

There is a distribution that allows us to describe this situation. It can be used when you believe that there is proportional variation—in other words, when you think it is equally likely that the variable will be *x*% higher or *x*% lower than the central trend value. It is called the **lognormal** distribution.

To use the lognormal distribution you need to specify two numbers, just as with the normal distribution. These two numbers are the median or middle value m of the distribution and the CV γ. Remember that the CV is a measure of *proportional variation* and is measured in percentage terms. So for instance, if $\gamma = 25\%$ then it means that there is a typical proportional variation of 25%, either higher or lower.

The lognormal distribution is based on the mathematical fact that if X is subject to proportional variation then the natural logarithm of X is subject to absolute variation. The *natural logarithm* transformation is denoted by "ln," and there is a function in Excel called LN. It is not essential you understand exactly what natural logarithms are. The point is that when a business variable is subject to proportional variation, it will be much more reasonable to suppose that $\ln X$ has the normal distribution than X itself.

DEFINITION

A business variable X has the **lognormal** distribution with median m and CV γ if $\ln(X)$ has the normal distribution with parameters

$$\mu = \ln(m) \text{ and } \sigma = \sqrt{\ln(\gamma^2 + 1)}.$$

We can then calculate the probability that X is less than some value v by the chance that $\ln(X)$ is less than $\ln(v)$. There is no need to memorize these formulas as all calculations are carried out automatically in the provided template lognormal.xls. This template is set out in a similar manner to normal.xls and gives the probability of the original variable being within any range x–y, and various percentiles of the original variable. You only need to input the median or central value m and the CV γ.

The mean of the original variable X will be larger than m and is given by

$$\text{mean} = m \times \sqrt{\gamma^2 + 1}.$$

The standard deviation of the original variable X will be the mean times the CV γ. Again, these are produced automatically by the template and need not be memorized. There is an internal function in Excel called LOGNORMDIST that directly calculates probabilities associated with the lognormal distribution. However, it requires you to know the mean μ and standard deviation σ of $\ln(X)$. In practice, it is more common to know the middle or median value and the CV.

EXAMPLE 3 (Continued) *Versace stock levels*

In the original formulation of this problem the trend demand level was 1550 and the standard deviation was 220. The CV is 220/1550 = 14.2%. Rather than assume that demand is normal, a more realistic assumption is that demand is lognormal with a median or central value of 1550 and a CV of 14.2%.

A diagram of the lognormal distribution is quite similar to the normal distribution but is slightly asymmetric, as presented below. The mean and standard deviation are a little larger than the earlier values: the mean is 1565.5 and the standard deviation is 222.2. The median demand of 1500 and the current stocking level of 1600 are also displayed on the graphic.

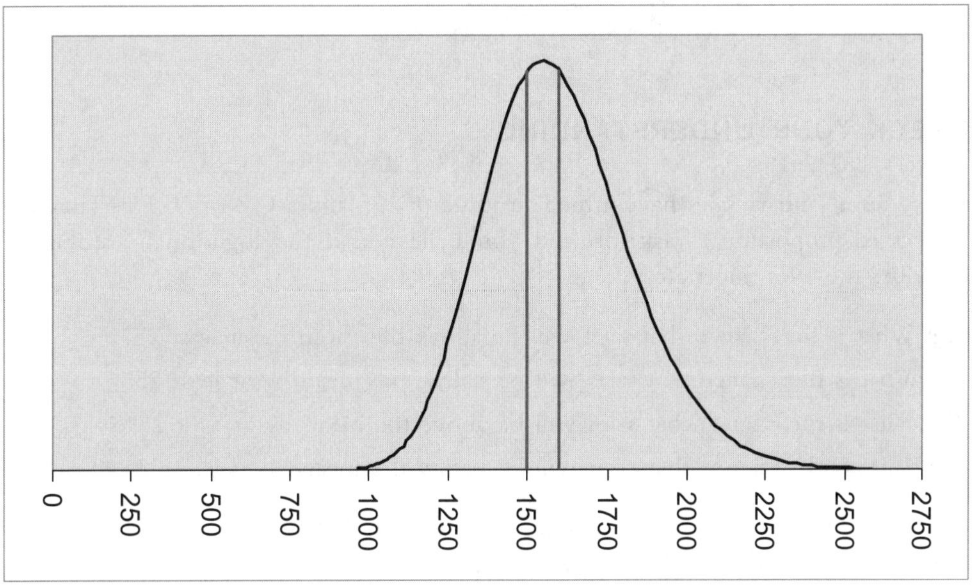

The key probability in assessing the stocking level of 1600 was the chance of not selling the last bag. Using lognormal.xls, we find that this probability is 58.89% and the MV is $22.95 (compared to $22.60 in the earlier formulation).

	Profit	Chance
Sell	$265.00	41.11%
Discount	–$146.00	58.89%
	$22.95	

The value of stocking that leads to a zero mean on the last bag is now 1633, instead of 1632. So practically speaking, in this example it does not make much difference whether we use the normal or lognormal distribution.

There tends to be more of a practical difference between the two distributions when you are interested in unusually high or low outcomes. For instance, the table below shows the extreme percentiles for the Versace example. In both cases, the central median demand is 1550 and the CV is 14.2%. If we were interested in the extremes then the highest percentile of demand under the lognormal distribution (2153) is quite a bit higher, that is, more extreme absolutely, than for the regular normal distribution. The lowest percentile of demand under the lognormal distribution (1116) is quite a bit higher, that is, less extreme absolutely, than for the regular normal distribution.

	Lognormal		Normal	
10%	1293	1858	1268	1832
5%	1229	1955	1188	1912
1%	1116	2153	1038	2062

It is a feature of the lognormal distribution that the highest outcomes tend to be more extreme than the lowest outcomes. This is worth knowing and taking account of and will be clearly visible when you collect data.

Check Your Understanding

Q6. Your January sales have a median value of 125 and a CV of 10.5%. They are subject to proportional variation and you believe that the lognormal distribution describes the sales uncertainty.

(a) What is the chance that sales will be above the mean by at least 25?

(b) What is the chance that sales will be below the mean by at least 25?

(c) What is the chance that sales will be above the mean by at least 25%?

(d) What is the chance that sales will be below the mean by at least 25%?

Q7. Monthly sales are described by the numbers below. We assume that each monthly sales figure is described by the lognormal distribution

	Median	CV
Jan	125	10.5%
Feb	102	11.0%
Mar	122	10.9%
Apr	135	10.9%
May	155	10.0%
Jun	134	9.2%
Jul	131	8.7%
Aug	147	8.5%
Sep	176	9.5%
Oct	187	11.4%
Nov	199	11.8%
Dec	235	13.9%

(a) What are the mean and standard deviation of sales each month?

(b) What is the chance that sales will be between 100 and 150 in each month?

7.8. SUMMARY

Many business outcomes depend on anticipating how large some variables will be, for instance, revenue, costs, or demand. These variables can take an almost infinite number of possible values so they are not described by a probability distribution but by a curve.

The **normal distribution** is the most common and useful of the so-called *continuous* distributions. It is specified by its mean μ, a standard deviation σ, and the characteristic bell shape of the curve. Probabilities are areas under the curve.

To calculate these areas/probabilities in Excel, use the function NORMDIST. An alternative way to arrange the calculation is to change the x-value to a z-value and then use the standard normal distribution. In Excel, the function NORMSDIST gives probabilities associated with the standard normal distribution.

The **lognormal distribution** is a more realistic distribution for describing common business outcomes like demand and revenue. It is appropriate when the variable has an asymmetric distribution and where the variability of the outcome is due to proportional variation. Proportional variation means that the variable is equally likely to be x% higher or x% lower than the central trend value.

It will give practically different results to the normal when the CV is large—say around 20% or higher—or when you are interested in extreme outcomes. To specify the particular lognormal distribution in an application you only need to know the middle or median value m and the CV γ. There is a function LOGNORMDIST in Excel, but the template lognormal.xls is preferred.

The normal and lognormal distributions are two of the basic building blocks of quantitative analysis. They allow us to put numbers to the chance of various outcomes that involve "how much." The other major building blocks are the binomial and Poisson distributions, which describe business outcomes that involve "how many," and the notion of MV. In the next chapter you will learn how to fit these basic elements into a coherent framework, known as decision trees.

EXERCISES

E1. Use the function NORMSDIST to calculate the following.

(a) The time T taken by a delivery vehicle to make a certain type of delivery run is normally distributed with a mean of 382 min and a standard deviation of 21 min. What is the probability that the run will take more than 7 h?

(b) Profit P is normally distributed with a mean of \$76,500 and a standard deviation of \$3200. What is the probability that profit will be less than \$75,000?

(c) Revenue R is normally distributed with a mean of \$187,500 and a standard deviation of \$2600. Costs are \$181,000. What is the probability of a profit?

(d) Monthly loss of stock due to pilfering is normally distributed with a mean of \$28,500 and a variance of 4,500,600. With a new security system, pilfering this month has dropped to \$22,000. Do you think the new security system worked?

E2. An aptitude test, when applied to the general population, gives scores that are normally distributed with a mean of 570 and a standard deviation of 60.

(a) What proportion of people sitting the test will score less than 500?

(b) What is the probability that a person scores between 570 and 600?

(c) For the subpopulation of people who are already successful managers, the mean score is 605 with a standard deviation of 48. What are the answers to parts (a) and (b) for this subpopulation?

E3. Daily turnover (or volume) in a particular stock is known to be normally distributed with a mean of $135 million and a standard deviation of $33 million.

(a) How likely is it that the turnover tomorrow will exceed $200 million, assuming that you have no extra information about tomorrow that you could use to predict volume?

(b) How many of the 247 trading days during the year will see volumes greater than $200 million? Give the answer in terms that a nonspecialist would understand.

E4. General Management Aptitude Test (GMAT) scores of candidates who choose to sit the test are known to be normally distributed with a mean of 580 and a standard deviation of 55. Entry to a certain business school requires a score of at least 650.

(a) What is the chance of a person who sits the test being admitted?

(b) A person scores 700. How unusually well have they performed? Your answer will require some calculations but express your final answer in nontechnical terms.

(c) What proportion of those admitted to the business school would you expect to have a score over 700? *(Harder)*

(d) The top 5% of students score above what GMAT score?

E5. The fuel economy of a particular Valiant model is supposed to be 18.9 km/L. In fact, economy varies somewhat from car to car and is normally distributed with a mean of 18.9 and a standard deviation of 0.57.

(a) What proportion of cars has fuel economy over 20 km/L?

(b) Your car has a fuel economy of 18.22. How unusually bad is it?

(c) Suppose that fuel economy can be accurately measured during production. Those with a fuel economy of over 19.5 are labeled as "economy guaranteed." What proportion of "economy-guaranteed" cars would have fuel economy over 20 km/L? *(Harder)*

E6. The amount of money spent by a customer entering a supermarket is normally distributed with a mean of $68 and a standard deviation of $16. What is

(a) the typical range of customer expenditure?

(b) the probability that a customer spends over $100?

(c) the chance a customer spends $100 to the nearest dollar? *(Harder)*

(d) The lowest spending 5% of customers spend less than what amount?

E7. The yearly profit at a company is uncertain but the expected profit is $150M and the uncertainty as measured by standard deviation is $55M. The Chief Executive Officer (CEO) is on an incentive scheme. If the profit exceeds $200M he or she receives a $100,000 bonus. If it exceeds $250M, he or she receives $500,000. *(Harder)*

(a) Describe the range of likely profits.

(b) Assuming that the profit has a normal distribution, what is the probability that profit will exceed $250 million?

(c) What is the mean bonus the CEO can expect to receive?

(d) The contract is actually for 3 years. Assuming inflation of 5% per year, what is the mean bonus in the second and third years?

E8. I am bidding on a job by closed tender. The person who bids the lowest wins the job. I have judged that the break-even point for this job will be $245K, so I have bid $257K to include a profit margin.

From historical data, I have determined that the lowest competing bid has a normal distribution with a mean 7% higher than my break-even point and is 1.5% of my break-even point.

(a) What is the probability that I win the job?
(b) Taking into account both the chance of me winning the job, and the profit enjoyed if I do win it, what is my mean profit?
(c) What would be my best bid?

E9. You have surveyed 250 potential customers on your airline and the maximum amount they would pay for a return airfare to Bali. The data are in Q9.xls. The mean is 1618.9 and the standard deviation is 19.0. You may assume that the reserve price is normally distributed across the population of all potential customers and use the above sample mean and standard deviation in place of the theoretical standard deviations for the normal distribution. Your break-even price is $1545 and your current fare is $1610.
(a) What is the probability that a customer will fly with you? You may assume that if their reserve price is higher than your fare, then they will fly with you.
(b) How much do you make when a customer flies with you? Hence, what is your mean profit?
(c) Use Solver to find the fare which maximizes your mean profit.
(d) *(Harder)* Try and calculate answers to the previous questions but using the observed data rather than the normal distribution.

E10. Revenue for January is normally distributed with a mean of $345.5K and a standard deviation of $75.9K. Based on historical seasonal patterns the revenues for the other months are higher than the revenues for January by the amounts in the table below. So for instance, February revenue is normally distributed but with a mean and standard deviation 6% higher than in January.

Jan	Feb	Mar	Apr	May	Jun
0%	6%	4%	8%	11%	13%
Jul	**Aug**	**Sep**	**Oct**	**Nov**	**Dec**
9%	10%	13%	17%	22%	33%

What is the chance that
(a) January revenue exceeds $500K?
(b) February revenue exceeds $500?
(c) Half year's revenue exceeds $3M?
(d) Yearly revenue exceeds $6M?
(e) What is the CV of monthly, half yearly, and yearly revenues?

E11. Monthly demand for umbrellas is highly unpredictable but the best trend estimate available for next month is 78,850. There is a typical uncertainty of 28% in this figure, either higher or lower. The distribution can roughly be assumed to be lognormal with the previous stated median and CV.
(a) What are the mean and standard deviation of demand?
(b) What is the chance that demand will exceed 100,000?
(c) What is the chance that demand will be less than 50,000?
(d) What demand can you be 90% sure of exceeding?
(e) You have a production capacity of 80,000 for next month. What is the chance you will be able to satisfy the demand?
(f) What would be the distribution of the demand for umbrellas measured in *dozens*?

E12. You are running a start-up company that is backed by a $10M venture capital. The current valuation of the company is $22.4M. Both you and the venture capitalist believe that there should be an underlying 10% growth rate per month.

The valuation of the company in the future is, however, uncertain and depends on a range of patents and labor agreements as well as the usual issues of logistics and demand. You are prepared to assume that future valuations are subject to proportional variation. Three months into the future the valuation has an unpredictability of 30%, and 1 year into the future it had an unpredictability of 60%. The venture capitalists will pull out if the valuation falls below $12M.

(a) What is the median and CV of the valuation after 3 months? Therefore, what is the chance the backers pull out after 3 months?

(b) How about after a year?

(c) What assumed growth factor would keep the chance of the company failing at the end of the year to below 1%?

CHAPTER 8

Making Complex Decisions with Trees

8.0. INTRODUCTION: WHAT IS THE ISSUE?

Earlier chapters introduced some basic tools for analyzing simple business decisions. The key ones were mean value (MV), conditional probability, and some standard distributions like binomial or normal for obtaining these probabilities. In a real situation, a manager will have a business process that evolves over time. At various points of this process there are sources of uncertainty that are outside the manager's control but also opportunities to make decisions that make better outcomes more likely and the worst outcomes less likely. And to be quantitative, the manager will have to carefully account for the various costs and revenues that may accrue along the way. Without a formal structure for setting out the problem, it is very easy to mix up the accounting, or the treatment of uncertainty or the logical relationships between the decisions and uncertain outcomes. Decision trees provide such a formal structure.

Let's introduce the main ideas through the GamerCorp case. This is quite a complex case so we will use a slightly simplified version. But by the end of the topic, you might like to read the full case and attempt an analysis.

Case Briefing: GamerCorp Releases Their New Gaming Console

GamerCorp designs platforms for electronic games. They are at the final stages of developing the new platform and could easily release it by July 2009, summer being the standard release period for gaming consoles. The concern is that the main competing company, Sonic Consoles, may release a new platform at the same time.

Data-Driven Business Decisions, First Edition. Chris J. Lloyd.

Product Background

Early product uptake is incredibly important in the game console industry. If the new console does not have a high take up and consumers instead wait for the new Sonic console, then GamerCorp lose the customer for several years—perhaps permanently. Very few consumers would have both products.

GamerCorp is very confident that Sonic Consoles will not release a new platform for the coming summer, since it is too soon after their previous generation console. But there is a fair chance that they may release a new-generation platform for the following standard release point—Christmas 2009.

If GamerCorp goes ahead and releases this summer then they can expect high sales, as there has not been a new console released by either of the main players for several years. To simplify this issue they have classified the sales outcomes into high, medium, and low. Their best assessment of the likelihood of these outcomes is also given.

Low	Medium	High
m$50	m$450	m$850
30%	45%	25%

However, only 65% of this is marginal profit and there are essential marketing costs of $55M worldwide to account for. So in the case of a low sales outcome, GamerCorp would have a marginal profit of $32.5M but face a loss of $22.5M after accounting for marketing. On the other hand, in the best case outcome of high demand they would make just under half a billion dollars over the life cycle of the product.

Release Now or Later?

However, the new console does not incorporate some of the latest technical developments that the company has been researching and testing. A further 3 months would give them time to include these features in the new console and would also mean that game developers would have more time to release and also market games for the new console.

Inclusion of the new features would cost a further $25M so the total fixed cost of release would then be $80M instead of $55M. But it would also mean the product would be more successful. The likely demand outcomes for low, medium, and high sales would improve to 20%, 35%, and 45%, respectively.

But the risk is that with the delay, Sonic Consoles also releases their new platform at around the same time. GamerCorp is worried about this competition scenario. Why? Because if they are the only new console then they have a virtual monopoly with respect to new customers who will naturally purchase the latest technology. Whereas, if Sonic enters the market at the same time as them, then they lose this huge advantage.

GamerCorp assesses that they would need to spend an additional $50M in revised marketing depending on the features of the new Sonic product. Under the competition scenario, sales would be lower even with the extra revised marketing. The likely probabilities for low, medium, and high sales would reverse to 45%, 35%, and 20%, respectively.

How likely is it that Sonic Consoles will release their new platform? GamerCorp is not sure but think that 35% is a reasonable estimate of the chances. They are not very confident about this figure, however. What should they do? How critical are the various figures to the conclusion?

8.1. Elements of Decision Trees

Decision trees are useful for problems that involve a sequence of decisions and uncertain outcomes. The tree represents the logical (usually temporal) relationship between the decisions and outcomes. At each node, the business process can follow several paths—represented by branches in the tree. **Decision nodes** are points where the manager has control over the path taken by the business process. **Outcome nodes** are points where the manager does not have control. These have to be handled by assigning probabilities to each path. Square nodes represent decisions and circular nodes represent random outcomes.

It is essential that probabilities of each and every random outcome are specified. It is also essential that the costs or payoffs associated with the outcomes are known. In most cases there are also costs or payoffs directly associated with the decision—for instance, a decision to go ahead and release the console, which involves marketing costs.

We will illustrate the main elements and concepts with the GamerCorp example, which is rather a simple problem compared with many decision tree problems. We will complicate the story a little later.

Step 1: Set Out the Logical Relationship between the Decisions and Outcomes in a Tree

Constructing the tree is the most important part of the problem. You need to carefully go through the story and think exactly what the decision points are, what the random outcomes are, and how they are logically related, that is, what depends on what. It is worth being very careful and methodical during this step.

For GamerCorp, the immediate problem is a decision of whether to release now or later. So the first node of the decision tree is a **decision node**. The branches coming out of the decision node list all the possible decisions at that point—here only two, but sometimes more. For most but not all trees, the first node is a decision.

Following a decision to Go Now, we have to worry about the product outcome being high, medium, or low. We represent this as an **outcome node** with three branches (high, medium, and low).

If we release later, then we will be immediately exposed to the possibility of competition from the new Sonic console. This is represented as an outcome node with two branches. Finally, for competition or no competition, we are still worried about the final product outcome. So we add additional product outcome nodes with three branches on both the competition and no competition paths.

The story is now finished, which is represented by a triangular node at the right-hand end of each path. In any decision tree, you will end up at one of these **terminal nodes**. The aim is to select the path at the decision nodes to give you the best chance of ending up at the highest payoff terminal nodes.

The decision tree just described is represented below. All the graphics in this chapter are created using the Treeplan Excel add-in.

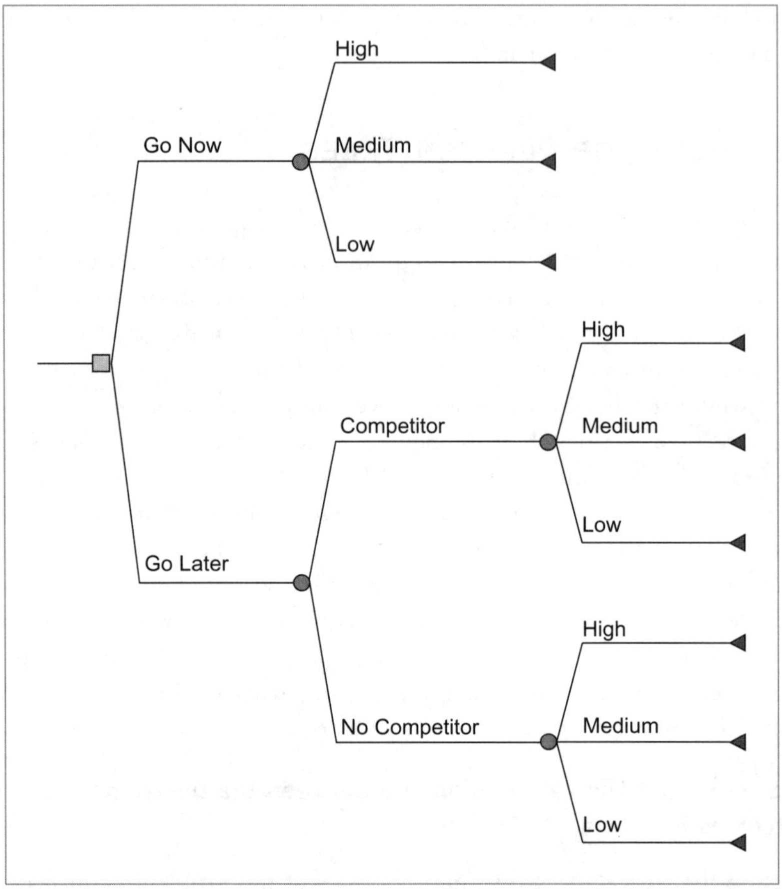

Step 2: Assign Costs/Payoffs to All Branches in the Tree

You first need to decide whether your basic performance measure is payoff or cost as well as the monetary units. In some problems it is easier to list payoffs and maximize them—in others it is easier to list costs and minimize them.

In the GamerCorp story, let's measure performance by the payoff in units of $1M. Once you have your performance measure, you go through each branch of the tree and assign a monetary value. You should think how much money is gained or lost *at each point of the story*. But we do not do any accounting yet. Do not try to add up any profits and losses. This happens later.

If you are using Treeplan, you will find that each branch has an initial value of 0, in blue font. These values should be replaced by the values appropriate to the business problem. Let's do this for GamerCorp, working in time order, meaning from left to right.

To start with, you will have to spend $55 in marketing if you release now. This cost is placed on the decision labeled Go Now. If, on the other hand, we decide to Go Later then the cost will be $80. Both these costs are entered as negative numbers because we are measuring payoff in this example.

There is no direct cost associated with the no competitor branch. This cell can be left blank, or you could leave the value 0. In the graphic below I have deleted the 0 and left the cell blank. For the Competitor branch there is the extra $50 for revised marketing.

	Low	Medium	High
Sales	m$50	m$450	m$850
Raw profit	m$32.5	m$292.5	m$552.5

The outcome node with High, Medium, and Low branches appears at three places in this decision tree. We need payoffs for these branches. According to the problem description, we obtain sales as listed in the table above, but only 65% of this is raw profit. The raw profits are also listed in the table. These figures are added to the High, Medium, and Low branches everywhere they appear. In more complicated problems the payoffs for High, Medium, and Low could potentially be different in different parts of the tree, that is, depending on the earlier decisions and outcomes. But in this problem, they are the same.

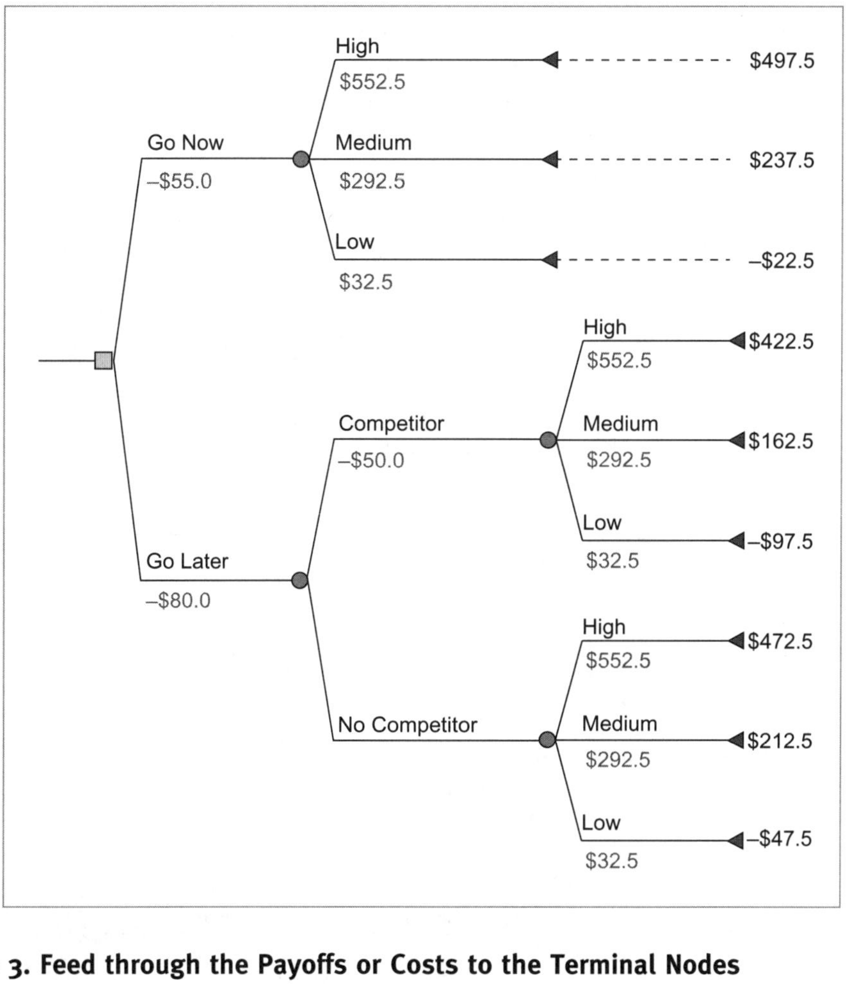

Step 3. Feed through the Payoffs or Costs to the Terminal Nodes

This is where the accounting gets done! Each terminal node has a unique path leading to it, which represents a unique story. Each unique story has its own final payoff displayed in bold black font if you are using Treeplan. The payoff of that node is just the sum of the payoffs along the path leading to it.

For instance, the bottom right terminal node represents the path

> We decide to go later with the product; we are lucky that there is no competition from Sonic, but unfortunately we still end up with the low sales outcome.

In this case we are spending \$80 in marketing, and then only receiving 65% of \$50 in return. The payoff in this case is –\$47.5. For more complicated stories it is easy to get confused about which payoffs and costs to include with each possible story. If you have the tree and if you have carefully included each payoff or cost at each step of the story, then you cannot get the accounting wrong. For this tree, there are nine terminal nodes, nine possible stories, and nine terminal payoffs, all represented in the diagram above (and below).

Step 4. Include the Probabilities of All Random Outcomes

For each circular outcome node you need a probability for every branch leaving it. They are placed above the branch name and are in green font. These probabilities have to add up to 100%. In general, these probabilities should be conditional on all random outcomes to the left.

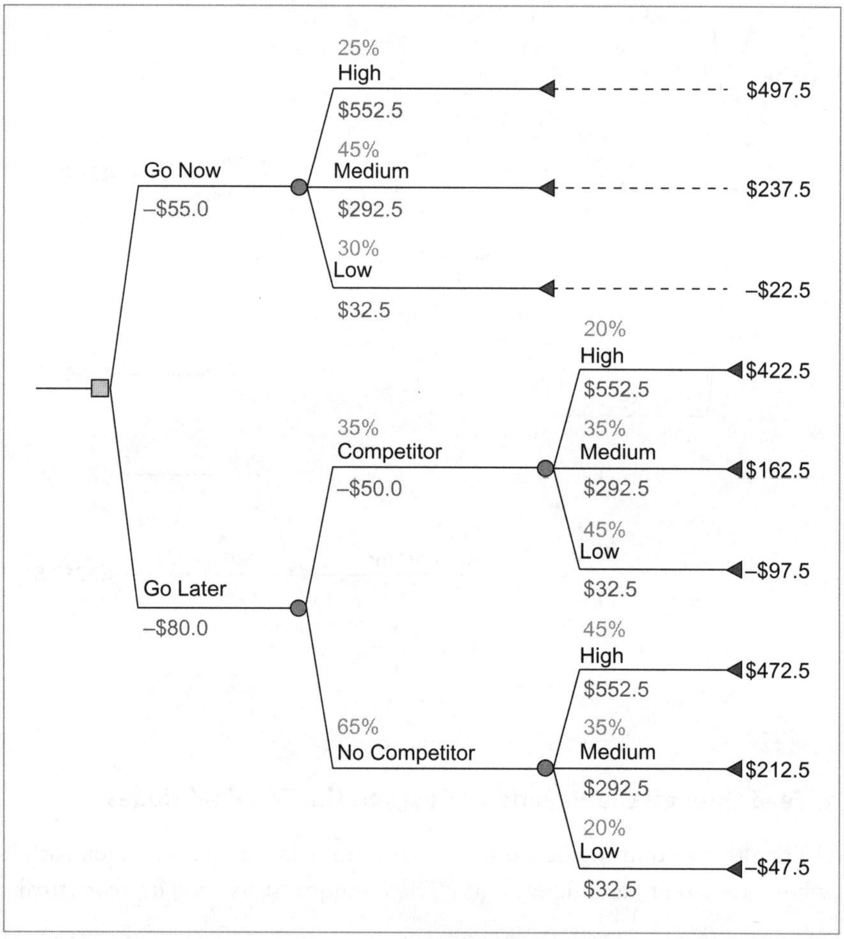

For instance, looking at the bottom right outcome node, the probabilities of the three product outcomes are 45%, 35%, and 20% for high, medium, and low, respectively. These are conditional on no competition from Sonic. In practice, it is conditional probabilities that are usually available. You can usually say to yourself, "If this happens then the chances of the next outcome will be this." The word "if" means "conditional on." You have been thinking about and using conditional probabilities all your life without realizing it. The probabilities described in the story are set out in the table below. These are the probabilities that are added to the tree at the appropriate nodes.

	High	Medium	Low
Go now	25%	45%	30%
No Comp	45%	35%	20%
Comp	20%	35%	45%

The previous diagram now has *all* the elements given in the GamerCorp problem. It includes the logical relationship between the decisions and the random outcomes, the costs of all outcomes and decisions, and the probabilities of the outcomes. It remains to *solve the tree.*

8.2. Solving the Decision Tree

The tree is solved automatically by the Treeplan add-in. It is important, though, to understand how this works.

Starting from the right of the tree we *value each node* by the values of the nodes that directly follow it. If the node is an outcome node, then it is valued by the MV of the nodes coming into it. If it is a decision node then it is valued by the maximum* value of the nodes coming into it.

*If you use costs then value node by minimum.

All these node values are displayed in Treeplan in orange. As an example, consider the lower right outcome node of the GamerCorp tree, which represented the case where we go later and there is no competition. The sales outcome node has been valued at $277.5. Why? There are three nodes with values $472.5, $212.5, and –$47.5 coming into it. These happen to be terminal nodes but it makes no difference what kind of nodes these may be. The probabilities of the three branches are 45%, 35%, and 20%, respectively. Combining these three probabilities with the three node values gives the MV $277.5. This represents the mean payoff if you Go Later and do not face competition. If you do face competition then the mean payoff is $97.5, and if you Go Now the payoff is $224.5. All these figures, remember, are net of the costs that can be incurred at various points.

The competition outcome node can then be valued by looking at the two nodes coming into it, whose values are $97.5 and $277.5. The probability of each of these is 35% and 65%, respectively, giving a MV of $214.5.

We now move to the decision node at the left. There are two outcome nodes coming into this, with values $224.5 and $214.5. We would choose the larger of these whose value is $224.5M. The Treeplan software indicates the optimal decision by a little number in the decision box. Decisions are numbered 1, 2, 3. … from upper to lower. The number "1" indicates the first or uppermost decision, which here is to Go Now (decision label 1) rather than Go Later (decision label 2).

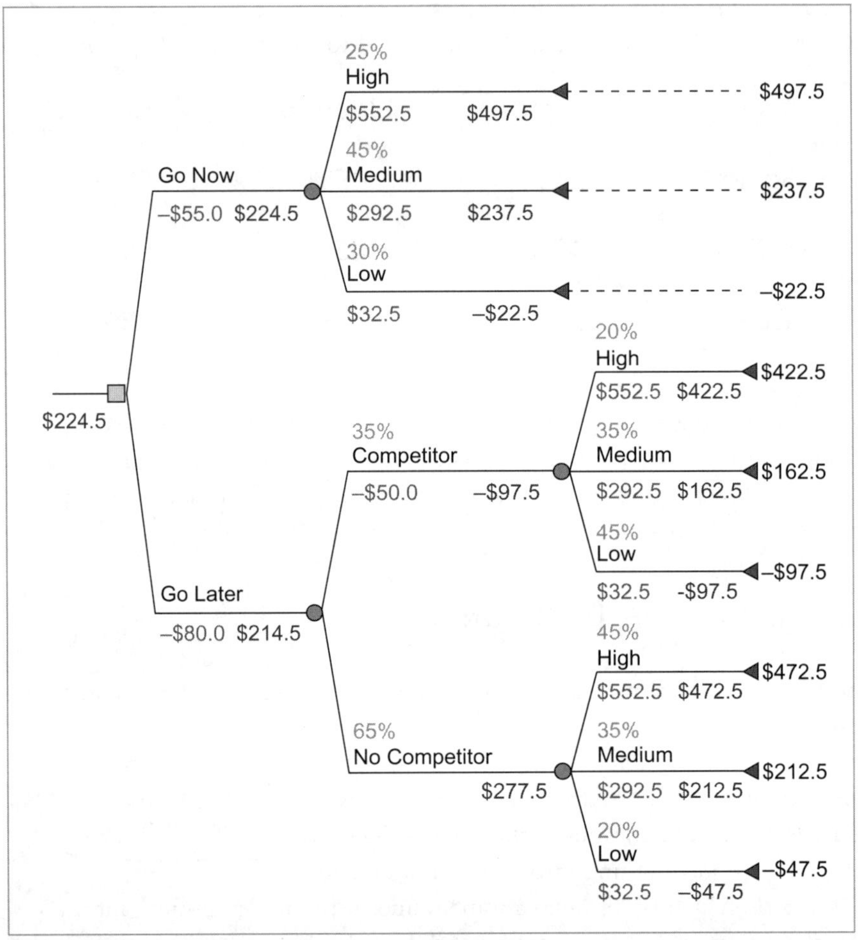

This completes the main task of the exercise, which is to *identify the optimal decision and its mean payoff.* This tree indicates that we should go ahead now and take a MV payoff of $224.5M. This is $10M better than the other option of delaying release and risking competition with Sonic.

However, mean payoff is only one way of looking at the value of a decision. While we have used the mean as the criterion to arrive at the best decision, it is still worthwhile looking at the range of payoffs and probabilities that this optimal decision delivers to us.

Risk Assessment

The MV of the decision to Go Now is $224.5M. This corresponds to the left distribution in the table below. There is a 30% chance of a loss and a 25% chance of a big win.

For the Go Later option there are six possible payoffs given in the right distribution of the table below. These are obtained from the six terminal nodes in the decision tree. They have been arranged from worst to best. The six probabilities are obtained by multiplying the probabilities along the branches leading to the node. For instance, the chance of the worst possible outcome of –$97M is 35% of 45%, which is 15.75%. This outcome occurs when there is competition and we get low sales. The mean of Go Later payoff distribution is $214.5M.

Mean is only one (important) aspect of the payoff distribution. It relates to *long-run average payoff.* But for this particular problem, and for most business problems, we are not so much interested in the long run as in taking the most justifiable option in the current circumstances. So it is also important to consider the riskiness of the payoff. For instance, we would surely rather a guaranteed payoff of $224.5K than the risky payoff distribution for Go Now.

Go Now		Go Later	
Chance	**Payoff**	**Chance**	**Payoff**
30%	-$22.5	15.75%	-97.5
45%	$237.5	13.0%	-47.5
25%	$497.5	12.25%	162.5
		22.75%	212.5
		7.0%	422.5
		29.25%	472.5
MV	$224.5	MV	$214.5
σ	$192.4	σ	$217.0

One way to measure riskiness of a payoff distribution is the standard deviation σ from Chapter 5. This is a single positive number that measures uncertainty of a payoff or probability distribution. The standard deviation of the Go Now option is $192.5 and the standard deviation of the Go Later option is $217.0. So the Go Now option is not only a higher mean payoff strategy but is less risky—at least if we use standard deviation as the risk measure.

If a single number is judged to be too crude a measure of risk, then one can look at specific and pertinent details of the payoff distribution. For instance, the *probability of a loss* is often of interest. For the Go Later option, there is a 28.75% chance of a loss—slightly less than the 30% if we Go Now. There is a 36.25% chance of a big win—greater than the 25% chance if we Go Now. So if we were particularly keen to avoid a loss, or to get a big win, we might decide to Go Later, despite the lower MV.

The most effective graphical comparison of two payoff distributions is the cumulative distribution function (from Chapter 5), which in business decision contexts is called the **cumulative risk profile** (CRP). The CRP is the probability of getting a payoff equal to or smaller than any specified payoff. You can use the probability_distribution.xls template to produce the table of these cumulative probabilities, presented below. The CRP is usually plotted as a *step function* graph with the cumulative probabilities on the vertical axis and the payoffs on the horizontal axis.

Go Now		Go Later	
Pr(≤)	Payoff	Pr(≤)	Payoff
30%	-$22.5	15.75%	-97.5
75%	$237.5	28.75%	-47.5
100%	$497.5	41.00%	162.5
		63.75%	212.5
		70.75%	422.5
		100%	472.5

Generally speaking, you would rather a payoff distribution whose CRP is *below* a competing payoff distribution. Why? Because it is then less likely that our payoff falls below any specified target. This may perhaps seem an obtuse way to think of things, but you just need to remember that in judging the CRP of a payoff distribution, *lower is better.* You can sometimes be lucky and find that one profile is completely below another, which means that this strategy dominates the other. When a strategy is dominant, not only will its mean be higher, but it is also preferable in terms of any sensible measure of risk.

In the case of comparing Go Now and Go Later strategies we are not in that simple situation. The earlier observation that the chance of a loss is (slightly) less for the Go Later strategy can be seen where the two CRP graphs cut the vertical axis. At this point Go Later is slightly better (lower). The observation that the chance of a "big win" is slightly higher is also visible in this plot—around a payoff of $300–$400—where Go Later is again lower. Looking at the graphs overall though, it is not all that clear which is better.

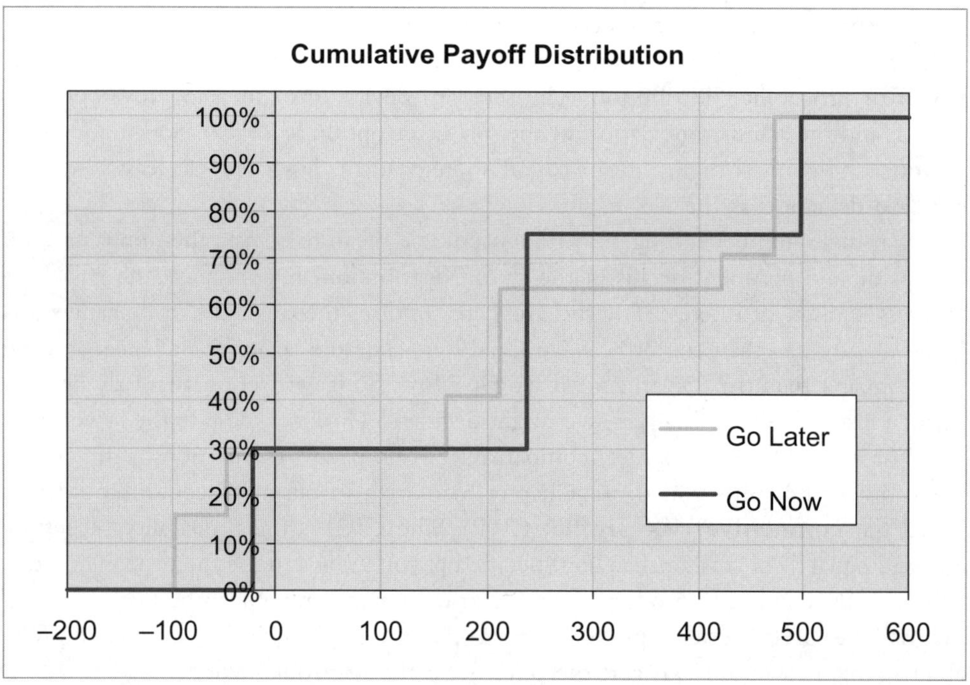

A clearer picture of the payoff distribution can often be obtained by assuming that the payoff distribution is *normal* with the mean and standard deviation calculated from the payoff tables. This is not as crazy as it might sound. Remember that the decision tree is an approximation to the problem—we often arbitrarily break the random outcomes into crude categories such as High/Medium/Low when this outcome would really be a continuum of possible payoffs. So the lumpiness of the payoff distribution is an artifact of our crude description of the problem. We can correct for this crudeness at the end of the analysis by using a payoff distribution that matches the one we have calculated in its mean and standard deviation, but which follows a nice smooth curve. Normal distributions are nice and smooth,

The template normal.xls in chapter 7 is already set up to produce a graphical comparison of two normal distributions. It is just a matter of entering the correct means and standard deviations. The plot below, which we already saw in the last chapter, shows that the Go Now option is better (lower) if you are worried about negative or low outcomes, while the Go Later option is better (lower) if you are more interested in the highest outcomes. The risk-averse manager would Go Now. The manager who especially valued the highest outcomes would Go Later. The manager who just "played the mean" would take the higher MV of 224.5 and Go Now.

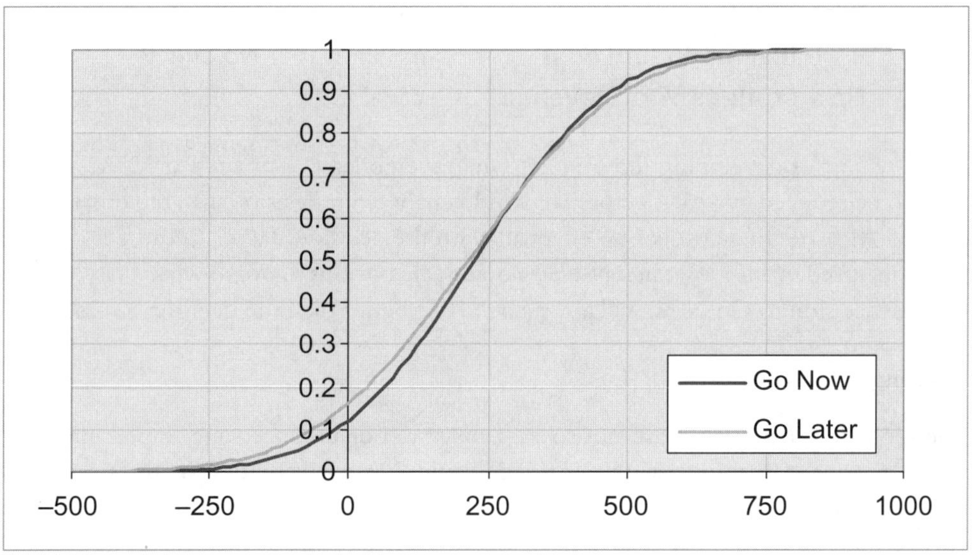

Sensitivity Analysis

The conclusion of the analysis is only as good as the numbers that you put into it. While you will presumably put the best available estimate for all these numbers, they could well be slightly wrong. So it is good practice to vary some of the numbers, especially the ones you are least confident about, to see how much the decision is affected.

One key number in the story is the chance of Sonic releasing early and providing competition. If this were lower than 35% you may well go later. This is easy to enter into the tree. You should make sure that the cell containing 65% always contains 100% minus the cell containing 35%. You can then vary the 35% to see at what point the decision changes.

You will find that the tipping point is 29.4%. So you can assert that your decision to Go Now depends on the chance of competition being larger than 29.4%. You best guess is 35%, so you are recommending Go Now.

In the same way, one can find tipping points for various other figures in the story. This can easily be achieved using Goalseek. You simply create a cell that contains the value of the Go Now node minus the value of the Go Later node. Goalseek will then vary any cell you like to target a difference of zero, the tipping point. This has been set up in the spreadsheet ex1 gamercorp.xls. The difference between the two decisions is in cell X5. The various numbers that drive the decision and that you might consider varying are in red.

The table below shows the point at which the decision changes to Go Later when other relevant variables are changed. If the cost of the extra revised marketing when there is competition was lower, it would have to be much lower—$21.4M instead of the estimated $50M.

Issue	Assumed	Tipping Value
Chance of competition	35%	29.4%
Extra marketing	m$50	m$21.4
Development cost	m$25	m$15
Initial marketing cost	-m$55	No effect!
Raw profit as % of Revenue	65%	85%

The cost of developing the product when we go later, estimated at $25M, would have to be reduced to $15M before we would change our decision. On the other hand, the $55-M marketing cost has no effect at all on the decision. Why? Because it is a cost that is incurred *whether we go now or later*. You can change this figure to whatever you like, and the decision to Go Now will always be $10M better than the decision to Go Later.

Pushing a Bit Further

Some of the other figures are not so easy to vary. For instance, one important set of numbers for the analysis was the 45%, 35%, and 20% probabilities for the three sales outcomes under the competition and no competition scenarios. These probabilities reverse under the two scenarios. What if we are interested in the importance of the 20% figure? We could change it to 15% but then the three probabilities do not add up to 100%! If you change one probability then you have to change (at least one of the) others. If you just change one of these figures in your Treeplan tree then you will get an error.

One sensible way to deal with probabilities is to change one, but keep all the rest of the probabilities in the *same ratios*. For example, consider the 20% figure, which leaves 80% for the other two sales outcomes. The 80% is split into 35% and 45%, a ratio of 7:9. We can code the cell containing 35% to instead contain a fraction 7/16 of the remaining 80%, while the cell containing 45% contains a fraction 9/16 of the remaining 80%. If you change the 20% to 15% then the 35% changes to 37.2% and the 45% changes to 47.8%. The value of the Go Later node increases to $220.6M and we are now only $3.9M better off with the Go Now decision. We can then use Goalseek to find the point at which the decision changes.

The tipping points, using this method, are given in the table below. The least important figure is the 35% figure for medium sales. This can be varied almost down to zero without affecting the decision. The most delicate figure is the 45%. This only needs to be 54.4% for the decision to reverse.

Key input	Assumed	Tipping Value
Pr(Low|Comp)	45%	54.4%
Pr(Medium)	35%	1.7%
Pr(High|Comp)	20%	11.8%

8.3. MULTISTAGE DECISION TREES

EXAMPLE 1 *Jazz festival*

It is March, and you are promoting an open air jazz festival, scheduled for next September, 6 months from now. It will cost you \$80K to commit to the venue and band bookings. The festival will bring you \$300K marginal profit provided the weather is fine. If, on the other hand, it rains and the festival is washed out then you will lose the \$80K set-up costs. Bureau of Meteorology reports allow you to estimate the chance of rain on a randomly chosen day in September to be 35%.

You have the option of insuring against the misfortune of rain. The policy specifies that the insurance company will pay you \$250K if the festival is washed out. The cost of the policy is \$100K. The contract can be signed up until 2 weeks before the festival.

It is a relatively easy calculation to compare the MV of the decision to insure with the MV of the decision not to insure. You will find that the insuring involves a loss of mean payoff. This is typical of insurance decisions. Your MV is reduced when you take an insurance policy but your risk is also reduced. From the insurance company's point of view, they must charge more than the "fair" MV of the policy payout in order to make a profit. There is no real need for a decision tree to solve this problem. You could just write down the payoff table for the two decisions.

So let's continue the story ...

A long-range weather forecaster claims to be able to better predict the chances of rain over 2 weeks than 6 months. Specifically, this forecaster claims that 2 weeks in advance he can predict whether a day will have significant enough rain to wash out the festival. He tends to be conservative in his predictions though—he will only predict rain 25% of the time.

He claims 80% accuracy, backed up by historical records of his performance. Specifically, he claims that if he predicts rain then there is an 80% chance it will rain while if he predicts no rain (hereafter called "fine") then there is an 80% chance it will be fine. So you now have the option of using the forecaster to get a better idea of whether it will rain. If he predicts rain, then the chance of rain is 80% rather than 35%, and this may make it very worthwhile to get insurance.

Unfortunately, the forecaster will not offer his services for free. He wants \$20K for his prediction. He will even give you back half of this cost—\$10K—if his prediction is for rain, which is the forecast you don't want to hear. Should you use the forecaster?

First, we construct the decision tree for this problem. The first decision is whether to even go ahead and promote the festival or to abandon the project now and save the $80K. If you go ahead then you have three decision options—go ahead without insurance, take out insurance, or pay for the forecaster. This is set out in the first two decision nodes in the tree below. If you prefer, you could instead think of this as four possible initial decisions. It ultimately makes no difference.

If you use the forecaster then he will predict rain or not. After his prediction you will have an option to go ahead without insurance (to "risk it") or to take insurance. This is where the potential value of the forecaster lies—in affecting your decision to insure or not. There are three levels of decision in this problem—to promote at all, if you promote to use the forecaster, and after the forecaster to insure or not. This is the basis of the name **multistage decision tree**. The whole tree is displayed below.

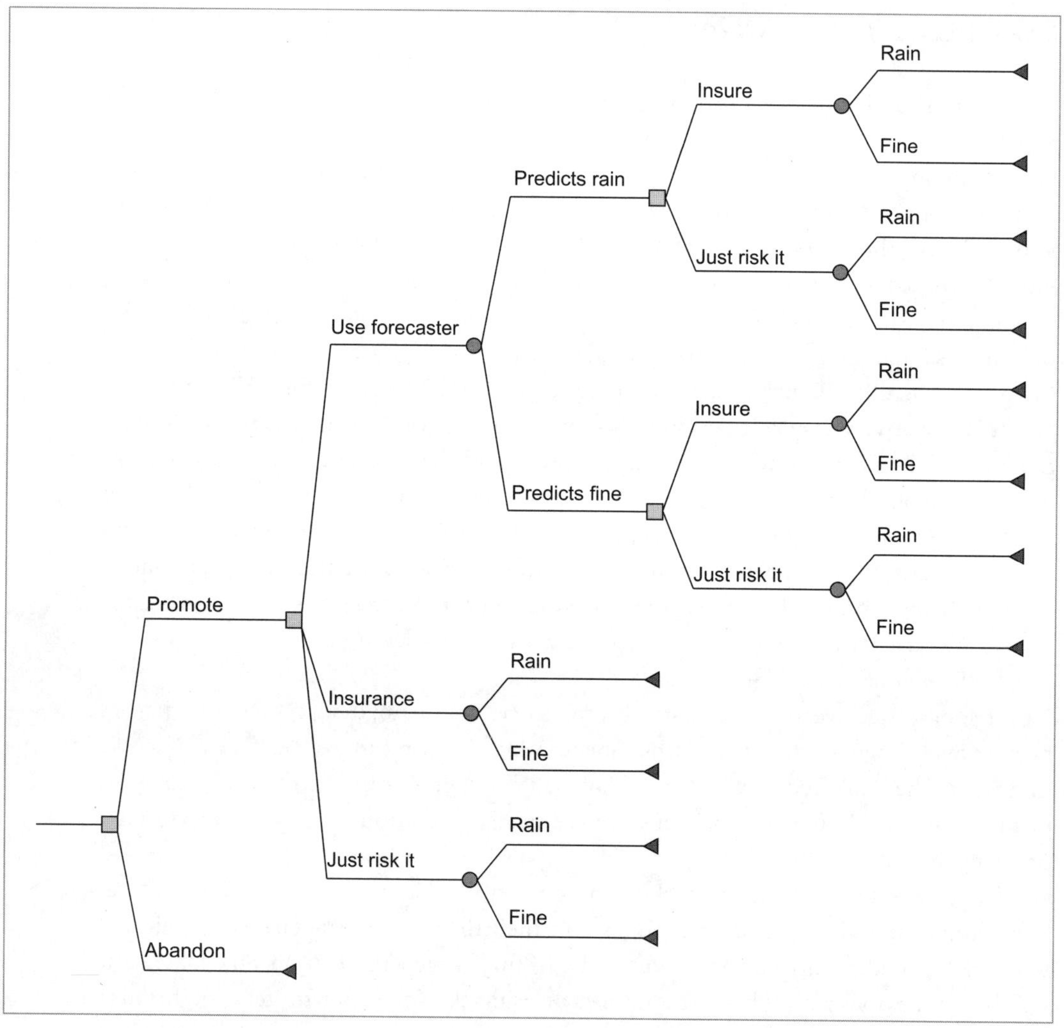

We will use payoffs in units of $1K as the performance measure. You only incur costs of $80K if you decide to promote, which will be added as a value of –80 on the "Promote" branch. If you insure it costs $100K. If you use the forecaster you pay another \$20K initially but you get back \$10K if he predicts rain. So there will be a value of –20 on the "Use Forecaster" branch and a value of +10 on the "Predicts Rain" branch. You receive \$300K if the festival runs with fine weather and nothing if it rains and this is repeated across all the Rain/Fine nodes that are to the right of a "Just risk it" decision. But if you are insured, you receive \$250K when it rains (and \$300K when it is fine). These numbers are all added into the tree at the appropriate branches.

The probabilities of rain or fine weather are 35%/65% if you do not use the forecaster. They are 80%/20% if you do use the forecaster. This is where the forecaster narrows the probabilities for you. You also need the probability that the forecaster predicts rain, given as 25% in the case.

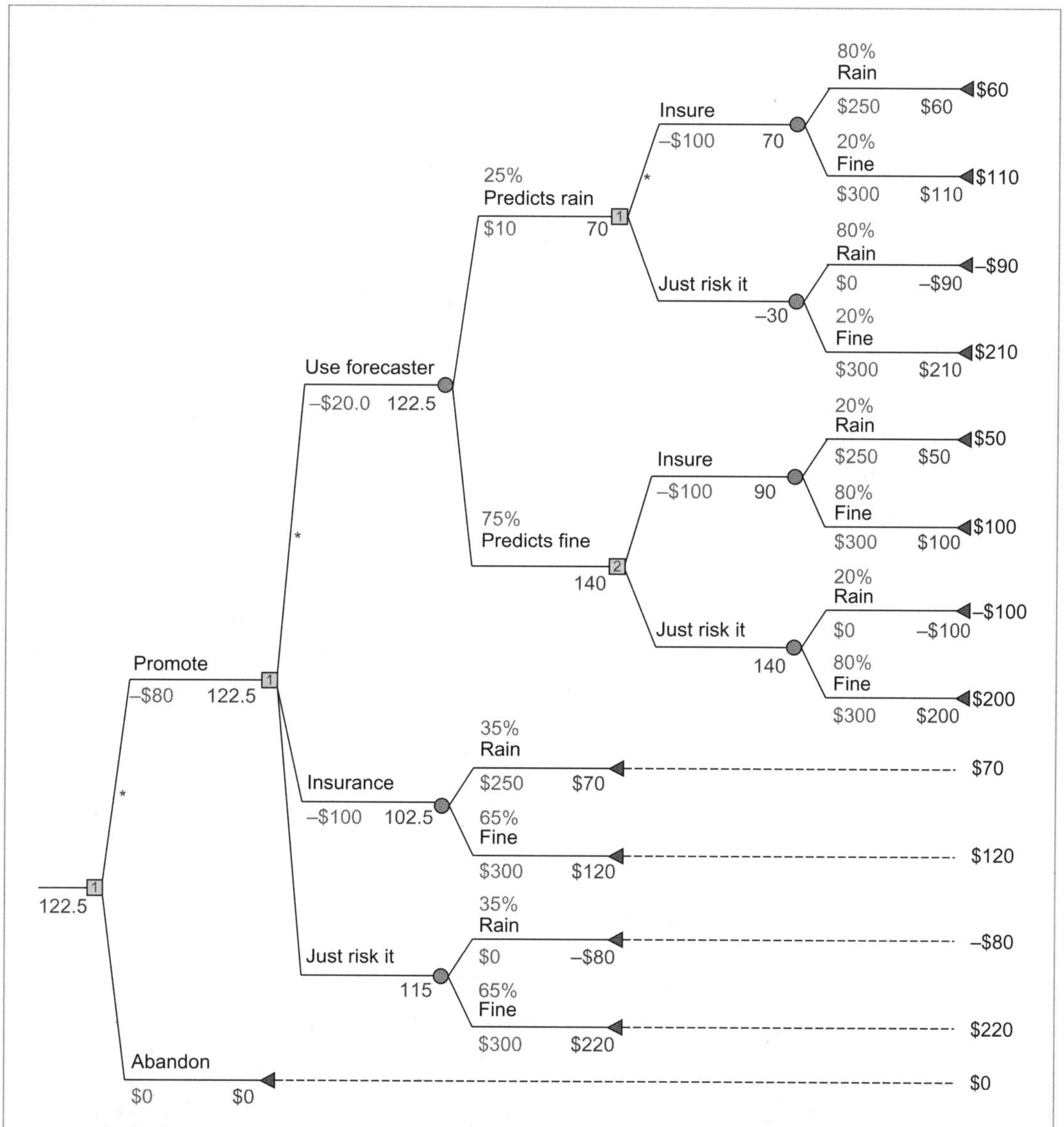

The decisions are indicated by the number in the decision box. I have also added a small ★ to make the indicated decision path clearer. According to the decision tree, you should pay for the forecaster and then take out insurance only if he predicts rain. The MV of this decision strategy is $122.5K, which is higher than the next best alternative of going ahead without insurance. The MV of taking out insurance is $102.5K, about $12.5K less than the $115K MV if you just risk it. As suggested in the preamble, it is natural that insurance involves sacrificing some mean payoff. The benefit is that you get reduced risk. With insurance, the worst possible outcome is $70K, whereas without insurance you can lose $80K.

CHECK YOUR UNDERSTANDING

Q1. You are considering going to court to sue your employer for an injury at work. You are asking for $500K. Your lawyers suggest that there is about a 50% chance that you will be awarded this amount. There is a 30% you will be awarded only medical costs of $100K. But there is also a 5% chance that you will lose and be $50K out of pocket for your own legal costs. Finally, there is a 15% chance that you will completely lose and have to pay your employer's legal costs of $150K on top of your own costs. Set this up as a (very simple) decision tree and give the best decision.

Thinking about Risk

With the optimal strategy, the worst possible payoff is rather bad. You could lose $100K. This is the outcome if the forecaster predicts fine weather and he is wrong. To examine the issue of risk in more detail, we need to see the full payoff distribution of each decision. The overall payoff tables are displayed in the table below. As explained in the previous section, these are obtained by reading off each terminal value that can be reached by that decision. The probabilities of these payoffs are obtained by multiplying probabilities along the branches leading to that node.

The chance of losing $100K is 15%, much less than the chance of losing $80K if you just go ahead. So not only are we obtaining a higher MV with the forecaster (by $7.5K), but we are reducing our risk significantly. This is only possible, of course, because we can take out insurance when the forecaster predicts rain, which has a faint odor of the unethical!

Prob	Insure Payoff	Risk it Payoff	Prob	Forecast Payoff
35%	$70	-$80	15%	-$100
65%	$120	$220	20%	$60
			5%	$110
			60%	$200
MV	$102.5	$115		$122.5

Thinking about Incentives

The value of the forecaster is that when he predicts rain we can take out insurance. It would be worrying if there was any incentive for the forecaster to not predict rain. But his payment structure gives exactly this incentive! He has to pay you back $10K whenever he predicts rain.

The forecaster receives $20K in the 75% of cases where he predicts fine weather and $10K in the 25% of cases where he predicts rain. His mean payoff then is $17.5K. I think there would be good sense in offering to pay a flat fee of $17.5K to the forecaster to remove this perverse incentive. It means he can focus on his core skill. And it would not cost either you or him anything in MV. You can check this yourself by modifying the tree appropriately—just replace the $20K charge by $17.5K and remove the $10K refund.

Pushing a Bit Further

You can do a sensitivity analysis to see which numbers might conceivably be different and change the decision. There is no reason to change the insurance payoff or the forecaster's fees, which are known numbers. The $80K cost of promoting the festival would also be well known. The main dollar figure that is uncertain is the $300K marginal profit if the festival goes ahead in fine weather. You can check for yourself that this figure *makes no difference to the decision at all.* The MVs of all three decisions change but the *relative* values do not. The reason is that all the costs savings are being delivered by the insurance company's $250K payout, which is a fixed amount.

The *probabilities* would be well worth varying. For instance, the 35% figure for the probability of rain is key. If this were sufficiently small you would just go ahead and risk it without forecasting or insurance. While the 80% figure is a measure of how accurate the forecaster is, if this were much lower than 80% then forecasting would not be worth the cost.

There is a technical problem in varying the 80%, 25%, and 35% figures. These numbers are logically dependent on each other. We encountered a similar problem in the previous section where probabilities had to add up to 100%. These three numbers do not have to add up to 100% but they are related in a more subtle way.

Think of it this way. The forecaster will predict rain 25% of the time and 80% of these occasions he will be correct and it will actually rain. He will predict fine weather 75% of the time and 20% of the time he will be wrong and it will rain. So the chance that it will rain is

$$80\% \text{ of } 25\% + 20\% \text{ of } 75\% = 35\%.$$

This agrees with the probability of 35% for rain given in the case. However, if I change the 80% figure to 90% then we get

$$90\% \text{ of } 25\% + 10\% \text{ of } 75\% = 30\%,$$

which is the wrong answer. The forecaster *cannot actually affect the chance that it will rain.* He only predicts it better than others. So I cannot just change the 80% figure to 90% without changing the 25% figure as well. I have to change the 25% figure so that we get the correct answer, 35%, for the chance of rain. How to change it is not too difficult to analyze. Some algebra shows that if we change the figure 80% to another value p, then the 25% figure must change to

$$(p - 0.65)/(2p - 1).$$

This has been coded into the spreadsheet ex2 jazz festival.xls in cell AA9. We can now vary the 80% figure while respecting the objective weather data that predict a 35% chance of rain in September. You will find that the decision changes when the forecast accuracy is 75.3%—not much smaller than the claimed accuracy of 80%. At this point the MV using the forecaster is identical to the MV of just risking it. If his accuracy is any lower than 75.3% then his forecasting would not be worth the money he is charging. So it looks as though you might want to evaluate this accuracy claims pretty thoroughly and critically.

8.4. VALUING A DECISION OPTION

It can never be a bad thing to have an extra decision option. At worst, it is not the best decision and would be worth zero. Some decisions, such as using the forecaster, cost money. In this case, you might still like to know how much the forecasting option is worth.

A decision option is represented as a branch on a decision tree. How much is that branch worth? We can answer this question with some simple verbal reasoning.

First, what is the MV of the decision tree with the cost of the decision option set to zero? Call this MV_1. This measures our payoff or utility if we could take that decision for free. Second, what is the MV of the decision tree with the decision option completely unavailable? This would be the MV of our next best decision option. Call this MV_2. The difference between these two (MV_1—MV_2) is the value of the decision option. It is the difference between having the decision option for no cost and not having the option at all. Notice that since having an extra decision option cannot possibly make MV lower, $MV_1 \geq MV_2$.

It is obvious from this analysis that if the decision is not one you would exercise if it were free, then MV_1 would equal MV_2 and so the value of the decision option is zero. This certainly makes sense.

To reiterate, we measure the value of a decision option by the difference between MV with this decision option included free and the MV with the decision option excluded. To calculate this is very easy once the decision tree had been set up. To calculate MV_1, set the cost on that decision branch to zero. The value at the root of the tree is MV_1. To calculate MV_2, set the cost on that decision branch to an extremely large number. This effectively removes the decision branch from the tree. The value at the root of the tree is MV_2.

Value of Sample Information

A special application of this idea is to a decision option that is associated with the purchase of better information about an uncertain business outcome—for instance the long-range weather forecast of the chance of rain in September. In this case, we call the value of the decision option the **MV of sample information**—denoted VSI.

EXAMPLE 1 (Continued) *Jazz festival*

What is the value of the improved assessment of the chances of rain that the forecaster is offering you? This would place an upper bound on how much you would pay for this information.

Remove the \$20K cost and the \$10K refund from the tree. This gives the MV if the forecaster offered his services for free. You will see that $MV_1 = 140$. Now replace the cost of \$20K by a, very large number. You will find that the MV for the tree is $MV_2 = 115$, being the MV obtained by taking the best decision (to just risk it) if the forecasting were not available.

The difference is \$140K—\$115K = \$25K.

Pushing a Bit Further

A sensible question is to ask how this changes if the main accuracy figure of 80% changes. I have already set up the sheet so that when this figure is changed the 25% figure automatically changes to respect the 35% overall chance of rain as explained earlier. It is easy but tedious to repeat the calculation for VSI with different values for the 80% accuracy of the forecaster. The value of his forecasting is plotted against the accuracy below. The cost he is charging is \$20K if the forecast is for fine and \$10K if it is for rain. The MV is

$$\$20K \times \Pr(\text{Predict rain}) + \$10K \times \Pr(\text{Predict fine}),$$

and this actually varies as well because Pr(Predict rain) in cell AA10 also varies. The chart shows this mean cost as a dotted line. When the accuracy is greater than 75.3%, the value of the forecaster is larger than the cost and so it is worthwhile using his services (as concluded earlier).

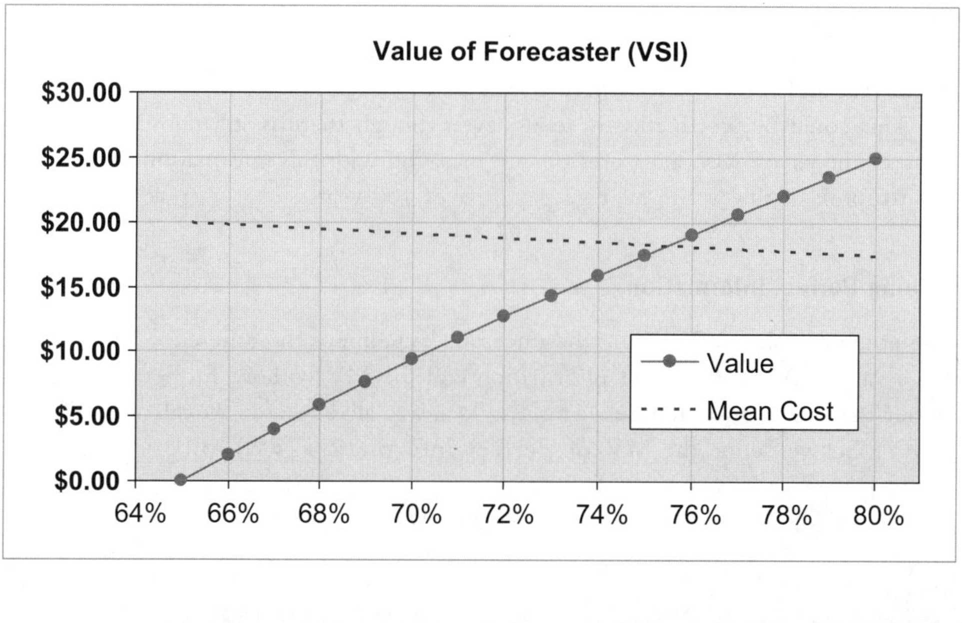

8.5. THE COST OF UNCERTAINTY

Uncertainty in a business outcome typically costs you money. It does not make you money. If you knew what the business outcome was going to be then you could make the right decision now. Uncertainty means your decision could end up being an unfortunate one.

In the GamerCorp example, the uncertain outcome is the possibility of competition from Sonic if you delay release. There is also uncertainty about your sales (which could be high, medium, or low). In the jazz festival example, the uncertain outcome is the weather. In other examples, the uncertain outcome might be how much a competitor will bid on a tender or the outcome of a clinical trial for a new drug you are thinking of investing in.

How much does the uncertainty cost you? This places an upper bound on what you would pay for *any* information, even perfectly accurate information, on that uncertain outcome.

What If I Knew the Outcome?

This depends on your decision options!

The way to assess this quantitatively is to look at what you would do, and what would be the mean payoff, if you could be told the uncertain outcome in advance. One way of thinking about this is to imagine there is a hypothetical forecaster with near-clairvoyant powers of prediction. This removes the uncertainty completely. You then ask *with this perfect prediction, what decisions would I take and what would the mean payoff be?*

We will call this payoff MV_0. We interpret this as the MV with perfect information about the uncertain event.

Note that we do not assume that the uncertain event's probabilities changes. Some people find this hard to understand. Think about the jazz festival example. We are not saying that anyone can actually change the weather. There is still a 35% chance of rain. Rather, we are imagining that someone can predict exactly whether it will rain or not. So out of 100 years he will correctly identify the 35 years where it will rain and the 65 years where it will be fine.

This could be worth money to us, even though there is still rain 35 times out of 100. The payoff MV_0 measures our mean payoff with this information. You might like to think of this as the average payoff over 100 years.

Valuing Perfect Information

The potential value of knowing the uncertain outcome is the difference between the mean value MV_0 with perfect information and the MV without further information (about the uncertain outcome). This last MV was already used to calculate VSI—it is MV_2. So we define the **MV of perfect information** (VPI) to be

$$VPI = MV_0 - MV_2.$$

You can think of this either as the *value of knowing* the uncertain outcome or the *cost of not knowing* the uncertain outcome. It really amounts to the same thing.

There are three MVs that we calculate when faced with a decision problem whose uncertain outcome may be costing is money. These are

- MV_0—what we achieve with perfect foresight of the uncertain outcome.
- MV_1—what we achieve with offered free information.
- MV_2—what we achieve if we just accept the outcome uncertainty.

It is always the case that

$$MV_0 \geq MV_1 \geq MV_2.$$

Therefore, VPI is always greater than VSI.

Notice that VPI, like VSI, *depends on the decision options that are available.* If knowing the uncertain outcome in advance would not lead to any other action, then there is no value at all in knowing the uncertain outcome. You may not like some of the outcomes but *uncertainty* about the outcome only costs you money if the bad outcomes could be avoided or mitigated by a decision.

EXAMPLE 1 (Continued) *Jazz festival*

Suppose that the perfect forecaster tells you it will rain. What will you do? I would take out insurance and receive a final payoff of \$70K. What if he told you it will be fine? Then you would go ahead and receive \$220K. Remember, we are not saying that the chance of rain has changed. So there is still a 35% chance of rain and 65% chance of fine.

Therefore the MV is

$$\$70\text{K} \times \Pr(\text{Rain}) + \$220\text{K} \times \Pr(\text{Fine}) = \$167.5.$$

Another way you can obtain this value is to use the spreadsheet ex2 jazz festival.xls. Remove the costs of the forecaster and then change his accuracy from 80% to 100%. You will find the MV of the tree is 167.5. To find the VPI we compare this figure with MV_2 = 115 calculated earlier to obtain

$$\text{VPI} = \$167.5 - \$115 = \$52.5.$$

This is the absolute maximum you would ever pay for weather prediction. This particular forecaster is worth \$25K, which we calculated earlier. He is charging \$17.5K in MV.

EXAMPLE 2 *GamerCorp*

There are two uncertain events we can think about here. Let's look first at the uncertain event of possible competition from Sonic.

If someone could tell us that there definitely *will not* be competition then we would delay and go later and receive \$277.5M in MV. This number comes from the value of the No Competition branch in the full tree given earlier. If someone could tell us that there definitely *will* be competition then we would go now and get \$224M.

We are not saying that prediction changes Sonic's behavior. So the chance of competition is still 35%. The MV is

$$MV_0 = 35\% \times \$277.5M + 65\% \times \$224M = \$258.95M.$$

Compare this with the MV of the best decision if we do without this perfect information, which is the MV of the tree MV_2 = \$224.5M. So

$$VPI = \$258.95M - \$224.5M = \$34.45M.$$

How about the uncertain outcome of sales being High/Medium/Low? If we know in advance that the sales will be high or medium or low then what would we do? Do we really have the option of doing anything? Not in the story as told. We could consider the option to drop the product but then we would be out of business. For the sake of going through the calculation, let's suppose that this was the only available option.

If we know in advance that the sales will be high then we should go now and receive \$497.5 (because it is better than either \$422.5 or \$472.5).

If we know in advance that the sales will be medium then we should go now and receive \$237.5 (because it is better than either \$162.5 or \$212.5).

If we know in advance that the sales will be low then we should ... drop the product and take 0 (because it is better than either −\$22.5 or −\$47.5). So

$$MV_0 = 25\% \times \$497.5 + 45\% \times \$237.5 + 30\% \times 0 = \$231.25,$$

and so

$$VPI = \$231.25 - \$224.50 = \$6.75M.$$

The conclusion is that information about whether or not Sonic will compete is much more critical than information about the final sales. Of course, in the final analysis we only care about sales. But the decision options that are available to us in response to sales are quite restricted. So the *uncertainty* about sales is not a major issue.

CHECK YOUR UNDERSTANDING

Q2. You are considering going to court to sue your employer for an injury at work. You are asking for \$500K. Your lawyers suggest that there is about a 50%

chance that you will be awarded this amount. There is a 30% chance that you will be awarded only medical costs of $100K.

But there is also a 5% chance that you will lose and be $50K out of pocket for your own legal costs. Finally, there is a 15% chance that you will completely lose and have to pay your employer's legal costs of $150K on top of your own costs.

The uncertain outcome here is the outcome of the case. Calculate the VPI under the following circumstances.

(a) There are no court costs.

(b) There are court costs of $20K. These are not accounted for in the original description of the problem. Do you think VPI will be higher or lower than (a)?

(c) The company offers you a settlement of $225K. Do you think VPI will be higher or lower than (b)?

(d) The company offers you a settlement of k$300. What is the VPI now?

8.6. SUMMARY

Decision trees are a formal framework for thinking about and analyzing complex quantitative decisions. The existence of this framework can be helpful in directing your thinking to the most important issues that need to be addressed.

The key elements are

- The logical relation between the available decisions and uncertain outcomes that you care about, represented as a tree.
- The payoffs associated with all uncertain outcomes and decisions.
- The probabilities of the uncertain outcomes (conditional on all previous outcomes.

The tree is constructed in Treeplan by moving from the first decision or outcome node forward through the story, tracing through every possible sequence of outcomes and decisions.

The tree is solved by moving from right to left, calculating the MVs of all outcome nodes and selecting the maximum payoff for all decision nodes. The "best" decision appears at the root of the tree and is the one that leads to the highest mean payoff or the lowest mean cost. Risk can be assessed by looking at the **CRP**. If risk is an issue you may choose a slightly suboptimal decision if it is much less risky.

Valuing Information

When a decision depends on an uncertain outcome about which you may be able to gather further information, then there are three key numbers that are relevant to assessing the value of such information. These are

- MV_0—what we achieve with perfect foresight of the uncertain outcome.
- MV_1—what we achieve with offered free information.
- MV_2—what we achieve if we just accept the outcome uncertainty.

The MV of sample information (VSI = MV_1—MV_2) measures the value of specific information that may reduce the uncertainty. You need to have the figures for how accurate this information is, for instance the accuracy rates of the forecaster. You should not pay more than VSI for the offered information.

The MV of perfect information (VPI = MV_0—MV_2) measures the maximum potential payoff of completely eliminating uncertainty about the outcome. Thought of differently, it is the cost of uncertainty. You should not pay more than VPI for any information concerning the uncertain outcome.

EXERCISES

E1. A new householder is currently considering insuring the contents of her house against theft for 1 year. She estimates that the contents of her house would cost her $40,000 to replace.

Local crime statistics indicate that there is a probability of 3% that her house will be broken into in the coming year. In that event her losses would be 10%, 20%, or 40% of the contents with probabilities 0.5, 0.35, and 0.15, respectively.

An insurance policy from company A costs $300 a year but guarantees to replace any losses due to theft. An insurance policy from company B is cheaper at $150 a year but only replaces a fraction (40%) of any loss suffered. Assume that there can be at most one theft a year.

(a) Draw the decision tree.

(b) What would be your advice to the householder if her objective is to maximize mean monetary value (MV)?

E2. You own a tract of land which has recently become of interest to a local natural gas company, HiTech. HiTech has offered you $180,000 for exploration rights and the option for future development. This option gives HiTech the right to buy the site in 1 year's time for an agreed value of $3.2 million. The market value of the site if there were no gas is $1.2 million. HiTech agrees with this estimate but says they are not interested in the site if there is no gas. However, if gas is found on the site then it would be worth $6 million according to HiTech.

You suspect that HiTech's interest in the site indicates a good chance that gas may be present and therefore you have gone out and got expert advice. The result of this advice is an estimated 60% probability that the site has natural gas and confirmation that $6 million is a reasonable assessment of the value of the site if gas is present.

So you are considering developing the site yourself. The initial step would be to contract for the exploration phase yourself. This would cost $300,000. By law, the results of this investigation would have to be revealed to HiTech in any future negotiations.

(a) What should you do? Accept HiTech's offer or contract for exploration yourself?

(b) If there were no laws about having to reveal the exploration results to HiTech, and if in fact HiTech did not find out that you had done any exploration, what would be the overall MV of the land? So how much does the law preventing your confidential exploration cost you?

E3. You own a grandfather clock that is 115 years old. You would like to sell it and you have three options. You could use an Internet auction website that charges a flat fee of $25 for each item sold. You could use a local auction house that charges a fee of 3% of the selling price of the item or you could use a national auction house that charges a fee of 5% of the selling price of the item. The probabilities for the number of bidders using each method are given in the table below.

	6 Bidders	8 Bidders	10 Bidders
Internet	30%	50%	20%
Local	50%	40%	10%
National	15%	25%	60%
Mean SP	$605.48	$763.43	$921.38

The more bidders there are the higher the mean estimated selling price (ESP). You have determined that the mean selling price can be predicted from a simple formula:

$$\$\text{Selling Price} = 0.065 \times (\text{Age} - 70)^2 \times (1 + 0.6 \times \text{bidders}),$$

so for a 115-year-old clock we have the mean selling prices in red in the table above.

(a) Draw a decision tree and use an MV criterion to decide which type of auction to choose.

(b) If you could get perfect information about the number of bidders there would be *on the Internet*, what would you be willing to pay for it?

E4. A company is trying to decide whether or not to bid on a certain contract. They assess the labor and material costs of this job at $127K.

The bidding process has two stages. Preparing a bid to the first stage will cost $10K. The main purpose of this stage is to establish the credentials and reliability of the company as a serious bidder for the job. There is a 40% chance that their bid will be put on the short list from the first stage. Otherwise it will be rejected.

Once short-listed, they may proceed to the second stage. At this stage they must supply further information about their bid, including, most importantly, their bid price. Proceeding to this second stage costs $5K and after this their bid will be accepted or rejected.

There is obviously a trade-off between how high they bid and their chance of winning. There are three possible bids under consideration: $155, $170, or $190. Based on analysis of previous bidding behavior and outcomes they assess the chance of these alternative bids being accepted as 90%, 75%, and 35%, respectively.

(a) What should they do? Explain your answer using a decision tree.

(b) What is the maximum amount they should pay for information about whether they will be short-listed or not, prior to making their initial bid?

(c) Give tipping point values for the 90%, 75%, and 30% figures.

E5. Russian Mining Industries (RMI) is considering digging in search of uranium in a new location in Ukraine. They believe that there are two possible outcomes: either the mine contains large reserves of uranium, yielding a profit of $10 million, or that it contains small reserves of uranium, yielding a profit of $1 million. Based on data from recent years, RMI has found that out of 100 similar locations in Ukraine, 30 contained large reserves of uranium and 70 contained small reserves. They are prepared to consider these data as representative of the likelihood of large or small reserves for the Ukraine site.

Alternatively, RMI may choose to continue digging in one of its new mines in the more remote area of Rostov, where there is an equal probability of making profits of either $2 million or $6 million. Not digging is not an option, since this alternative is dominated by the other options.

If RMI is solely interested in maximizing the mean profit, what should it do? What is the mean profit under this policy?

A geologist has offered his services to RMI. For a fixed fee, the geologist is willing to carry out several tests and issue a report stating his beliefs regarding the capacity of the Uranium reserves in the Rostov mine (but he is not willing to analyze the Ukraine mine). Based on his past performance, out of all the large reserve mines he has assessed, the geologist identified 5/6 of them correctly as a large reserve. Out of the small reserve mines, he identified 6/7 correctly as a small reserve.

(a) What is the probability of the geologist producing a positive report, that is, one which predicts the site will be a large reserve?

(b) After a positive assessment from the geologist, what would be the probability that the Rostov mine is a large reserve and, therefore, what would be its MV?

(c) How valuable is the geologist's service? Describe this by adding appropriate decision branches to your previous decision tree. Copy your decision tree into your answer booklet with all nodes, branches, and values.

(d) Consider the upside figure of $10 for the Ukraine mine. If this were sufficiently low, you would always go with the Rostov mine and if it were sufficiently high you would always go with the Ukraine mine. For what range of values of this figure, then, is the geologist's service worth anything at all?

(e) A new test, capable of accurately (100% success) predicting the amount of uranium reserves, has just been developed. What is the maximum RMI would pay for testing the Ukraine location?

There are further decision tree questions provided in electronic format.

CHAPTER 9

Data, Estimation, and Statistical Reliability

9.0. Introduction: What Is the Issue?

One of the first things we do with business performance data is to summarize it. We might break it up into groups and look at how the performance measure differs between the groups. This is known as **descriptive statistics**. Tables of means and standard deviations allow us to extract the main patterns and features in what would otherwise be a meaningless spreadsheet of numbers. So, one function of the descriptive statistics is to convert data into information that can be understood. This facilitates communication of the main patterns to a third party. Another person may not have access to the raw data or the inclination to look at it, but descriptive statistics will convey the main patterns and relationships.

However, there is a much deeper reason that we might calculate summary statistics, such as the average customer satisfaction for different age groups. We do it because we think it tells us something fundamental about how age affects customer reaction. The sample means suggest something about the underlying structure of the business or, more accurately, about the business process that generated the data. Inferring something about the process fundamentals from data is known as **inferential statistics**.

This chapter is about a *coherent conceptual basis for inference and data analysis.* You could do data analysis without reading this chapter, but you would just be applying recipes. Specifically, a recurring theme in data analysis is that statistics such as sample averages should always be accompanied by an indication of their measurement error—which in data analytic jargon is called **standard error**. Without this chapter you would have no idea why there is any measurement error in the sample average. Nor would you have an answer to the question "Error in measuring what?"

Many textbooks stress the notions of sample and population in explaining the foundational ideas of data analysis. Unfortunately, in many business contexts these

Data-Driven Business Decisions, First Edition. Chris J. Lloyd.

notions are of no use—often there is no obvious population. Sometimes the "sample" is not a sample at all. It is the whole population.

As an example, in Chapter 1 we looked at some data on the salaries of 273 NTC employees, as well as their gender, age, and experience. Below is a table of the average salary broken into age and experience groups (using Pivotables). The overall average salary is \$74.3K but increases from \$51.1K for the youngest age group to \$95.0K for the 45–49 age group, and then falls to \$78.8K for the oldest age group. It also increases with experience in a similar manner—from \$54.3K to \$94.4K for the group with 25–29 years of experience and then falls to \$79.4K for the group with 30–34 years of experience.

However, if you look *within an experience group*, salary does not seem to be greatly affected by age. For instance, in the 10–14 years experience group, the salary is around \$80K regardless of age. We can argue to ourselves that this makes sense because once someone has a certain level of experience it should make little difference how old they are. We are trying to infer something fundamental about how age and experience drive the performance measure—here salary. We are not just describing the data we have. We want to say something deeper and more actionable.

	Experience (in years)							
Age	0-4	5-9	10-14	15-19	20-24	25-29	30-34	ALL
15-19	\$51.1							\$51.1
20-24	\$54.0	\$64.5						\$58.3
25-29	\$56.3	\$69.0	\$79.2					\$70.7
30-34	\$63.1	\$72.9	\$79.1	\$87.6				\$80.2
35-39		\$76.1	\$81.3	\$88.9	\$89.8			\$86.9
40-44				\$88.0	\$92.9	\$90.5		\$90.2
45-49					\$94.0	\$95.2		\$95.0
50-54							\$81.7	\$81.7
55-59							\$77.8	\$77.8
60-65							\$78.7	\$78.7
ALL	\$54.3	\$68.4	\$79.3	\$88.3	\$91.4	\$94.4	\$79.4	\$74.3

So it is natural that we would want to know how reliable the patterns we see are. All of the averages in this table have an intrinsic measurement error, called **standard error**. For most of these numbers it is around \$2. It can be very easily calculated and you will be given the formula in this chapter.

However, it is completely unclear here what the population and sample are. The 273 employees were actually the entire workforce of NTC, the particular company involved. If you think of the population as all employees across the country then you have to start thinking about which companies and employees are included. You have to think how this "sample" of 273 happened to end up working for NTC. What about if there were no comparable companies? In this case the population is NTC and so the sample is the whole population again.

If this sounds confusing to you, it should. Yet this is how most statistics courses ask you to think. Luckily, there is no need to talk about samples or populations at all in explaining the fundamental principles of data analysis. I will instead build the theory on the idea of the **data-generating mechanism (DGM)**. This links the data to the business process that generated it. Ultimately, it is the business process that you want to understand.

9.1. DESCRIBING THE PAST AND THE FUTURE

Descriptive statistics is about describing the data we already have—the past. Probability is about saying what might happen in the future. **Inferential statistics** is about linking the past with the future behavior of an uncertain business variable.

We already know how to describe past data and future likely behavior.

PREVIOUS DEFINITIONS

The **data distribution** describes *observed behavior of a business variable*. It is a list of all observed values of the variable together with the number or proportion of times that they occurred.

The **probability distribution** describes the *likely behavior of a business variable*. It is a list of all possible values of the variable together with the chance that they will occur.

The probability distribution can be conceptualized as a chart. The mean μ is the central value of the variable—a compromise value that measures central or typical performance. The standard deviation σ is the spread of the chart and measures the uncertainty of the variable. The probability distribution of a variable is usually *unknown*. Therefore, these important numbers μ and σ will be unknown. As will the probability of the variable being within any specified range of interest.

The data distribution can also be summarized as a chart. The sample mean measures the center of the distribution. The sample standard deviation s measures the observed variability. Once we collect past data on the variable then the data distribution is *known*. Therefore, the sample mean and sample standard deviation will be known. The proportion of cases where the variable is within a specified range of interest will also be known.

What is the connection between the probability and data distribution? We rather hope that one tells us about the other.

EXAMPLE 1 *Defective computer chips*

Your plant assembles computers. The key component is the central processing unit (CPU) chip which, while thoroughly tested, can still be defective. The plant assembles 1500 computers per week and so requires 1500 CPU chips. Suppose that the engineers who designed the production and quality control process at the CPU manufacturing plant know that on average, 1 in 750 chips will be defective. Provided that defects in one manufactured chip do not affect defects in another chip, the number of defective chips we will receive in a week is binomial with $n = 1500$ and $p = 1/750$. The mean of this probability distribution is $\mu = 2$ while the standard deviation is $\sigma = 1.407$.

In this example, then, we are supposing that we knew the probability distribution, whereas in practice we often do not. The list of probabilities is in the table below.

Probability Distribution		Data Distribution	
# defective	**chance**	**# observed**	**Rel.Freq**
0	0.135	6	0.115
1	0.271	13	0.250
2	0.271	16	0.308
3	0.181	8	0.154
4	0.090	6	0.115
5	0.036	2	0.038
6	0.012	1	0.019
7	0.003	0	0.000
8	0.001	0	0.000
9	0.000	0	0.000
..	..	..	..

Now suppose that we had records on the past year and had counted up how many defective chips there were in each week, discovered later when the machines are repaired under warranty. The serial number of each repaired computer can be traced back to the week the computer was assembled. So for each week you can record how many of the 1500 chips used in assembly were defective. These data are also displayed in the table, both as a frequency and as a relative frequency. The left half of the table is the probability distribution and the right is the data distribution.

It looks like the two distributions are quite close. The sample mean of the data distribution is 2.10, because there was a total of 109 defects in 52 weeks. This compares with a mean of $\mu = 2$ for the probability distribution. The standard deviation s can be calculated using frequency_distribution.xls and is 1.418, which is close to the standard deviation $\sigma = 1.407$ of the probability distribution. This similarity of the two distributions is confirmed and made more visual if we plot both on the same chart.

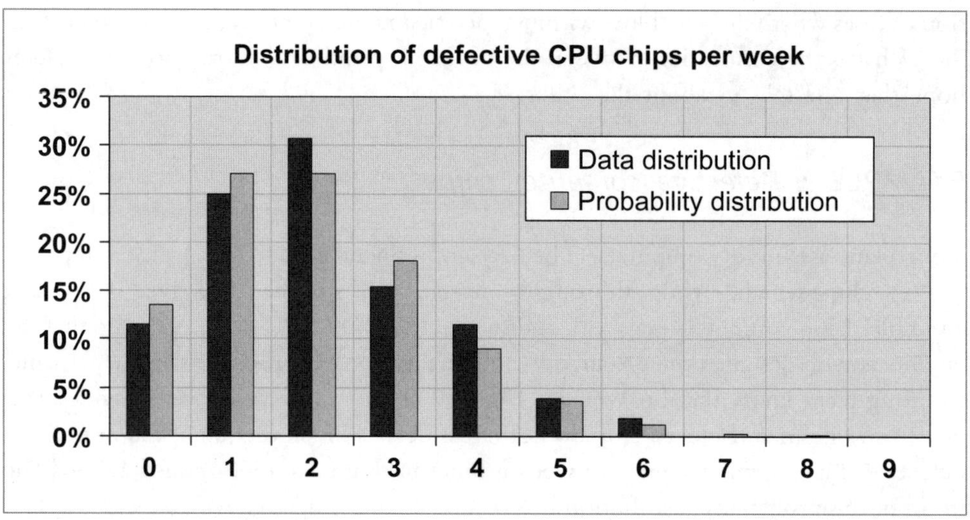

It should hardly be a surprise that they are close. When we assert that the probability of 0 defective chips is 0.135, what else do we mean other than we expect this to happen about 13.5% of the time? Out of 52 weeks this would mean about seven times. It actually happened 6 times out of 52, a relative frequency of 0.115.

9.2. How Were the Data Generated?

The numbers in your spreadsheet were generated by a business process. You should never lose sight of this. This is the golden thread that links the analysis of your numbers to management decision making.

Think about the computer chip example, where the performance measure is the number of defective chips in a week. Each week, the business process generates chips that are put into 1500 computers. The chance of any chip being defective is 1 in 750. This business process is quite a simple one and results in a simple binomial distribution for the performance. But every business process, however complicated, determines a probability distribution for the performance variable.

We collect data over 52 weeks. These data are generated by the business process of CPU chip manufacture. We might also think of the data as being *generated by the probability distribution*—here binomial. The fact that the probability distribution generates the data links the data back to the business process. Of course, the reason we want to know about the business process is that we care about future performance. Future performance will again be mediated by the same probability distribution. So it is the unknown probability distribution that is the central player and the focus of our interest. It generated the past data and it will generate future outcomes.

These ideas apply to any business process, no matter how complicated. The data are produced by a **DGM**, which is formalized as a probability distribution for the performance variable. The data reveal some of the features of this probability distribution, which tells us about future performance, since this will be generated by the same mechanism.

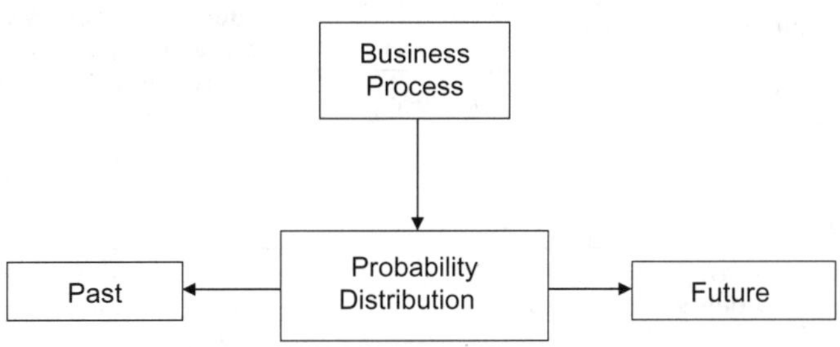

The key to inferential statistics is the connection between the probability distribution and the past data it generated. While the arrow of causality goes from the probability distribution to the data, nevertheless we can infer quite a lot about the cause from seeing the effect. In management terms, we can infer something about business fundamentals from the appearance of interesting patterns in the data generated by our business, with a view to understanding and managing future performance.

9.3. Law of Large Numbers

If a variable is random, then we can never know its value exactly. The best we can ever know is its probability distribution.

The Law of Large Numbers (LLN; also sometimes called the Law of Averages) is a mathematical result that connects the data distribution and the probability distribution that generated it. It applies to any uncertain variable X, where we have observed X a large number of times.

> The LLN says that the data distribution will be close to the probability distribution that generated it, for a sufficiently large sample.

It is rather hard to see how we could give the probability distribution its name if this were not the case. For instance, if $\Pr(X = 2) = 0.15$ then we would surely expect to see around 15% of values equal to 2, at least in the long run!

One might set this out schematically below. The probability distribution can be summarized in terms of its mean μ, its standard deviation σ, and various probabilities of interest. For instance, if X was profit we might be interested in the chance that profit exceeds some value, such as \$1000K. All these quantities are typically *unknown*. The data are generated by the probability distribution and is *known*. It can be summarized in terms of its sample mean, its sample standard deviation, and various proportions of interest. For instance, we could count up the proportion of times that profit exceeds \$1000K. For every quantity that summarizes the probability distribution on the left, there is an analogous and observable quantity on the right.

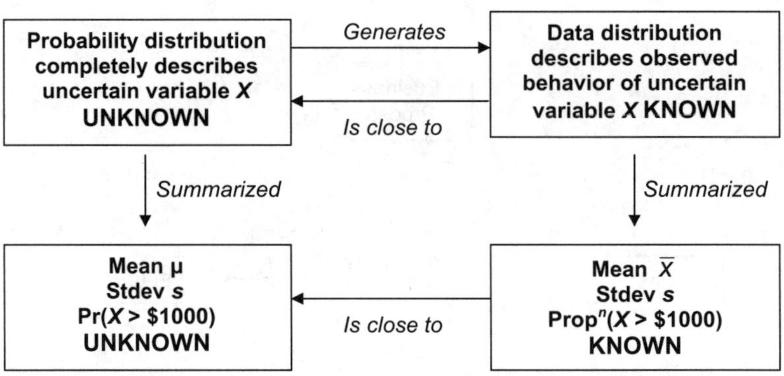

Now the LLN says that the data distribution will be close to the probability distribution. It implies that everything on the right-hand side will be close to the analogous quantity on the left-hand side. Therefore, if you did not know the true quantities on the left, you may be able to infer quite a lot about them from the observable quantities on the right.

In this chapter we mainly concentrate on the sample mean and how close it is to μ. We care about μ because it is the true mean of the underlying business process. Indeed, one interpretation we gave for μ earlier is that it is the long-run average value. In this chapter we can say much more, though. We can say how close the sample average is to μ. We can calculate this measure of error from the same data we used to calculate the sample average.

9.4. THE VARIABILITY OF THE SAMPLE MEAN

This is probably the most sophisticated concept in the book. Everyone seems to be comfortable with the concept of data being variable. But many people consider it silly to talk about the variability of the sample mean. There is only one value of the sample mean. It is not variable at all?!

EXAMPLE 1 (Continued) *Defective computer chips*

We already saw 1 year of data earlier. The spreadsheet example 1(defective chips).xls has 2 years of data. The data distribution is roughly similar to the probability distribution and the sample mean is 2.05, still close to $\mu = 2$, in fact slightly closer. The value μ here is a key issue for our business. It is the long-run theoretical mean number of defectives per week, generated by our production process and supply chain.

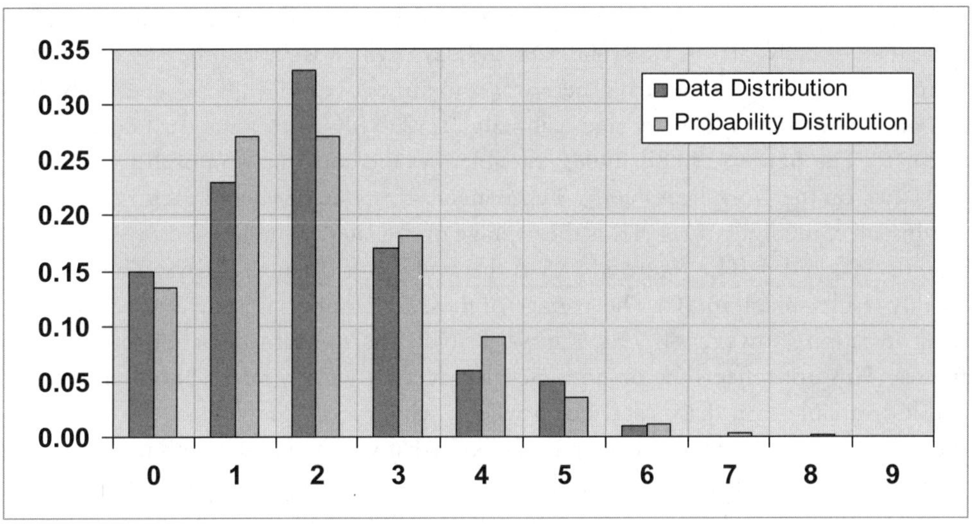

It is important to realize that the sample mean—the figure 2.05—is variable. You can see very well that the data are variable. You cannot see the variation in the sample mean though, for the simple reason that there is only one figure. But since the sample mean is calculated from the data and the data are variable, does it not follow that the sample mean is also variable?

One trick to see the sample mean vary is to simulate data using the DGM. We could wait for another 2 years of data, but a quicker way is to use the computer.

Click on the worksheet *generate* in example 1(defective chips).xls and generate a new sample of 2 years of data by simply activating any cell and hitting *delete*. You will see the sample mean change, because the data have changed. Each time you generate a new sample you generate a new sample mean. If you do this several times you will develop a feel for how far the sample mean typically differs from the theoretical value $\mu = 2$. You will find that it is usually within 0.1 or 0.2. If someone could have told us this earlier then we would have looked at our original sample of mean of 2.05 in a new light. We could say to ourselves

> The sample mean will typically be within 0.1 or 0.2 of the theoretical mean μ. So the theoretical mean μ is probably within 0.1 or 0.2 of the sample mean of 2.05.

From the observed sample mean of 2.05, and a figure for its variability, we could infer a plausible range for μ. But this all requires a reliability assessment that we obtained from the simulation. Luckily there is no need at all to do a simulation of your business process! We will later have a simple formula for the reliability of the sample mean. In this particular example it gives the answer 0.138, confirming our informal judgment of 0.1–0.2.

EXAMPLE 2 *Deepwater Bay real estate, 1995*

The spreadsheet **example 2 (hkre).xls** contains 1 year of daily sales data at a real estate agency in Deepwater Bay, Hong Kong, during 1995. Each daily sales figure is converted to US$1000 at the exchange rate of January 1 of that year. Our performance measure here, then, is daily sales in US$1000. On 267 days, which is 73% of the 364 days, there were no sales. On the other days there was sometimes over $1000K of sales. Daily sales are extremely erratic. The average daily sales is $290.8K, with a standard deviation of $520.4K. The figure $290.8K itself is variable. Let me convince you of this.

Click on the worksheet *weekly*. This contains the average sales of each 7-day week. For instance, the figure $380.1K is the average of the sales of the first 7 days—0, 0, 995, 685, 0, 981, and 0. The figure $114.1 is the average of the next 7 days. There are 52 weekly results in column C. The average of these 52 numbers is again 290.8. The standard deviation, however, is 192.7, way less than the standard deviation of the daily figures. This just reflects the obvious fact that average weekly sales is more predictable and less variable than daily sales. For 6 weeks, which is around 11% of the 52 weeks, there were no sales. It is of course quite unlikely that you would sell nothing in a whole week, only an 11% chance compared with a 73% chance of selling nothing in a day.

Continue to fortnightly data. The mean is 290.8 and the standard deviation is further reduced to 143.6. There was not a single fortnight period where there was no sale. The average daily sales over a fortnight is becoming much more predictable.

For average daily sales over a month the average is 290.0 (only because the months do not have the same number of days) and the standard deviation of the 12 figures is 101.8. Finally we can calculate the four quarterly figures whose mean is 290.8 and whose standard deviation is 71.7. Let us put these empirical facts in a table and look at the pattern.

The variability decreases systematically as we look at average daily sales over a week (average of 7 days), a fortnight (average of 14 days), a month (average of around 30 days), and a quarter (average of 91 days). Whether you measure variability by standard deviation, or by the range of data from smallest to largest, or by the percentage of days where there was no sale, the conclusion is the same. Average daily sales become more predictable and less variable as we move from days, to weeks, to months, and to quarters.

Period	Mean	Std. Dev	Ran ge	No Sales	n
Daily	290.8	520.4	0 to 2300	73%	1
Weekly	290.8	192.7	0 to 900	11%	7
Fortnightly	290.8	143.6	80 to 680	0%	14
Monthly	290.0	101.8	100 to 450	0%	~30
Quarterly	290.8	71.7	230 to 386	0%	91
Yearly	290.8	?	?	?	364

We now look at the last line and ask about the 290.8 figure, which is the average of 364 daily sales. How variable is it? Again, we do not see its variability because there is only one value and we cannot calculate the standard deviation of one value. We would be quite wrong to think that it is not variable at all though. Why would weekly or monthly sales be variable but yearly sales not?! But there is a decreasing pattern in variability and we would reason that it must be much less variable than the quarterly figure. We might even try to extrapolate how standard deviation *s* decreases as the number of days being averaged increases from 1 to 7, to 14, to 30, to 91, and to 364. A figure around \$20–\$30 looks about reasonable but it is hard to be sure.

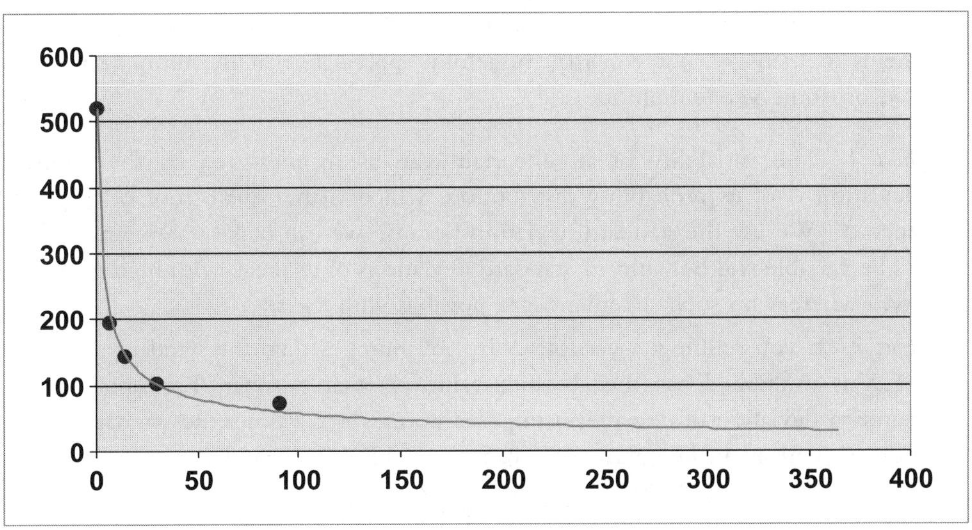

But there should be no doubt in any reasonable person's mind that (a) the yearly average *is* variable even though this variability is implicit and cannot be seen directly,

(b) it is *less* variable than an average taken over a shorter period such as a week or a month, and (c) this variability apparently follows a regular mathematical pattern.

CHECK YOUR UNDERSTANDING

Q1. In the specific context of the Deepwater Bay real estate data, try to write down a clear, nontechnical explanation of the following concepts.

- The performance measure
- The DGM
- The probability distribution
- The mean μ
- The variability in the sample mean

9.5. THE STANDARD ERROR OF THE MEAN

We have seen that a sample average is variable even though its variation cannot be directly seen. It is variable as a consequence of being calculated from data that are variable. Mathematically then, the issue becomes one that can be stated quite exactly. If we start with a performance measure X that is variable, if we observe this variable many times and then calculate the sample average, then how variable is the average? We expect that it will be much less variable than the individual performance values. For instance, in the real estate example the daily sales had a variability of about \$540K but it looked like the sample average has a variability of around \$20–\$30K.

We need a formula for the variability of the sample mean. I will describe the bare bones of the mathematical argument here. There is no need to commit these arguments to memory, but you may hopefully appreciate that the ultimate formula is based on some very simple ideas.

Fact 1 The variability of an uncertain variable is measured by the standard deviation σ of its probability distribution, which is the square root of the variance σ^2. We use the standard deviation because we can make statements such as "The variable will be within 2 standard deviations of its mean with high probability," whereas no such statements are possible with variance.

Fact 2 If you multiply a variable X by any number then the standard deviation of X is multiplied by (the absolute value of) that number. For instance, the standard deviation of demand in imperial pounds is 2.2 times the standard deviation of demand in kilograms. We can write this as a formula

$$\text{Std.Dev}(aX) = |a|\,\text{Std.Dev}(X),$$

which can be proven mathematically from the definition of standard deviation. This can also be written as

$$\text{Var}(aX) = a^2\text{Var}(X).$$

Next we consider what happens if we add two unpredictable quantities, X_1 and X_2. Let us suppose that the two quantities are independent to the extent that there is no tendency for one variable to follow the other. So, for instance, it will not be the case that one variable is systematically smaller than average when the other is larger so that their variations cancel each other out.

Fact 3 It can be shown that the variance of the sum equals the sum of the variances of the two variables. We can write this as a formula

$$\text{Var}(X_1 + X_2) = \text{Var}(X_1) + \text{Var}(X_2).$$

The same is true of the sum of three or more variables. The variances add. Notice that this means that *it is not true* that the standard deviations add. The standard deviation of the sum is always less than the sum of the standard deviations. This is the key reason why sample averages work.

The Standard Error of the Mean

Armed with facts (1–3), we can demonstrate an incredibly important fact. Suppose that we have an uncertain variable X with standard deviation σ. We observe this variable many times—the data. Call these observations X_1, X_2, $\ldots X_n$. Each of these observations is generated by the DGM and so each has a standard deviation σ. We then seek a formula for the standard deviation of

$$\bar{X} = \frac{1}{n}(X_1 + X_2 + \ldots + X_n).$$

The conclusion is that

$$\text{Stdev}(\bar{X}) = \sigma / \sqrt{n}.$$

This is an incredibly important conclusion. It says that a sample average has a standard deviation less than that of a single observation. So we *do* reduce variability by calculating an average, *but only by a factor* $\sqrt{n}$. For instance, to double the accuracy we need a sample *four* times larger, not two times larger. To get an extra decimal point of accuracy—to reduce variability by 10 times—requires a sample 100 times larger.

In practice, σ is usually unknown because the probability distribution is unknown. However, it can be replaced by our best estimate of σ from the data—the sample standard deviation s. This gives us a measure of the reliability of the sample average that can be calculated from the known data. It is called the **standard error of the sample mean** and is given by the formula

$$\text{Std.err}(\bar{X}) = \frac{s}{\sqrt{n}}.$$

EXAMPLE 1 (Continued) *Defective computer chips*

The DGM was a binomial process with $n = 1500$ and $p = 1/750$. The mean weekly defective rate is $\mu = 2$ and the standard deviation is $\sigma = 1.407$. From 2 years of data the sample average was 2.05. Two years of data means n = 104 weeks and so the standard deviation of the sample average is

$$\text{Stdev}(\bar{X}) = \frac{1.407}{\sqrt{104}} = 0.138.$$

As pointed out above, though, the standard deviation of 1.407 would not be known in practice. We can instead use the sample standard deviation s = 1.464, which gives

$$\text{Std.err}(\bar{X}) = \frac{1.464}{\sqrt{n}} = 0.144.$$

This is the figure we use to measure typical error in the sample average. From 2 years of data we can say that our best estimate of the weekly defective rate is 2.05 with a standard error of 0.144. Taking 2 standard errors as a reasonable range we might assert that the true defective rate μ should lie within the range 2.05 plus or minus 0.29, which is 1.76–2.34.

EXAMPLE 2 (Continued) *Real estate in Deepwater Bay*

During 1995, the sample mean daily sales was 290.8 and the standard deviation was 520.4. This is an average of 364 days. The standard error of the mean is therefore

$$\text{Std.err}(\bar{X}) = \frac{520.4}{\sqrt{364}} = 27.3.$$

So there is an intrinsic error of $27.3K in the yearly average of $290.8K. The fundamental mean daily sales might differ from our best estimate by as much as $50K. So if we had been aiming at a benchmark of $300K for mean daily sales then we might be disappointed with the $290.8K figure but we would have little reason to infer that we were systematically underperforming.

CHECK YOUR UNDERSTANDING

Q2. If you throw a fair die once, what is the probability distribution of the result? What are the mean and standard deviation (you can use a template)?

Therefore, suppose you threw a die 100 times and calculated the average results. What would be the likely range for this average? What sort of result for the average might lead you to think that the die was actually biased?

Q3. I have surveyed 100 customers on their satisfaction with service on a scale of 1 to 10, 10 being good. The sample average $\bar{x}$ of the 100 survey results is 7.3. The sample standard deviation of the 100 survey results is 2.1.

We would like to know the underlying mean level μ of customer satisfaction. How accurate an estimate of μ is $\bar{x}$? What is a plausible range of possible values for the underlying mean satisfaction μ of all customers? How many customers would you need to survey to make the estimator 10 times more accurate?

EXAMPLE 3 *Stock indices and share portfolios*

The NASDAQ index measures the overall performance of a collection of high technology based stocks. The DJ index measures performance of a set of blue chip stocks and the S&P500 measures a wider range of general stocks. Stock indices are much less volatile than individual stocks over almost any time period. For instance, a typical weekly change in the DJ index is around 2%, while individual stocks could easily change by 5%.

A share portfolio tries to mimic the reduced volatility of an index by spreading the investor's money across a range of stocks that cover most industries. For instance, if you put one-third of your money in GE, one-third in Walmart, and one-third in Cisco then even if one stock goes down, another might go up to offset it. Portfolios are designed to be less volatile than investing all money in an individual stock.

What has this got to do with the standard error of the mean?

All stock indices are a special kind of **weighted average** of a set of shares. So the percent growth or *return* on an index is a weighted average of the returns on the shares. The same is true of a portfolio. The return on a share portfolio is a weighted average of the returns on the shares in the portfolio. In the financial context, volatility is measured by the standard deviation of the returns. So when we talk about the volatility of an index or of a portfolio we are talking about the standard deviation of a (weighted) average.

The formula for the standard error of the mean says that the variability of an average is smaller by a factor of $\sqrt{n}$ than the individual numbers that are averaged. There are several reasons why this result does *not* apply exactly to indices or portfolios of stocks. First, they involve weighted rather than simple averages. Second, the stocks being averaged are not repeated observations on a performance measures. Each stock return has its own characteristics and its own standard deviation. There is not a single σ but rather there is a different σ for each stock. Third and most important, the stocks being averaged are *not* independent but are (typically positively) correlated. So when one goes up or down the others tend to go up or down.

Nevertheless, it can be shown mathematically that the standard deviation of the weighted average will still be less than the average standard deviations of the things being averaged. So the volatility of the portfolio or index will be less than the average volatility of the stocks involved. While the formula

$$\text{Stdev}\left(\bar{X}\right) = \sigma / \sqrt{n}$$

does *not* apply, the main conclusion about averages being less variable does still hold. A formula for the volatility of a portfolio of stocks will be given in Chapter 13 and you will use it to construct portfolios that clearly dominate putting all your money in any individual stock.

9.6. THE NORMAL LIMIT THEOREM

In an earlier example we measured average daily real estate sales at \$290.8K and found the standard error of this figure was \$27.3K. If we think of 2 standard deviations as including most of the probability then we could quote a reasonable range of \$290.8K plus or minus \$54.6K. It turns out we can be more specific about this than "reasonable range." We can actually put a number on how plausible this range is. In this instance it is 95% plausible.

It is a mathematical fact that the implicit variability of the sample average tends to follow a distribution we have already seen—the normal distribution. The mean of this normal distribution is the true mean μ and the standard deviation of this normal distribution is $\sigma/\sqrt{n}$.

Since the variation of the sample mean is not directly observable, it is rather hard to give a simple demonstration of this fact. The earlier explanation of looking at weekly, fortnightly, and monthly averages was sufficient to see that the standard deviation was decreasing. But it is too crude to see the detailed shape of the distribution because there are not enough data. For instance, there were only 12 monthly averages and it is not possible to look at 12 numbers and see if they look normally distributed. You need many hundreds to get a reasonable idea of the shape of a distribution.

EXAMPLE 4 *Average result of throwing dice*

If I throw a die once then the distribution is very simple. Each of the values 1–6 is equally likely. The mean $\mu = 3.5$ and the standard deviation σ turns out to equal 1.707.

If I throw two fair dice and calculate the average then the distribution is set out in the table below. This is obtained by looking at all $6^2 = 36$ possible outcomes and seeing what the average is in each case. For instance, an average of 2 is obtained from the outcomes (13), (22), or (31), so the chance is 3/36.

x	1	1.5	2	2.5	3	3.5	4	4.5	5	5.5	6
prob	1/36	2/36	3/36	4/36	5/36	6/36	5/36	4/36	3/36	2/36	1/36

The shape of this distribution is triangular, in the left plot below. The mean is again 3.5 and the standard deviation is $\sigma/\sqrt{2} = 1.208$. It does not look much like a normal distribution but it is closer than the distribution of a single toss, which was exactly flat.

If we throw three dice and calculate the average then there are $6^3 = 216$ possible outcomes. It is tedious to list all these possibilities and the average values for each possible outcome but the result is the distribution in the right plot. It looks slightly more concentrated around the mean of 3.5 and its standard deviation is $\sigma/\sqrt{3} = 0.986$, which is smaller. The distribution is also finer because there are more possible values that the average can take. And the shape of the distribution is starting to resemble the normal distribution.

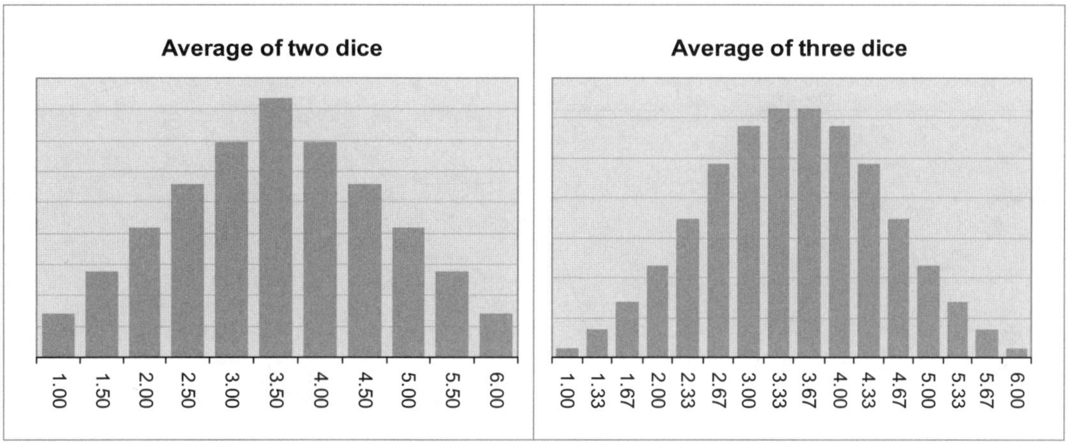

This trend continues as we take the average of a larger number n of dice. The mean is always 3.5 but the standard deviation gets smaller according to the formula $\sigma/\sqrt{n}$, the distribution becomes finer, and the shape looks more and more like a normal distribution.

These patterns were first observed over 200 years ago and are not specific to the example of throwing dice. The same patterns occur much more generally. They are formalized in a mathematical result[1] called the **normal limit theorem** (NLT; also called the central limit theorem). The larger the sample size, the closer in shape to normal will be the distribution of the sample mean. The normal distribution is like the universal constant of statistics. It is to probability what the speed of light is to physics—something built deeply into the nature of the world.

Why would you care about any of this?

Because you can now use normal probabilities to describe the error in the sample mean. Because a normal variable is within 2 standard deviations of its mean 95% of the time, we can say that the sample average will be within 2 standard errors of the true mean μ 95% of the time. So once we observe the sample mean and its standard error we can say that the true mean μ will be within 2 standard errors of the sample mean with probability 95%.

These ideas will not be fully exploited until the next chapter.

How Accurate Is the NLT?

The LLN says that the data distribution and probability distribution will be approximately equal, the approximation being better the larger the sample size. The NLT

[1] This was proven by Carl Gauss so the normal distribution is also known as the *Gaussian* distribution.

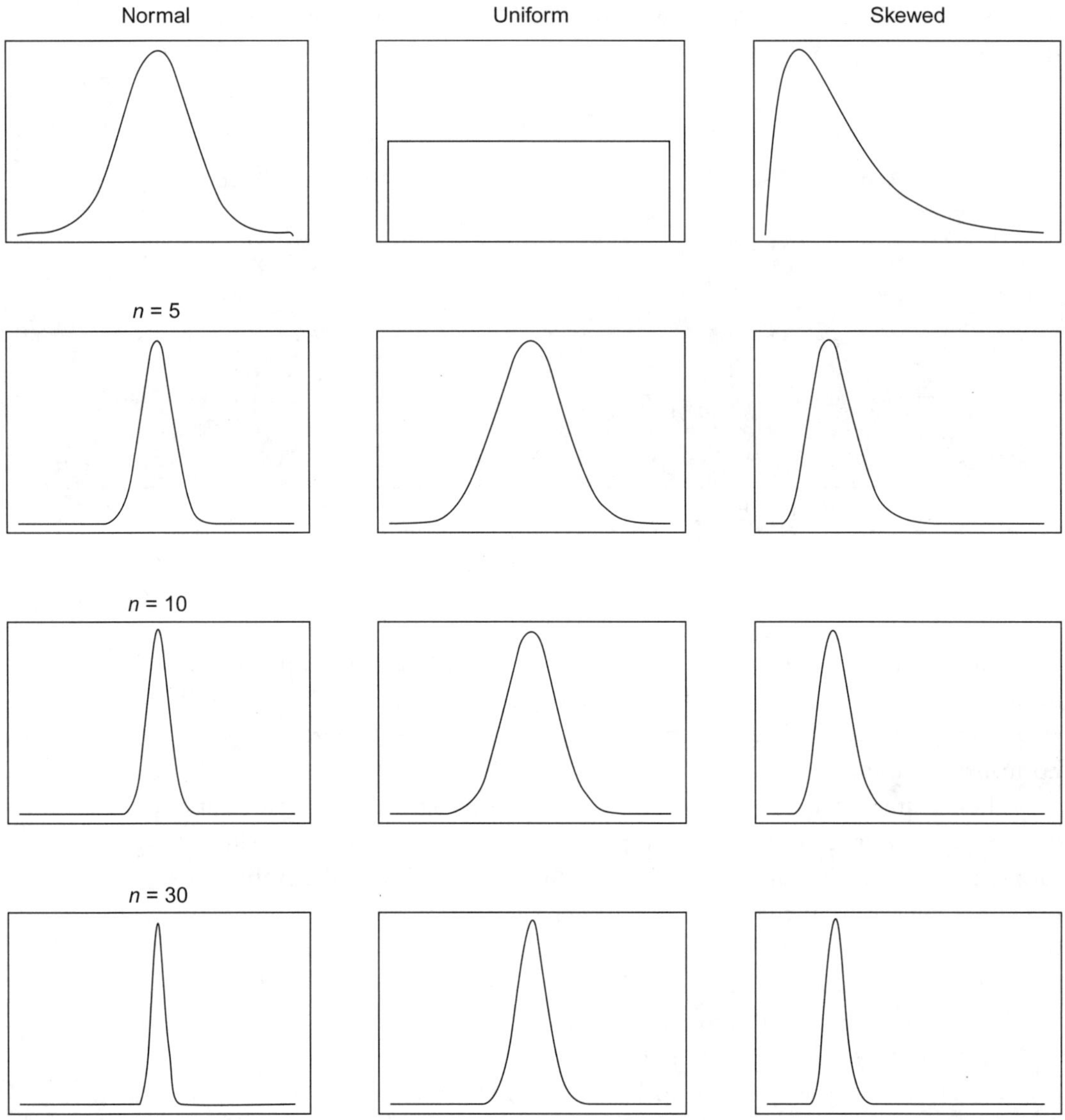

says that the distribution of the variations in the sample mean will be approximately normal, again the approximation being better the larger the sample size. The NLT is an approximation but it is a practically useful one.

First, the NLT applies almost regardless of the distribution of the underlying variable X. It works for dice or for prices of apartments. The bottom line is that the NLT *does* apply to business data and any average that we calculate in a business context will be bound to follow the pattern of the NLT.

However, it is true that for a given sample size n, the sample mean will have a distribution that is more normal if the original distribution (i.e., the distribution of a single value revealed by the data distribution) is more normal. But even a bad distribution like a fair die works very well after about $n = 25$ or so.

Accuracy in Pictures

Below is a pictorial representation of how the NLT works for different underlying distributions of the performance measure *X*.

In the first column, the distribution of *X* is normal right from the start. In this case the NLT is not an approximation. It is exactly correct and the average has an exact normal distribution with standard deviation $\sigma/\sqrt{n}$. In the middle column, the distribution of X is uniform—equally likely to be any value within some specified range. Not many business variables would have such a distribution so this is really a stress test of the NLT. You can see that even for $n = 5$ the average looks roughly normal, though not until about $n = 10$ are the calculations based on the normal practically accurate. In the right column, the original distribution is **skewed**. Many business variables have a distribution that is skewed, for instance demand or revenue or any variable that is lognormal. Averaging does produce a more normal distribution but the skewness is still apparent for moderate sample size *n*.

In practice, you will be able to use the NLT with confidence so long as *n* is about 25 or larger. If the data distribution looks reasonably normal it will be accurate for a much smaller sample sizes than this.

Check Your Understanding

Q4. Recall the defective computer chip example where we thought that the mean defective rate $\mu = 2$ per week. You monitor the sample mean over the year and note the following results that were available at the end of various periods of time.

Time period	Sample mean	Sample Std dev *s*
One week	2.38	1.423
Four weeks	2.27	1.422
13 weeks	2.29	1.410
52 weeks	2.31	1.415

What is the standard error of these sample means? How far above the hypothesized mean of $\mu = 2$ is the sample average, if you count this in terms of standard errors? In other words, calculate how far above 23 each sample mean is and divide by the standard error. Do you still think that $\mu = 2$ is reasonable?

Q5. Still thinking about the defective computer chip example, the number of defectives in a week was thought to be binomial with $n = 1500$ and $p = 1/750$ so the mean $\mu = 2$ is known, as is the standard deviation $\sigma = 1.407$.

The purpose of this question is to directly investigate how accurate the NLT is by comparing the answer we get with the NLT with the exact answer. This question is a little harder than most.

Suppose that you collect data for 52 weeks and calculate the average defectives per week. Using the NLT,

- What is the standard deviation of this sample mean?
- What is the chance that the sample mean is between 2.25 and 1.75?

Let's look now at the exact answer. In 52 weeks there are $52 \times 1500 = 78{,}000$ computers assembled. So the number of defectives in a year is binomial with $n = 78{,}000$ and $p = 1/750$. Now if the sample average was 2.25 then this would mean $52 \times 2.25 = 117$ defectives in the year, and if the sample average was 1.75 then this would mean 91 defectives in the year. So the sample mean is between 2.25 and 1.75 when there are between 91 and 117 defectives.

Since it is not clear whether we should include the 117 or 91 in this calculation we will calculate both. Using the bino_calculator template,

- What is the probability of the number of defectives in the year being between 91 and 117 inclusive?
- What is the probability of the number of defectives in the year being between 91 and 117 exclusive?

How close are these two answers to the NLT approximation?

9.7. Samples and Populations

We commonly want to know something about a population of customers who are too numerous to sample exhaustively. We might be interested in some performance measure X such as customer satisfaction on a 1–5 scale. So we take a sample of size n from a much larger population of N and measure their satisfaction. In many cases, N could be many millions while the sample size n may only be a few thousand or even a few hundred.

As mentioned in the introduction to this chapter, statistical theory is traditionally taught in terms of samples and populations. While this is not an appropriate basis for inferential statistics in general, sampling from a population is one very important application of the theory.

The DGM here is the process of selecting the sample from the population. One method of selecting the sample is to choose customers entirely at random. This is not always easy to achieve. If you have a list of all the customers in the population then you can use random numbers to select the customers in the sample. Sometimes, though, more elaborate methods must be used. Let's suppose then that we do manage to get a **random sample**. What this means is that every customer from the population has the same chance of being sampled. In other words, each has a probability $1/N$ of being sampled first, a probability $1/N$ of being sampled second, and so on.

Let's look at the first measurement of customer satisfaction, X. The first measurement is equally likely to be the customer satisfaction of any of the N customers. This defines a probability distribution for X. The mean μ of this probability distribution turns out to equal the mean of the whole population. This is why many textbooks, and even some computer programs, call μ the **population mean**.

The standard deviation σ of the probability distribution turns out to be the standard deviation of the population (but with the annoying difference that the $N-1$ in the denominator of the usual calculation is replaced by N). This if often called the **population standard deviation**.

The bottom line is that for sampling populations of customers the parameter of interest μ is the average satisfaction (or more generally the average performance measure) of all customers. The average of our sample of n tells us about this wider average. The formula for the standard error of the mean

$$\text{Stdev}(\bar{X}) = \sigma / \sqrt{n}$$

still applies and since we do not know the population standard deviation σ we replace it with the standard deviation s of the sample as usual.

Sampling without Replacement

There is an annoying exception, however. It is a very common exception, albeit one that can often be ignored in practice.

Sampling of populations is usually **without replacement**, by which we mean that the n customers in the sample must all be *different* customers. Market research companies cross customers off their survey list after they have sampled them once—at least for that survey. They do not sample the same person twice.

What this means is that the n observed values of X are *not* independent. If I sample a very hostile customer then this customer cannot be sampled again. Therefore the pool of remaining customers is less hostile on average. So the next customer I survey will be more likely to be nonhostile. This is what we mean by dependence. One measurement being high or low alters the chance that other measurements will be high or low. Of course, if the population was very large, removing one person from the population to be sampled would hardly matter and we could ignore the whole issue.

Nevertheless, the previous formula for the standard error of the sample average is definitely *wrong* if sampling is without replacement. The correct formula is instead

$$\text{Stdev}(\bar{X}) = \frac{\sigma}{\sqrt{n}} \times \sqrt{\frac{N-n}{N-1}},$$

which is always smaller than $\sigma/\sqrt{n}$—which of course is a good thing. So it is better to sample without replacement, which is presumably why it is done.

However, if the sample size n is much smaller than the population size N then the correction factor is very close to 1.0 and you can ignore it and use the simpler formula $\sigma/\sqrt{n}$. On the other hand, if you sample the whole population so that $N = n$ then the standard deviation of the sample mean equals zero—which makes sense because you then know the average μ of the population without any error at all.

The NLT still applies when sampling is without replacement. So the sample average still has an approximate *normal* distribution but with the standard error given by the modified formula. Remember though that, as before, the NLT is only an approximation. It is a good approximation if the sample size is larger than about 25. It may not work well if the sample is too small. However, for sampling without replacement, the NLT will also work poorly if your sample is too large, specifically if n is too close to the full population size N. The number of nonsampled customers (N–n) should also be at least 25. But let's face it! If you only needed another 25 customers you would just sample the whole population and be done with it.

Does the Size of the Population Matter?

People often argue that political polls cannot possibly be accurate summaries of the opinions of very large populations. For instance, if I ask 1000 randomly chosen Europeans to rate the performance of the European Union president on a scale of 1–10 then how could this possibly be a reliable estimator of the many *hundreds of millions* of people in Europe?

This plausible complaint is actually entirely wrong. It really does not matter how big the population is. Surveys of Europe are *not* less accurate than surveys of Canada. Europe's larger population does not matter.

This conclusion follows from the standard error formula above. The only point where the population size N enters is the correction term $(N-n)/(N-1)$. So long as the population size is large, this factor is very close to 1.0. It makes no practical difference whether N equals 1 million or 300 million. The correction term will basically equal 1 when the population size is large.

In this case the standard error is $\sigma/\sqrt{n}$. So it is the size of the sample n that is important in judging the accuracy of a survey. The size of the population simply does not matter—so long as it is much larger than n and so long as you have a properly random sample.

9.8. SUMMARY

In data analysis and inferential statistics, we want to infer something about the DGM. The DGM is formalized by the unknown probability distribution of the performance measure X. A key aspect of this unknown distribution is the mean μ. This represents the fundamental or trend or long-run level of performance.

The data distribution describes the data but it also tells us about the unknown probability distribution. In particular, the sample mean tells us about the unknown mean μ. The **LLN** says that the data distribution will be close to the probability distribution for a large enough sample. This applies in particular to the sample average, which will be close to the unknown mean μ.

The **standard error of the mean** measures the intrinsic, implicit variability of the sample mean. It is calculated as the standard deviation s of the data divided by the square root of the sample size. To double the accuracy of the sample mean you need to quadruple the sample size.

The **NLT** says that for a moderate-sized sample (say 25 or more), the variations of the sample mean from the true mean are governed by the normal distribution.

This allows us to make specific and accurate statements about how close the true mean is likely to be to an observed sample mean. For instance, normal variables are within 2 standard deviations of their mean about 95% of the time. So the sample mean will be within 2 standard errors of the true mean μ, 95% of the time.

In the special case of sampling a database of customers, the formula for the standard error needs to be slightly modified. However, in most cases in business the modification is very minor and the regular formula works fine.

EXERCISES

E1. You measure demand for your product during the month of March across the 128 stores in your franchise. Write down a clear, nontechnical explanation of the following concepts.

- The performance measure
- The DGM
- The probability distribution
- The mean μ
- The variability in the sample mean

E2. You have surveyed 250 people on their degree of satisfaction with their last experience at a call center. The satisfaction measurement is on a scale 1–10, with 10 being best. The data are below.

Rating	1	2	3	4	5	6	7	8	9	10
Frequency	14	2	4	17	24	40	47	23	39	40

(a) What is the mean satisfaction level?
(b) What is the standard error of the mean?
(c) If you surveyed another 250 people randomly selected from the same population as the original, then how much would you expect the sample mean to vary from the sample mean of the original sample?
(d) In order to estimate the mean satisfaction with typical accuracy of 0.05, how large a sample would you roughly need?

E3. A survey of 10,000 consumers on the amount they spent during the last month on chocolate has given a mean of \$6.54 and a standard deviation of \$8.57.
(a) What is the typical range of customer expenditure?
(b) What is your estimate of the underlying mean level of expenditure per customer and how accurate is the estimate?
(c) Suppose you wanted to estimate the underlying mean level of expenditure per customer with a typical accuracy of 25 cents. What size sample should you have taken?

E4. Measured radiation levels at 10 randomly selected times in a nuclear power plant were 1.231, 1.244, 1.231, 1.232, 1.231, 1.233, 1.249, 1.233, 1.247, and 1.246. The long-term safe dose is 1.2335.
(a) What are the sample mean and the standard error of the mean?
(b) Does it appear that the radiation levels are too high on average?
(c) The measurements only exceed the benchmark safe level of 1.2335, 4 times out of 10. Doesn't this suggest that the mean level is actually less than the benchmark?

E5. From 52 weeks of data your average sales were \$337.8K per week with a standard deviation of \$38.8K.

(a) What is the standard error of the mean?

(b) At the start of the year you determined that \$18M was a reasonable benchmark for expected sales over the year. How far short of this target did you fall in statistical terms?

E6. You want to measure the amount of lead content in fuel. The legal limit is 75 μg/L. Fuel samples vary in their measured lead content due to variations in the production and refinement process, not to mention the measurement errors. The result is that the measured lead content has a standard deviation of 0.710 μg/L.

(a) Suppose you take 100 samples and calculate the average. What will be the typical error in this measurement?

(b) How many samples would you need for the typical error to be 0.1 μg/L?

(c) How about 0.01 μg/L?

E7. You are managing a call center and measuring the number of calls handled during a 16-h day. The system records the start and finish times of each call. The data headed "calls" list the number of calls that finished during each minute of the working day, that is, $16 \times 60 = 960$ min. You are interested in the average calls per minute.

(a) For each 60-min period of the data, calculate the average calls per minute and give a standard error for this figure.

(b) Produce a graphic that describes call load trends over the day but also gives an indication of the measurement error.

E8. You have data on a particular share over an entire year. There are 48 half-hourly prices for each of the 252 trading days, 12,096 numbers in all. You calculate the percentage change between successive numbers—representing the return on an investment (ignoring transaction costs). There are 12,095 of these numbers. The average is 0.000523% with a standard deviation of 0.023%. Notice that this is a return on half an hour's investment. Expressed as a per day rate this is 0.0251% with a standard deviation of 1.1%. For the rest of this question, growth is always to be measured in units of "percent increase per day."

(a) How sure are you that the value of the share is *systematically* growing, that is, is there really a trend?

(b) Suppose you calculated the return over the day. Each day's return is (roughly) the average return over the 48 half-hour periods. You then have 252 numbers corresponding to each of the trading days. What would be the mean and standard deviation of these 252 numbers?

E9. In 1994, Australia eliminated 1- and 2-cent coins. It was intended that transactions will be rounded to the nearest 5 cents. So if the bill is for \$5.02, the shopkeeper will lose 2 cents. If you did 10,000 transactions in a week, you could lose \$200. Or you could just as easily gain \$200.

But haven't you just added an unnecessary variability to store profits? Should shopkeepers be worried about this unknown and possibly large loss or win that gets added to their revenue? For example, consider a large supermarket that does, say, one transaction each minute, 12 h a day, 7 days a week, 365 days a year, for a total of 262,800 transactions in a year.

(a) What is the *range* of possible losses or gains over this period?

(b) What can you say about the *likely* loss or gain?

(c) What are the mean and standard deviation of the loss or gain?

(d) What can you say about the average loss or gain per transaction?

(e) Therefore, what can you say about the total loss or gain, bearing in mind that this will be the average loss or gain times the number of transactions in a year (262,800)?

E10. Recall the defective computer chip example where the underlying performance measure was the number of defectives in a week. The probability distribution was binomial with $n = 1500$ and $p = 1/750$ so the mean $\mu = 2$ is known, as is the standard deviation $\sigma = 1.407$.

The purpose of this question is to directly investigate how accurate the NLT is by comparing the answer we get with the NLT with the exact answer. This question is a little harder than most.

Suppose that you collect data for 52 weeks and calculate the average defectives per week. Using the NLT,

- What is the standard deviation of this sample mean?
- What is the chance that the sample mean is between 2.25 and 1.75?

In 52 weeks there are 52 × 1500 = 78,000 computers assembled. So the number of defectives in a year is binomial with $n = 78{,}000$ and $p = 1/750$. Now if the sample average were 2.25 then this would mean 2.25 × 52 = 117 defectives in the year, and if the sample average were 1.75 then this would mean 91 defectives in the year. So the sample mean is between 2.25 and 1.75 when there is between 91 and 117 defectives in the year.

Since it is not clear whether we should include the 117 or 91 in this calculation we will calculate both.

Using the bino_calculator template,

- What is the probability of the number of defectives in the year being between 91 and 117 inclusive?
- What is the probability of the number of defectives in the year being between 91 and 117 exclusive?

How close are these two answers to the NLT approximation?

CHAPTER 10

Managing Mean Performance

10.0. Introduction: What Is the Issue?

You manage a chain of supermarkets and care about maintaining minimum standards of customer satisfaction. In the past you occasionally surveyed customer satisfaction on a scale of 1–10, 10 being good.

As manager, you have set a minimum target for all stores in the chain: the mean satisfaction level of customers should be at least 7.5. To monitor this you intend to regularly survey customers across the chain and compare each store with this benchmark. One typical set of results for "Store X" is displayed in the chart below, which summarizes responses of 100 customers for a single survey last year, prior to the recent changes.

Data-Driven Business Decisions, First Edition. Chris J. Lloyd.

The sample mean for these data is 7.11, below the 7.5 target. If it was just one customer who responded 7, you would presumably not infer that Store X was underperforming. If there were 1000 customers in the survey you would probably be convinced. So the size of the survey is important. This survey involved 100 customers. How accurate is the 7.11?

The accuracy matters because you are going to be doing this many, many times. There are more than 80 stores in the chain and you are going to be surveying each store every month. This means around 1000 store surveys will be carried out during the year. If you send out the management consultants to every store that "fails," you could spend a lot of money. More to the point, if stores were really performing at your target level of 7.5 then roughly half can be expected to fail just by bad luck! So you would need to do a huge amount of intervention and further training—perhaps needlessly.

Clearly then you need to build in a margin of error and lower the "pass mark" below 7.5. If you go too far below 7.5 though, many underperforming stores may go undetected. So there are two types of errors to worry about—ignoring a real problem on the one hand or needlessly ringing alarm bells on the other. There are no easy answers, but any decision should take into account how reliable or unreliable the survey results are.

Here are the kinds of questions that you need to be asking and answering in order to properly manage mean customer satisfaction.

- *What do we mean by "the mean satisfaction level of customers"?* This is not as obvious as you might think because the population of customers is not easy to identify and the way customers are surveyed does not give every customer the same chance of being counted.
- *How will management know when a store is underperforming?* You need an objective rule for saying when a store requires intervention and when it does not. Remember, if a store passes this month you can always pick up poor performance next month.
- *What are the costs of false alarms?* This is probably easy to identify. For instance, the intervention might be a program of retraining of frontline staff, which costs \$17.5K. This cost will be incurred for every store where intervention is required.
- *What are the costs of missing a problematic store?* This means a poor customer experience at those stores, the cost of which is more difficult to estimate. You might assign an opportunity cost of lost monthly sales depending on how far below 7.5 the customer rating is, and multiply this by the typical number of customers per month at that store.
- *How costly is data collection?* There is some (small) cost involved in collecting the survey data. Part of the cost is just paying the interviewers but there is also the irritation factor with customers being harassed as they leave the store.

This management issue involves both trade-offs and uncertainty in flagging those stores that need an intervention. The key to treating problems like this systematically and quantitatively is to appreciate that each store's sample mean is only an estimate of their fundamental mean performance and to measure the intrinsic error of this estimate, using the standard error (SE) formula from the last chapter.

10.1. BENCHMARKING MEAN PERFORMANCE

There is a wide range of apparently different problems that can be dealt with using the techniques of this chapter. Here is one example for you to consider.

EXAMPLE 2 *Deepwater Bay real estate*

A real estate firm in Deepwater Bay, Hong Kong, has sold 108 properties during 1995. This is the same firm mentioned in the previous chapter, except that there we list sales per day for the 364 days of the year. Here we are listing the sale price of the 108 apartments that sold. In later chapters we will try to explain the sale price of each apartment in terms of various features such as their size and age. For the present, though, we are just interested in the mean sale price for 1995. Why? Because there is always interest in the underlying market level and whether it is rising or falling.

At the end of 1994, a mean price of $940 in units of US$1000 was projected for 1995. This is a reference figure that was obtained by a detailed analysis of the real estate market in Hong Kong in 1994 and projected trends for Deepwater Bay. It is a par figure deemed to be a relevant benchmark for comparing later prices. If we accept this, then there is obvious interest in knowing the answer to the following question: *Has the underlying market increased from the 1994 reference figure determined to be 940?*

The average sale price for the 108 apartments sold was $979.9. This is certainly above the benchmark of 940. But is this sufficient to conclude that we have systematically outperformed the benchmark? An accountant would say that you have. There is nothing at all wrong with accountancy. However, if you want to say something deeper about the fundamental performance of the business it is not enough to just compare $979.9 with $940. You need to say something about the accuracy of the $979.9 figure.

Other Success Measures

You do not have to measure sales success by the sample mean. Indeed, it is very common in the real estate industry to use median sale price, that is, the sale price for which half the sales are higher and half are lower. The reason median is used in real estate is that sales are often highly variable due to the range of different properties on the market. The median is not much affected by one or two extremely high or low sales and is thought to better reveal the fundamental price level. There is nothing wrong with using the median, but you could not use the formulas given in this chapter.

Recall the chain of supermarkets and customer satisfaction on a 1–10 scale. There are different ways to summarize the results for a store. You might be especially interested in the proportion of customers who rate you below 7 (which was 37% for Store X). This ignores the upside—for instance, all those 28 customers who rated you 10. To account for this, you might create a kind of Net Promoter Score (NPS) by subtracting the proportion of negative responses (1–6) from the proportion of positive responses (9–10), giving a score of 33%—37% or −4% for Store X.

These are just two plausible ways of converting the 1–10 rating distribution into a final success measure. But we are supposing that you are primarily interested in *mean satisfaction*. There is no reason why you must always look at the mean. But it does have the virtue that it takes full account of each customer's response. For instance, if a customer changed their response from 6 to 1 then neither of the previous measures would be affected at all.

In this chapter, we will always be monitoring mean performance.

Framework for Monitoring the Mean

The problems in this chapter have several key features in common. First and foremost, you are interested in a particular performance measure X. Second, you are interested in monitoring *mean* performance rather than some other summary measure of X. There is a critical distinction between the mean μ of the data-generating mechanism (DGM) and the sample mean of any data we have seen. The sample mean tells us something about the fundamental mean μ.

To monitor μ we collect some performance data and calculate the sample mean. We then compare the sample mean with a benchmark or reference value. A larger difference between the sample mean and reference level means stronger evidence that the true mean deviates from the reference level. At the end of the day, you have to make a yes or no conclusion that you have met the performance benchmark or not. So there is always the chance of making an error, even with the best analysis. We explain these essential elements in a little more detail:

A Measured Variable X This is a performance measure we want to manage, predict, or monitor. Typical examples might be weekly revenue, or apartment sale price, or customer satisfaction, or customer service time.

The DGM The business process produces observable outcomes of the performance measure. It results in a probability distribution of the performance measure X. For customer satisfaction, "How likely is it that customers will rate me 1 or 2 or 3...." These probabilities describe all we can know about X. However, the DGM is typically extremely complicated and so this probability distribution is unknown to us.

The Mean Performance μ This is the mean of the unknown probability distribution of the performance variable X. In simple language it is the underlying trend or fundamental level of performance. Since the probability distribution is unknown *the mean* μ *is also typically unknown.*

Another way to understand it is this: μ is the long-run average performance we would get if we could somehow observe the performance, a very large number of times. So by asking about μ we are asking about what results we would probably get if we could, at perhaps great expense, collect a much larger sample than the one we have.

A Reference or Benchmark Level μ_0 for the Mean This is a prespecified value that we want to compare mean performance with. It will be determined by background knowledge of the problem and managerial judgment, not by the data. It can be a par value, a fair value, a hypothesized value, a regulatory value, or a competitor's value—depending on the context. *The reference level* μ_0 *is always known.*

A Suspected Deviation from Benchmark We either suspect or want to detect if the mean deviates from the benchmark μ_0 in one particular direction. For instance, we might suspect that, or want to detect if, the mean is larger than the reference/benchmark level ($\mu > \mu_0$). In other examples we might suspect that, or want to detect if, the mean is smaller than the reference/benchmark level ($\mu < \mu_0$).

A Sample of Performance Data In order to reveal the probability distribution of X we collect data $X_1, X_2, \ldots, X_n$ where n is the number of measurements of X. This might involve surveying many customers, recording the sale prices of many apartments, or listing the revenues of many stores in your chain. To use the formulas in this chapter, these data should be **independent**, which means that there is no tendency for one data value to affect another. If this is not the case then more complicated methods are required.

From these data values we can calculate the sample average $\bar{X}$ and the sample standard deviation s. These numbers measure the center and the spread of the data, and by implication the mean and standard deviation of the unknown probability distribution.

A Decision Rule On the basis of the sample mean, sample standard deviation, and sample size, we have to make an unequivocal decision. Either the mean μ equals the benchmark or it deviates from the benchmark. We are not allowed to sit on the fence and say, "We don't know." The decision is based on seeing how far the sample mean deviates from μ_0, while taking into account its intrinsic error.

CHECK YOUR UNDERSTANDING

Q1. Consider the quantities $\bar{X}, \mu, \mu_0$? What does each of these mean in simple words? Which will be known in practice and which will be unknown? Which one are we primarily interested in?

Q2. At the beginning of this section we described a supermarket chain. The management surveys customer's satisfaction levels on a 1–10 scale, and have set a minimum target for all stores of a score no lower than 7.5. How do the concepts of (1) random sample, (2) true underlying mean, (3) reference level, and (4) decision rule relate to this story?

10.2. The Statistical Size of a Deviation

We would like to know whether μ deviates from the benchmark μ_0, either higher or lower depending on the context. Since μ is unknown we replace it with our best estimate, the sample mean $\bar{X}$.

The difference between $\bar{X}$ and μ_0 tells us about the likely difference between μ and μ_0. But how far from μ_0 should $\bar{X}$ be before we are convinced that μ differs from μ_0? This obviously depends on how close we think $\bar{X}$ is to μ. The **standard error of the mean** $\bar{X}$ is given by

$$\text{Std.err}\left(\bar{X}\right) = s/\sqrt{n}.$$

It measures intrinsic variability of the sample mean $\bar{X}$. It also quantifies the typical error of the sample mean as an estimator of μ.

We have to take account of this error in evaluating any deviations of $\bar{X}$ from μ_0. We would expect $\bar{X}$ to differ from μ by 1 SE. This is what an SE means! So if $\bar{X}$ deviates from μ_0 by 1 SE then there is really no credible evidence at all that μ differs from μ_0. Two or more SEs would be another story.

We can count how many SEs $\bar{X}$ is away from μ_o by calculating the ***t*-statistic**

$$t = \frac{\bar{X} - \mu_o}{s/\sqrt{n}}.$$

The *t*-statistic measures the difference between the sample mean $\bar{X}$ and the benchmark μ_o in units of statistical measurement error. The *t*-statistic can be interpreted similarly to a standardized *z*-value. Any value between ±1 is completely usual. Any value larger than ±2 is unusual.

EXAMPLE 1 (Continued) *Supermarket chain (example 1 [customers].xls)*

The sample mean customer satisfaction at Store X is 7.11. What does this say about Store X? Well, it seems to have performed below target but it could just be the particular 100 customers surveyed. It could be bad luck. A different set of 100 customers might give a quite different answer.

The chart does not provide us with much guidance. There is a wide range of responses and it is not obvious that the results are inconsistent with Store X performing to a mean satisfaction level of 7.5. Here is an interesting empirical fact: *Statistical conclusions are usually much stronger than human intuition*. It may often look like your data are consistent with target standards and that a shortfall in performance could occur by chance, but the correct statistical calculation often reveals that it could not. Data analysts are typically easier to convince than the layperson.

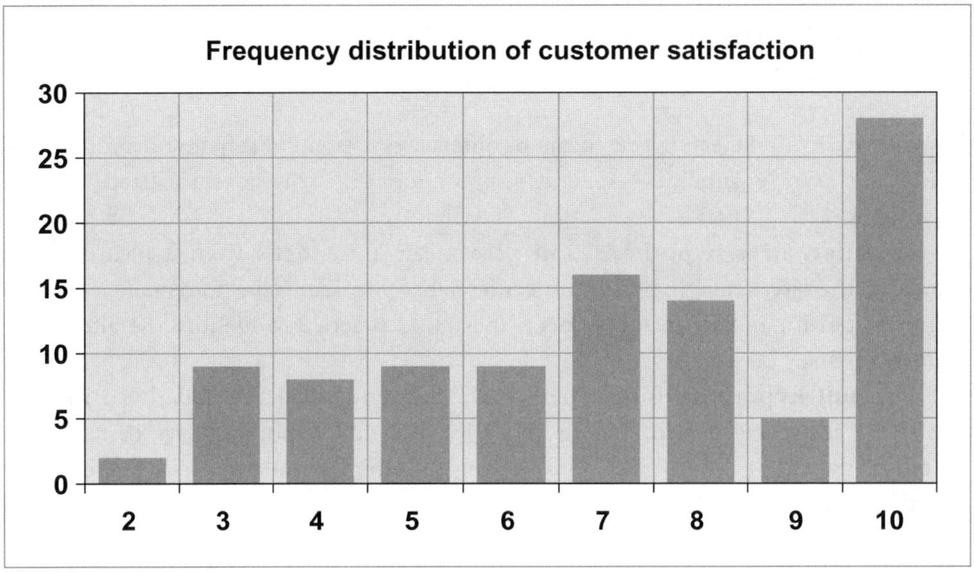

Let's calculate the *t*-statistic for this problem. To calculate the *t*-statistic we also need the sample standard deviation of the data, which is the spread of the above chart. So the variability of the performance is important in assessing the sample mean. For these data, $s = 2.45$. Since the sample size is $n = 100$, the standard error of the mean is $s/\sqrt{100} = 0.245$.

The sample average 7.11 differs from the benchmarks of 7.5 by 0.39. In units of SEs this is

$$t = \frac{7.11 - 7.5}{0.245} = \frac{-0.39}{0.245} = -1.59.$$

The sample mean is 1.59 SEs *below* target. This is in the "gray area" between 1 and 2, and we need to leverage some earlier theory to make our final conclusion. However, even at this stage we can assert that the performance of Store X is below target by a fair bit more than you would ordinarily attribute just to bad luck.

CHECK YOUR UNDERSTANDING

Q3. In each case below, give a rough sketch of what a histogram of the data would look like, calculate the SE, and calculate the *t*-statistic.

- The sample average is 107.9, the standard deviation is 7.4, the reference level is 100, and the sample size is 500.

- The sample average is 10.83, the standard deviation is 0.014, the reference level is 10.81, and the sample size is 50.
- The sample average is 290.75, the standard deviation is 520.38, the reference level is 278.1, and the sample size is 364.

10.3. Decision Making, Hypothesis Testing, and *p*-Values

We are trying to detect if the mean μ differs from μ_0 in one particular direction. There are two possibilities—it does or it doesn't. This is formalized as two hypotheses.

The **alternative hypothesis** is that the mean μ *does* differ from μ_0. Much more generally, the alternative hypothesis specifies what you are trying to detect, what you are interested in, and what you suspect. It is good practice to identify the alternative hypothesis first.

The **null hypothesis** is that there is no deviation—that the underlying mean μ equals the reference level μ_0. More generally, the null hypothesis says that there is no effect, that what you suspect or are trying to detect is not true. In a single phrase it is the *status quo*.

EXAMPLE 1 (Continued) *Supermarket chain*

The management wants to detect underperformance relative to the 7.5 benchmark, so the hypotheses are

$$\text{Null } H_0: \mu = 7.5 \text{ versus Alternative } H_1: \mu < 7.5.$$

We earlier found that the sample mean was 1.59 SEs below target. The *t*-value of −1.59 is suspiciously low. To quantify how suspiciously low it is we ask

> How likely is it that we could get an outcome as low as this just by chance if the store is meeting the 7.5 benchmark?

p-Values: How Extreme Is a *t*-Value?

The normal limit theorem says that $\bar{X}$ has an approximate normal distribution with a mean equal to the true mean μ and a standard deviation equal to the SE, here 0.245. If the store is meeting the 7.5 benchmark then this mean $\mu = 7.5$. So $\bar{X}$ is approximately normal ($\mu = 7.5$, $\sigma = 0.245$).

Recall that you can convert a general normal variable into a *standard* normal by subtracting off the mean and dividing by the standard deviation. So

$$(\bar{X} - 7.5)/0.245$$

has an approximate standard normal distribution. But this is just the t-statistic! So, we have shown that if the null hypothesis is true then the t-statistic has an approximate standard normal distribution. It should really be called a z-statistic. It is only for historical reasons that it is called t.

We can now answer the question about how unusual a t-value is. It has a standard normal distribution. Depending on whether we are looking for the mean being lower or higher than the benchmark we will be anticipating that the t-value is negative or positive. It is simplest to simply ignore the sign of the t-value and then calculate the chance of being more extreme, that is, larger than the observed value. So in general we calculate

$$1 - \text{NORMSDIST}(t\text{-value}),$$

provided you always take the t-value to be a positive number. This is called a ***p*-value**. It measures how unusually extreme the t-value is, assuming the null hypothesis is true. If it is sufficiently unlikely, you would naturally conclude that the null hypothesis is false.

EXAMPLE 1 (Continued) *Supermarket chain*

We want to measure how low the t-value of −1.59 was. Ignore the sign of the t-statistic and just think of it as 1.59. The standard normal distribution tells me how likely it is to get an outcome as *extreme* as 1.59, that is, 1.59 or larger. It is

$$=1 - \text{NORMSDIST}(1.59),$$

which gives the answer 0.056, or about 1 in 18. This is the first p-value you have seen. You will see literally hundreds of these by the end of this book! It measures here how unusually small the sample mean of 7.11 was. The answer is that it would happen by bad luck about 1 in 18 times (because 0.056 is about 1/18). So it looks like Store X is probably underperforming. Or to put it more accurately, if it isn't underperforming then it has been rather unlucky with the survey. How unlucky? A 1 in 18 shot.

Significance Levels

So what is our final decision about Store X? It depends on what level of proof we require, which ultimately will depend on issues outside the data, such as the costs involved in making an error.

A way of formalizing "level of required proof" is to specify the so-called **significance level**. This is a probability that we set, usually a fairly low one. If the p-value for Store X is less than this significance level then we will say that it has failed to meet the benchmark. For instance, we might set a significance level of 0.1. Only if the p-value is less than 0.1 will we conclude that what we suspected is true (the alternative), otherwise we will conclude that the effect is not present (the null).

Type of Errors: False Alarms

There are two possible errors that we could make—rejecting the null hypothesis when it is true or accepting the null hypothesis when it is false. The first of these is called a type I error, the second a type II error. Type I errors are "false alarms." In the context of the customer satisfaction example, a type I error occurs when we say a store is underperforming but it actually was not.

You might expect that if we have a low level of significance then there will be a small chance of this happening. For instance, if I set the significance level at 0.01, then I would only say a store underperforms if their mean satisfaction is so low that the p-value is less than 0.01. For Store X, we would not have concluded that they underperform with this significance level.

In fact the significance level *equals* the chance of a type I error. So at the moment you set your significance level, you automatically set the false alarm rate. If you only want to falsely identify stores as underperformers 10% of the time, then choose a significance level of 0.10.

EXAMPLE 1 (Continued) *Supermarket chain*

Let us suppose that the management chooses a significance level of 10%. This ensures that compliant stores will only fail the test 10% of the time. This is a management decision, not a data-driven conclusion. For Store X, we can now make a decision. Since the p-value 0.056 is smaller than 0.1 we say "OK. The mean of 7.11 is too unlikely for me to accept as just bad luck. I will say that Store X is underperforming." To put it more formally, we conclude the alternative hypothesis H_1.

It is worth thinking here whether a 10% significance level is reasonable. Remember that each store will be tested 12 times in the year. There is a 90% chance that a compliant store will pass each test. However, the chance of passing all 12 tests during the year is $0.90^{12} = 0.282$. So there is a 71.7% chance that a store, which is meeting the management benchmark, will fail the test sometime during the year. This sounds impractically high.

It looks like it would be sensible, then, to choose a much smaller significance level here—because this is a repeated testing regime. For instance, with a significance level of 1%, the chance of passing the whole year is $0.99^{12} = 0.886$, and so there is only an 11.4% chance of a compliant store failing. This is more consistent with the original notion of aiming for 10% false alarms.

With a 1% significance level, Store X passes the test since the *p*-value of 0.056 is not less than 0.01. It looked pretty likely that they were actually underperforming but we will get another 11 chances to detect this if it is true.

Let's summarize and generalize the statistical concepts that have just been introduced in the context of the customer satisfaction example.

Null Hypothesis The status quo. In symbols, $\mu = \mu_0$.

Alternative Hypothesis That the true mean deviates from the benchmark, either lower ($\mu < \mu_0$) or higher ($\mu > \mu_0$). What we suspect or are aiming to detect.

Test Statistic A measure of how far the sample mean $\bar{X}$ deviates from the benchmark in statistical units. It is only worth calculating if the sample mean deviates from the benchmark in the anticipated direction. You can then just ignore the sign of the *t*-statistic.

***p*-Value** A measure of how improbably large the value of *t* is assuming the null hypothesis is true. The smaller the *p*-value the more improbable it is that the observed deviation occurred just by chance. You calculate the *p*-value from the *t*-value by

=1 – NORMSDIST(*t*-value).

Significance Level A value chosen by the analyst, setting a level of proof required to reject the null. If the *p*-value is smaller than the significance level then you conclude that the observed deviation indicates a real deviation, that is, you decide on the alternative hypothesis. The significance level determined the chance of making a type I error (false alarm).

What about the *t*-Distribution?

If you have done a statistics course before you will have heard of the **Student's *t*-distribution**. This is a distribution defined by a bell-shaped curve very similar to the normal. In fact, there is not one *t*-distribution. There are lots of them, depending on another number called the *degrees of freedom*. In practice, I think that the standard normal distribution is fine for calculating the *p*-value, but you will find that many computer programs (and most textbooks) use this slightly different distribution.

The rationale for the *t*-distribution is to account for the "fudge" of replacing σ by s in the SE. However, the use of this distribution is ill conceived. First, if the sample size is reasonably large then the difference between the two approaches is very small. In the customer satisfaction example, you get the *p*-value 0.058 instead of 0.056. This is hardly going to affect a business decision! Second, when the two approaches give different results there are much more modern and accurate methods of calculating the *p*-value than using the *t*-distribution.

Check Your Understanding

Q4. For the customer satisfaction example, a survey of Store Y gave the results below. How would you assess Store Y against the benchmark of 7.5?

Response	1	2	3	4	5	6	7	8	9	10
Freq	0	8	6	4	12	30	73	65	37	15

10.4. Confidence Intervals

Hypothesis testing is used for a rather special task. You have a benchmark value for the underlying mean level of performance μ, a suspected deviation from this benchmark, and a requirement to make a decision.

There is a much simpler question that we can ask about μ. *What is a plausible range for μ after seeing the data?* The answer to this question is very easily calculated from the sample mean and its SE.

DEFINITION

A **confidence interval (CI)** for an unknown quantity is an interval that contains the unknown quantity with a prespecified probability.

CIs almost always have the same form:

- You will have **an estimate** of the unknown quantity.
- You will have **an SE**, which measures the *intrinsic precision* of the estimate.
- You add and subtract a certain number Q of SEs to and from the estimate, to obtain the interval. A general form for a CI is

$$\text{estimate} \pm Q \times \text{SE(estimate)}$$

The number Q is obtained from the standard normal distribution. If you want a 95% interval then the number Q is chosen such that the chance of a standard normal variable being within the interval (−Q, Q) is 95%. For instance, if you want a 95% interval use Q = 2. The table below gives appropriate values of Q for other levels of confidence. The more confidence required, the wider the interval will have to be. For instance, for a given set of data a 99% CI will be wider than a 90% CI. The most commonly quoted CI is the 95% one, perhaps because it corresponds to 2 SEs.

Confidence	Q
99%	2.58
95%	2.00
90%	1.65
75%	1.15
50%	0.68

More data typically result in a narrower interval—because the SE tends to get smaller. So for instance, a 95% CI for the mean based on 1000 data values will be twice as narrow as a 95% CI based on 250 data values. Remember that four times the data means double the accuracy.

For the special case of estimating the mean μ from the sample mean $\overline{X}$ a general form for the CI for μ is

$$\overline{X} - Q\frac{s}{\sqrt{n}},\ \overline{X} + Q\frac{s}{\sqrt{n}}.$$

EXAMPLE 2 (Continued) *Deepwater Bay real estate*

We had data from 108 apartment sales in Deepwater Bay, Hong Kong, during 1995. The performance measure here is apartment sale price and μ is the underlying mean level, which is a kind of measure of market strength.

The sample mean sale price was \$979.9 and the standard deviation was \$264.3. There was interest in a benchmark target value of \$940K.

The standard error of the mean is $s/\sqrt{n} = \$264.3/\sqrt{108} = \$25.4$. We will look at a 75% CI. Using $Q = 1.15$,

$$(979.9 - 1.15 \times 25.4,\ 979.9 + 1.15 \times 25.4)$$

gives the interval (950.7, 1009.1). We are 75% sure that this interval contains the true mean market level μ. Notice that this interval does not include the benchmark value 940. One might almost conclude, then, that we are 75% sure that μ is not equal to 940. For subtle reasons this statement does not always follow from the previous two. But you would not go terribly wrong assuming that it does. Nevertheless, if you want to do a test then I think it is better to construct a *t*-statistic and do the formal test, rather than a CI.

If we want to increase the confidence of the interval then we have to make it wider. A 95% interval uses $Q = 2$ and gives the range (930.1, 1029.7), which does include the benchmark value 940.

Of course, to test the benchmark value 940 we can and should calculate a *t*-statistic and *p*-value. You will find that the *t*-value is 1.57 and the *p*-value is 0.058. So there is reasonably strong evidence that the mean is above 940.

10.5. One-Sided and Two-Sided Tests

Both the previous tests were so-called one-tailed tests. This means that the alternative hypothesis is of the form $\mu < \mu_0$ or $\mu > \mu_0$. Remember that we suspect the alternative may be true, so for one-sided tests we anticipate that the true mean differs from the reference level *in a particular direction.*

In other circumstances, we may not have any idea how the underlying mean might differ from the reference level. For example, we might have data on the rate of defectives using a competing production method and we might not know whether the defective rate is going to be less or greater than the historical rate. In this case we would want to do a "two-tailed test." A two-tailed test is simply a test where the alternative hypothesis is of the form $\mu \neq \mu_0$.

> To perform a two-tailed test, all steps are identical to the one-tailed test except at the last step, just **DOUBLE THE *p*-value.**

What is the logic of this? Suppose that we calculate the *t*-statistic and obtained the answer 1.9. The *p*-value was defined in Section 10.3 to be the probability of the observed value "or more extreme." Certainly, obtaining a value larger than 1.9 would be more extreme. But for a two-tailed test, obtaining a value of −1.9 or smaller would also be more extreme, because these values would also be telling us that the underlying mean $\mu \neq \mu_0$. We therefore calculate the probability of getting a value larger than 1.9 or smaller than −1.9, and because the normal distribution is symmetric, this is just twice the probability of getting a value larger than 1.9.

10.6. Using StatproGo

When the raw data are available, rather than just the frequency distribution, you can use StatproGo to automate all these calculations. Choose StatproGo then Statistical Inference, and then One-Sample Analysis.

The first dialog boxes ask you to identify the column of numbers containing the observations. You are then presented with the left box below. You can produce a CI by checking the box and then choosing a level of confidence. To do a hypothesis test of the mean, check the lower box.

In this case you will be presented with the dialog box on the right. The top part of this box identifies the mean of Store X as the "population" parameter. As explained in the previous chapter, this concept is not widely applicable to business data and it is better to think of the mean μ as the trend or fundamental level of performance. The dialog box allows you to specify the alternative hypotheses, which is what you are looking for. In the customer satisfaction example we are trying to detect when the mean is *less than* 7.5. Type the value 7.5 in the box "Value of population parameter under null."

The output appears as in the table below. You should recognize the mean and standard deviation in the top section. The next section gives the CI with confidence 75%, because I chose 75 as an option in the first dialog box. The SE is 0.245. The

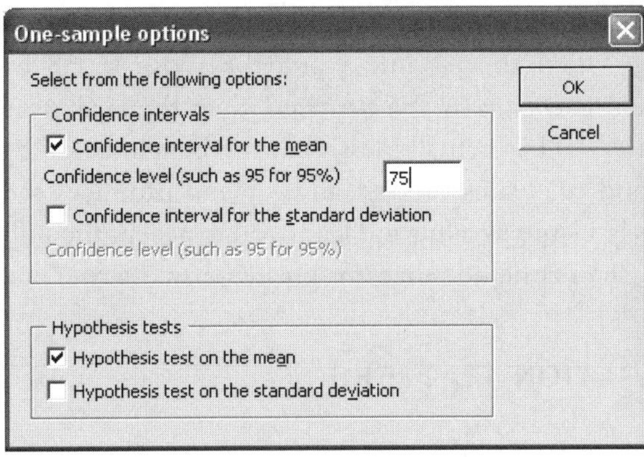

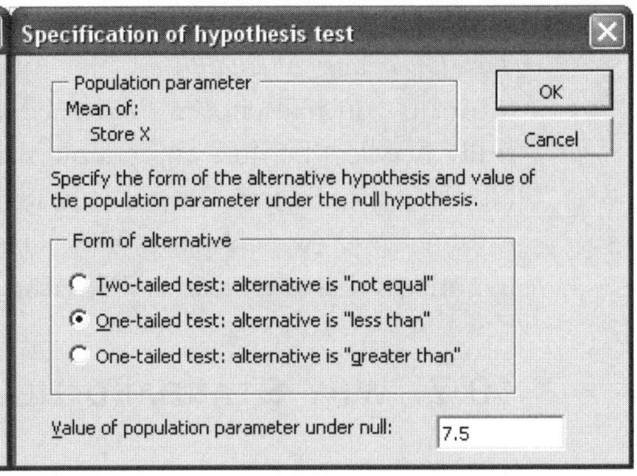

lower and upper limits are obtained by adding and subtracting 1.15 SEs to and from the sample mean. StatproGo actually uses a slightly different number to 1.15, based on the aforementioned *t*-distribution but you will get almost identical answers if you use the recommended value 1.15 (unless the sample size is very small). You can alter the cell containing 75% to produce any desired CI you choose.

Results for one-sample analysis for Store X	
Summary measures	
Sample size	100
Sample mean	7.110
Sample standard deviation	2.453
Confidence interval for mean	
Confidence level	75.0%
Sample mean	7.110
Std error of mean	0.245
Lower limit	6.828
Upper limit	7.392
Test of mean against 7.5 versus one-tailed alternative	
Hypothesized mean	7.500
Sample mean	7.110
Std error of mean	0.245
t-test statistic	-1.590
p-value	0.058

The lower section of the output gives the result of the hypothesis test. It lists the benchmark value 7.5, the sample mean 7.11, the SE 0.245, and from this calculates the *t*-statistic as −1.59, as obtained earlier. It calculates the *p*-value as 0.058. This differs slightly from our earlier calculation of 0.056, again because of the fact that StatproGo uses the *t*-distribution instead of the normal distribution.

StatproGo does not make a formal decision for you but just gives you the *p*-value, which is really the bottom line.

If, in the "Specification of hypothesis test" dialog box, you had instead chosen *Two-tailed test: alternative is "not equal"* then the p-value would be twice 0.058 or 0.116. If you had chosen *One-tailed test: alternative is "greater than"* then the analysis is really needless because the sample mean 7.11 is actually less than the benchmark 7.5. Nevertheless, StatproGo goes ahead and calculates the test anyway and produces the p-value 0.942 (which is 1–0.058). This is a large p-value and leads you to accept the null hypothesis that the mean is 7.5, rather than conclude that it is greater than 7.5.

10.7. Why Standard Deviation Matters

The formula for the t-statistic includes the sample standard deviation s. It follows, then, that we cannot answer any question about the mean without also knowing s. The other number that is important is the sample size n.

To put it in simple terms, if performance variability (as measured by s) is smaller then we will be able to make more accurate inferences about the mean. If the sample size is larger, then we will also be able to make more accurate conclusions. This is embodied in the key formula of the last chapter

$$\text{Std.err}\left(\bar{X}\right) = s / \sqrt{n}.$$

This SE appears on the denominator of the t-statistic so a given observed deviation from the target will be judged as more significant the smaller this SE is.

To illustrate these points, below is the frequency distribution for Store X next to another Store Y. Very few people would look at these charts and say

> It is dead obvious that Store Y is underperforming compared to the target of 7.5. But I am not quite sure about Store X.

For Store X, the t-statistic was 1.59 and the p-value was 0.058. With a 1% significance level (which was suggested earlier on the basis that each store is tested multiple times per year), we would say Store X gets the benefit of the doubt. For Store Y, the *t*-statistic is 2.594 and the *p*-value is 0.0047. So we would say Store Y fails and needs an intervention. One reason for this is that for Store Y the standard deviation is much smaller (1.731 compared to 2.453) but the main reason is that the sample size for Store Y is 250, whereas for Store X there were only 100 customers surveyed.

The *t*-statistic takes proper account of both how variable the performance measure is and how much data you have collected. It is impossible to do this using visual expert judgment. You need to calculate the *p*-value.

10.8. Assessing Detection Power

In the customer satisfaction example, the main reason for the test is to identify underperforming stores. You would like to catch as many as possible. But you are constrained by the possibility of false alarms. As we have seen, the chance of a false alarm can be completely controlled by choosing a significance level. For instance, if you choose a significance level of 1% then there is a 1% chance that stores who are meeting the benchmark will be incorrectly identified and attract an intervention in any given month.

Once I choose the significance level, I have formalized completely the testing regime. I can then ask about the chance of detecting a store that is underperforming—which was the whole reason for the exercise. This obviously will depend on how bad the store really is. If its true mean satisfaction μ is 7.4999 then it is hardly different from a store whose mean μ is 7.5, and I know that the chance of such a store failing the test is only 1%. If the mean level is much lower than 7.5, though, I will have a better chance of detecting it.

How about if a store had a mean satisfaction of 7.0? Would I catch them? Remember that in statistical analysis we like to measure things in terms of SEs. So the first thing to do is to measure the difference between 7.0 and 7.5 in units of SEs. If the SE were 0.245 then we calculate

$$(7.5 - 7.0)/0.245 = 2.041.$$

This is a little like a *t*-statistic but it is not calculated from any data. It is a way of measuring how far a hypothesized level of performance is from the benchmark.

PROBABILITY OF DETECTION

In general, if we have a benchmark μ_0 and a level of performance μ_1 that you want to detect then we measure the deviation by

$$\delta = (\mu_1 - \mu_0)/\text{SE}.$$

If your test has been chosen to have a significance level α then a formula for the chance of detecting the deviation δ is

$$\text{NORMSDIST}(\text{NORMSINV}(\alpha) + |\delta|)$$

where | . | just means ignore the sign of the thing inside. This formula is coded into the template detection.xls.

EXAMPLE 1 (Continued) *Supermarket chain*

If I had a testing regime that allowed α = 1% false alarms and I was interested especially in detecting low satisfaction levels of μ_1 = 7.0 then the chance of this would be

$$\text{NORMSDIST(NORMSINV}(0.01) + 2.041),$$

which gives the answer 0.3876. You will detect a store whose mean level has fallen to 7.0 with a probability of 38.76%. It will pass the testing regime with a probability of 61.24%. Which sounds bad. But recall again that each store is to be tested 12 times. So the chance that it passes all 12 tests is 0.6124^{12}, which is 0.00278. You will definitely detect these stores during the year.

How about a store with a mean level of 7.4—only slightly below the target of 7.5? Will we catch them? You calculate δ = 0.408 and the chance of detection is only 2.75%, so there is a 97.25% chance of them passing any single survey. Even with 12 surveys the chance is 0.9725^{12} = 0.715 that they pass them all. So it looks like we will not detect stores with a mean level of 7.4.

All this assumes, of course, that the SE is 0.245, which came from a sample of n = 100. If we instead took a sample of size n = 500 then the SE would be $2.45/\sqrt{500} = 0.110$. We then find δ = 0.913. The chance of detecting a store with μ_1 = 7.4 is now 7.87%, which means the chance of passing the year is 0.9213^{12}, which is 37.4%. It looks like we will be able to detect such stores with this much larger sampling effort. We would have to wonder whether this effort was worth it. Five times the sample is costly and the benefit of detecting 7.4 instead of 7.3 appears to be quite small.

The worksheet detection probabilities in example 1 (customers).xls has been set up to display how this detection probability increases from 1% as the true customer satisfaction falls further and further below the target of 7.5. You can change the significance level α and see how the curve changes. You can also change the sample size, currently n = 100, to see how much more detection this "buys" you and at what levels of satisfaction the extra detections kick in.

10.9. Summary

When you are interested in how mean performance μ relates to a benchmark μ_0 you first need to establish the hypotheses.

- The **alternative hypothesis** is what you suspect is true and are probably trying to detect or demonstrate, either H_1: $\mu > \mu_0$ or H_1: $\mu < \mu_0$.
- The **null hypothesis** is the status quo, here H_0: $\mu = \mu_0$.

You make a formal decision by comparing the sample mean to the benchmark and calculating a ***t*-statistic**

$$t = \frac{\bar{X} - \mu_0}{s/\sqrt{n}}.$$

which measures how far $\bar{X}$ deviated from μ_0 in units of statistical variation.

The t-value is converted into a ***p*-value** with the formula

1—NORMSDIST(t-value),

ignoring the sign of the t-value so long as it points in the direction you were trying to detect. If it points in the other direction, there is no need for a statistical analysis and you conclude the status quo H_0.

The p-value

- measures how improbably extreme the t-statistic is. Therefore it measures how likely it is that the sample mean would differ from the reference value by the observed amount or more, just by chance.
- measures the weight of the evidence against the null hypothesis. The smaller the p-value is, the more unlikely it is that the observed data would occur assuming the null hypothesis is true.
- is used to make a test decision. If the p-value is too small then the null hypothesis is rejected. How small is too small is set by the decision maker and is called the significance level.
- is just doubled if you are doing a two-sided test.

The significance level is a cut-off value for the p-value.

- If the p-value is smaller than the significance level then you reject the null hypothesis and conclude the alternative.
- The significance level automatically sets the probability of rejecting the null hypothesis when it is true. It is the false alarm probability.
- A smaller value for the significance level makes it harder to reject the null hypothesis and therefore less likely that you will decide that the effect you were looking for (the alternative hypothesis) is present.

CIs give a plausible range for an unknown parameter. A CI for the mean μ has the general form

$$\bar{X} - Q\frac{s}{\sqrt{n}}, \bar{X} + Q\frac{s}{\sqrt{n}}$$

where Q is chosen to give the prespecified level of confidence. All calculations to this point are automated in StatproGo or in the provided template one_sample_template.xls.

If you are using a significance level α, then the probability of detecting a given deviation from benchmark can be calculated using the formula

$$\text{NORMSDIST}(\text{NORMSINV}(\alpha) + |\delta|)$$

where

$$\delta = (\mu_1 - \mu_0)/\text{SE}.$$

EXERCISES

E1. Calculating *p*-values from *t*-values. You only bother to calculate the *t*-statistic if the data point in the direction of the alternative. For instance, if you were trying to detect a mean less than 100 and the sample mean turns out to be 103, then there is no need to do a test. Obviously, there is no evidence from the data that the mean is less than 100! Only if the sample mean turned out to be less than 100 would you bother doing any statistical analysis at all.

If the sample mean turned out to be 97.5 and the SE was 1.2 then you would calculate the *t*-statistic to be (97.5–100)/1.2 = −1.75. To assign a *p*-value to this *t*-value you want to know that chance of the sample mean differing by more than 1.75 SEs in the anticipated direction (which here happens to be negative). So, *ignore the sign* of the *t*-statistic and just calculate $\Pr(Z > 1.75)$. Using Excel,

$$\Pr(Z > 1.75) = 1\text{—NORMSDIST}(1.75) = 0.0401.$$

This is quite a small *p*-value and constitutes moderate evidence that the true mean is less than 100. Depending on your significance level, you would formally conclude that the mean is less than 100 if the *p*-value was smaller than the chosen significance level.

For two-sided tests, you always calculate the *t*-statistic since you are interested in a departure in either direction. Again, ignore the sign of the *t*-statistic to calculate the *p*-value, and at the last step, double the *p*-value. In the previous example, the *p*-value would be 0.0802.

(a) Testing H_0: $\mu = 50$ against H_1: $\mu > 50$. You observe a sample mean of 53.5 with an SE of 2.9. What is the *p*-value and what does it mean? What is your decision with a significance level of 10%?

(b) Testing H_0: $\mu = 750$ against H_1: $\mu < 750$. Observe a sample mean of 702 with an SE of 26.5. What is the *p*-value? What is your decision with a significance level of 5%?

(c) Testing H_0: $\mu = 750$ against H_1: $\mu < 750$. Observe a sample mean of 757 with an SE of 17.5. What is the decision? What is your decision with a significance level of 20%?

(d) Testing H_0: $\mu = 500$ against H_1: $\mu \neq 500$. Observe a sample mean of 557 with an SE of 22. What is the decision? What is your decision with a significance level of 20%?

(e) Testing H_0: $p = 0.7$ against H_1: $p < 0.7$. Observe a sample proportion of 65.7% with an SE of 4.4%[1]. What are the *p*-value and your conclusion with a significance level of 10%?

(f) Testing H_0: $p = 0.9$ against H_1: $p \neq 0.9$. Observe a sample proportion of 93.7% with an SE of 2.2%. What is the p-value? What are the p-value and your conclusion with a significance level of 10%?

E2. You have surveyed 250 people on their degree of satisfaction with their last experience at a call center. The target level for mean satisfaction of all customers is 7.0. The satisfaction measurement is on a scale 1–10, with 10 being best. The data are below. The mean of these data is 6.89 and the standard deviation is 2.41.

Rating	1	2	3	4	5	6	7	8	9	10
Frequency	14	2	4	17	24	40	47	23	39	40

(a) How much evidence is there that average customer satisfaction has fallen below the target value?

(b) If you had surveyed 2000 people and obtained the same mean and standard deviation, then how, if at all, would your answer to part (a) change?

E3. Complaints at a call center have historically arrived at a rate of 2341 per week. Over the past 12 weeks, the number of complaints has been 2337, 2345, 2361, 2335, 2366, 2357, 2349, 2352, 2346, 2366, 2354, and 2334.

(a) Do you think that the underlying complaint rate has increased? You will have to choose your own significance level.

(b) On the basis of the rule that you use to decide part (a), what is the chance of you falsely concluding that complaint rates have increased?

E4. The data file Q4.xls contains data on customer satisfaction of 10 stores in a chain. The target level is 7.5 and the stores have been surveyed in February, April, and June (with training and intervention in between if required). Different numbers of customers were involved in each survey.

(a) For each store and month, calculate a p-value for testing whether the store fails to meet the 7.5 target.

(b) Using a significance level of 1%, which stores would have received interventions?

(c) Looking at the data, what significance level do you think was being used?

E5. The data in Q5.xls are the same data on Store X and Store Y that were discussed in the text. For Store X there were 100 customers surveyed with a sample mean of 7.11. For Store Y, there were 250 customers surveyed with a sample mean of 7.22. We compared this with a target benchmark of 7.5. There is another way to look at these, though. If we classify a score of 1–6 as negative, a score of 7–8 as neutral, and a score 9–10 as positive then we could calculate the percentage positive minus the percentage negative. This is a kind of NPS. The management has set a benchmark for NPS of 0.1, which means 10% more positive than negative responses. They do not want NPS to fall below 0.1.

(a) Recode the data as −1 if the response is negative, +1 if it is positive, and 0 if it is neutral. You can use IF, VLOOKUP, or simply sort the data and do the coding manually.

(b) Calculate the average of the recoded data and format the result as percent. This is actually the percentage of positives minus the percentage of negatives.

[1] The formula for the standard error of a sample proportion will be given in a later chapter.

(c) Test whether the mean NPS is below the target of 0.1. Using a significance level of 5%, would you say Store X or Store Y is underperforming?

E6. Again, thinking about Store X and Store Y, a reasonable manager would wonder about the financial effects of different ratings. Previous studies have suggested that the customers that give various ratings will, on average, spend the amounts tabulated below over the next week. (The small values represent a small chance of them actually coming to the store).

(a) Calculate 75% CIs for the mean value of Store X and Store Y customers.

(b) For each store, test whether their mean value deviated from \$200.

Rating	1	2	3	4	5	6	7	8	9	10
Value	\$5	\$5	\$10	\$10	\$25	\$100	\$200	\$200	\$250	\$300

E7. The data in Q7.xls give the daily sales at a real estate agent in Deepwater Bay, Hong Kong. This is the same data that we examined in Chapter 9. There is interest in the underlying mean level of sales and also in a benchmark value of \$300K per day.

(a) Imagine it is February 1. Calculate a 90% CI for the mean sales. How would this change on February 2, February 3, and so on? Produce a CI for each remaining day of the year.

(b) Imagine it is February 1. Test whether the mean sales differ from \$300K per day. Repeat this for each remaining day of the year. At what points is it clear that the mean sales deviate from the benchmark?

E8. The 108 apartment sales Q8.xls have been listed together with their area in square feet. Obviously, area will have a big effect on price. Use Pivotables to break the data up into ranges of areas from 750 to 1000 ft^2, from 1000 to 1250 ft^2, and so on.

(a) Give a 95% CI for the mean price of an apartment in each size category.

(b) Display the relationship of mean price to size category on a graph, taking care to also display the uncertainty in the mean price.

E9. *(Harder)* Continuing with the problem of detecting customer satisfaction falling below 7.5, suppose you want to make sure that you detect levels as low as 7.0. The typical standard deviation of customer satisfaction is around 2.0. So your SEs $s/\sqrt{n}$ will roughly equal .

(a) If you take a sample of size 50 and use a significance level of 10% then what is the chance of detecting a store with level 7.0 in a single survey?

(b) If you take a sample of size 250 and use a significance level of 1% then what is the chance of detecting a store with level 7.0 in a single survey?

(c) Produce a table showing the chance of detecting a store with level 7.0 in a single survey for the significance levels 10%, 5%, 2%, and 1%, and for sample sizes 50, 100, 150, 200, and 250, 16 combinations in all.

(d) One way to judge the success of the testing regime is to look at the chance of detection minus the chance of false alarm. The larger this value, the better. For each possible sample size, what significance level would you use?

(e) Suppose you have decided on a 5% significance level and you are determined to achieve a detection level of 90%. What sample size should you choose? You can use Goalseek for this.

(f) Set up the table so that you can easily alter the provided figures of 7.0 for the detection target and 2.0 for the typical standard deviation.

E10. *(Harder)* You are designing a monitoring protocol for an industrial process. A key feature of the process is that mean sulfur emission level should not exceed 1.22 mg/kg, though variations from this level over short periods of time and from sample to sample are both common and quite permissible. From historical data, it is known that the sulfur content of a random sample of 1 kg of emission material has a standard deviation of 0.0084 mg/kg. You want to be able to detect if the mean level goes higher than 1.22. Obviously, if the mean level is 1.22001 then this will be very hard to detect. But if the mean level goes as high as 1.225 then you want to be able to detect that there has been a rise with high probability.

(a) Suppose that you took n = 50 samples of material. What would be the standard error of the mean?

(b) Based on your answer to part (a), how large would the average sulfur content of the 50 samples have to be before you would say there is a rise in the sulfur level above 1.22? It will be up to you to set this level.

(c) What is the probability of a "false alarm" using your critical level in (b)?

(d) Suppose that the mean level were actually 1.225. What is the probability that the mean level would be as high as, or higher than, the critical level you came up with in part (c)?

(e) Using Excel, experiment with how the sample size and your chosen critical value affect these calculations. These are the only two things that you can control. What sample size would you need in order to be 99.9% sure of detecting a mean rise to 1.225?

CHAPTER 11

Are These Customers Different? Did the Intervention Work? Looking at Changes in Mean Performance

11.0. Introduction: What Is The Issue?

How do the purchasing habits of male and female customers differ? How many products do they typically purchase on a shopping trip? How much do they spend per purchase?

A telephone company mails advertising brochures to a randomly selected group of customers. How effective is the mail-out? This involves a comparison of the behavior of customers who did and did not receive the brochure.

We are interested in some performance variable X, such as the number or value of purchases per customer, customer satisfaction, or total customer waiting time in connecting to a phone consultant. Specifically, we are interested in whether or not the mean performance depends on a **two-level factor** like gender (male or female), day type (weekend or weekday), and strategy (advertise or don't advertise). And if it does depend on this factor, how large is the difference? And just as importantly, how reliable is our assessment?

EXAMPLE 1 *U.S. Labor Census revisited*

In Chapter 2 we looked at the Bureau of Labor Statistics in the United States. The data described almost 8000 people who were classified as full-time workers in the

Data-Driven Business Decisions, First Edition. Chris J. Lloyd.

previous year. The main variables recorded were salary in units of earnings per hour (EPH), educational achievement such as high school diploma (HS) or a bachelor's degree (UNI), as well as age and gender.

One issue of interest was the gender gap. Using Pivotables it is easy to break the data up into males and females. You will find that males have an average EPH of \$17.77 compared to the average female EPH of \$15.36, a difference of \$2.41. The difference, however, is not uniform across age groups. If you break up the data by age as well, you will find that for 21-year-olds, males and females have almost identical salaries. In fact, males earn slightly less in this age group. As the age increases, however, a gap starts to appear.

This is graphically represented below. You can produce this graph yourself by generating a Pivotable with age in rows, gender in columns, average EPH in the data field, and creating a line graph.

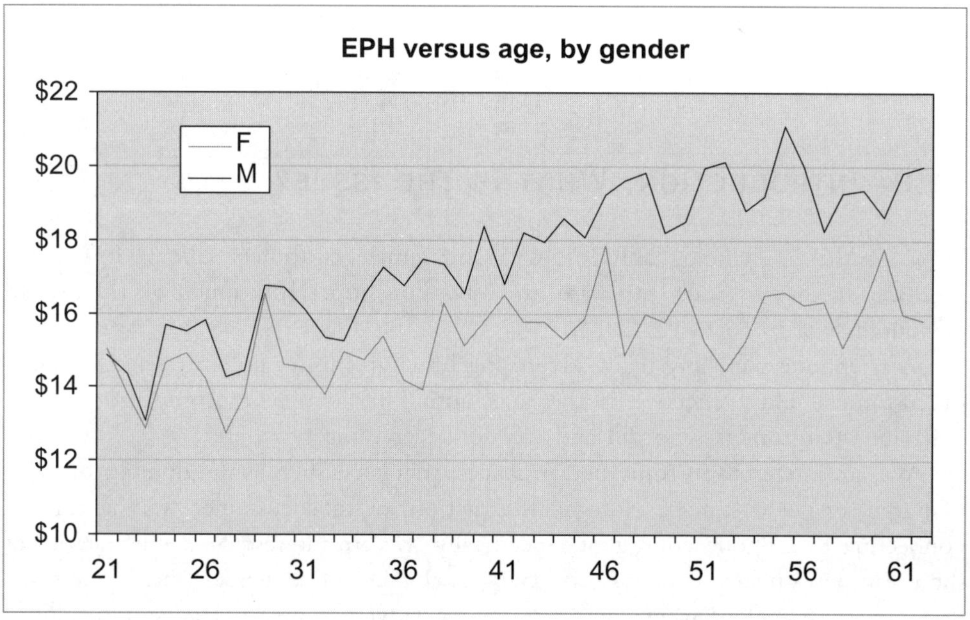

Every point on this graph represents a sample average—of that particular gender and age group. If you really bought into the message of the previous two chapters then you will immediately want to know how much intrinsic error there is in all of these figures. We cannot take sample averages at face value until we know how accurate they are.

If we are primarily interested in the gender *difference* then we might plot the gender difference against age. This is just a plot of the gap in the graph above. Each point on this graph is now *a difference in two means*. We need a measure of error for these numbers as well.

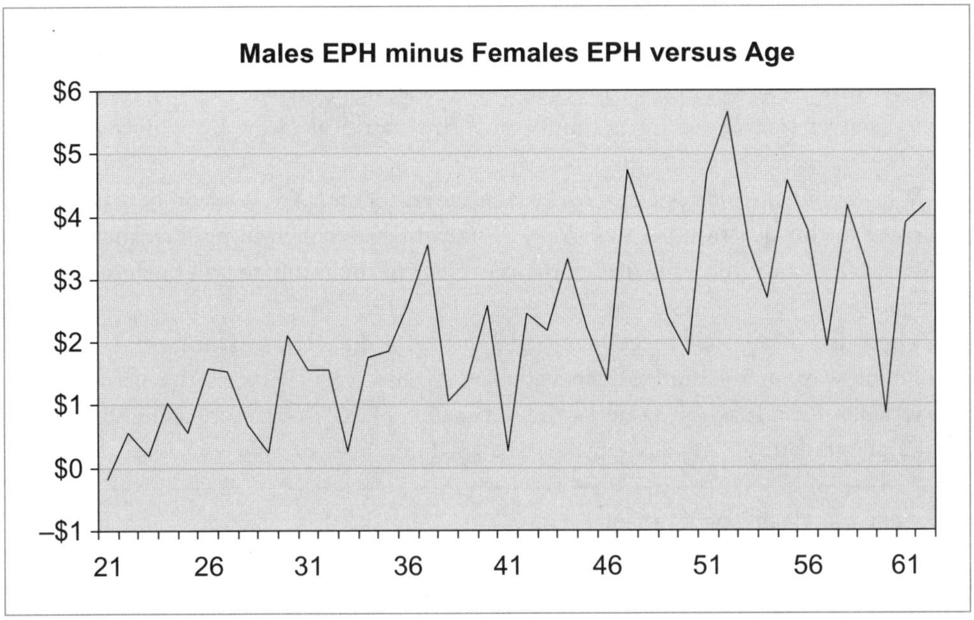

11.1. How Variable Is a Difference?

You could skip the mathematical details in this section, but the basic ideas are not difficult to explain. The payoff is an appreciation for what lies behind the formulas.

Let's start off with a very simple but abstract problem. We have two variable business numbers X_1 and X_2. These could be individual performances outcomes or the average performance of two groups. It makes no difference to what is about to be asserted.

> Standard deviation squared is named "variance" but is not itself of much use in business.

Suppose we knew the statistical variability of both these numbers. We use standard deviation to measure statistical variability. Let σ_1 and σ_2 be the standard deviations of the variables X_1 and X_2, respectively. How variable is the total of X_1 and X_2? Since we are adding two variables with error, you would expect the errors to accumulate. So you might guess that the answer is $\sigma_1 + \sigma_2$. This is not a bad guess but it happens to be wrong. It turns out that variability does not add in this simple way. Rather the *square* of the variability adds.

For any two *independent* variables X_1 and X_2,

$$\text{Stdev}^2(X_1 + X_2) = \text{Stdev}^2(X_1) + \text{Stdev}^2(X_2).$$

Since we measure statistical variability by standard deviation and not by standard deviation squared, a more useful form for this equation is

$$\text{Stdev}(X_1 + X_2) = \sqrt{\sigma_1^2 + \sigma_2^2}.$$

It is important that the two numbers be independent, otherwise one variable could, for instance, always tend to be low when the other was high so that the variability of the total would tend to be less.

The formula is extremely important because it always gives an answer smaller than $\sigma_1 + \sigma_2$. Statistical errors do not simply add. There is some error reduction just from the process of adding, or indeed from averaging. *Maximum* error, which computer scientists care about, does simply add. But statistical error, by which we mean typical or most likely error, does not.

What about the *difference between* two numbers X_1 and X_2? We will be particularly interested in this question because $X_1 - X_2$ measures a change in performance. When assessing any change in performance the reliability of the estimate will be an important consideration.

There is a neat trick to get the variability of a difference. Think of $X_1 - X_2$ in a different way, as the sum of the variables X_1 and $-X_2$. What is the variability of the variable $-X_2$? It is the same as the variability of X_2! Variability is blind to sign. So the above formula applies equally well to differences of two variables.

For any two *independent* variables X_1 and X_2,

$$\text{Stdev}(X_1 - X_2) = \sqrt{\sigma_1^2 + \sigma_2^2}.$$

The main application of this result is in comparing the mean performance for different subgroups of data. In this case, X_1 is the sample mean of the first group and X_2 is the sample mean of the second group. The variability of these is each measured by their *standard error* (SE), which is calculated as the standard deviation of that group divided by the square root of the number of individuals in the group. So the difference between the two sample means will have the variability

$$\text{Std.Error } (\bar{X}_1 - \bar{X}_2) = \sqrt{\{\text{SE}(\bar{X}_1)\}^2 + \{\text{SE}(\bar{X}_2)\}^2}$$

This will always give an answer that is larger than either SE but smaller than the sum of the SEs.

EXAMPLE 1 (Continued) *U.S. Labor Census*

Let's confine attention to the youngest age group, 21–25 years, and assess the difference in male (M) and female (F) salaries (measured in EPH). The data are on a worksheet "Age 21–25" of ex1 (census).xls. Using Pivotables you can easily calculate the mean, standard deviation, and number of individuals in the two gender groups. The results are in the table below.

Gender	Mean	Stdev	Number	Std.Error
F	$14.146	$7.033	354	$0.374
M	$14.754	$7.349	424	$0.357
All	$14.477	$7.209	778	$0.258

The SEs were each obtained by dividing the standard deviation by the square root of the number of individuals in that group. The difference between average EPH for males and females is $0.608 or 61 cents to the nearest cent. This is a small amount but how reliable is this number? It is obtained by subtracting \$14.146 from \$14.754. These have the intrinsic errors 35.7 cents and 37.4 cents, respectively. The intrinsic variability of the difference is therefore

$$\begin{aligned}\text{Stdev}(\bar{X}_{\text{MALES}} - \bar{X}_{\text{FEMALES}}) &= \sqrt{\{\text{SE}(\bar{X}_{\text{MALES}})\}^2 + \{\text{SE}(\bar{X}_{\text{FEMALES}})\}^2} \\ &= \sqrt{0.374^2 + 0.357^2} = 0.517\end{aligned}$$

(Note that this is smaller than 37.4 cents + 35.7 cents = 73.1 cents.) We assess the error in the estimated 61-cent salary difference as 52 cents to the nearest cent. So the 61 cents is poorly estimated. In fact, we cannot even be sure that the trend male salary really is greater than the female salary for this age group. The mean difference is just too poorly measured.

11.2. Describing Changes in Mean Performance

When you spend money on some kind of business intervention you will want to know if it has been effective and, if so, how effective it has been. You decide if it has been effective with a hypothesis test. You measure how effective it has been with an estimate and a confidence interval (CI).

The key formula for this chapter is

$$\text{Std.Error}\ (\bar{X}_1 - \bar{X}_2) = \sqrt{\{\text{SE}(\bar{X}_1)\}^2 + \{\text{SE}(\bar{X}_2)\}^2}$$

for measuring the error in a change or difference of sample means. The two sample means will typically be the average performance under two scenarios, for instance no advertising compared with advertising at a given level.

SEs can be used for tests and CIs, and there is a pattern to how SEs are used that is repeated throughout the book. Once you get the pattern, all the formulas start to make sense.

In general, there will be an unknown business fundamental or "parameter" that we want to say something about. In the previous chapter this was just a fundamental mean level of performance μ. There will also be an estimate of this fundamental. In the previous chapter this was the sample mean. Finally we need an SE for this estimate—the standard error of the mean in the last chapter.

To test whether the fundamental deviates from a benchmark value we measure the statistical deviation with

$$t = \frac{\text{estimate} - \text{benchmark}}{\text{SE(estimate)}}.$$

If the *t*-statistic is much greater than 1 then the estimate deviates from the benchmark by statistically more than one would expect by chance. This can be turned into a *p*-value by calculating

$$1 - \text{NORMSDIST}(t\text{-value}).$$

and ignoring the sign of the *t*-value.

> If you want to say something about the likely range of the fundamental then you just add and subtract an appropriate number Q of SEs to and from the estimate to obtain a CI of the general form
>
> $$\text{estimate} \pm Q \times \text{SE(estimate)}.$$

In this chapter we are interested in a difference in mean performance. If we call the mean performance under the two management conditions μ_A and μ_B then the fundamental parameter of interest is $\mu_A - \mu_B$. Very often we will want to test whether the difference differs from *zero* so the benchmark is often (but not always) 0. The estimated change in performance is the difference in sample means. We have a formula for the SE of this estimate and so the t-statistic has the form

$$t = \frac{\overline{X}_A - \overline{X}_B - \text{benchmark}}{\text{SE}(\overline{X}_A - \overline{X}_B)}.$$

If we just want to give a range for the change in performance then we give a CI for $\mu_A - \mu_B$ in the form

$$\overline{X}_A - \overline{X}_B \pm Q \times \text{SE}(\overline{X}_A - \overline{X}_B).$$

EXAMPLE 1 (Continued) *U.S. Labor Census (ex1 [census].xls)*

For the age group 21–25 years we are interested in the fundamental mean difference between earnings of males and females. Consider the hypotheses

$$H_0 : \mu_{\text{MALES}} = \mu_{\text{FEMALES}} \text{ versus } H_1 : \mu_{\text{MALES}} > \mu_{\text{FEMALES}}.$$

Another way to write this is

$$H_0 : \mu_{\text{MALES}} - \mu_{\text{FEMALES}} = 0 \text{ versus } H_1 : \mu_{\text{MALES}} - \mu_{\text{FEMALES}} > 0.$$

Our estimate of the excess male salary was \$0.608. The SE of this figure was \$0.517. So the t-statistic is

$$t = \frac{\overline{X}_{\text{MALES}} - \overline{X}_{\text{FEMALES}} - \text{benchmark}}{\text{SE}(\overline{X}_{\text{MALES}} - \overline{X}_{\text{FEMALES}})} = \frac{0.608 - 0}{0.517} = 1.176.$$

This means that average male salaries exceeded average female salaries by slightly more than you would expect by chance. The p-value is

$$= 1 - \text{NORMSDIST}(1.176),$$

giving the answer 0.120, so the chance of seeing male salaries exceed female salaries by this magnitude by pure chance is around 12%. This suggests that there probably is a real difference but we cannot really be sure.

By way of contrast, for the age group 26–30 the sample means for males and females are in the table below, together with the SE obtained from the standard deviation divided by the square root of the number.

The difference is \$1.243, which is double the difference that we saw for the youngest age group. The intrinsic variability of the difference is

Gender	Mean	Stdev	Number	Std.Error
F	$14.406	$7.161	361	$0.377
M	$15.649	$7.880	473	$0.362
All	$15.111	$7.598	834	$0.263

$$\text{Stdev}(\bar{X}_{\text{MALES}} - \bar{X}_{\text{FEMALES}}) = \sqrt{0.377^2 + 0.362^2} = 0.523,$$

so the error in the $1.243 figure is 52.3 cents. There now seems to be compelling evidence for a real difference in genders since the apparent difference is more than twice the intrinsic error. To be specific the *t*-statistic is

$$t = \frac{\bar{X}_{\text{MALES}} - \bar{X}_{\text{FEMALES}} - \text{benchmark}}{\text{SE}(\bar{X}_{\text{MALES}} - \bar{X}_{\text{FEMALES}})} = \frac{1.243 - 0}{0.5327} = 2.377.$$

The *p*-value associated with this *t*-value is very small, 0.009 to be exact, so there is less than a 1% chance of a difference of this magnitude occurring by pure chance. So there *is* a real difference and we should give a plausible range for this difference. For instance, a 75% CI is obtained by adding and subtracting 1.15 SEs to the estimate and is

$$\bar{X}_{\text{MALES}} - \bar{X}_{\text{FEMALES}} \pm 1.15 \times \text{SE}(\bar{X}_{\text{MALES}} - \bar{X}_{\text{FEMALES}}) = 1.243 \pm 1.15 \times 0.523 = (0.641, 1.844).$$

So we are 75% sure that the fundamental trend difference between males and female salaries for this age group is between 64 cents and $1.84.

Check Your Understanding

Q1. What is the yearly depreciation on the sale price of a Mitsubishi Magna? You have data on the sale price of 27 2-year-old Magnas and 38 3-year-old Magnas. The data are given in the table below.

	Number	Mean	Std. Dev
2 years	27	18,550	1560
3 years	38	15,680	1120

(a) Calculate the SEs for the mean sales price for 2- and 3-year-old cars.

(b) Calculate the difference in the mean sale price of 2- and 3-year-old cars and calculate an SE for this figure.

(c) Conventional wisdom has it that yearly depreciation on a Magna is $1500. You have always thought that it was greater than this. How much support do the data provide for your position?

11.3. Example 2: Is Product Placement Worth It?

A particular fizzy beverage, Duo, is sold in supermarkets across the country. It is a popular beverage and average weekly sales per store is around $20,000K. There is a

45% margin on the product, that is, every extra dollar of sales gives you an extra 45 cents profit, other things being equal.

One important determinant of sales is where the product is displayed on the shelf. For one particular supermarket chain that stocks your product, the charge for preferential product placement (PP) is in increments of $10,000—from $0 right up to $50,000 per week—if you are displayed at the end of an aisle on the top shelf, right opposite the checkout.

You have data on the 270 supermarkets within this chain and have total sales over the past week. More details of the background of this case are in the case Duo Beverages. Open the worksheet "basic data" in ex2 (duo).xls. The variable Sales gives the total sales of your drink for each supermarket in the chain. The variable Placement gives the PP spend at that store for that week. Sales vary widely from $12,655 to $145,022. Most of this is due to placement that can multiply sales by a large factor but, even among the stores where you spent nothing on placement, sales varied from $12,655 to $36,965, mainly because some stores are just much larger and in more populated areas than others.

What is the effect of placement? The first thing to do is to use Pivotables to break the stores into different groups and see how sales depends on PP spend. The table below gives the average sales, the standard deviation of sales, and the number of stores within each PP expenditure group. Some simple calculations suggest that spending $10,000 *is* worth it.

PP spend	Mean Sales	Stdev Sales	Number	Std.Error
$0	$23,405	$6,483	23	$1,352
$10,000	$48,446	$7,261	18	$1,712
$20,000	$67,640	$5,386	28	$1,018
$30,000	$89,571	$7,109	116	$660
$40,000	$109,699	$6,551	69	$789
$50,000	$128,058	$6,171	16	$1,543

Why? Looking at the highlighted part of the table, for stores where you spend $10K, mean sales are $48,446 compared to $23,405 for stores where you spend nothing—a difference of $25,040. Remember, though, that only 45% of this is extra profit, which translates into $11,268, which is $1268 more than the $10,000 you spend. Thought of another way, you get a 12.68% return on your $10K investment in PP.

As usual, we want to measure the intrinsic accuracy of the conclusion. We have SEs for all the means involved in the last column. These were obtained in the usual way—dividing the standard deviation by the square root of the sample size. They measure the intrinsic error of the figures in the mean sales column.

The table below shows the calculations. The column "Impact" contains the mean sales for each PP expenditure level minus the mean sales without ($23,405). For instance, the Impact of $10K expenditure we already saw is $25,040. The right-hand columns measure impact after accounting for the 45% margin. You will see that the figure $11,268 has an SE of $981. Let's see how this was calculated. First, consider the figure \$25,040 = \$48,446 − \$23,405. From the table above the error in the \$48,446 figure is \$1712 and the error in the \$23,405 figure is \$1352, so the error in the difference is

$$\sqrt{1352^2 + 1712^2} = 2181.$$

	Before 45% margin		After 45% margin		
PP spend	Impact	SE (Impact)	Impact	SE (Impact)	T-value
k\$10	\$25,040	\$2,181	\$11,268	\$981	1.29
k\$20	\$44,235	\$1,692	\$19,906	\$761	-0.12
k\$30	\$66,166	\$1,504	\$29,775	\$677	-0.33
k\$40	\$86,294	\$1,565	\$38,832	\$704	-1.66
k\$50	\$104,652	\$2,051	\$47,094	\$923	-3.15

Using the 45% margin the impact becomes 0.45 × \$25,040 = \$11,268. The SE is reduced by the same 45% factor—the SEs and standard deviation both rescale in this simple way. And 45% of \$2182 is \$981.

So our final conclusion is that spending \$10,000 on PP leaves you \$1268 in front with an SE of \$981. As a percentage, you are 12.7% in front with an SE of 9.8%. So we would be fairly confident that we are really in front. The *t*-value measures how far \$11,268 is above the \$10,000 cost in units of intrinsic errors and is

$$t = \frac{11268 - 10000}{981} = 1.29.$$

The *p*-value is 0.0981 so there is a 9.81% chance of being in front by this amount just by chance. We might consider doing a two-sided test here—since it is not obvious whether we would finish in front or not. In that case the *p*-value would be double this, or 19.62%. We would have to say that even though we appear to be in front, the evidence is not compelling.

You can repeat this whole calculation for the other levels of PP expenditure and you will obtain the *t*-values in the right-hand column. For the higher levels of placement expenditure you are behind, because the net impact is less than the PP spend. Moreover, the *t*-values are quite large and negative for the two highest levels of expenditure. It looks like you definitely lose money at these higher spend levels.

Using the Par Value Data

There is a great deal of variability in weekly Sales, around \$7000 even within the same PP spend group. This is due to differences in locations and sizes of the stores. It is good practice to try and account for this kind of variability if you can. The result can be smaller SEs and a cleaner or even a very different conclusion.

There are data available for this purpose in the worksheet "extended data." The new variable Par Sales is an estimate of baseline or expected sales for that store for that week. You will learn methods for making such an estimate in the later chapters of this book. The beverage company would have plenty of data available to create such an estimate. They would need to particularly take into account seasonal effects as well as the overall size and past record of that store. So we have a figure Par Sales (what we expect with no PP) and Actual Sales (which is just the Sales figures we were using before).

This allows us to immediately calculate the *excess* sales for each store, notionally due to the PP, by subtracting the par value from actual sales. Again breaking the data up into the different PP spend groups, we can look now at average Excess Sales and how this is affected by the spend.

PP spend	Par Sales	Actual Sales	Excess Sales
$0	$20,334	$23,405	$3,071
$10,000	$18,514	$48,446	$29,932
$20,000	$18,267	$67,640	$49,373
$30,000	$19,698	$89,571	$69,873
$40,000	$19,708	$109,699	$89,992
$50,000	$18,842	$128,058	$109,216

Let's have a quick look at the $10K figures. It seems like we are in front again. Why? Because you get an extra $29,932 of sales on average. Remember, though, that only 45% of this is extra profit, which translates into $13,469, which is $3469 more than the $10,000 you spend. Thought of another way, you get a 34.9% return on your $10K investment in PP.

We need to repeat this calculation for the other levels of PP expenditure but we also want to give SEs for our results. The first thing to do is to calculate Excess Profits (EPs) for each store by multiplying the Excess Sales by 45%. This is done in Column G of the worksheet. We can then calculate the mean and standard deviation of EPs for each PP spend group, from which we can calculate SEs in the usual way.

PP spend	Mean EP	Stdev EP	Number	Std. Error
$0	$1,382	$1,993	23	$416
$10,000	$13,469	$2,854	18	$673
$20,000	$22,218	$2,171	28	$410
$30,000	$31,443	$2,176	116	$202
$40,000	$40,496	$2,136	69	$257
$50,000	$49,147	$1,730	16	$432

Let's look again at the $13,469 EP figure for the $10K expenditure group. The SE for this figure is $2854/\sqrt{28} = 673$. This is the formula for the standard deviation of a sample mean from the last chapter. This is a smaller SE than we were getting earlier, and is even smaller for the other PP groups. This is the payoff for having the Par Value numbers.

You might have thought that we have to use the formula for the SE of a difference in means, since the excess Sales are calculated by subtracting Par Sales from

Actual Sales. However, we were able to calculate the EP for each of the 270 stores in a single Column G. This single column of numbers has an average of \$13,469. So there is surely no reason not to use the formula from the last chapter for a single sample mean. In fact, you would be wrong to use the earlier formula for the standard deviation of a difference between two means. This is a tricky point that will be explained in detail in the Matched Pairs section below.

So our estimated effect of spending \$10K on PP is that we get a net EP of \$13,469 – \$10,000 = \$3469 or 34.7%, with an SE of \$672, which is 6.7%. This is clearly a real effect, then. In fact the *t*-statistic is

$$t = \frac{\bar{X}_1 - \bar{X}_2 - \text{benchmark}}{\text{SE}(\bar{X}_1 - \bar{X}_2)} = \frac{13649 - 10000}{673} = 5.16,$$

which is a huge value for a *t*-statistic. There is no realistic chance at all that the EP here is an artifact of chance. So we would be interested in a plausible range for the mean EP. A 95% CI is

$$\$13,649 \pm 2.0 \times \$673 = (\$12124,\ \$14815).$$

Subtracting the \$10K cost, we are in front by an amount of \$3649 with a 95% CI (\$2124, \$4815), or when expressed as a percentage, we get (21.2%, 48.1%) as an interval for the return on the \$10K investment.

We can repeat this calculation for the other levels of PP expenditure to get the results below. The calculations are in the worksheet "second analysis." For instance, spending \$40K on PP results in an extra \$40,496 EP, which is only \$496 after we subtract the \$40K cost. The error in this figure is \$257, so the \$496 figure is unlikely to have occurred by chance. The *t*-value is 1.93. If we spend \$50K on PP, it appears that we do not get our money back. We end up with a negative EP of –\$953 per store after subtracting the \$50K cost. The *t*-statistic is −1.97, which suggests this is a robust statistical result.

PP spend	Adjusted EP – PP spend	T-value	Low(95%)	High(95%)
\$0	\$1,382	3.33	\$551	\$2,213
\$10,000	\$3,469	5.16	\$2,124	\$4,815
\$20,000	\$2,218	5.41	\$1,397	\$3,039
\$30,000	\$1,443	7.14	\$1,039	\$1,847
\$40,000	\$496	1.93	-\$18	\$1,010
\$50,000	-\$953	-1.97	-\$1,718	\$12

Pushing a Bit Further

It looks like the Par Value data resulted in smaller SEs, larger *t*-statistics, and clearer evidence that PP expenditure is working. We are not finished, however. Benchmarking performance with some kind of Par Value measure is a good idea. But it has to be done right. If you look at the first row of the table above you will see something strange.

For those stores where there was no PP expenditure last week, we obtained an average EP of $1382. The *t*-value for this is 3.33, which means that it cannot be explained by luck. This doesn't make any sense! The Actual Sales of the 23 stores that did no advertising were systematically higher than their own Par Value Sales—by $3071, which means $1382 extra profits. Why would they outperform their own Par Value Sales when these Par Values are supposed to estimate sales with no PP expenditure? There can only be one explanation. There is something wrong with our Par Values! Perhaps they have not properly accounted for recent growth in market share or general economic conditions. In any case, they have been set too low. What to do?

Luckily, we have an estimate of how wrong these par values are—$1382. This is one reason for including the zero PP spend stores in the analysis: to check that the Par Values are correct and to correct them if they are not. One simple way to correct them is to simply adjust all our Excess Sales downwards by this amount. There are other ways we could do it, but this is the simplest. As usual, we will want to take account of the variability of all the numbers involved. Let's revisit the calculation for $10K PP expenditure and then it can be rolled out across the other categories.

Originally we estimated EP of $13,469 but we now adjust this down by $1382 to get $12,087. This is a difference of two numbers, each with errors. The error in the $13,496 figure was $673 and the error in the $1382 figure was $416, so the error in the difference is

$$\sqrt{673^2 + 416^2} = 791.$$

To compare our adjusted EP to the benchmark expenditure of $10K in statistical units we calculate

$$t = \frac{12087 - 10000}{791} = 2.64.$$

So we are still very confident that expenditure of $10K is "worth it." The return on investment is about 20.9%, with an SE of 7.9%. A 75% CI for the mean EP is

$$\$12,087 \pm 1.15 \times \$791 = (\$11178,\ \$12996).$$

Repeating these calculations for the other expenditure categories, we find that we are very near breakeven for $30K and are very likely losing money at $40K. We are clearly behind with a $50K spend. The statements are based on the sign and size of the *t*-statistics.

	Adjusted Excess Profit		Test and CI's		
PP spend	Mean	Std.Error	T	Low(75%)	High(75%)
$10,000	$12,087	$791	2.64	$11,178	$12,996
$20,000	$20,836	$584	1.43	$20,164	$21,507
$30,000	$30,061	$462	0.13	$29,529	$30,592
$40,000	$39,114	$489	-1.81	$38,552	$39,676
$50,000	$47,765	$600	-3.73	$47,075	$48,455

11.4. PERFORMING THE *T*-TEST WITH STATPROGO

All the calculations in the previous section can be performed using StatproGo. As an example, let's recreate the analysis from the Par Value data that gave the *t*-value of 2.64 above and the 75% CI ($11,178, $12,996).

Choose StatproGo, then Statistical Inference, and then Two-Sample Analysis. You will be asked where the data area is, and then whether the data are stacked or unstacked. The idea of stacking was described in Chapter 2. If the data are in two separate columns then they are *unstacked*. If the data are in a single column with a second column labeling the sample each value belongs to then the data are said to be *stacked*. Our data are stacked.

Next, select the coding variable. This is the variable that defines the groups—here Placement.

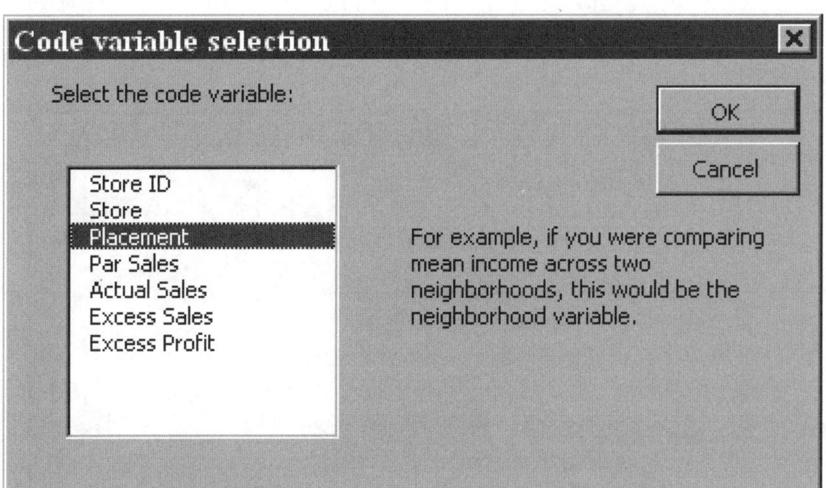

Then select the two groups of data you want to compare. Here we want to compare the $0 and $10,000 groups.

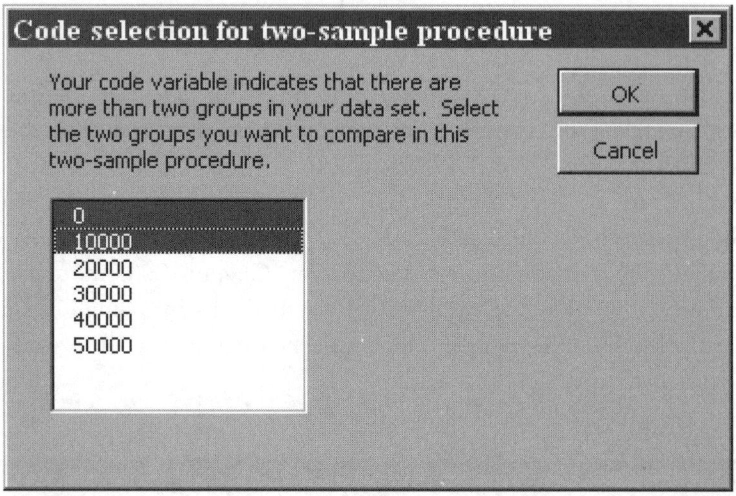

In the next box, select EP as the variable to analyze. Then in the next box, check the *Confidence interval for the difference between means* and *Hypothesis test on the difference between means* as desired. I have chosen a 75% CI.

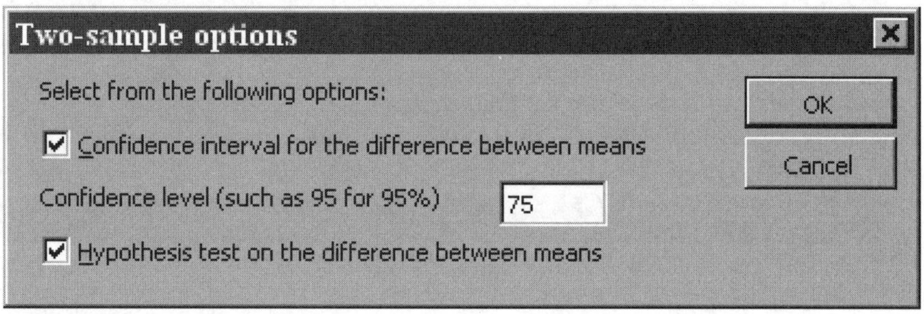

Now comes the most important box, where we define the hypotheses we are testing. Unfortunately, StatproGo often defines the unknown parameter to be the reverse of what we would naturally choose. The "population parameter" here is the mean EP for the \$0 stores minus the mean EP for the \$10,000 stores. This is kind of backwards but we have to live with it.

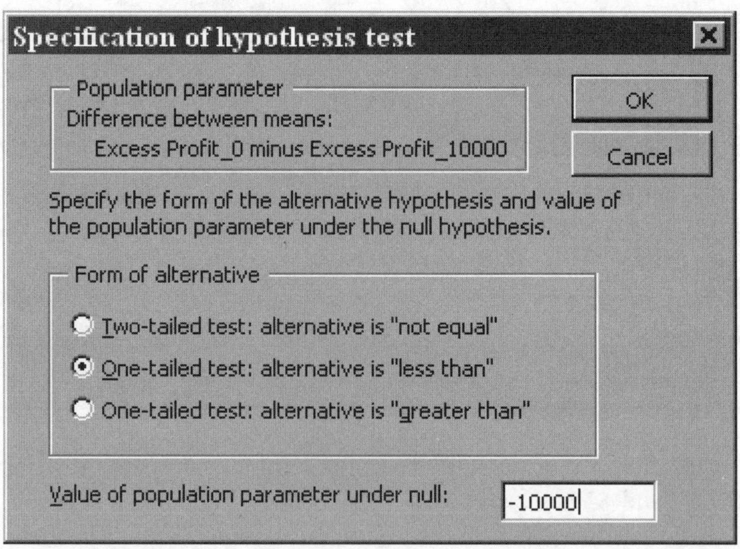

The unknown parameters here are the mean EP for the \$0 group and the mean EP for the \$10,000 group. Let's denote these by $\mu_{\$0}$ and $\mu_{\$10,000}$. The alternative hypothesis is always what we are tying to detect. We are trying to detect if we are in front so we hope that

$$\mu_{\$10,000} - \mu_{\$0} > 10,000.$$

But in terms of the reverse parameter assumed by StatproGo, we are trying to detect if

$$\mu_{\$0} - \mu_{\$10,000} < -10,000.$$

Therefore, in the dialog box, check the button "One-tailed test: alternative is less than" and put −10,000 in the "Value of population parameter under null" box.

The output is below. Make sure that you can recognize the mean EP difference, SEs, confidence limits, and *t*-statistic that we calculated above. There can be slight differences between the direct calculations above and the output of StatproGo. This is because StatproGo uses the so-called Student's *t*-distribution instead of the standard normal. For reasonable-sized data sets though, you should not see much difference. For instance, in the output below you will see that the 75% confidence limits differ only slightly from what we calculated above by \$1.

Two-sample analysis for Excess Profit_0 minus Excess Profit_10000		
Summary stats for two samples		
	Excess Profit_0	Excess Profit_10000
Sample sizes	23	18
Sample means	1382	13469
Sample standard deviations	1993	2854
Confidence interval for difference between means		
Confidence level	75.0%	
Sample mean difference	-12087	
Std error of difference	791	
Lower limit	-12997	
Upper limit	-11177	
Test of difference against -10000 versus 1-tailed alternative		
Hypothesized mean difference	-10000	
Sample mean difference	-12087	
Std error of difference	791	
t-test statistic	-2.64	
p-value	0.007	

Some additional output that is labeled "Test of equality of stdevs" is not displayed here but will be explained later.

11.5. DIFFERENT STANDARD DEVIATIONS

The main formula of this chapter is

$$\text{Std.Error}\left(\bar{X}_1 - \bar{X}_2\right) = \sqrt{\text{SE}^2(\bar{X}_1) + \text{SE}^2(\bar{X}_2)}.$$

Substituting the formulas for the SE of the two means gives the more explicit form

$$\text{Std.Error}\left(\bar{X}_1 - \bar{X}_2\right) = \sqrt{\frac{s_1^2}{n_1} + \frac{s_2^2}{n_2}},$$

where n_1 and n_2 are the two sample sizes and s_1 and s_2 are the standard deviations of the two samples. Many statistical packages use a different formula for the SE, based on an additional assumption.

The Classical *t*-Test

Suppose we knew that the true standard deviations of the two samples were equal—in other words there really is no difference in the underlying variability of the performance variable under the two sets of conditions. In this case, it seems strange to have two separate standard deviations in the formula. It would make more sense to rewrite the formula above as

$$\text{Std.Error}\left(\bar{X}_1 - \bar{X}_2\right) = \sqrt{\frac{s^2}{n_1} + \frac{s^2}{n_2}} = s\sqrt{\frac{1}{n_1} + \frac{1}{n_2}},$$

where s is now some single estimate of the assumed common variability of the performance measure. You might take the average of s_1 and s_2 for this. It turns out that a better estimate is

$$s = \sqrt{\frac{(n_1 - 1)s_1^2 + (n_2 - 1)s_2^2}{n_1 + n_2 - 2}}.$$

This is called the **pooled sample standard deviation** and it is a compromise between the standard deviation of the two samples (it will always be somewhere between the two). This gives a different *t*-statistic with a different standard error of the mean difference on the denominator. This statistic and the test based on it are often called the **classical *t*-test.**

EXAMPLE 2 (Continued) *Duo beverages*

We earlier calculated an SE of \$791 for the adjusted EP of \$12,087. This is a difference of two numbers each with errors. The mean \$13,496 was from $n_1 = 18$ stores with a standard deviation of \$2854 and the figure \$1382 was from $n_2 = 23$ stores with a standard deviation of \$1993. Using the above formula the pooled sample standard deviation is

$$s = \sqrt{\frac{(18-1)\times 2854^2 + (23-1)\times 1993^2}{18+23}} = \$2376$$

and so the error in the \$12,087 difference is

$$\$2376\sqrt{\frac{1}{18}+\frac{1}{23}} = \$747$$

instead of the previous figure of $791.

In most cases, there is very little difference between results using the classical or nonclassical SE. The only time there is a difference is when the two standard deviations are very different—precisely when the assumption of equal variability would be suspect! So when the results differ, the nonclassical answer is to be believed. You might legitimately wonder why anyone would use the classical test. There is a philosophical objection too. If you suspect that mean performance might be different in the two groups then why would you assume that the variability is the same?

Nevertheless, the classical method is the standard method in most textbooks and appears in most common software. The method that does not assume equal variability is to be preferred. StatproGo does not perform the classical *t*-test. It has only been included in the book for completeness.

Sample Sizes

If you are trying to detect a change in mean performance then you would like the standard error of the mean difference to be as small as possible. The formula

$$\text{Std.Error}\left(\bar{X}_1-\bar{X}_2\right)=\sqrt{\frac{s_1^2}{n_1}+\frac{s_2^2}{n_2}}$$

gives a clue how to do this. You would obviously like the standard deviations s_1 and s_2 to be as small as possible. This is determined by the variability of your performance measure. It may well be worth trying to reduce the variability of your performance measure, but you would not do this simply to reduce the SE of your data analysis! The only other numbers in the formula are the sample sizes. These might well be worth choosing since they are part of your data collection process.

The formula above implies that you should choose sample sizes in proportion to the variability of the two samples. For instance, if you were only going to collect 120 data values and if you thought the performance measure was twice as variable in one group as the other then you would take 80 samples from the more variable group and 40 from the less variable group.

In general if you are going to collect n_{TOTAL} samples and if you know the standard deviation of the two groups then you should choose samples sizes

$$n_1 = n_{\text{TOTAL}} \times \frac{s_1}{s_1+s_2}, \quad n_2 = n_{\text{TOTAL}} \times \frac{s_2}{s_1+s_2}.$$

The same principle works for more than two groups. If you want to allocate your total sampling effort across several groups and you know, or have a rough idea, of the standard deviations for each group then the number of samples you should allocate to each group is

$$n_{\text{GROUP}} = n_{\text{TOTAL}} \times \frac{\text{stdev of group}}{\text{total of all stdevs}}.$$

EXAMPLE 3

You want to measure customer satisfaction across five different age groups on a 1–10 scale and you will be ultimately interested in comparing all the different age groups. Past surveys suggest that there is more variability in the response of younger customers. In fact the last survey gave the following results:

Group	21-29	31-39	41-49	51-59	60+
Stdev	3.76	2.33	2.10	1.87	2.36

You have a budget to survey 1500 customers and the ability to target customers in different age groups from customer records. The total of the standard deviation is 12.42. Express each standard deviation as a percentage of this total, in the row "%" in the table below. This gives the percentage of the 1500 surveys that should be allocated to each age group.

Group	21-29	31-39	41-49	51-59	60+	Total
Stdev	3.76	2.33	2.10	1.87	2.36	12.42
%	30.3%	18.8%	16.9%	15.1%	19.0%	100%
Number	454	281	254	226	285	1500

CHECK YOUR UNDERSTANDING

Q2. What is the yearly depreciation on the sale price of a Mitsubishi Magna? In Q1, you calculated the estimates and SEs below. The SE of 350.92 was calculated without the equal variance assumption.

	Number	Mean	Std. Dev
2 years	27	$18,550	$1560
3 years	38	$15,680	$1120

(a) Recalculate the SE under the equal variance assumption.

(b) What does the equal variance assumption mean in this context?

(c) With the benefit of hindsight, if you were going to the trouble of gathering data on 65 sales, what would have been a better allocation of the 65 samples to the two groups and how much of a difference would this have made?

Testing Standard Deviation

One will occasionally be specifically interested in whether an intervention affects variability of performance rather than mean performance. In other words the parameters of interest will be the standard deviations σ_1 and σ_2 under the two sets of conditions, not the means.

StatproGo automatically outputs information about the standard deviations of the two samples. Returning to the earlier example where we were comparing \$10K spend on EP compared with \$0K spend on PP, the output below includes a test of the equality of the standard deviations of the two samples. This output is always produced, regardless of whether you ask StatproGo to calculate a test, or a CI, or both.

The main statistic of interest is the ratio of the standard deviations. Here the standard deviation of the \$10K data is a factor 1.432 higher than the standard deviation of the \$0K data (because 2854/1993 = 1.432). The *p*-value of 0.125 just below this measures how unlikely it is that this would occur by chance. The smaller this *p*-value, the less likely it is that one would see the standard deviations being as different as they are if the true standard deviations are in fact the same. If the *p*-value is sufficiently small, then you may conclude that the true standard deviations σ_1 and σ_2 are not the same.

Two-sample analysis for Excess Profit_0 minus Excess Profit_10000		
Summary stats for two samples		
	Excess Profit_0	Excess Profit_10000
Sample sizes	23	18
Sample means	1382	13469
Sample standard deviations	1993	2854
Test of equality of stdevs		
Ratio of sample stdevs	1.432	
p-value	0.125	

11.6. Analyzing Matched-Pairs Data

A furniture retailer wants to assess customer reaction to sales staff. They are specifically interested in whether staff might be more or less effective with male or female customers. In many cases, sales staff deal with husband–wife pairs. On 45 randomly selected occasions, a married couple is interviewed about their reactions to the sales experience but the husband and wife are surveyed separately. Are sales staff more effective with males or females?

We would naturally look at the average satisfaction of the males, the average satisfaction of the females, and subtract one from the other. We could calculate an SE and then do a test or make a CI for the mean difference. There is a special feature of the data, though, that makes the SE formula used so far in this chapter *completely wrong*. The reason is there is a natural pairing of the two data sets because males and females are married pairs. It is very easy to spot this situation (if you just take 5 s to think about it) and the alternative analysis is also very easy. In fact, it is an analysis that you have already done in the last chapter.

What Are Matched Pairs?

Husband and wife are interviewed separately and their score recorded on a scale of 1–50. Each of the 45 occasions involved a different salesperson and couple.

Data are matched pairs if...they come in pairs! It will not always be as obvious as a married couple. You can immediately know if you have matched pairs by asking yourself, "Does this number go with the number next to it, or do they just happen to be sitting next to each other in the spreadsheet?" For a start, this will only be possible when the two groups have the same number of observations. When they do have the same number, which is quite common, you may have to stop and ask the question above.

The file ex4 (couples).xls contains the survey results for the furniture store. If you look at the data you can see that each pair of numbers in Columns B and C is a married pair. If it was not made obvious in the spreadsheet then you would need to ask more about the nature of the data, to identify if they were paired. You might expect husbands and wives to give similar satisfaction ratings, since they are not only married but have just both experienced the same interaction with sales staff. If you plot the satisfaction of wives against that of their husband then you do see a strong positive relationship.

After reading this chapter so far you would probably think of testing whether the mean satisfaction for husbands is greater than the mean satisfaction for wives using the methods described earlier. You would calculate the mean and standard deviation for husbands and wives. Using the sample size of $n = 45$ you would calculate an SE for each. The difference in the mean levels of satisfaction turns out to be very small. For husbands the mean score is 41.71 and for wives it is 41.04, a difference of only 0.667.

You would then need an SE for the 0.667 figure. You might be tempted to calculate

	Husband	Wife	Difference
Number	45	45	
Mean	41.71	41.04	0.667
Std.Dev	3.31	2.86	
Std.Error	0.494	0.426	??

$$\text{Stdev}(\bar{X}_{\text{HUSBANDS}} - \bar{X}_{\text{WIVES}}) = \sqrt{\{\text{SE}(\bar{X}_{\text{HUSBANDS}})\}^2 + \{\text{SE}(\bar{X}_{\text{WIVES}})\}^2}$$
$$= \sqrt{0.494^2 + 0.426^2} = 0.653$$

and conclude that the observed difference of 0.667 is very similar to the intrinsic error of 0.653, and so there is no clear difference. You would be *wrong* to calculate SE this way. Let's see why.

Why the Usual SE Formula Is Wrong

The formula for the SE of a difference of means was based on the basic result for the variability of the difference of any two quantities. It was expressed as:

> For any two *independent* variables X_1 and X_2
>
> $$\text{Stdev}(X_1 - X_2) = \sqrt{\sigma_1^2 + \sigma_2^2}.$$

The key phrase in this statement is "two *independent* variables." If the two variables are *dependent* then all bets are off. For instance, if one variable tends to be higher or lower when the other is higher or lower then the variability of the difference would be less, potentially much less, than this formula predicts. This is exactly what we have with husbands and wives. The variability of the 0.667 figure is actually much less than 0.653. This is good news from the point of view of analyzing the data and getting a clear conclusion.

How You Analyze Matched Pairs

If we are interested in the difference between husband and wife responses, why not just look at the difference directly? For each couple we have two measurements, the husband rating and the wife rating. So for each couple we can calculate the husband's score minus the wife's score. For instance for couple 1, the husband's rating was 41, the wife's rating was 38, so there was a higher rating of 3 units for the husband than the wife. For the second couple the husband gave a rating 2 units lower than the wife.

Husband	Wife	Diff
41	38	3
33	35	-2
41	43	-2
38	39	-1
43	41	2
--	--	--
--	--	--

This gives us a single set of 45 numbers; each represents how much higher the husband scores the salesperson than the wife. A negative value means the wife scores higher than the husband.

We then want to know which of the following two hypotheses are true:

Alternative (H_1): There is an underlying tendency for husbands to give higher ratings than wives. This means the mean difference in scores is positive.

Null (H_0): There is no underlying tendency for husbands and wives to give different ratings. This means the mean difference in scores is zero.

The 45 differences are in Column C in the spreadsheet. The average of this column is 0.667. The point is that this 0.667 arises from an average of a single column of numbers. *This is now a one-sample problem!* We can use the methods of the last chapter to test whether the mean of a variable—here the excess satisfaction rating of husbands over wives—deviates from zero. So the relevant formula for the SE is

$$\text{Stdev}\left(\bar{X}_{\text{difference}}\right) = s / \sqrt{n},$$

where s is the standard deviation of the differences. Using the function STDEV on Column C, you will find that the standard deviation is 2.164 and so the SE of the 0.667 figure is

$$2.165 / \sqrt{45} = 0.323,$$

which is less than half of the 0.653 figure we mistakenly calculated earlier. The 0.667 difference now looks much more reliable. It appears that husbands *do* react more positively than wives. The difference may be very small but it is not due to chance.

General Method

In general, whenever you have matched pairs you should combine the pair of measurements into a single measurement. The most common way to do this is to calculate the simple difference of the two numbers. Another common way is to calculate the percent difference between the two values—though this leaves a choice of which of the two numbers to use for the denominator.

StatproGo will perform a matched-pairs analysis using the simple difference. Choose StatproGo, then Statistical Inference, and then Paired Sample Analysis.

Check Your Understanding

Q3. In each case described below, would a one-sample matched pairs or a two-sample procedure be appropriate? Give a general description of the correct analysis.

(a) A manager is going to be evaluated by the profit growth he or she has overseen and whether or not profit growth is in line with the industry average of 4.5%. There are 33 stores that have been under the manager's control during the past year and you have data on the profit in the previous year and the profit in this year. The average profit last year was \$1,255,655 per store. The average profit this year was \$1,304,555 per store.

(b) A second manager is being compared with the first. This second manager is in charge of 45 stores and these have their profit growth measured. The average profit growth for the 45 stores is 4.81% compared with an average profit growth of 4.26% for the first manager. How much better has the second manager performed?

(c) A supermarket surveys 100 customers on satisfaction. The average result on a standard 1–5 scale is 3.89. A week after an employee retreat on customer focus, 100 further customers are surveyed. The average result is 3.97. Was the training effective in increasing customer satisfaction?

(d) The fuel efficiency of 625 cars in your rental fleet is measured. The average value is 10.75 L/100 km. They are all services and their fuel efficiency is checked. The mean is 10.24 L/100 km.

11.7. SUMMARY

We often want to compare how a business performance variable X differs between two sets of conditions. For instance, how does company profit/revenue/sales performance differ before/after an advertising campaign, and how does customer reaction differ between two demographic groups?

We measure the difference between conditions by the difference in the mean outcome $\mu_1 - \mu_2$ and estimate this by the difference in the sample means. If the two samples are independent then the SE of the difference in sample means is given by

$$\text{Std.Error}\ (\bar{X}_1 - \bar{X}_2) = \sqrt{\{\text{SE}(\bar{X}_1)\}^2 + \{\text{SE}(\bar{X}_2)\}^2}$$

This is called the **two-sample** SE. This SE can be used to test whether the mean difference $\mu_1 - \mu_2$ differs from a benchmark value. The t-statistic is

$$t = \frac{\bar{X}_1 - \bar{X}_2 - \text{benchmark}}{\text{SE}(\bar{X}_1 - \bar{X}_2)}$$

and measures how much the difference in sample means deviates from the benchmark in statistical units. In many cases, you want to test whether the means differ at all and so the benchmark is zero. The p-value is calculated from the t-value exactly as for the one-sample problem—just use the normal distribution. The p-value is used the same way in all cases—reject the null hypothesis if the p-value is less than the chosen significance level.

The SE of the difference in means can also be used to create a CI for $\mu_1 - \mu_2$, which has the form

$$\bar{X}_1 - \bar{X}_2 \pm Q \times \text{SE}(\bar{X}_1 - \bar{X}_2),$$

where Q is chosen to be larger for more confidence. Values of Q for different levels of confidence were given in the previous chapter.

Data are **matched pairs** when each number in one sample pairs with a number in the other sample. Data like these should *not* be analyzed using the two-sample t-test. Instead you should combine each pair of measurements into a single measurement that measures the effect you are interested in—most often some kind of difference or ratio of the two numbers. You can then use **one-sample methods** on the resulting single column of numbers.

In Excel StatproGo, select the menu Statistical Inference and then either Two-Sample Analysis or Paired Sample Analysis.

EXERCISES

E1. In 2002, term 1, I had 155 students enrolled in my course. The raw exam scores had a mean of 69% and a standard deviation of 6.7%. In term 2, I taught the same course with the same assessment tasks to 77 part-time students. The raw exam scores had a mean of 75% and a standard deviation of 9.9%.

(a) What would you say about a person who scored 77% in term 1? How would this change if the same score was attained in term 2? (Use z-scores.)

(b) Is there really any difference in the underlying mean level of the two classes? How sure are you?

(c) How might your answer to (b) affect the way you scaled the final marks?

E2. I have 1 year of weekly data on the number of defective components per thousand supplied to a customer. The mean is 7.7, the standard deviation is 4.6, and the standard error of the mean is 0.638. The benchmark defective rate is 8.5.

(a) Explain, in words that would be understood by a nonexpert, what the 4.6 and 0.638 figures tell us.

(b) What assumptions underlie the interpretation of the figures in part (a)?

(c) Is the customer receiving better than the benchmark? Since 7.7 is less than 8.5, is this a question even worth asking?

(d) Suppose that the 8.5 figure comes from last year's database across 28 customers, and includes $28 \times 52 = 1456$ recorded defective counts per 1000, the average of which was 8.5 and the standard deviation of which was 5.1. Is the customer receiving better quality than last year?

E3. In each case, samples from two populations are described. Specify the hypotheses you would test, calculate the t value and, if necessary, calculate a p-value.

(a) Sample 1 of size 50 has a mean of 6.75 and a standard deviation of 2.25. Sample 2 of size 75 has a mean of 5.98 and a standard deviation of 3.26. You want to detect whether the true mean of population 1 is larger than that of population 2.

(b) Sample 1 of size 500 has a mean of 123.6 and a standard deviation of 12.2. Sample 2 of size 20 has a mean of 128.9 and a standard deviation of 13.7. You want to detect whether the true means of the two populations differ.

(c) Sample 1 of size 45 has a mean of 0.77 and a standard deviation of 0.023. Sample 2 of size 35 has a mean of 0.68 and a standard deviation of 0.042. You want to detect whether the true mean of sample 1 is less than that of sample 2.

---

[1] They had been given a $10 discount voucher redeemable against their next bill, provided that they answer the second survey.

(d) Sample 1 of size 5 has a mean of 55.75 and a standard deviation of 4.32. Sample 2 of size 7 has a mean of 61.83 and a standard deviation of 5.68. You want to detect whether the true means of the two samples are different.

E4. In each case, samples from two populations are described. Calculate a CI for the mean with the indicated confidence level.

(a) Fifty customers in week 1 have an average satisfaction of 3.81 with a standard deviation of 1.31. Seventy-five customers in week 2 have an average satisfaction of 3.52 with a standard deviation of 0.96. What is the change in customer satisfaction with 90% confidence?

(b) Seventy-eight three-bedroom houses sold in Eastern Melbourne during January–February had an average sale price of $732K with a standard deviation of $121K. During the same period and over the same region, 66 four-bedroom houses had an average sale price of $866K with a standard deviation of $164K. What is the difference in mean value of a four- and three-bedroom house? Make a statement with 95% confidence.

(c) One hundred and forty customers sampled during normal times at a supermarket experienced an average waiting time of 5.014 min with a standard deviation of 4.293 min. Another 98 customers sampled at peak times (when there are both more customers but also more staff) experienced an average waiting time of 5.480 min with a standard deviation of 4.284 min. Make a statement about the extra waiting time experienced by customers at peak times that you can be 99% confident about.

E5. A company uses paint primer on metal frames to reduce rust. It is important that the thickness of the coat of the primer, when properly applied, should not be too thin or water may penetrate and cause rust. It is also important that it is not too thick or it will flake off and also be unsightly. It has been determined by experts that the most desirable paint thickness is 1.2 thousandths of an inch. A new method of applying the paint is being considered, which is hoped to be better than the existing method. A sample of 50 metal frames are treated with primer applied using the old method and another sample of 60 metal frames are treated with primer applied using the new method. The thickness is measured using a highly accurate laser technique.

(a) Does the standard method tend to result in coats of primer that are too thick?

(b) Does the standard method tend to result in coats that are thicker than those produced using the new method?

(c) Does the new method tend to result in coats of primer that are closer in thickness to the ideal than those produced using the standard method?

E6. The call center data are in Q6.xls. Suppose there is interest in comparing males to females. For the exercises below, practice using both StatproGo and Pivotables to do (part of) the calculations.

(a) Give a 90% CI for the difference in mean rating of males and females.

(b) Give a 90% CI for the difference in mean service time of males and females.

(c) Give a 90% CI for the difference in mean holding time of males and females.

(d) Comparing male and female consultants rather than customers, evaluate the difference in service times of male and female consultants.

(e) Create a variable that measures whether the consultant and client are the *same gender*. Evaluate the difference in mean rating for these two groups.

(f) Why is the answer to (e) not a sensible way to check whether matching the gender of the customer and the consultant is a good idea? Perform a better analysis.

E7. As part of a market research exercise, randomly selected customers are asked to choose between one of two massage and manicure packages. To further tease out the difference in values, they are asked to mark how much they would pay for each of the packages on a line marked $0–$50. The marks are then coded into numbers to the nearest dollar. The data for 45 customers are in Q7.xls.

(a) Are these data matched pairs or not? How would you know?

(b) Calculate the mean and standard deviation of the dollar amounts for each package. Create a data distribution for both packages and put them on one chart.

(c) Give a 75% CI for the difference in the dollar values of the two packages.

(d) How many of the customers preferred package 1? Supposing for the sake of argument that there is no difference in the values of the two packages, how likely is it that this would occur by chance?

E8. Worksheet Q8.xls contains survey results of customer satisfaction with their experience at a call center, measured on a 10-point scale, with 10 being the best rating possible. The benchmark value for mean customer satisfaction is 6.0 and it is the aim of the management that the underlying mean should not fall below this level. An individual customer rating of 4 or lower is considered particularly undesirable, as other research suggests you are highly likely to ultimately lose such customers.

There were three surveys. The first was of 500 randomly selected customers. For this first survey, your mean is 6.15, slightly above the benchmark. Nevertheless, soon after this survey was completed, you sent your staff on a training course in customer relations, and 1 month later a second survey of 250 customers was taken. Finally, some time after that, staff were required to take a second training course to consolidate the learning outcomes of the first course. The same 250 customers from survey 2 were surveyed a second time[1] to gauge their reaction

(a) Before the first training course, how strong is the evidence that your call center was performing better than the benchmark in mean satisfaction?

(b) After the first training course, how strong is the evidence that your call center was performing better than the benchmark in mean satisfaction?

(c) How much did the first training course increase mean customer satisfaction? Give an estimate and a measure of reliability.

(d) How much did the second training course further increase mean customer satisfaction over the first course? Are you even sure that it had an effect?

(e) How much effect did the first training course have on the proportion of your customers who rate you at level 4 or lower?

E9. A power company has 133 main transformers in their grid. There is inevitably some loss of power when it is transformed to a different voltage and this loss tends to increase over time unless the transformers are upgraded. The upgrade involves a combination of maintenance, repair, and replacement of components where necessary. One expects that power loss will decrease after upgrade but it is possible that power loss for a particular machine can be worse after upgrade.

There are two upgrade protocols called A and B. The difference between these two protocols is technical and involves the target outputs of various components within the system and the tolerances that should be assumed. These technical details are not important for you to answer this question. But we are interested in how the two protocols perform in practice.

The operations manager selected 75 machines to be upgraded using protocol A and the remaining 58 machines to be upgraded using protocol B. The efficiency of the machines is measured before and after the upgrade. Efficiency is a measure of the extent to which the machine minimizes power loss. An efficiency of 100 represents the efficiency of a brand new machine operating at peak level. However, it is possible for the efficiency of a particular machine to be greater than 100.

There is further interest in measuring the effect of a so-called extended upgrade to a machine that involves more thorough maintenance, repair, and replacement of worn components than a standard upgrade. The machines have been given an extended upgrade following their standard upgrade and the efficiency was measured again.

The worksheet Q9.xls has the efficiency data for all 133 machines. There are three measurements. Initial is the efficiency before the upgrade. Standard is the efficiency after the standard upgrade. Extended is the efficiency after the extended upgrade. For example, the machine with ID = 23 began with 92% efficiency, which increased to 98.7% after upgrade using protocol A and further increased to 100% when given the extended upgrade using protocol A.

(a) What is the effect of upgrade protocol A on the mean efficiency? How sure are you that the upgrade is effective at all?

(b) What is the effect of upgrade protocol B on the mean efficiency? How sure are you that the upgrade is effective at all?

(c) After the standard upgrade using protocol A, what is the effect on the mean efficiency of the extended upgrade?

(d) After the standard upgrade using protocol B, what is the effect on the mean efficiency of the extended upgrade?

(e) What evidence is there for a difference in the effect of the standard upgrade with protocol A compared to the standard upgrade with protocol B?

E10. You have been asked to analyze the performance of two leading coffee shop chains that are considering merging. Toward the potential merger, the two chains are keen to provide evidence of higher revenue, profitability, and continuous growth. You have collected data on the quarterly revenue for different shops across the chains.

The worksheet Q10.xls has observations on the different shops in Victoria. The names of the two chains involved are suppressed here for confidentiality reasons, but the first 75 are from the chain labeled A, and the next 58 are from another chain labeled B. The quarterly revenue in Australian dollars was observed for both chains in the first quarter (Q1), second quarter (Q2), and third quarter (Q3) of 2008.

For example, shop ID = 1 belongs to chain A and had a revenue of $801.8K in Q1, $896.49K in Q2, and $882.97K in Q3.

(a) What is the change in mean revenue for chain A between Q1 and Q2? What is the uncertainty in this estimate? How sure are you that this is a real difference?

(b) What is the change in mean revenue for chain B between Q1 and Q2? What is the uncertainty in this estimate? How sure are you that this is a real difference?

(c) With 90% confidence, what change is there in the mean revenue for chain A between Q2 and Q3?

(d) What evidence is there that chain B had a higher mean revenue than chain A in Q1?

(e) Assess the evidence for the proposition that the increase in revenue between Q1 and Q2 was larger than that between Q2 and Q3 for chain A.

CHAPTER 12

What Is My Brand Recognition? Will It Sell? Analyzing Counts and Proportions

12.0. Introduction: What Is The Issue?

How do the purchasing habits of male and female customers differ? The standard way to look at this would be to compare the mean purchase of males and females using the methods of the previous chapter. The *mean*, though, does not tell you much about extremely high and low purchasers and how this might relate to gender. One way to look at this would be to divide the data into different levels of purchase—for instance the highest 10%, the next highest 10%, and down to the lowest 10%—and then look at the numbers of males and females in each group. The key numbers, then, would be the *percentages* of males and females. Gender is not a number, though. It is an attribute.

There are many business variables that are non-numeric. Rather, the variable is something that is true or false, that is present or absent, and that requires a yes or no answer. Gender is one example but there are many others. Can customers name your brand without prompting? Are they satisfied? Do they prefer Coke to Pepsi? Was the item defective? Did the seller of a car secure the servicing contract? Did my product sell at this price? Do you agree with the proposition? This chapter is about analyzing this kind of non-numeric "yes–no" data.

The analysis of "yes–no" data is slightly different from the analysis of a numeric outcome such as revenue or sales. For a start, it does not immediately make sense to talk about mean gender, let alone the standard deviation of gender! It makes much more sense to count up the number of males and females and to report these as proportions or percentages. With our focus, then, on *proportions* rather than on means,

Data-Driven Business Decisions, First Edition. Chris J. Lloyd.

most of the ideas from the last chapter carry through—ideas such as standard errors (SEs), confidence intervals, SE of a difference, null and alternative hypotheses, and *t*-statistics.

GATORADE VERSUS POWERADE: CASE BRIEFING

Brands are worth money. Brand recognition is a measure of the extent to which customers think of your brand with no other prompting than being told to consider a general product category.

Gatorade conducted regular surveys on their brand recognition in Australia, as well as the brand recognition of their main competitor—PowerAde. The survey involved asking the customer to name any products that came to mind when they are told the product category "Sports Drinks." Roughly 100 customers are surveyed by phone each week, which adds up to a large sample of around 5000 per year.

During the 2008 summer holidays (January and February) there was a series of advertisements that appeared during major sporting telecasts such as the Test cricket series and the Australian Open Tennis.

Hans Refsing is a market research analyst employed by Pepsi Australia. He is looking at a spreadsheet that has data for the last 8 weeks of 2007. Following up on the 2008 advertising campaigning, Hans has also extracted data for the first quarter of 2008.

Hans has been asked to address several issues. First and foremost, he is asked to summarize the 2007 data into a simple table or chart. The key issue is to put a range on the brand recognition of Gatorade and PowerAde and also to compare the two products. Second, he is to produce a chart that shows how Gatorade brand recognition has varied over this 13-week period. Looking at the resulting chart there are some fairly stark changes over the period. From a peak of 86% in mid-February, Gatorade brand recognition seems to have declined steadily to 71% but has bounced back by 10% the last week.

What is driving these movements? Before giving an interpretation of these trends and looking deeper for the reasons, he needs to assess the changes statistically and also assess the general levels of brand recognition compared with what it was last year.

Further details of the background are available in the full case.

12.1. How Accurate Are Percentages?

How often have you heard a claim like "78% of survey respondents accept the proposition that human activity is the major contributor to global warming ..."? If you are lucky, then the statement might be followed by "... with a 2% margin of error."

In earlier chapters, we had numeric performance measures on n independent individuals. For instance, we might measure the satisfaction or total purchases of a sample of customers; we might measure the sale price of 108 apartments; or we might measure the stock returns on 250 consecutive trading days in a financial year.

In this chapter, we suppose that we measure a **binary attribute**, rather than a numeric variable. Some attributes are inherently binary like gender. Another example is whether or not a customer can spontaneously name your brand. Binary attributes can also arise from ordinal or numeric measurements. For instance, we might record *whether or not* customers respond 4 or 5 on a 5-point scale, classifying these as satisfied; we might record *whether or not* each of 108 apartments sold for more than the reserve price; or we might record *whether or not* today's return on a stock was greater than the market return. So an original numeric measurement can become binary if we decide to look at it that way.

The general formulation is that we have n measurements of a binary attribute of interest, such as a customer's response to the question, "Are you satisfied with your sales experience?" We count how many y have the attribute out of n. You might like to think of y as standing for "Yes, they have the attribute." So the data here are very simple—much simpler than a column of numeric measurements. We simply have two numbers—y and n.

EXAMPLE 1 *Call center data*

The M-Tel call center data have been well described in earlier chapters. The main performance variable was customer satisfaction on a standard 1–5 scale. We also had the time in seconds that the customer was kept on hold, the time in seconds they spoke to an operator, and their gender.

One issue we examined was the extent to which time spent on hold affects their ultimate satisfaction with the call center experience. The standard way to look at this would be to divide the data up into different holding time groups and see how *mean* satisfaction varied across these groups. We would expect to see mean satisfaction decrease as holding time increased.

How Does Holding Time Affect Customer Positivity?

However, the management were especially interested in whether customers have a genuinely positive experience or not. So they classified a response of 4 or 5 as positive and a response of 1–3 as not positive. The worksheet *EMS data* in ex1 (call centre).xls has a column "positive," which uses the IF function to recode the satisfaction rating as 1 if the rating is greater than 3 (i.e., 4 or 5) and as 0 if otherwise. With this binary attribute as our chosen success measure, we would want to look at the *proportion* of customers who responded positively and examine how this varies across the different holding time groups.

It is easy to use Pivotables to break the data up by the rating being positive or not. Out of $n = 1120$ customers, $y = 557$ gave a positive satisfaction rating. As a percentage this is 49.7%—almost exactly half. You should immediately wonder how reliable this figure is. If means are variable then surely so are proportions. We can use Pivotables to further break the data into different holding times. We use the grouping facility to group times into 60-s intervals. In the table below, the holding times over 3 min have been joined into a single group "Over 3 min."

	0-1 mins	1-2 mins	2-3 mins	over 3 mins	Overall
Positive	212	273	61	11	557
Number	330	542	193	55	1120
%	64.2%	50.4%	31.6%	20.0%	49.7%

The proportion of positive responses is well over 50% for those who had the shortest holding time, but way less than 50% for those who had to wait over 3 min before being answered.

The Data-Generating Mechanism

Each individual either has the attribute or not. The key number, then, is the probability p that an individual has the attribute. The number p is unknown and is the focus of our interest, in the same way that the unknown mean μ was our focus in previous chapters. You can think of p as the underlying, or true, or trend, or fundamental probability of an individual having the attribute.

The data-generating mechanism (DGM) may be very complex. For instance, if the binary attribute is whether or not supermarket customers are satisfied then the business process that generates a satisfied or unsatisfied customer includes how the customer came to arrive in the store and be surveyed, the day of the week, the attitudes of the check-out staff, the weather, and the customer's mood. The fundamental parameter p describes the bottom line of this process as the overall probability a customer will be satisfied.

In other cases, the DGM may be very simple and we can give p a clearer interpretation. For instance, we might randomly sample a known database of our customers during the last 12 months and record "M" if they are male. In this case, the probability p that a customer has the attribute is equal to the proportion of males in the customer database or "population."

Even in many market surveys, we do not have a clearly defined population of customers that we sample. Moreover, the attribute measured is not something that is fixed liked gender. The same customer may be satisfied today but very unsatisfied tomorrow. So the proportion of the population with the attribute may be different tomorrow.

The common interpretation of p given in traditional textbooks, as *the proportion of the population with the attribute* will, in most business contexts, not hold much water. As with the mean, you are better of thinking about p as the unknown, fundamental, or trend probability of the attribute.

SE of a Proportion

The key to the SE formula for a proportion (to be given below) is that individuals are **independent**, just as it was important in previous chapters. For instance, if we were sampling customers who were in the same family about whether or not they recognize a particular brand, then the methods of this chapter could not be used without considerable modification.

The key to understanding data that come in the form of counts is the **binomial** distribution. Since each individual will either have or not have the attribute, and since the individual responses are independent, the binomial distribution describes the probability distribution of the number of individuals y that have the attribute of interest out of the sample of n. The number of individuals n is known but the probability of a "success" p isn't.

Even though p is unknown there is an obvious way to estimate it—by the proportion of individuals in the sample who have the attribute, that is, y out of n expressed as a proportion or percentage. This is denoted by

$$\hat{p} = y/n$$

This is the first example of a notation that we will find useful in later chapters. The p with a "hat" above denotes a data-based estimate of the unknown quantity beneath the "hat," in this case p. In the same spirit, an alternative notation for the sample mean would be $\hat{\mu}$. The sample standard deviation s could be denoted $\hat{\sigma}$, since it is a data-based estimate of the unknown true standard deviation σ. How good an estimate of the fundamental p is the sample proportion $\hat{p}$?

Since y is binomial its mean is np. So the mean of y/n must be p. This means that the sample proportion with an attribute is an unbiased estimate of the true probability p of having the attribute. It does not tend to be systematically too high or low. It would be pretty strange if this was not the case! This is a minimal requirement and does not mean that it is a particularly good estimate. So how accurate is it as an estimator of p? Recall that the variance of y, which has a binomial distribution, is $np(1 - p)$. So the standard deviation of $\hat{p}$ is

$$\text{Stdev}(\hat{p}) = \frac{\text{Stdev}(y)}{n} = \frac{\sqrt{np(1-p)}}{n} = \sqrt{\frac{p(1-p)}{n}}.$$

This formula describes how far the sample proportion $\hat{p}$ varies about its mean p. Notice that there is a $\sqrt{n}$ on the denominator so again we have the principle that to double the accuracy you will need four times the sample.

The formula in its present form is not ready for use, because it involves the unknown p. So we replace p by its estimate.

The SE of a proportion is calculated as

$$\text{Std.Error } (\hat{p}_1 - \hat{p}_2) = \sqrt{\{\text{SE}(\hat{p}_1)\}^2 + \{\text{SE}(\hat{p}_2)\}^2}$$

It measures the intrinsic measurement error in any sample proportion.

This is the key formula for this chapter. The reason for the "$n - 1$" in the denominator is not important. It is closely related to the "$n - 1$" in the formula for a sample standard deviation. The rough reason is that for a sample of $n = 1$ you cannot assess variability and so the sample size only starts to "count" from $n = 2$. This makes almost no difference to the calculated value, of course.

EXAMPLE 1 (Continued) *Call center data*

The proportion giving a positive response was 557/1120 = 49.7%. The intrinsic error in this figure is measured by

$$\text{Std.Error}(\hat{p}) = \sqrt{\frac{0.497(1-0.497)}{1120-1}} = 0.0149,$$

so the intrinsic error in the 49.7% figure is 1.49%. If we think of 2 SEs on either side as defining a plausible range of variation then a plausible range for the fundamental probability of customer satisfaction is roughly 50% plus or minus 3%. This is a range of 6%, rather wide considering there are 1120 customers that have been sampled. You will find throughout this chapter that the accuracy is rather disappointing, as soon as we focus attention on binary attributes rather than numeric performance measures.

We earlier broke the data down into different holding times and within each group we can calculate the proportion of customers who are satisfied. The proportions are in the table below and seem to systematically decrease as the holding time increases. Each of these figures has its own intrinsic variability. We might expect that the percentages will be more reliable if they are calculated from a larger number of customers. For instance, the 11/55 = 20% figure would be the least reliable since it is based on only 55 customers.

	0-1 mins	1-2 mins	2-3 mins	over 3 mins	Overall
Positive	212	273	61	11	557
Number	330	542	193	55	1120
%	64.2%	50.4%	31.6%	20.0%	49.7%
SE	2.64%	2.15%	3.36%	5.44%	1.49%
Low	61.6%	48.2%	28.3%	14.6%	48.2%
High	66.9%	52.5%	35.0%	25.4%	51.2%

Using the SE formula for each subgroup gives the SEs listed in the table. For instance, for the "Over 3 min" group we calculate

$$\text{Std.Error}(\hat{p}) = \sqrt{\frac{0.20(1-0.20)}{55-1}} = 0.0544,$$

which is indeed the largest of the SEs, mainly because the least customers were in this group. A nice way to represent these data is to plot the proportions with 1 SE on either side. The proportion minus 1 SE is called "low" in the above table and the estimate plus 1 SE is called "high."

This plot conveys very simply not only the consistent way in which longer holding times lead to lower proportions of satisfied customers. It tells you how strong the effect is (positive responses reduce from 64% to 20%) as well as the error in each point on the plot. The calculations for all SEs and the plot are on the worksheet *holding*1.

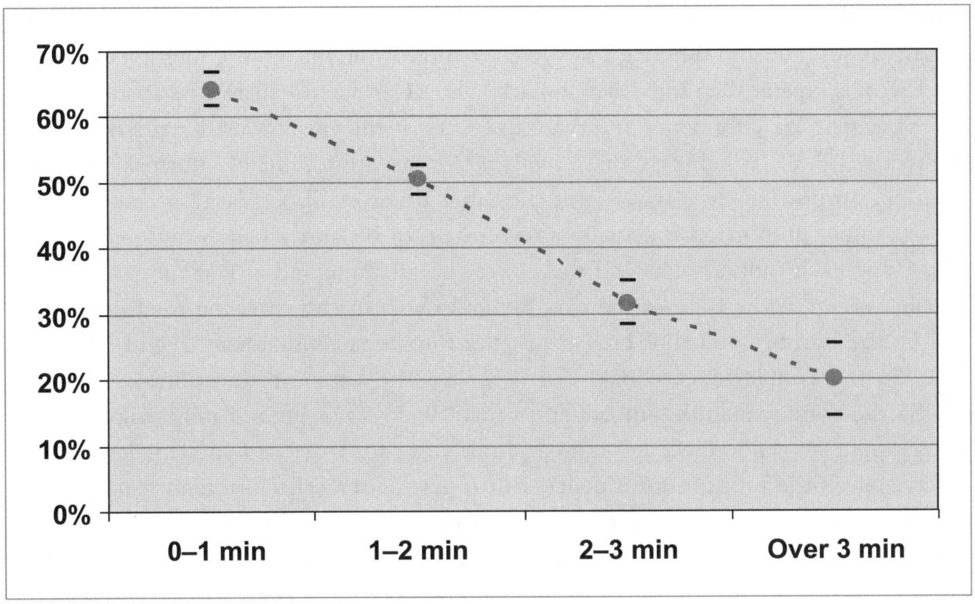

CHECK YOUR UNDERSTANDING

Q1. From 12,546 Ford Falcons sold in 2007, 2335 were returned for repairs under the 3-year warranty and 1234 were returned more than once. *Give estimates and SEs relevant to the situation and the questions below.*

(a) What is the probability that a car will be returned for repair?

(b) What is the probability that a car will be returned for repair more than once?

(c) Of those cars that are returned at least once, what proportion of cars is properly repaired?

Q2. The call center data in Q2.xls describes 1120 customers to a call center. We are interested in the relationship between gender and service time. Imagine breaking the 1120 customers into 10 groups of 112. The column "service_group" contains a label saying which decile of service time the customer was in. For instance, the lowest 112 service times have been labeled "1," the next 112 have been labeled "2," and so on. The longest 112 service times have been labeled "10."

(a) Use Pivotables to tell you how many males and females are in each service group. There are 112 customers in each of these groups.

(b) Report the proportion of males in each of these groups. There is an obvious trend in these figures. What does it mean in simple words?

(c) Report an SE for the proportions in part (b).

(d) Produce a graph that displays how the proportion of males decreases as the service time increases, and also shows the error bars 1 SE on either side of the estimate.

12.2. TESTS AND CONFIDENCE INTERVALS FOR PROPORTIONS

The sample proportion is supposed to estimate the unknown probability p. We have a simple formula for its SE. It would be nice if we could use SEs of proportions in the same way as SEs of means. For instance, we might want a 95% confidence interval for p. Can we just add and subtract 2 SEs like we did for the mean? We might want to test whether p is greater than some benchmark value. Can we calculate a t-statistic?

The basis for confidence intervals and tests of the mean was the **normal limit theorem** (NLT), which says that *sample means* are approximately normal. We have a sample proportion here that is not the same thing at all. Or is it?

A sample proportion *is* actually an average—of 0's and 1's. It is quite easy to see this. Code each individual as 1 if they have the attribute and as 0 if they don't. The sample average is the total of the data divided by n. In this case, the total of the data will be the number of 1's. Which is just the number of individuals Y with the attribute. So the sample mean equals Y/n, which is the sample proportion!

So the comment in the introduction that "It does not immediately make sense to talk about mean gender" was not quite right. If you code males as 1 and females as 0 then the average is the proportion of males. But it gets better. The formula for the SE of a sample mean also works for binary attribute data. You just treat the 0's and 1's like ordinary data. You calculate the sample standard deviation s of the 0's and 1's and then use the formula $s\sqrt{n}$. Lo and behold, this actually gives you the exactly the same answer as

$$\text{Stdev}(\hat{p}) = \sqrt{\frac{\hat{p}(1-\hat{p})}{n-1}}.$$

EXAMPLE 1 (Continued) *Call center data*

We earlier used Pivotables to divide the data into different holding time groups of 60 s and counted the number of positive and negative responses in each group. The results were in the worksheet *holding1*, where we also calculated SEs using the formula above.

Let's confirm that we can get the same answers using the formula $s\sqrt{n}$ for the standard error of the mean. This time, we will use Pivotables to calculate the average of the variable "positive" (which you recall are 1's and 0's) for each group, the standard deviation of this same positive variable (this is s in the discussion above), and the count of ID (which is the number of individuals n in each group). We can then calculate the standard error of the mean ($s\sqrt{n}$). The results are in the worksheet *holding2*. Pivotables creates groups of equal width and cannot create the larger holding time group for "Over 3 min." This was done manually.

You will see that the averages of the variable *positive* are exactly the sample proportions of positive customers that we calculated before and also that the SEs agree exactly with what we calculated earlier. The point being that the methods for means can be used for sample proportions as well. You could even use StatproGo on each holding group if you preferred.

Formulas for Tests and Confidence Intervals

We can use SEs in the by now familiar manner to both test and generate confidence intervals for the unknown fundamental of interest, here the unknown probability p that an individual has a binary attribute.

If we want a confidence interval for the unknown probability p then simply add and subtract the appropriate number of SEs to and from the estimate:

$$(\hat{p}-Q\times SE(\hat{p}), \hat{p}+Q\times SE(\hat{p})).$$

If we want to test whether or not the unknown probability p deviates from a benchmark p_0 then we calculate how far the sample proportion deviates from the benchmark in units of SEs, that is, we calculate

$$t=\frac{\text{estimate}-\text{benchmark}}{\text{SE(estimate)}}=\frac{\hat{p}-p_0}{SE(\hat{p})}$$

and convert this into a p-value as explained in the previous two chapters, that is, we ignore the sign of t and, provided it points in the expected direction, we calculate

$$=1-\text{NORMSDIST}(|t\text{-value}|).$$

What Does the SE Really Mean Again?

The data are generated by a mechanism that makes the individual presence or absence of the attribute unpredictable. This induces unpredictability in the sample proportion with the attribute. As with the sample mean, you may sometimes be deceived into thinking that the sample proportion is a fixed number. But it could easily be different if, for instance, different individuals had been chosen for your sample.

The spreadsheet NLT_proportions.xls is designed to aid your understanding of why a proportion is variable and how the SE formula describes this variation. The spreadsheet allows you to set a true proportion p with the attribute. For instance the attribute might be brand recognition. You can also select a size for your sample. The spreadsheet will then generate a sample of individuals who do or do not have the attribute, calculate the proportion and its SE, and display the sample proportion on a graph. You will find that the sample proportion is mostly within 1 SE of the true proportion p and nearly always within 2 SEs. You will also find that the SE in cell E4 is always very close to the standard deviation in cell E8. Remember that the difference between these two is that the SE uses the best estimate of p in place of the unknown true p.

The fact that these variations follow the normal distribution cannot be easily seen. However, if you generate 100 samples you should find that around 68 times the proportion will be within 1 SE and that around 95 times, the proportion will be within 2 SEs. The values 68% and 95% are characteristic of the normal distribution.

EXAMPLE 1 (Continued) *Call center data*

If we want 75% confidence intervals for the true probability p of a customer being satisfied then we add and subtract $Q = 1.15$ SEs to and from the sample proportion. The results for each holding time group are in the table below and coded in the worksheet *holding2*. If we wanted to test whether the probability of a customer being satisfied deviates from $p_0 = 50\%$, then we can calculate a *t*-statistic:

$$t = \frac{\hat{p} - 0.5}{\mathrm{SE}(\hat{p})}$$

The table below lists *t*-statistics for each holding time group and also overall. If we want to detect deviations from 50% in either direction then this means a two-sided test. So to calculate a *p*-value we would calculate

$$1 - \mathrm{NORMSDIST}(|t\text{-value}|)$$

and then double it. Looking at the results in the table, we can conclude that for the 0–1 min holding time group, the probability of a customer being satisfied is definitely different from (greater than) 50% ($p = 0.000$) and for the 2–3 min and over 3 min groups, it is definitely different from (less than) 50%. For the 1–2 min group it is statistically very close to 50% and there is no evidence that it deviates from 50% ($p = 0.864$).

	0-1 min	1-2 mins	2-3 mins	over 3 mins	Overall
%	64.2%	50.4%	31.6%	20.0%	49.7%
SE	2.64%	2.15%	3.36%	5.44%	1.49%
low (75%)	61.2%	47.9%	27.7%	13.7%	48.0%
high (75%)	67.3%	52.8%	35.5%	26.3%	51.5%
T-statistic	5.39	0.17	-5.48	-5.51	-0.18
P-value	0.000	0.864	0.000	0.000	0.858

12.3. Assessing Changes in Proportions

We have been looking at binary performance attributes, which are summarized by the sample proportion of individuals with that attribute, together with an SE. In the previous chapters we were interested in how *mean* performance differed between market segments or before and after some intervention. When the performance measure is a binary attribute, we are interested in how the probability of having the attribute differs.

The general problem is that we have two sample proportions—for instance the proportion of satisfied males and females as well as their SEs—and we want to say something about the difference between genders.

In the previous chapter, it was pointed out that for any two unpredictable quantities X_1 and X_2 with standard deviation σ_1 and σ_2, the standard deviation of the difference is

$$\mathrm{Stdev}(X_1 - X_2) = \sqrt{\sigma_1^2 + \sigma_2^2},$$

provided the two variables are *independent*. This was used to give a formula for the SE of the difference in two means. The same applies to a difference of two sample proportions.

If we have two independent samples and have measured a binary attribute on each then we can estimate the probability of having the attribute for each sample by the sample proportion and its SE. We will often want to compare the two sample proportions. The SE of the difference between the two sample proportions is

$$\text{Std.Error } (\hat{p}_1 - \hat{p}_2) = \sqrt{\{SE(\hat{p}_1)\}^2 + \{SE(\hat{p}_2)\}^2},$$

provided again that the two sample proportions come from *independent* data sources. The SE can be used to give a confidence interval for the difference in probabilities or to test if the two probabilities are equal.

As a very simple example, for the call center data there were 378 out of 786 males who responded positively. This is a sample proportion of 48.1% with an SE of 1.78%. There were 179 out of 334 females who responded positively—a sample proportion of 53.6% with an SE of 2.73%. The difference between the positivity rates is 53.6% − 48.1% = 5.5%, in favor of females. The intrinsic variability of this difference is

$$\text{Std.Error } (\hat{p}_M - \hat{p}_F) = \sqrt{0.0178^2 + 0.0273^2} = 0.0326.$$

So the error in the 5.5% figure is 3.26%. It looks like the gender difference is probably real. The *t*-statistic is 5.5/3.26 = 1.69.

EXAMPLE 1 (Continued) *Call center data*

Does Holding Time Really Affect Satisfaction? Earlier we broke the holding times into four categories, namely 0–1 min, 1–2 min, 2–3 min, and over 3 min. There are many other ways to categorize the time spent on hold. The simplest is to take the 1120/2 = 560 shorter holding times and call these "short" and call the other 560 holding times "long." This is recorded in the variable "wait" in the worksheet EMS data(2). Using Pivotables, you will find that there were 336 positive responses from the short hold group but only 221 from the long hold group. The calculations for the sample proportions and their SEs are in the table below.

	Long	Short	Diff
Positive	221	336	
Number	560	560	
%	39.5%	60.0%	-20.5%
SE	2.07%	2.07%	2.93%

The difference between the two proportions is 20.5%. The SE of this figure is 2.93%. So there is no question that the length of holding time has an effect on the probability of customers returning a positive rating. It is hardly worth calculating the *t*-statistic of 20.5/2.93 = 7.02 here.

Are Males Less Patient Than Females? Let's pursue this idea of breaking the data up into different hold time groups but this time we will create five groups, from the shortest 20% of calls to the longest 20% of calls. There will be 224 customers in each group. This is coded into the variable "hold_group" in the worksheet <u>EMS data(2)</u>. For each hold group, we can look at how many of the 224 customers gave a positive response. We are going to go one step further, though, by further dividing the data up by gender.

	Females		Males	
Hold_group	**Positive**	**Number**	**Positive**	**Number**
Level 1 (8-49secs)	23	38	118	186
Level 2 (50-70secs)	32	56	106	168
Level 3 (70-91secs)	49	81	60	143
Level 4 (91-124secs)	46	78	63	146
Level 5 (125-447secs)	29	81	31	143

For instance, among the 38 females who were in the shortest holding group, 23 or 60.5% were positive, whereas for the 186 males in the same holding group there were 118 or 63.4% who were positive. Each of these figures has its own SE. The table below shows the percent positive for both genders and all five holding time groups, with SEs for each figure.

	Females		Males	
Hold_group	**%**	**SE**	**%**	**SE**
Level 1	60.5%	8.04%	63.4%	3.54%
Level 2	57.1%	6.67%	63.1%	3.73%
Level 3	60.5%	5.47%	42.0%	4.14%
Level 4	59.0%	5.61%	43.2%	4.11%
Level 5	35.8%	5.36%	21.7%	3.46%

It looks like the percentage of positive responses decreases as holding time increases, but that it decreases more for males. This can be seen clearly by plotting the percent positive against the holding group, for both males and females on the one chart. It appears as though holding time only really affects the satisfaction of females if they are in the longest holding group.

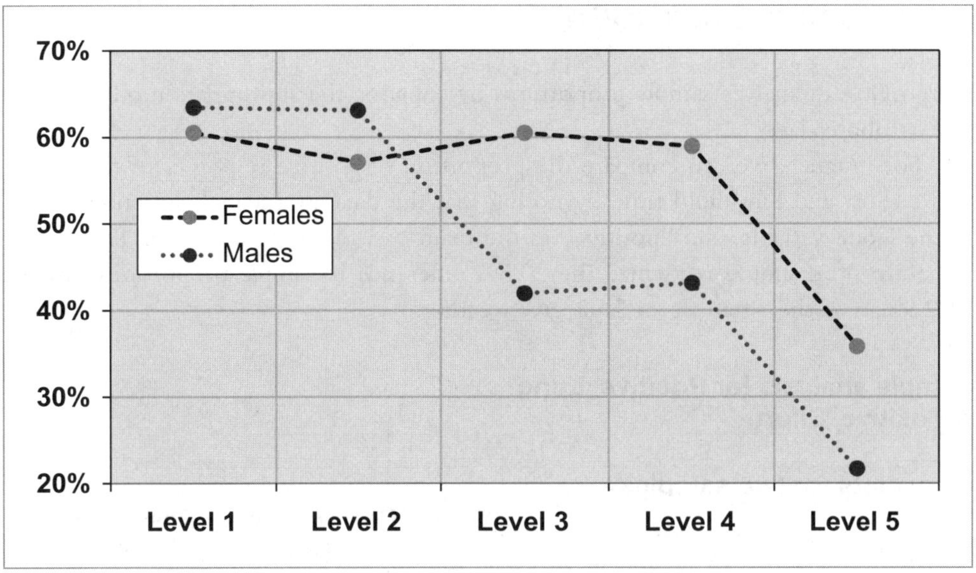

Are these differences real, though? We can use the main formula of this section—the SE of a difference between two proportions—to assess the difference between these two graphs at each holding time level. The table below gives the positive rate for males minus the positive rate for females. It also gives the SE and finally, a *t*-statistic for testing whether there is a difference. For example, for holding group 1 the difference is 63.4% − 60.5% = 2.9%, the SE of this difference is

$$\text{Std.Error}\ (\hat{p}_M - \hat{p}_F) = \sqrt{0.0804^2 + 0.0354^2} = 0.0878,$$

and so the *t*-statistic is 2.9/8.78 = 0.33. So there is no statistical difference between the positive response rates of males and females for customers that are in the shortest holding time group. The same is true of the second holding group. Males have a higher rate of positive response but compared to the SE we would say there is no clear difference. For the three longest holding groups, though, the results are clear. Males have a lower rate of positive response and the *t*-statistics clearly indicate that the conclusion is statistically reliable.

Hold_group	%	SE	T
Level 1	2.9%	8.78%	0.33
Level 2	6.0%	7.65%	0.78
Level 3	-18.5%	6.86%	-2.70
Level 4	-15.8%	6.95%	-2.28
Level 5	-14.1%	6.38%	-2.21

We might summarize the results as saying something about the patience of males and females. If we interpret the word "patience" to mean having a negative reaction to waiting for something, then males appear less patient than females. Their satisfaction clearly declines in holding group 3 (which is only a modest wait of 70–91 s). And it declines by more for the longest holding times. All these calculations are in the worksheet *holding3*.

12.4. USING STATPROGO

StatproGo can analyze sample proportions by applying the appropriate module to the 0–1 attribute data.

For instance, we can compare the proportion of positive responses of those who had a short and long hold time by noting that the data are stacked, selecting "wait" as the Code variable, and "positive" as the main variable to be analyzed. The output is below. You should recognize the 20.5% difference in sample proportions, the SE of 2.9%, and the *t*-statistic of 7.02 given earlier.

Two-sample analysis for Positive_Long minus Positive_Short		
Summary stats for two samples		
	Positive_Long	Positive_Short
Sample sizes	560	560
Sample means	0.395	0.600
Sample standard deviations	0.489	0.490
Confidence interval for difference		
Confidence level	95.0%	
Sample mean difference	-0.205	
Std error of difference	0.0293	
Lower limit	-0.263	
Upper limit	-0.148	
Test of difference against 0 versus two-tailed alternative		
Hypothesized mean difference	0.000	
Sample mean difference	-0.205	
Std error of difference	0.0293	
t-test statistic	-7.02	
p-value	0.000	

12.5. ALTERNATIVE METHODS

The methods based on the NLT are *approximate* and if the number of individuals n is large then you can expect good accuracy. For instance, your 90% confidence intervals will really contain the correct value with a probability of 90%, not 88% or 93%. If n is small the methods will not be accurate. How large should n be before the results can be trusted?

A Slight Improvement

Before answering this, it is worth mentioning that a simple adjustment to the standard method makes it work better for any sample size. The adjustment is to use a different estimate of p in the SE, namely $(y + 2)/(n + 4)$ instead of y/n. The theory for this is complicated and also rather ad hoc. But the bottom line is that it makes the standard method work better when the sample size is small and has hardly any effect when the sample size is large.

For instance, from $y = 20$ successes from $n = 100$ trials the estimate of p used in the SE formula is 21.15% rather than 20.0% and the SE is 4.10% rather than 4.02%. This adjustment is coded into the template estimating_p.xls. It is not coded into StatproGo.

Conditions for Accuracy

How large should n be for the approximation to be practically adequate? It was claimed in an earlier chapter that the NLT mostly works fine for $n = 25$ or so. But it depends on the basic performance measure and how close its distribution is to normal. Unfortunately, when the performance measure is a binary attribute, we are about as far from normal as you can get. So you probably want to have at least $n = 50$ individuals before you would rely on the NLT-based methods given so far being accurate. It is actually even a little more complicated than this. It not only depends on the number of individuals n but also on how common the attribute is.

Under the following easily identified conditions *the standard methods are not accurate and should not be used.* All these simple checks involve multiplying a probability by the sample size n.

> *Confidence Interval for* p. If you have calculated an approximate confidence interval (p_L, p_U) then to check its accuracy, calculate the following four numbers:
>
> $$np_L, n(1-p_L), np_U, n(1-p_U).$$
>
> If either np_L or $n(1 - p_L)$ is *less than 5*, then the accuracy of the lower limit is barely reasonable. If either is smaller than 2, the accuracy is poor. If either np_U or $n(1 - p_U)$ is *less than 5*, then the accuracy of the upper limit is barely reasonable. If either are smaller than 2, the accuracy is poor.
>
> *Testing* p. If the null value is p_0 then calculate the numbers np_0, $n(1 - p_0)$ and if either of these are *less than 5*, then the accuracy of the NLT method is barely reasonable. If either is smaller than 2, the accuracy is poor.
>
> *Confidence Intervals or Tests of* $p_1 - p_2$. Check to see whether the interval for p_1 is accurate using the above check as well as the interval for p_2. If either is inaccurate then the methods in this chapter for assessing changes or differences in sample proportions will also not be accurate.

These accuracy checks have been coded into the *approximate* worksheet of estimating_p.xls. Any figures that are likely to be inaccurate will appear in a pale gray font.

If the NLT Method Is Not Accurate

For calculating intervals for a single probability there is an exact method that does not involve any approximation. The details are complex but the resulting intervals have been coded into the worksheet "*exact*" in the estimate_p.xls template. For testing a single probability, there is also an exact method that is easy to explain.

Suppose we are testing the alternative H_1: $p < 0.5$, for instance to see if a coin is tail biased. We observe the number of heads and count, say, 44 out of 100. A p-value is supposed to measure how unusually low the proportion of heads is. One way to do this is to calculate an SE and a t-statistic, but a more direct way here is simply to calculate the chance of a fair coin showing heads 44 or fewer times out of 100. We can use BINOMDIST directly for this. This has also been coded into the spreadsheet Exact. There is one p-value for testing if p is greater than the reference and another for testing if p is less than the reference.

There do exist methods for two-sided p-values when NLT methods are not accurate, as well as for comparing two sample proportions, but they are highly complex and cannot be easily coded into Excel. Therefore, the worksheet Exact does not have any such output.

EXAMPLE 2 *Price sensitivity of olive oil (ex2 [olive oil].xls)*

You surveyed some 500 customers in a supermarket about whether they would buy your brand of olive oil. They are shown a 4-L can of your branded product (and offered a taste) and quoted a price. They are also reminded of the market dominating brand and its current price of $14.40 for a 4-L container. They are then asked to rate the chance that they would buy your brand on a 1–5 scale, from "definitely not" to "definitely would."

There are many ways to look at these data but you decide to convert a response of 3–5 into a positive response and 1–2 into a negative response. You can then use Pivotables to calculate the proportion of positive responses for each offered price as well as an SE.

Price	Y	N	Estimate	SE	Low (75%)	High (75%)
$12.50	32	36	88.9%	5.2%	79.9%	94.6%
$12.75	28	36	77.8%	6.9%	69.4%	86.2%
$13.00	26	36	72.2%	7.5%	63.3%	81.1%
$13.25	30	37	81.1%	6.4%	73.1%	89.0%
$13.50	29	36	80.6%	6.6%	72.4%	88.7%
$13.75	20	37	54.1%	8.2%	44.5%	63.6%
$14.00	17	36	47.2%	8.3%	37.5%	56.9%
$14.25	20	36	55.6%	8.3%	45.9%	65.2%
$14.50	8	36	22.2%	6.9%	13.8%	30.6%
$14.75	12	36	33.3%	7.9%	24.1%	42.6%
$15.00	13	36	36.1%	8.0%	26.7%	45.5%
$15.25	12	36	33.3%	7.9%	24.1%	42.6%
$15.50	11	36	30.6%	7.7%	21.4%	39.7%
$15.75	8	30	26.7%	8.1%	16.9%	36.4%

The proportion of positive customers is supposed to indicate the market share that might be achieved. However, it is well known that the chance of a customer actually buying the product is way less (probably around four times less) than the proportions you will see in such a survey, as customers tend to be more comfortable with a positive than a negative response. Nevertheless, research suggests that a predictable proportion of positive responses will convert into actual sales.

A nice way to present the results is to plot the proportion of positive responses against the offered price. In addition, one should give a statistical range for each of these proportions. Since there are only 30–37 individuals within each price quote group, it is safer to use exact intervals rather those based on the approximate NLT.

The figures in the table above are for 75% intervals. For instance if you type 32 and 36 into the Exact worksheet of estimating_p.xls and 75% for the coverage then the interval is (79.9%, 94.6%) to accompany the estimate of 88.9%. This has been done for each price and the results are listed in the table under the headings Low and High. The pattern is displayed in a plot below. It appears that the positivity seems to steadily decline from $12.50 to $14.25. For the price $14.50, which is the first time the price is higher than the $14.40 price of the dominating brand, positivity drops drastically. Thereafter, the price appears to be fairly insensitive to the offered price, though presumably it would eventually decline to zero if the quoted price were high enough.

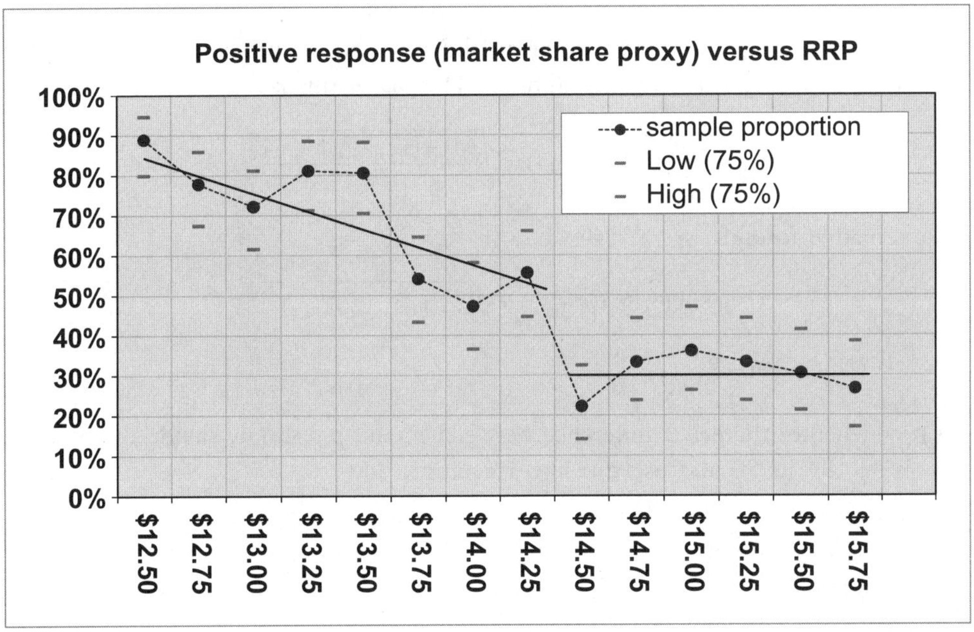

I have drawn in the trendlines suggested by this discussion. The best price for your product would depend on the marginal profit of your product but the data suggest that you should set your price just lower than the dominating brand. Further details are in the case "Spanish Olive Oil."

CHECK YOUR UNDERSTANDING

Q3. You conduct a soft drink survey of 78 people with the following results.

- Sixty say they would purchase the old formula.
- Sixty-two say they would purchase the new formula.
- Thirty-two prefer the old formula.

Calculate 99% confidence intervals for the relevant proportions and check that conditions are such that these intervals are accurate.

12.6. SUMMARY

In general we have n_1 independent individuals who may or may not possess a certain binary attribute. We find that y_1 have the attribute. We have an estimate and an SE

$$\hat{p}_1 = y_1/n_1, \ \mathrm{SE}(\hat{p}_1) = \sqrt{\hat{p}_1(1-\hat{p}_1)/n_1}.$$

We have n_2 independent individuals who may or may not possess a certain binary attribute. We find that y_2 have the attribute. We have an estimate and an SE

$$\hat{p}_2 = y_2/n_2, \ \mathrm{SE}(\hat{p}_2) = \sqrt{\hat{p}_2(1-\hat{p}_2)/n_2}.$$

The difference $\hat{p}_1 - \hat{p}_2$ is an estimate of the difference in the probability of having the attribute under the two sets of conditions. The SE of this is

$$\text{Std.Error } (\hat{p}_1 - \hat{p}_2) = \sqrt{\frac{\hat{p}_1(1-\hat{p}_1)}{n_1} + \frac{\hat{p}_2(1-\hat{p}_2)}{n_2}}.$$

An alternative formula is

$$\text{Std.Error } (\hat{p}_1 - \hat{p}_2) = \sqrt{\{\mathrm{SE}(\hat{p}_1)\}^2 + \{\mathrm{SE}(\hat{p}_2)\}^2}$$

This SE can be used to

- test whether there is a difference between p_1 and p_2. Simply divide the estimate $\hat{p}_1 - \hat{p}_2$ by its SE and use this like a *t*-statistic and
- construct a confidence interval in the usual way. Simply take the estimate $\hat{p}_1 - \hat{p}_2$ and add or subtract Q to and from the SEs, where Q comes from the normal distribution.

Proportions of binary attributes can be treated like sample means if the attribute is coded as 1/0. In this case the sample average of the 0's and 1's is the proportion with the attribute and the formula $s\sqrt{n}$ for sample means can be used as an alternative route to the SE of the proportion.

When the sample size is small or when the proportions involved are close to 0 or 1, the approximate methods can be inaccurate. There are better but more complicated methods available. Some are coded into estimating_p.xls.

EXERCISES

E1. From a sample of 1215 moviegoers, it was found that 226 of 771 male respondents agreed with the proposition that "There is too much advertising prior to main features," while for females the number who agreed was 111.

(a) How much evidence is there that males and females differ in their attitude to advertising at movies?

(b) Estimate the overall proportion of the moviegoing population who agree with the proposition.

E2. A survey of 1547 customers involved several questions that required yes/no answers. The surveys were administered by six different interviewers. The results below relate to the question, "I think that luxury cars are not worth the money."

Interviewer	1	2	3	4	5	6
Agree	38	60	14	102	68	65
Disagree	127	221	102	323	202	225

(a) How much evidence is there that interviewer 3 is different from the other five treated collectively?

(b) Would it be reasonable to combine the data into a single result, namely 347 agree out of 1547 surveyed?

E3. From a survey of 557 people, 378 said they preferred your product to your leading competitor. On a repeat survey of 335 people taken a week later, 241 said they prefer your product.

(a) Based on the first survey, estimate the proportion of the underlying population who prefer your product. Give an SE and a 95% confidence interval. Give your answer in terms that would be understood by someone not knowing any statistics.

(b) Are the two surveys in agreement statistically? What would it mean if they were not?

E4. Two surveys have been taken to estimate the degree of brand recognition of Soapy Detergent. The first survey was conducted over 1 week and out of the 1265 customers surveyed, 487 named the brand without prompting. A second independent survey was taken a month later. No new advertising campaign to increase brand recognition has been undertaken. In this second survey, 995 customers were surveyed and 401 named the brand without prompting.

(a) How much evidence is there that the underlying population who can name Soapy Detergent without prompting has changed from the first survey to the next?

(b) Estimate the proportion of the underlying population who can name Soapy Detergent without prompting. Give an SE and a 95% confidence interval. Give your answer in terms that would be understood by someone not knowing any statistics.

E5. On the basis of surveys over the past 6 months, 1222 of 3265 customers mentioned Fluffysoft detergent among the best known three brands without prompting. Brand recognition of Fluffysoft detergent is an important bottom-line issue for the company. It is estimated that each extra 1% of customers who mention Fluffysoft brand among the first three will add \$12,000 to profit.

Fluffysoft had paid for an advertising campaign that involves free giveaways over the year at randomly selected retail locations. The cost of the campaign is \$20,000. After 1 month, they survey 375 randomly selected customers and find that 165 can name Fluffysoft unprompted among the first three recognized brands.

(a) On the basis of the historical data, what proportion of customers recognizes Fluffysoft and how accurate is this figure?

(b) Has the advertising campaign definitely increased Fluffysoft's brand recognition? How sure are you?

(c) Is the advertising campaign worth the cost? Answer this question by performing a hypothesis test at significance level 5%.

(d) Calculate a 90% confidence interval for the *net payoff* of the advertising campaign.

E6. One hundred people are randomly selected from those walking into the Victorian Market and were asked if they favored a ban on all guns. Fifty-five people indicated that they favored a ban. The political party doing the survey claims that over 50% of voters support a ban on guns.

(a) Determine a 90% confidence interval for the proportion supporting a ban.

(b) Is the claim of the political party upheld at the 10% significance level?

(c) A second company performed a survey at the same time as the first, but at Footscray Market. They surveyed 150 people and found that 71 supported a ban on guns. Are the two surveys consistent with each other?

(d) How many more people would you need to survey to double the accuracy?

E7. Customers of a Cable TV network were surveyed in 2002 on their degree of satisfaction or dissatisfaction with programming. The acronym VD is the standard for "very dissatisfied," and so on. The data tabulated below are for customers on the "standard," that is, the minimum package. There were 1030 such customers for the 2002 survey. The survey was repeated in 2003 with roughly double the sampling effort. These figures are also recorded in the table and the 2026 customers recorded here are again those on the standard package.

	VD	D	N	S	VS	Total
2002	113	165	245	375	132	1030
2003	206	355	447	695	323	2026

It may be assumed that customers surveyed are a random and representative sample of all network customers. The frequencies can easily be converted to percentages by dividing by the total numbers on each survey, but these have been left blank in the data table above. Remember that any quoted percentages or proportions should be given a measure of reliability.

(a) What proportion of standard package customers in 2002 have a negative reaction to programming? (By negative, I mean D or VD).

(b) What proportion of standard package customers in 2003 have a positive reaction to programming? (By positive, I mean S or VS).

(c) Has the proportion of standard package customers who have an extreme reaction to programming, that is, VD or VS, changed from 2002 to 2003? By how much? How sure are you?

(d) Given that customers are positive, how has the probability of being very satisfied changed from 2002 to 2003?

E8. You have surveyed 437 single adults between the ages of 25 and 35 and asked them how much, on average, they spend on fresh meat. You record this as a yearly spend, and you record the gender of the respondent as well.

(a) Use the methods of the last chapter to compare the mean spend for males and females.

(b) Divide the data up into the following expenditure groups: \$0, \$1000–\$1999, \$2000–2999, \$3000–3999, \$4000–4999, \$5000–5999, \$6000–6999, and \$7000+. Pivotables will do most but not all of this. Count up how many males and females there are in each of these groups.

(c) Produce a graphic that shows how gender depends on expenditure. Your graph should include some indication of reliability.

(d) For each expenditure group, use the Exact template to test the hypothesis that the proportion of males differs from 50%.

E9. A theory in physics predicts that in 26.2% of cases a certain atomic reaction will produce a neutrino. An alternative theory predicts that it is 26.4%. Roughly how many experiments will need to be performed to decide which of the theories is correct?

E10. Answer these three questions in as clear and simple terms as you can.

(a) What is an SE?
(b) What does a *t*-statistic actually measure? How is it interpreted?
(c) What does a *p*-value mean? How do you use it?

CHAPTER 13

Using the Relationship between Shares to Build a Portfolio

13.0. Introduction: What Is the Issue?

What is the relationship between the current 10-year bond interest rate and the level of the national stock market index? Most people know that the relation is negative—when one goes up the other tends to go down. I need to decide how much of my assets to put in stocks and how much to put in bonds. Even though stocks usually give a better average return than bonds, I want to reduce my risk by investing in both. How much will I reduce my risk and how should I allocate my money? To answer this you need to know more about the relationship of stock and bond prices than that they are negatively related. You need a numerical measure of the relationship, of the extent to which one variable varies with the other.

Most business problems require an understanding between the relationships of the main driving variables. Indeed, this will be the main topic for the rest of the book—understanding, measuring, and appreciating the implications of the relationships between business variables.

This chapter serves as a nice entry into this general area. It also covers some financial concepts and some applications of the mean and standard deviation in the context of finance. The new element will be how to measure the relationship between the returns on two financial assets, using **correlation**. This allows us to construct a financial portfolio. Correlation is used much more widely than in finance, though, and will be explained in more detail in the following chapter.

Data-Driven Business Decisions, First Edition. Chris J. Lloyd.

EXAMPLE 1 *Oil and airlines*

Southwest Airlines (SWA) is a passenger airline within the United States. As of December 31, 2009, it operated 537 Boeing 737 aircraft and provided service to 68 cities in 35 states. It was founded in 1967 and is headquartered in Dallas, Texas. A major cost input for airlines, perhaps *the* major cost, is fuel. So you might expect SWA to do poorly when oil prices rise.

If you measure company performance by share price, then you might expect to see SWA shares fall whenever people believe oil prices will rise in the short or medium term. What the market believes about future oil prices is measured in the oil futures market.

The file oil&airlines.xls contains weekly data on oil futures and on SWA airlines share price (adjusted for splits and dividends) for the period January 1989–January 1995. This includes the oil shock of 1990, where oil increased from $18 to $38 per barrel and then fell back to $17 per barrel. A plot of the data is below. The share price of SWA increased from $1.31 to $5.78 over these 6 years, including a peak of $11.07.

Whereas, oil did not increase overall. There are two reasons you might invest in oil. In the long term, you might think it will go up. Though you should keep firmly in mind that the oil future at any point in time represents what the entire market of interested investors think the future price will be. The second reason, though, is that even if it doesn't go up overall, it might provide some insurance against oil price fluctuations adversely affecting my airline share price. This is the notion of hedging.

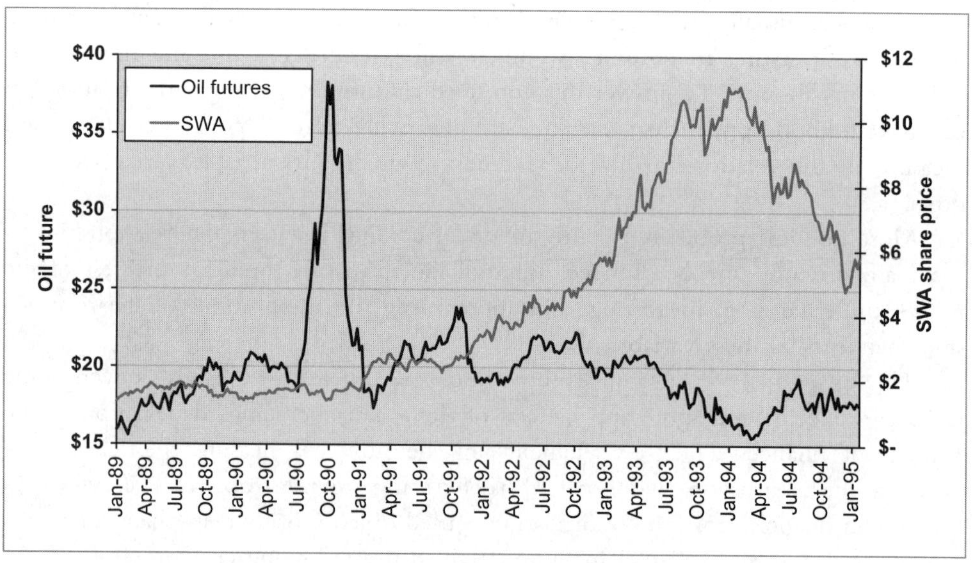

This sounds a little like betting on both red and black at the casino. Why would you bother? But the key difference with financial investments is that they tend to go up over time. So you will still make money with this apparently defensive strategy of insuring against oil price rises.

What is amazing is that you can actually end up making higher returns than putting all your money in SWA.

13.1. How to Measure Financial Growth

The actual value of a share price does not tell you much, if anything, about the company. It depends on how many shares there are. You make money when the share price changes and when the share pays a dividend.

This chapter is not about the dividend payoff from shares which, ultimately, underlies their value. It is about the variations on the value of the share itself, most of it completely random from day to day or from week to week.

Ordinary Returns

To look at share price data the first thing to do is to calculate the growth of the share from period to period. In financespeak these are called **ordinary returns** or often just returns. The (ordinary) return on an investment is just the percentage change. If the value of a share changes from V_1 to V_2 then the return is

$$\text{ordinary return} = V_2/V_1 - 1.$$

EXAMPLE 1 (Continued) *Oil and airlines*

> Quoted share prices can be in fractions of a cent because they are adjusted for splits and dividends.

For instance, from the end of the first week of 1989 to the end of the second week, the SWA share value changed from \$1.317 to \$1.416, a return of

$$1.416/1.317 - 1 = 0.0752$$

or 7.52%. It is good practice to always quote such figures as a percentage. You can achieve this in Excel by just formatting the cell as a percentage.

You can easily calculate the return for *each week* of oil and for each week of SWA. There are 316 such weekly returns rather than 317 because you cannot calculate the return on the first week without knowing the prices in the week prior to the available data.

The weekly ordinary returns are listed in the worksheet <u>*returns*</u> of the file oil&airlines.xls. If you plot the returns of SWA against time you get the graphic below. Each point represents the percent growth of SWA during that particular week. The main thing to notice about this plot is that it is completely chaotic.

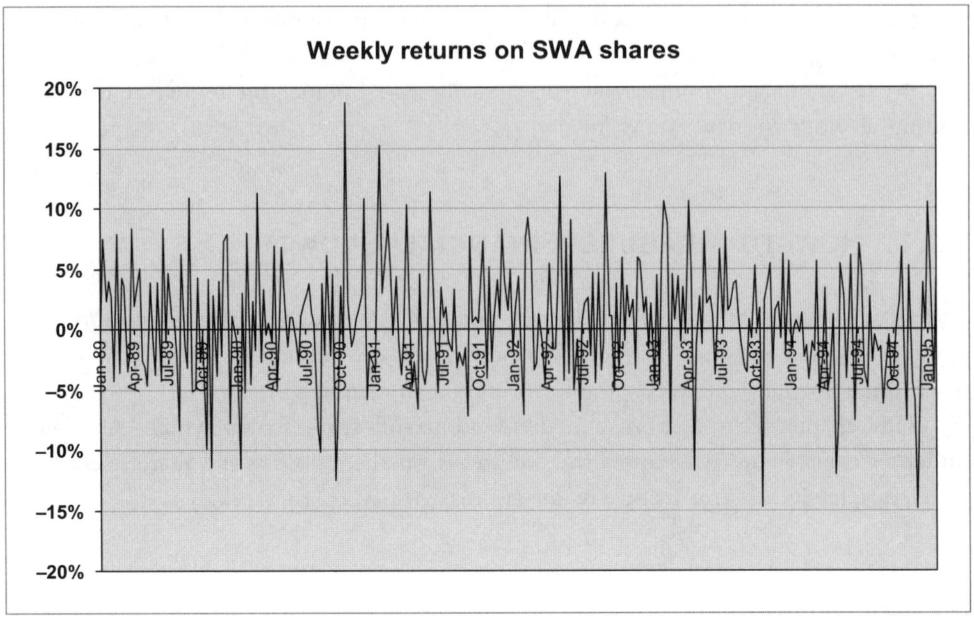

It seems that there is no pattern to when the stock price might go up or down, nor how much. If you think there is a pattern then *can you tell me what the next return will be*? This is an important lesson to learn. If you are ever tempted to think stock prices follow some simply predictable path, come back and have a look at this graph. The same is true of the plot for oil futures or for any other freely traded equity. Price changes are chaotic and very close to being completely unpredictable.

Average Yearly Growth

Suppose a share grows from V_1 to V_2 over a period of Y years. What yearly growth rate (GR) does this amount to? This depends on the factor by which the investment has grown and the number of years. If the growth factor V_2/V_1 is called F then the average yearly growth factor is $F^{1/Y}$ and the GR is

$$\text{GR} = F^{1/Y} - 1.$$

EXAMPLE 1 (Continued) *Oil and airlines*

In Excel type: = 4.387∧(52/317).

From the first week of 1989 to the first week of 1991, SWA grew from \$1.317 to \$1.654, a growth factor of 1.256 over 2 years. To turn this into a yearly growth factor F we reason that 2 years of such growth would multiply the value by F^2, which should equal 1.256. Therefore F must equal

$$1.256^{1/2} = \sqrt{1.256} = 1.121,$$

and so GR = 0.121, which means 12.1% per annum growth. The average yearly growth for the entire 6 years is based on SWA growing from $1.317 to $5.778, which is a factor of 4.387. This was for 317 weeks, which is $Y = 317/52$ years. So the equivalent yearly growth factor is

$$4.387^{52/317} = 1.275,$$

which means an average of 27.5% per annum GR. Put another way, an investment that grows at 27.5% per annum will grow by a factor of 4.387 over 317 weeks. For oil futures, the per annum growth is only 1.60% per annum.

The Paradox of Average Returns

The 316 weekly returns for Oil and SWA are in the worksheet *returns* of the file oil&airlines.xls. You might naturally want to look at the average of the 316 returns for SWA. The result is that the average weekly growth is 0.592%. If you compound 0.592% growth 52 times, this implies a yearly growth factor of

$$1.00592^{52} = 1.3623,$$

which means 36.2% per year. This is the wrong answer! We just calculated above that the yearly growth was 26.5%. For Oil the situation is even worse. The average weekly growth is 0.089%, which implies a yearly growth of 4.73%, almost three times higher than the correct growth of 1.60% that we just calculated.

It gets even more bizarre. If I have a share that increases from $100 to $125 then the increase is 25%. If it decreases back to $100 then this is a 20% drop. The average of 25% and −20% is +2.5%. So even though the share finished where it started the average growth is positive!

Log Returns

Analyzing financial data requires looking at the mean of the period returns. But ordinary returns lead to absurd results—for instance that the average return is positive even when there is no actual growth in the value of the share. For this and other reasons, an alternative growth measure is common in financial analysis, called **log returns**.

> Another name is continuously compounded returns.

If the value of a share changes from V_1 to V_2 then the log return is

$$\text{Log return} = \text{LN}(V_2/V_1),$$

where LN means natural logarithm and is a standard function available in Excel. Log returns give similar numbers to ordinary returns. For instance, growth from $100 to $125 is a log return of

$$\text{LN}(125/100) = 0.223$$

or 22.3%, while the fall from \$125 to \$100 is a log return of

$$\mathrm{LN}(100/125) = -0.223$$

or −22.3%. So the average log return is exactly zero.

The upshot of all this is that it is better to measure growth using log returns than ordinary returns, even though they are not as easy to explain or understand. At the end of the day, a given log return can be converted back into an ordinary return using the formula

$$\text{return} = e^{\text{log return}} - 1,$$

where e is the number 2.7183. … The Excel function EXP( ) calculates power to the base e. For instance, a log return of 10% means an ordinary return of EXP(0.1) − 1, which gives 0.10517 or 10.517%.

EXAMPLE 1 (Continued) *Oil and airlines*

The log returns for both Oil and SWA are on the worksheet *log-returns* of the file oil&airlines.xls. The average log returns are 0.032% for Oil and 0.468% for SWA. To work out the yearly log return from the weekly return is very simple. You just multiply by 52—unlike ordinary returns. This gives 1.59% for Oil and 24.33% for SWA. To convert these log returns back into an ordinary returns we calculate

$$\mathrm{EXP}(0.0159) - 1 = 0.0160$$

for Oil, which means 1.60% growth and we calculate

$$\mathrm{EXP}(0.2433) - 1 = 0.275$$

for SWA, which means 27.5% growth—the correct answers!

13.2. RISK AND RETURN: BOTH MATTER

Ultimately investors want growth in value. There is also the question of risk. If I offered you 10% guaranteed you should prefer this to a return that is equally likely to be anywhere from 5% to 15%. The pursuit of low risk, though, is more than just a psychological effect. It is actually just as important as growth and there is a natural exchange rate of one for the other.

The riskiness of a stock is measured by the standard deviation of the period on period returns. Risk should be interpreted as a percentage and you should format the cells as percentage in Excel.

The standard deviation measures how much variation there is in the return from one period to the next. For instance, if the standard deviation on daily returns of Microsoft (MSFT) shares is 2.25% then this means that you can easily see the return tomorrow of 2.25% and a return the next day of −2.25%. And remember that this variation is almost entirely unpredictable.

EXAMPLE 1 (Continued) *Oil and airlines*

The standard deviation of the returns for Oil and SWA has been calculated on both ordinary and log returns in the spreadsheet. It makes little difference whether you use ordinary or log returns, though in principle log returns are better. Overall, oil futures are less volatile than SWA, despite the extremes of the 1990 oil shock.

	OIL	SWA
Ordinary returns	3.40%	5.06%
Log returns	3.43%	5.05%

On the other hand, Oil had a much lower average return (1.59% per annum) than SWA (24.33% per annum). It would have made life easy if SWA had a lower volatility than Oil. It would then be better than Oil both in terms of growth and risk. So you might think that you should put 100% of your money in SWA. You would actually be *quite wrong* in this conclusion.

Anyway, we are not in this situation and it looks like we will have to choose whether we want high-growth SWA or low-risk Oil. It is not a choice of one or the other, though. There is always the option of putting some of our money in both and getting performance somewhere in between.

EXAMPLE 2 *Ten big stocks*

The file big10.xls contains daily share prices for 10 large U.S. companies for the 2-year period 1997–1998. There were 504 trading days in this period, which gives 503 daily returns for each of the 10 stocks. These are all calculated on the worksheet *returns*.

It is a simple matter to use StatproGo to list the average and standard deviations of these 10 columns. The table below has omitted three of the companies that were in the middle of the pack with respect to both risk and return. This highest growth company was Yahoo (YHOO). Unfortunately it was also the most risky. The second highest growth was achieved by AOL, which also had the second highest risk. At the other end, the lowest risk share was Merck (MRK), which was one of the lowest in growth.

	YHOO	AOL	MSFT	INTC	MRK	BAC	CT
Mean (return)	0.74%	0.57%	0.24%	0.12%	0.13%	0.06%	0.16%
Stdev (risk)	4.91%	3.76%	2.25%	2.53%	1.91%	2.32%	3.97%

It starts to look like the situation with SWA and Oil was not a special case—that high-growth stocks tend to also be those with high risk. We can look at this by plotting the risk against the return for these 10 stocks. The graphic is below and it is indeed the case that high/low growth goes with high/low risk. If you want the high-average growth of YHOO you can have it, but you will have to take the risk.

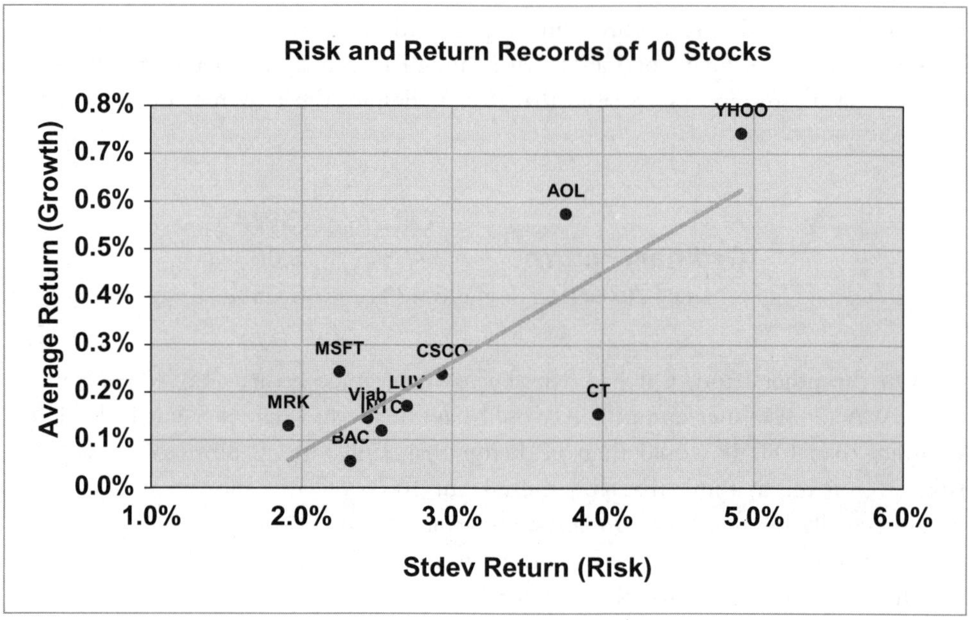

Stocks with high risk and return are top right and stocks with low risk and return are bottom left. Ideally you would like to be the high return and low risk—which is top left. With this in mind, we can also classify the performance of stocks by seeing how far above and to the left they are relative to the trendline. It looks like MRK and MSFT were good stocks over this period, as are YHOO and AOL. It also seems that Capital Trust (CT) was poor. In fact, CT had a higher volatility than AOL but had four times less growth.

In interpreting this plot, you should not lose sight of the fact that it is historical and both the risk and return of these stocks may be quite different in the future to what might have been seen in even the recent past. We will return to this point in the last section of this chapter.

13.3. Correlation and Industry Structure

The share prices of companies within the same industry should tend to move in tandem. Most bad news for Microsoft should also be bad news for Cisco. For companies in completely different industries you might expect share prices to be close to independent. With Oil and SWA, we argued in the introduction that they might tend to move in opposite directions.

To look at this, you calculate returns for the two stocks in question. If you plot them both against time you get a graph that is dominated by the chaos we saw when we plotted just SWA returns against time—it is very hard to see whether returns on one asset tend to follow or go against returns on the other. A much more sensible way to look at the relationship between two shares is to scatter-plot the returns of one against the other.

EXAMPLE 1 (Continued) *Oil and airlines*

A scatter plot of SWA returns against Oil returns is displayed below. There is no time element in the plot anymore. Each point corresponds to a particular week and tells you what happened to Oil and SWA that week. A point in the far top right would mean that both assets increased by a large amount. There was no such week. Nor was there a single week where they both went down by a large amount, which would be in the bottom left quadrant.

There are, however, plenty of weeks where one w ent up and the other went down by a large amount—in the top left or bottom right quadrants. So it looks like the relationship between SWA and Oil is *negative*, as we anticipated from the structural fact that Oil is a cost input into airlines.

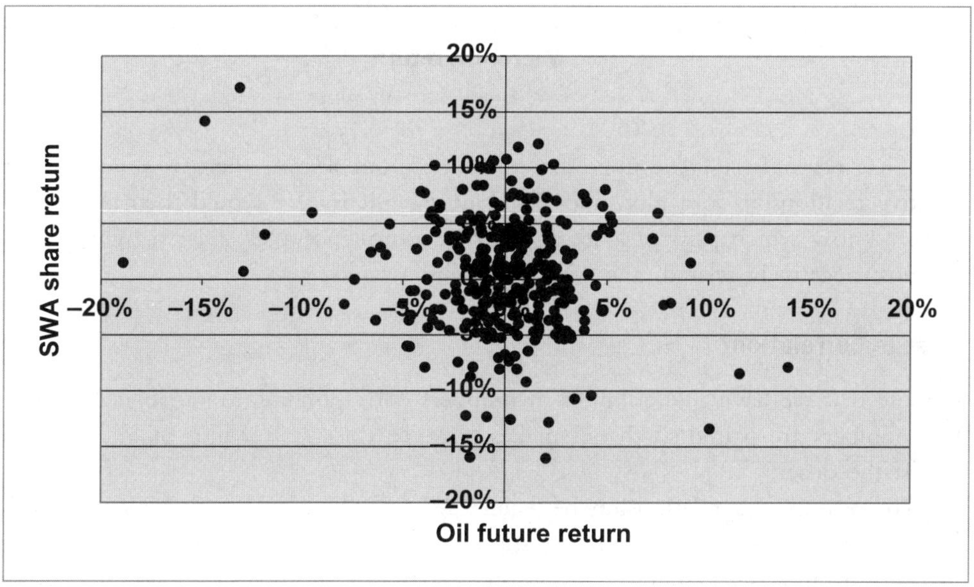

EXAMPLE 3 *Cisco and MSFT*

Cisco (CSCO) makes IT networking products including routers, home networking, and security products. MSFT sells the operating system and office applications. You would expect that both are driven almost entirely by the number of computers that are moving. Any news that is good for the computer industry will be good for both. You would only expect to see one go up and the other go down if there was some important news specific to the company—for instance, if Bill Gates perished.

The mean daily return for CSCO is 0.248% and for MSFT is 0.244%. Both have quite similar volatilities. The extent to which one share follows the other is displayed in the plot below. These stocks are *positively* related. There is not a single day when CSCO went up by 5% that MSFT went down by 5% or vice versa.

There is one peculiar day when MSFT went up by 9.23% and CSCO went down by 2.30% (can you see it?) on April 18, 1997.

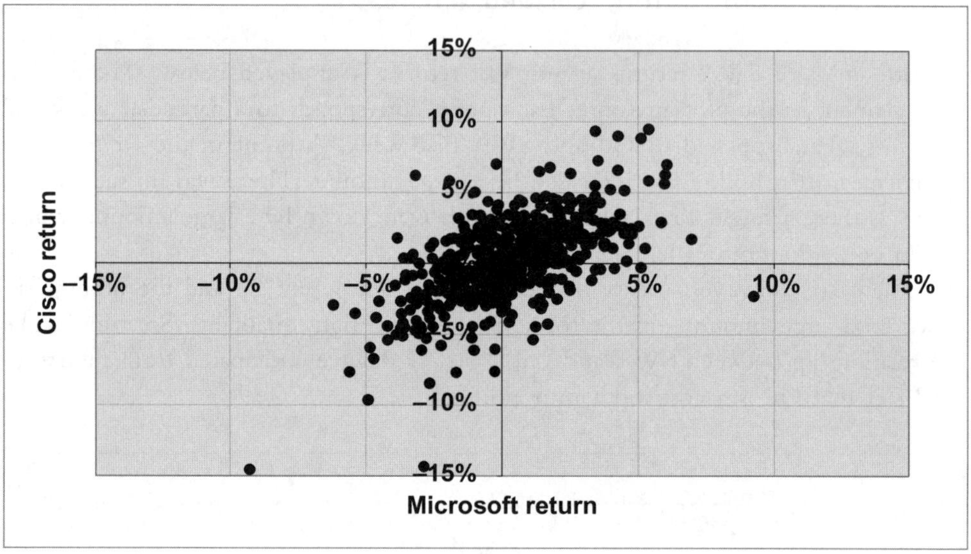

What we need is a number that measures both *whether* there is a positive or negative relationship in a plot, and also *how strong* it is. We would then be able to quickly know which pairs of a set of stocks are most positively related, which pairs are most negatively related, and which are least related.

What Is Correlation?

Suppose that we have two columns of numbers corresponding to variables X and Y. The numbers are paired so that it makes sense to do a scatter plot of one column against the other.

To measure the relationship between the two variables, we first convert both columns into z-scores. This removes the effect of the units of measurement. If we change currency the z-scores will not be affected at all. We then plot one set of z-scores against the other. The plot will look identical to a plot of X against Y except that the scale of the axes will be different. Both variables will be centered at zero and both with a range between about –3 and 3.

Positive relationships are characterized by points in the top right (high–high) or bottom left (low–low) quadrants. These points agree in their X- and Y-values. A simple way to measure the extent of the agreement is by multiplying their z-scores.

For instance, for a point with both *z*-scores of 3 the product would be 9. A point with both *z*-scores of −3 would also give a product of 9. These points strongly agree. Whereas, points in the bottom right or top left will give a large negative value when we multiply their *z*-scores. A point with one *z*-score of +3 and the other point with a *z*-score of −3 will have a product of −9. Such a point shows disagreement between *X* and *Y*. Each point, then, has an agreement number. We finally calculate the average agreement over the whole plot.

The **sample correlation** of a scatter plot is

$$r_{XY} = \frac{1}{n-1}\sum_{i=1}^{n} Z_{xi}Z_{Yi},$$

where Z_{xi} are the *z*-scores associated with the *x*-sample and Z_{Yi} are the *z*-scores associated with the *y*-sample. Remember that *z*-scores are obtained by subtracting off the mean (of that variable) and dividing by the standard deviation.

Apart from the division by "$n - 1$" rather than by n, this is the average of the agreement scores. This formula can only be used when $n > 1$, which makes sense because it is nonsense to talk about the relationship in a plot with one point.

There is no need to calculate the *z*-scores in practice. In Excel you can use the function **CORREL(X,Y)**, where X is a range of cell references containing the *x*-values and Y is a range of cell reference containing the *y*-values. For instance, CORREL(A1:A10,B1:B10) calculates the correlation of data from 10 cases stored in Columns A and B.

EXAMPLE 1 (Continued) *Oil and airlines*

If you go to the spreadsheet *returns* and type

= CORREL(B4:B319,C4:C319)

you get the answer −0.146. This says that the relationship between returns on Oil futures and SWA is negative. What does the −0.146 figure mean, though? Is this a strong or weak negative relationship? Looking at the plot, the relationship appears rather weak.

Properties of Correlation

Correlations are always between −1 and +1. This is very handy because the extremes of +1/−1 correspond to a perfect positive/negative linear relationship. By positive, we mean the line slopes up and by negative, we mean the line slopes down. So if you get a correlation of −0.9 you can anticipate that the scatter plot will show points clustering closely around a downward sloping line. Correlation is very poor at detecting or measuring the strength of nonlinear relationships. We talk more about this in the next chapter, but it is not important for share price data.

Zero correlation means there is neither a positive nor a negative relationship in the plot. This could mean that there is no relationship at all—apparent as a random cloud of points in the scatter plot. Or it could mean that there is some strange, nonlinear relationship that could not be characterized as positive or negative. Again, this does not happen for share price data. A correlation of zero for share price data means that there is hardly any relation between the two share returns.

Correlation is unaffected by the units chosen to measure X and Y. To this extent it measures the intrinsic association of the variables, unaffected by scale. It measures the relationship that you see in the plot, and is not affected by the labels on the axes. A correlation does not have any units itself. It is a pure number.

EXAMPLE 1 (Continued) *Oil and airlines*

The correlation of returns of Oil and SWA was −0.146. This is a very weak negative relationship. It is much closer to 0 than to −1.

What Does a Given Value of r_{XY} Mean?

Open the file correlation.xls, which allows you to generate scatter plots of X against Y and see what the correlation is. The purpose of this spreadsheet is to help you get a feel for correlations. I suggest you spend 5 min experimenting with this tool so that you can develop experience and intuition about what a given correlation of, say, 0.7, means.

CHECK YOUR UNDERSTANDING

Q1. Consider the two stocks in a similar industry such as YHOO and Xerox. Suppose we are interested in the performance of these stocks on the first and second trading days of each month.

Think about the returns on these two stocks on the first or second trading day of the month. Let

- Y_1, Y_2 be the return on YHOO on the first and second day, respectively.
- X_1, X_2 be the return on Xerox on the first and second day, respectively.

Which of the four variables—Y_1, Y_2, X_1, and X_2—are positively associated, negatively associated, and independent? To decide if two variables are dependent or independent, ask yourself the question, *Would knowing one variable help me to predict the value of the other?* If not then they are independent.

EXAMPLE 2 (Continued) *Ten big stocks*

With 10 stocks there are 45 pairs that we could look at and ask, "Are they negatively or positively related, and if so, how strongly?" StatproGo has a module for calculating the correlation of all pairs from a set of variables. Go to StatproGo then to Summary Stats, and then to Correlations, Covariances. Select all the variables to include and the correlation of each pair will be computed and set out in a table.

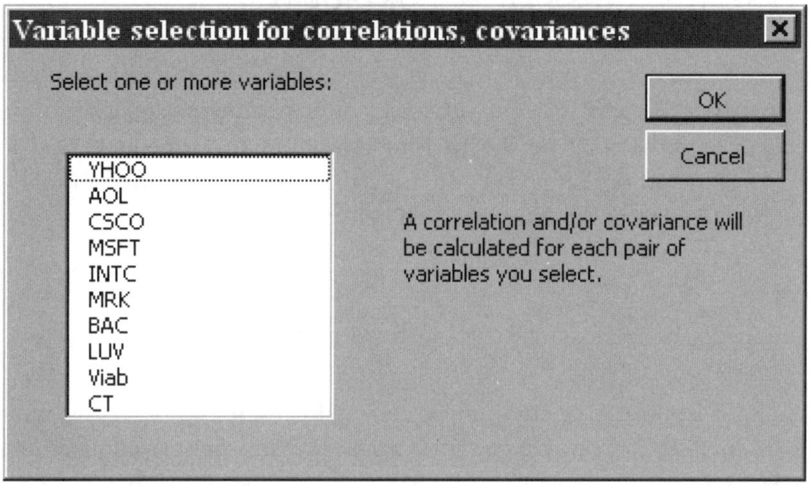

The results are in the table below and also in the worksheet *correlations*. Notice first that the cells along the diagonal have been left empty. The correlation of a share with itself is always +1.

Notice how the largest positive correlations are between companies within the same sector, for instance CSCO, MSFT, and Intel (INTC). The correlations are quite strong—about 0.6 where, you recall, 1.0 is the maximum possible. YHOO and AOL are also quite strongly positively correlated. It is also noteworthy that there is not a single negative correlation in the table. Negatively correlated stocks are very hard to find, because all shares tend to move up and down together in response to overall good or bad news about the economy.

	YHOO	AOL	CSCO	MSFT	INTC	MRK	BAC	LUV	Viab	CT
YHOO		**0.47**	0.39	0.34	0.28	0.20	0.22	0.29	0.14	0.06
AOL	**0.47**		0.44	0.41	0.31	0.31	0.29	0.33	0.20	0.09
CSCO	0.39	0.44		**0.59**	**0.59**	0.41	0.36	0.36	0.21	0.16
MSFT	0.34	0.41	**0.59**		**0.62**	0.43	0.35	0.34	0.23	0.10
INTC	0.28	0.31	**0.59**	**0.62**		0.37	0.37	0.30	0.21	0.10
MRK	0.20	0.31	0.41	0.43	0.37		0.39	0.34	0.24	0.08
BAC	0.22	0.29	0.36	0.35	0.37	0.39		0.34	0.25	0.17
LUV	0.29	0.33	0.36	0.34	0.30	0.34	0.34		0.23	0.07
Viab	0.14	0.20	0.21	0.23	0.21	0.24	0.25	0.23		0.04
CT	0.06	0.09	0.16	0.10	0.10	0.08	0.17	0.07	0.04	

One stock has very low correlations with all other stocks—CT. This is the same stock that we earlier identified as having a poor performance in terms of risk and return. However, low correlation with other stocks is, as we shall later see, a good thing. So some limited exposure to CT might still be a useful part of a portfolio even though it seems to be poor in terms of risk and return.

13.4. The Riskiness of a Portfolio

An important use of correlation is in calculating the risk of a combination of two variables X and Y. For instance, suppose there are two investments under consideration. Let X be the percent return on investment X, and let Y be the percent return on investment Y. Suppose that I put a% of my money in investment X and 1 − a% in investment Y. Then the return on my total investment will be

$$\text{Return} = aX + (1 - a)Y.$$

For example, if I put 40% of my money in X, which goes up 10%, and the remaining 60% in investment Y, which goes up 20%, then my combined investment increases by

$$0.4 \times 10\% + 0.6 \times 20\% = 16\%.$$

So the practical question is, "What are the return and risk of the portfolio assuming I know the returns and risk of the two investments?" The mathematical question is, "What are the mean and standard deviation of $aX + (1 - a)Y$ if I know the mean and standard deviation of X and Y?"

The *mean growth* on a combined investment is easy. If investment X has mean return μ_X and investment Y has mean return μ_Y then the mean return on the combined investment is

$$\text{Mean Return} = a \times \mu_X + (1 + a) \times \mu_Y,$$

which will always be somewhere between μ_X and μ_Y. So if I want a higher mean return then I put more of my money in the higher mean growth share. No surprises here.

What about volatility? This will surely depend on the riskiness of the two investments, call them σ_X and σ_Y. It will also depend on the relationship between the two stocks. Ideally we would like a negative relationship between the stocks. We measure the type and strength of relationship by r_{XY}. Here is the formula for calculating riskiness of a combined investment.

The square of the risk of a two-stock portfolio investment is

$$\text{Stdev}^2(aX+(1-a)Y) = a^2\sigma_X^2 + (1-a)^2\sigma_Y^2 + 2a(1-a)\sigma_1\sigma_2 r_{XY}$$

and the square root of this will be the standard deviation or *volatility risk.*

If the correlation r_{XY} is negative then one share will go up when the other goes down and the riskiness should be less. In this case, the last term in this expression will be negative and measures the effect of **hedging**.

EXAMPLE 1 (Continued) *Oil and airlines*

Using weekly log returns the risk and return of Oil and SWA are in the table below. The correlation of returns was −0.146. With these five numbers we can work out the riskiness of any combination of the two stocks. Remember that the idea of putting money in Oil was not only that it is less risky than SWA, but that the negative relationship might lead to an even lower volatility.

	Mean	Stdev
SWA(X)	0.468%	5.05%
OIL(Y)	0.031%	3.43%

Let's suppose that we put half our money in each, so $a = 0.5$ and $(1 - a) = 0.5$. We will take X to be SWA and Y to be Oil. The mean growth will be halfway between the growth of SWA and Oil, which in this case is 0.249%.

How about risk? The formula for the squared risk of the combined investment gives

$$\begin{aligned}\text{Stdev}^2(0.5X+0.5Y) &= 0.25\times 5.05^2 + 0.25\times 3.43^2 + 0.5\times 5.05\times 3.53\times(-0.146)\\ &= 9.315+(-1.268)\\ &= 8.047.\end{aligned}$$

The square root of this is 2.837%. This is the volatility of the investment.

Stop and compare this with the volatility of SWA and the volatility of Oil. It is not halfway between 5.05 and 3.43. So it is *not true* that the volatility of an equally weighted portfolio of two stocks is the average of the volatility of the two stocks. It can actually be less than either. In this case, putting half your money in SWA and the other half of your money in Oil is actually less risky than putting all your money in the less risky asset Oil! And this effect is not all due to hedging. If the correlation of the two assets was zero then the −1.268 term would not be in the above calculation and you would get the answer $\sqrt{9.315} = 3.052$. But this is still less risky than oil.

Spreading investments across multiple assets tends to give you a lower volatility. This is termed **diversification of risk**. If you can also find stocks that are negatively related then you can obtain an even lower risk. This is called **hedging of risk**. The formula we are using includes both the effects of diversification and of hedging.

You might wonder, then, if we could get an even lower risk by allocating our money across SWA and Oil differently, that is, by putting some other fraction into Oil than 50%. If you open the worksheet *portfolio* in oil&airlines.xls you can alter the number in cell A3 to try and make the risk of the portfolio in cell D5 as small as possible. The key formula of this section has been coded into cell D6, which contains the so-called variance, which is Stdev^2.

You should find that putting 34% of your money in SWA and 66% in Oil results in the lowest possible risk of 2.634%. There is a better way to discover this than trial and error.

Using Solver

Solver is a tool that comes with Excel that allows you to change the values of one or more cells to produce a desired result in a target cell. The desired result can be used to maximize the value in the target cell, to make the target cell equal to a specified value, or to minimize the value of the target cell. In our case, we want to minimize the value of the target cell D6 (or D5).

Solver is found in the Analysis section under the data ribbon in Excel 2007 (and in the Tools menu for Excel 2003). The dialog box is displayed below. Our target cell is D5 and we want to minimize it. The cell we change is A3. Click *Solve* and you should find that the cell A3 changes to 0.338. This will only work if the cells are all linked correctly.

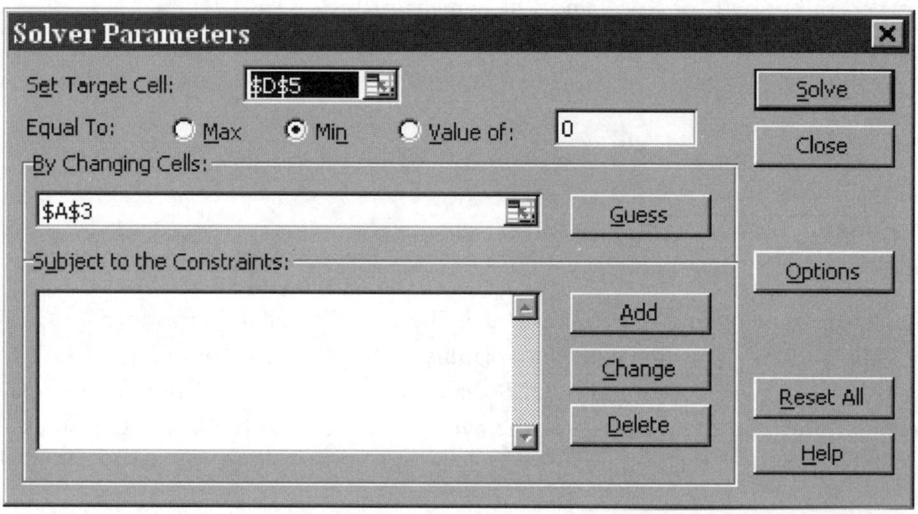

Here is another interesting calculation you can do with Solver. Instead of minimizing the risk we can set it to equal the risk of Oil, which was 3.43%. If you check the button "Value of:" and enter 0.0343 in the value box then you will find that the allocation is 67.6% to SWA and 32.4% to Oil. This gives a risk of 3.43% and a mean growth of 0.326%. Notice that this growth is way higher than the growth of Oil, but with the same risk. This shows that *nobody in their right mind could put all their money in Oil*. You get a higher mean return with the same risk by putting two-thirds of your money in SWA and one-third of your money in Oil.

All these calculations, of course, assume that the five figures we are using are appropriate for making future investment decisions. We will return to the issue of how you get the five numbers at the end of this chapter.

EXAMPLE 2 (Continued) *Ten big stocks*

We can do a similar exercise with any pair of stocks. Let's look at MSFT and CSCO. These are in the same industry and have a strong positive correlation of 0.591 so there will be no hedging of risk happening here. The relevant mean and standard deviation are in the table below.

	Mean	Stdev
MSFT	0.244%	2.25%
CSCO	0.238%	2.93%

If we put 80% in MSFT and 20% in CSCO then we obtain a growth of 0.243%, almost as good as putting all our money in MSFT. But we get a volatility of 2.20%, which is less volatile than either stock. Think about this. We put 20% of our money in the more risky CSCO and the volatility goes ... down! This is an effect of diversification, even though the positive correlation of 0.591 works against this to some extent. The calculation is in the worksheet <u>portfolio</u> of big10.xls.

CHECK YOUR UNDERSTANDING

Q2. For the oil–airlines example, we calculated the variance of the portfolio using the general formula

$$a^2\sigma_X^2 + (1-a)^2\sigma_Y^2 + 2a(1-a)\sigma_1\sigma_2 r_{XY}$$

and obtained the answer 8.040. This was less than the variance 11.87 for oil future returns and less than the variance 25.48 for airline returns.

(a) If the returns on the two investments were uncorrelated then what would the variance be? Would the variance still be less than the variance of either alone?

(b) What important principle of statistics could help you to anticipate the answer to part (a) without doing the calculation?

13.5. Balancing Risk and Return

We have seen that spreading money across two assets can give better results than either asset can achieve on its own. For instance, you can get a much lower risk than either investment. But the aim of the game is not to minimize risk per se. It is to get high return *and* low risk. There are two performance measures here—risk and return. We need some way to combine them into a single performance measure.

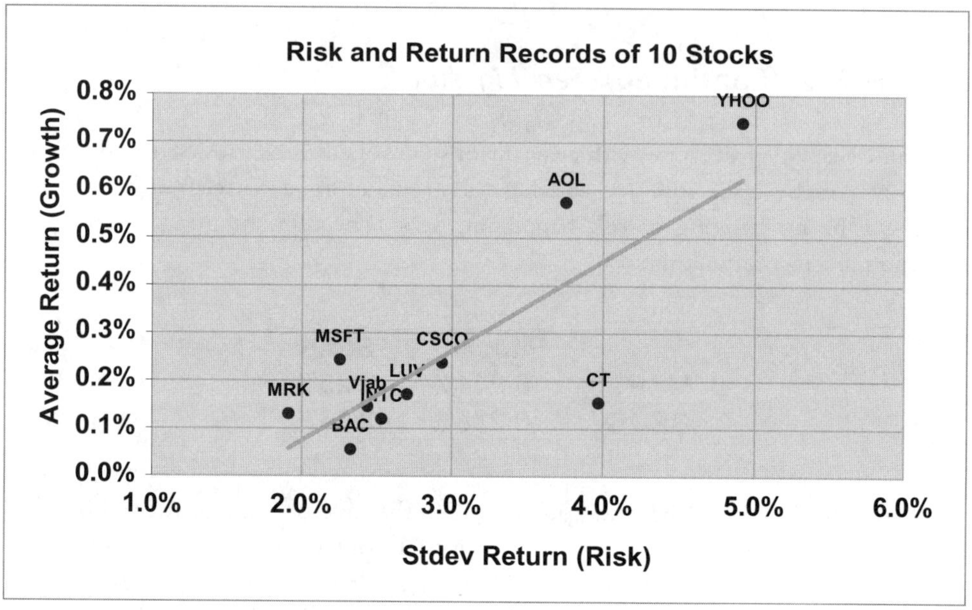

The clue to how to do this is in the earlier plot of return and risk of the 10 stocks. It looks like there might be an increasing linear relation between mean and standard deviation, of the form

$$\text{mean} = m x \text{Stdev} + b.$$

The intercept b represents the mean growth of a zero-risk asset—the so-called **risk-free rate (RFR)**, often taken to be the interest rate on a treasury bond (TB). So

$$\text{mean} = m x \text{Stdev} + \text{RFR}.$$

We would like the slope m of the line to be as large as possible, so that the mean return increases as fast as possible as the risk increases. A little bit of algebra allows us to express the slope as

$$\frac{\text{mean} - \text{RFR}}{\text{stdev}}$$

This is known as the **Sharp ratio**. It is a measure of how fast the mean return on an investment increases compared to the risk involved. It is a single numerical measure of the quality of an investment. No one in their right mind would accept less than the RFR. So on the numerator is the excess return over this RFR. As soon as you pursue a higher growth you accept some risk. This goes on the denominator. So the Sharp ratio measures how many percent of excess return you obtain for each extra 1% of risk.

EXAMPLE 2 (Continued) *Ten big stocks*

During 1997–1998 the RFR was around 4% per annum, which is 0.08% per week. All terms in the Sharp ratio must be measured in the same units—here in units of return per week, because the data are weekly.

The Sharp ratios are in the table below. YHOO has the highest ratio, not because it had the highest return but because it has the best combination of return and risk, as measured by the Sharp ratio. BAC has a negative Sharp ratio because it returns less than the RFR.

	YHOO	AOL	MSFT	INTC	MRK	BAC	CT
Mean (return)	0.74%	0.57%	0.24%	0.12%	0.13%	0.06%	0.16%
Stdev (risk)	4.91%	3.76%	2.25%	2.53%	1.91%	2.32%	3.97%
Sharp Ratio	0.136	0.133	0.075	0.018	0.029	-0.008	0.020

EXAMPLE 1 (Continued) *Oil and airlines*

The RFR during 1989–1996 varied but we will take a central figure of 0.02% per day, which means 5.1% per annum. From the return and risk of SWA and Oil we can calculate the Sharp ratio of both. SWA has a way higher Sharp ratio than Oil.

	SWA	OIL	50–50
Mean	0.47%	0.03%	0.25%
Stdev	5.05%	3.43%	2.84%
Sharp	0.0887	0.0031	0.0808

We calculated the return and risk of a 50:50 portfolio earlier. The portfolio is an investment like anything else, and its Sharp ratio is calculated using its mean and risk. It turns out that the Sharp ratio for the portfolio is 0.0808—not as good as SWA. This does not mean we should put 100% of our money in SWA, though. We just have not got the balance right.

If you put 80% in SWA and 20% in Oil then the Sharp ratio is 0.0902, which is better than SWA. This is very close to the best allocation possible. You can find the best allocation by using Solver and maximizing the Sharp ratio of the portfolio. The worksheet *portfolio sharp* is set up for you to do this.

What Is a Reasonable Value for the Sharp Ratio?

There is no simple answer to this question. For starters it depends on whether you are measuring daily, or weekly, or monthly, or yearly returns. The Sharp ratio for a given stock will be higher when considered over a longer period. This actually carries a message—that longer-term investments are better than shorter-term ones!

For per annum returns, it is not unusual for Sharp ratios to equal around 1, meaning that you get an extra 1% per annum growth for each extra 1% per annum risk. But this varies over time. Sharp ratios tend to be higher in boom times.

You should make sure that when you are comparing stocks and portfolios you use the same period of return and the same period of time for each—for instance, weekly from 1989 to 1996. Subject to this, you want the combination of stocks with the highest Sharp ratio.

13.6. CONTROLLING RISK WITH TBs

There is a correct way to allocate your money across two stocks, once you know the means, risks, and correlation. The optimal portfolio has its own mean and standard deviation, which delivers the best of trade-off risk for return. But what if you just don't like the return and risk of the portfolio? For instance, you might have wanted a higher return (accepting that this will involve higher risk) or you might have wanted a lower risk (accepting that this will involve less return). You can use TBs to increase or decrease your return and risk to match your individual risk preference.

To do this you put a certain proportion a of your money in the portfolio (with the relative amounts in the two stocks determined by the optimal Sharp ratio) and the rest of your money $1 - a$ in the TB. Your investment then has three components, the TB and the two risky investments X and Y.

The mean of this investment will be

$$\text{Mean Return} = a \times \mu_{PORT} + (1 - a) \times \text{RFR},$$

where μ_{PORT} is the return on your portfolio. The risk of the investment is

$$\text{Stdev} = a \times \sigma_{PORT},$$

where σ_{PORT} is the risk of the portfolio.

The larger the allocation ***a*** to the risky portfolio, the higher your return and risk. The smaller the allocation ***a***, the lower your return and risk.

The resulting investment has a very attractive property. There will be no other combination of the three investments that has a higher growth for the same risk. If you wanted to target a particular risk, then this strategy will achieve it with the maximum growth possible. There will be no other combination of investments that has a lower risk for the same growth. If you wanted to target a particular GR, then this strategy will achieve it with the minimum risk.

EXAMPLE 1 (Continued) *Oil and airlines*

We earlier determined that the original 50:50 allocation across SWA and Oil was not a good balance and gave a worse Sharp ratio than SWA alone. We found that the best allocation across SWA and Oil, in terms of maximizing the Sharp ratio, was 80:20.

	SWA	OIL	80–20
Mean	0.468%	0.031%	0.380%
Stdev	5.05%	3.43%	4.00%
Sharp	0.0887	0.0031	0.0902

This has a risk of 4.00%. What if you wanted less risk—say no more risky than Oil alone, which has a risk of 3.43%? We could alter the 80:20 mix to achieve this. In fact we did this earlier and got a mean growth of 0.327% with 68% in SWA and 32% in Oil. This is called "naïve target" in the table below. We necessarily sacrifice some of our optimized Sharp ratio when we deviate from the 80:20 mix. There is a better way to achieve the target risk of 3.43% that does not involve fiddling with the 80:20 mix. You put some of your money in TBs instead.

	Optimal	Naïve target	Optimal target
SWA	80%	68%	68.6%
Oil	20%	32%	17.2%
TB			14.2%
Mean	0.380%	0.327	0.330%
Stdev	4.00%	3.43%	3.43%
Sharp	0.0902	0.0893	0.0902

But how much? From the formula

$$\text{Stdev} = a \times \sigma_{\text{PORT}},$$

we can easily target a standard deviation of 3.43% starting with the standard deviation of 4.00% for the portfolio. If we put 85.8% of our money in the portfolio then the standard deviation is 0.858 × 4.00 = 3.43%. The mean return is then 0.330%—slightly better than 0.327%. The calculations are set up for you in the worksheet *treasury bonds* and summarized in the table above.

This investment requires each $1000 to be split up as follows: You invest $858 in SWA and Oil in the ratio of the optimal portfolio, which is 80:20. So $686 of the $858 goes into SWA and the remaining $172 goes into Oil. The remaining $142 is invested in TBs.

You might like to calculate the Sharp ratio of the total investment. You will find it is 0.0902—exactly the same as for the optimal portfolio. In fact, you can allocate your money between the optimal portfolio and TBs how you like and the Sharp ratio is always 0.0902. This is another argument in favor of using the Sharp ratio. It measures the trade-off possible between risk and return. You can then make your personal choice about how much return to trade for risk by allocating more or less money to TBs.

What about if you wanted more growth, say you wanted 0.400% growth? You can use Solver to target the cell C10 to equal 0.0040. The result is that you put 1.054 into the portfolio and −0.054 in TBs!? Does it make sense to talk about negative allocations? Yes it does! In this case, it would mean borrowing $5.4 for every $100 you want to invest (at the RFR) and then putting the whole $105.4 into the Portfolio. In practice, of course, you cannot borrow money at the RFR. Your cost of capital will be higher, depending on who you are and your credit rating.

Where Do We Get the Five Numbers?

Designing optimal combinations of stocks requires you to know the mean return of each stock, the standard deviation or volatility of each stock, and the correlation of the returns.

Structural Correlations Of these, the correlation is probably the easiest to estimate. You can just use historical correlations. There is reason to believe that historical correlations will persist into the future because they measure the structural relationship between companies and sectors. For instance, all companies within a sector will tend to be highly correlated. There are more sophisticated methods of estimating correlations than just using the correlations of historical returns. So-called *linear factor models* attempt to explain the correlations between stocks by a small number of unobserved structural factors.

Volatilities Volatility risk of each stock could be estimated by historical returns—for instance, the standard deviation of the last year of weekly returns. But there is no guarantee that next year's volatility will be similar to last year. You might have good reason to think that next year will be more or less risky than last year. Actually, this is not such a problem for portfolio theory because it is only the *relative* volatilities that matter in determining the best allocation. So if all stocks have 10%

higher volatilities next year then the best allocation is not affected. However, if the relative volatilities change—for instance, you expect big changes in commodity price volatility—then this will have an effect.

There are several ways of objectively assessing how risky a particular share might be in the future. If the share is traded on the options market, then it is possible to infer what the market believes about the share's future volatility from its option price. Unless you think you know better than the market, you might take this market-based estimate as your own. These are called *implied volatilities.*

Mean Returns: Potential Growth The hardest numbers to get are the mean returns for each stock. These are supposed to represent the most likely return on the stock next year. Certainly, history will be of absolutely no help to you here. To get reliable numbers for the mean returns you will have to do your homework on the company, its management, and the prospects for the sector. Warren Buffet and the good folks at Berkshire-Hathaway are very good at this!

The biggest limitation on optimal portfolio construction is in getting the numbers, especially the means. But once you have these numbers, there is no question about how you should allocate your money. You allocate it to maximize the Sharp ratio. Any other allocation is simply wrong—assuming you believe your own numbers.

What about More Than Two Stocks?

If you have more than two stocks then you need to decide how much of your money to invest in each. To determine the best allocation, you need to know the mean return for each, you need to know the volatility risk of each, and you need to know all the correlations. The historical figures were given for the 10 stocks examples. The best portfolio will allocate more money to stocks that are high return, are low risk, and are lowly correlated with other stocks.

To find the best portfolio you need a formula for the mean and volatility of a portfolio. The mean is easy. If you put 10% in one stock, 30% in a second stock, and 60% in a third stock then the mean return is 10% of the first mean plus 30% of the second plus 60% of the third. The volatility is more complicated—it depends on the volatilities of all the stocks and all their pairwise correlations. The formula will not be given here, but can be written simply in *matrix* form.

Once you have the mean and standard deviation, the Sharp ratio is defined in the same way, and you can optimize the allocation to each stock by maximizing the Sharp ratio. You can use Excel Solver for this or there are direct mathematical formulas.

Other Types of Risk

We noted that CT looked like a poorly performing stock but that it had low correlation with other stocks and so could be potentially useful in a portfolio. It rose to as high as $12 during 1997–1998 but fell to $6 at the end.

You might like to check the CT share price now. In mid-2010 it was about \$1.80 compared to heights of about \$40. This company was in the business of selling subprime loans and their derivatives. The historical standard deviation does not measure this kind of risk. It measures the sensitivity of the share price to the random fluctuations of the market. Portfolio theory would not protect you from the global financial crisis (GFC) unless you realized, better than the rest of the market, that these assets were highly risky.

13.7. Summary

The most common measure of association between two variables is the **correlation**. This number is between −1 and+1, representing the extremes of a perfect linear negative or positive relationship, respectively. Correlation is independent of the units of measurement.

Investment quality is measured by the mean and standard deviation of the returns. The mean represents growth and the standard deviation represents volatility risk. If we have two possible investments X and Y with mean return μ_X and μ_Y and risk σ_X and σ_Y, respectively, and if their correlation is r_{XY} then we might consider putting a proportion $\boldsymbol{a}$ of our money in X and a proportion $1 - \boldsymbol{a}$ of our money in Y. In this case the mean of the combined investment is

$$a\mu_X + (1-a)\mu_Y$$

and the squared risk of the combined investment is

$$\text{Stdev}^2(aX + (1-a)Y) = a^2\sigma_X^2 + (1-a)^2\sigma_Y^2 + 2a(1-a)\sigma_1\sigma_2 r_{XY}.$$

Different values of $\boldsymbol{a}$ lead to a different trade-off between mean performance and risk. The minimum risk investment is *not* obtained by putting all your money in the less risky asset.

The quality of an investment with mean return μ and risk σ is measured by

$$\frac{\text{mean} - \text{RFR}}{\text{stdev}}$$

known as the Sharp ratio. It measures how much excess return over the RFR you obtain for each unit of risk.

TBs can be used, in combination with a risk portfolio, to target any desired mean or any desired risk. You should leave the relative allocation across the risky assets at the values that optimize the Sharp ratio. The desired mean or risk can then be targeted by putting the appropriate proportion of your money in a TB. The Sharp ratio of this three-way investment is the same as the optimized Sharp ratio.

EXERCISES

E1. There are two possible investments you are considering. Throughout this question we measure return on investment in units of percent per annum. Shares in Solid Pty. Ltd. have returns whose mean has been assessed as 5.5 with a standard deviation of 2.1. On the other hand, you could invest in Avago Co., whose shares enjoy an expected long-term return of 12.5 but with a larger standard deviation of 7.5. The correlation between the returns of the two investments is 0.098.

(a) What does the positive correlation imply in words?

(b) Calculate the mean and standard deviation of the return on a portfolio that has 50% of your money invested in each company.

(c) Calculate the mean and standard deviation of the return on a portfolio that has 95% of your money invested in Solid. Pty. Ltd. Do you notice anything about this portfolio compared to a 100% investment in Solid Pty. Ltd?

E2. Suggest two publicly traded shares that you might expect are negatively related. Explain why you would expect this. Download some share price data from Yahoo, calculate the returns, and see if you were right!

E3. What if X does not vary at all? What is the correlation of X and Y in this case? It is difficult to decide because the z-values from the x sample will be undefined because the denominator S_X of the z-values will be zero. However, by convention we say that the correlation of any variable with any constant equals *zero*.

(a) Suppose that you are considering an investment in a stock whose mean return is 10.5 but whose standard deviation of return is 12.5. On the other hand, you can put some of your money in a totally risk-free asset (a TB), whose return is 5.5. If you put 25% of your money in the risk-free asset then what is the mean and standard deviation of your combined investment?

(b) In general, suppose that you put a proportion $\boldsymbol{a}$ of your money in a risky asset whose Sharp ratio is S and the rest in a risk-free asset. What is the Sharp ratio of this combination of two assets?

E4. You are considering investing in two possible shares. This is as an alternative to a risk-free 12-month TB, which returns 3.5%.

The first is Russian Rouble Roulette (3R), which has very high growth prospects, around 16% over the RFR. Bet Your Shirt (BYS) Pty. Ltd. has a much lower expected growth than 3R.

The table below gives figures describing the likely *annual returns* for these two investments. These figures may be taken as true and correct for the purposes of the required calculations. Obviously, most stocks will tend to go up and down together as general business conditions vary. Your assessment of the association of these particular stocks is summarized by the figure 0.12, being the correlation of annual returns.

	Mean	Stdev
3R	19.6%	22.3%
BYS Pty. Ltd.	6.6%	3.7%

(a) Describe *in quantitative but nontechnical terms* what the table of means and standard deviations says about the returns on each investment.

(b) Suppose you put 99% of your money into BYS and 1% in 3R. What will be the mean and standard deviation of the annual return, both correct to two decimal places?

(c) Give a short assessment of this statement: "BYS is a perfectly respectable investment with a good return. Putting 1% of your money into 3R may give you a higher mean growth, but why would you expose yourself to the extra risk?" (50 words maximum)

(d) Compare the portfolio in (b) with a 100% investment in BYS using the Sharp ratio.

(e) Which combination of 3R and BYS gives the best trade-off between the mean growth and the risk as measured by the Sharp ratio? Describe this portfolio.

(f) You have $50,000 total investment, and you are going to spread your money across BYS, 3R, and a risk-free asset. You want a mean growth of 7%. How do you allocate your funds and what is the associated risk?

E5. The file Q5.xls has recent weekly data on three shares—MSFT, General Electric (GE), and a medical supply and insurance company MDT.

(a) Calculate log returns of all these shares.

(b) Calculate mean returns, volatility risk, and correlations for all these stocks.

(c) Consider putting money in MSFT and MDT only. What is the best combination?

(d) Suppose that you do not believe that the high growth in these three stocks can persist. You decide that the future GRs will be exactly three times lower than the historical average returns, which were achieved during the recovery from the lows of the GFC. What is the best allocation now?

(e) Using the deflated growth figures, suppose you wanted to target 12% growth. How much money would you put in TBs, MSFT, and MDT?

(f) Repeat parts (c), (d), and (e) for portfolios of MSFT and GE.

(g) Repeat parts (c), (d), and (e) for portfolios of MDT and GE. (You will find that there are some negative allocations of money to one of the stocks. Your instructor will explain what this means in the real world!)

(h) Which would be the best way of obtaining 12% growth?

CHAPTER 14

Investigating Relationships between Business Variables

DEEPWATER BAY REAL ESTATE: CASE BRIEFING

Justin Ho is a HK property developer and investor considering investing in the area of Deepwater Bay. He needs to be able to identify apartments that are selling at or below their fair market price. He is also interested in redeveloping apartments into different configurations and wants to maximize their resale value.

Justin obtains data on 108 properties that had sold during 1995. The total sales was over $105M. There was a wide range of prices that had been realized—from about $600K to $2M, expressed in 1995 U.S. dollars.

The main features that are likely to drive the value of an apartment are its total floor area, its age, the number of bedrooms and bathrooms, and the number of dedicated car spaces.

Justin wants to know which apartment features are the strongest drivers of price. He has an idea of what he thinks these should be but wants confirmation from the data, if for no other reason than to confirm to himself that these data are to be trusted.

He is to prepare a short report that describes which features are the most important drivers of price and what their effect on price is. Are there any obvious but easily measured features of the apartments that you can think of that Justin should make an extra effort to collect?

14.0. INTRODUCTION: WHAT IS THE ISSUE?

You sell apartments in Deepwater Bay, Hong Kong, and you need a sensible way of estimating values before you can consider offers or set a reserve for auction. The main features that impact on price are its age, the number of bedrooms and bathrooms, and whether or not it comes with a dedicated car space. Which of these features most strongly affect the price?

Data-Driven Business Decisions, First Edition. Chris J. Lloyd.

Can a county's trade deficit this quarter be predicted from the trade deficit last quarter? How about the quarter before that? In other words, is there a relationship between current behavior and previous behavior that could be used to predict future behavior?

How does a car's market value depend on miles traveled and age? Older cars automatically have more miles so isn't the dependence on age mostly due to the miles and not age per se? Can we ever untangle this?

Most business problems require some understanding of the relationships between variables. In this section we look again at the use of correlation as a general measure of association between any two business variables, how it is interpreted, and whether a given correlation is to be believed.

14.1. Measuring Association with Correlation

Two variables X and Y are dependent if the value of one affects the likely values of the other. They are **positively associated** if large values of one variable make larger values of the other more likely. They are **negatively associated** if large values of one variable make smaller values of the other more likely.

In the previous chapter we used correlation to measure the strength and nature of the relationship between returns on two shares. Correlation is a general measure of association and can be used to measure the association between any two business variables, not just returns on stocks.

The **sample correlation** of a scatter plot is

$$r_{XY} = \frac{1}{n-1}\sum_{i=1}^{n} Z_{xi}Z_{Yi},$$

where Z_{xi} are the z-scores associated with the x sample and Z_{Yi} are the z-scores associated with the y sample.

Correlation is not the only measure of association but it is by far the most common. Let's remind ourselves of its properties. First, it is unaffected by units so if I want to know how the area of an apartment affects its price, I can measure area in square feet or square meters and price in U.S. dollars or HK dollars and the correlation will not change.

Correlation is on an absolute scale from −1 to 1. The closer to ±1, the closer the relationship is to being perfectly linear. The sign of the correlation tells you if the relationship is positive or negative.

In Excel, the function CORREL(xrange,yrange) calculates the correlation of any two sets of numbers. If you want to calculate the correlation of many variables with each other then you can use StatproGo. Select Summary Stats, then Correlations, Covariances, and the correlations will be output as a table.

EXAMPLE 1 *Hong Kong real estate*

You have the sale price of 108 apartments sold in Hong Kong together with five features that you think are relevant to the price—the floor area, the number of bedrooms and number of bathrooms, as well as the age and the number of car spaces. We are most interested how these variables are related to price but there are also relationships between these five variables. For instance, we can expect that larger apartment will have more bedrooms.

The data are in ex 1 hkre.xls. Using StatproGo you can obtain the correlations in the table below. These describe the relationship of each variable with each other variable—15 pairs in all.

	BEDS	BATHS	CARS	AGE	AREA	PRICE
BEDS	1					
BATHS	0.393	1				
CARS	0.066	0.275	1			
AGE	0.279	-0.124	-0.120	1		
AREA	0.239	0.614	0.433	-0.292	1	
PRICE	0.254	0.561	0.549	-0.391	0.828	1

The strongest predictor of price is area because the correlation of 0.828 is the largest for this feature. You can check the spreadsheet and the comment in the first cells to see that the area is measured in units of square feet and the price has been converted to U.S. dollars. However, this has no effect at all on the correlation.

The next strongest predictor is the number of bathrooms, then car spaces, then age (which has a negative effect on price), and finally the number of bedrooms. Each of these figures describes a plot. Two of them are below.

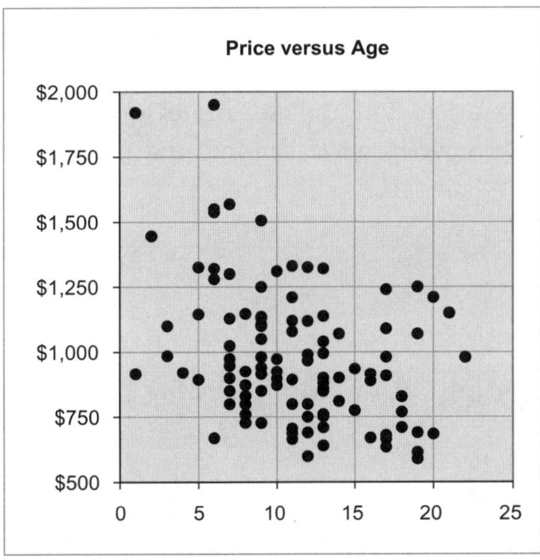

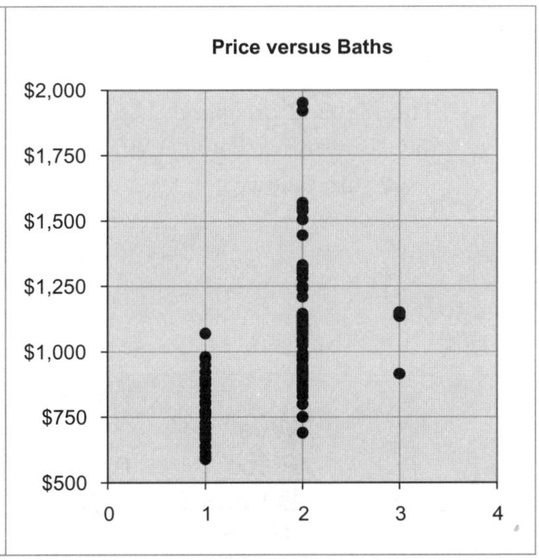

You can see the negative relationship of price with age clearly, and see that it is fairly weak. The numerical measurement is –0.391. The plot of the price against the number of bathrooms is much harder to judge, because the apartments had either one, two, or three bathrooms and so the x variables stack up in columns. This is why it is useful to have an objective numerical measure, precisely for those cases where visual judgment is suspect. The correlation of this plot is 0.561. The relationship is judged to be considerably stronger than the negative association with age.

There are also other relationships that we get from the correlation table. Looking at the AREA row, we see that it is positively related with beds, baths, and cars. No real surprises there. You would expect larger apartments to have more rooms and, since these tend to be more upmarket and expensive, it is no surprise that they have more car spaces. The negative relationship of area with age is unexpected. This says that older apartments are smaller, or to put it another way, larger apartments are newer.

In fact, looking at the AGE row we see that older apartments tend to not only be smaller but they have more bedrooms and fewer bathrooms. The age variable gives us a view into the past. This might say something about the changing circumstances of typical Hong Kong families in the period from 1975 to 1995.

EXAMPLE 2 *Pricing policy*

You manufacture an innovative kind of spanner that costs \$4.45 to produce. The recommended retail price (RRP) is determined on a weekly basis. There is not much seasonality in the sale of basic tools. Since the launch of the product roughly 2 years ago you have increased your pricing from around \$8 to \$11.50. For each week, you have also determined the number of spanners sold. This allows you to calculate the profit from the formula

$$\text{Profit} = \text{number sold} \times (\text{RRP} - 4.45).$$

The file ex 2 pricing.xls has 2 years of these data. You can use StatproGo to tabulate the correlations between the four variables week, price, demand, and profit. The results are below.

	Week	Price	Demand	Profit
Week	1			
Price	0.917	1		
Demand	-0.757	-0.953	1	
Profit	0.639	0.319	-0.039	1

The variable Week here just labels the weeks 1, 2, 3, and so on. Positive correlations with Week indicate that the variable is increasing over time. Looking at the first column we can see that prices increase over time (because management thought the market could bear higher prices), that demand decreased but that profit increased. Pricing has a strong effect on demand as you would expect. The correlation of −0.953 says that increasing price produces an almost linear reduction in the units sold.

Let's focus on the bottom line—the Profit row. The correlations suggest that profit increases with price and decreases with demand. If we take this to its logical conclusion, it suggests that we should increase prices as high as we like and we will get less demand and also get more profit. This sounds like utter nonsense—and it is. The problem is that some of these relationships are not linear and could never be linear.

The plot of demand against RRP *does* look linear. Though, if you think about it, the relationship cannot continue as a line indefinitely since linear demand would eventually be negative if the price was high enough. But over the range of prices charged, demand does follow a decreasing linear trend. The plot of profit versus RRP is *not linear* and logically it never could be. If you charge too much for your product you lose demand and profit, while if you charge too little you lose margin. There is always a best price somewhere in between, which looks like somewhere just less than $10 according to this plot.

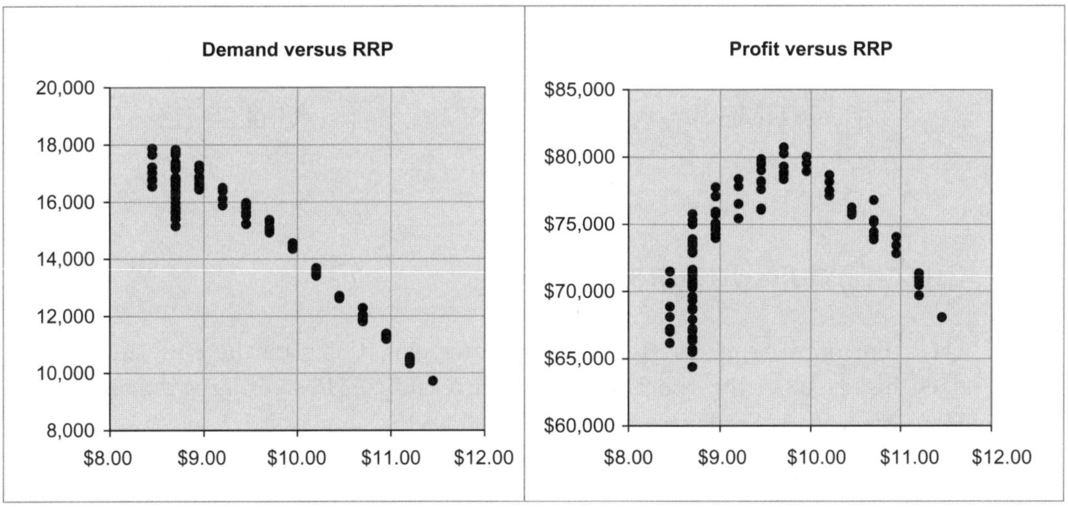

In this case you make a serious error in using correlations because some of the key associations cannot be linear. Whenever you are interested in optimizing some business output, such as profit, you will nearly always find that there is a nonlinear relationship with the key inputs. Rest assured that even though this is a limitation of correlation, we can handle situations like this, and you will find out how in the later chapters on multiple regression.

Neither can correlation tell you which variables drive which, though typically common sense does. In this case, RRP varies over time in a manner *which management decides by policy*, so this is really a decision variable. Price affects the main uncertain variable here, namely demand. You also wonder whether there might be some underlying growth in demand as the product becomes more widely known. Even though the correlation suggests that demand has gone down over time, this might be because of the increasing price and the underlying level of the demand might actually be increasing, and this is supporting the price (and profit) increase. You would hope so! Finally, once we have demand, the profit is determined mathematically by the unit price and the simple rules of accounting.

All of this has been represented in a flow diagram below. It is always a good idea to map out which variables drive which. This is also a good opportunity to stop and think whether you have missed any important variables. For instance, if you are spending lots of money on advertising, and if this varies over the 100 weeks of data, then this might have been worth recording. If unit cost was changing from $4.45, you would also need to account for this.

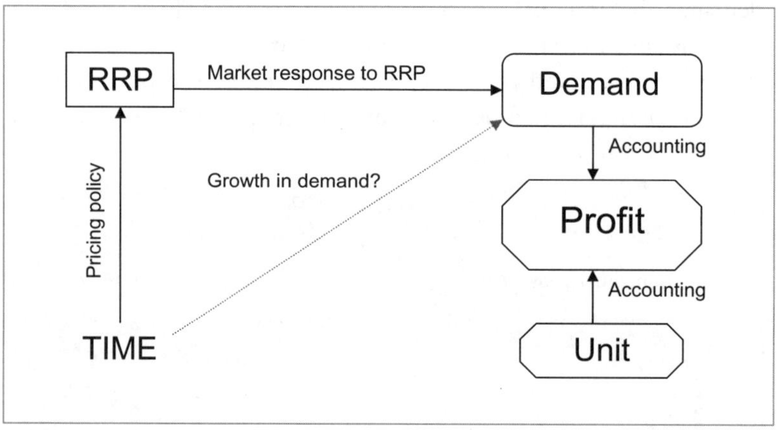

Check Your Understanding

Q1. For the data in Q1.xls, create a scatter plot. Calculate the correlation. What does this say about the association between X and Y? How strong is the association? How can you reconcile this with plot?

14.2. Looking at Complex Relationships

Correlations tell you about the relationship in a scatter plot. When the performance variable is driven by more than one possible input the scatter plot can be misleading. Therefore the correlation can be misleading.

This is represented schematically in the diagram below. The variable Z drives both X and Y. If we see a correlation between X and Y, it may mainly be due to the variable Z. Such a variable is called hidden or confounding. In economics it is called endogenous.

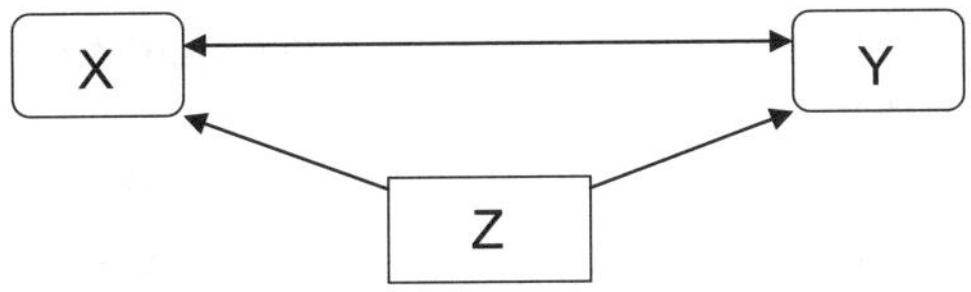

For instance, there is a positive correlation between income and height. You can get data from almost any country and see it for yourself in a plot. Do you really think taller people are paid more? The hidden variable in this case is gender. Males are taller than females on average and they are paid more than females on average. Never mind whether you think this is fair. It is a fact. And you would kind of miss the point if you interpreted the data as evidence of height discrimination!

EXAMPLE 2 (Continued) *Pricing policy*

If we plot demand versus time we can see a clear decreasing relationship. The correlation is −0.757. The relationship is obviously nonlinear, but let's focus on an even more important point. The RRP was being systematically increased over this period. So some or perhaps all of the reducing demand might be due to increasing price. If we wanted to measure the underlying growth in demand for the spanner we would want to separate this from the effects of our pricing policy. To put it more clearly, if we look at those weeks where the pricing was constant, is there evidence for decreasing demand?

There were 13 distinct prices charged during the 100 weeks of data. If we break the data up into these groups and calculate the correlation of demand and week within each group then we get quite different results. For instance, the lowest RRP of $8.45 was charged for 8 of the 100 weeks. The particular weeks and the demand are in the table below.

Week	7	8	12	14	16	17	20	34
Demand	16544	16802	16806	16755	17220	17029	17659	17870

It looks like demand increases over these particular 8 weeks. The correlation is actually 0.91. If I do this for each of the 13 unique prices we get the 13 correlations below. Every correlation is positive and large! This is the opposite conclusion we got before. What it means is that underlying demand is strongly *increasing* over time. The only reason we saw demand apparently decreasing was that we were increasing prices strongly.

If we wanted to summarize the relationship of demand and time in a single number we might use the average of these 13 correlations, giving 0.868. In fact, even though demand decreased at an average rate of 56 per week, when the changing RRP is allowed for, it was actually increasing at an average rate of 51 per week.

RRP	# Weeks	Correl
$8.45	8	0.91
$8.70	35	0.97
$8.95	11	0.84
$9.20	4	0.75
$9.45	9	0.94
$9.70	6	0.90
$9.95	3	1.00
$10.20	4	0.70
$10.45	4	0.72
$10.70	6	0.85
$10.95	3	0.96
$11.20	5	0.74
$11.45	2	1.00

You will find out how to calculate these **slopes**, which are an alternative measure of relationship, in the next chapter.

Excel

Pivotables breaks data up into groups but it will not calculate correlations for each group. It will only calculate means, standard deviations, and counts. The template grouped correlation.xls can be used to for this purpose. To use it just drop the *Z*, *X*, and *Y* data into Columns D, E, and F. The template breaks the data up into groups with similar values of *Z*.

You have two options. You can just choose how many subgroups you want and the template will define these groups automatically based on the values of the *Z* variable. For instance if you choose 10 groups then the template takes the lowest 10% of *z* values for the first group, the next lowest 10% for the second group, and so on. Or you can define your own group labels and type them into Column C.

The calculations for the pricing example are in the worksheet *grouped* of ex 2 pricing.xls. There is other output in the template that will be explained later.

Moving Correlations

The grouping template should work for most applications. There is another useful way to account for the hidden variable *Z*. There is no template provided for this but it is easy to do. Here are the steps.

- Put *X*, *Y*, and *Z* in adjacent columns.
- Sort on *Z* from smallest to largest.
- Choose a number of cases that you want in each group. I suggest an odd number, say around 11.
- Calculate the correlation of *X* and *Y* for the first 11 cases, which will be the 11 smallest values of *Z*. Next, calculate the correlation for cases 2–12, then for cases 3–13, and so on. You can easily do this by dragging the formula down.

- Plot these correlations against the center of each group. For instance, plot the first correlation of cases 1–11 against the sixth value of *Z*.

EXAMPLE 3 *Sale price of used motorcycles*

The main determinants of the selling price of a motorcycle are its age and its mileage. The file ex 3 motorcycles.xls contains the sale prices of 135 motorcycles sold at auction, their age in years, and their mileage. No motorcycle was less than 3 years old.

The relationship between all variables is extremely strong. Miles traveled has a negative effect ($r = -0.983$), as does age ($r = -0.932$). Not surprisingly, there is a strong positive relationship between miles and age ($r = 0.941$). This makes us wonder about how much of the calendar time age depreciation on the price of the motorcycle is due to the larger mileage. If you were trying to value the motorcycle, it would be important to separate these effects. In terms of the hidden variable idea, we want to know the relationships between X = price and Y = age, controlling for the variable Z = miles.

The worksheet *moving correlations* has the calculations. The data are first sorted with respect to miles. I used a "window" of 23 so the first correlation measures the association of price and age for the 23 motorcycles with the least miles, the second correlation measures the association of price and age for motorcycles 2–24, and so on. A plot of these moving correlations against the mileage is below.

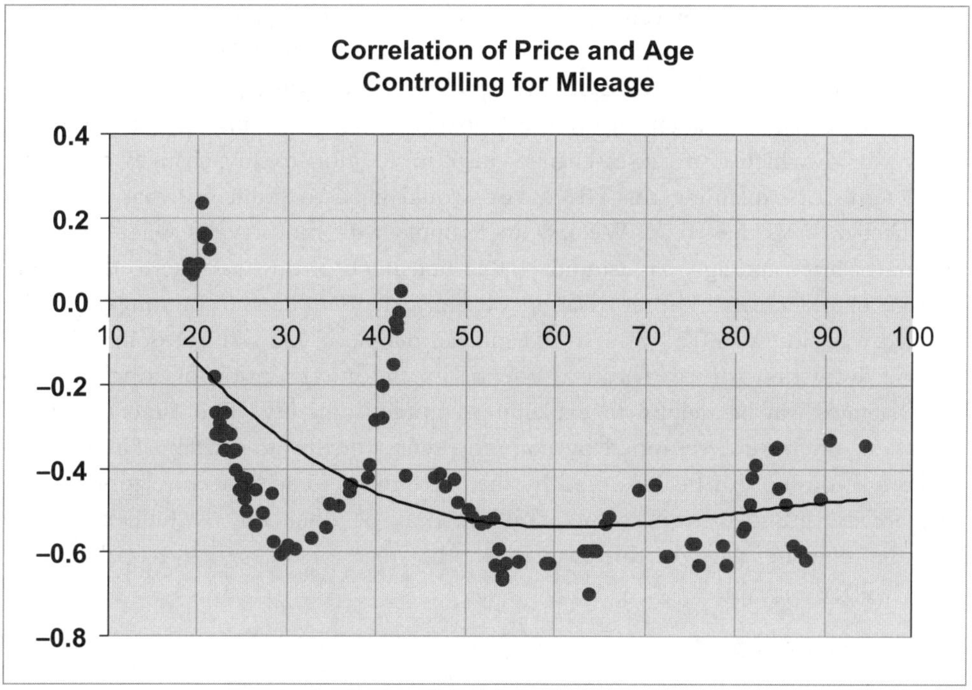

You can ignore most of the detailed features in moving correlation plots. To do this it is helpful to add a trendline. We will have more to say about this in the next chapter. The main conclusion from this plot is that

Curve added as visual aid: *Add trendline.*

the correlation of age and price is much weaker than the figure −0.932. A more reasonable figure looks like somewhere around −0.5. Moreover, the correlation seems to be weaker for motorcycles with lower mileage. In simple words, for motorcycles with low mileage, the age had very little effect on price (over and above the mileage). For motorcycles with higher mileage, there seems to be a stronger penalty for age.

14.3. INTERPRETING CORRELATIONS

How do you convey correlations to others? If you can do this well, you should understand the concepts better yourself.

Validity and Causality

If a correlation is large then we would like to say that changes in *X* will cause large changes in *Y*, either positive or negative depending on the sign. This may not be the case, and suggesting that it is can be extremely misleading.

Firstly, *Y* may cause *X* rather than *X* cause *Y*. This is not often an issue in business but there are public policy contexts where it is key. For instance, if you plot official interest rates against gross domestic product growth (for whatever country you come from) then there is a strong positive correlation. Higher interest rates are associated with higher growth. So why not increase interest rates to get higher growth? The direction of causation is the reverse! Central banks raise interest rates *in response to* excessive economic activity, with a view to cooling the economy.

Especially when other variables are involved, careful interpretation is required. Even if there is some causal relationship between *X* and *Y*, changing *X* may cause a change in *Z*, which also causes changes in *Y* in addition to any changes caused by *X*. In terms of explaining this effect, you would need to point out that not all of the effect on *Y* is due to *X*. We saw an example with motorcycles where the correlation of price and age was around −0.932 but much of this was due to the higher mileage of older cars. The correlation of age and price after accounting for miles traveled was close to −0.5. You would mislead people if you did not point this out. Making distinctions of this nature is essential to the interpretation of correlation.

Diagrams can be helpful in explaining complex causality. The direction of the arrow can often be determined by common sense (not by the data!). The strength of the relationship can be measured by the correlations. The best correlations to use here are the grouped correlations. This can only be done for *one* hidden variable with the template. Later in this chapter, another tool for doing this (partial correlations) will be explained.

EXAMPLE 3 (Continued) *Sale price of used motorcycles*

If you use the grouped correlation template with 10 subgroups then you get a better estimate of the direct relationship of price with age and miles. Treating miles as the grouping variable, the average grouped correlation of age and price is −0.26, and treating age as the grouping variable, the correlation of miles and price is −0.64. The correlation of age and miles is 0.94.

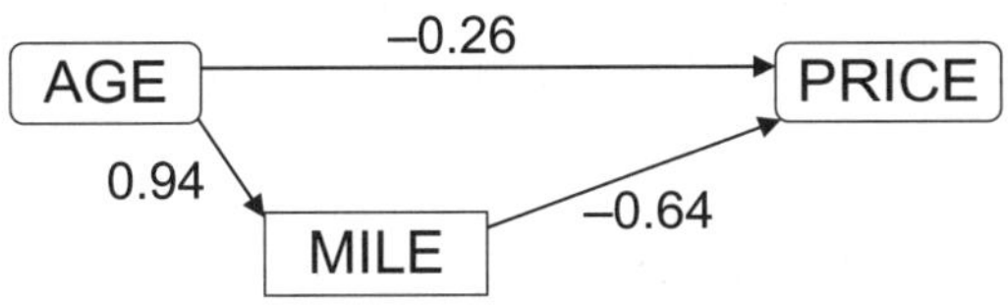

The diagram above tries to represent these relationships. The directions of the arrows are clear—age causes mileage. Age and mileage drive price. Positive and negative relationships can be drawn in different colors. In addition, it can be helpful to move the variables closer together if they are more strongly related.

Practical Meaning

A common way of interpreting a given correlation $\boldsymbol{r}$ is to square it and interpret this as the "percent of variability of one variable that is explained by the other." So if $r = 0.9$ then $r^2 = 0.81$, and we say that 81% of the variation of Y is explained by X. There is a mathematical basis for this claim. We will not prove it here but let's look at a demonstration.

EXAMPLE 3 (Continued) *Sale price of used motorcycles*

A plot of mileage versus age is below. The correlation is 0.941. This means an r-squared of 88%. I claim that I can explain 88% of the variation in miles by age. What this means is that if I tell you the age of a motorcycle then the uncertainty in its mileage reduces by 88%.

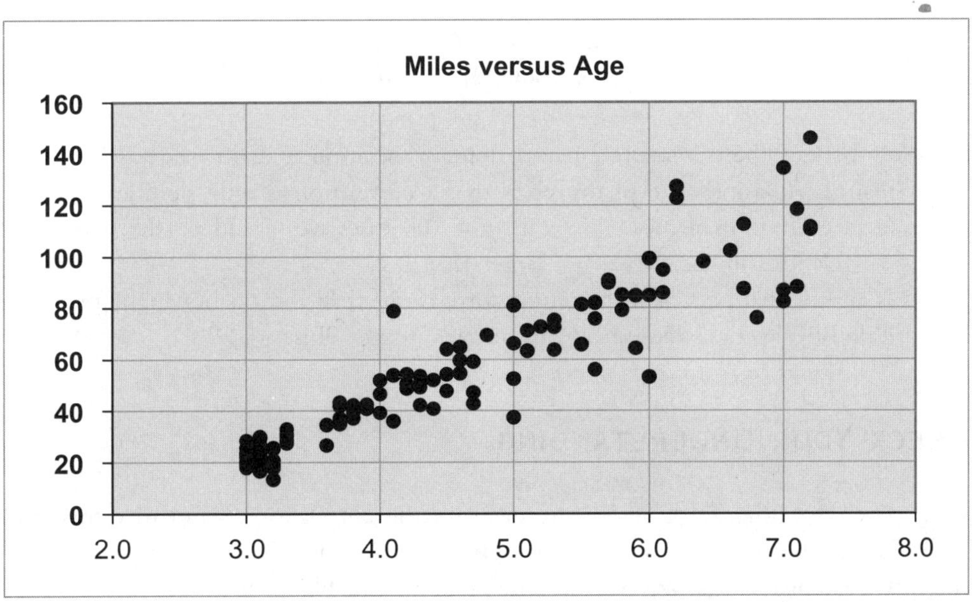

You can see this in the plot. If I tell you nothing about a motorcycle then the mileage is very uncertain indeed. If I tell you the age of the motorcycle then there is much less uncertainty—visible in the plot as the vertical spread of the points at a given age. If the points lay exactly on a line, then there would be zero uncertainty at a given age. In this case, correlation equals ±1 and $r^2 = 100\%$.

CHECK YOUR UNDERSTANDING

Q2. For the Hong Kong real estate data, list the five factors in order of the values of r^2. Taken together, do you notice something strange about these numbers?

Standard Error and Significance

You can see correlation in a scatter plot. However, there is always a degree of unreliability in anything that we see in data. If the correlation is quite weak then there is the distinct possibility that it may have appeared by pure chance and there is really no relationship between the variables.

There is a simple formula for the standard error of a correlation. It is

$$\mathrm{SE}(r) = \frac{\sqrt{1-r^2}}{\sqrt{n-2}}.$$

This formula cannot be used when $n = 2$. The reason is that when there are only two points in a plot, the correlation is automatically 1 because the points lie on a line. So it makes sense that we could not evaluate the reliability.

If you are trying to test whether the true correlation is zero then you can calculate a t-statistic:

$$t = \frac{\text{estimate} - \text{reference}}{\mathrm{SE}(\text{estimate})} = \frac{r\sqrt{n-2}}{\sqrt{1-r^2}}.$$

We only believe there is really an underlying association if this t-value is large, say larger than 2. A simple rule of thumb is that a correlation is only significant if it is larger in magnitude than $2/\sqrt{n}$. So with $n = 100$ cases we would not be convinced of any correlations unless they were larger than 0.2.

It is an essential part of interpreting correlations that you do not highlight those that are statistically indistinguishable from background noise.

CHECK YOUR UNDERSTANDING

Q3. For the Hong Kong real estate data, list the correlations, standard errors, and t-statistics of the five factors explaining price. How about the associations between these five factors? Could any of these be attributed to blind chance?

14.4. WHAT IS AUTOCORRELATION?

Many business variables are measured every day or week or month. Such data are called *time series*. For instance, share prices are measured virtually continuously, but daily and weekly data are readily available. Standard economic indicators such as trade balances and the consumer price index are measured monthly. Sales and revenue within a business can easily be organized into daily, weekly, or quarterly form.

One of the questions we naturally ask about time series is whether present values depend on past values. This can be investigated by seeing if there are any correlations between the past and present values. If so, then future values could be predicted from present and previous values. Autocorrelations are just ordinary correlations applied to this question.

If you have a time series then you can create a new variable containing the previous values by copying the column of values and moving it down one cell. The first cell will be blank and the last cell must be deleted since it has no partner. For instance, if your weekly data is denoted by $X_1, X_2, \ldots, X_{52}$ then the column containing last week's values would be $\star, X_1, X_2, \ldots, X_{51}$, where $\star$ denotes a missing value. This is called **lagging** the variable. The lag-1 autocorrelation is the correlation of

$$X_2, X_3, \ldots, X_{52} \text{ and } X_1, X_2, \ldots, X_{51}.$$

A large positive correlation indicates that high values in one period are typically followed by high values in the next period. A large negative correlation indicates that high values in one period are typically followed by low values in the next period. Similarly, you can look at the relationship between this week and 2 weeks ago by looking at the correlation of

$$X_3, X_4, \ldots, X_{52} \text{ and } X_1, X_2, \ldots, X_{50}.$$

This measures the extent to which values of the series are associated with values two time periods ago. Continuing to higher lags gives a picture of the extent to which the time series value in a particular period depends on the recent or remote past.

Excel

There are no standard Excel functions for doing this. StatproGo has two modules that are useful. First, there is a module for creating the lagged data. Just choose Data Utilities and then Create Lagged Variable(s). You can choose lag 1, lag 2, or larger. We will find this is useful in Chapter 19 when we use multiple regression to analyze time series data. Second, there is a module specifically for autocorrelation. Just choose Summary Stats and then Autocorrelations and decide how many lags you want to consider. The autocorrelations of different lags are output in a table and also in a plot.

EXAMPLE 4 *U.S. unemployment*

The file ex4 US unemployed.xls contains 10 years of monthly data on the numbers of unemployed persons in the United States, measured in thousands. There is also a second series that removes seasonal patterns in unemployed. The raw data and the adjusted data are represented in the plot below. We will look at the seasonally adjusted series only.

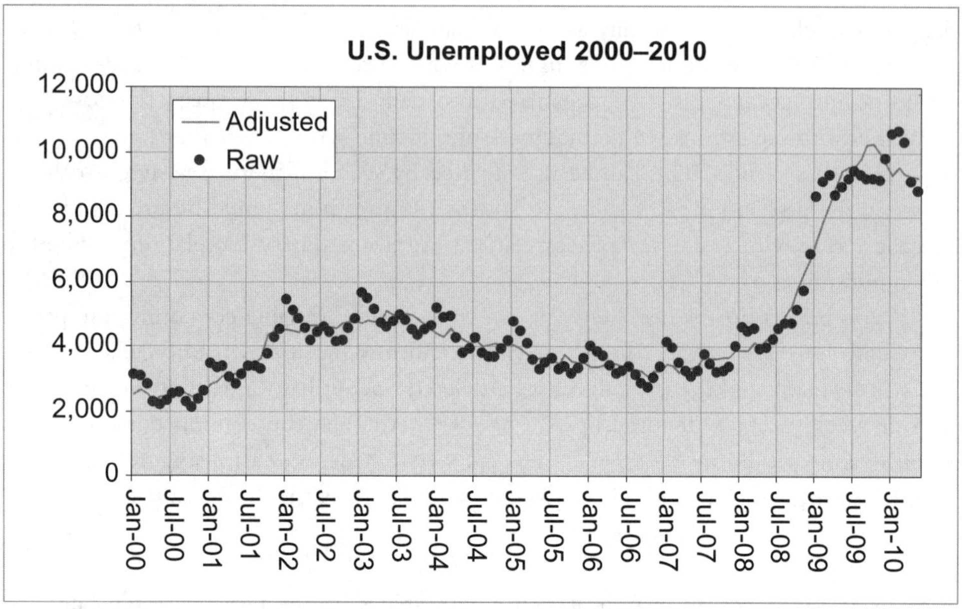

Especially looking at the adjusted series, you would think that the number of unemployed in the previous few months tells you quite a lot about the number this month, and by extension the numbers next month. The first few records of the lagged data are displayed below. These can be quickly obtained using Data Utilities, then Create Lagged Variables(s).

Date	Adjusted	Lag1	Lag2	Lag3	Lag4
Jan-00	2527	*	*	*	*
Feb-00	2655	2527	*	*	*
Mar-00	2521	2655	2527	*	*
Apr-00	2298	2521	2655	2527	*
May-00	2460	2298	2521	2655	2527
Jun-00	2442	2460	2298	2521	2655
Jul-00	..	..	..	..	..

If you plot last month's unemployment against this month's unemployment you get the plot below. The correlation of this plot is 0.970, which is the lag-1 autocorrelation. We can do the same for lag 2, lag 3, and so on.

All the autocorrelations are high, even down to lag 12 and beyond. The actual values and a plot will be given below. But there is another way to look at unemployment data and that is to look at monthly changes in the numbers. These might not be quite as predictable as the actual level you would think. The numbers are on the worksheet changes, and we can use the StatproGo module Autocorrelation on these alternative figures.

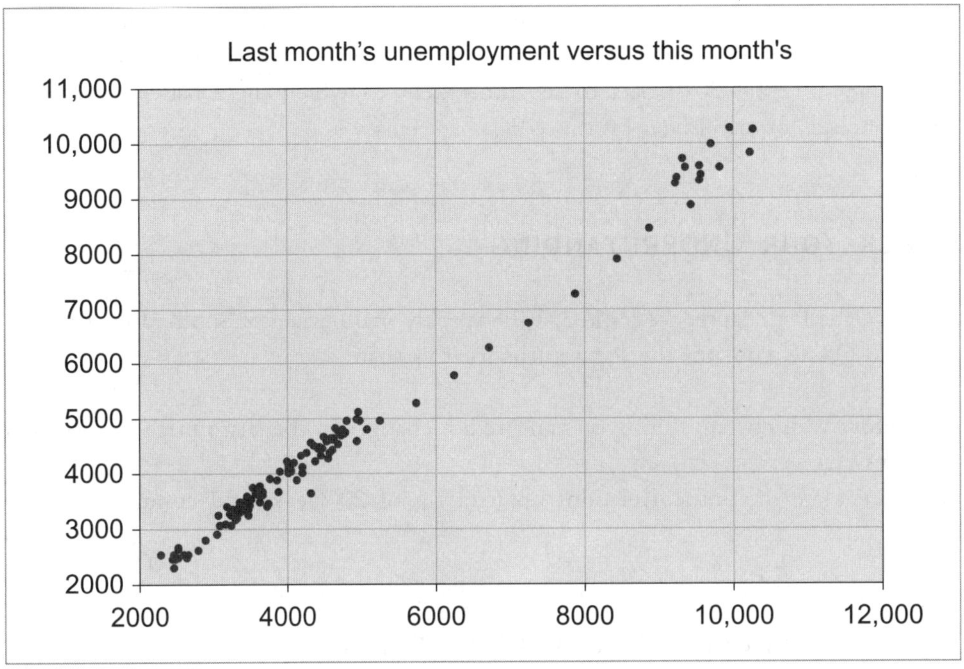

It is revealing to plot autocorrelations against the lag. This gives an idea of the *persistence* of the series. The left plot for the actual numbers of unemployed displays high persistence. Even 12 months away, there is a correlation of over 0.3. The weekly changes in numbers are not nearly so predictable. The correlations die out after about lag 8. The standard errors of these figures are around 0.09, so even the lag-8 autocorrelation of 0.127 is not all that large statistically.

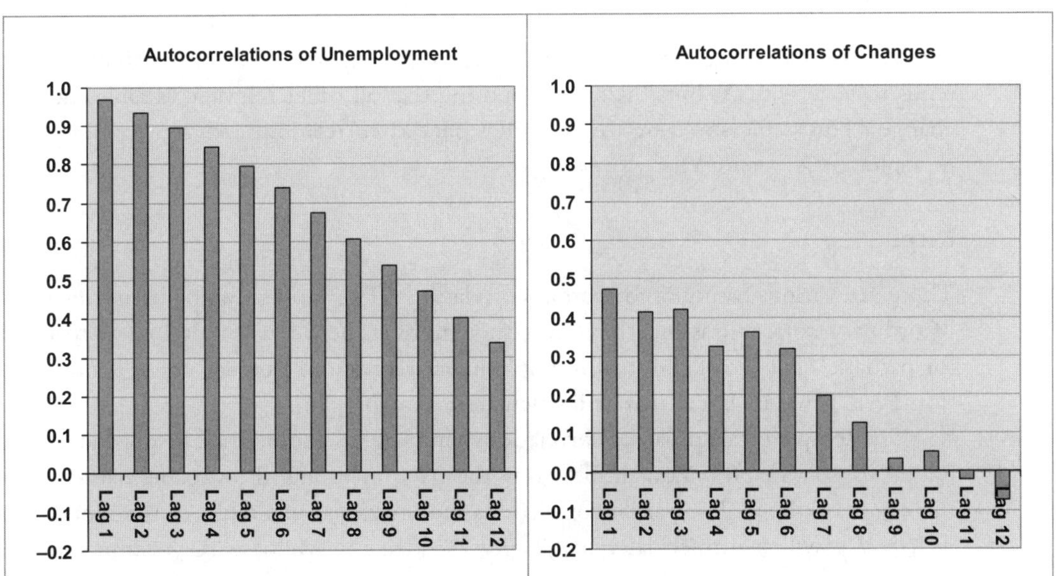

These data include the global financial crisis, which was the largest shock to the U.S. economy in 80 years. You might like to reanalyze these data yourself after removing the 2008–2010 data to see the extent to which these patterns represent general trends or are driven by the GFC.

CHECK YOUR UNDERSTANDING

Q4. In the last chapter we looked at the weekly share prices of South West Airlines. The file Q4.xls contains the log returns for this share.

(a) How well do you think you can predict changes in the share price from recent previous changes?
(b) Calculate the autocorrelations up to a lag of 20 weeks and comment on the result.

14.5. UNTANGLING RELATIONSHIPS WITH PARTIAL CORRELATION

With a web of variables that possibly affect each other there are conceptually two types of association.

The first is the *apparent* relation between the variables. This is measured by the ordinary correlation, and you can see it in a plot of *X* versus *Y*. These are also known as **marginal** correlations. To what extent does *Y* tend to vary with *X*, acknowledging that many other variables may also change at the same time? How much does the age of a motorcycle reduce the price? We know that much of it will be due to increased mileage but the marginal correlation still gives the bottom line measure.

The second is the direct relation between the variables. To what extent does *Y* tends to vary with *X*, but this time supposing that all other relevant variables do not change? This is measured by the so-called **partial** correlation, and you cannot see it in a plot of *X* versus *Y*.

Excel

There are various formulas for partial correlations. The most meaningful are in terms of ordinary correlations but they are rather messy. There is a simple matrix formula for partials. They also fall out of multiple linear regression. But alas, there is no function PARTIAL in Excel that will calculate them for you.

The template called partial correlations template.xls can be used to produce them for up to 10 variables. You simply copy the data, including the variable names, into the *data* worksheet. The partial correlations should appear in a table on the worksheet *partial*. We will see much later in Chapter 18 that the Multiple Regression module of StatproGo also produces partial correlations.

EXAMPLE 1 (Continued) *Hong Kong real estate*

We earlier gave the ordinary or marginal correlations of all six variables. We noted that area was the strongest factor affecting price, and that larger apartments tended to be newer. Since people would typically prefer newer apartments, the apparently high marginal correlation of price and area might exaggerate the role of area.

It is worth reminding ourselves of the marginal correlations for comparison with the partial correlations that we are about to calculate.

	BEDS	BATHS	CARS	AGE	AREA	PRICE
BEDS	1					
BATHS	0.393	1				
CARS	0.066	0.275	1			
AGE	0.279	-0.124	-0.120	1		
AREA	0.239	0.614	0.433	-0.292	1	
PRICE	0.254	0.561	0.549	-0.391	0.828	1

The partial correlations are in the table below. Just ignore the numbers on the diagonal for now. Look at the price line, since PRICE is the performance measure of interest here. We want to know how the five features affect it. The strongest partial correlation is again AREA but it is 0.67—considerably less than the marginal correlation of 0.828. Another interesting figure is 0.07 for BATHS. This says that the number of bathrooms has almost no association at all with price, after accounting for the other variables. It does not say that a bathroom is worth nothing. Rather it says that if you have an apartment of a given size with a given number of bedrooms, there is no extra value in squeezing another bathroom into it. To this extent, it is then rather surprising that BEDS does have a distinct positive partial correlation of 0.24. This suggests that it *is* worthwhile squeezing in an additional bedroom. It might suggest that there is some kind of mismatch between the stock of apartments and the market.

	BEDS	BATHS	CARS	AGE	AREA	PRICE
BEDS	**31.7%**	0.29	-0.15	0.43	-0.07	0.24
BATHS	0.29	**44.6%**	0.00	-0.02	0.32	0.07
CARS	-0.15	0.00	**33.1%**	0.18	-0.05	0.42
AGE	0.43	-0.02	0.18	**33.1%**	0.06	-0.38
AREA	-0.07	0.32	-0.05	0.06	**72.0%**	0.67
PRICE	0.24	0.07	0.42	-0.38	0.67	**77.4%**

Partial correlations can be statistically assessed in the same way as ordinary correlations. The formulas for the standard error and *t*-statistic have the same form.

Partial correlations larger in magnitude than $2/\sqrt{n}$ reflect associations that would be unlikely to occur by pure luck.

Multiple *r*-Square

The remaining figure in the PRICE line is 77.4%. This measures how much of the variation in prices can be explained by, or attributed to, the five measured features *in combination*. Recall that the marginal correlation with AREA was 0.828, and so area alone explains $0.828^2 = 68\%$ of the variations in prices. We only get another 9.4% with the four other factors.

The PRICE line tells you most of what you need to know about the drivers of price. How much each directly affects price is measured by the partial correlations. How useful all variables are together is measured by the multiple *r*-squared. We will meet multiple *r*-square again when we learn about multiple linear regression in Chapter 17.

Interpreting Partial Correlations

Partial correlations are often quite different to marginal correlations so it is important to understand and be able to explain the difference.

Marginal correlation describes how *Y* varies with *X*. Since other things may be varying at the same time, it is more of an empirical bottom-line measure. If the correlation is high then you can assert that in the future you will expect to see *Y* move when *X* moves.

Partial correlation describes how *Y* varies with *X*, imagining all other relevant variables could be held fixed. This measures the direct effect of *X* on *Y* and is useful for understanding fundamentals. In practice, it may not be possible to have all the other variables fixed. This does not mean that it is silly to imagine what would happen if they were fixed.

You can square partial correlations and interpret them as the *proportion of remaining variation explained, in addition to all the other variables*. This is not quite as easy to explain or understand.

EXAMPLE 1 (Continued) *Hong Kong real estate*

For the variable CARS the partial correlation is 0.416 so the partial r^2 is 17.3%. What does this mean? Using the above rubric it measures how much of the remaining variation CARS can explain, that is not explained by the four variables AREA, AGE, BEDS, and BATHS. Let's confirm this assertion from the numbers. There is no need to do these calculations in practice, much less explain them to a client. The point is to confirm the statement about squared partial correlations that was made above.

First, we look at how much can be explained with just these four variables. You can check this by putting PRICE, AREA, AGE, BEDS, and BATHS into the template. You will find that the multiple r^2 for PRICE is 72.7%. So we can explain 72.7% of the variations in prices using these four variables.

This leaves 100% − 72.7% = 27.3% unexplained. The squared partial correlation of 17.3% for CARS says that if we add CARS into the mix then we will be able to explain 17.3% of this remaining 27.3%, which is 4.7%. So we will be able to explain the 72.7% we have now, plus 4.7%, which is 77.4%. This is precisely what we saw when we considered all five factors.

Limitations of Partial Correlation

You might have been wondering why the grouped correlation template is not sufficient for untangling relationships. It has advantages and disadvantages. One advantage of partial correlations is that they implicitly adjust for *all* other variables at the same time, whereas grouped correlations only account for *one* hidden variable *Z*. A second advantage is that partial correlations often give a stronger result (i.e., a larger correlation) than do grouped correlations. The reason for this is that each grouped correlation limits attention to a subset of the data, which reduces the ability to "see" the association.

There are two disadvantages of partial correlations compared to grouped correlations. First, like marginal correlations, partial correlations are only able to detect linear associations. Any kind of curvilinear relationship will be ignored. Whereas, grouped correlation can actually be used to measure curvilinear relationships. You can learn about this idea in one of the exercises. Second, partial correlation assumes that the association between *X* and *Y* can be measured with a single number. We will sometimes find interesting patterns in the grouped correlations that a single number suppresses.

For example, we saw earlier in Example 3 that the effect of age on price of a motorcycle appeared to be less for low-mileage motorcycles than for high-mileage motorcycles. This pattern was interesting and potentially important. We will encounter this idea again when we look at **interactions** in Chapter 20. Partial correlation is blind to these interactions.

CHECK YOUR UNDERSTANDING

Q5. Thinking about the motorcycle data,

(a) Do you think the partial correlations of Price with age and mileage will be less or more than the marginal correlations?
(b) Use the template to calculate them and see if you were right.
(c) How well could you predict prices from knowing their age and mileage?
(d) Can you think of an example where the partial correlations would be much stronger than the marginal correlations?

14.6. SUMMARY

The most common measure of association between variables is **correlation**. This number is between −1 and +1, representing the extremes of a perfect linear negative or positive relationship, respectively. Correlation is independent of the units of measurement. The squared correlation measures proportion of variation in one variable that can be explained by the other. It is typically expressed as a percentage.

The statistical reliability of a correlation depends on its size and the sample size though the formula

$$\text{SE}(r) = \frac{\sqrt{1-r^2}}{\sqrt{n-2}}.$$

This gives a *t*-statistic for testing whether the correlation is real. A rough rule of thumb critical value for significant correlation is

$$r_{\text{CRIT}} = \frac{2}{\sqrt{n}}.$$

Autocorrelations are measures of the degree to which time series data can be predicted by past values. They are ordinary correlations of the series with lagged versions of the same data.

Partial correlations describe how two variables affect each other, imagining all other relevant variables could be held fixed. Squared partial correlations measure the *proportion of remaining variation explained, in addition to all the other variables.*

In combination with ordinary marginal correlations, they are useful for untangling which variables really depend on which.

Excel

Compute ordinary correlations using

CORREL(yrange,xrange).

If you have many variables use

StatproGo then Summary Stats then Correlation, Covariance.

Partial correlations cannot be obtained with standard Excel. Use the provided template to compute them.

EXERCISES

E1. Below are some (fictitious) correlations between all pairs of three variables. The means and standard deviations are also given. Imagine that they were obtained from a sample of 35 randomly chosen individuals.

	Income	Education	Age
Income($1000)	1.0	0.43	0.22
Education(years)	0.43	1.00	-0.58
Age(years)	0.22	-0.58	1.00
Mean	45.2	11.3	47
Stdev	8.5	3	12

(a) Which, if any, of these correlations are significantly different from zero?
(b) What does "significantly different from zero" mean in simple words?
(c) How large a sample of individuals would be required for a correlation of 0.1 to be significant?
(d) If the units of Age changed to months then which figures would change and how?

E2. In each case below you are given a correlation describing the relationship between two variables. You may suppose that you have no prior expectations about whether the relationship between the two variables is positive or negative so that a two-sided test is appropriate. You are given a significance level as well. Make a formal decision about whether or not there is a relationship between the variables and, if you decide there is, describe how strong the relationship is in common nontechnical terms.
(a) From a sample of 100, the correlation between X and Y is 0.54. The standard deviation of Y is 20. The significance level is 5%.
(b) A sample of 1000 returns on a stock is weakly related to 1000 returns of another stock on the previous day. The correlation is 0.08. The standard deviation of Y is 20. The significance level is 1%.
(c) The scores of 25 students on the midterm test appear to be related to their scores on the final exam. The correlation is 0.22. The standard deviation of exam results is 12%. The significance level is 10%.

E3. Try to explain and interpret the following facts.
(a) Those with a higher IQ also have a larger shoe size.
(b) Taller people are paid more.
(c) Murder rates are higher in those states that have higher numbers of people sentenced to the death penalty.
(d) More people die while playing lawn bowls than while playing any other sport.
(e) Among low drinkers, complete abstinence from alcohol is associated with higher death rate.
(f) Dog food price is associated with fillet steak price.
(g) Inflation-adjusted dog food price is associated with inflation-adjusted motor car price.
(h) People on antibiotics are more likely to die from a serious infection than those who are not.

E4. Optus has just introduced a system where prospective customers are run through a credit checking company and if they fail the credit check they are required to pay a significant deposit to cover possible defaults. Looking at the data after 6 months, it is found that there is a positive correlation between the deposit and the chance of defaulting. Does this mean the deposit scheme is a failure?

E5. The data in Q5.xls describe a survey of 100 households, their yearly salary, and how much they spend on various classes of goods and services.
(a) Calculate the correlation of the four variables salary, culture, sports, and dining. It is easiest to use StatproGo. Which variable has the strongest association with culture and how strong is it?

(b) Why might you expect sports and culture to have a negative correlation?

(c) Calculate culture, sports, and dining as a percent of salary, to create three new variables.

(d) On the basis of two relevant correlations, how would you summarize the relationship of sports expenditure to salary?

(e) How about dining?

E6. The data in Q6.xls are the pricing data. The variables are week (measuring time), RRP, demand, and profit.

(a) Calculate the correlations and explain in simple words what each one means, including cases where the correlation is misleading.

(b) Which of the correlations are statistically significant? Give the standard errors, t-statistics, and p-values, and explain what these mean.

(c) Calculate partial correlations of week, price, and demand (i.e., exclude profit). What do these indicate? Why are the marginal and partial correlations of demand with time so different? Is there growth in demand or not?

(d) Using the grouped template, create labels 1–13 for the 13 distinct prices charged and examine the relationship of demand and week. What do the grouped correlations look like? Do they agree with the partials?

E7. Using the same data as for Q6.xls, we noted that the relationship of profit to time was nonlinear and the correlation of 0.639 was completely misleading. You can use the grouped correlation template to investigate curvilinear relationships

(a) Copy the profit and week data into Columns X and Y. Copy the week data into Column Z. So the X and Z variables here are the same. The grouped correlations now represent correlations of profit and week over narrow ranges of weeks. Over these shorter periods, the relationship is less curvilinear.

(b) Experiment with the number of groups to obtain the cleanest picture of how profit varies over time.

E8. The data in Q8.xls contain weekly data on the Hang Seng Index from 1990 to 2001.

(a) Calculate the log returns.

(b) Create lag_1 and lag_2 versions of log returns.

(c) Plot returns against lag_1 returns. Is there any relationship?

(d) Plot returns against lag_2 returns. Is there any relationship?

(e) Use StatproGo to calculate autocorrelations up to lag 20. How would you interpret these results?

E9. The data in Q9.xls contain daily data on the Hang Seng Index from 1997 to 2001. Investigate the autocorrelations in this data up to lag 31. Are any of these significant? Look at the plots that go with any significant autocorrelations and comment on the reliability of the autocorrelations.

E10. The data in Q10.xls give labor force numbers in the United States from 2000 to 2010. They have been seasonally adjusted.

(a) Check that the figures have been adjusted with an appropriate Pivotable.

(b) Examine the autocorrelations.

(c) Calculate monthly changes and exam the autocorrelations.

(d) Investigate what partial correlations say about the changes up to lag 9.

CHAPTER 15

Describing the Effect of a Business Input: Linear Regression

DUO BEVERAGES: CASE BRIEFING

One important determinant of sales in supermarkets is where the product is displayed on the shelf. The impact on sales can be huge, sometimes resulting in a fivefold increase. Such positioning does not come free of course. Supermarkets are well aware of the effect on sales and charge for this preferential shelf space.

Simon Templeton is a product manager for General Foods. One of the many products Simon is responsible for is a lemon-flavored fizzy beverage called Duo. It is a popular beverage and average weekly sales for a typical-sized supermarket is around $20,000K. There is a 45% margin on the product, that is, every extra dollar of sales gives you an extra 45-¢ profit.

Wellmark, the largest supermarket chain, is your most important retail outlet. They have 270 stores across the country. Charges for product placement (PP) have recently increased. The charge for preferential PP is in increments of $10,000 from $0 right up to $50,000 per week, depending on the position and amount of the shelf.

If Simon chooses the maximum level of PP then he knows that sales will increase significantly. But paying $50K for a single store when typical sales are only $20K sounds like a bad deal. Even if sales did increase by five times to $100K, only 45% of extra $80K sales would be extra profit, so it would not be worth the $50K cost. But it really depends on what the effect of the shelf placement will be, at the different expenditure levels.

Simon has a database of total weekly sales for each of the 270 supermarkets in the Wellmark chain. He extracts the sales of Duo over the past week. These are in the worksheet "basic data" in duo.xls. Sales vary widely from $12,655 to $145,022. What do the data suggest about the best level of expenditure on PP?

Data-Driven Business Decisions, First Edition. Chris J. Lloyd.

15.0. INTRODUCTION: WHAT IS THE ISSUE?

Correlations and partial correlations measure the nature and strength of the relationship between variables. They have the advantage of being unit free and being on an absolute scale from −1 to +1. Notwithstanding their interpretation in terms of variation explained, correlation is ultimately a mathematical measure of association, not a practical business measure.

To put it more plainly, it is one thing to say that there is a positive correlation between an apartment price and its area. It is helpful to know that area has the highest correlation among various features that you consider important. But ultimately you want to know *what* the relationship is, not how strong it is. If you tell me the area then I should be able to give you an estimated price. Correlation doesn't do this.

Because business variables are partly unpredictable, any equation I use to make predictions will not give the exactly correct answer. We want to find a rule that will give as accurate a prediction as possible, subject to the inevitable random variations that we see in real data. As always, we will also quantify the accuracy of every conclusion we make, with a relevant standard error.

15.1. LINEAR RELATIONSHIPS

The relationship between an input variable x and an output variable y is **linear** if it can be described by an equation of the general form

$$y = mx + b,$$

where m and b are two known numbers. The graph of a linear function is, not surprisingly, a line. Each choice of m and b corresponds to a different line.

The most important number in a linear relationship is the value m. The practical interpretation of m is that it measures *the effect of the input* x *on the output* y. Specifically, m gives the change in y when you increase x by one unit. For instance, if $m = -2.5$ then for each unit increase in the input variable x, the output y *decreases* by 2.5 units. A common name for m is the **slope** or **gradient** because geometrically it measures the slope of the line.

Only for linear functions is the slope constant. Asserting that whenever you change x by one unit, y will change by the same amount is an assumption—one that characterizes a linear relationship. The assumption can be checked and nonlinear relationships can be modeled, albeit with some increase in conceptual and computational complexity. We will certainly do this in later chapters.

The second number that defines a linear relationship is b, which in most contexts is far less important than the slope. It is known as the **y-intercept** or the **vertical intercept**. A more practical interpretation is as the **baseline** performance. Specifically, it gives the output y when the input x equals 0.

EXAMPLE

Salaries typically increase with the experience of the employee. Suppose that within a particular industry is the following equation:

$$\text{Salary} = 35 + 0.6 \times \text{Exp}.$$

The slope here is $m = 0.6$. In order to interpret it, we need to know the units that salary and experience were measured in. Unlike correlation, the slope does depend on units. Let's suppose that salary was measured in units of \$1000 per annum and experience is measured in years. The slope of 0.6 then means that for every year of extra experience, they can expect to have an extra \$600 per annum wage. If they have 10 years extra experience they can expect an extra \$6000. The baseline $b = 35$ measures the value of salary (y) when experience (x) equals zero. This is the starting salary for someone with no experience.

Salaries typically increase with the age of the employee. Most of this is presumably due to the increased experience. Suppose that there is a linear relation between experience and age of the form

$$\text{Age} = 20 + 1.0 \times \text{Exp},$$

where experience and age are both measured in years. The slope $m = 1$ says you gain 1 year of experience for each year that you are older. The baseline $b = 20$ says that someone with no experience will be aged 20—in other words this is the starting age for this industry.

If older people have more experience and if more experienced people get higher salaries then older people will get higher salaries. We can quantify this by noting that Exp = Age − 20 and substituting this into the first equation to obtain

$$\text{Salary} = 35 + 0.6 \times \text{Exp} = 35 + 0.6 \times (\text{Age} - 20) = 23 + 0.6 \times \text{Age}.$$

The slope is again $m = 0.6$ but this now says that you get an extra \$600 for each year of age (rather than experience). The baseline $b = 23$ measures the salary for someone of age zero. This is a nonsensical interpretation of b because someone of age zero would not have a job. You can still think of b as baseline in a more general sense—being a number you start with in the formula. You then add \$600 for every year of age.

In the real world salary will not follow a strict relationship (unless they are in a regulated economy where they are guaranteed a salary increment of \$600 each year). More likely, if you look at the salaries of many people in the same industry you will see a tendency for salary to increase with age. You might like to have an idea of how salary depends on age, acknowledging that there will not be a perfect linear relationship. This is the whole point of the techniques in this chapter.

CHECK YOUR UNDERSTANDING

Q1. Sketch the graphs of the following lines. It will help you to identify the slope, the y-intercept, and the x-intercept in each case.

(a) $y = 2x - 4$
(b) $y = 3(x - 2)$
(c) $q = 50(1 - p/10)3$

Q2. Demand Q is negatively associated with price. For every increase of \$1 in price, demand decreases by 10 units. When price is zero, the demand is 100 units. What is the demand equation?

15.2. THE LINE OF BEST FIT

If you plot a business output Y against a business input x you will often see a relationship but it will not be perfect. It will be *noisy*. There will be random deviations from any underlying trend. You have seen many examples in the previous chapter—demand versus recommended retail price, motorcycle price versus mileage. Provided that the relationship looks roughly linear, we would like to summarize the relationship with a line. The line needs to go through the middle of the data in some sense, otherwise it will not be a fair summary.

EXAMPLE 1 *Okun's Law (ex1 [okuns law].xls)*

When unemployment (UE) goes up, there are less people in the workforce so you expect national measures of output to go down. If UE goes up from 5% to 6%—a rise of 1%—you might guess that gross domestic product (GDP) will go down by 1%. There are reasons why it might not be exactly 1%, though. First, the least productive workers might become unemployed first. In this case, GDP would drop by less than the full 1%. On the other hand, when people are unemployed they spend less and this leads to reduced demand across the economy, which leads to lower output—the so-called *multiplier effect*. This argument suggests that it might be more than 1%. There are competing forces at work and the "exchange rate" between increases in UE and drops in GDP is an empirical question.

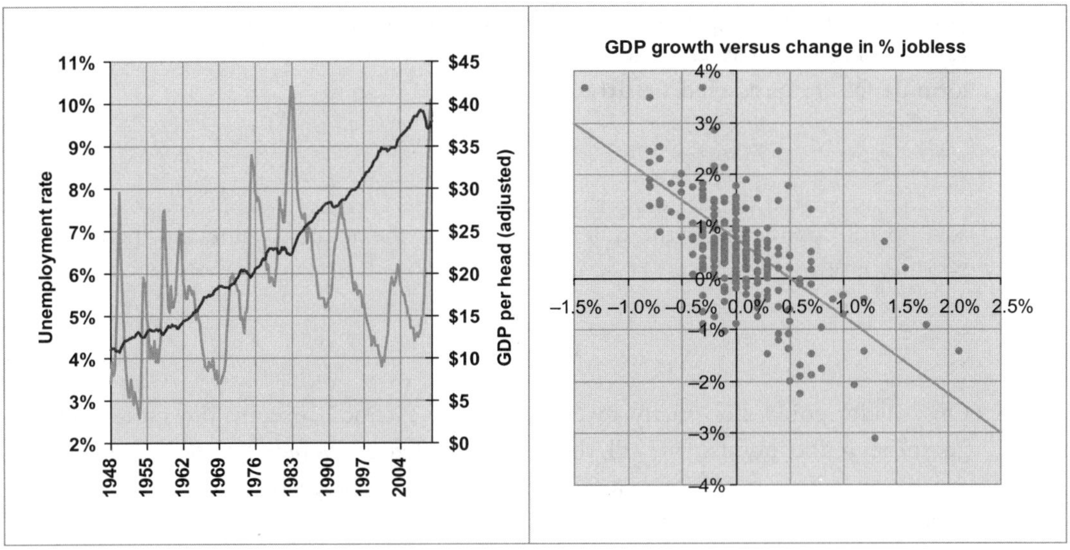

Above left is a plot of the GDP and UE history of the United States based on quarterly data from 1948 to 2010. For each quarter, we have the UE rate and the GDP per head of population, in units of $1000 per annum, adjusted for inflation, purchasing power parity, and seasonality factors. You can see the peaks in UE that correspond to well-known financial crises. In contrast, GDP per head seems to march upwards with only small hills and valleys. But it does appear that there are small drops in GDP when there are spikes in UE. There is a better way to look at this.

The right plot shows the *proportional change* in GDP per head versus the *change* in the UE rate. The time order of the data has now been lost. The predictions of Okun's Law are broadly confirmed. In the bottom right are years where the UE rate increased and GDP growth was consequently negative. In the top left are years where the UE rate fell and GDP growth was positive. The correlation is −0.610. But this does not tell us how much impact an extra 1% in UE has on GDP growth. We can estimate this by imagining a line going from the top left to the bottom right corner, as shown in the right plot. As the quarterly change in UE moves from −1.5% to +2.5%, the GDP growth moves from +3% to −3%. So the slope of this line is

$$(\text{change in } Y)/(\text{change in } X) = -6\%/4\% = -1.5.$$

This line, however, is only a guess. We need an objective method of finding a line that goes through the middle of the data points.

Least Squares

Ideally a line that describes the data well will be close to all the data points. If the data points are noisy there will be a limit to how close they can all be to the same line.

First, how close is a single point to the line? A line is defined by its slope and intercept. Suppose we consider the line $y = mx + b$ as a summary of the relationship.

For each data pair (x_i, y_i) we can substitute the value x_i to arrive at a predicted y-value. Using the "hat" notation to represent an estimate of the thing underneath, a formula for the predicted or **fitted value** is

$$\hat{y}_i = mx_i + b.$$

The error of prediction is the difference between the actual y-value and the predicted y-value, in symbols

$$e_i = y_i - \hat{y}_i.$$

Only if the points lie exactly on a line, and we choose exactly the correct line to go through the points, will all these errors be zero. When the points do not lie exactly on a line, it will be impossible to reduce all these errors to zero. So we will have to settle on the line that makes the errors *collectively as small as possible.*

There are many ways we could measure the collective size of the errors. The most obvious is just the average error, ignoring the sign. This is called mean absolute error (MAE). A second method, which is ultimately the one we will use, is to calculate the average of the *squared errors* and then take the square root. This is just another measure of the typical error and is called *root mean square error* (RMSE). A formula for it is

> The $n - 2$ rather than n relates to the fact that two points will fit a line exactly.

$$\text{RMSE}(m, b) = \sqrt{\frac{1}{n-2}\sum_{i=1}^{n} e_i^2}.$$

We can then ask, what line minimizes this measure of how close the points are to the line? We can try different values of (m,b) until RMSE is as small as possible.

EXAMPLE 1 (Continued) *Okun's Law*

Open the file least squares.xls. You will find that the Okun's Law data are in Columns B and C. It has been set up for you already with a possible line

$$\text{GDP change} = -1.5 \times (\text{Change in UE rate}) + 0.5\%.$$

So the slope is -1.5 and the intercept b is 0.5%. You will see that the seventh row of data (0.70%,1.40%) has been highlighted. If the line was correct then the change in GDP from a 1.40% change in UE should be

$$-1.5 \times (1.4\%) + 0.5\% = -1.60\%.$$

It was actually 0.70% so there is a rather large error of 2.30%. This has been highlighted on the plot as a bold vertical line, measuring how close this particular point is to the line. Many of the points are much closer than this.

The MAE is 0.601. This measures how close the points are to this particular line on average. The other measure we use, RMSE, equals 0.799. You can now play with the two buttons to change the line and see how the RMSE and MAE change. Try and make the RMSE as small as you can.

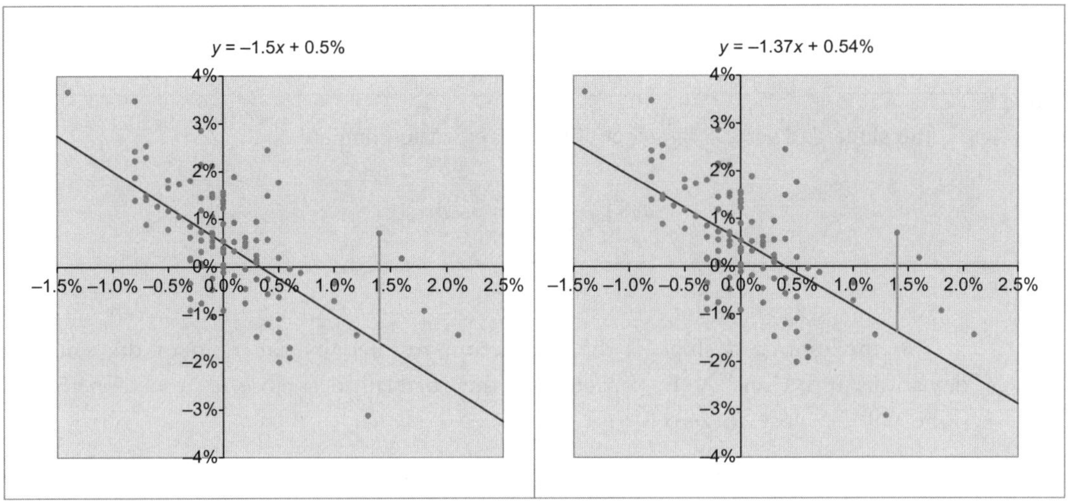

You will find that the best fitting line is

$$\text{GDP change} = -1.37 \times (\text{Change in UE rate}) + 0.54\%$$

displayed in the right plot. The RMSE is 0.796. This line actually fits the highlighted seventh row worse than the original line, but overall it fits the 248 data points better than any other line.

So what does this mean in terms of Okun's Law? We have estimated from this plot that each increase of 1% in the UE rate is associated with a 1.37% decrease in GDP growth. The multiplier effect dominates.

The other number 0.54% measures the mean GDP growth when the change in UE rate is zero. You might think of this as measuring GDP growth in stable conditions of equilibrium. Remembering that the GDP measure was per head, this would be due to productivity improvements from technical advances and management practices. The GDP data was quarterly, so this says that underlying mean productivity growth in the U.S. economy is 0.54% per quarter, which means 2.19% per annum.

15.3. Computing the Least Squares Line

The line that is closest to the points as measured by RMSE is called the *least squares (LS) regression line*. You will no doubt be relieved to hear that there is no need to copy every data set into the LS template and fiddle with the buttons to find the line that gives the smallest RMSE. There are direct formulas for finding the slope and intercept of the best fitting line.

The same five numbers that we needed for an optimal portfolio.

These formulas depend on five numbers: the mean and standard deviation of the x-values, which tells you about the distribution of the x-values; the mean and standard deviation of the y-values, which tells you about the distribution of the y-values; and the correlation of X and Y, which tells you about the strength of the relationship between X and Y.

The slope and vertical intercept of the LS regression line are

$$\hat{m} = r_{XY}\frac{S_Y}{S_X}, \quad b = \bar{y} - \hat{m}\bar{x}.$$

So the estimated slope is the correlation rescaled by the ratio of the standard deviations and Y and X. In particular, if the correlation is close to zero then the LS slope will be close to zero.

EXAMPLE 1 (Continued) *Okun's Law*

The means and standard deviation of the change in GDP and the change in UE Rate are in the table below. The correlation was –0.610.

	GDPperHead	UERate
Mean	0.509%	0.025%
Stdev	1.002%	0.446%

The LS slope is

$$\hat{m} = r_{XY}\frac{S_Y}{S_X} = -0.610 \times \frac{1.002}{0.446} = -1.372,$$

and the LS intercept is

$$\hat{b} = \bar{y} - \hat{m}\bar{x} = 0.509\% - (-1.372) \times 0.025\% = 0.543\%.$$

So the LS line is

$$\text{GDP change} = -1.372 \times (\text{Change in UE rate}) + 0.543\%.$$

Excel Functions

There are standard functions in Excel that will calculate the slope and intercept of the LS line. The slope is calculated from

$$= \text{SLOPE(yvalues,xvalues)}.$$

Unlike CORREL, the order of the y-values and x-values is important for slope. The intercept is calculated from

$$= \text{INTERCEPT(yvalues,xvalues)}.$$

There is an even quicker way to obtain the LS line if you have already produced a scatter plot of X against Y with Y on the vertical axis. Just right click on any point, and then click on *Add Trendline*. A linear trendline is selected by default. Click the button Display Equation on Chart (in Excel 2003 you will have to first click the Options tab).

EXAMPLE 2 *Duo beverages: spending on PP*

In Chapter 11, we looked at a case where the sales manager of a drink called Duo has to look at the effectiveness of PP on sales. There are five levels of PP spend that have been tried in the past, across some 270 stores. There is a 45% marginal profit on each item sold. So for instance if you spend \$10,000 on PP and sales increased from \$20,000 to \$40,000 then the extra \$20,000 sales means an extra \$9000 in profits, which does not cover the \$10,000 PP spend. In the previous analysis, we looked at mean sales for each PP spend group and followed through the implications for profit.

There is another way to look at the data. Below are plots of sales versus the expenditure on PP as well as "marginal" profit, being 45% of sales minus the PP spend. By "marginal" profit I mean profit that ignores the fixed costs. It is fine to ignore these since they will be present regardless of how much we spend on PP.

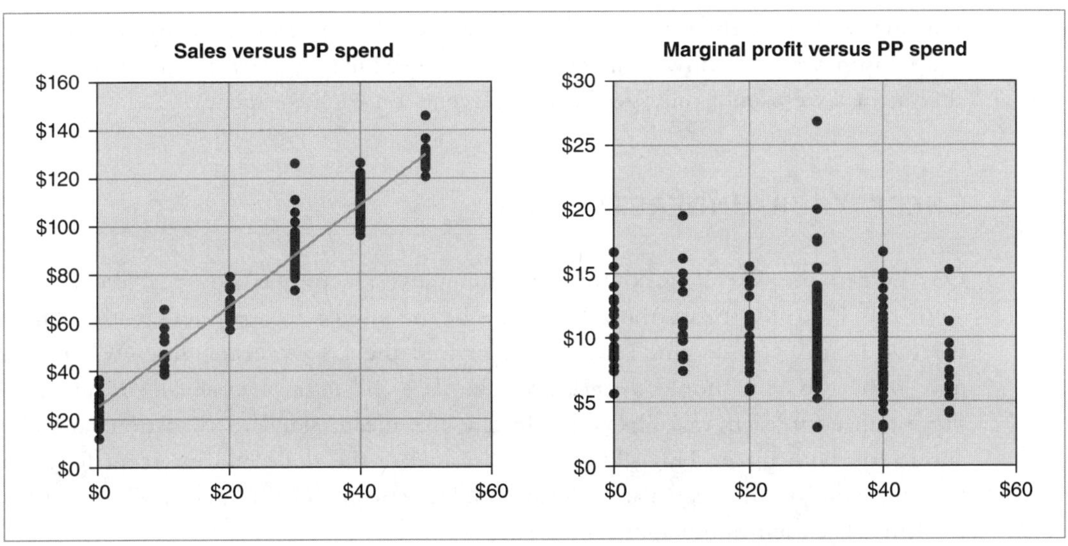

Very clearly PP has a huge impact on sales and they appear to increase more or less linearly as the PP spend increases. The vertical variation is mainly due to differences between stores. The impact on profit is far less clear. There appears to be very little effect on profit. This is not so surprising if one considers that the supermarket would charge the maximum amount that they can for PP subject to the client (here Duo) just ending up in front.

Since the relationship of sales and PP demand is so regular, it suggests that we could assume that there is a linear relationship and estimate what this relationship is. The LS line is

$$\text{Sales} = 25.721 + 2.104 \times (\text{PP Spend}).$$

This has been added to the left plot using Add Trendline. We could get the same intercept and slope using either the five key numbers or the Excel functions INTERCEPT and SLOPE.

The interpretation of these numbers is key to assessing the value of PP. The vertical intercept $b = 25.721$ measures the mean sales if you spend \$0 on PP. So baseline sales are \$25,721 per week without PP. Therefore, the remaining part of the formula measures the extra sales due to PP spend.

The slope parameter $m = 2.104$ says that for every \$1 you spend on PP you get an extra \$2.104 in sales. This sounds great, but remember that only 45% is profit. So you only get an extra $0.45 \times 2.104 = 94.7$ cents, which, unfortunately, does not cover the cost of the \$1. It looks like PP is not worth the money according to this calculation—but it is clearly a line ball.

Another way to look at this would be to fit a line to the marginal profit plot. It appears to slope downwards slightly, and if you use Add Trendline you will find that the LS line is

$$\text{Marg Profit} = 11.575 - 0.053 \times (\text{PP Spend}).$$

This means that baseline profit is \$11,575 per week. For each \$1 you spend on PP you end up 5.3 cents down on the whole deal—which agrees with our earlier conclusion that we would only get back 94.7 cents on each \$1 spent.

CHECK YOUR UNDERSTANDING

Q3. Open the Excel workbook containing the Deepwater Bay real estate data. Your task is to investigate the relationship of the sale of an apartment with each of the five factors. To do this I want you to find the LS regression line. When you have done this you should *describe what the slope and intercept mean in this context.* I suggest that for each variable you calculate the mean, standard deviation, and the correlation with price. This allows you to calculate the slope and intercept for each feature. Confirm the calculation using the functions SLOPE and INTERCEPT. Explain what each number means in simple words.

15.4. The Regression Model

Anyone can draw a line through a scatter plot. What would be more useful, though, is to say how accurate your conclusions were. In order to do this, you need to make some very plausible assumptions about the data-generating mechanism. These assumptions can be checked and we will certainly do so in later chapters.

These assumptions are called the **regression model**. They amount to a simple conceptual model for how the scatter plot of points appeared in your Excel spreadsheet. There are two reasons for introducing these assumptions now. First, it is a mathematical fact that, with these assumptions, the LS regression method that we have been using is the best method of estimating the true underlying line. How best? Best in terms of the estimated line being closest to the true line on average. In particular, using maximum error or average error will give regression lines that are not as close to the true line.

Second, under these assumptions we can give standard errors for the various conclusions that we can make from an LS line.

Assumption 1. Linearity The first assumption is the most important—that the underlying relationship between Y and X is indeed a line. By relationship we mean how the mean of Y depends on X. We can write this assumption as

$$\mu(Y \mid x) = mx + b,$$

where $\mu(Y|x)$ is shorthand for the mean of the distribution of Y when the value of X is x. This represents the true underlying relationship between Y and X. The true intercept and slope are b and m. We never know this true underlying relationship because the data do not follow the true line exactly.

To handle this logically we need a clear idea of why the data do not follow the true linear trend. The simplest idea is to imagine that the business response Y gets disturbed from its trend value by factors outside our control. So instead of seeing the line you see

$$Y = mx + b + \varepsilon,$$

where ε is a random error with a mean of zero. The response Y will try to follow the line but gets "knocked" randomly up or down by the random error ε. Since the random errors have a mean of zero, the response Y will follow the underlying linear relationship on average, but a given set of data will not follow the line exactly.

Assumption 2. Independence The error disturbances ε are supposed to be independent. Recall that two variables are independent if the values of one variable do not likely affect the values of the other. In this case we are saying the disturbances of one point have no effect on the disturbances of the other points. For instance, if one point is above the line, this does not make it any more or less likely that the next point will be above the line.

You will often be able to see the failure of this assumption in a data plot. If the data tend to clump together then the most sensible explanation is some form of dependence. An example is in the right plot below. The points tend to clump together. Whereas, in the left plot, the points do not clump and seem to fall randomly above or below the general trend. You could not apply some of the remaining formulas in this chapter to the right hand plot. You could apply them to the left hand plot.

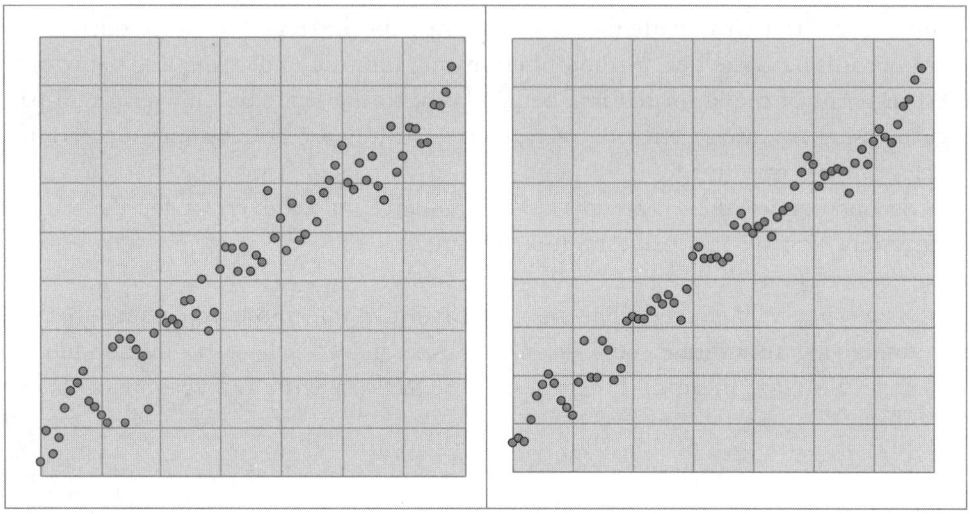

The typical context where this assumption might be called into question is for time series data. There are certainly methods for analyzing data of this kind, and we will see some of them in Chapters 19 and 20.

Assumption 3. Constant Variability The typical size of the underlying error disturbance ε is measured by the standard deviation σ of ε. Like the true slope and intercept, it is unknown. The third assumption of the regression model is that σ is the same, regardless of the value of x. Such an assumption is not appropriate if the data exhibit proportional error, for then the disturbances would be larger for larger values of Y.

Ideally, we expect to see the variations of the points from the line following a uniform pattern from left to right, as in the left plot. In other words, no matter where you are to the left or to the right of the linear relationship, the disturbances to the data have the same average size.

The left plot below displays a situation where the constant variability assumptions apparently fails. There is much more variability to the right of the plot—when Y is larger. When Y is smaller at the beginning of the plot, there is hardly any variability. You would be wrong to apply the remaining formulas in this chapter to data like these. We can deal with data of these kinds, but you will again have to wait until later chapters to find out how.

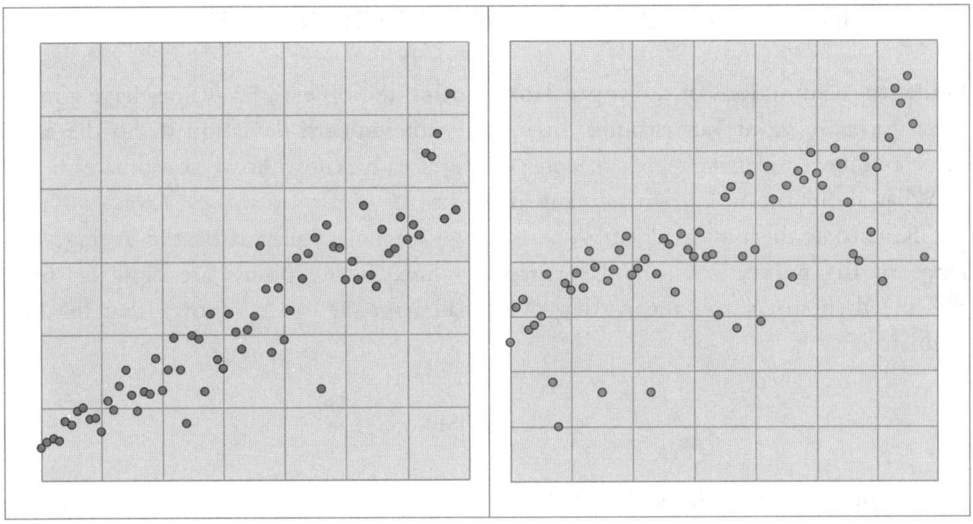

Assumption 4. Normality of the Noise Ideally, we want the error disturbance ε to have a normal distribution. The idea is that the further away from the line you move, the less points there are—with most of the data within 1 standard deviation (σ) of the line.

It is quite difficult to see if this assumption is reasonable from looking at a raw data plot. The right hand plot shows a situation where it looks like the assumption fails. There seems to be more data above the linear trend but with a smaller number of points well below the linear trend. There is a lack of symmetry in the way the points scatter about the trendline.

This fourth assumption is actually *not* essential to the regression model. Provided that you have a reasonable large data set, you could still apply most of the remaining formulas of this chapter.

CHECK YOUR UNDERSTANDING

Q4. Look at each of the plots below. Which, if any, of the four regression model assumptions do you think might fail for these plots?

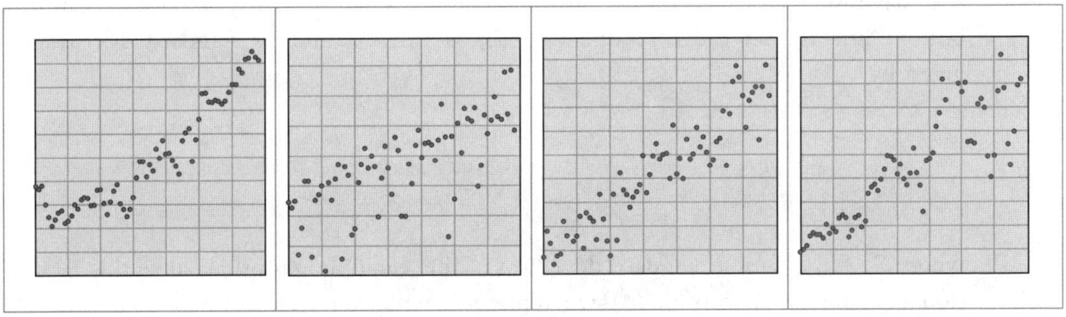

15.5. How Reliable Is the Regression Line?

Under the assumptions of the **regression model**, the observed *Y*-values have a mean equal to $mx + b$ but vary around this mean with standard deviation σ. So there are three numbers to estimate: m, b, and σ. We already know how to estimate m and b. What about the unknown standard deviation σ?

Since σ is the typical disturbance size, we might estimate it by the average distance of the points from the LS regression line. If the points are close/far from the line then surely this means that σ is small/large. It can be shown that the best estimate is

$$\hat{\sigma} = \text{RMSE}.$$

This is the measure of how close the points are to the line that we used in defining the LS line. So our estimate of the typical size of the disturbance is simply our RMSE measure of the typical distance of the points from our best fitting line.

This is a number that we will want to know. It is one thing to quote a line that describes the relationship between, say, the area of an apartment and its price. But surely you would also want to know how close the prices are to the line. This measures the variability of realized apartment prices about their fair market value. Thought of another way, it is an estimate of the typical error we make if we use the linear rule to predict the sale price of these apartments.

Another value we get from the regression model is an assessment of how reliable the LS line is itself. Of the two numbers that define the line, the slope is almost always the more important. It describes how much effect the input X has on the output Y. So we would really like to know how reliable our estimate of this slope is.

The LS estimate of the slope is given by

$$\hat{m} = r_{XY}\frac{S_Y}{S_X}.$$

You might remember from the last chapter that the correlation coefficient has its own standard error. The other terms in the above formula are also unreliable and have standard errors. The mathematical details are fairly complex, but the bottom line is that the LS slope estimate is variable and its standard deviation is given by

$$\frac{\sigma}{S_X\sqrt{n-1}},$$

where S_X is the sample standard deviation of the x sample. As usual, since this expression contains an unknown (σ) we replace it with our best estimate (which is the RMSE) to obtain **the standard error of** $\hat{m}$.

The standard error of $\hat{m}$ is given by

$$\mathrm{SE}(\hat{m}) = \frac{\hat{\sigma}}{S_X\sqrt{n-1}}.$$

This serves the same purpose as the standard error of any other estimated quantity, namely to describe the intrinsic or implicit variability—in this case of the estimated slope. As usual, since there is a $\sqrt{n}$ on the denominator, we have the principle that to double the accuracy we have to take four times the sample. This principle applies to virtually all of statistics, no matter what you are estimating. Second, the term S_X being on the denominator means that the standard error will be smaller if S_X is bigger. Larger standard deviation is usually undesirable. But in this case, more variability in the x-values means that you will be able to estimate the slope more accurately. For instance, if you were trying to estimate how much area affects the value of an apartment, you would be better off getting two apartments of very different sizes than two apartments that had almost the same size. Standard errors can be used in the usual way, to generate confidence intervals for the true slope and to test hypotheses about the slope.

EXAMPLE 1 (Continued) *Okun's Law*

For this data set we found that the estimated slope was −1.372. How accurate is this figure? We need three numbers to use the formula for the standard error of the slope. The RMSE of the best fitting line was 0.796%. This measures the typical error we would incur if we tried to predict this quarter's change in GDP from the change in the UE rate using the LS equation

$$\text{GDP change} = -1.372 \times (\text{Change in UE rate}) + 0.543\%.$$

The figure −1.372 in this equation has its own standard error. The standard deviation of UERATE(x) was $S_X = 0.448\%$ and the sample size was $n = 248$. So the standard error of the slope is

$$\mathrm{SE}(m) = \frac{\sigma}{S_X\sqrt{n-1}} = \frac{0.796}{0.448\sqrt{247}} = 0.114.$$

This is the error measure that goes with the −1.372 figure. We could add and subtract 2 standard errors to give a 95% range for the true underlying slope.

Using StatproGo

The regression model gives us measures of uncertainty. These numbers are not easily produced in ordinary Excel but are output automatically by StatproGo.

Select Regression Analysis and then Multiple. Multiple regression allows us to evaluate multiple input variables at the same time. We are currently learning how to analyze the effect of a single input variable, which is called simple regression. We will use the Multiple Regression module right from the start, which will mean we will be familiar with much of the output when we move to the more complex (but more interesting) context of multiple input variables.

The first dialog box identifies the data area. If you activated any cell in a rectangular data area, then this area will be chosen by default. This is the case for all StatproGo routines. The next dialog boxes ask you to specify the *Y* variable (called the response variable) and the x variable, called the explanatory or predictor variable.

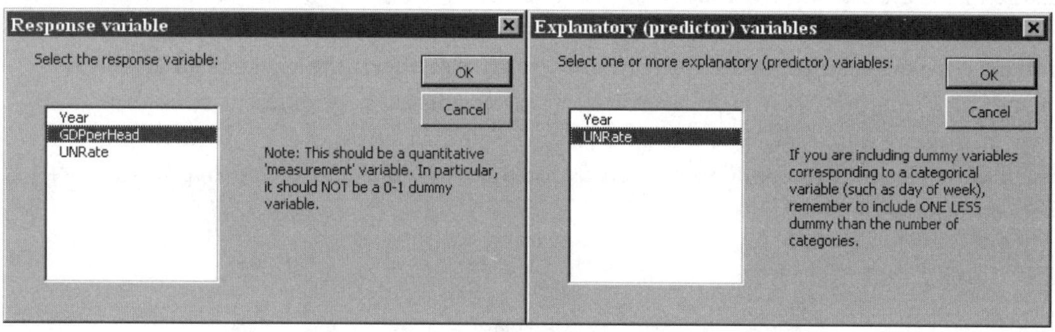

The next dialog box asks you about diagnostic options. You can ignore this by clicking OK for now. The output for the Okun's Law data is below. I changed the format of some of the numbers to percent because our *Y* variable here is the change in GDP.

Results of multiple regression for GDPperHead							
Summary measures				Predicted Value:		0.543%	
Adj RSquare		37.0%		Pred Error		0.799%	
Model Error		0.796%		Trend Error		0.071%	
p-value		0.0000					
Regression coefficients							
	Coefficient	Std Err	t-value	p-value	Lower	Upper	Partial
Constant	0.543%	0.051%	10.7	0.000	0.444%	0.643%	
UERate	-1.372	0.114	-12.1	0.000	-1.596	-1.148	-0.610

Let's identify the relevant numbers in this output. The lower section with the title *Regression Coefficients* tells us about the fitted line. The LS intercept of 0.543% is labeled *Constant* and the LS slope of −1.372 is labeled *UERate*, which was the name given to the x variable. The standard error of the LS slope is sitting right next to it (0.114) and a 95% confidence interval for this slope is given as (−1.596,−1.148). The partial correlation is given as −0.61. This is just an ordinary marginal correlation here because there is only one input x variable. But with multiple input variables it is the partial correlation that we saw in the previous chapter.

The other figure you should recognize is 0.796%, which was our RMSE and the estimate of σ. In the StatproGo output it is called *Model Error.*

There are some other figures that can also be explained at this point. You will notice that there is a standard error figure 0.051% sitting next to the baseline estimate 0.543%. We will not look at the formula for this standard error as it is a little more complicated than the formula for the standard error of the slope. As always, though, this standard error measures the intrinsic error in a number we have calculated from data—here 0.543%. There is a 0.051% error in this figure. Remember that this figure measured underlying GDP growth when the economy is in stable equilibrium (when the UERate is not changing).

There is also a figure called Adjusted r^2. Recall that we use the square of the correlation coefficient to measure the percent of variation explained. In this case, the squared correlation is $r^2 = 0.610^2 = 37.2\%$. The adjusted r^2 is (as the name suggests) a slight adjustment to the ordinary r^2, and in this case equals 37.0%. The reason for this adjustment will be explained in Chapter 17. For now, we can look at the two figures in the Summary Measures section and see how well the line performs. The adjusted r^2 expresses this in terms of variation explained. We would like this to be as high as possible. Here it is only 37.0%. The Model error expresses this in terms of the typical error you would make if you use the line to predict GDP growth. We would like this to be as small as possible.

Finally, there is some other output that will not be discussed now. This has been de-emphasized with a paler font.

EXAMPLE 2 (Continued) *Duo beverages: spending on PP*

The StatproGo output for Duo beverages is given below. The estimated slope is 2.104 and intercept is 25,721, as we calculated earlier. The error in the 2.104 figure is 0.032. So it is known reasonably accurately.

The RMSE is 6768, which measures the variability in sales after taking account of the differing expenditure in PP. In other words, if we use the LS equation

$$\text{Sales} = 25.721 + 2.104 \times (\text{PP Spend})$$

to predict sales, we will be wrong on average by \$6768, either too high or too low.

Results of multiple regression for Sales							
Summary measures				**Predicted Value:**		25721.43	
Adj RSquare	94.0%			Pred Error		6793.0	
Model Error	6768			Trend Error		582.5	
p-value	0.0000						
Regression coefficients							
	Coefficient	Std Err	t-value	p-value	Lower	Upper	Partial
Constant	25721.4	1020.5	25.2	0.000	23712.1	27730.7	
PP	2.104	0.032	64.9	0.000	2.040	2.168	0.970

You will recall that the profit margin on Duo beverages was 0.45% and that it looked like the slope of 2.104 was not sufficient to make p "worth it". Our reasoning was that $0.45 \times 2.104 = 94.7$ cents, which is less than the \$1 spent. Looking at this a little more abstractly, we were calculating $0.45 \times m$ and seeing if it was greater than 1. This is identical to seeing if m is greater than the reciprocal of 0.45, which is 2.222. This is the breakeven point at which PP expenditure becomes worth it.

So we can now look at our estimate of 2.104 and how it compares to this natural benchmark of 2.222, taking into account the standard error 0.032. The t-statistic for measuring this deviation is

$$t = \frac{\text{estimate} - \text{benchmark}}{\text{SE(estimate)}} = \frac{2.104 - 2.222}{0.032} = -3.65.$$

So statistically, the estimated slope of 2.104, which measures how effective PP expenditure is in terms of increasing sales, is well below the point where we break even. Another way of looking at the same thing is to note that the 95% interval (2.040,2.168) does not contain the breakeven value 2.222. There is some statistical robustness to the claim that sales do not rise fast enough with PP expenditure to offset the cost. We will return to this example in a later chapter and give a yet more refined analysis.

Testing Whether an Input Has an Effect

One thing we do with estimates and standard errors is test. We just calculated a t-statistic above and decided that PP was not effective. Even before we do this, one of the first things we can look at is whether the input variable x has any effect on the output variable y at all.

When the slope is zero the input x has no effect on the output y. This is the null hypothesis, and the alternative hypothesis is that the input x does have an effect on the output y. So we want to compare the estimated slope to a benchmark of 0. A t-statistic for measuring this is

$$t = \frac{\text{estimate} - \text{benchmark}}{\text{SE(estimate)}} = \frac{\hat{m}}{\text{SE}(\hat{m})}.$$

If you look in the StatproGo output in the column labeled "t-value" you will see the ratio of the slope estimate to its standard error. This is testing whether the input has any effect at all. For the Duo example, the t-value is

$$2.104/0.032 = 64.9,$$

which is a truly huge value! The p-value in the output converts the t-value to a measure of evidence using 1 – NORMSDIST(t). However, by default all tests in StatproGo are two-sided, so the p-value is doubled. In this case the p-value is very close to zero anyway, so the doubling has no visible effect. But in less clear-cut examples it would be important. If you were testing for a slope being positive then you could halve the p-value to make it one-sided. In the present example this would be appropriate, as we can be sure that if PP expenditure has any effect on sales, it will surely be positive.

There is no question at all that PP has an effect on sales. We knew this anyway so it is a rather silly thing to test. Nevertheless, in other contexts it may not be so obvious whether all inputs have an effect on the output and this is the standard output of StatproGo and most regression packages.

The attentive student may have been wondering why we couldn't test whether X had an effect on Y by using the correlation and the t-statistic based on it

$$t = \frac{r\sqrt{n-2}}{\sqrt{1-r^2}},$$

as given in the previous chapter. The answer is that you can. Let's see what we get with the Duo example. The correlation was 0.970 and the sample size was 270. If you substitute this into the formula for t you get the answer … 64.9! This is not such a surprise when you recall that the LS slope was just the correlation rescaled by the standard deviations. Slopes are closely related to correlations and so testing whether the slope is zero should be, and is, identical to testing whether the correlation is zero.

CHECK YOUR UNDERSTANDING

You have fitted a simple linear regression on a scatter plot of 28 data points and obtained an LS estimate of the slope equal to 0.75. The standard error is 0.022.

(a) Is the slope significantly different from zero?

(b) Give a 95% confidence interval for the slope. Would a 99% interval be wider or narrower?

(c) There are theoretical reasons beforehand to expect that the slope will be equal to 1.0. Is the slope significantly different from 1.0? This will require you to slightly extend the theory given in the lecture notes.

15.6. SUMMARY

The effect of an input variable X on an output variable Y can be measured by how much Y changes when X is changed by one unit. When the answer does not depend on x, the relationship is linear and summarized by an equation of the form

$$y = mx + b,$$

where m and b are two known numbers. A common name for m is the **slope** or **gradient**. It measures *the effect of the input* x *on the output* y. A common name for b is the ***y*-intercept** or **vertical intercept**. It measures output y when the input x equals 0.

LS Regression Line

Noisy scatter plots can be summarized by a linear function. The LS line is the one that is closest to all the points in terms of the RMSE. The slope and intercept of this LS line are given by

$$\hat{m} = r_{XY}\frac{S_Y}{S_X}, \quad b = \overline{y} - \hat{m}\overline{x}.$$

Regression Model

We assume that the data are generated by completely random disturbances from a true underlying line of typical size σ. With these assumptions we can estimate the reliability of the line by

$$\hat{\sigma} = \text{RMSE}$$

and the reliability of the LS slope by

$$\text{SE}(\hat{m}) = \frac{\hat{\sigma}}{S_X\sqrt{n-1}}.$$

The standard error is used in the usual way for tests and confidence limits.

Excel

LS line from raw data: Standard functions are SLOPE and INTERCEPT.
LS line from plot: Right click on any point and then click on Add Trendline.
Regression model output: StatproGo and then Regression Analysis_Multiple.

EXERCISES

E1. Demand Q is negatively associated with price P. For every increase of \$5 in price, demand decreases by 40 units. When price is \$10, demand is 50 units. What is the demand equation?

E2. **(a)** What would be the slope of this line?
(b) What would be the formula for this line?

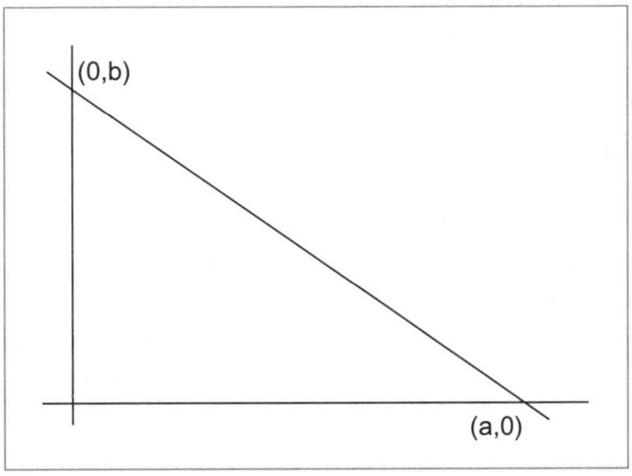

E3. You have data relating the selling price of 150 homes to their appraised value (before sale). The correlation between these two variables is 0.8412. A table of means and standard deviations is given below:

Summary measures for selected variables		
	Value	**Price**
Count	150	150
Mean	132.21	133.07
Standard deviation	12.99	14.64

(a) What is the LS regression line?
(b) What does the estimated slope indicate in terms of the accuracy of price appraisal?
(c) The minimized RMSE (also called Model Error by StatproGo) is 7.640. What is a standard error for the slope and what does it mean?
(d) Is it plausible from these data that sale price and appraised price are mutually consistent?

E4. Below are some (fictitious) correlations between all pairs of three variables. The means and standard deviations are also given. Imagine that they were obtained from a sample of 35 randomly chosen individuals.

	Income	**Education**	**Age**
Income($1000)	1.0	0.43	0.22
Education(years)	0.43	1.00	-0.58
Age(years)	0.22	-0.58	1.00
Mean	45.2	11.3	47
Stdev	8.5	3	12

(a) What would be the slope and intercept of a regression predicting Income from Age?
(b) What would be the slope and intercept of a regression predicting income from Education? Does this parameter have any sensible meaning?
(c) If the units of Age changed to months then how would the slope of the regression of Income on Age change?

E5. For the PP expenditure data on Duo beverages, the slope was 2.104, the intercept was 25,721, and the RMSE was 6768. The standard deviation of the PP spend is $12,734 and there are 270 stores in the database.

(a) Give a prediction of sales when the PP spend is $30,000.

(b) Give 1 standard deviation range for the answer to (a).

(c) Give a 1 standard deviation range for the net profit when the PP spend is $30,000. To do this, multiply by the 45% margin and subtract the cost.

(d) Calculate a standard error for the slope of 2.104.

(e) Give a 75% interval for the effect of PP spending on Sales.

E6. Below is some output from a regression model of the amount spent on pay TV optional extras using the number of optional extras purchased in the previous year as the predictor. There were 83 individuals in the database. The mean expenditure was $20.02 with a standard deviation of $14.06. The mean number of optional purchases last year was 2.783, with a standard deviation of 1.828.

Results of multiple regression for Expend							
Summary measures				**Predicted Value:**		12.261	
Adj RSquare	13.1%			Pred Error		13.36	
Model Error	13.19			Trend Error		2.75	
p-value	0.0008						
Regression coefficients							
	Coefficient	Std Err	t-value	p-value	Lower	Upper	Partial
Constant	12.261	2.648	4.63	0.000	6.992	17.529	
PP	2.787	0.797	3.50	0.001	1.202	4.372	0.363

(a) Is the number of previous options purchased a significant predictor of expenditure this year? How sure are you?

(b) How would you explain the regression equation in simple words?

(c) How accurate is the regression equation either in terms of typical prediction error or in terms of variation in options explained?

(d) Predict the expenditure of a customer who purchased five optional extras last year.

(e) Suppose I did not give you any figures in the Summary Stats section. How could you calculate the correlation of Expenditure with Number last year?

E7. A survey of 200 randomly chosen consumers was presented with the proposition "luxury cars are not the worth the money." They responded to this proposition on a 5-point scale, 5 meaning strongly agree and 1 meaning strongly disagree. There are two main explanatory variables, the respondent's age and the number of months since the respondent bought a car. The data are in Q7.xls.

(a) Use StatproGo to produce regression output for predicting the response from age. Use it a second time for predicting the response from months.

(b) Based on the output, which is the better predictor of response, and how good a predictor is it?

(c) Predict the mean response of those customers who last purchased a car 12 months ago.

(d) You have not covered the theory for this yet, but use StatproGo again to create a regression model that uses both months and age at the same time to predict the response. You can achieve this by selecting both months and age as explanatory variables. Does this model look much better than the separate models?

E8. The motorcycle data describing the price of auctioned motorcycles, their age, and their mileage are in Q8.xls.

(a) Use StatproGo to produce regression output for predicting the price from age. Describe in simple words the effect of age on the price of a motorcycle.

(b) Use StatproGo to produce regression output for predicting price from mileage. Describe in simple words the effect of mileage on the price of a motorcycle

(c) Suppose you have a motorcycle that is 2 years old with mileage of 20,000. Predict its price using its age.

(d) For the same motorcycle in (b), predict its price using its mileage.

(e) Which of the two models is most accurate?

(f) What do the two models say about the price of a new motorcycle?

(g) You have not covered the theory for this yet, but use StatproGo again to create a regression model that uses both mileage and age at the same time to predict price. You can achieve this by selecting both mileage and age as explanatory variables. Does this model look much better than the separate models?

CHAPTER 16

The Reliability of Regression-Based Decisions

16.0. INTRODUCTION: WHAT IS THE ISSUE?

You have data on 108 apartments sold in Deepwater Bay in 1995. There is a clear positive association between sale price and area. The correlation is 0.828 and the least squares regression line is

$$\text{Price} = 122.2 + 0.4913 \times \text{Area}.$$

There are various reasons why this regression equation might be useful. In this particular example, it can answer at least three pertinent questions.

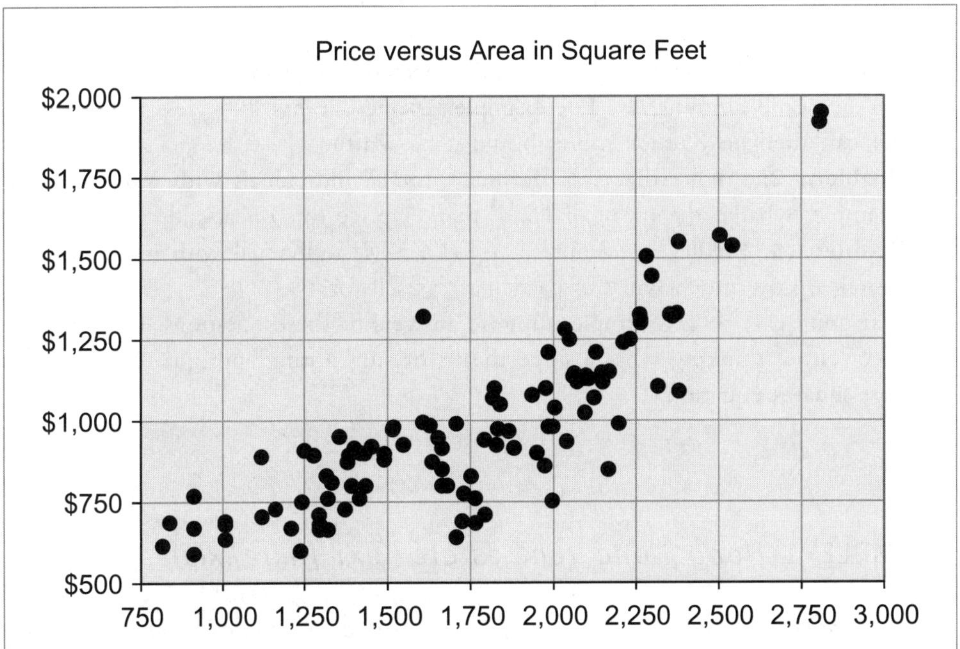

Data-Driven Business Decisions, First Edition. Chris J. Lloyd.

What is the value of an extra 100 ft^2 of floor space? The branch office is having a sales review. Even though there was no apartment of exactly 1500 ft^2 in their database, what is the fair market price for such apartments? A client comes into the office with an apartment of a certain size and wants you to quote a range for likely sale price. What do you quote?

It is quite easy to give numerical answers to these questions. However, a proper statistical answer will not only give a best estimate, but will also evaluate the accuracy of this estimate. These accuracy estimates depend on the assumptions of the regression model. So a really thorough statistical answer would also verify the appropriateness of these assumptions.

16.1. Three Kinds of Questions That Regression Answers

Suppose that we have two business variables X and Y and are mainly interested in predicting the value of Y as well as changes in the value of Y. We have fitted a least squares regression model to the data and have obtained the linear equation,

$$y = \hat{m}x + \hat{b},$$

either from StatproGo or from the formulas given in the previous chapter.

There are at least three typical problems of prediction that may be of interest in applications.

Problem 1: Predict the average or expected *change* in output Y if input x changes by some amount Δx. For example, if one car has 4000 less mileage than another car, then how much more should it be worth?

Problem 2: Predict the *mean* output Y for *all* individuals with input value x. For example, what is the mean or "fair" market price for 5-year-old cars?

Problem 3: Predict *actual* output Y for a *single* individual with input value x. For instance, how much will this particular car sell for?

It is quite easy to give simple numeric answers to these questions. It is simply a matter of either thinking what a slope means or substituting appropriate values into the least squares equation.

EXAMPLE 1 *Hong Kong real estate (ex1 [hkre].xls)*

Our LS prediction equation relates Y (price measured in units of \$1000) to X (area measured in units of ft^2). The equation is

$$\text{Price} = 122.2 + 0.4913 \times \text{Area}.$$

Problem 1: *What is the market value of 100 ft^2 of floor space?* To answer this question, we ask what the typical change in Price would be if area changed by 100 units (which is 100 ft^2).

The general regression equation $y = \boldsymbol{m}x + \boldsymbol{b}$ describes the effect of the input x on the output y. The slope measures the change in output per unit change in input. So an increase in the input from x to $x + \Delta x$, which an increase of Δx, induces a mean change in output of $\boldsymbol{m}\Delta x$. We can estimate this from the regression because it gives us an estimate of $\boldsymbol{m}$.

In our example we have $\Delta x = 100$ and $\widehat{m} = 0.4913$ so the difference in mean price between one apartment and another of similar quality with an extra 100 ft^2 is

$$\widehat{m}\Delta x = 0.491 \times 100 = 49.1.$$

Remember that prices are measured in units of \$1000, so this values 100 ft^2 at \$49,130. The answer depends critically on the fact that the regression equation is *linear*. It is only because the equation is linear that we can give a single numeric measure of the effect of changing x.

Even if the linearity assumption is correct, the answer \$49,130 is only an estimate based on 108 apartments sold in 1995. If a different 108 apartments had been sold that year, we would have obtained a different slope and a different answer. But how different? How accurate is the estimate \$49,130? What we need is a *standard error and a confidence interval for* $\mathbf{m}\Delta\mathrm{x}$.

Problem 2: *What are 1500 ft^2 apartments worth on average, or if you prefer, what is their fair market price?* We want to estimate the mean (i.e., the central, typical or expected) price for those apartments whose area is 1500 ft^2. A naïve method would be to take all the apartments that are 1500 ft^2 and calculate the average sale price. But what if there are no apartments of this exact size?

Since we have the linear regression equation, we do not have to search for 1500 ft^2 apartments. It is just a matter of substituting Area = 1500 into

$$\text{Price} = 122.2 + 0.4913 \times \text{Area}$$

to obtain the answer 859.2. The central or fair market price is \$859,200. *If* we had many apartments of this size, we would expect some of them to sell for more than this, and some to sell for less, but we would expect the average price to be around \$859,200.

How accurate is this figure though? Remember, it has been calculated from data on 108 apartments. If a different 108 apartments had sold, then we would get a different LS line and a different answer. There is an intrinsic inaccuracy in our \$859,200 estimate, but how much? What we need is a *standard error and a confidence interval for the mean of* Y *when* x = *1500.*

Problem 3: *A client walks in with a 1500-ft^2 apartment to sell. She asks you straight up: What can you sell it for?* She is asking us to predict the price (y) for an apartment whose area (x) is 1500 ft^2. This is *almost* the same as asking for the mean or fair market price of such an apartment.

Certainly, to quote a best estimate, we would again just substitute Area = 1500 into our regression equation,

$$\text{Price} = 122.2 + 0.4913 \times \text{Area},$$

to obtain the answer \$859,200. This is our best guess for the price of this particular apartment—the same answer as we obtained for the previous question concerning the fair market price of 1500-ft^2 apartments.

How accurate a *prediction* is this? There are two issues. First, the figure 859.2 is an estimate of the mean or fair price for 1500-ft^2 apartments. There is error associated with this figure. Second, even if by some miracle, our estimate of the fair price is exact, we can never predict the price of a particular apartment exactly. It depends on who bids on the day.

Therefore, to answer the question "how accurate is our prediction," we need to know both the intrinsic variability of the fair market figure \$859,200, as well as the intrinsic variability of apartment prices around their fair market price. This gives rise to a *standard error of prediction* and a *prediction interval.*

CHECK YOUR UNDERSTANDING

Q1. The motorcycle data contain auction prices for 134 motorcycles, as well as their mileage in miles. Give single numeric answers to the following questions and say what kind of an interval would describe the accuracy of this estimate.

(a) There is a cycle coming up for sale that has 22,000 mi on the clock. What will it sell for?
(b) Typical mileage per year is 15,000 mi. If this is the case, then what is the typical yearly depreciation due to mileage?
(c) The auctioneer wants a best estimate for the value of cycles with only 10,000 mi on the clock.

Q2. You have surveyed several hundred customers and have established a regression relationship between the customer's age and their weekly expenditure on certain items. Which would be more useful do you think—a confidence interval for the mean or a prediction interval? Try to think of a scenario to justify your answer. There is no clearly correct answer here. It may depend on the business context that comes to your mind.

Q3. You have collected data on male wage earners from the Australian Bureau of Statistics (ABS), and you have plotted the relationship of per annum income to age in years. There is an increasing relationship.

(a) You want to predict the per annum income of an individual aged 47 years. Would you want a prediction interval or a confidence interval for the mean?
(b) You want to estimate the average extra per annum income due to one extra year of age. Would you want a prediction interval or a confidence interval for the mean?

(c) You want to predict the average income of 45-year-old Australians. Would you want a prediction interval or a confidence interval for the mean?

The formulas for the different kinds of standard errors and intervals all rely on the regression model assumptions that were explained in the previous chapter. So before using them, we will want to check that the assumptions seem to be satisfied. Methods for checking the regression assumptions will be given in the last section of this chapter. For now though, let us press on and find the standard error formulas for the three key types of questions.

16.2. Estimating the Effect of a Change

Suppose that X is related to Y though an underlying linear trend $y = \mathbf{m}x + \mathbf{b}$. Then as the input X changes, the output Y changes in an easily predictable way, governed by the slope parameter $\mathbf{m}$. For every unit of change in X, the output changes by $\mathbf{m}$ units. So an increase in the input from x to $x + \Delta x$, an increase of Δx, induces a mean change in output of $\mathbf{m}\Delta x$. We estimate this by

$$\text{Estimated change in } Y = \widehat{m}\Delta x,$$

where $\widehat{m}$ is our least squares estimate of $\mathbf{m}$. The StatproGo output lists this estimate, as well as its standard error. The standard error of the estimated change in Y is

$$\text{SE(Estimated change in } Y) = \text{SE}(\widehat{m}) \times \Delta x.$$

> When we ask about the effect of increasing X by Δx, the estimated effect is the slope estimate $\widehat{m}$ multiplied by Δx. The standard error is the standard error of $\widehat{m}$ multiplied by the same multiplier Δx.

EXAMPLE 1 (Continued) *Hong Kong real estate*

We earlier estimated the value of $100\,\text{ft}^2$ of floor space by

$$\widehat{m}\Delta x = 0.491 \times 100 = 49.1.$$

The standard error of $\widehat{m} = 0.491$ is listed in the StatproGo output as 0.032. So the error in valuing of $100\,\text{ft}^2$ is

$$\text{SE}(\widehat{m}) \times \Delta x = 0.032 \times 100 = 3.2.$$

Remember, prices here are measured in units of \$1000, so our estimate of the value of 100 ft^2 of floor space is \$49.1 K, with an error of \$3.2 K.

Continuing this example, suppose that it turned out that in this year's database the area measurement mistakenly includes the area of the car parking space for those apartments that have them. The area of a car space is quite standardized at 116 ft^2. All the apartments with car spaces should therefore have their floor space measurement reduced by 116 ft^2. What effect will this have on their expected price? They will go down by

$$\widehat{m}\Delta x = 0.491 \times 116 = 55.95,$$

and the intrinsic error in this estimate is

$$\mathrm{SE}(\widehat{m}) \times \Delta x = 0.032 \times 116 = 3.7.$$

CHECK YOUR UNDERSTANDING

Q4. The motorcycle data contain auction prices for 134 motorcycles, as well as their mileage in miles. Typical mileage per year is 15,000 mi. If this is the case, then what is the typical yearly depreciation due to mileage, and how accurate is your estimate? Give a 75% interval for the depreciation.

16.3. ESTIMATING THE TREND MEAN

According to the regression model, the performance measure Y follows a linear trend of the form

$$Y = \boldsymbol{m}x + \boldsymbol{b} + \varepsilon,$$

where ε is a random disturbance with a mean of zero. Another way to think of this is that the mean of Y depends on x according to the equation

$$\mu(Y \mid x) = \boldsymbol{m}x + \boldsymbol{b},$$

but actual values of Y are subject to random errors of typical size σ. The notation $\mu(Y|x)$ is our notation for the mean of Y when the input variable equals x. There are many business contexts where we would like to know the mean performance when the business input takes a specified value.

Suppose we are interested in mean performance when the input variable X equals some prespecified value v. This means that we want to know

$$\mu(Y \mid v) = \boldsymbol{m}x + \boldsymbol{b}.$$

If we have estimated the parameters $\boldsymbol{m}$ and $\boldsymbol{b}$ by least squares then we can estimate the mean value of Y by

$$\hat{\mu}(Y \mid v) = \hat{m}x + \hat{b}.$$

But how accurate is this answer? It must have some intrinsic error because of it is calculated from the scatter plot, which, according to the regression model, is contaminated by random disturbances. Formally, these disturbances ε are assumed to have the same standard deviation σ. What does this imply about the variance of the prediction? The answer can be embodied in a formula

$$\text{SE}(\hat{\mu}(Y \mid v)) = \hat{\sigma}\sqrt{\frac{1 + z_v^2}{n}}$$

known as the **standard error of the trend mean**. The number z_v is a kind of z-score associated with the prespecified value v. It says how extreme the value v is compared with the x-values in the data set. Specifically,

$$z_v = \frac{v - \overline{x}}{s_x}.$$

So the more extreme the value v is, the larger z_v will be, and the larger the standard error. This makes sense—if you try to estimate the price of extremely large or small apartments, you will expect to do it less accurately.

To simplify this formula further, let us suppose that the value v is about one standard deviation from the mean of the x-values—in other words, $z_v = \pm 1$. In this case, we have

$$\text{SE}(\hat{\mu}(Y \mid v)) = \hat{\sigma}\sqrt{\frac{2}{n}}.$$

This is probably a good compromise formula to take, so long as you keep in mind that the real standard error will be less if you are estimating near the very center of the x-sample (since z_v will be close to zero), and will be somewhat larger if you are estimating toward the extremes of the x-sample. For instance, if $z_v = 2$, then the 2 inside the square root should really be a $1 + 2^2 = 5$. If z_v is even larger than 2, then you will seriously underestimate the standard error. However, large values of z_v mean we are extrapolating outside the regular range of the x-sample. It is bad practice to do this anyway, as there is no reason to assume that the linear relationship would persist under conditions that have never been empirically tested.

EXAMPLE 1 (Continued) *Hong Kong real estate*

We earlier asked *What are 1500-ft² apartments worth on average, or of you prefer, what is their fair market price?*

We answer this by substituting v = 1500 into our regression equation

$$\text{Price} = 122.2 + 0.4913 \times \text{Area}$$

to obtain the answer 859.2, so the fair market price is \$859,200. To obtain a standard error for this, we look at the value v = 1500 compared with the sample of apartments, whose mean size was 1756 ft², with standard deviation 445 ft². So z_{1500} equals −0.552. This is a smallish apartment but is not at all unusual. To assess the accuracy of the 859.2 figure, we need the estimate of σ, which is labeled Model error in StatproGo, and here equals 149. So the standard error of the estimate fair price is

$$\text{SE}(\hat{\mu}(Y \mid v)) = \hat{\sigma}\sqrt{\frac{1+z_v^2}{n}} = 149\sqrt{\frac{1+0.552^2}{108}} = 16.4.$$

There is an intrinsic \$16.4 K error in the \$859.2 K figure, which on a practical level is rather small. If we use the rough formula, we get the answer

$$\text{SE}(\hat{\mu}(Y \mid v)) = \hat{\sigma}\sqrt{\frac{2}{n}} = 149\sqrt{\frac{2}{108}} = 20.3.$$

So this rough formula really only gives a ballpark figure, both here and in other examples.

We can use the standard error in the usual manner for tests and confidence intervals. For example, suppose management had a benchmark or target price of \$875 K for 1500-ft² apartments. This figure might have come from an exhaustive study of the Hong Kong property market. Our "fair market price" of \$859.2 K is really an estimate of the price *we* are able to achieve for 1500-ft² apartments. In terms of standard errors, we are

$$T = \frac{\text{estimate} - \text{benchmark}}{\text{SE(estimate)}} = \frac{859.2 - 875}{16.4} = -0.97,$$

or slightly less than one standard error below the target. The p-value associated with this is

$$1 - \text{NORMSDIST}(0.97) = 16.6\%$$

for a one-sided test and 33.2% for a two-sided test. So it is not at all unusual for the mean trend sale price to deviate from the benchmark by this amount. While the lower than targeted sale price might be disappointing, there is no reliable evidence that we are actually underperforming.

CHECK YOUR UNDERSTANDING

Q5. The motorcycle data contain auction prices for 134 motorcycles, as well as their mileage in miles. The auctioneer wants a best estimate for the mean market value of cycles with only 10,000 mi on the clock. Give a 90% confidence interval for this quantity.

16.4. PREDICTION

According to the regression model, the performance measure Y follows a linear trend of the form

$$Y = \boldsymbol{m}x + \boldsymbol{b} + \varepsilon,$$

where ε is a random disturbance with a mean of zero. If we want to estimate or predict the performance of an unseen case, we need to first estimate the trend level $\boldsymbol{m}\mathrm{x} + \boldsymbol{b}$. However, in evaluating the accuracy of this prediction, we will need to take account of both the intrinsic error in this trend estimate, and the fact that the actually performance of the unseen case will be subject to the additional error ε.

To predict the performance $Y(v)$ of an unseen case whose x-value equals v, the obvious estimate is

$$\hat{Y}(v) = \hat{m}v + \hat{b},$$

which is formally no different to the trend estimate. The typical error of this when used as a prediction, rather than as a trend mean estimate, however, is not the same. It can be shown that

$$\left\{\mathrm{SE}(\hat{Y}(v))\right\}^2 = \{\mathrm{SE}(\hat{\mu}(Y \mid v))\}^2 + \hat{\sigma}^2$$

The first term on the right-hand side is due to intrinsic error in estimating the trend mean. The second term is due to the random disturbance ε. Expressing this in terms of SE rather than SE^2 and using our earlier formula for the standard error of the trend mean, we obtain

$$\mathrm{SPE}\left(\hat{Y}(v)\right) = \hat{\sigma}\sqrt{1 + \frac{1 + z_v^2}{n}}.$$

SPE stands **for standard prediction error**, to distinguish this from the earlier formula for standard error of the trend mean. It is worth noting that this formula can never give a smaller answer than $\hat{\sigma}$, and for large sample sizes, it gives an answer very close to $\hat{\sigma}$. In fact, for most practical purposes, we can just take the model error $\hat{\sigma}$ to be a measure of the typical prediction error.

EXAMPLE 1 (Continued) *Hong Kong real estate*

We earlier considered a situation where a *client walks in with a 1500-ft² apartment to sell. She asks: What can you sell it for?*

This is asking for a prediction for a specific apartment. Our best estimate is the fair market price calculated earlier from substituting $v = 1500$ into our regression equation,

$$\text{Price} = 122.2 + 0.4913 \times \text{Area},$$

given that the fair market price is \$859,200. To obtain a standard error, we need the value z_{1500}, which still equals −0.552. So the standard prediction error is

$$\text{SPE}\left(\hat{Y}(v)\right) = \hat{\sigma}\sqrt{1 + \frac{1 + z_v^2}{n}} = 149\sqrt{1 + \frac{1 + 0.552^2}{108}} = 149.94.$$

So the error in the prediction is now \$149.9K. This is almost entirely made up of the unavoidably random nature of sale prices—as measured by the model error $\hat{\sigma} = 149$. This is typically case, except small data sets.

CHECK YOUR UNDERSTANDING

Q6. The motorcycle data contain auction prices for 134 motorcycles, as well as their mileage in miles. The regression output is below. There is a cycle coming up for sale that has 22,000 mi on the clock. What will it sell for and how accurate is your estimate?

16.5. PREDICTION ERRORS AND WHAT THEY TELL YOU

You can use a linear regression model to understand the effect of X on Y or to predict Y for a given value of X or to estimate the trend mean—*provided the regression model is correct.* Regression relies on a set of assumptions that come down to a simple proposition; the performance measure Y follows a linear trend $Y = \boldsymbol{m}x + \boldsymbol{b}$, but is disturbed from this trend by totally unpredictable random errors. If these assumptions are false, then our standard errors and even our main predictions could be completely wrong. Luckily, the veracity of the regression model can be checked.

Residual analysis is the main method for doing this. In the world of *multiple* regression where there are many input x variables (see next chapter), it is the only feasible tool. When there is a single input x variable as in this chapter, plotting the data can work just as well. Nevertheless, we introduce the ideas in this simpler context.

Fitted Values

For each observed individual x-value x_i, we can predict the corresponding Y-value Y_i from the linear rule:

$$\hat{Y}_i = \hat{b} + \hat{m}x_i.$$

Of course, we do not really need to predict these Y-values, because we have observed them. The point is to test the model on known cases. The predicted values are called **fitted values**.

Residuals

The error of prediction is the difference between the actual value Y_i and the fitted value. These prediction errors are called **residuals** and denoted by

$$e_i = Y_i - \hat{Y}_i.$$

After fitting a model, every data point (x_i, Y_i) has a fitted value and a residual e_i measuring how well this point fits the general trend. Geometrically, a residual measures how far a point lies above or below the LS line. If you recall the explanation of the least squares procedure in the previous chapter, it was these vertical errors that we try to minimize in finding the best line.

The average of the residuals is automatically zero. The data points are distributed in a balanced way above and below the line. This is just a consequence of the LS line being chosen to go through the middle of the data.

Residual Analysis 1: Detecting Unusual Cases

A large residual indicates that the Y-value deviates greatly from the value that we predict from the general trend. Therefore, we can use residuals to *detect points that do not fit the general pattern of the data.*

Some residuals will be positive, some negative, some large, some small. The typical size of the residuals is output from the regression model—the RMSE estimate $\hat{\sigma}$ labeled model error by StatproGo. This can be used to benchmark residuals as statistically large or small.

If a residual is many multiples of $\hat{\sigma}$, then it fits the trend of the data very badly. If it is only about as large as $\hat{\sigma}$, then it fits the general trend about as well as a typical point. This suggests rescaling residuals to obtain what are called **standardized residuals**. These are given by the formula

$$s_i = e_i/\hat{\sigma}.$$

If a point has a standardized residual of −1.5, then it falls below the general trend by one-and-a-half typical model errors. It is low, and rather unusually low. If a point has a standardized residual of 3.5, then it really does not fit the general pattern at all.

Standardized residuals are rather like z-scores. Recall that z-scores measure how far an x-value stands out from the mean in units of standard deviations. Standardized residuals measure how far a point (x, Y) stands out from the general linear trend in units of model errors.

A standardized residual larger than 2.5 or smaller than −2.5 means that the case deviates from the trend by a statistically large margin. In the simple context of a single input variable x, you will be able to see that the point stands out from the linear trend and is visually exceptional. You would not need residuals to identify it. When there are multiple input variables, it is much harder to see such exceptional cases in a plot.

Exceptional points deserve investigation. For instance, it may correspond to a week in which sales were significantly higher than the established trend. The reason for unusually high or low performance may become apparent when the case is investigated in detail. This not only explains what is happening in the business but may indicate that there are other important variables that you need to measure and include in the business analysis.

However, if too many points have large residuals then it means that there is something systematically wrong with the model. The model is supposed to summarize the data. If too many points "do not fit," then it has failed. To put it another way, if one or two points do not follow the trend, we should look at why not. If very many points do not follow the trend, then we are probably not describing the trend correctly.

Residual Analysis 2: Detecting Trend in the Residuals

Another way of thinking of residuals is as estimates of the disturbance ε_i that disturbed the Y_i from the general trend. Remember that the regression model assumes that these disturbances are completely random with no pattern at all. Therefore, we can use the residuals collectively to assess the validity of the regression model assumptions about the noise. Ideally, the residuals should be completely and utterly random.

The first and most important use of residuals is to detect if the relationship of Y with x may be curvilinear rather than linear. The way to detect this is to plot the residuals against x. The trend in this plot measures the way in which the relationship between Y and x deviates from linearity.

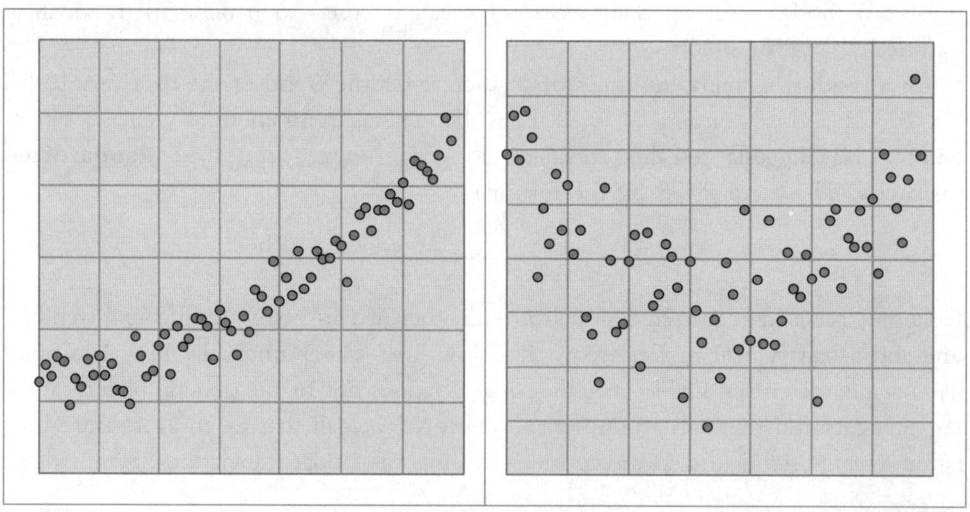

The left plot above is a plot of Y versus X, and the right one is a plot of the residuals versus x. There is a clear "smile" shape in the right plot. If you look carefully at the left plot, you can see that it was not quite a straight line, but it is much more obvious in the residual plot. If we use a line to describe a relationship that is not a line, then we will be systematically wrong in our predictions. We will also be wrong when we quote the slope parameter $\boldsymbol{m}$, since a curvilinear trend means that it simply is not true that change in x by one unit always induces the same change in Y.

Getting the shape of the relationship wrong is the most serious error in regression modeling. It means that your main conclusions will be wrong. At this stage, we do not have a method of describing curvilinear relationships. Rest assured that we will be able to handle curvilinear relationships in the next chapter through multiple regression

Residual Analysis 3: Variability Trends and Clumping

The next most important assumptions of the regression model are that the disturbances are uniform in their typical size (measured by the parameter σ) and that they are independent. These assumptions can be assessed by plotting the *residuals against the fitted values*. The horizontal axis has the fitted value, measuring the typical size of the performance being predicted, and the vertical axis the size of the prediction error.

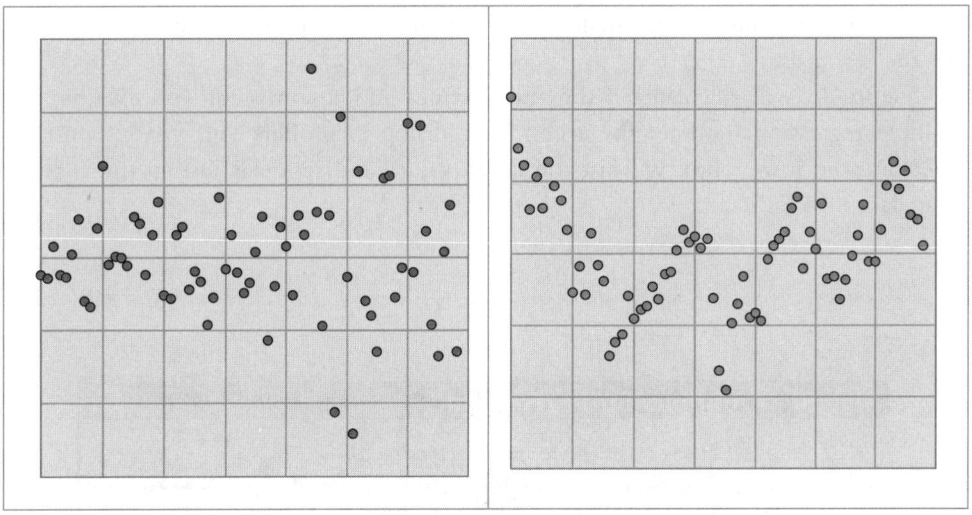

The left plot show a pattern of increasing variability. When performance is low (at the left), the errors are smaller than when performance is high. This might occur for instance if errors were *proportional*. For instance, it might be the case that there is an inevitable 5% variability in auction price of an apartment. So if we tried to predict the price of a \$1 M apartment, there would always be \$50 K uncertainty in our predictions. If we used the same model to predict the price of a \$500 K apartment, then the error would only be \$25 K. If this were the case, then we would expect to see a residual plot like the left one above.

The right-hand plot shows "clumping" of the prediction errors. This is usually caused by dependence between the cases, and is common in time series. The plot also shows some curvilinear trend, so it is problematic in two ways.

Neither nonuniform variability nor clumping makes the LS equation wrong. The estimated slope and intercept are still valid as are your predictions. However, standard errors and prediction errors will be wrong, the more so depending on the extent of the nonuniformity and/or clumping.

Some methods of dealing with these two problems are covered in Chapters 19 and 20. For now, we are just focusing on how to detect such problems with residuals.

EXAMPLE 1 (Continued) *Hong Kong real estate*

Our LS prediction equation relates Y (price measured in units of \$1000) to X (area measured in units of square feet). The equation is

$$\text{Price} = 122.2 + 0.4913 \times \text{Area}.$$

By substituting the areas of the 108 apartments into this equation, we can calculate 108 predicted prices of each of these apartments. You might think of these as fair market values based on their size. We can then compare each sale price with its fitted price to see how much more or less than fair market value each sold for. These are just the residuals.

StatproGo will calculate all the fitted values and residuals for you. Within the multiple regression module, the second last dialog box offers you various options. Checking the lowest box will list the fitted values and residuals just to the right of your data.

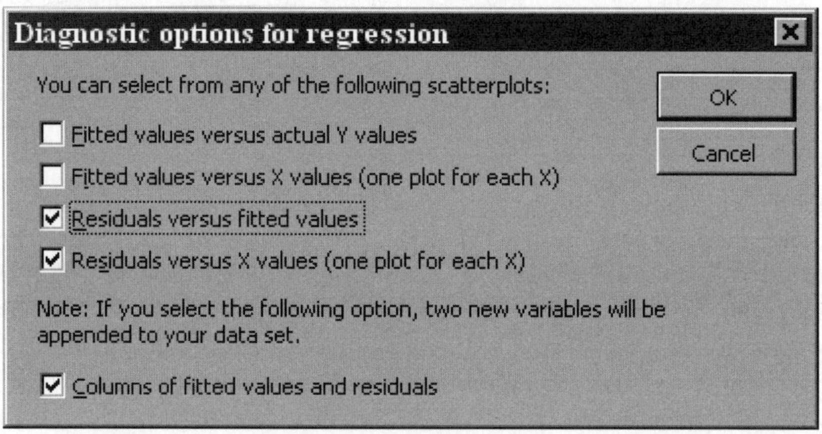

If you check the second lowest box, StatproGo will also plot residuals against the input x variables (one for each x variable, but there is only a single x variable in this chapter). If you check the third lowest box, you obtain a plot of the residuals against the fitted values.

StatproGo does not calculate or plot standardized residuals. You need to calculate these yourself by dividing each residual by the model error—here \$149.0. Standardized residuals do not have any units, and you should format them as pure number with one decimal point for ease of interpretation.

Below are two plots that give information about the adequacy of the model. The left plot shows that the residuals depend on the size of the apartment. It is clear that the smallest and largest apartments are mostly selling for more than their "fair market value," while middle-sized apartments are selling for less. This just means that we are making systematic errors in our assessment of fair market value. The linear model is wrong—or at least not quite right.

The right plot shows standardized residuals versus fitted values. The vertical axis says how far away statistically each apartment is from the assessed fair market value, which is on the horizontal axis. There are two apartments (with IDs 95.143 and 95.058) with standardized residuals of 3.0 and 2.8, respectively. This is most likely caused by the model systematically failing to properly value these two large and high-value apartments.

There is also an apartment in the middle of the plot (with ID 95.171) that has a standardized residual of around 2.7. This looks like a genuinely unusual apartment. It stands out from the other apartments, and we will not be able to "fix" this with any kind of curvilinear model. The most likely reason this apartment is so expensive is because of other features. Indeed, one of the reasons for identifying unusual cases is to find out what caused it and then to measure this in the future.

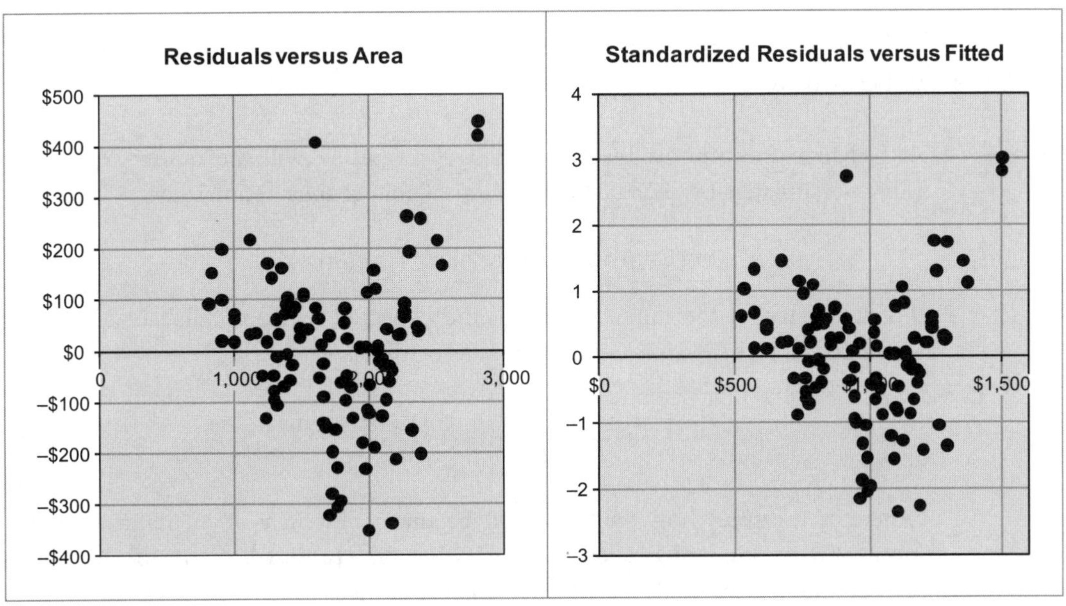

There is also some tendency in the right-hand plot for the variability to be higher toward the right than the left—over and above the trend and outliers that we have noted. All in all, the simple linear model relating price to area is not a good description of the data.

The attentive reader will no doubt have noticed that both these two plots look the same, even though we have focused on different aspects and interpretations. This is only the case when there is a single input x variable. When there are several x variables, plotting residuals against fitted values (the right plot) will give a different view to the other plots.

CHECK YOUR UNDERSTANDING

Q7. The motorcycle data contain auction prices for 134 motorcycles, as well as their mileage in miles. The regression output was obtained in an earlier exercise.

(a) Use StatproGo to calculate the fitted and residuals values.
(b) Plot residuals against mileage. Is there any systematic trend in this plot?
(c) Calculate standardized residuals.
(d) Select any point among the residuals and sort this data area with respect to fitted value. So the data are now ordered from the lowest value/mileage cycle to the highest.
(e) Now select the standardized residuals only (i.e., a single column) and create a scatter plot. This plots the standardized residuals against the row number, which here means the rank of the value of the cycle; that is, 1 is the predicted cheapest and 134 is the predicted most expensive cycle. Are there any outliers or any nonuniform variability in this plot?

16.6. SUMMARY

After a regression model is fitted and accepted, there are three typical questions that it can be used to answer:

1. If I change the input x by Δx, then by how much will the output Y change? This is estimated by $\hat{m}\Delta x$. The accuracy of this change estimate is

$$\text{SE(Estimated change in } Y) = \text{SE}(\hat{m}) \times \Delta x.$$

2. For this value of the input x, what is the expected or mean value of Y? This is estimated $\hat{\mu}(Y \mid v) = \hat{m}v + \hat{b}$. The accuracy of this is

$$\text{SE}(\hat{\mu}(Y \mid v)) = \hat{\sigma}\sqrt{\frac{1+z_v^2}{n}},$$

where z_v measures how far v is from the mean of x in units of standard deviations of x—a kind of z-score. This is called the **standard error of the trend mean** and will typically be much smaller than $\hat{\sigma}$.

3. For this value of the input x, what is my prediction of Y? This is estimated by $\hat{Y}(v) = \hat{m}v + \hat{b}$, which is numerically the same as a trend estimate. However, the accuracy is

$$\text{SPE}\left(\hat{Y}(v)\right) = \hat{\sigma}\sqrt{1 + \frac{1 + z_v^2}{n}}$$

and is known as the **standard prediction error**. It will typically be just slightly larger than $\hat{\sigma}$.

The standard errors are used in the usual way to calculate t-statistics and confidence intervals. The estimates and standard error formulas rely on the regression model being correct.

Residual analysis is used to assess the veracity of the regression model. After fitting a regression model, every data point has an associated fitted value and residual. Fitted values are predictions of what Y_i would be if it followed the LS linear trend. Residuals are the difference between the observed value Y_i and what it is predicted to be. Geometrically, it is the vertical distance of the point to the line. Fitted values and residuals are output by StatproGo.

Plotting residuals against x-values can reveal deviations from linearity in the relationship between the y output and the x input. Any trend suggests that the true relationship of Y and x is not linear. If the relationship is not linear, then all the estimates will be incorrect.

Standardized residuals are residuals divided by the estimate of σ and are on an absolute statistical scale. They measure how far a point stands out from the general trend. Standardized residuals outside the normal range of −2.5 to 2.5 indicate a point that fits the model unusually badly.

Plotting standardized residuals against the fitted values can reveal points that are outliers as well as nonuniform variability and clumping. Badly fitting points often deserve further investigation. Many badly fitting points suggest that the model is missing something important. Nonuniform variability and/or clumping invalidates the standard error formulas. Handling such problems requires more advanced methods (Chapters 19 and 20).

EXERCISES

E1. What type of statistical interval would be relevant to informing the following questions?

(a) You have a regression model of house values on several variables, including area of the house. You are considering extending your home by 800 ft^2, and you are interested in assessing the increased value of your home after the renovation. *Will the added value exceed the renovation costs?*

(b) You have a regression model of total trip times of delivery vehicles on total distance of trip, number of deliveries, and so on. Payment is to be made according to the expected trip duration. In other words, the output of the regression model is used as a benchmark. A delivery driver thinks that the benchmark is too low for a particular trip. *Could his assessment and your assessment both be reasonable?*

(c) You have a regression model of house values on a range of relevant variables. You are interested in bidding on a house and have come up with a valuation from the regression model. You are only interested in bidding if the house is a bargain. *Where should you stop bidding?*

(d) You have a regression model for monthly telephone bills based on the number of people living in a household and their ages. It is based on a large database of households across Melbourne. You have two kids aged 12 and 17 and the regression predicts a monthly bill of \$176. *What bills do you expect over the coming months?*

(e) You have a regression model for demand for water on population size, in a moderate-sized country town. It is estimated that the population will increase by 25,000 over the next decade. *What are the implications for water demand?*

(f) As in part (e), you have a regression model for monthly telephone bills on the number of people living in the house and their ages. It is based on a large database of families across Melbourne. You have two kids aged 12 and 17, and the regression predicts a monthly bill of \$176. Your bills have been consistently running at \$210 per month. *Are your kids overusing the telephone?*

E2. The file Q2.xls has some fictitious data on IQ measured on individuals measured first at age 16, and then again at age 20.

(a) Is there any evidence that the intercept differs from zero? What does the intercept mean here in simple words?

(b) Is there any evidence that the slope differs from 1.0? What would it mean if it did?

(c) Calculate residuals for this model. Plot these residuals against the IQ at age 16. What do you notice?

(d) Fred and Jim both did the test at aged 16. Fred got 98 and Jim got 112. Predict both their scores if they are 20.

E3. The file Q3.xls has real data on student exam results in a statistics course at a well-known business school. The first score is the result in a midterm exam. The second score is their results in the final exam, which, by school policy, is scaled so that the mean is between 74 and 76.

(a) Plot the final score versus the midterm and add a trendline.

(b) Fit a regression of final score on midterm score. How good is the model overall? What would it mean in practice if the model was highly accurate? Would this be a good thing or a bad thing?

(c) Test whether the intercept equals zero. What does a nonzero intercept mean? Does it matter?

(d) Test whether the slope equals 1. What does the slope indicate? Is this a good thing or a bad thing?

(e) Which student performed most outstandingly in the final compared with expectations based on the midterm result?

(f) Examine appropriate residual plots to see if the model has any defects.

E4. The HK real-estate data are in Q4.xls. Use regression and residual analysis to examine the effect on price of the stated feature change, and whether or not the feature has a simple linear effect on price:

(a) Apartment is 5 years older.

(b) Apartment has two more bedrooms.

(c) Apartment has one less bathroom.

E5. A construction manager wants to relate time to project completion (in weeks) to the total value of the project. Project value is routinely used to contract a construction time for the client. The contracted time need not be the time the project manager actually thinks the project will take. The data comprise the past 76 projects whose values vary widely from \$0.88 M to \$5.14 M.

(a) Fit the LS line to these data.

(b) What is a simple interpretation of the intercept?

(c) How much extra time to completion does an extra \$100,000 of value imply, on average? How certain are you?

(d) The value of a project, previously budgeted at \$1.2 M, has now been revised at \$1.4 M (because the client has made some variations). How much longer do you estimate it would take? How certain are you?

(e) The next project is valued at \$2.5 million, and the contract is just about to be signed and will include a penalty clause for exceeding time. What construction time should you contract?

(f) A little later, you are trying to set long-term planning parameters, and, as a benchmark, you are interested in the average construction time for projects of value \$1 million. How much time do such projects typically take? How certain are you?

(g) Do any projects standard out from the general trend?

E6. The worksheet Q6.xls contains data on 141 countries. The variables recorded are average life span (which is estimated by actuarial analysis from currently estimated death rates, GDP per head of population and the freedom index, which measures economic freedom, a high number meaning less freedom. Because GDP varies by such a huge amount from country to country, it is common to transform GDP onto a stretched scale, called log(GDP). This has the effect of spreading out the large number of countries with low GDP so they can be better distinguished on a plot. For example, the left plot shows GDP against the freedom index. Clearly, countries with a higher freedom index (less freedom) have a lower GDP. The right plot replaces GDP with log(GDP). We can now see more clearly the relationship for low GDP countries as the scale has been stretched out. The purpose of the exercise is to look at the relationship between log(GDP), freedom, and life span, and to identify countries that do not fit the general pattern.

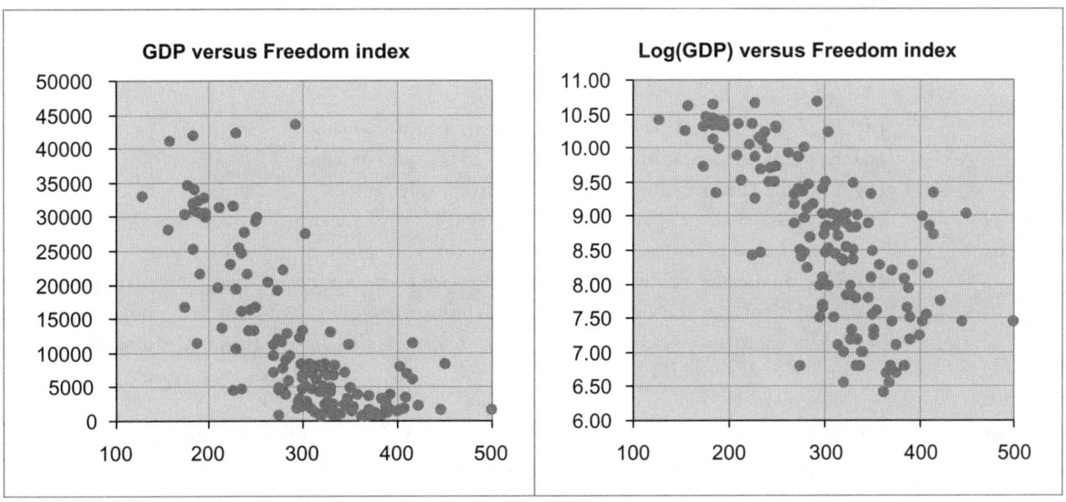

(a) Fit a regression that explains lifetime in terms of log(GDP). Which countries have a standardized residual smaller than −2. What does this mean in simple words? What do you think the reason might be?

(b) Remove the countries identified in part (a). Fit a regression that explains lifetime in terms of log(GDP) to this reduced list of countries. Look at the residual plot. What does it indicate about the relationship? Why do you think that the relationship is curvilinear?

(c) Fit a regression that explains log(GDP) in terms of the freedom index. What does the slope coefficient say about the way freedom is associated with higher log(GDP)? Which countries have the highest/lowest GDP after taking account of the effects of freedom?

E7. The file Q7.xls contains the weekly share price of three companies, General Electric, Walmart, and Cisco. It also has data on the Standard and Poor's 500 stock index, as well as the return on a U.S. 1-month treasury bond, expressed both as a yearly and, more pertinently, a weekly rate (since the data are weekly).

Go to worksheet returns and double click the formulas to compute the weekly growth in stock price for all three stocks and for the S&P500 market index. Next, go to worksheet Excess returns and click on the formulas to subtract off the risk-free rate from each return. These are called excess returns, and measure the return over and above the risk free return on a TB.

(a) Plot the excess return of GE against the excess return of the market. Fit a regression to describe this relationship. The slope coefficient is known as the "beta" of a stock—here GE. What is your estimate of the beta for GE and what is the uncertainty in your estimate?

(b) Suppose that the market index went up or down by 10% in a week. What would be your prediction for the change in the value of GE? Therefore, is GE more or less volatile than the market?

(c) Repeat this for Walmart and Cisco. Which is the most/least volatile stock of the three? Why might you expect these results?

E8. The HK real-estate data are in Q8.xls, where area is measured in units of 1000 ft^2. Using simple linear regression you can obtain the following equations:

$$\text{PRICE} = 122{,}026 + 491.4 \times \text{AREA},$$

$$\text{AREA} = 1340.4 + 155.8 \times \text{BEDS},$$

$$\text{AREA} = 2059 - 27.9 \times \text{AGE}.$$

(a) Explain the meaning of the 491.4 in simple words.

(b) Explain the meaning of the 155.8 in simple words.

(c) Explain the meaning of the 27.9 in simple words.

(d) Suppose that an apartment was a year older. How much smaller would you expect it to be? Therefore, how much less do you think it would be worth?

(e) Do a simple regression explaining price in terms of age. This suggests that apartment depreciates quickly with age. However, we know from part (d) that older apartments are smaller and so some of this has nothing to do with age per se. What would be your best guess about the reduction in price due to age per se.

(f) Suppose that an apartment had an extra bedroom. How much larger would you expect the apartment to be. Therefore, how much more would you expect it to sell for?

E9. The data in Q9.xls list demand and price data for a spanner over 50 weeks. These are actually the second 50 weeks of 1000 weeks of data that you saw in the previous chapter.

(a) Fit a simple regression for predicting demand from week and interpret the intercept and slope.
(b) Fit a simple regression for predicting demand from price and interpret the intercept and slope.
(c) Fit a simple regression for predicting price from week and interpret the intercept and slope.
(d) From parts (b) and (c), it appears that each week, the price goes up by 5.1 cents on average and that each $1 increase the demand should go down by 2935. Therefore, you would expect demand to have been going down over this period, because of the pricing policy. This does not mean there is any underlying trend in fundamental demand. What would you estimate the growth in fundamental demand to be?

E10. The file Q10.xls has data pertaining to valuation of 146 apartments in central business district of Washington, DC, during 2003. There is information on the size of the apartment and the number of bedrooms. In addition, you have a real estate consultant's valuation of the value of the property just prior to sale. Finally, you have the actual sale price. We will analyze these data thoroughly in the next chapter.

(a) How much does the valuer appear to value area?
(b) How does the market value area? Does this differ significantly from the valuer?
(c) How much does the valuer appear to bedrooms?
(d) How does the market value to bedrooms? Does this differ significantly from the valuer?
(e) How good a job of predicting the apartment price does the valuer do? In particular, perform appropriate tests on the slope and intercept to detect any systematic biases in the valuation.

CHAPTER 17

Multicausal Relationships and Multiple Regression

RIGHTWAY MEATS: CASE BRIEFING

A major supermarket chain, Rightway, has recently opened a new store in a newly redeveloped shopping mall. The main competing supermarket chain, WellMark, already had an outlet in the same mall.

Store manager Chris Judson is looking at sales in the meat section over the past year. He has collected 48 weeks of data on total sales in units of kilogram during the first full year of operation. He adjusts these for seasonality by dividing by an industry index for fresh food and then plots them against time. It appears that sales have increased steadily over this first year, no doubt driven by customers learning of the new store.

The shopping mall is essentially a duopoly. The most obvious determinant is the price you charge and the price charged by your direct competitor. Chris knows this and has been monitoring price movements both of Rightway and of the competition. He has the price of a typical basket of meat products at Rightway for each week, measured in \$/kg, as well as the price of the same basket of goods for WellMark. A "basket" of goods is a standard cross-section of products in a category. The data for the WellMark are collected by sending one of his employees there to survey prices of the meat items in the standard basket. Price surveillance is standard practice for large competing retailers.

What is the underlying sales growth of the meat section? How sensitive is demand to price, and what pricing policy should Rightway pursue?

Data-Driven Business Decisions, First Edition. Chris J. Lloyd.

17.0. INTRODUCTION: WHAT IS THE ISSUE?

Most business performance outcomes are driven by more than one factor. For instance, demand for my product depends not only on the price that I charge but also on the price my main competitors charge, as well as general economic conditions, seasonal effects, and the growth trajectory of the business. The value of an apartment depends on many factors, including configuration, size, age, and view. An employee's salary depends on age, experience, education, and level of responsibility.

When there are several drivers of performance, simply plotting the business performance against each driver can easily give you a misleading impression of how these drivers affect performance. The basic problem is that when all the drivers can and do change simultaneously, it is difficult to isolate the effect of each one separately—certainly with a plot.

EXAMPLE 1 *Washington, DC, apartments*

You have some data on the sale price of 150 apartments sold in Washington, DC, in 2003. The key features of the apartment are the total area and the number of bedrooms. If you plot sale price against each of these inputs, then you get the graphics below. Note that price is measured in units of \$1000, and area is measured in units of 100 ft². The trend lines suggest that an extra 100 ft² is worth \$4760, which means \$47.60 per ft². While an extra bedroom is worth \$10,158, at least on average. One of these numbers is, in an important sense, just plain wrong. Can you guess which one?

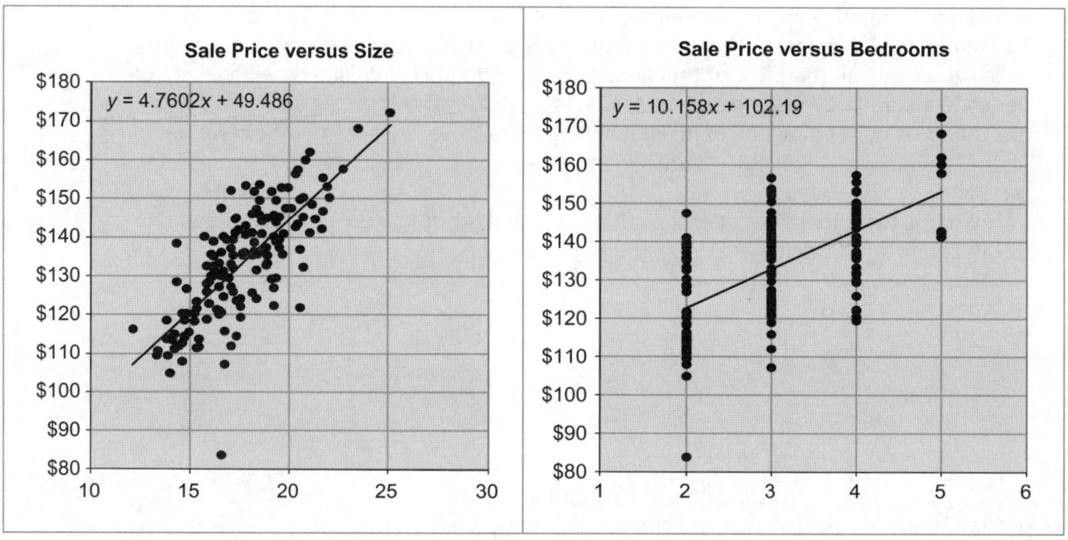

We can look at this is more detail with a Pivotable. Look at the table below, which categorizes the 150 apartments by the number of bedrooms and then area in categories of 200 ft^2.

Area	2	3	4	5	Overall
12-14	$113				$113
14-16	$116	$126	$120		$119
16-18	$128	$132	$129		$131
18-20	$144	$141	$138		$140
20-22		$146	$146	$150	$147
22-24			$150	$163	$159
24-26				$172	$172
Overall	$120	$135	$140	$156	$133

In the body of the table, looking across the rows there is very little increasing tendency, certainly way less than $10 K per bedroom. For instance, looking at middle-sized apartments between 1800 and 200 ft^2, the price of two-, three-, and four-bedroom apartments are almost the same and appear to slightly decrease with more bedrooms! The lack of clear tendency to increase from left to right is apparent across the whole table. In words, *there is little value in an extra bedroom for a given-size apartment*. The increase in price with the number of bedrooms that we saw in the earlier plot may well be measuring the value of the extra area, rather than an extra bedroom per se.

As you look down the columns, there is a very strong effect of area, of around $5 K to $10 K for each 200 ft^2 category. So it looks like area drives price much more strongly than the number of bedrooms. The earlier plot of price versus area is probably a reasonably fair indication of the value of area, but the plot of price versus bedrooms was, in a sense at least, misleading, because most of the effect, perhaps all, was just the extra area of the bedroom.

You might find my argument unconvincing. You might instead argue that the figure $10,158 is the correct value of an extra bedroom because an extra bedroom does imply extra area. I agree that in this sense the $10,158 figure is the bottom line figure. But imagine you were trying to value an apartment and you knew its size and number of bedrooms. You would add $47.60 for each square foot of area. Would you then add the $10,158 for each bedroom? This $10,158 includes the extra area associated with an extra bedroom. So you are double-counting the area, and you will end up with too high a valuation.

If you want to understand how a set of business inputs affect performance you cannot look at each one in isolation. You need to look at them in combination. The tool for doing this is multiple regression. Why can't we just use a Pivotable analysis as we did above? With only two business inputs you can. But with many business inputs, it is very difficult to do a tabular analysis. For instance, if we had the number of bathrooms and the age of the apartment as well, we would have to create a table that covered all combinations of age, area, beds, and baths. Not only would the table be hard to understand, but you would find that most of the cells in the table would be empty—there would not be any apartments with that combination of features.

Multiple regression avoids both these problems. It can deal with as many input variables as you like, it is simple to understand, and you do not need to worry about having too few apartments in the cells. In addition, you get a simple formula for prediction and standard errors for all your conclusions.

17.1. MULTILINEAR RELATIONSHIPS

A linear function (of several variables) is a formula that does not involve any powers or logs or other transformations of the basic input variables. To put this more mathematically:

DEFINITION

A **multilinear relationship** between an output Y and inputs $X_1, X_2, \ldots, X_p$ is a formula of the form

$$Y = \boldsymbol{b} + \boldsymbol{m}_1 X_1 + \boldsymbol{m}_2 X_2 + \ldots + \boldsymbol{m}_p X_p.$$

The parameter $\boldsymbol{b}$ is called the *intercept* parameter. It measures the output Y when *all input variables* equal zero. In many examples, this will not make sense, and $\boldsymbol{b}$ is better thought of as a *baseline* level for Y. The parameters $\boldsymbol{m}_1, \boldsymbol{m}_2, \ldots, \boldsymbol{m}_p$ are called *slope* parameters. They measure the effects of the input variables on the output and are usually of primary interest. What do we mean by *the effect of an input variable on the output* Y when there are multiple variables that drive the output Y?

Let us think about a couple of examples. Cars devalue with age. Each year, they are worth \$m less. Part of this is their increased mileage, and part of it is the age itself. If we needed to value a car, we might want to separate out the age and mileage effects. We can do this by asking "how much does the value of a car go down if it is 1 year older but has the same mileage?" and "how much does the value of a car go down if it has 1000 mi more but the same age?" As another example, experience is one driver of salary. To measure this, I would want to know how salary increases per extra year of experience, other factors such as education level and responsibility level held fixed.

In almost every business context, when we ask about the effect of one input on performance, we are asking about how the performance changes when this variable changes, but the others do not. With a multilinear relationship, the slope parameter measures just this. For example, the slope parameter $\boldsymbol{m}_1$ measures the change in output Y per unit change in input variable X_1 *with all other variables* $X_2, X_3, \ldots, X_p$ *being held constant.* In simple words, it measures the pure effect of input variable X_1.

EXAMPLE 2 *NTC salary data*

The file ex2 salary.xls lists the annual salary, education level, experience, and age of 274 employees of a training company. These data are from the NTC pay equity case where the key interest was in how gender affects salary. The gender of each employee has not been recorded here but will be investigated in a later chapter. For now, we want to look at how age, experience, and education affect salary.

If you plot salary against each variable and add a trendline, you will find the slopes that describe the effect of each input variable. For instance, each year of age adds $1503 to salary, while each year of experience adds $1808. Each level of education subtracts $3235 to salary. Huh?! How could education *reduce* your salary? Let us put this to one side for now and look at a multilinear equation that might describe the drivers of salary.

The business output Y to be explained here is salary and the three drivers are age, experience and education. Consider the linear equation

$$\text{Salary} = 13{,}670 - 85 \times \text{age} + 2180 \times \text{exp} + 2873 \times \text{educ}.$$

Multiple regression produces multilinear equations of this form, based on historical data. In fact, we will later obtain just this equation using multiple regression.

How Does Age Drive Salary?

The equation tells us that if Fred is a year older than Jim and both have the same experience and education levels, then Fred will have an annual salary of $85 less. In practical terms then, age has almost no effect on salary. Nevertheless, if you plot salary against age you see a very strong positive relationship—an extra $1503 per year of age on average. If the above equation is correct, this must all be due to older employees having more experience and getting paid more for the extra year of experience, not the extra year of age.

How Does Experience Drive Salary?

The formula also says that the effect of an extra year of experience is to add $2180 to the annual salary (provided age and education are held constant), significantly larger than the $1808 that the raw data plot suggests.

How Does Education Drive Salary?

Finally, the formula also says that the effect of another year of education is to add $2873 to annual salary (with age and experience held constant). This is almost the exact reverse of the data plot which said that salary reduces by $3235.

Why Might Education Look Like It Reduces Salary?

Suppose that employees with more education happened to be younger. This is probably true in many workplaces. Specifically, suppose that employees with one extra level of education are on average 2.8 years younger. They will probably have 2.8 years less experience. So their salary is \$2873 more for the extra level of education, but it will also be 2180 × 2.8 = \$6104 less because of the reduced experience. So in total, they will tend to earn \$6104 − \$2873 = \$3232 less. This does not mean education is a bad idea. This is pretty much what we saw in the data. Most people would agree that the \$2873 figure measure the education effect and that the −\$3223 figure mixes up the effects of experience and education.

Predicting Salary

We can also use the formula to predict the salary of a specific person, or to predict what would happen to salary under rather complicated scenarios. For instance.

Am I Better Off Spending a Year Increasing My Education by One Level?

The way to look at this is to see what would happen to my salary if I go back to school and compare it with what would happen if I do not. If I go back to school, then at the end of the year my age and education level would both increase each by 1 year/unit. So my salary would increase by −\$85 + \$2873 = \$2788, whereas if I do not go back to school, then my age and experience will increase by 1 unit. So my salary would increase by −\$85 + \$2180 = \$2095. The difference is \$2788 − \$2180 = \$608. I am \$608 per annum better off taking a year out to increase my education. The educational bonus of \$2873 more than offsets the experience bonus of \$2180 that you forgo.

Is it reasonable to add a fixed bonus of \$2180 for each year of experience? Wouldn't the first few years of experience be more valuable than the last few? The multilinear equation assumes that each year of experience has the same effect. Is it even reasonable to just add up the effects of experience, age, and education? The multilinear equation assumes that it is. These assumptions may be wrong. There are ways of checking them, and there are more complex formulas that can be used. We will build up to this as we go.

CHECK YOUR UNDERSTANDING

Q1. As manager of a delivery company, you have developed an equation to predict the average speed of a delivery run. The average speed is equal to the distance of the delivery run in kilometers divided by the total time in hours from leaving the depot until returning to the depot. You obtain the following formula $S = 58.5 - 2.3 \times T - 3.2 \times N_D$, where S is speed of delivery run in kilometer per hour, T is tonnage of delivery vehicle, and N_D is the number of delivery stops.

(a) What is the average speed of a delivery run for a 4-ton truck making three delivery stops?
(b) Describe the effect of tonnage. Why would this have an effect?

(c) Describe the effect of the number of delivery stops in simple words. Does this sound reasonable?

Q2. You have an equation for monthly demand Y of your product of the form:

$$Y = 15,000 - 700X_1 + 800X_2 + 100X_3,$$

where the driving variables are

$$X_1 = \text{price of my product in dollars,}$$

$$X_2 = \text{price of main competing product dollars, and}$$

$$X_3 = \text{time measured in months from some baseline date.}$$

(a) What does the baseline/intercept mean?
(b) What is the effect of your pricing policy?
(c) What is the effect of your competitor's pricing policy?
(d) Is there growth in demand?
(e) What will happen if I raise my price by \$1 but my competitor matches? Does this make you think twice about the equation's correctness?

17.2. MULTIPLE REGRESSION

Multiple regression is a technique for developing a multilinear equation from historical data, analogous to drawing a least squares line through a scatter plot. It is based on a set of assumptions about how $X_1, X_2, \ldots, X_p$ affect the likely value of Y. The first and key assumption is that

$$Y = \boldsymbol{b} + \boldsymbol{m}_1 X_1 + \boldsymbol{m}_2 X_2 + \ldots + \boldsymbol{m}_p X_p + \varepsilon,$$

where ε is a random error with mean zero. The response Y "tries" to follow the multilinear relationship but is disturbed from the trend by uncontrollable factors, resulting in a random error ε. Since the random errors have mean zero, the response Y will follow the underlying linear relationship on average, but a given set of data will not follow the trend exactly.

We make the same assumptions about the random errors that we made in the simpler context of a single input variable. The assumptions are collectively called the **multiple regression model**. In order of importance we assume the following:

A2. Independence Assumption: The error disturbances ε are independent. For instance, if one point is above the trend, this does not make it more or less likely that another point will be above the trend.

A3. Variance Assumption: The underlying error disturbance ε has the same standard deviation σ, regardless of the values of $X_1, X_2, \ldots, X_p$.

A4. Normality Assumption: The error disturbance ε has a *normal* distribution, and so errors will seldom be outside the range -3σ to 3σ.

Fitting the Regression Model

To start with, we need data on how the output Y has been related to the inputs X_1, X_2, … , X_p in previous cases. We want to describe the pattern of observed dependence with a multilinear rule

$$Y = \boldsymbol{b} + \boldsymbol{m}_1 X_1 + \boldsymbol{m}_2 X_2 + \ldots + \boldsymbol{m}_p X_p,$$

so we need to choose values for the unknown parameters $\boldsymbol{b}$, $\boldsymbol{m}_1$, $\boldsymbol{m}_2$, … , $\boldsymbol{m}_p$. For any choice of these numbers, we can calculate fitted values for each of the observe Y-values by substituting in the input X-values for that case. The best choice for the parameters $\boldsymbol{b}$, $\boldsymbol{m}_1$, $\boldsymbol{m}_2$, … , $\boldsymbol{m}_p$ makes these fitted values as close as possible to the observed values. The closeness of the fitted values and observed values is measured by

$$\text{SSE} = \sum_{i=1}^{n} \left(Y_i - \hat{Y}_i\right)^2,$$

which is the sum of the squared errors.

There are direct formulas for these optimal values, which are known as the **least squares estimates**. The typical size σ of the error is estimated by

$$\hat{\sigma} = \sqrt{\frac{\text{SSE}}{n - p - 1}},$$

where $\boldsymbol{p}$ is the number of input x variables. As with simple regression, this measures the average observable difference between the fitted or predicted y-values, and the actual observed y-values. It is called *model error* in StatproGo. There are also simple and direct formulas for the standard error of each slope estimate and of the intercept estimate. These measure implicit unseen variability in our best estimates of the true slopes and intercept. Standard errors can be used in the usual way to test hypotheses and construct confidence intervals.

To fit a multiple regression using StatproGo, select Regression Analysis then Multiple. This is the same procedure we have used for simple regression. The only difference is that we now select several input x variables rather than one.

EXAMPLE 1 (Continued) *Washington, DC, apartments*

We have data on sale price of apartments, their size, and number of bedrooms (as well as the valuation by a consultant which we ignore for now). We saw earlier that each square foot adds \$47.60 to the price while each extra bedroom adds \$10,158. We wondered whether most or all of the value of a bedroom was just the extra area. A Pivotable analysis suggested that for a given-sized apartment, the number of bedrooms has very little effect on price.

To investigate this using multiple regression, we imagine that the value of apartment follows a multilinear rule

$$\text{Sale price} = b + m_{\text{AREA}} \times \text{area} + m_{\text{BED}} \times \text{beds}.$$

To use StatproGo, designate Price as the response variable, and the variables Area and Beds as the explanatory variables. To select more than one variable, you will need to hold down the control key while you select.

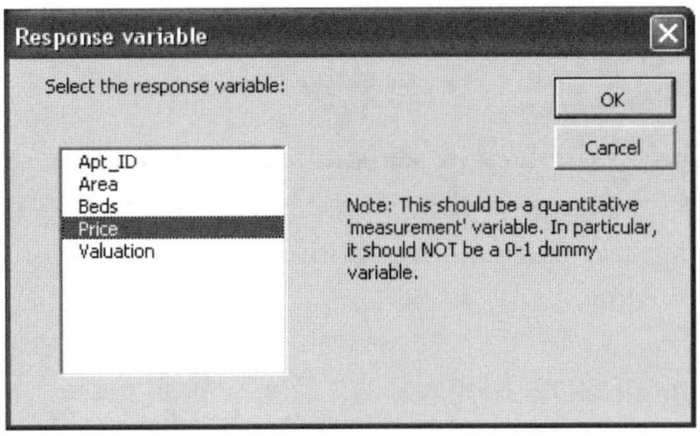

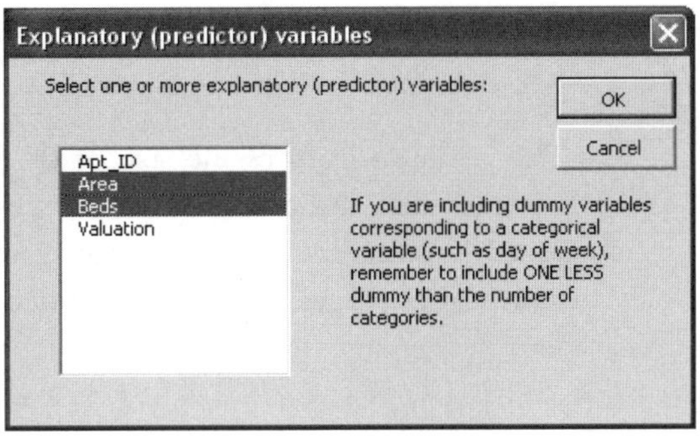

The output is below. Let us go through each number and make sure we know what it means.

Results of multiple regression for Price				
Regression coefficients				
	Coefficient	Std Err	t-value	p-value
Constant	49.095	6.747	7.3	0.000
Area	4.813	0.555	8.7	0.000
Beds	-0.178	1.491	-0.1	0.905

Using the historical data, our best valuation formula is

$$\text{Sale price} = \$49{,}095 + \$4813 \times \text{area} - \$178 \times \text{beds}.$$

Each extra 100 ft^2 of area adds \$4813 to the price, so the value of space is \$48.13 per ft^2, which is fairly similar to what we got from the naive plot of price against area. However, each extra bedroom subtracts \$178 from the price, very different from the \$10,158 that we got from the naive plot of price against bedrooms. The \$49,095 is not really meaningful, as it formally values an apartment with zero area and zero bedrooms. It is best thought of as baseline figure to which we add or subtract amounts depending on the number of bedrooms and floor area.

t-Values and *p*-Values

The effect of an input X_i is measured by the slope parameter $\boldsymbol{m}_i$. When this parameter equals zero, the input has no effect. Especially when there are many inputs, knowing which of them have an effect and which do not is one of the aims of regression.

We have LS estimates of each of the slopes $\boldsymbol{m}_i$, which measure the observed effect of the input X_i. We have a standard error measuring the statistical uncertainty in each estimated effect. We can decide whether $\boldsymbol{m}_i$ equals zero by comparing the estimate with its standard error, that is, by calculating

$$t = \frac{\widehat{m}_i}{\mathrm{SE}(\widehat{m}_i)}.$$

The *t*-value measures the size of the observed effect in statistical units. A *t*-value of 2 means that the observed effect is twice as large as the measurement error. The *t*-value is converted into a *p*-value using the normal distribution. By convention, statistical packages report a two-sided *p*-value

$$p = 2 \times (1 - \mathrm{NORMDIST}[|t|]).$$

p-Value is the chance of seeing an observed effect as large as what one sees in the data by sheer chance. The larger the *t*-value, the smaller the *p*-value. Formally, we test the hypotheses

$$\text{Hypothesis } 0: m_i = 0 \text{ versus Hypothesis } 1: m_i \neq 0,$$

which in words mean

Hypothesis 0: X_i has *no* effect versus Hypothesis 1: X_i *has* an effect.

We reject the null hypothesis and conclude the X_i has an effect if the *p*-value is smaller than a chosen significance level α.

EXAMPLE 1 (Continued) *Washington, DC, apartments*

The reliability of the key figures \$4813 and \$178 are described by the standard errors, *t*-values and *p*-values.

The \$4813 figure has an intrinsic error of \$555. The *t*-value columns contain the estimate divided by its standard error, which is used to test whether or not the input has any effect. For the input variable *area*, the *t*-value is 8.7 and the *p*-value is close to zero. The large *t*-value and small *p*-value mean that area *does* have an effect. The \$178 figure has an intrinsic error of \$1491. The *t*-value is −0.1 and the *p*-value is 0.905. A small *t*-value and large *p*-value mean that the number of bedrooms is not a significant driver of price.

The regression analysis agrees with the Pivotable analysis, and it is saying the same thing. It is area, not the number of bedrooms, that drives price. For a given-sized apartment, there is no reliably statistical evidence that bedrooms affect price.

The raw estimate is negative, but the error in this figure is so large that a more sensible conclusion is that there is no apparent relationship between price and bedrooms, after taking account of area.

Some Economics of Valuation

Imagine for a moment that apartments tended to be worth more if they had more bedrooms *even if they were the same size*. We just decided this is not the case. But what if it was? What would you do if you were a developer with 2000 ft^2 to develop? You would include an extra bedroom. The cost of a few plaster walls and power sockets is really very small, once you are building already. So, over time, the stock of available apartments would change to have more bedrooms, exactly up to the point where there was no market premium for an extra bedroom. Any bedroom premium (or indeed penalty) represents a mismatch between the existing stock of apartments and what is desired by the market. Any such premium or penalty will be exploited by developers, and the "market inefficiency" should disappear.

Economics is just one of the reality checks that we can use to inform our approach to regression modeling. If we obtained a regression with a really large bedroom coefficient, then we would suspect something was wrong, either with our model or with the data.

How about bathrooms? The premium for an extra bathroom could be a little larger, because the cost of a bathroom is considerably higher than a bedroom, perhaps around $10,000. A developer would only spend the extra $10,000 on a bathroom if the market premium was larger than $10,000. We would not be surprised to find, even controlling for floor area, that apartments with a second or third bathroom sold for more than those with one.

Pushing a Bit Further

The third variable in the data file is the valuation of a real estate consultant called Jim. For a fee, Jim gives a prediction of the sale price 3 weeks prior to sale. Jim has access to extra relevant information about both the specific apartments he is valuing and more general market information. There are several interesting questions that we can ask and answer using regression.

- Does Jim perform as well as a regression?
- Does Jim value area and bedrooms correctly?
- How much better could we do if we use Jim's valuation in addition to the area and number of bedrooms?

Does Jim Perform as Well as the Regression? We know that Jim has access to more information about the apartments than their size and number of bedrooms. Provided this information is used correctly, we would expect Jim to outperform the regression.

It is an easy matter to calculate the difference between Jim's valuations and the actual prices for our 150 cases. If we are going to make a fair comparison with the regression, then we should measure the typical error by

$$\sqrt{\frac{\text{sum of errors}^2}{n-p-1}} = \sqrt{\frac{2502.484}{150-1-1}} = 4.113,$$

since this is how we measure regression model error. This is calculated on the worksheet *consultant.* So the typical error of Jim is \$4113. This compares very favorably with the typical error in the previous regression, which was \$9534. Jim is more than twice as accurate.

If you fit a regression for predicting price from Jim's valuation, then you get an even smaller model error of \$3906. The regression uses Jim's valuation not at face value but instead predicts price using the formula

$$\text{Sale price} = -\$6860 + 1.043 \times \text{valuation}.$$

You might think of this as a method of correcting Jim's prediction for small systematic errors that he seems to be making. If no correction were required, then the intercept would be zero, and the slope would be one. The p-value for testing the intercept is 0.033, which suggests that it is not zero. The estimated slope is larger than 1. Standard regression output only tests if the underlying parameter differs from *zero*. To test a different value, you have to calculate the t-statistic yourself. In this case, we calculate

$$t = (1.043 - 1)/0.024 = 1.801,$$

which gives a p-value of 0.072. This is again fairly small. In summary, it appears that Jim's valuation does require correction.

Regression coefficients				
	Coefficient	Std Err	t-value	p-value
Constant	-6.860	3.189	-2.2	0.033
Valuation	1.043	0.024	44.1	0.000

Does Jim Value Area and Bedrooms Correctly? The "correct" valuation is what the market says. We obtained these numbers earlier with a regression of sale price in terms of area and beds. The result was \$4813 per 100 ft^2 and −\$178 per bedroom. We can look at how Jim implicitly values area and bedrooms by fitting a regression with valuation as the y variable. The results are below.

Results of multiple regression for Valuation				
Regression coefficients				
	Coefficient	Std Err	t-value	p-value
Constant	58.701	6.127	9.6	0.000
Area	4.094	0.504	8.1	0.000
Beds	1.191	1.353	0.9	0.380

Jim values floor area at \$4094 per 100 ft^2 and bedrooms at \$1191. It seems then that Jim undervalues space and overvalues bedrooms. We decided that bedrooms have no practical value over and above their area. Jim, who does better than our regression overall, seems to disagree! Who is right? Since Jim predicts better than our regression, are we wrong about bedrooms being worth nothing?

There are two points to make. First, while Jim does better than our regression, Jim has extra information available and his superior performance will largely be driven by this extra information. So he may still be wrong about bedrooms, and beat our regression despite incorrectly valuing bedrooms.

Second, Jim may not actually be valuing bedrooms this way. If we had access to all the other variables Jim uses, and fitted a regression explaining Jim's valuations using all these variables, then we may well find that the above figure of \$1194 is quite different to the figure Jim implicitly uses.

Can We Do Even Better Using Jim's Valuation in Addition to the Area and Number of Bedrooms? To answer this, we fit a regression that predicts from the valuation, the area, and the beds. If Jim uses information in the best way, then we would not expect to do any better by adding the information of area and beds that Jim already uses.

The regression has a model error of \$3838, which is slightly better than the \$4113 using the valuation directly, or the \$3906 using the valuation as a regression input variable. The parameter estimates are in the table below.

Results of multiple regression for Price				
Regression coefficients				
Constant	-10.121	3.462	-2.9	0.004
Area	0.683	0.269	2.5	0.012
Beds	-1.380	0.602	-2.3	0.023
Valuation	1.009	0.037	27.6	0.000

If Jim were using all information correctly, then we would expect the constant, the area slope, and beds slope to all be zero. What is interesting in this output is that the *p*-values for area, beds, and the constant are all small, suggesting that the true parameters are not zero. In terms of final model accuracy, the improvement is modest—from \$4113 to \$3838, which is a 7% improvement. But there is strong statistical evidence, as measured by three small *p*-values, that there is something systematically wrong with the method used by Jim.

The valuation formula implied by this model is

$$\text{Sale price} = -\$10{,}212 + 1.009 \times \text{valuation} + \$683 \times \text{area} - \$1380 \times \text{beds}.$$

The −\$10,212 corrects for Jim's tendency to overvalue apartments overall. The \$683 corrects for Jim's tendency to undervalue area. The −\$1380 corrects for Jim's tendency to overvalue bedrooms.

CHECK YOUR UNDERSTANDING

Q3. In Chapter 14, we looked at some data on 134 motorcycles, their price at auction, their age in years, and their mileage. The same data are in Q3.xls. Fit a multiple regression model that described the effect of mileage and age on price.

(a) What is the depreciating effect of mileage and how accurately can you estimate this?
(b) What is the depreciating effect of age and how accurately can you estimate this?
(c) How much do motorcycles typically vary from their "fair price"?
(d) How does mileage depend on age? What do the slope and intercept mean in simple words?

17.3. MODEL ASSESSMENT

The first regression model is seldom the best one. Regression models can even be seriously misleading if you are not careful. There are several tools for assessing a regression model. Once you are satisfied that you have found the best regression model, and only then is it worth using the model for describing the effects of the inputs or for making predictions.

Fitted Values and Residuals

For each known case, we can use the regression model to predict the y-value. These are called fitted values. The reason for predicting known cases is to compare the predictions with the actual values, and thereby assess the model. Ultimately, the model is evaluated by seeing how close the fitted values are to the observed values. The prediction errors are called **residuals** and denoted by

$$e_i = Y_i - \hat{Y}_i.$$

Overall Measures of Model Accuracy

A model is good if the fitted values are close to the observed, or, equivalently, if the residuals are collectively small. This gives rise to two measures of overall accuracy.

If you plot the actual values against the fitted values, then you will hope to see a perfectly straight line. In practice, the predictions will not be perfect, and you will instead see points scattered about a line. We can measure the strength of the relationship between the actual and fitted values by the correlation of this plot. We noted in Chapter 14 that the square of the correlation is interpreted as variation explained.

The left plot below shows the relationship between the actual prices and the predicted prices of the DC apartments (using area, beds, and Jim's valuation). The correlation in this plot is 0.9657 and the squared correlation is 93.26%.

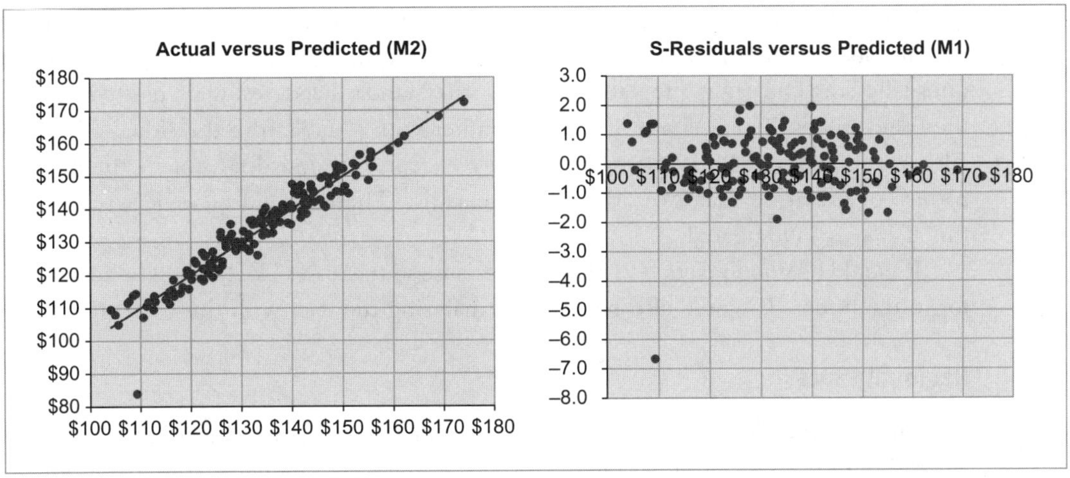

A higher value for r^2 means that the predictions are close to the actual y-values. So you might think this is a sensible measure of overall model quality. There is a problem though. Whenever you add a variable, it is a mathematical fact that r^2 always increases, even if the extra x variable is unrelated to Y. To correct for this natural but misleading tendency of models with more variables to always appear better, an adjustment is made to r^2. This is known as **adjusted r^2** and is always a little smaller than ordinary r^2. The formula depends on r^2, the number of cases n, and the number of x variables p, and is not worth remembering. For the example above, adjusted r^2 equals 93.1%, slightly less than 93.26%.

The second measure of how close the fitted values are to the actual values is based on measuring the average size of the residuals. This is measured by

$$\hat{\sigma} = \sqrt{\frac{\sum e_i^2}{n - p - 1}}.$$

For the present example, it equals 3.838. StatproGo outputs this number, labeled as model error, and adjusted r^2 in the Summary Measures section at the top of the output. If you look at worksheet *consultant + area + beds(M2)*, you will see both these values. In words we would say that 93.1% of the variation in prices is explained by this model (i.e., by area, beds and Jim's valuation), and the typical difference between predicted and actual is \$3.838 in units of \$1000. The higher the adjusted r^2, the lower the model error.

Finding Outliers

Adjusted r^2 and model error are overall average measures of model success. Much more can often be gleaned from looking at the *pattern* of the prediction errors. As in the previous chapter, to detect points that do not fit the general pattern of the data, we rescale the residuals by the model error. These are called **standardized residuals** and are given by the formula

$$s_i = e_i / \hat{\sigma}.$$

If a point has a standardized residual of −1.5, then it falls below the general trend by one and a half times as much as a typical point. It is below trend and rather unusually so. The right plot above shows the standardized residuals plotted against the fitted values. There is one very clear outlier with a standardized residual of −6.67. The apartment (ID 2003.060) is completely exceptional and does not fit the general pattern of valuation that 149 other apartments do. There would be a clear reason for this if it was investigated.

It would be good practice to identify the cause so that cases like this can be accounted for in the future. It would also be worth reanalyzing the data with this case excluded.

Residual Plots

Patterns in the residuals plots can be used to identify whether the input x variables affect the output in a nonlinear manner. The simplest technique is to plot the residuals against each x variable. Any trend in these plots suggests that the x variable affects Y according to a curvilinear rule.

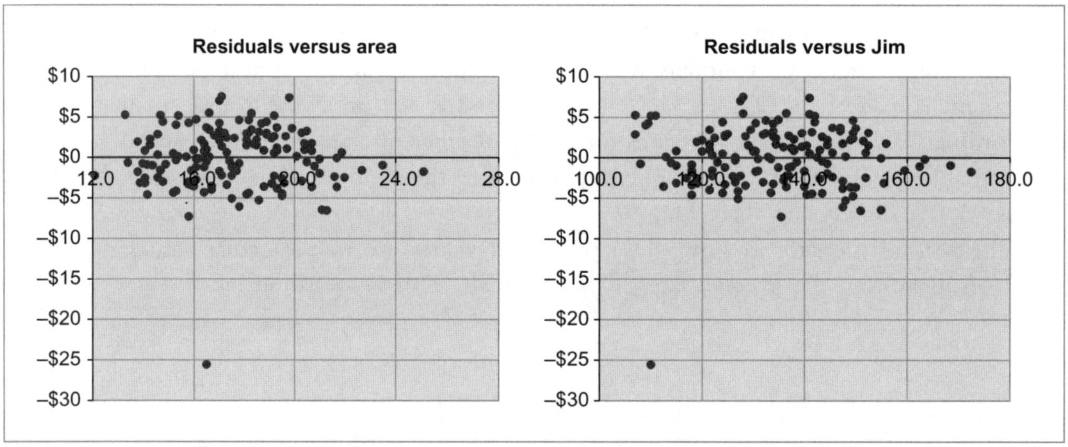

Above is a plot of the unstandardized residuals against the area variable and also against Jim's valuation. We could also plot residuals against beds, but this plot has not been presented. Both these plots look quite random. There is no tendency for residuals to be systematically positive or negative for certain values of area of Jim's valuation. If there were, then it would mean that we are making systematic errors, and we should be able to do better. A nonrandom residual plot means that there is something wrong with the model, but it also means that we can do better!

The only anomalous feature of the residuals plots are the clear outlier, which we already identified in the previous plot.

EXAMPLE 2 (Continued) *NTC salary data*

The file ex2 salary.xls had the annual salary of 274 employees of a training firm, as well as their education level, experience, and age. We can use multiple regression to explain salary in terms of these three drivers.

Results of multiple regression for salary				
Summary measures				
Adj R-Square	71.7%			
Model Error	7.197			
p-value	0.0000			
Regression coefficients				
	Coefficient	Std Err	t-value	p-value
Constant	13.672	8.966	1.5	0.128
age	-0.085	0.203	-0.4	0.676
exp	2.180	0.217	10.0	0.000
education	2.874	0.475	6.0	0.000

The overall quality of the model is measured by the first two numbers. We can explain 71.7% of the variation in salary with the variables age, experience, and education. The typical difference between the predicted and actual salaries is \$7197, called model error.

The coefficient section says that the best multilinear equation is

$$\text{Salary} = 13{,}670 - 85 \times \text{age} + 2180 \times \text{exp} + 2873 \times \text{educ}.$$

It also says that age does not appear to have any clear effect on salary, after accounting for experience and education. However, all this interpretation of the model is premature, until we have looked at the residual plots.

The plots below display a clear curvilinear trend for both age and experience. The plot against education looks fairly random and has not been presented. The trend in the age and experience plots means that we can do better! With the current model, actual salaries tend to be lower than predicted for those who are young and inexperienced, above predicted for those who have middle age and experience and lower than predicted for those who are older and very experienced. If we can see this systematic error, we should be able to correct the model to not make the error! We see how to do so in the next section.

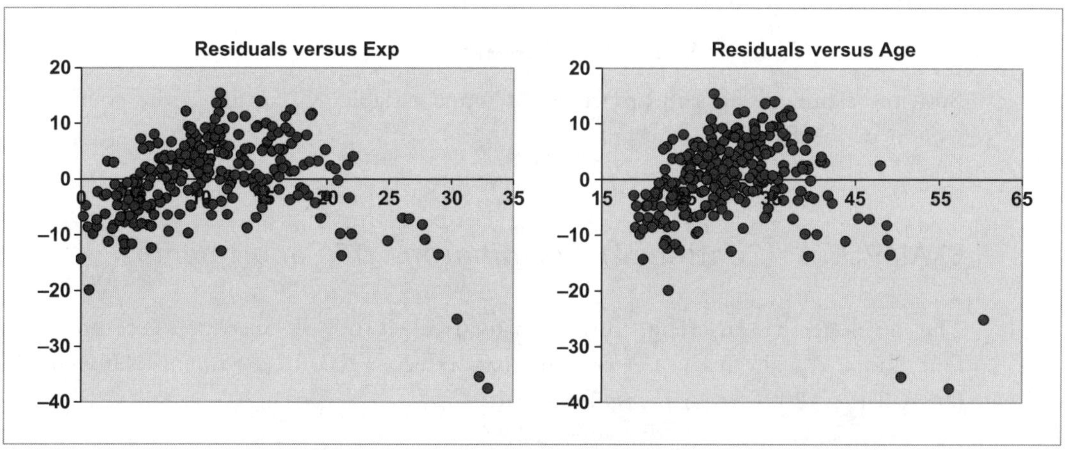

CHECK YOUR UNDERSTANDING

Q4. Recall the data on 134 motorcycles, reproduced in Q4.xls. Fit a multiple regression model that describes the effect of mileage and age on price. However, this time, make sure to save the residuals and fitted values.

(a) Plot the residuals against mileage and age. Does this look acceptable?
(b) Calculate standardized residuals. Calculate standardized residuals. Which cycle was the most underpriced and overpriced compared with its "fair market price," and how unusual were these sales?
(c) Plot standardized residuals against fitted values. Any comments?
(d) Plot standardized residuals against the rank of the fitted value. To do this, just reorder the residuals with respect to the fitted values (using the sort button), and then plot the standardized residuals against nothing. They will be automatically plotted against row number, which, since the data have been sorted with respect to fitted value, is the rank of the fitted value. What does the plot indicate?

17.4. PREDICTION AND TREND ESTIMATION

It would be silly to use start making predictions for the salary data. The model is systematically wrong. But for the DC apartments data, the model looked confirmed, apart from one outlier.

As for simple regression, there are three kinds of prediction that we make from the output of a regression.

Impact of Changing Inputs

The first type relates the effect on Y of changes in one of the input variables. Recall that the impact of variable X_i is measured by the slope $\boldsymbol{m}_i$. If we increase input variable X_i from x to $x + \Delta x$, an increase of Δx, then we expect a mean change in output of $\boldsymbol{m}_i\Delta x$. We estimate this by

$$\text{Estimated change in } Y = \widehat{m}_i \Delta x.$$

The standard error of this change estimate is

$$\text{SE(Estimated change in } Y) = \text{SE}(\widehat{m}_i) \times \Delta x.$$

Both the estimate and standard error for input variable X_i appears in the coefficients section of the StatproGo output.

EXAMPLE 1 (Continued) *Washington, DC, apartments*

The developer has an architectural plan for twelve 1600-ft^2 apartments spread across four floors. An alternative set of plans has sixteen 1200-ft^2 apartments. How much less will the 1200 ft^2 apartments be worth?

The model with Jim's valuation would not be directly useful because when the area changes, Jim's valuation would also change. Even though it has poorer overall accuracy, the appropriate model to use is the first model that used area and beds as the input variables. This describes, after all, the values of area and beds in the market. It gave a figure of \$4813 per 100 ft^2, with a standard error of 555 ft^2. The smaller apartments are 400 ft^2 smaller. So their value will be 4 × \$4813 = \$19,252 less, with standard error 4 × \$555 = \$2220.

Estimating the Trend Mean

The regression model says that the mean value of Y follows the trend

$$\boldsymbol{b} + \boldsymbol{m}_1 X_1 + \boldsymbol{m}_2 X_2 + \ldots + \boldsymbol{m}_\mathrm{p} X_\mathrm{p}.$$

We can estimate this by replacing each slope by its LS estimate. To state this more formally, the mean business performance when the input variables $X_1, X_2, \ldots, X_\mathrm{p}$ take the values $v_1, v_2, \ldots, v_\mathrm{p}$ is

$$\widehat{\mu}(Y|v_1,v_2,\ldots,v_p) = \hat{b} + \widehat{m}_1 v_1 + \widehat{m}_2 v_2 + \ldots + \widehat{m}_p v_p.$$

To estimate the trend for a particular constellation of input x variables, we just substitute the values of the x variables into the multilinear formula. This is easily done in Excel using the function SUMPRODUCT. We need a standard error for this trend estimate. For each of the x variables, we can measure how close the value v_i is to the center of the X_i variable data by counting up how far away it is from the sample mean $\overline{x}_i$ of that variable in units of standard deviations. Call this

$$z_i = | v_i - \overline{x}_i | / s_i.$$

Then an approximate formula for the standard error of the trend estimate is

$$\mathrm{SE}\{\widehat{\mu}(Y|v_1,v_2,\ldots,v_p)\} = \hat{\sigma}\sqrt{(p\overline{z}^2+1)/n},$$

where $\overline{z}$ is the average of $z_1, \ldots, z_\mathrm{p}$. A further approximation is to assume that the average of the z-values equals 1, which is to say that we are extrapolating to a set of values for the input variables, which deviate from the center by a typical amount. In this case, we have

$$\mathrm{SE}\{\widehat{\mu}(Y|v_1,v_2,\ldots,v_p)\} = \hat{\sigma}\sqrt{(p+1)/n}.$$

This formula is coded into StatproGo. It will always be considerably smaller than the model error $\hat{\sigma}$, because of the $\boldsymbol{n}$ in the denominator. If we want to estimate the trend right in the center of the x variables (where all the z-values equal zero), then the formula is even simpler:

$$\mathrm{SE}\{\widehat{\mu}(Y|v_1,v_2,\ldots,v_p)\} = \hat{\sigma}\sqrt{1/n}.$$

EXAMPLE 1 (Continued) *Washington, DC, apartments*

We will focus on an apartment that has just come onto the market. It is on the large side, with an area of 2500 ft^2 (which means 25 in units of 100 ft) and three bedrooms. Jim estimates that the apartment will sell for \$155 K.

Our estimate of the fair market price is

$$\text{Sale price} = -\$10{,}212 + 1.009 \times 155 + \$683 \times 25 - \$1380 \times 3 = 159.18,$$

some \$4180 higher than Jim. To assess the error in this trend estimate, we measure how typical this apartment is in terms of the three input variables. Using the mean and standard deviations, we find that

$$z_{\text{AREA}} = 3.17,\ z_{\text{BEDS}} = 0.05,\ z_{\text{JIM}} = 1.54.$$

The calculations are on the worksheet *consultant + area + beds(M2)*. The mean value is $\bar{z} = 1.59$, and so

$$\text{SE}\{\hat{\mu}(Y|25,3,155)\} = \hat{\sigma}\sqrt{\frac{p\bar{z}^2 + 1}{n}} = 3.838\sqrt{\frac{3 \times 1.59^2 + 1}{150}} = 0.915,$$

so the error in the estimate of \$159,180 K is \$915. Using the simplified formula,

$$\text{SE}\{\hat{\mu}(Y|25,3,155)\} = \hat{\sigma}\sqrt{\frac{p+1}{n}} = 3.838\sqrt{\frac{4}{150}} = 0.627,$$

so the error is estimated at \$627. This is coded into StatproGo but is only a ballpark figure, as illustrated by this example.

Predicting a New Case

To predict the actual output Y of an unseen case when the input variables take the values v_1, v_2, … , v_p, we again just substitute in the values of the input x variables. Formally,

$$\hat{Y}(v_1, v_2, \ldots, v_p) = \hat{b} + \hat{m}_1 v_1 + \hat{m}_2 v_2 + \ldots + \hat{m}_p v_p,$$

which is identical to the trend estimate. In assessing the accuracy of this prediction, we acknowledge that there are two sources of error. First, the trend mean has error. Second, the business performance has unavoidable error σ even if the mean trend is known perfectly. This leads to the formula

$$\text{SPE}\left\{\hat{Y}\left(v_1, v_2, \ldots, v_p\right)\right)\} = \hat{\sigma}\sqrt{1 + \frac{p\bar{z}^2 + 1}{n}},$$

and for a set of input x-values that deviate from the center by a typical amount, this simplifies to

$$\text{SPE}\{\hat{Y}(v_1, v_2, \ldots, v_p))\} = \hat{\sigma}\sqrt{1 + \frac{p+1}{n}}.$$

There is no need to memorize this formula. It is coded into StatproGo. It will usually be just a little larger than the model error $\hat{\sigma}$.

EXAMPLE 1 (Continued) *Washington, DC, apartments*

We focus on the same apartment with an area of 2500 ft^2, three bedrooms, and valued by Jim at \$155 K. Our estimate of the sale price of this particular apartment is

$$\text{Sale price} = -\$10{,}212 + 1.009 \times 155 + \$683 \times 25 - \$1380 \times 3 = 159.18.$$

We earlier calculated that $\bar{z} = 1.59$, and so

$$\text{SPE}\{\hat{Y}(25, 3, 155)\} = \hat{\sigma}\sqrt{1 + \frac{p\bar{z}^2 + 1}{n}} = 3.838\sqrt{1 + \frac{3 \times 1.59^2 + 1}{150}} = 3.945,$$

so the error in the estimate of \$159.180 K is \$3945. Using the simplified formula

$$\text{SPE}\{\hat{Y}(25, 3, 155)\} = \hat{\sigma}\sqrt{1 + \frac{p+1}{n}} = 3.838\sqrt{1 + \frac{4}{150}} = 3.889,$$

so the error is estimated at \$3889. This is coded into StatproGo.

Using StatproGo

StatproGo output us automatically set up to perform prediction or trend estimation. You will see a red "1" to the left of the constant. Simply enter the values for the input variables below the "1" and next to the appropriate variable. For instance, in the example below, we are predicting the price of the apartment that is 2500 ft^2 with three bedrooms and which Jim values at k\$155.

The prediction appears in the top right—here \$159,180 K. The prediction error using the simplified formula is \$3889 and the trend error using the simplified formula is \$627, as obtained above.

	Results of multiple regression for Price				
	Summary measures		Predicted Value:		159.18
	Adj R-Square	93.1%		Pred Error	3.889
	Model Error	3.838		Trend Error	0.627
	p-value	0.0000			
	Regression coefficients				
		Coefficient	Std Err	t-value	p-value
1	Constant	-10.121	3.462	-2.9	0.004
25	Area	0.683	0.269	2.5	0.012
3	Beds	-1.380	0.602	-2.3	0.023
155	Valuation	1.009	0.037	27.6	0.000

CHECK YOUR UNDERSTANDING

Q5. Recall the data on 134 motorcycles and the multiple regression that you already fitted in Q3 and Q4. The output is in Q5.xls.

(a) Cycles typically travel 11,000 mi in a year. Taking this as a benchmark figure, what is the typical mileage depreciation suffered by a cycle in a year (separate from any direct age depreciation)?
(b) You want to know the fair market price of cycles that are 3 years old with 50,000 mi? What is your estimate and its accuracy?
(c) You want to predict the price of a cycle that is for sale. It is 4 years old and has only traveled 25,000 miles. What is your prediction and its accuracy?

17.5. SUMMARY

A **multilinear relationship** between an output Y and inputs $X_1, X_2, \ldots, X_p$ is a formula of the form

$$Y = \boldsymbol{b} + \boldsymbol{m}_1 X_1 + \boldsymbol{m}_2 X_2 + \ldots + \boldsymbol{m}_p X_p.$$

The parameter $\boldsymbol{b}$ measures the output Y when all input variables equal zero. The slope parameter $\boldsymbol{m}_J$ measure the effect of changing input X_J by one unit on the output Y, assuming all other inputs are held fixed.

The **multiple regression model** assumes that Y follows a multilinear trend but is disturbed by random noise. In symbols,

$$Y = \boldsymbol{b} + \boldsymbol{m}_1 X_1 + \boldsymbol{m}_2 X_2 + \ldots + \boldsymbol{m}_p X_p + \varepsilon,$$

where ε has mean zero and typical size σ. The disturbances ε are assumed completely random, independent, and uniform.

The intercept and slopes are estimated from historical data by minimizing the total squared difference between the predicted and actual y-values. This is done automatically by StatproGo. Under the regression model assumptions, StatproGo also produces and estimate of σ (called model error), and standard errors for the intercept and for all the slopes.

The model can be used to predict by substituting x-values into the multilinear formula. For estimating the mean output Y, the standard error is approximately

$$\mathrm{SE}\{\hat{\mu}(Y|\nu_1,\nu_2,\ldots,\nu_p)\} = \hat{\sigma}\sqrt{(p+1)/n}.$$

This is often called **standard error of trend**. For predicting a specific Y, the **standard prediction error** is approximately

$$\text{SPE}\left\{\hat{Y}(v_1, v_2, \ldots, v_p)\right\} = \hat{\sigma}\sqrt{1 + \frac{p+1}{n}}.$$

As with simple regression, **residuals** are prediction errors. When divided by the model error, they are called **standardized residuals**. Unusual or aberrant cases are identified by large standardized residuals. Systematic errors in the basic prediction formula of the model are detected by plotting residuals against each X-value. Any trend in these plots indicates a curvilinear effect of that input variable.

More subtle issues, such as dependence of the disturbances and nonuniform variability, are revealed by plotting residuals against fitted values.

EXERCISES

E1. Below is some output from a regression model of amount spent on pay TV optional extras using the number of optional extras purchased in the previous year as the predictor.

Results of multiple regression for Expend						
Summary measures						
Adj R-Square	0.121			Last year	Expend	
Model Error	13.19		Mean	2.783	20.019	
			Std.Dev	1.828	14.064	
Regression coefficients						
	Coefficient	Std Err	t-value	p-value	Lower	Upper
Constant	12.261	2.648	4.63	0.000	6.992	17.529
Number Last Year	2.787	0.797	3.50	0.001	1.202	4.372

(a) Is the number of previous options purchased a significant predictor of expenditure this year? How sure are you?
(b) How would you explain the regression equation in simple words?
(c) How accurate is the regression equation either in terms of typical prediction error or in terms of variation in expenditure explained?
(d) Predict the expenditure of a customer who purchased five optional extras last year.
(e) What would be the correlation of Expenditure with Number last year?

E2. A survey of 200 randomly chosen consumers was presented with the proposition *luxury cars are not worth the money*. They rated their degree of agreement with this proposition on a 5-point scale, 5 meaning strongly agree and 1 meaning strongly disagree. There are two main explanatory variables: the respondent's age and the number of months since the respondent bought a car. Below is some output from two regression models.

Results of multiple regression for Response						
Summary measures						
Adj R-Square	0.011					
Model Error	1.395					
Regression coefficients						
	Coefficient	Std Err	t-value	p-value	Lower	Upper
Constant	2.220	0.4190	5.30	0.000	1.393	3.046
Age	0.0154	0.0086	1.79	0.074	-0.0015	0.0323

Results of multiple regression for Response						
Summary measures						
Adj R-Square	0.008					
Model Error	1.397					
Regression coefficients						
	Coefficient	Std Err	t-value	p-value	Lower	Upper
Constant	2.687	0.192	14.00	0.000	2.308	3.065
months	0.0110	0.0069	1.60	0.111	-0.0025	0.0245

(a) Based on these two simple regression models, which is the better predictor of response, and how good is it?

(b) Predict the mean response of those customers who last purchased a car 12 months ago.

(c) Using multiple regression, describe the effects of age and months since last purchase on consumer response to the proposition. The data are here.

(d) Give a predicted response for a 50-year-old who last bought a car 3 years ago. How accurate is the prediction?

Results of multiple regression for Response						
Summary measures						
Adj R-Square	0.053					
Model Error	1.365					
Regression coefficients						
	Coefficient	Std Err	t-value	p-value	Lower	Upper
Constant	0.825	0.606	1.36	0.175	-0.370	2.021
Age	0.0322	0.0100	3.23	0.001	0.0125	0.0519
Months	0.0248	0.0080	3.12	0.002	0.0092	0.0405

E3. A company wants to estimate the repair costs on its fleet of cars. They run the following regression with repair costs over a year (REPAIR) as the dependent variable, and the age of the car at the start of the year (AGE) and thousands of kilometers driven during the year (KMS) as the independent variables. Read the Excel output and answer the questions below.

Descriptives	REPAIR COST	KMS	AGE
Mean	1688.87	16.37	1
Standard Deviation	111.68	4.34	0.85
Range	343	16.2	2
Minimum	1518	8.4	0
Maximum	1861	24.6	2
Count	15	15	15

Results of multiple regression for Repair Cost						
Summary measures						
Adj R-Square	0.781					
Model Error	52.27					
Regression coefficients						
	Coefficient	Std Err	t-value	p-value	Lower	Upper
Constant	1180.9	73.3	16.1	0.000	1021.3	1340.6
KMS	26.68	3.70	7.2	0.000	18.61	34.75
AGE	71.13	19.046	3.7	0.003	29.65	112.61

(a) Explain the regression equation.

(b) How much more does this model estimate that repair costs are for a 2-year-old car as opposed to a 1-year-old one? (Find a point estimate and an interval estimate.)

(c) Is this a good model? How can you tell? (What other information would you like?)

(d) How much would you expect the annual repair bill to be for a new car (0 years old when bought) that is driven 13,000 km during the year?

(e) A colleague suggests that repair costs are mostly related to whether a particular car is a "lemon"—that is, some cars are more prone to need repair than others, even though age and kilometers are the same. How would you reply based on the model above?

E4. The data in Q4.xls give data on 76 building renovation projects. You have calendar date when the contract was signed with the client. The performance variable is the number of weeks taken from signing the contract to completion (when the client signs off). The main explanatory variable is the value of the contract. Value of the project is measured in units of \$100,000. The aim is to understand why projects take the amount of time that they do.

(a) Fit a simple linear regression of weeks predicted by value. Explain all relevant features of the output.

(b) Plot the residuals against value. What does it indicate?

(c) Plot the residuals against calendar data. What does this indicate? What do you think is the cause of this effect?

(d) In Column A, you will find a variable Time, which measures month after January 2003 when the contract was signed. Include this second variable in the regression and interpret the output.

(e) Looking at the residuals, is this model validated?

E5. The data in Q5.xls give weekly demand for a spanner, as well as the recommended retail price. The unit cost of the spanner is $4.45, so the profit can easily be calculated (excluding fixed costs).

(a) Perform a multiple regression for predicting demand using week number and price. Interpret both the slope coefficients in simple words. What is the estimated growth?

(b) Examine the residual plots and comment on whether the regression model seems to be satisfied.

(c) Perform a multiple regression for predicting profit using week number and price. Interpret both the slope coefficients in simple words. Why does this suggest that the model is nonsense?

(d) Look at the residuals plots and confirm that there is something seriously wrong with this model.

CHAPTER 18

Product Features, Nonlinear Relationships, and Market Segments

PAY EQUITY AT NTC: CASE BRIEFING

NTC are being accused of gender discrimination. They do not believe that they systematically discriminate against female employees. In fact, they even have some affirmative action built into their hiring protocols.

You are a quantitative consultant advising NTC. The professional body representing the plaintiffs is basing its claims on a data file that was freely provided by NTC. It gives the characteristics of 273 employees across the company, suitably stripped of identifying details to preserve confidentiality. The database includes all current employees, excluding senior management and nonprofessional staff.

Breaking the data down into males and females you find that males are paid around $10,000 per annum more on average than females. This is way more than the $4200 per annum being claimed. However, there are other things to consider, such as the experience and education of the employees, as well as their age—though age is not a legally valid consideration in employment decisions any more than gender.

You are to write a report that anticipates some of the uses that the prosecution might make of the data if the matter actually proceeds to court. You should list the possible analyses—from least to most sophisticated—as well as a critique that you can present in court. Ultimately, you need to understand exactly which features drive salary, to account for any gender differences that may be explained by these other features and to assess any differences between males and females that may remain.

18.0. INTRODUCTION: WHAT IS THE ISSUE?

Business performance outcomes are typically driven by several factors, and these factors can interact in complex ways. For example, if we increase our advertising

Data-Driven Business Decisions, First Edition. Chris J. Lloyd.

expenditure in a period of strong economic growth, then it will not be obvious whether advertising or general economic conditions are driving our observed profit performance. Multiple regression is the tool to untangle this.

But the techniques presented so far are limited. How does gender affect buying habits? How does leather trim affect car value? Gender and leather trim are not numbers. So it is not immediately obvious how we could include them in a regression analysis. That is one area where we need to expand our use of regression—to situations where one of the input variables is a **binary trait** rather than a numeric measurement.

Just as important, not all input variables have a simple linear effect on the output. For instance, years of industry experience undoubtedly contributes to higher salaries, but each year of experience is surely not worth the same amount. The first year of experience in an industry is probably highly bankable, but going from 15 to 16 years is probably not so important. Yet the regression models we have considered so far would require us to associate a fixed-dollar increase in salary for each year of experience—the slope.

If regression were not able to deal with more complex dependencies, then it would not be nearly as useful. Luckily, it is rather easy to use regression to include binary features and also to measure the complex nonlinear effects that some input variables may have.

EXAMPLE 1 *Northside car auctions*

The data in ex 1 car auctions.xls is from the Northside car auctions case. It lists the sale price of 134 cars of the same make, sold at auction. For each car, you have recorded the mileage and the age in years, as well as the presence of three optional features, namely extra airbags, leather trim (rather than cloth), and tinted windscreen.

A plot of price versus both age and mileage reveals some interesting features. Price tends to decrease with age, more or less linearly; however, mileage seems to reduce price is a nonlinear manner. Depreciation for cars with low mileage is less than for cars with high mileage.

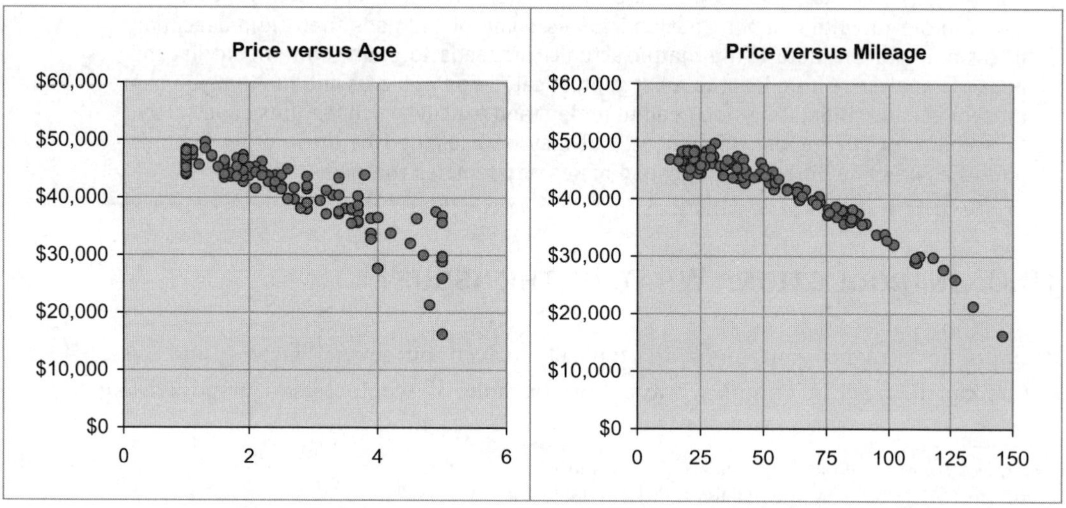

We also have the optional features that we believe should add value to the car, but there is currently no way to include these yes–no variables. Moreover, we have the old problem of untangling effects. The table below shows the average mileage, age, and price of cars with and without airbags. While cars with airbags sold for $2493 more than those without on average, the cars with airbags had almost 10,000 less mileage. So most of the price difference will be the mileage, not the airbags.

	Mileage	Age	Price
Airbags (N0)	53.60	2.38	$41,614
Airbags(YES)	43.75	1.99	$44,107
Difference	-9.85	-0.38	$2,493

Regression is ideally suited to untangling these kinds of complications. But we do not yet know how to include airbags into the regression. Moreover, if the effect of mileage is not linear, we will need to take this into account in adjusting the valuation of airbags. What we need is a regression model that includes both curvilinear effects of mileage, as well as the optional features.

18.1. ACCOUNTING FOR YES–NO FEATURES

Binary traits are characteristics that an individual case either has or has not. Gender is a binary trait, and so is a customer's decision to purchase or his or her response to a yes–no satisfaction survey.

To include binary traits into a regression, just code each case as "1" if it has the trait and "0" if it doesn't. The input x variable becomes a column of 1's and 0's and is called a **dummy variable**. If you include the dummy variable in your regression, you will obtain a slope estimate for the binary trait. What does this mean? Remember that in general, a slope estimate says how the output changes when the input variable changes by 1 unit. When the input variable is coded as 0 or 1, changing from 0 to 1 means changing from not having the trait to having the trait. So the slope measures the increase in the output when you change from not having the trait to having the trait. In simple language, it measures the average business performance value of the trait.

Regression will output a standard error, confidence interval, t-statistic, and p-value for the trait. The p-value can be used to test whether or not the trait has any effect at all on performance.

EXAMPLE 1 (Continued) *Northside car auctions*

On the worksheet *regression data* in file ex 1 car auctions.xls, you will find that the three features of airbags, leather trim, and tinting have been coded as 0 or 1, depending on whether or not the car has the feature. We can now include these three variables in a multiple regression, together with age and mileage. The output is below. Overall, the model explains 92.9% of the variation in car prices using the five listed features.

The value of airbags is now estimated at \$606 with a standard error of \$295. The *p*-value is small, so we are confident that airbags do add to price—though we were never in any doubt of this anyway. The estimate of \$606 is much, much lower than the naïve estimate of \$2493 from the Pivotable because it takes into account that the cars with airbags had less mileage. But is this model acceptable as a description of the data?

Regression coefficients				
	Coefficient	Std Err	t-value	p-value
Constant	51118.5	333.2	153.4	0.000
Air	606.0	295.5	2.1	0.042
Ltrim	866.6	302.1	2.9	0.005
Tint	222.2	287.6	0.8	0.441
Miles	-225.6	14.9	-15.1	0.000
Age	936.9	349.5	2.7	0.008

There are several features of this output that should make us very nervous. First, tinting appears to be worth only \$222, which is way too low, and the *p*-value associated with this feature suggests that it has no clear effect at all. Second, the constant \$51,118 values a car with no features, zero miles, and zero years of age—that is, a new car. If you read the case describing these data, it is clear that this is also way too high. Worst of all, look at the age slope. It says that if a car is 1 year older, it will be worth \$937 *more*! These are not classic cars—they are at most 5 years old—so we know that this conclusion must be wrong. And the *p*-value of 0.008 is telling us that this reversed age effect is statistically real.

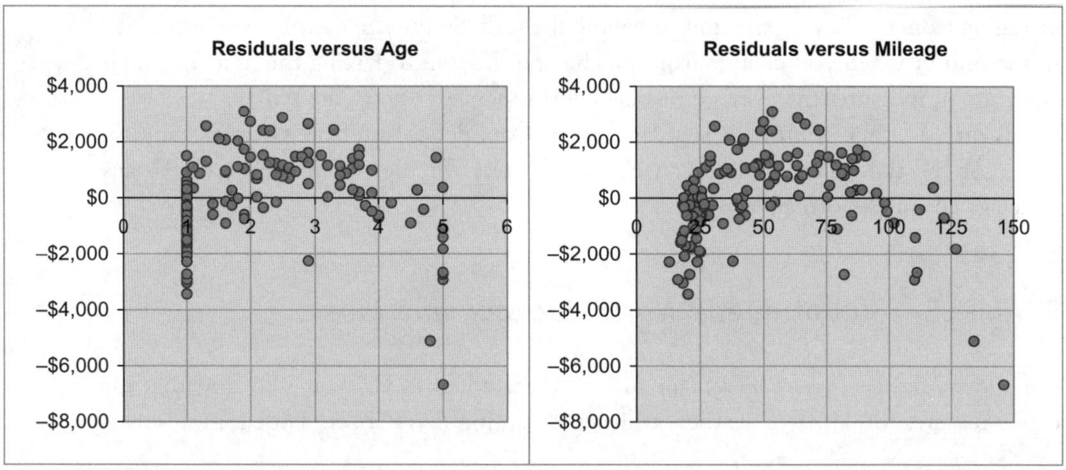

There is something seriously wrong with this model, and it is revealed when we plot residuals against age and mileage. In both plots, there appears to be a clear curvilinear trend. Young and old cars tend to sell for less than we predict, while middle-aged cars tend to sell for more than we predict. This means that our prediction formula is systematically wrong. Similarly for mileage, there are even clearer systematic deviations from our model.

When you see residual plots like this, *all the output from the regression is just wrong*, and there is no need to dissect it in detail. The value of airbags is not $606, any more than it was $2493. The value of tinting is not $222. Age does not have a positive effect on price. This model needs open-heart surgery.

Check Your Understanding

Q1. The workbook Q1.xls contains data of the annual salaries of 273 employees that we have seen several times now. The age, experience, and education level of each employee are recorded. This time, however, we also have the gender of each employee.

(a) Use Pivotables to measure the difference in mean salaries of males and females.
(b) By dragging in appropriate icons into the Pivotable, compare the males and females in terms of their age, experience, and educational attainment. How might this explain the difference in salaries?
(c) Create a dummy variable for whether or not someone is male. You can either use the IF function in Excel or use the Data Utilities in StatproGo.
(d) Fit a multiple regression that describes salary in terms of age, experience, education, and gender. What is the estimated salary difference between males and females now? Why is it different?
(e) Check residual plots. Is the model acceptable?

18.2. Quadratic Relationships

A linear function has the special property that for each unit increase of the input variable x the output Y changes by the same amount, denoted $\boldsymbol{m}$. There are many business contexts where the input has a more complicated and therefore nonlinear effect on the output. It appears from the previous example that the effect of mileage on car price is one of them.

There are many mathematical ways to describe nonlinear relationships. One of the simplest and most flexible methods is to use quadratic functions.

DEFINITION

A **quadratic relationship** between an output Y and input X is a formula of the form

$$Y = \boldsymbol{b} + \boldsymbol{m}_{\mathrm{L}} X + \boldsymbol{m}_{\mathrm{Q}} X^2.$$

The feature that makes it quadratic is the appearance of the X-squared term.

Interpretation of Parameters

The baseline $\boldsymbol{b}$ still measures the output Y when the input variable X equals zero. So this does not change from a linear function.

The interpretation of the two coefficients $\boldsymbol{m}_{\mathrm{L}}$ and $\boldsymbol{m}_{\mathrm{Q}}$ is not as simple as for linear relationships. This is just an inevitable consequence of the relationship being more complex.

The so-called **linear coefficient** $\boldsymbol{m}_{\mathrm{L}}$ measures the slope when $X = 0$. In simple words, it measures the incremental effect of increasing X from a baseline value of zero. Of course, if it makes no sense for X to equal zero (for instance if X is price), then neither $\boldsymbol{b}$ nor $\boldsymbol{m}_{\mathrm{L}}$ will make much sense when interpreted this way.

The so-called **quadratic coefficient** $\boldsymbol{m}_{\mathrm{Q}}$ measures the degree of nonlinearity in the relationship. In particular, if $\boldsymbol{m}_{\mathrm{Q}} = 0$ then the relationship is a simple line. When $\boldsymbol{m}_{\mathrm{Q}}$ is positive, the value of Y becomes large as X increases. When $\boldsymbol{m}_{\mathrm{Q}}$ is negative, the value of Y becomes large and negative as X increases.

EXAMPLE 2 *Advertising, price, and growth*

Suppose that we are interested in describing how weekly profit Y depends on two inputs that are within our control, namely price charged and weekly advertising expenditure. We expect that the effects of price will be nonlinear. Why? Because if we make the price too low or too high, our profits will suffer. Somewhere in the middle, we will get the best profit, so the relationship of profit to price will be "hill-shaped." Similarly with advertising, there are diminishing returns in how advertising affects demand, so too much advertising eventually becomes unprofitable. Let us also include a third variable, time, to measure growth in profits.

We need to specify the units of all of these. We will measure profit and advertising in units of \$1000. We will measure price in units of 1 cent, imagining for the sake of argument that the product is a packet of potato crisps. We will measure time in weeks, with time = 0 representing the beginning of the period of interest. Here is a possible formula that describes how the three input variables, time, price, and advertising, affect weekly profit:

$$\text{Profit} = -121 + 0.65 \times \text{Adv} - 0.006 \times \text{Adv}^2 + 4.10 \times \text{Price} - 0.0084 \times \text{Price}^2 + 0.68 \times \text{Time}.$$

Let us look at what the formula means. First, there are three parts in the formula: one depending on advertising, another on price, and another in time. As with multilinear relationships, each part of the formula describes the effect of that input variable, assuming the others are held fixed. So let us look at the advertising part of the formula $0.65 \times \text{Adv} - 0.006 \times \text{Adv}^2$. The number 0.65, which is the linear coefficient, measures the incremental effect of advertising when advertising expenditure is zero. In other words, it measures the extra profit that we get from the very first dollar we spend on advertising. We get 65 cents of return on investment (ROI), which is a huge dividend. The number −0.006 is the quadratic coefficient and indicates that the positive effect of advertising on profits *reduces* as we spend more and more.

To say much more, we really need to see a picture. Create a column of values from 0 to 100 representing different advertising expenditures that we might consider. In the column next to it, calculate 0.65 × Adv − 0.006 × Adv^2, and then plot this against the amounts of advertising. The plot is the left one below. We can see that at an expenditure around 55 (which means $55K per week), profit starts to reduce. So our best level of advertising is identified as $55K. All of this supposes that price is held constant.

Let us look next at the price assuming that advertising is held constant, which is described by the formula 4.10 × Price − 0.0084 × Price^2. The linear coefficient is 4.10, but this is not easily interpretable because it makes no sense to set the price equal to zero. If it did, the number 4.10 would say that starting from a price of $0, if we increase the price by 1 cent, we will expect to make extra 4.1 cents of profit. Of course, we would actually be making a loss at this price. But the linear coefficient does say that at low prices, it will be worth our while to increase price, but only up to a point! The quadratic coefficient of −0.0084 says that eventually, profit will start to go down if we raise prices too high. A graph of the effect of price on profit is in the right plot below. It looks like the price giving the highest profit is somewhere around 250 cents.

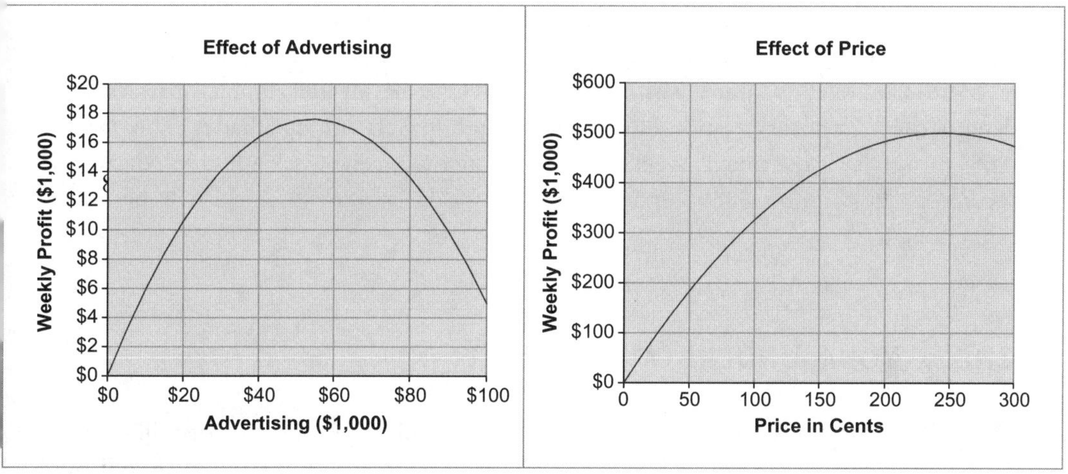

Finding the Optimum

It would be nice if we could quickly find the "top of the hill" in such examples, since these correspond to the best setting of the input variable. There is a simple formula for finding the best setting using the quadratic and linear coefficients. The formula is

$$X_{\text{BEST}} = 0.5 \times \boldsymbol{m}_{\text{L}} / \boldsymbol{m}_{\text{Q}}.$$

Typically, input variables in a business context are positive. So this formula will only give a positive and, therefore, sensible answer when $\boldsymbol{m}_{\text{L}}$ and $\boldsymbol{m}_{\text{Q}}$ have the opposite sign. When $\boldsymbol{m}_{\text{L}}$ is positive and $\boldsymbol{m}_{\text{Q}}$ is negative, then the graph is *hill shaped*, and the formula above gives you the value of X, which corresponds to the top of the hill. When m_L is negative and m_Q is positive, then the graph is *valley shaped*, and the formula above gives you the value of X, which corresponds to the bottom of the valley. This might be of interest if the Y variable were cost, and you want to find the x-value, which minimized cost.

EXAMPLE 2 (Continued) *Advertising, price, and growth*

Let us apply this to price and advertising. Both of these are hill shaped. For advertising, we calculate

$$X_{\text{BEST}} = -0.5 \times 0.65/(-0.006) = 54.2,$$

which tells us that the optimum level of advertising is \$54.2K. To find the optimal price, we calculate

$$X_{\text{BEST}} = -0.5 \times 4.8/(-0.0084) = 244,$$

so the optimal price is \$2.44. These calculations are all in ex2.xls.

Finally, the time part of the formula is 0.68 × Time. This is not quadratic—it is linear. So it is quite permissible to have some of the input variables still described by a linear relationship, even though others are quadratic. The figure 0.68 measures how much weekly profit increases each week. It says that this week's profit will be \$680 higher than last week, and next week will be \$680 higher again.

CHECK YOUR UNDERSTANDING

Q2. The workbook Q2.xls contains data on monthly sales (in units of millions) of a retailing chain over 5 years. The seasonally adjusted sales are in Column E and our performance measure of interest.

(a) Right click on any part of the seasonally adjusted line on the graphic. Select add Trendline then polynomial of degree 2 (which is a quadratic). Also select the option "Display equation on chart."
(b) Here x is time measured in months with time = 0, meaning the first month of January 3. According to the quadratic, what was the growth rate in sales at the beginning of the series?
(c) Is the growth increasing or decreasing?
(d) By substituting an appropriate value into the formula, what is your estimate of the underlying sales in January 2008?

18.3. QUADRATIC REGRESSION

To include quadratic effects in a regression model, you simply create a new column containing the squared *X*-values and then include both *X* and X^2 as predictor variables. StatproGo will estimate a prediction formula of the form

$$Y = \boldsymbol{b} + \boldsymbol{m}_{\mathrm{L}}X + \boldsymbol{m}_{\mathrm{Q}}X_2 + \text{other input variables.}$$

In particular, it will estimate the **linear coefficient** $\boldsymbol{m}_{\mathrm{L}}$ and the **quadratic coefficient** $\boldsymbol{m}_{\mathrm{Q}}$. While these two numbers are not as simple to interpret as a single slope, we saw how to interpret them in the previous section.

EXAMPLE 1 (Continued) *Northside car auctions*

In the worksheet *quadratic regression* in file ex 1 car auctions.xls, you will see that I have created two new variables called age2 and miles2, which contain the squares of the age and mileage, respectively. You can use StatproGo to fit a multiple regression model, which includes the three 0–1 coded optional features, a quadratic effect in age (using two variables age and age2), and a quadratic effect in miles (using miles and miles2).

The adjusted r^2 is now 97.4%, considerably higher than the 92.9% we achieved with straight linear effects. This is one strong clue that we have a better model. Let us look at the output in detail.

Results of multiple regression for Price				
Regression coefficients				
	Coefficient	Std Err	t-value	p-value
Constant	47318.6	382.0	123.9	0.000
Air	597.3	181.5	3.3	0.001
Ltrim	774.1	185.1	4.2	0.000
Tint	494.0	179.2	2.8	0.007
Miles	-5.7	29.0	-0.2	0.845
Age	-318.5	753.0	-0.4	0.673
Miles2	-1.3	0.2	-8.2	0.000
Age2	9.8	105.7	0.1	0.926

Airbags are worth $597, not very different from the $606 that we obtained from the previous wrong model. But we only find out that the $606 was close to the mark after we have done the quadratic regression. Other estimated features have completely changed. Tinting is now valued at $494—a much more reasonable value—and a new car without features is valued at $47,318—which is just about right if you read the case background.

Checking for Model Defects

Before we spend too much time looking at this output though, let us make sure that there is nothing obviously wrong with the model. Because as we saw earlier, if the model has systematic defects, then the output will be completely misleading.

The way we detect defects in the model is to look at residual plots. The plots below look quite random. There are no apparent trends, which means that this model is not making any systematic errors in predicting car values, in the way that the previous linear model was. This means that the quadratic model is sufficient to describe the effect of age and mileage on price. In particular, there is no more exotic kind of relationship than quadratic at play.

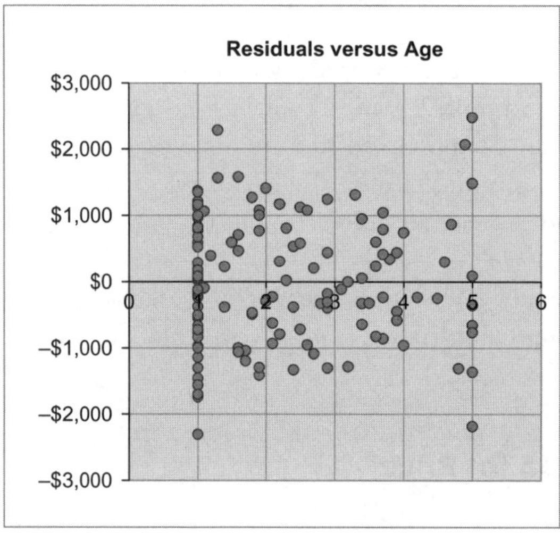

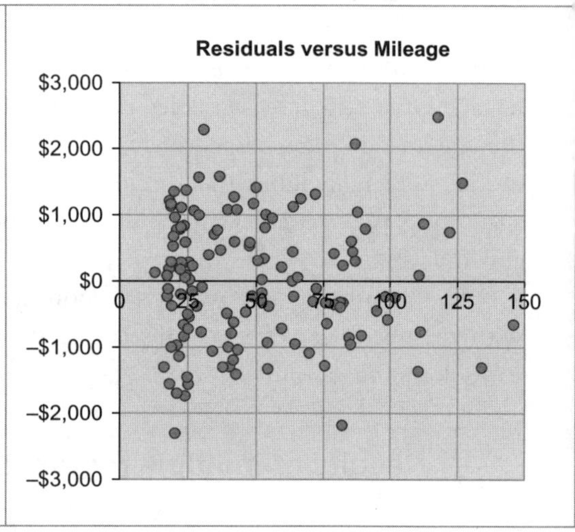

Looking for a Simpler Model

Since we are now confident that the model is not grossly wrong, it is worth looking at the output in more detail. The large *p*-values tell a story. They tell us that the associated variables do not seem to have any effect on price. The largest *p*-value of 0.926 is for age2, which refers to the quadratic coefficient m_Q for age. It appears that this term is not statistically different from zero. This simply means that there does not seem to be any nonlinear effect of age on price. So the next step in describing these data would be to remove the age2 term.

If you remove the term age2, you will find that the resulting model has one rather large *p*-value (0.645) for the term miles. This suggests that the linear coefficient m_L for mileage is zero. Removing this term, we end up with the model below, where all *p*-values are small. This means that all the terms in the model have a clear effect on price, and removing any of them would result in a significantly poorer valuation model.

Results of multiple regression for Price				
Regression coefficients				
	Coefficient	Std Err	t-value	p-value
Constant	47201.2	243.2	194.1	0.000
Air	597.8	178.6	3.3	0.001
Ltrim	770.6	182.8	4.2	0.000
Tint	499.1	174.9	2.9	0.005
Age	-330.9	144.6	-2.3	0.024
Miles2	-1.3	0.0	-29.1	0.000

Assessing the Model

Let us finish this example by summarizing the final model, whose main output is displayed above. The adjusted r^2 for this model is 97.4%, very high in an absolute sense. However, it is virtually identical to the adjusted r^2 before we removed the insignificant *age2* and *miles* terms. So in terms of explanatory power, this model is no better than the original one. The payoff is that we have a *simpler model*. We have dropped two terms from the prediction formula for the same, or slightly better, explanatory power.

Explaining the Valuation Formula

The estimated values of airbags, leather trim, and tinting are \$598, \$449, and \$771, respectively. These values for airbags and tinting are consistent with the cost of having these features added after sale. The costing for leather trim may seem rather low, less than what you could reasonably expect to pay for a new leather interior. But these are 1- to 5-year-old cars! The leather trim will be worn and should be less valuable than brand new leather fittings. A value of \$771 seems about right.

Each year of age subtracts \$331 from the price. As for all regression models, this assumes that all other variables, especially mileage, is held constant. So if you have two cars each with 50,000 mi travel, and one is 2 years older than the other, the older one is worth \$662 less (with standard error of \$290).

Understanding the Model Formula

The overall prediction formula is

$$\text{Price} = \$47{,}201 + \$598 \times \text{Air} + \$771 \times \text{LTrim} + \$499 \times \text{Tint} - \$331 \times \text{age} - \$1.35 \times \text{miles}^2.$$

Suppose we want to predict the price of a 3-year-old car that has traveled 80,000 mi with all optional features. We can use the StatproGo output and place 1 next to each of the optional features, 3 next to age, and $80^2 = 6400$ next to miles2. The predicted price is \$39,442, with a prediction error of \$986.

	Regression coefficients				
		Coefficient	Std Err	t-value	p-value
1	Constant	47201.2	243.2	194.1	0.000
1	Air	597.8	178.6	3.3	0.001
1	Ltrim	770.6	182.8	4.2	0.000
1	Tint	499.1	174.9	2.9	0.005
3	Age	-330.9	144.6	-2.3	0.024
6400	Miles2	-1.35	0.05	-29.1	0.000

What is the effect of mileage? It is the $-1.35 \times \text{mi}^2$ part of the prediction formula. At this stage, it is helpful to give an additional interpretation of the linear and quadratic coefficients of a quadratic.

Pushing a Bit Further

If X has a quadratic effect on an output variable Y, then the incremental effect of X is not a single number—it depends on the value of X. The *incremental effect on* Y *per unit change in* X is measured by

$$\text{effect of } X = \boldsymbol{m}_{\text{L}} + 2\boldsymbol{m}_{\text{Q}}X.$$

If the quadratic coefficient $\boldsymbol{m}_{\text{Q}}$ is zero, then the effect of X is a single number $\boldsymbol{m}_{\text{L}}$. This is a linear relationship, not a quadratic one.

For the car auction data, we have the reverse situation. The linear coefficient is zero, which is a rather uncommon situation. What this means is that the incremental effect of an extra 1000 mi on price is

$$\text{effect of miles} = 0 + 2 \times (-1.35) \times \text{miles} = -2.7 \times \text{miles}.$$

So, in particular, there is no mileage depreciation for a new car, when miles equals 0. When mileage is 50,000, the depreciation rate is $2.7 \times 50 = \$135$ per 1000 mi. Why per 1000 mi? Because mileage was measured in these units. When mileage is 10,000, the rate is $2.7 \times 100 = \$270$ per 1000 mi. The rate of mileage depreciation per 1000 mi increases with mileage.

Check Your Understanding

Q3. Recall the data in Q2.xls and the data description given there.

(a) Create a column Time^2, and use StatproGo to fit a quadratic regression.
(b) Give a confidence interval for the growth at the beginning of the series?
(c) Is the growth increasing or decreasing? How sure are you?
(d) By substituting an appropriate value into the formula, what is your estimate of the underlying sales in January 2008?
(e) What is the growth rate at the end of the series?

18.4. ALLOWING FOR SEGMENTS AND GROUPS

Dummy variables are a way of coding binary traits so that they can be included in a regression model. Dummy variables can also be used to include group labels into a regression. For instance, executive salaries might depend on the industry sector (which is a group label, not a number). Car value might depend on whether it is four-door, two-door, or two-door convertible (which is a group label, not a number). Sales revenue of your product might depend on the month of the year (which is a label, not a number).

In general, you might identify K different groups that can affect your output measure Y. For instance, there are $K = 12$ months in the year, which affect sales. There might be $K = 5$ industry sectors that you want to account for. To include this information in your regression model, you create a dummy variable for the trait of group 1 membership, another dummy variable for the trait of group 2 membership, and so on, K dummy variables in all.

EXAMPLE 3 *Pay scales*

The file ex 3 pay scales.xls lists the weekly salary of 256 employees, their gender, their job grade, and how long they have been in that job grade. Gender is a trait and is coded as a dummy variable. Job grade ranges from 1 to 8, but these are just labels for the increasing levels of responsibility. It makes more sense to think of the 8 job grades as 8 groups. Below are the first 10 records. Most of the employees are female.

Rate	Waiting	Gender	Grade	Male	Grade1	Grade2	Grade3	Grade4	Grade5	Grade6	Grade7	Grade8
$747	1.5	F	2	0	0	1	0	0	0	0	0	0
$842	0.5	F	3	0	0	0	1	0	0	0	0	0
$747	2.5	F	2	0	0	1	0	0	0	0	0	0
$624	0.8	F	2	0	0	1	0	0	0	0	0	0
$612	0.5	F	1	0	1	0	0	0	0	0	0	0
$990	2.5	F	6	0	0	0	0	0	0	1	0	0
$814	1.5	F	5	0	0	0	0	0	1	0	0	0
$1,238	2.0	F	7	0	0	0	0	0	0	0	1	0
$795	2.5	F	2	0	0	1	0	0	0	0	0	0
$894	1.5	M	4	1	0	0	0	1	0	0	0	0
..	..	.	..	..	..	..	..	..	..	..	..	..

The first four columns contain the basic data. The first employee is a female who is paid $747 per week, is in job grade 2, and has been in this grade for 1.5 years. The rest of the columns are dummy variables that have been generated from the basic data. The gender trait is coded as a dummy variable called Male. The grade label is coded using eight dummy variables labeled Grade 1 to Grade 8.

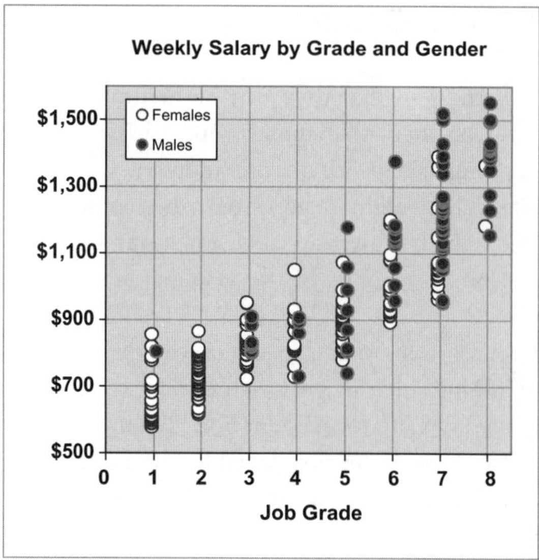

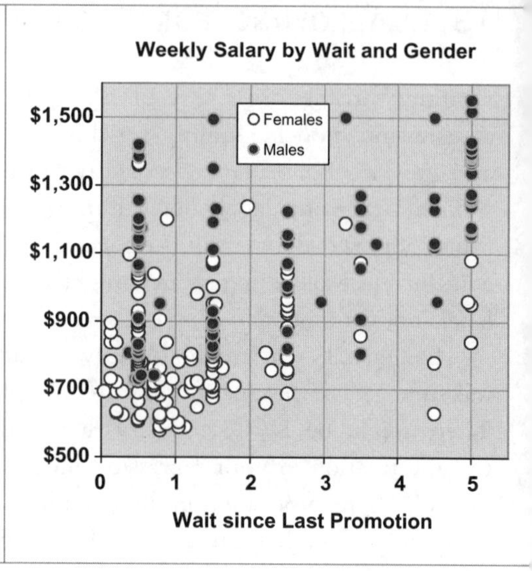

The left plot shows the strong effect of grade on weekly salary. Within each grade, you can compare males and females by recognizing the different plotting symbols. The effect of waiting time on salary is in the right plot. This seems to have a much weaker effect, though on the bottom left of the plot, there are a large number of females who have low salaries and have recently been promoted (short waiting time).

The average salary of males is $295 higher than the average salary of females. This is not automatically an evidence of gender discrimination. Some of the difference is explained by males being employed at higher grades than females. The table below shows that if you look within each grade, the differences are much smaller.

	1	2	3	4	5	6	7	8	All
Females	$665	$725	$830	$834	$887	$1,006	$1,093	$1,274	$833
Males	$804		$835	$824	$919	$1,131	$1,213	$1,376	$1,128
Difference	$139		$5	-$10	$32	$125	$120	$102	$295

Of course, if males are promoted to higher grades faster than females, then this could be evidence for gender discrimination as well. So the waiting time to promotion variable is another *Y* variable that we would want to analyze.

How to Include Group and Segments in a Regression

You can use StatproGo to create dummy variables from any grouping or segmenting variable. An example was a job grade that had $K = 8$ levels. First, select

StatproG0 → Data Utilities → Create Dummy Variable(s)....

Select the column containing the grouping variable, for instance, job grade. Statpro then creates *K* dummy variables automatically. The names of these variables will all begin with the name of the original grouping variable, followed by the underscore "_" character, followed by the group labels.

To include grouping variable in the regression, you

- choose one group to be the baseline. Ultimately, it does not matter which group you choose, so choose the group that you think makes most sense to compare the other groups with. For instance, you might omit the group that you know has the lowest performance;
- fit a multiple regression that includes the dummy variables for all groups except the **baseline**. There will be $K - 1$ of these.

If you try to include all K dummy variables, you will generate an error. If you try to include the original group variable in addition to the dummies, you will also generate an error. Only $K - 1$ dummy variables can be used in the regression.

Parameter Interpretation

For each dummy variable you include in the model, you obtain an estimated slope coefficient in the multiple regression output. The interpretation of these slopes is easy: *They measure the difference in performance for that group compared with the baseline group.*

For instance, suppose response was sales and the grouping variable was day of the week. You would then generate seven dummy variables for each day of the week and include six of them in the regression. If you decided to omit Monday, then Monday becomes the baseline and so the regression estimate for

- *Tuesday*—measures mean Tuesday sales minus mean Monday sales,
- *Friday*—measures mean Friday sales minus mean Monday sales,

and so on. Ultimately, it makes no difference which group you choose as the baseline. It will not affect the overall fit of the model, or your predictions, or the estimates of any other variables. If you change the baseline, all that happens is that the interpretation of the dummy variable slopes changes. There is usually a natural choice for the baseline group.

EXAMPLE 3 (Continued) *Pay scales*

Suppose we are interested in the issue of gender discrimination. We would want to estimate the mean difference in the salary of males and females, but adjusting for other relevant factors. Job grade is certainly relevant, and time since last promotion should also be (less) important, since salary can increase within a grade if someone has more experience.

We have a dummy variable called Males, which records if the employee is male. The regression estimate associated with this will measure the salary premium for males—how much more males get paid than nonmales (i.e., females). We could fit a multiple regression that treats waiting time and grade both as simple numerical variables. The adjusted r^2 is 82.1%, and the estimated coefficients are in the table below.

Results of multiple regression for Rate				
Regression coefficients				
	Coefficient	Std Err	t-value	p-value
Constant	526.7	14.1	37.2	0.000
Waiting	30.8	4.6	6.7	0.000
Grade	75.0	3.3	22.6	0.000
Males	59.6	16.0	3.7	0.000

The difference in salaries between males and females is now estimated at $59.6 after adjusting for job grade and waiting time in grade. This is way less than the naïve estimate of $295. However, we are treating job grade here as a number rather than as a group label. If we fit a regression model with all grade dummy variables included except Grade 1, then we get an adjusted r^2 of 84.8% and coefficients as listed below.

Regression coefficients				
	Coefficient	Std Err	t-value	p-value
Constant	631.9	19.5	32.4	0.000
Waiting	26.9	4.4	6.2	0.000
Males	46.9	15.0	3.1	0.002
Grade_2	60.9	22.4	2.7	0.007
Grade_3	150.8	24.9	6.1	0.000
Grade_4	168.0	26.6	6.3	0.000
Grade_5	209.8	24.3	8.6	0.000
Grade_6	356.4	26.3	13.5	0.000
Grade_7	433.9	24.5	17.7	0.000
Grade_8	613.0	30.9	19.9	0.000

The estimated level of gender discrimination is now $46.9. The *t*-value is high (3.1) and the *p*-value is small (0.002), so we are very confident that the gender difference is not just statistical bad luck. There is a systematic difference in the pay of males and females, even after adjusting for different job grade and the waiting time in that grade.

The waiting time coefficient estimates that each year an employee is in the same grade, their salary increases by $26.9. This is a much clearer effect than the gender effect (since its *t*-value is 6.2). When they get promoted into the next grade, their salary moves into a different range. This is described by the grade coefficients. It is very easy to summarize the grade coefficients in a chart. Just mark out the seven labels and coefficients and choose a column chart. The left chart below describes the effect of job grade on salary. The model does not assume a linear effect, or a quadratic effect of job grade. It allows each job grade to be associated with it own salary level.

No analysis is complete without checking residuals. One of the residual plots is below right. There does not seem to be any clumping, but there is a slight suggestion that variability may be larger to the right of the plot than to the left. There are a couple of employees with standardized residuals larger than three. It would be worth checking these individuals to see why they were paid so highly or lowly. This might bring to light some other variables that need to be included in the analysis.

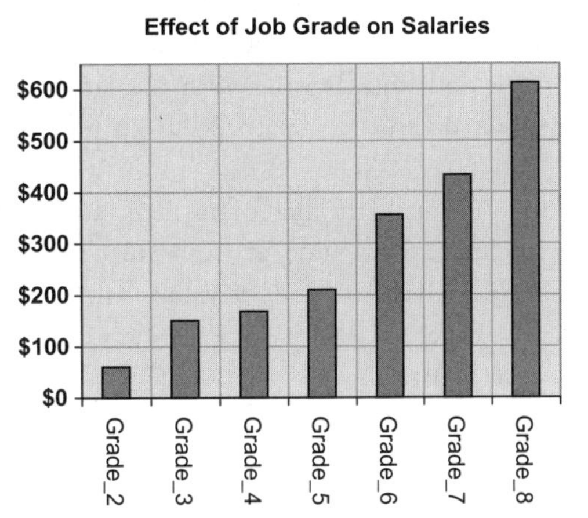

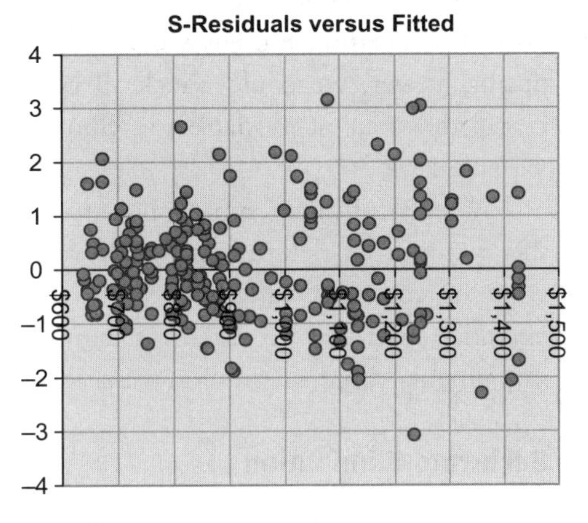

CHECK YOUR UNDERSTANDING

Q4. The file Q4.xls is taken from the Forbes survey of CEO compensation. The *Y* variable in the first column is total compensation. The predictors are age, industry sector, and having an MBA. Industry sector is a segmenting or grouping variable. I have already created 10 dummy variables for these 10 different sectors. Using the dummy variables, fill in the actual industry sectors in Column D. You might want to sort the data by each dummy variable.

Q5. The file Q5.xls is taken from the Forbes survey of CEO compensation. The *Y* variable in the first column is total compensation. The predictors are age, industry sector, and having an MBA:

(a) Use Statpro to create dummy variables for the categorical variable "industry sector." Also, create a dummy variable for the binary trait MBA.
(b) Fit a multiple regression that allows for age, MBA, and industry sector to affect compensation. Leave out food industry as the baseline.
(c) State the meaning of some of the industry sector coefficients.
(d) Why does an MBA not seem to add to salary?

18.5. AUTOMATIC MODEL SELECTION

With the inclusion of dummy variables for grouping variables and possible quadratic effects, it is possible to have a very large number of input variables available for multiple regression. For instance, you might be trying to explain monthly revenue in terms of your pricing, your competitor's pricing, the advertising budget, underlying growth, and the month of the year. This sounds like only five variables, but we would want to allow for possible quadratic effects in the first four variables, so there will be two variables (X and X^2) for each of these. The month of the year is a grouping variable, and so we will need to create 12 dummy variables and use 11 of these (see Chapter 20). So there will be 2 + 2 + 2 + 2 + 11 = 19 variables in all. Since each input variable could either be in the model or not, there are $2^{19} = 524{,}288$ possible regression models we could fit! Which one is the best? With enough computing power, we could check all possible models and find the one with the largest r^2 and the smallest model error. Some packages can do this for up to 20 or so input variables.

A less ambitious approach is to step through a small number of models, using the p-values to determine which variable to include or exclude at each step. We want all included variables to "be significant" (i.e., have a small p-value) and all excluded variables to be "not significant" (i.e., have a large p-value). StatproGo implements three of these automatic partial search algorithms.

Backward Elimination

1. Begin with all variables in the model. Remove the least significant x variable if its p-value is larger than a specified cutoff value, often 0.2.
2. Continue removing insignificant x variables *one by one*. The procedure terminates when all variables are significant compared with the chosen cutoff value—that is, all p-values are less than the chosen cut-off.

Forward Selection

1. Begin with the single x variable that has a high correlation with Y. At each step, consider adding just one of the remaining variables. Add the one that has the smallest p-value, provided that its p-value is less than a prespecified value.
2. Continue checking the list of omitted variables to see if any one of them can be usefully added to the model. At the end of the procedure, none of the omitted variables would be significant if added to the model.

Stepwise

At the end of the forward algorithm, no excluded variables are useful. However, you may find that some of the included variables are insignificant, even though when they first entered the model, they were significant. Similarly, at the end of the backward algorithm, all the variables are significant, but some of the ones you excluded early on in the algorithm could still be useful.

There is a hybrid algorithm that combines backward elimination and forward selection to try to avoid such problems. At each step, you can enter a new x variable or remove an existing x variable. You must prespecify a p-value for entering and a p-value for leaving.

In StatproGo, just select Regression Analysis and then either Backward, Forward, or Stepwise. The first dialog boxes require you to list the input x variables and the y variable, just as you do for any multiple regression. There is then an extra dialog box that asks you for the p-value levels where you will decide to exclude or include a variable.

EXAMPLE 4 *Deepwater Bay Apartments*

We have seen the data in ex 4 HKRE.xls several times now. There are 108 apartments sold in Deepwater Bay Hong Kong. This time, there is an extra variable describing the apartments—the floor they were on. Higher floors typically mean a better view, which means a higher price. Let us try to look for the most flexible model possible so that we do not miss any important patterns in the data. We can use a little economics and common sense to guide our thinking.

- In an efficient market, we would expect value to be linearly related to area, so any curvilinear effect will mean there is a market opportunity. Therefore, we consider possible curvilinear effects of area on price by including both sqft and sqft^2 in the regression.
- Older apartments will be worth less, but we expect that depreciation will level off. The loss of value during the first few years will be more than the loss of value, for, say, a 20-year-old apartment. We consider possible curvilinear effects using age and age2.
- Apartments that are higher will have a higher view and presumably be worth more. But would you really care much if you were on floor 21 compared with floor 20? There will probably be diminishing premiums for each extra floor. So we will allow for curvilinear effects by using both floor and floor2 in the regression.
- Car spaces come on a separate title and are freely tradable in the market, so three car spaces should necessarily be worth three times as much as one car space. Therefore, we include cars as a simple linear variable.
- In principle, bathrooms could add value over and above the extra floor space. There is no reason though why three bathrooms would be worth three times as much as two bathrooms. We will use dummy variables for BATHS_2, BATHS_3, and leave out BATHS_1 as the baseline.
- In principle, bedrooms probably should not add to value over and above any extra floor area. Any significant effects will indicate a market opportunity for developers to build more apartments of that type. We will use dummy variables for BEDS_3, BEDS_4, and BEDS_5 (baseline 2).

There are 12 variables in total, which means about 4000 possible models. The original data are on the worksheet *basic data*, and the extended data with the squares and dummy variables are on the worksheet *regression data*.

To select a model, I chose the stepwise procedure and included the 12 variables above. Be careful not to include BEDS, BATHS, BED2, or BATHS1. StatproGo then asks you for cutoff *p*-values for deciding when a variable is useful or not. Remember that a small *p*-value means that the variable is useful. The smaller you make the cutoff, the harder it is for a variable to be included in the model, and the simpler the final model will be. In business contexts, I think a cutoff of around 0.2 is reasonable. This means that the input variable's effect is clear enough that it would only occur one in five times by pure luck. When using stepwise, you have to choose two cutoff *p*-values, one to determine when to drop a variable (*p*-to-leave) and another to decide when to include a variable (*p*-to-enter). You must choose *p*-to-enter smaller than *p*-to-leave. I suggest using 0.19 for *p*-to-enter.

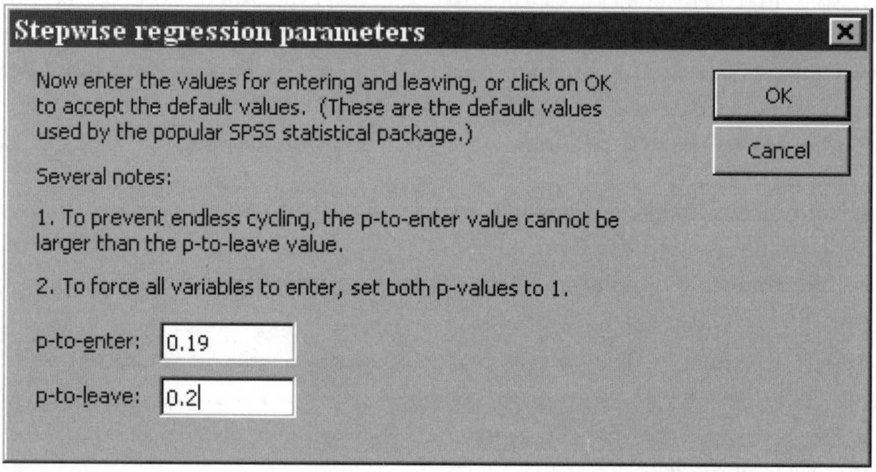

The final model has adjusted r^2 of 83.6% and a model error of \$107.0K. The coefficients are below. It appears as if there is market demand for three-bathroom apartments, and that it would be worth building small en suites with your three- and four-bedroom apartments. It also appears that there is a premium on larger apartments, and, as a developer, you would be better off designing larger apartments than smaller ones. Each floor adds about \$9760 to the price, and each car space is worth almost \$300K. These effects are described for you graphically on the worksheet *final model*.

Results of multiple regression for price				
Regression coefficients				
	Coefficient	Std Err	t-value	p-value
Constant	1147.0	148.3	7.7	0.000
SQFT	-677.7	166.6	-4.1	0.000
SQFT2	298.5	46.7	6.4	0.000
CARS	133.9	35.7	3.8	0.000
AGE	-26.0	10.0	-2.6	0.011
AGE2	0.67	0.42	1.6	0.111
Floor	9.76	4.21	2.3	0.023
BATHS_2	69.57	28.0	2.5	0.015
BATHS_3	93.03	60.3	1.5	0.126

CHECK YOUR UNDERSTANDING

Q6. Below is the output from halfway through the stepwise procedure. What would be the automatic next step if *p*-to-leave = 0.1 and *p*-to-enter = 0.05?

	Coefficient	Std Err	t-value	p-value
Constant	6.305	0.086	73.5	0.000
X2	0.099	0.050	2.0	0.051
X3	0.080	0.028	2.9	0.005
X6	-0.025	0.009	-2.8	0.006
X7	0.096	0.032	3.0	0.004
X8	0.069	0.020	3.5	0.001
X9	0.116	0.009	13.6	0.000
X12	0.001	0.000	2.1	0.041
X14	0.079	0.027	3.0	0.004
X15	0.045	0.023	2.0	0.052
X16	0.088	0.039	2.2	0.028

18.6. SUMMARY

Binary traits can be included in a regression by coding them as 0–1 dummy variables. The coefficient in the output then measures the value of the trait.

Curvilinear effects of an input variable are described using **quadratics**. They are fitted by including both X and X^2 in the regression model. The **linear coefficient** $\boldsymbol{m}_{\mathrm{L}}$ measures the slope when $X = 0$. The **quadratic coefficient** $\boldsymbol{m}_{\mathrm{Q}}$ measures the degree of nonlinearity in the relationship. In particular, $\boldsymbol{m}_{\mathrm{Q}} = 0$, then the relationship is a simple line. The *incremental effect on* Y *per unit change in* X is measured by

$$\text{effect of } X = \boldsymbol{m}_{\mathrm{L}} + 2\boldsymbol{m}_{\mathrm{Q}}X.$$

For hill- or valley-shaped effects, the top of the hill or the bottom of the valley occurs at the input value:

$$X_{\mathrm{BEST}} = -0.5 \times \boldsymbol{m}_{\mathrm{L}} / \boldsymbol{m}_{\mathrm{Q}}.$$

Grouping or **segmenting** variables are included in regression by creating a dummy variable for each group and including all but one of these dummies in the regression. The one left out becomes the baseline. The coefficients in the output measure mean performance for that group compared with the baseline group.

When there are many potential variables that could be included in regression, there is a huge number of possible models. StatproGo includes three **model selection algorithms** that search for the best model. The algorithm is controlled by selecting a cutoff significance level for a variable being included or excluded from the model. A common cutoff level is $P = 0.2$.

EXERCISES

E1. You monitor weekly profit and are able to choose the amount of expenditure on advertising each week. The relationship between marginal profit and advertising is

$$\text{Marginal Profit} = 227{,}000 + 2.24 \times \text{Adv} - 0.000013 \times \text{Adv}^2.$$

Your net profit is marginal profit minus the weekly cost of advertising. Both profit and advertising are measured in units of U.S. dollars.

(a) How does your net profit depend on advertising?
(b) What net profit do you make with no advertising?
(c) How much ROI do you get back on the first $1 spent on advertising?
(d) How much ROI do you get back on the 25,000th dollar spent on advertising?
(e) What level of advertising maximizes net profit?
(f) How would the equation change if profit and advertising were measured in units of $1000?

E2. You have the following model relating monthly sales of your product to (a) the price of your product in units of $1, (b) the price of your only major competitor in units of $1, (c) your expenditure advertising this month in units of $1000, (d) your expenditure advertising last month in units of $1000, (e) your expenditure advertising 2 months ago in units of $1000, (f) calendar time (measured in months with month = 0 representing 6 months ago, i.e., month = 6 represents now).
You arrive at the following formula based on multiple regression:

$$\text{Sales} = 14{,}200 - 700 \times \text{my price} + 500 \times \text{their price} + 300 \times \text{advertnow} + 800 \times \text{advertlast} + 100 \times \text{advertlast} - 2 + 125 \times \text{month} - 4.5 \times \text{month}^2.$$

(a) If the price of your product is $19.95 and your major competitor is $18.50 and if you spend $3000 per month on advertising, then what is your predicted sales this month?
(b) What will be your predicted sales in 6 months' time?
(c) Describe all the elements in the prediction formula in nontechnical terms.

E3. A regression of salary on age gives the output below.

Results of multiple regression for salary				
Summary measures				
Adj R-Square	71.5%			
Model error	4.877			
Regression coefficients				
	Coefficient	Std Err	t-value	p-value
Constant	-7.53	4.27	-1.76	0.08
age	3.786	0.260	14.56	0.000
age2	-0.041	0.004	-10.72	0.000

(a) What is the formula relating salary to age? What would be the predicted salary of someone of age 30?

(b) According to this model, what age is associated with the highest salary?
(c) How well can you predict salary from someone's age alone?
(d) If these data were used in an age discrimination case, then how might one explain the apparent association with age and claim that there is, in fact, no age discrimination?

E4. Below is a regression model for the salaries (in units of US$1000) of 455 employees in an organization on various factors thought to be of interest, namely gender, age, education, and experience. Exp2 means the square of experience. So a quadratic effect of experience is assumed by this model. Age has been categorized into six age groups. These have been coded as dummy variables and age group 40 taken as baseline.

Results of multiple regression for salary				
Summary measures				
Adj R-Square	86.8%			
Model error	3.319			
Regression coefficients				
	Coefficient	Std Err	t-value	p-value
Constant	22.045	3.834	5.7	0.000
experience	2.827	0.160	17.6	0.000
education	1.597	0.244	6.5	0.000
Exp2	-0.055	0.006	-8.9	0.000
Gender_Male	1.637	0.473	3.4	0.001
Agegroup_20s	-0.143	1.579	-0.1	0.928
Agegroup_30s	0.127	1.339	0.1	0.924
Agegroup_50s	-6.069	3.192	-1.9	0.058
Agegroup_60s	1.775	3.762	0.5	0.637
Agegroup_teens	0.530	2.136	0.2	0.804

(a) Predict the salary of a male in his 50s with 18 years of experience and level 12 education. Give an interval that would be likely to contain the salary of this individual.
(b) How much evidence is there that males are paid more than females? How accurately can this alleged bias be estimated?
(c) How accurate is this regression model?
(d) Suppose you included the dummy for females instead of for males. Which coefficient and slope estimate would change and how?
(e) What does the large *p*-value for teens indicate? What is your overall view of the effect of age on salary?
(f) Suppose you used the oldest age group (60s) as the baseline. What would be the slope estimate for the coefficient labeled Agegroup_20s, and what would it mean?

E5. Below are some general questions about regression models and their interpretation:
(a) A regression model has an adjusted r^2 of 72% and a model error of 3450. What do these figures tell you about the prediction accuracy of the model? Is it a good model?

(b) A multiple regression model produces a strong positive slope estimate for input variable x_1,and a strong negative slope estimate for input variable x_2. Yet when you look at a plot of y against x_1 and a plot of y against x_2, there appears to be no relationship. Is there really a relationship between y and x_1 and/or x_2 or not?

(c) A multiple regression model of y on x_1 and x_2 produces a significant and positive slope estimate for x_2, and a very small and insignificant slope estimate for x_1. Yet when you look at a plot of y against x_1, there is a strong positive association. Is there really a relationship between y and x_1 or not?

(d) A multiple regression model includes categorical input variables for gender and age group. You have used dummy variables to include these input variables. The baseline for gender is female and for age group is the youngest age group. You decide to change the baseline for gender to males and for age group to the oldest age group. Which aspects of the regression model will change? The slope estimates? The constant? Their standard errors? The model error? The predictions? The adjusted r^2?

CHAPTER 19

Analyzing Data That Is Collected Regularly Over Time

GASTHOF INTERNATIONAL: CASE BRIEFING

Gasthof International is a franchise chain of lodge style hotels with 68 locations spread across 12 European countries. Typical sales revenue is around €7 million per month. Business travelers are the main customer base though there is also a significant holiday market that is strongly seasonal with peaks in the summer holiday months as well as Christmas.

Arturo Leon has recently taken up the role of sales and development manager and has been given the impression that sales have been growing steadily and that monthly sales are increasing by roughly €32,000 each month. Gasthof has apparently defied the global financial crisis.

He has been provided with data on monthly sales for the past 6 years. A simple plot of the monthly sales reveals a very strong and consistent seasonal component in the sales, though there is also some obvious growth, which on first view looks extremely steady. Looking a little more carefully at the growth, he focuses on the August figures and sees that year-on-year growth has been around €300,000–400,000 but that more recently, August 2008 was around €600,000 higher than the previous August. This suggests that the growth may be increasing. However, looking at other months besides August gives a different message.

Arturo wished he could somehow remove the regular seasonal effect from the data. Everyone knows that business is good in July, August, September, and December. If he could remove this from the data, then perhaps he could better see what was really going on underneath.

Data-Driven Business Decisions, First Edition. Chris J. Lloyd.

19.0. INTRODUCTION: WHAT IS THE ISSUE?

Business and industry performance data are often collected at regular time intervals, most commonly monthly or quarterly. Such data are called **time series data**, and looking at a time series of your business is an important view of your business. As soon as you have the time element in mind, several obvious questions arise. What is the growth rate? Can I predict performance next month? Does changing this management variable affect performance immediately, or does it have a delayed effect spread over several periods?

In most industries there is a predictable pattern to performance over the year—a **seasonal pattern**. This is outside the control of any manager and is part of the business environment. It also obscures assessments of the underlying performance level, growth in the performance level, and deviations from the underlying level.

Naive methods of estimating the seasonal pattern fail dismally. Regression is one systematic way of measuring the seasonality, the performance level, and the growth rate. It also provides predictions of performance into the future.

EXAMPLE 1 *Quality Kitchens meatloaf*

Quality Kitchens is a brand of meatloaf manufactured by Amalgamated Food Products (AFP). It is a consistently profitable item with a 40% marginal profit. Sally Franklin has 5 years of monthly profit data. There are several drivers of profit described in the full case, but for the moment, we will just focus on one of them—promotional budget. This measures how much AFP spends each month on promotional offers to retailers. The final profit measure is net of the cost of these promotions, and so is the bottom line figure.

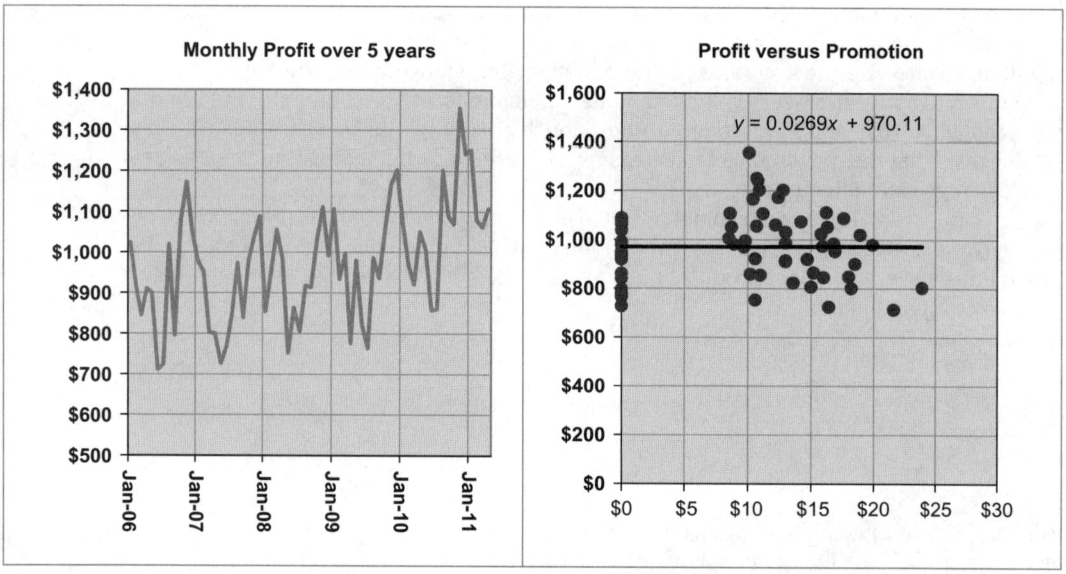

Above left is a plot of monthly profit over time. There is clear repeating pattern over the year with a peak in November to December and a trough in June to July. On top of this, it looks like profitability is increasing over time. One possible driver is promotional spend. The right plot does not lend much support to this possibility. It suggests that promotional spend has almost no effect at all on profits. We know by now that this could be misleading. What if promotion was higher in the less profitable months? This would make it look less effective than it really is. Regression will untangle this.

EXAMPLE 2 *Employment in Wisconsin food sector*

File ex 2 food.xls contains monthly data on the number of people employed in the food industry in Wisconsin from 1995 to 2000. There is a clear seasonal effect, which has been exaggerated by the choice of vertical scale. Sales are highest in August and September, and lowest around February and March.

There are several reasons we might analyze these data. We might want to predict employment for the next few months of the year 2000. We might want to measure the underlying *growth rate* of employment. We might want to identify particular months that deviated from the expected pattern. All these issues require us to take account of the two major patterns in this time series: trend and seasonality.

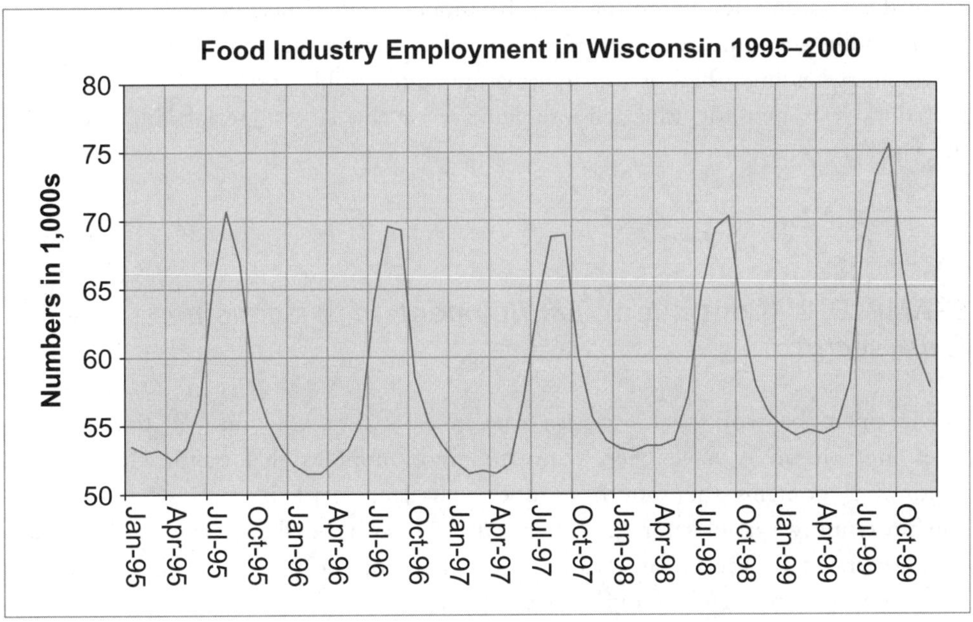

19.1. MEASURING GROWTH AND SEASONALITY

As a manager, you should be interested in how performance changes—hopefully increases—over time. If you have time series data, you can use regression to measure the rate of increase, also known as **growth rate**.

The simplest model for growth is a linear function of the form

$$Y = \boldsymbol{b} + \boldsymbol{m}T,$$

where T is a variable that measures time. For time series, you will commonly set $T = 0$ at the beginning of the series, so that $\boldsymbol{b}$ represents the performance Y at the beginning of the series.

The parameter $\boldsymbol{m}$ measures the growth rate *per unit of time*. It is common to count T in the same units as the data is recorded. For instance, if you have weekly or monthly or quarterly data, then you let T be the number of weeks or months or quarters since the start of the series. Then $\boldsymbol{m}$ measures the weekly or monthly or quarterly growth rate. It makes no ultimate difference how you measure time so long as you keep in mind the units you have used.

The other key feature we see in time series data is a **seasonal pattern**. For instance, if the data are monthly, then you will expect to see a characteristic pattern of sales across the 12 months, superimposed on any growth that may or may not be present.

Month is not a number—it is a label! So we must use dummy variables for the 12 months if we are going to use this information in a regression. You create dummy variables—one for each month—using StatproGo and Data Utilities. You then include 11 of the 12 dummies in the model. The month omitted becomes the baseline that other months are compared with. While it makes no ultimate difference which month is chosen as baseline, there is usually a natural and sensible choice. For ease of interpretation, it is best to either choose January or the lowest performing month of the year.

EXAMPLE 2 (Continued) *Employment in Wisconsin food sector*

If you open the worksheet *regression data* in ex 2 food.xls, you will find that the dates in Column A have been converted into numbers that StatproGo can use. Column B contains the month number (1 = Jan, 2 = Feb, etc.). Columns E–P contain dummy variables for the 12 months. These have labels that were automatically generated by the Create Dummy Variables routine in Data Utilities. Column C measures how many months have passed since January 1995. It has been labeled Time.

To fit a model that measures both trend and seasonality, we use the Multiple Regression module with Food as the response. The explanatory variables are Time and 11 of the monthly dummies. Let us leave out January as the baseline.

Results of multiple regression for Food				
Summary measures				
Adj r^2	95.6%			
Model Error	1.415			
p-value	0.0000			
Regression coefficients				
	Coefficient	Std Err	t-value	p-value
Constant	51.5	0.7	74.9	0.000
Time	0.069	0.011	6.4	0.000
Month_2	-0.61	0.89	-0.7	0.500
Month_3	-0.44	0.90	-0.5	0.627
Month_4	-0.57	0.90	-0.6	0.530
Month_5	0.04	0.90	0.0	0.960
Month_6	3.32	0.90	3.7	0.001
Month_7	11.57	0.90	12.9	0.000
Month_8	16.68	0.90	18.6	0.000
Month_9	16.43	0.90	18.3	0.000
Month_10	7.34	0.90	8.2	0.000
Month_11	3.03	0.90	3.4	0.002
Month_12	0.92	0.90	1.0	0.312

In terms of overall explanatory power, this model is very good with an adjusted r^2 of 95.6% and a model error of 1.415. In other words, 95.6% of the observed pattern of employment can be reproduced by this model with a typical error of 1415 people, either too high or too low.

Growth is measured to be 0.069 per month, with an error of 0.011, which is 0.826 per year, with an error of 0.129. We are very sure that there is growth because the *t*-value is 6.4. The monthly dummy coefficients measure how much lower or higher each month is than the baseline—chosen as January. So November is 3.03 higher than January, while December is only 0.92 higher. The error in all these figures is 0.9.

You might wonder why we need regression to estimate the seasonal effects. Couldn't we just calculate the average employment numbers for January, for February, and so on, and then subtract off the January average if we wanted to measure everything compared with January? The problem with this is that does not adjust for the growth in the data. Since December comes 11 months after January for each of the 5 years, it has 11 months advantage of growth and will tend to be $11 \times 0.069 = 0.757$ higher. This is over and above any December sales peak that might really be present. The same is true for November, which has 10 months growth advantage over January.

For the present data set, this is not a huge issue, but it does make some difference. The left plot below shows the naïve monthly averages compared with January and the regression estimates on the same chart. The naïve method says that December is 1.68 higher than January, whereas the (more correct) regression estimate says that it is only 0.92 higher.

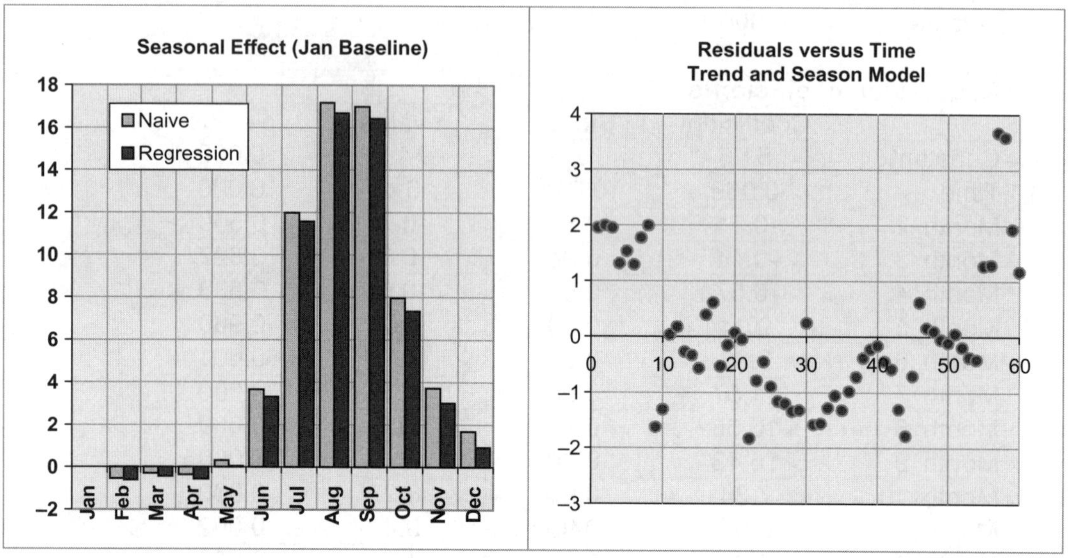

Of course, we are not finished with regression until the residual plots look random. The only x variable that it makes sense to plot the residuals against here is the time variable. The right plot suggests that there is a curvilinear trend in time. Employment numbers do not increase by a fixed number each month. So the current model is not acceptable. It summarizes the growth rate in a single number when this is not supported by the data. The model being wrong means that the seasonal effects cannot be trusted. Predictions will definitely be adversely affected. We need a better model.

CHECK YOUR UNDERSTANDING

Q1. The workbook Q1.xls contains data on passenger numbers on trans-Atlantic flights for a U.S. airline. There is huge seasonality in these data and an apparent upward trend.

(a) Complete the column time to measure the number of months, the column months to give a month number, and then use StatproGo to generate 12 monthly dummy variables.
(b) Fit a multiple regression model that estimates both trend and seasonality, treating January as the baseline.
(c) What is the yearly growth rate?
(d) Plot residuals against time. What does it suggest?

19.2. How Is the Growth Rate Changing?

When the residual plot against time contains trend, it means that the growth rate may not be constant. The next simplest model for growth after a linear function is to allow a quadratic function of time. This is a formula of the form

$$Y = \boldsymbol{b} + \boldsymbol{m}_{\mathrm{L}}T + \boldsymbol{m}_{\mathrm{Q}}T^2,$$

where T still measures time in the units of the time series. The baseline $\boldsymbol{b}$ still measures performance at $T = 0$. The linear and quadratic coefficients can also be meaningfully interpreted.

The linear coefficient $\boldsymbol{m}_{\mathrm{L}}$ measures the growth rate at the beginning of the series, that is, at time $T = 0$. In simple words, it is the *initial growth rate*. The parameter $\boldsymbol{m}_{\mathrm{Q}}$ measures the *nonlinearity of growth*. A large T-value and a small p-value mean that there really is nonlinear growth in the data.

Recall that for a general quadratic function the *incremental effect on* Y *per unit change in* X is measured by $\boldsymbol{m}_{\mathrm{L}} + 2\boldsymbol{m}_{\mathrm{Q}}X$. Here, the input variable X is time T, and the incremental effect per unit change in X means growth rate. So for a quadratic growth model,

$$\text{Growth at time } T = \boldsymbol{m}_{\mathrm{L}}T + 2\boldsymbol{m}_{\mathrm{Q}}T.$$

The most interesting time to measure growth is at the end of the time series. So if you enter the last value of T into this formula, you get the most recent growth rate. For instance, if you have 5 years of monthly data, then you will have the number 0–59 for the time variable, and you substitute $T = 59$ into the above formula.

EXAMPLE 2 (Continued) *Employment in Wisconsin food sector*

If you open the worksheet *quadratic growth*, you will find that Column D contains the squares of the numbers in Column C. The column has been labeled time2, meaning *time squared*. It sounds very strange to talk about time squared in a business context. The reason we introduce this variable is not because we think time squared has any business meaning. We use it because we suspect that we have nonlinear growth, and we want a simple mathematical way to describe it. There are other ways to do this, and you will learn an alternative nonlinear growth model in the next chapter.

To fit a regression model that allows for nonlinear growth and seasonality, you just add the variable time2 to the previous model. You still have the choice of which of the 12 monthly dummies to leave out, and it makes no difference to the final results which one you leave out. The model output is below.

The adjusted r^2 is now 98.3%, and the model error has reduced from 1.145 to 0.875. This is one indication that the nonlinear growth is real and important. The *T*-value associated with time2, which we generically call $\boldsymbol{m}_Q$, is 8.8, so there is no question that there is curvilinear growth. The earlier residual plot pointed toward this. The large *T*-value confirms it.

The linear term $\boldsymbol{m}_L$ equals −0.149, and means that at the start of the series, which was January 1995, underlying employment numbers were falling at a rate of 149 per month with a standard error of 26. The growth rate at any time *T* is

$$\text{Growth at time } T = -0.149 + 0.0074 \times T.$$

Specifically, at the end of the data series, when $T = 59$, we get an estimated growth rate of 0.287. Compare this with the single growth figure of 0.069 from the linear model. We have identified that growth has switched from −149 per month to 287 per month. This is something worth knowing!

Results of multiple regression for Food				
Summary measures				
Adj r^2	98.3%			
Model Error	0.875			
p-value	0.0000			
Regression coefficients				
	Coefficient	Std Err	t-value	p-value
Constant	53.6	0.5	111.0	0.000
Time	-0.149	0.026	-5.8	0.000
Time2	0.0037	0.0004	8.8	0.000
Month_2	-0.572	0.554	-1.0	0.307
Month_3	-0.371	0.554	-0.7	0.506
Month_4	-0.478	0.554	-0.9	0.393
Month_5	0.148	0.554	0.3	0.790
Month_6	3.427	0.555	6.2	0.000
Month_7	11.678	0.555	21.0	0.000
Month_8	16.782	0.556	30.2	0.000
Month_9	16.518	0.556	29.7	0.000
Month_10	7.407	0.557	13.3	0.000
Month_11	3.069	0.558	5.5	0.000
Month_12	0.923	0.559	1.7	0.105

How about predicting the future? It is not good statistical practice to predict too far into the future, because this assumes that the trends we have seen in the past will necessarily persist. But a few months into the future does not stretch credulity too far. For example, we might want to predict employment numbers for the first 3 months of 2000. For January 2000, the variable time = 60, so time2 = 3600. The month is January, so there is no extra dummy coefficient to add. You will find that the predicted level is 57.94. For February, time = 61 so time2 = 3721, and we need to subtract the February index of 0.572. This leads to a prediction of 57.67. For March, the prediction is 58.17, and you will find the appropriate numbers entered in the worksheet *trend2 + season*.

But is this all premature? We have not checked the residuals yet. If you check the residual plots for this quadratic model, you will find that there is no any obvious trend. However, the plot does look slightly "clumpy." There are ways of dealing with this that we will touch on later in this chapter. Whether you go to this level of complexity depends on what you are using the model for. If you need to get standard errors correct, or if you want to do prediction, then you would need to worry about the clumping.

Less ambitiously, a common purpose of trend and seasonal models like the one above is to *seasonally adjust* the data. If this is the sole purpose, then the model we have just fitted is quite adequate.

CHECK YOUR UNDERSTANDING

Q2. Continuing with the airline example, Q2.xls contains the same data, including the time variable and the monthly dummies. The residual plot suggested a curvilinear trend.

(a) Fit a model that allows for seasonality and curvilinear trend.
(b) Is growth increasing or decreasing? How sure are you?
(c) What is the initial and final growth rate?
(d) At what month did the underlying level of passenger numbers peak?

19.3. SEASONALLY ADJUSTING DATA

Since the seasonal pattern in sales, revenue, or profit figures are not within a manager's control, it makes sense to remove the effect so that underlying levels of performance are better revealed.

The first step is to obtain seasonal indices that measure the seasonal pattern. We have already seen how to do this with regression. However, regression will produce seasonal coefficients that are all relative to a particular baseline month—the one that was left out. If you choose December instead of August as the baseline, the numbers will all be different. While this does not really matter, it would be nice to have seasonal indices that are relative to the year as a whole rather than relative to any specific month.

Centered monthly seasonal indices are obtained by taking each of the 12 seasonal index numbers from the regression, including the value zero for the baseline month, and then subtracting off the average of the 12 numbers. They can be interpreted as *performance for that month compared with the yearly average*. Some will be positive, and some will be negative. The average of the 12 centered indices is automatically zero. To **seasonally adjust** a time series, you subtract off the centered seasonal indices.

EXAMPLE 2 (Continued) *Employment in Wisconsin food sector*

For the quadratic trend model, with January as the baseline, the monthly coefficients are listed in the column Jan-Baseline in the table below. You can check these in the regression output on the worksheet *trend2 + season.* Notice that I have included January in this list with a coefficient of zero. This happened to be the month chosen as baseline in the regression model.

Month	Jan-Baseline	Centred
Jan	0.00	-4.88
Feb	-0.57	-5.45
Mar	-0.37	-5.25
Apr	-0.48	-5.36
May	0.15	-4.73
Jun	3.43	-1.45
Jul	11.68	6.80
Aug	16.78	11.90
Sep	16.52	11.64
Oct	7.41	2.53
Nov	3.07	-1.81
Dec	0.92	-3.95

The average of these 12 numbers is 4.88. If I subtract 4.88 from each of the 12 numbers, I obtain the numbers in the column labeled *Centered.* So December is 3.95 lower than the yearly average, while July is 6.80 higher than the yearly average. It is very common to plot these centered indices as a bar chart to summarize the seasonal pattern.

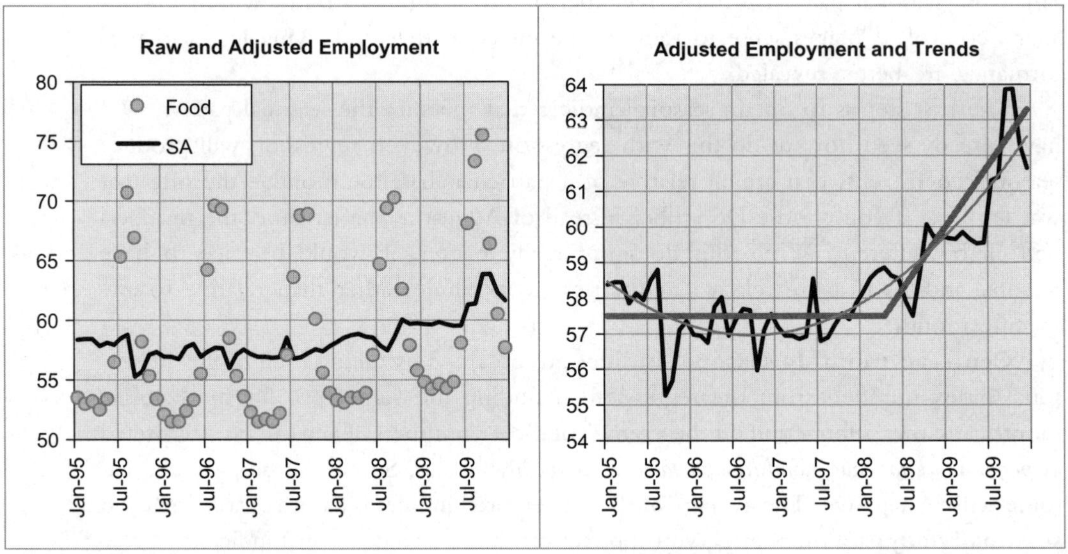

But the main use of these indices is not to present them in a graph but to use them to seasonally adjust the data. If you look in worksheet *SA*, you will find that the centered seasonal indices have been copied into Column D. They have then been subtracted from the data in Column C to produce seasonally adjusted employment numbers in Column E. In the left plot, I have plotted the original numbers and the seasonally adjusted series. Most of the variation in the original plot was due to the seasonality and has been removed. What is left is the underlying level of employment. We can see this better in the right plot, where the scale has been adjusted. It looks very much like there was no growth at all from January 1995 to around 1998. After that time, there was a very clear growth. It is not clear exactly where we changed from no growth to positive growth, but it is clear that we are growing strongly now! Just as importantly, we can see which months stand out from the general trend. There was a huge dip in September 1995 that was not apparent in the original plot. There is a big peak and drop at the end of the series that was also not visible in the unadjusted data.

The quadratic regression model assumes that the underlying level follows a quadratic curve. Under this assumption, we estimated the growth rate at the end of the series to be 0.287. This is not the only reasonable estimate, and it would not be unreasonable to use the linear trend in the plot above.

CHECK YOUR UNDERSTANDING

Q3. Continuing with the airline example, Q3.xls contains the last trend and seasonality model you fitted.

(a) Give a graphical presentation of the seasonal effect.
(b) Create seasonal adjusted numbers. Plot these on the same graph as the original data.
(c) What would you say about the growth trajectory?

EXAMPLE 1 (Continued) *Quality Kitchens meatloaf*

The data were monthly profit for a brand of meatloaf for over 5 years and are in the file ex 1 meatloaf.xls. Management also had control over how much they spend on promotional offers. A naive plot of profit versus promotional spend suggested that it had almost no effect. The slope coefficient was 0.0269, which means that for every $1 spent on promotion, we receive an extra 2.7 cents of profit. This is not a bad monthly return on investment. However, if you look at the full regression output for a regression of profit in terms of promotional spend, the standard error is 2.56, and the *T*-value is 0.01. The data are really saying that promotional expenditure has no clear effect at all on profit.

However, there is strong trend in the profit as well as a seasonal effect. Both of these could easily make promotional expenditure look worse (or indeed better) than it really is. If you open worksheet *regression data*, you will find that monthly dummies have been created, as well as a time and time2 variable. The output from a regression model that allows for nonlinear trend, seasonality, and promotion are in the table below.

Results of multiple regression for profit				
Summary measures				
Adj r^2	76.5%			
Model Error	69.1			
p-value	0.0000			
Regression coefficients				
	Coefficient	Std Err	t-value	p-value
Constant	950.7	46.6	20.4	0.000
Time	-3.0	2.0	-1.5	0.140
Time2	0.10	0.03	3.5	0.001
PROM	3.42	1.51	2.3	0.028
Month_2	-61.0	41.2	-1.5	0.145
Month_3	-101.3	40.0	-2.5	0.015
Month_4	-110.9	40.1	-2.8	0.008
Month_5	-139.5	42.6	-3.3	0.002
Month_6	-220.4	42.1	-5.2	0.000
Month_7	-220.7	42.4	-5.2	0.000
Month_8	-11.0	42.1	-0.3	0.796
Month_9	-88.4	45.0	-2.0	0.055
Month_10	27.6	43.8	0.6	0.531
Month_11	132.7	42.3	3.1	0.003
Month_12	69.0	42.1	1.6	0.108

The effect of promotion is now 3.42. For every $1 spent on promotional offers, we get $3.42 back in extra profit (after allowing for the $1 spent remember). The *p*-value is 0.028, so we are pretty sure that we are in front, though the standard error of $1.51 makes the $3.42 difficult to really interpret.

This model also generates seasonal indices. You can take the 11 coefficients, center them by subtracting off the average, and then subtract these off the original data to produce a seasonally adjusted series. This was not really the main point of this example though. The point was to estimate the effect of promotion, *allowing for trend and seasonality*.

19.4. Delayed Effects

Let us start this section by revealing more information about the earlier example on meatloaf and then fitting a regression, including the extra variables. I will then explain how the standard regression largely misses the point and show how to widen the scope of regression, yet again, to include delayed effects.

EXAMPLE 1 (Continued) *Quality Kitchens meatloaf*

We will now reveal several other variables that affect profit in this example. You can read about the full background in the case *Quality Kitchens*. The data are in ex 1B meatloaf.xls. The main variables are on the worksheet *data*. Plots of these variables are on the same sheet.

Marketing Variables

There are two controllable marketing variables that affect profit. One is promotional offers, as we have already seen. The other is advertising. There is a great deal of interest in determining whether a dollar of the marketing budget is better spent on promotion or advertising. Spending on both forms of marketing has been decreasing over time.

Economic Environment

There is an economic indicator of consumer's spending on discretionary goods. A high value means good economic times. It is believed that meatloaf is a *countercyclical* product—that people will buy more in bad times than good times. The indicator had increased steadily over time, which should be bad news for our product.

Seasonal Index

There is an industry-wide index that measures the seasonal variations in packaged food sales. This is a decimal number that represents a percentage effect. For instance, the January index is 0.096, which means that January sales tend to be 9.6% higher than the yearly average. Our first step will be to remove this seasonal effect by dividing the profit by 1.096 for January, and similarly for the other months. These index adjusted numbers are in Column G and called Profit(IA).

Why not use the data to obtained seasonal indices? The answer is that we could do this, but we will use the provided index to keep things a little simpler.

The worksheet *unlagged models* contains five progressively more complete regression models. Each gives an estimate of the effect of spending $1 on promotion and on advertising. The table below gives the main figures.

	PROM		ADV	
	Effect	T	Effect	T
Models 1 & 2	$0.14	0.1	-$0.24	-0.3
Model 3	-$0.07	0.0	-$0.25	-0.3
Model 4	$5.24	3.2	$1.26	1.9
Model 5	$5.50	3.5	$1.59	2.5

If you plot profit first against promotion, and then against advertising, you can get two slope estimates. These are models 1 and 2. The effect of promotion is 0.14 cents return on the dollar, but the *T*-value is incredibly small. Promotion has no clear effect at all. Advertising has a negative effect on profit, but again, the small *T*-value means it is more sensible to say it has no clear effect.

Model 3 includes both promotion and advertising in the same model. Both *T*-values are still very small, and it appears that neither form of marketing has an effect on profit. Model 4 includes time in the model—which accounts for the growth that was occurring over the 5 years of the data. Since marketing expenditure was decreasing over the same period, this was making both forms look bad. All of a sudden, we see that promotion increases profit by $5.24 and advertising by $1.26. Both *T*-values are fairly large. Marketing works big time!

Model 5 includes the economic index and a quadratic term in time. The effects of promotion and advertising become even clearer with larger *T*-values for both and slightly larger estimated effects. Residual plots look random. It looks like money spent on promotion is way more effective than money spent on advertising. But we have missed a critical issue.

Actions Have Effects Both Now and Later

Some management actions can have immediate effects. For instance, a price change will have an almost immediate effect on demand. Other actions have a delayed effect. For instance, when the FED changes interest rates, it takes a few months to flow through the economy. Marketing and advertising often has both an immediate and a delayed effect. If you are going to properly assess the effectiveness of your action, you need to account for its *total* effect, not just its immediate effect.

A Simple Model for Delayed Effects

Let us look at a simple model for how an actionable variable such as advertising might affect monthly revenue. Let ADV(now) be the amount spent on advertising this month and ADV(last) the amount spent last month. If advertising has a delayed effect, then revenue this month will be affected directly by advertising this month, but I will also get the delayed benefits of advertising last month. In an equation, suppose that

$$\text{Revenue} = \boldsymbol{b} + 1.56 \times \text{ADV(now)} + 0.35 \times \text{ADV(last)},$$

where $\boldsymbol{b}$ is the performance with no advertising at all. The immediate effect of spending $1 on advertising is to increase revenue by $1.56. The effect of $1 spent last month increases revenue this month by $0.35. It therefore follows that the $1 spent this month will increase revenue *next* month by another $0.35. So the total effect of $1 spent this month is $1.56 now, plus $0.35 next month, for a total of $1.91. If you just plotted revenue against advertising, you would miss the delayed effect and undervalue your advertising.

Using Regression

Regression can be used to estimate the immediate and delayed effects—to obtain the numbers 1.56 and 0.35 in the above example. The key trick is to include **lagged variables** in the regression. Advertising last month is an example of a lagged variable.

EXAMPLE 1 (Continued) *Quality Kitchens meatloaf*

The problem with promotional offers is that retailers stock up on your product at the cheap price. They store it and sell it for a higher margin next month. So you will not be surprised to see profits go *down* next month, even if they go up this month. Advertising on the other hand keeps on delivering. People will have an immediate response to a good advertising campaign, but you will get further benefits in the coming months.

We can estimate the delayed effects by creating variables that measure how much was spent on promotion and advertising last month. To do this, we just copy the spending this month and *move it down one cell*. These *lagged variables* are in worksheet *lagged regression data* in Columns D and F. If we include these two variables in the regression, we get the results below.

Results of multiple regression for Profit(IA)				
Summary measures				
Adj r^2	72.7%			
Model Error	49.5			
p-value	0.0000			
Regression coefficients				
	Coefficient	Std Err	t-value	p-value
Constant	2726.3	1278.8	2.1	0.037
PROM	5.16	1.09	4.7	0.000
PROM_Lag1	-2.23	1.12	-2.0	0.052
ADV	1.74	0.47	3.7	0.000
ADV_Lag1	2.17	0.47	4.7	0.000
ECON	-20.2	13.3	-1.5	0.134
Time	-2.5	1.5	-1.7	0.094
Time2	0.128	0.0	4.6	0.000

The stocking effect of promotional offers is clearly apparent. When you spend a dollar on promotion, you get an extra \$5.16 this month, but you lose \$2.23 next month for a net effect of \$2.93. For advertising, there is initial payoff of \$1.74 and an even bigger payoff of \$2.17 next month for a total effect of \$3.90. It looks like advertising is better than promotion.

The model also estimates an underlying quadratic time trend. At the beginning of the series, growth was −2.5 per month, but there is now (in month 59) a strongly positive growth of 12.59 per month. The economic indicator has a negative effect on profits, as anticipated.

Pushing a Little Further

It is always worth trying a few alternative models to see that the main conclusion of interest is robust. The worksheet *lagged models* contains two other models in addition to the one above that is labeled model 1.

Model 2 analyzes Profit rather than index-adjusted profit but instead includes the index variable in the regression. So instead of dividing profit by the index, we let the regression model use this variable in the best way it can. Model 3 includes 11 monthly dummies instead of the index variable. This effectively estimates the seasonal effect rather than accept the industry-wide index as the best description of the seasonal effect. Model 4 repeats this analysis, but uses Profit(IA) as the *Y* variable. This allows us to estimate any seasonal effects that may remain in Profit(IA) even though it has been index adjusted. The *p*-values for the monthly dummies are all large, which indicates that there is no apparent systematic seasonal effect in the index-adjusted profit. In other words, the index adjustment has performed its task.

For all four of these models, the main conclusions about marketing are hardly changed at all. Promotion is less effective than advertising. The economic index has a negative effect on profit. Finally, growth is curvilinear and has switched from negative at the start of the series to positive at the end.

Why stop at last month? Why not look back two or three? The answer is that you can. You simply include extra lags of the marketing variables. The lag-2 variables are shifted down by two cells, the lag-3 by three cells, and so on. There is a tool in Data Utilities called Create Lagged variables that will quickly create as many lagged versions of a variable as you desire.

In the present example, you will find that there is some evidence that the stocking effect of promotion persists for a second month but that the positive effects of advertising disappear after 2 months. This adds further weight to our conclusion that advertising is more effective than promotion.

Check Your Understanding

Q4. The numbers in Q4.xls are monthly building approvals in Victoria, Australia, and prime lending rate for housing loans.

(a) What is a naive estimate of the effect of rates on building approvals? What does this estimate ignore?
(b) Fit a regression model that allows for growth, seasonality, and a delayed effect of rates up to 3 months.
(c) Describe the effect of rates on building approvals.

19.5. PREDICTING THE FUTURE (USING AUTOREGRESSION)

There are situations when we are not so much interested in understanding the effects of the x variables, as just using them to get a prediction. Time series data are often mainly collected with a view to predicting the future. You would think that one of the most important pieces of data in predicting next month's sales is this month's sales—and you would be right. This suggests that we could use lags of the y variable to predict the y variable.

The so-called **autoregression** is a regression where lags of the y variable are included as explanatory variables. The payoff of these methods is first that the adjusted r^2 often increases by a great deal, and second, that residuals plots are no longer "clumpy." The downside is that the models are more difficult to explain and interpret.

EXAMPLE 3 *Predicting retail sales*

The data in ex3 retail.xls list 5 years of data on sales across a retail chain in the United States. The sales are in units of thousands of dollars per day per outlet in the chain. The number of chains varied from 15 to 20, but these details are not important to the ideas we will look at here.

If you look at worksheet *trend and season* you will find the output of a regression model that includes quadratic trend and monthly dummies. The overall r^2 is 97.4%, so it is a good model in an absolute sense. The monthly dummy coefficients have been used to produce a seasonally adjusted version of the data, and a chart of this is below left. There are some interesting features in the adjusted series, and these correspond to events that are described in the case, but do not matter here.

Unfortunately, when we look at the residuals, which are graphed in the right plot, we see a clear structure. This means that there is systematic deviation of the data from the model. Since the model already has a quadratic term in time, it is not clear where we should go from here.

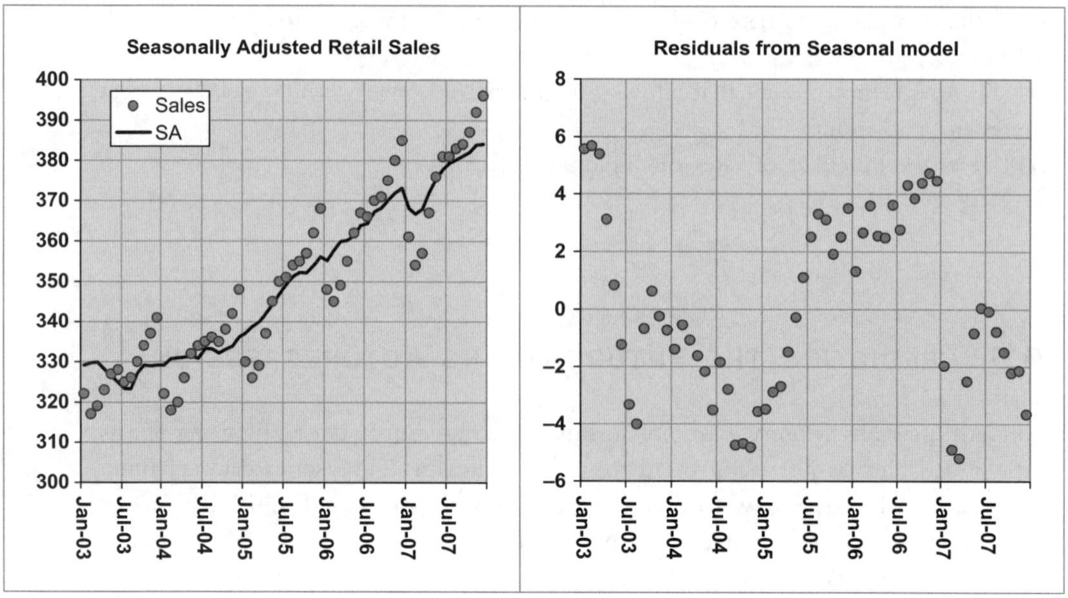

If the main aim was to produce a seasonally adjusted series, then the nonrandom residual plot does not matter greatly. It just means that the standard errors are unreliable. If, however, you were mainly interested in predicting the future, then any systematic pattern in the residuals is potentially useful. It means that we can use the pattern to get a better model.

One reason why we might see "clumping" in the residual plot is that the points are not independent. In simple words, this means if 1 month is above trend, then the next few months tend to be above trend. This would most likely be because there are other unmeasured variables that are driving the series. We can account for the tendency of the series to "follow itself" by using earlier values of the series to "explain" later values of the series.

To do this, create lags of the Sales variable itself. I have created three lags in the worksheet *autoregression*. You could include more, but you can check for yourself later that the fourth and later lags end up not being useful (large p-values). We include the time variable and the monthly dummies as before. If you use the backward algorithm, you will find that many of the monthly dummy variables are now dropped from the regression. The remaining variables and their estimated coefficients are listed below.

The most exciting aspect of this output is that adjusted r^2 is 99.7%! This is not so surprising when you consider that we are using the sales variable itself to estimate future sales. The high accuracy of the model is the upside. An additional upside is that the residuals are now nice and random, as displayed in the left plot below. It looks like there is no pattern at all, and so we have used all the patterns in the data that we can.

The downside is that the coefficients are no longer easy to interpret. In particular, the coefficient of 0.19 for the variable Time has nothing to do with growth, and the monthly coefficients are not simple seasonal indices.

Results of multiple regression for Sales				
Summary measures				
Adj r^2	99.7%			
Model Error	1.24			
p-value	0.0000			
Regression coefficients				
	Coefficient	Std Err	t-value	p-value
Constant	52.2	10.1	5.2	0.000
Time	0.19	0.04	5.2	0.000
Sales_Lag1	1.28	0.04	35.6	0.000
Sales_Lag2	-0.59	0.07	-8.9	0.000
Sales_Lag3	0.15	0.07	2.1	0.041
Jan	-23.51	0.79	-29.7	0.000
Mar	-4.04	1.68	-2.4	0.020
Jun	-1.65	0.77	-2.1	0.038
Jul	-3.89	0.73	-5.3	0.000
Sep	-2.88	0.64	-4.5	0.000
Dec	1.31	0.68	1.9	0.061

Bearing in mind then that the model is hard to interpret, let us look at how well it predicts. First, you can plot the fitted values and the actual values on the same chart, and see almost perfect agreement. This is shown in the right plot. Each fitted values is based on using the calendar information and the three previous sales results to predict the current monthly sales. How about predicting the future?

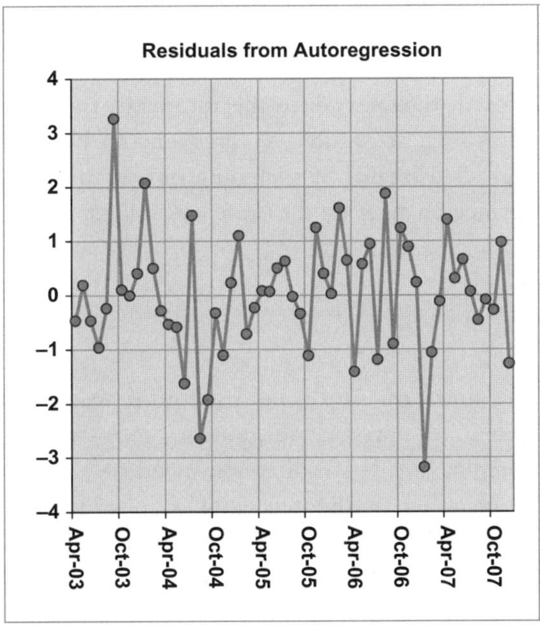

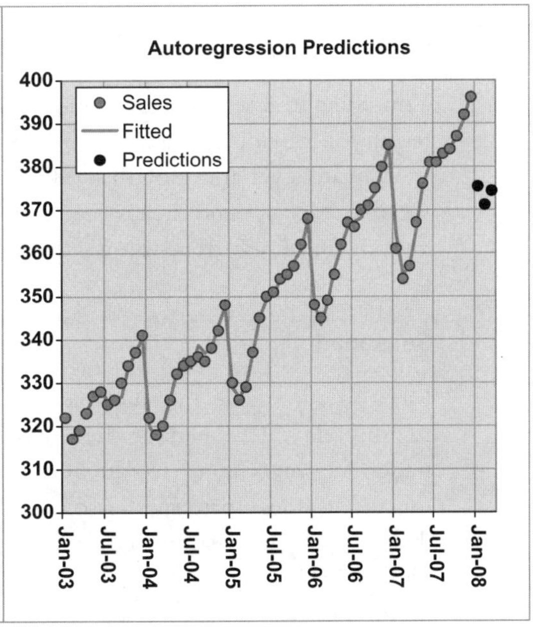

To predict the next month, which is January 2008, and is month 61, we set Time = 61, and the dummy variable Jan = 1. The three lagged variables are the last three observations, which are

$$\text{lag1} = 396, \text{lag2} = 392, \text{lag3} = 387.$$

This gives the prediction 375.4. The error in this prediction is 1.35, which is the prediction error listed by StatproGo. To predict the next month, which is February 2008 and month 62, we set Time = 62, we set Jan = 0 (since it is no longer January), and for the three lags, we use the last three sales figures, the last of this is our prediction for January 2008. Specifically, we set

$$\text{lag1} = 375.4, \text{lag2} = 396, \text{lag3} = 392.$$

The right plot displays these two, and a third prediction, after the end of the series. Since the overall model fit is so good, we would have high confidence in these predictions. Unfortunately, apart from the first prediction, it is complicated to give a prediction error for these numbers.

19.6. SUMMARY

Data that are collected regularly over time are called **time series**. Managers should care about time series because they give a historical record of the success of the business. The key elements of interest, and how we use regression to deal with them, are listed below.

Underlying Level of Performance and Growth Rate of Performance

You want to assess the level and the growth trajectory into the future. In the long term, you obviously want growth to be as high as possible. Regression can be used to estimate level and growth (collectively called **trend**) by including time as an input variable. Linear trend means that performance changes by the same amount each time period. Quadratic trend allows the growth rate to change.

Seasonality

Most products have a predictable **seasonal pattern**. This is not part of the manager's responsibility. It is part of the environment. But if you are going to see what the underlying level is, or if you need to predict into the future, you need to account for the seasonal pattern. Seasonality is included in the regression by including a dummy for each season. The most common form is monthly data, which involves including 11 monthly dummies. For quarterly data, you would include three quarterly dummies.

The estimates describe the seasonal effects. You can center these by subtracting off the average to obtain **centered indices**. To seasonally adjust the original data, you just subtract off the centered indices.

Management Variables

Management will presumably be making decisions about key variables, such as pricing and advertising, over time. These will affect performance over and above the growth and seasonality. To reveal the effects, you need to account for the growth and seasonality at the same time.

To use regression for this, you simply include the management variables in addition to the trend and seasonality terms. The regression model will untangle the trend, seasonality, and management variable effects.

Delayed Effects

The management variables do not necessarily have an immediate effect. Their total effect could be spread over several time periods. Delayed effects can be included in the regression by **lagging** the management variables. To lag a variable by k periods, you move the data down k cells. If this variable is included in the regression, it measures the effect on the output k *periods later.* If it is not included in the regression, then you are assuming that there is no such delayed effect.

EXERCISES

E1. You have data for relating monthly sales of your product to the price of your product in units of $1, the price of your only major competitor in units of $1, your expenditure advertising this month in units of $1000, your expenditure advertising last month in units of $1000, your expenditure advertising 2 months ago in units of $1000, calendar time (measured in months with month = 0 representing 6 months ago, i.e., month = 6 represents now). You arrive at the following formula based on multiple regression:

$$\text{Sales} = 14{,}200 - 700 \times \text{my price} + 500 \times \text{their price} + 300 \times \text{advertnow} + 800 \times \text{advertlast} + 100 \times \text{advertlast} - 2 + 125 \times \text{month} - 4.5 \times \text{month}^2.$$

(a) If the price of your product is $19.95, and your major competitor is $18.50, and if you spend $3000 per month on advertising, then what is your predicted sales this month?

(b) What will be your predicted sales in 6 months' time?

(c) Describe how pricing policy affects sales in nontechnical terms.

(d) Describe how advertising affects sales in nontechnical terms.

(e) Describe underlying trend and growth in nontechnical terms.

E2. The data in Q2.xls list monthly retail sales in units of $1000 across a small retail chain. There data plot displays clear trend and seasonality in the data.

(a) Convert the dates into a month number using the function MONTH(). Then use StatproGo to create 12 monthly dummy variables.

(b) Create a time variable starting at 0 and counting the months. Also create a time^2 variable to allow for possible nonlinear growth.
(c) Fit a multiple regression. Save fitted values and residuals.
(d) Create a chart of the centered seasonal indices.
(e) Seasonally adjust the data. Add the deseasoned series to the original raw data chart. Comment on what this appears to say about growth.
(f) What are the initial and final growth rates?
(g) Predict retail sales for the next month.

E3. The data in Q3.xls list passenger numbers on continental flights for a U.S. airline from 2002 to 2006. In addition, there is a dummy variable that indicates whether that month contained some or all of the 1-week Easter break (which is typically associated with less air travel).

(a) Fit a multiple regression that allows for curvilinear trend, seasonality, and the Easter break.
(b) Is the growth rate decreasing? How sure are you?
(c) What is your estimated growth rate at the end of the series?
(d) After seasonally adjusting the data, what would you say about the growth rate and the end of the series?

E4. The Metropolitan Transit Commission (MTC) operates trams, buses, and underground trains in a large metropolitan city. You have 6 years of monthly data in Q4.xls. It is important to be able to forecast passenger numbers for several reasons, for instance, to anticipate monthly revenue for financial control, and second, to decide on the amount of rolling stock to have available. The cost of traveling is uniform regardless of how far one travels, so passenger numbers are directly related to revenue.

(a) Fit a multiple regression that allows for curvilinear trend and seasonality.
(b) Seasonally adjust the data and comment on what it reveals.
(c) Compare naive seasonal estimated to regression estimates.
(d) What are the initial and final growth rates?
(e) Predict passenger numbers for the next 3 months.
(f) Evaluate the model.

E5. The data in Q5.xls list the number of monthly motor accidents in Manitoba, Canada, for the years 1988–1992. The most obvious pattern in the data it that accidents are very high in December and very low in April. Accidents must involve damage to property significant enough for an insurance claim and police to be called to the scene. Any injury to person automatically involves police presence and recording of the accident. So we can classify accidents as property only, those that involve injury, and those that involve death. For each type of accident, you are to

(a) produce a seasonally adjusted plot of accidents,
(b) evaluate the recent trend, and
(c) predict the number of accidents next month.

E6. The data in Q6.xls record monthly raw profit and monthly expenditure on promotional offers for a health drink, both in units of \$1000. The raw profit does not account for the cost of promotions.

(a) Based on a simple plot of raw profit versus promotion, give a naive estimate of the effect of promotions.
(b) Fit a multiple regression model that includes possible curvilinear trend in revenue, as well as lagged effects of promotions up to 3 months. How good is the model?
(c) Use backward to remove insignificant terms. What is your assessment of the effect of promotions?

E7. The data in Q7.xls record monthly profit and monthly expenditure on radio advertising for a chocolate bar, both in units of \$1000.

(a) Based on a simple plot of revenue versus advertising, give a naive estimate of the effect of promotional offers on profit.

(b) For a multiple regression model that includes possible curvilinear trend in revenue, seasonal effects and lagged effects of promotion up to 3 months. How good is the model?

(c) Use backward to remove insignificant terms. What is your assessment of the effect of promotion on profit?

(d) What marginal profit would be required to make advertising "worth it"?

CHAPTER 20

Extending Regression Models: The Sky Is the Limit

BUSINESS MODELING: CAREER BRIEFING

Do you care about what drives your business outcomes? Do you want to understand the impact of your actions? How about predicting what might happen if you make an intervention? Or just predicting the future? If you do, then you will need a **quantitative business model**.

A "model" is really just an equation that uses observed regularities and patterns in your business data to establish what variables affect which and how.

The basic regression models described up to this point are sufficient for most business applications. There are some occasions though when the patterns in your data will require some extended techniques. We cover a couple of the most important of these in this chapter.

Over the past 20 years, there have been big developments in modeling business processes. Regression is an old technique but is very widely applicable and is now easily available in desktop packages, like StatproGo. If you need something more sophisticated, there are plenty of new models available, but you will probably want to consult an expert.

20.0. INTRODUCTION: WHAT IS THE ISSUE?

The regression techniques we have used so far are pretty flexible in accounting for most of the ways business inputs can affect the business output. We can handle curvilinear effects, delayed effects, binary features, and segmenting variables. However, there are still some common patterns that we cannot handle with the methods so far. Here are a couple of examples.

Data-Driven Business Decisions, First Edition. Chris J. Lloyd.

Recall the example of real estate in Deepwater Bay. One extra variable that was not mentioned earlier is the floor or level that the apartment is on. Higher floors give better views and a higher price. We can easily add this floor variable into the regression, along with the other variables of area, age, beds, baths, and car space. Let us think a little about the area variable. This tells you the price of a square foot of area. Wouldn't it make sense that the cost of a square foot would be more if you were on a higher floor? With the tools introduced so far, we cannot allow for this very plausible possibility. We can include a term for area and a term for floor, but we cannot allow for the possibility that *the effect of area on price itself depends on floor level.*

Here is another simple example. Recall the Northside Car auctions data. After allowing for the effects of age and mileage, as well as the other features of tinting and airbags, we valued leather trim at $766.80. However, leather trim tends to deteriorate with age. Wouldn't it make sense that older leather trim would be worth less? With our present tools, we can add a certain amount for leather trim and subtract a certain amount for age. We cannot allow for the possibility that *the effect of leather trim on price itself depends on age.*

These kinds of relationships can be handled using **interactions**, which is one of two main topics in this chapter.

The other issue in this chapter concerns the central assumption of the regression model—the assumption of *multilinearity*. Simply said, this says that the output Y can be explained by *simply adding up the effects of each input variable.* The impact of each x variable is *additive*. Surely it is possible that some input variables could have a proportional rather than an additive effect on the output. For instance, if I increase my price by $1, the effect could be to reduce demand by a certain *percentage* rather than by a certain absolute amount. This could be quite important if, for instance, you wanted to know the effect of a price rise during the December. It would probably have a bigger effect than during slow months like February. The effect of seasonality itself could also be to increase or decrease sales by a certain *percentage* each month, not by a certain fixed amount.

Regression can be used to account for proportional rather than absolute effects of the input variables. This involves **transforming the y variable**.

20.1. Inputs That Have Varying Effects: Interactions

The core assumption of a regression model is that each input has an effect on the output and that these effects can simply be added up. For instance, if

$$Y = \boldsymbol{b} + \boldsymbol{m}_1 X_1 + \boldsymbol{m}_2 X_2$$

then increasing X_1 by one unit while holding X_2 fixed changes Y by $\boldsymbol{m}_1$ units. It does not matter what the value of X_2 is, so long as it is held constant. What if the effect of X_1 does depend on the value of X_2 though? As suggested in the introduction, wouldn't the value of an extra square foot of apartment space depend on the view?

There is a simple way to use ordinary regression to allow for this. All you have to do is *multiply the two* x *variables together*, and add this new variable into the regression. So in the case of two input variables, X_1 and X_2, you create a new column containing X_1 times X_2. The new variable is called an **interaction variable**. Multiple regression then produces a formula of the form

$$Y = \boldsymbol{b} + \boldsymbol{m}_1 X_1 + \boldsymbol{m}_2 X_2 + \boldsymbol{\alpha} X_1 X_2.$$

The interaction parameter α describes how one variable *influences the effect of the other variable* on Y.

Let us try to understand how interaction formulas work in the context of one concrete example. Suppose we are trying to explain an apartment's sale price. We have a variable *Area* measured in square feet and a variable *Floor* that gives the floor level of the apartment, with Floor = 0 meaning ground floor. The equation

$$\text{Price} = \$200{,}000 + \$200 \times \text{Area} + \$20{,}000 \times \text{Floor}$$

says that the price of apartment can be built up from a base price of \$200,000 by adding \$200 for each square foot of space and \$20,000 for each additional level. There is a single price of \$200 per square foot regardless of the level. There is a single premium of \$20,000 for each level regardless of area. This seems unrealistic. The price of space should increase with the floor level. In terms of the equation, the slope figure of \$200 should itself depend on the Floor level. The floor premium should also depend on the size. In terms of the formula, the \$20,000 slope should depend on area. The formula above does not allow for this possibility because there is no interaction term.

Here is another possible equation:

$$\text{Price} = \$200{,}000 + \$200 \times \text{Area} + \$20 \times \text{Floor} \times \text{Area}.$$

This again says that we can start with a base price of \$200,000 and add \$200 per square foot, but there is an additional term: \$20 × Floor × Area. If you were on the second floor, then this term is \$40 × Area. So you can expect to pay an additional \$40 per square foot, for the privilege of being on the second floor. Thought of another way, the value of area is \$240 per square foot for a second-floor apartment. If you are on the third floor, it is \$260, and on the fourth floor, \$280, and so on. The value of a square foot of space depends on the floor level and equals \$200 + \$20 × Floor.

What is the value of being on a higher floor? It depends on the area. For instance, if the area is $1000\,\text{ft}^2$, then the price is

$$\text{Price} = \$200{,}000 + \$200 \times 1000 + \$20 \times \text{Floor} \times 1000 = \$400{,}000 + \$20{,}000 \times \text{Floor},$$

so each floor adds \$20,000 to a ground floor price of \$400,000. For a 1500-ft^2 apartment,

$$\text{Price} = \$200{,}000 + \$200 \times 1500 + \$20 \times \text{Floor} \times 1500 = \$500{,}000 + \$30{,}000 \times \text{Floor},$$

so each floor adds \$30,000 to a ground floor price of \$500,000. In general, the value of an extra floor depends on area and equals \$20 × Area.

EXAMPLE 1 *Deepwater Bay real estate*

The data for this example are in ex1 hkre.xls. The 108 apartment sold in Deepwater Bay had prices that depend on area, the number of bedrooms and bathrooms, the number of dedicated car spaces, and the age. In addition, there is the variable Floor, which we did not have in earlier chapters.

Let us use the tools we have had up until now to create a valuation model for these apartments. We will allow for possible quadratic effects in Area, Age, and also Floor. A curvilinear effect in Floor would allow for the possibility that additional floors will have less value as you move higher up the building; we will use dummy variables for the number of bathrooms using BATH_1 as baseline and dummy variables for the number of bedrooms using BED_2 as baseline. If you run the backward algorithm with *p*-to-leave of 0.2, then you will obtain the model below, which is also on the worksheet *simpler model.*

Results of multiple regression for PRICE				
Summary measures				
Adj R-Square	83.0%			
Model Error	108.8			
p-value	0.0000			
Regression coefficients				
	Coefficient	Std Err	t-value	p-value
Constant	1147.0	148.3	7.7	0.000
SQFT	-677.7	166.6	-4.1	0.000
SQFT2	298.5	46.7	6.4	0.000
CARS	133.9	35.7	3.8	0.000
AGE	-26.0	10.0	-2.6	0.011
AGE2	0.7	0.4	1.6	0.111
FLOOR	9.8	4.2	2.3	0.023
BATHS_2	69.6	28.0	2.5	0.015
BATHS_3	93.0	60.3	1.5	0.126

The model is good in an absolute sense, since it explains 83% of the price variation across the 108 apartments. It has some interesting features. It seems that putting in two or three bathrooms adds value to an apartment, over and above the extra space that may be required. Each extra floor level adds \$9.8K to the value. Since the floor^2 term was dropped by the backward algorithm, the analysis supports a fixed floor premium. It does not support our idea that height premium decreases with higher floors.

Let us try for a better model. There is another driver of price in the data that we have not so far recognized. It was there all the time in the earlier chapters. If you plot residuals against the ID number, you will see an increasing tendency. The ID numbers of the apartments were assigned *in the order in which they were sold*. So ID number is actually like a time variable. If there is growth in the prices over time, we can use ID in the regression to measure this. If you look on worksheet *extended data*, you will see a Time variable, which is just the last digits of the ID variable. An actual time variable would have been better, but this is all we have.

In addition, we want to allow for the possibility that the price of area increases with floor, or, what amounts to the same thing, that the premium for being on a higher floor depends on the area. If you look on worksheet *extended data*, you will see that Column T has been labeled Floor*Area. It contains the floor level times the area. The two extra variables, Time and Floor*Area, can be added into the multiple regression. If you use the backward algorithm again, you end up with the model below.

There is a huge improvement in the adjusted r^2, which we can mainly attribute to including the Time variable. We know that it was due to this term because the T-value is so large. The Floor*Area term is also retained in the model.

Results of multiple regression for PRICE				
Summary measures				
Adj R-Square	95.3%			
Model Error	57315			
p-value	0.0000			
Regression coefficients				
	Coefficient	Std Err	t-value	p-value
Constant	1062921	81525	13.0	0.000
Time	1803	116	15.5	0.000
SQFT	-713	92.8	-7.7	0.000
SQFT2	0.300	0.0	11.5	0.000
CARS	172696	19408	8.9	0.000
AGE	-31503	5395	-5.8	0.000
AGE2	913	225	4.1	0.000
BEDS_3	24908	12808	1.9	0.055
BATHS_2	52477	15515	3.4	0.001
BATHS_3	88265	32425	2.7	0.008
FLOOR*AREA	2.89	1.29	2.2	0.027

Interpreting Interaction Formulas

We can use multiple regression to obtain an equation of the form

$$Y = b + m_1X_1 + m_2X_2 + \alpha X_1X_2 + \text{other terms.}$$

The trick, as always, is interpreting what the formula means. Let us use a little bit of basic algebra to rearrange the formula into the form

$$Y = b + m_2X_2 + (m_1 + \alpha X_2)X_1.$$

Let us think now what this says about the effect of variable X_1 on the output Y. As always, we interpret this to mean how Y would change if we increase X_1 by one unit and hold X_2 fixed. Look at the above formula and think of X_2 being a fixed known number. Then the slope for variables X_1 is the thing that X_1 is multiplied by, which here is $\boldsymbol{m}_1 + \alpha X_2$.

> For a model with an interaction term X_1X_2, the effect of input variable X_1 depends on the value of X_2 and is measured by $\mathbf{m}_1 + \alpha X_2$. The parameter $\mathbf{m}_1$ measures the effect of X_1 when $X_2 = 0$. This will only make sense if it makes sense for X_2 to equal 0.

Conversely, the effect of X_2 depends on the value of X_1 and is measured by $\boldsymbol{m}_2 + \boldsymbol{\alpha} X_1$, and so $\boldsymbol{m}_2$ measures the effect of X_2 when $X_1 = 0$.

EXAMPLE 1 (Continued) *Deepwater Bay real estate*

Let us just look at the area and floor part of the model and make sure we understand what it says. The valuation equation is

$$\text{Price} = 106{,}291 - 713 \times \text{Area} + 0.300 \times \text{Area}^2 + 2.89 \times \text{Floor} \times \text{Area} + \text{other terms}.$$

The effect of being on a higher floor is to increase the price by 2.89 times the area. For instance, a 2000-ft^2 apartment costs $2.89 \times 2000 = \$5780$ more for each floor higher. The area affects the floor premium.

Not only does area affect the floor premium, but the floor affects the value of area. Looking at the $2.89 \times \text{Floor} \times \text{Area}$ term, you need to add $2.89 \times \text{Floor}$ to the value of a square foot of space, depending on what floor you are on. For instance, if you are on the 10th floor, then you can add an extra \$28.9 per square foot to the base price per square foot.

The base price per square foot is complicated by the fact that the effect of area is quadratic. For a ground floor apartment,

$$\text{Price} = 106{,}291 - 713 \times \text{Area} + 0.300 \times \text{Area}^2 + \text{other terms},$$

since Floor = 0. The incremental effect of area is

$$\text{effect of Area} = \boldsymbol{m}_\text{L} + 2\boldsymbol{m}_\text{Q} \times \text{Area} = -713 + 0.600 \times \text{Area}.$$

So for a 1500-ft^2 apartment, the value of an extra square foot is

$$-713 + 0.600 \times 1500 = \$186.2$$

if it is on the ground floor. As you move up floors, you simply add \$2.89 for each floor.

Final Observation

Referring to the case, one of the purposes of the analysis was to advise the developer on what kinds of apartments to build. The analysis that includes time, and floor has thrown up a new and interesting feature—that there is a premium in building apartments with three bedrooms, as opposed to two or four or five, holding all other variables, most especially area, fixed. Since there is very little cost in doing this, it would seem that the developer could easily exploit this market opportunity in designing future developments. The BATH terms may also be worth exploiting, since the values associated with having a second bathroom ($52.5K) is probably well in excess of what it would cost to fit out an extra bathroom.

CHECK YOUR UNDERSTANDING

Q1. Apartment sale price is measured in units of $1000. I want to allow for the possibility that the value of an extra bedroom may differ, depending on the age of the apartment.

(a) What extra term should I add to a regression model?
(b) What term in the model would tell you the value of an extra bedroom on a new apartment?
(c) What would the coefficient of –0.7 for the interaction term in (a) mean?

Q2. Apartment sale price is measured in units of dollars, and area is measure in units of square feet. You fit a regression model and obtain a prediction equation of the form

$$\text{Price} = 400{,}000 + 450 \times \text{AREA} - 12{,}000 \times \text{AGE} - 2 \times \text{AGE} \times \text{AREA} + \text{other terms.}$$

(a) In simple language, what does the existence of the AGE*AREA term in the model allow for? There is no need to mention the coefficient of –2 in this answer.

(b) Describe how the value of a new apartment depends on area.

(c) Describe how the value of a 10-year-old apartment depends on area.

(d) Give a formula for the price per square foot and how it depends on age.

(e) Give a formula for the depreciation effects of age and how this depends on area.

EXAMPLE 2 *Northside car auctions*

You will recall that the data in ex2 northside.xls gave the sale price of 134 cars sold at auction, their mileage, age, and three optional features. One of the regression models we obtained earlier is displayed below.

Results of multiple regression for PRICE				
Summary measures				
Adj R-Square	97.4%			
Model Error	$968.4			
p-value	0.0000			
Regression coefficients				
	Coefficient	Std Err	t-value	p-value
Constant	$48483.7	$269.0	180.2	0.000
Miles	-$86.7	$13.0	-6.7	0.000
Age	-$251.7	$226.7	-1.1	0.269
Miles2	-$1.31	$0.09	-14.9	0.000
Air	$595	$179	3.3	0.001
Trim	$772	$183	4.2	0.000
Tint	$497	$175	2.8	0.005

Mileage had a clear curvilinear effect on price, age had a negative effect on price though a very weak one judging from the large *p*-value. The value of leather trim is $772.

It is surely possible that older leather trim would be worth less than newer leather trim. We can allow for this by creating a new column Trim*Age and adding this to the regression model. We can also do the same for Air and Tint, though it does not seem likely that age would reduce the value of these two features.

The worksheet *all variables* has the resulting regression output. As suspected, the Air*Age and Tint*Age terms have high *p*-values, as does the age and age2 terms. Using the backward procedure with *p*-to-leave equal to 0.2, we arrive at the model summarized in the table below.

Results of multiple regression for PRICE				
Summary measures				
Adj R-Square	97.5%			
Model Error	$939.7			
p-value	0.0000			
Regression coefficients				
	Coefficient	Std Err	t-value	p-value
Constant	$48,271.3	$270.5	178.5	0.000
Miles	-$94.4	$6.4	-14.9	0.000
Miles2	-$1.27	$0.08	-15.9	0.000
Air	$572	$174	3.3	0.001
Trim	$1,730	$357	4.8	0.000
Tint	$475	$170	2.8	0.006
Trim*Age	-$410	$132	-3.1	0.002

The adjusted r^2 is only slightly higher than the previous model; however, the model makes more sense and has the same number of terms (six). Air and Tint have a slightly lower value. Mileage is still curvilinear. Age has no direct effect but is part of the leather trim effect.

The value of leather trim is $1730 when it is new but is worth $410 less for each year of age. So it is worth $1320 after 1 year and virtually nothing after 4 years (compared with having standard cloth trim). If you look at the worksheet *final model*, you can estimate the price of any car by altering the red cells. Even though Age is not directly in the model, it does affect the value through the Age*Trim term.

Pushing a Bit Further

According to the model, a 5-year-old trim is worth −$322 that is, $322 less than cloth trim. This does not seem likely, since cloth trim wears out just as quickly as leather trim. If the model could somehow assume that the value of leather trim decreases with age but at a rate less than linear, we might be able to get a more sensible valuation.

There are many ways of doing this, all of which involve transforming the original x variables. We have already used one transformation, x^2, to allow for curvilinear effects. This is not appropriate here because it would make the age effect get bigger rather than smaller. A common transformation that makes variable have less effect at higher values is a **logarithmic transform**. This is the main topic of the next section below, but it is useful to introduce it here. If you look at the worksheet *pushing further*, you will find a column called LN(age). The Excel function LN calculates logarithms of any value. You do not need to understand what this means yet.

Instead of a term Trim*Age, we instead have a column Trim*LN(age). This will describe how the value of leather Trim changes with age, but because of the logarithmic transform, the effect of age will be less for higher ages. The value of trim will depreciate more slowly as it gets older.

The output is also given on the same sheet. The value of leather trim is

$$\text{Value of L-Trim} = \$1334 - \$807 \times \text{LN(AGE)}.$$

When Age = 5, this gives the answer $36—almost nothing in other words—but not negative. For the previous more standard model, the value of trim was

$$\text{Value of L-Trim} = \$1730 - \$410 \times \text{AGE}.$$

Both models have very similar r^2, and we could not really distinguish them on this basis. For models that have very similar fit quality, it is perfectly sensible to use common sense to decide between them. If you really know that trim cannot be worth less than cloth, then you would be better to use the log-based model. A plot of the estimated value of leather trim using the standard and logarithmic model is below. The quadratic mileage effect is also plotted.

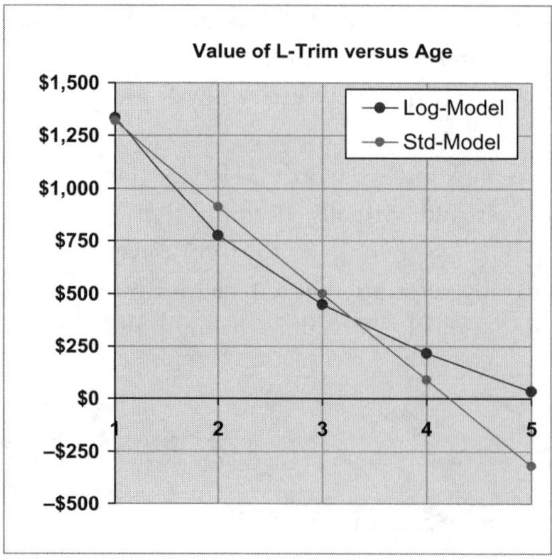

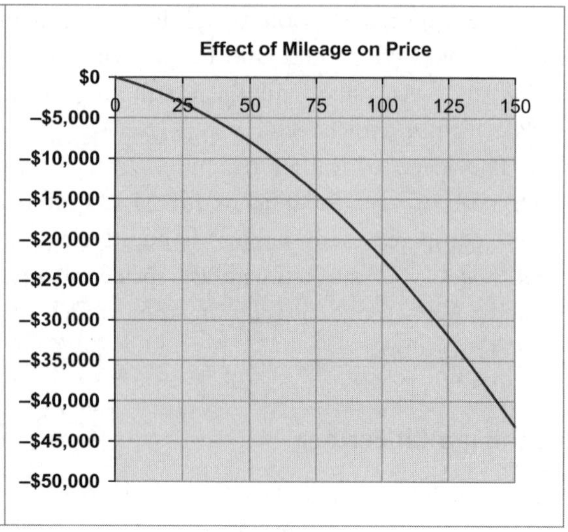

20.2. Inputs That Have Proportional Impacts

Imagine that I send mail-order catalogs to my customers and want to measure the effect of this on purchases that year. A standard regression model would allow me to estimate the effect of each mailing on purchases. However, I would expect that my high-spending customers would respond more to the mail than low-spending customers. If one customer spends \$500 per year and another \$5000 per year, then I would expect more impact on the higher spending customer, who clearly has more disposable money to spend. It may be that each catalog increases spending by say 10%. So the \$500 customer will spend \$50 more, and the \$5000 customer will spend \$5000 more. Standard regression would give me a single figure—like \$250 per mail. It is unable to give me a variable figure.

This sounds a little but like an interaction—the effect of the mail depends on the purchase. But purchase here is the y variable, and interactions are used only on x variables.

Logarithmic Transformation

In Chapter 13, we introduce the idea of log returns. We learned that if a share changes from V_1 to V_2 then the log return is

$$\text{Log return} = \text{LN}(V_1/V_2),$$

where LN means **natural logarithm**. This gives almost the same answer as the ordinary percentage change. For instance, growth from \$100 to \$105 means a return of

$$\text{LN}(105/100) = 0.0488$$

or 4.88%, while the percentage increase is 5.0%. It is a mathematical fact that an alternative expression for the log return is

$$\text{Log return} = \text{LN}(V_1) - \text{LN}(V_2).$$

This is easy enough to explain if you understand what logarithms are but is not pertinent to the main conclusion—which is this. *A small change in the logarithm of the value is approximately the same as the percentage change in the original value.*

As a simple example, suppose that the base purchase for a customer is V_1, and this increases to V_2 after a mail catalog. Suppose that the effect of the mail is to increase purchase by 10%. The table below shows the outcome for a low-, medium-, and high-value customer. The increase is \$50 for the low-value customer and \$500 for the high-value customer. The numbers in the columns LN(V_1) and LN(V_2) were obtained using the Excel function LN( ). These numbers do not mean anything sensible themselves. But the increase in the logarithm of the purchase is the same in each case—namely 0.095. You can interpret this as roughly 9.5%—though it was really 10%. We can adjust for this difference later. The point is that on the log scale, the mail catalog has a fixed effect of 0.095.

V_1	V_2	Increase	LN(V_1)	LN(V_2)	Increase
\$500	\$550	\$50	6.215	6.310	0.095
\$2,000	\$2,200	\$200	7.601	7.696	0.095
\$5,000	\$5,500	\$500	8.517	8.613	0.095

This has an enormous practical application. If we are interested in how a business input affects the business output in *proportional* rather than absolute terms, then we can look at how it affects the logarithm of the business output. In particular, if we believe that the business input has a fixed proportional effect on the business output, then we can use the equation

$$\text{LN}(Y) = \boldsymbol{b} + \boldsymbol{m}x.$$

The number $\boldsymbol{m}$ then measures how much LN(Y) changes when x changes by one unit. Since a change in LN(Y) is a proportional change in Y, this means that $\boldsymbol{m}$ measures the *proportional change in* Y *for a unit change in* X.

EXAMPLE 3 *Rightway meats*

The file ex3 rightway.xls contains data on 48 weeks of meat sales (in kilograms) in a Rightway supermarket that you manage. The main explanatory variables are the price charged for the meat and the price of the main competitor in the same mall. There is also some growth in the series. The raw data and some graphical summaries are in the worksheet *original data*.

To account for the growth in the series, we create a variable measuring time in weeks and use weeks, my price, and the competitor's price (called *their price*). The resulting output is on worksheet *analysis of sales*. The main output (below) says that weekly sales are growing at a rate of 17.2 kg per week. This sounds like a small amount, but it means that weekly sales 1 year from now will be about

52 × 17.2 = 900 kg higher. The model also says that if I raise my price by $1, then my weekly sales will go down by 412 kg. If the competitor raises prices by $1, then my weekly sales will go up by 217 kg. If we both raise our prices together by $1, then sales will change and go down by 195 kg (which equals 412–217).

Results of multiple regression for Sales				
Summary measures				
Adj R-Square	88.4%			
Model Error	83.2			
p-value	0.0000			
Regression coefficients				
	Coefficient	Std Err	t-value	p-value
Constant	5978.9	781.2	7.7	0.000
week	17.2	1.0	17.7	0.000
my prices	-413	57.6	-7.2	0.000
their prices	217	73.8	2.9	0.005

There is nothing terribly wrong with this model. The r^2 is high, and the residual plots look random. All the key inputs have a strong effect on sales (as measured by the high *T*-values).

There is another way to describe these data though. Economic theory says that growth is typically compound; that is, sales increase by a certain percentage each time period, not by a fixed amount. Economic theory also suggests that a change in price will cause a characteristic *percentage* change in sales.

We can produce a model that respects these two principles by repeating the previous analysis, but using LN(Sales) as the *y* variable instead of sales. The output is on the worksheet *analysis of ln(sales)*, and the main output is in the table below. The output has been slightly reformatted to help us interpret the model. Specifically, any number that refers to a change in the *y* variable—which is now log sales—has been formatted as a percentage, since we interpret it as a percentage effect on the original unlogged sales.

Results of multiple regression for Sales				
Summary measures				
Adj R-Square	88.5%			
Model Error	2.58%			
p-value	0.0000			
Regression coefficients				
	Coefficient	Std Err	t-value	p-value
Constant	9.0	0.2	37.1	0.000
week	0.539%	0.03%	17.9	0.000
my prices	-12.6%	1.8%	-7.0	0.000
their prices	6.2%	2.3%	2.7	0.009

Here is what the model says. Sales are growing at a rate of 0.539% per week. Multiplying this by 52 gives a rough yearly growth rate of 28%. If I increase my price by $1, then my sales will go down by 12.6%. If the competitor increase their price by $1, then my sales will go up by 6.2%.

The model error is 0.0258, which measures typical error in predicting log sales. We format this as 2.58% and interpret it as the typical proportional error if we use the model to predict unlogged sales.

CHECK YOUR UNDERSTANDING

Q3. In the following examples, explain what each coefficient on the right-hand side means in simple words.

(a) You record monthly revenue and try to explain it in terms of time (measured in months) and advertising budget in units of $1000. You decide to use a regression model for LN(revenue) and obtain the equation

$$\text{LN(revenue)} = 4.53 + 0.0043 \times \text{Time} + 0.022 \times \text{Advert.}$$

(b) You have a database on 309 existing customers, and you want to explain their expenditure this year. You have the gender of the customer and how many times you sent a mail catalog. The variable Male is a dummy variable for males, and the variable Mails counts how many mail catalogs you sent. You decide to use a regression model for LN(spend) and obtain the equation

$$\text{LN(spend)} = 2.05 + 0.13\ \text{Male} + 0.028 \times \text{Mails.}$$

(c) In a gender discrimination case, you have data on the salaries of 273 employees, as well as their gender and educational level. The variable Male is a dummy variable for males, and the variable Education measures the education level on a scale of 10–17. You decide to use a regression model for LN(salary) and obtain the equation

$$\text{LN(salary)} = 3.54 + 0.08\ \text{Male} + 0.015 \times \text{Educ.}$$

Expressing Conclusions on the Original Scale

The regression model not only produces measures of the effect of each input, it also produces predictions of the y variable. When the y variable has been subject to a logarithmic transform, StatproGo produces a prediction of log-y, next to the heading "Predicted Value." To convert this back into a prediction for y, we need to "undo the logarithm." The error in your final prediction of y is given by the prediction error, but this is interpreted as a *percentage error.*

There is one more point to make before we finish this section. We have been saying throughout that a change in log-y is *roughly* the same as the proportional change in y. The approximation is fairly accurate for changes of the order of 10% or less. For larger changes, it can be very rough indeed. To avoid this, you can calculate the *exact* proportional change from the log-scale change with the following simple formula:

$$\text{Exact proportional change} = \text{EXP(log change)} - 1.$$

EXAMPLE 3 (Continued) *Rightway meats*

The previously discussed output explaining sales in terms of growth is in the worksheet *analysis of LN(sales)*. Let us focus on the green-colored cells, which are not part of the StatproGo output but have been added manually.

If you look in the cell Q4, you will find that it applies the function EXP( ) to the prediction of log sales to the left of it. The spreadsheet has been set up to predict the sales next week (week 48) if both Rightway and their competitor set prices at \$16 per kilogram. The prediction is sales of 3717 kg.

The error in this prediction is 2.68% in cell P5. This is almost but not quite the same as the percentage error in sales. The cell Q5 contains EXP(2.68%) − 1 = 2.72%, which is the correct error to apply to the sales estimate of 3717.

The same formula can be used to adjust the main coefficient estimates of 0.539%, −12.6%, and 6.2%. These actually measure effects on log sales and are only approximately the same as percentage effects on sales. The three figures in Column S give the exact figures. For instance, the effect of increasing my price by \$1 is to reduce sales by 11.8% (not 12.6% as stated originally).

The *yearly* growth can be calculated by multiplying the weekly coefficient of 0.539% by 52, which gives exactly 28%, but again, this is an effect on the log scale. To convert it to an exact growth rate, we calculate

$$\text{EXP}(28.0\%) - 1 = 32.4\%.$$

CHECK YOUR UNDERSTANDING

Q4. In the previous three examples for Q3, express the meaning of the coefficients in terms of an exact rather than approximate percentage.

20.3. CASE STUDY: HOW EFFECTIVE ARE CATALOG MAIL-OUTS?

The data in ex4 maililng.xls have data for a mail-order stereo and PC company. Looking at the worksheet *basic data*, each row corresponds to 1 of 309 customers who were on their mailing list at the beginning of the year. There is plenty of information about these customers. The company has demographic information, including age, gender, number of children, and marital status. They have economic variables, such as home ownership and salary, and whether they live close to a physical stereo and electronics store. Most importantly, they have variables describing the expenditure of the customer last year and the number of mailing catalogs sent to them so far this year. The y variable here is the amount spent by the customer this year.

A Very Simple Model

As a first pass of the data, we fit a multiple regression model describing the Spend in terms of the 10 listed variables. The adjusted r^2 is 72.2%. The least useful variables are the amount spent by the customers last year, their marital status, their age, and home ownership. The key variable *mailings* returns a coefficient of 0.480, which means that each extra mailing leads to \$480 more spending by the customer.

Quadratic Effects

If age affects Spend, one would not expect it to be linear, the youngest and oldest might spend less than those in middle age. Salary may also have a nonlinear effect, for instance, if Spend increases with salary up to a certain point. Most importantly, we expect that the effect of mailings would wear off—that a certain number of mailings would be effective, but at some point, the catalogs would go straight into the trash. The worksheet *quadratic models* contains output from two models. Both have quadratic effects in salary and age. They differ in how they treat the mailings variable. The first model has a quadratic effect in mailings. The second treats mailings as a dummy variable.

The adjusted r^2 of both models are slightly lower than the previous linear model. As before, age, marital status, and previous spend are still not useful predictors of the spend. The quadratic model displays weak evidence of diminishing returns for mailings. The quadratic coefficient is negative, though the T-value of -1.0 is hardly convincing. The second model gives estimates of the effect of mailing two, three, or four times compared with once. This is presented in the left chart below. We can again see a tendency for the fourth mailing to be less effective than earlier mailings.

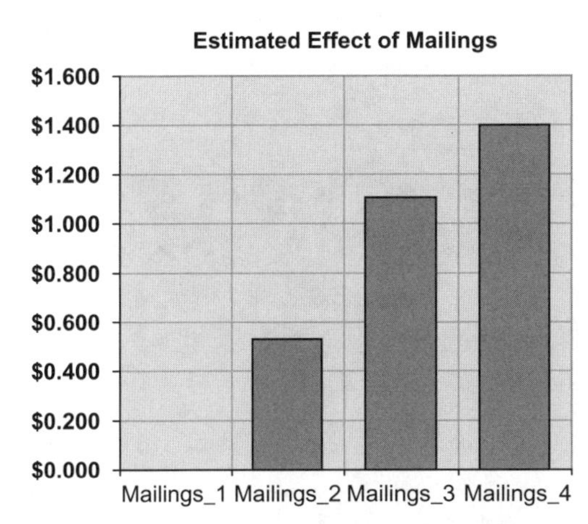

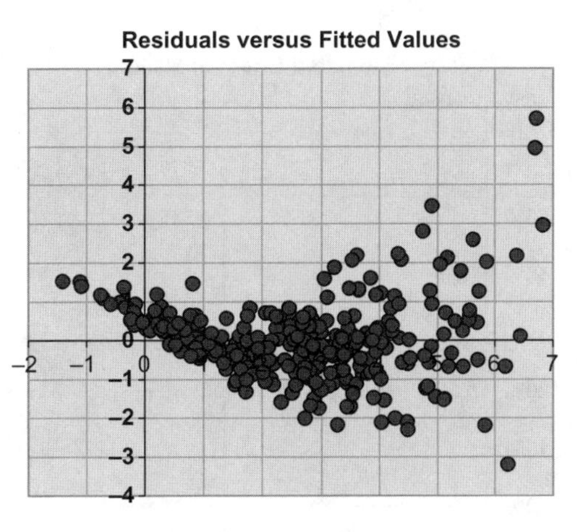

Model Assessment

Prior to this chapter, this is where we would have had to stop. Unfortunately, when we look at a plot of the residuals against fitted values, the model is revealed as completely defective. Looking at the left end of the plot, it produces some negative estimates of spend, the largest being –\$1403! There is also a clear structure in the plot. The third obvious feature is that there is more variability to the right than at the left—a kind of trumpet shape. This pattern is very common when the performance variable is subject to errors that are in proportion to the level of performance.

Log-Scale Analysis

The logarithmic transformation can correct all these problematic features. If we fit a regression model to LN(spend), then all predictions are automatically positive (after we apply the EXP() function). Proportional variation on the original scale, which produced the "trumpet" shape, translates into constant variation on the log scale.

The worksheet *log models* contains analogs of the two models that we just discussed, but with LN(Spend) as the y variable instead of Spend. They both have adjusted r^2 of around 85%. Both the outputs have had their formatting altered to reflect that coefficients now describe percentage effects on spend.

The first model has a quadratic trend in mailing. The quadratic term is now more clearly negative ($T = -2.4$), and the implied optimum number of mailings is 4.80 (using the optimum of a quadratic rule). The second model treats mailings as a dummy variable and gives a very similar level of fit. Before proceeding further though, we should look at the residual plots. The right plot below now looks both random and uniform in variation. The trumpet shape has gone. The left plot shows estimates of the mailing effect, but these now refer to effects on LN(spend), which are interpreted as percentage effects on Spend. The second mailing increases spend by 29%, the third by 51.3%, and the fourth by 62.4%. These effects are large enough that we should really convert them properly to proportional effects using the

$$\text{Exact proportional change} = \text{EXP(log change)} - 1$$

formula. These numbers are given in the spreadsheet.

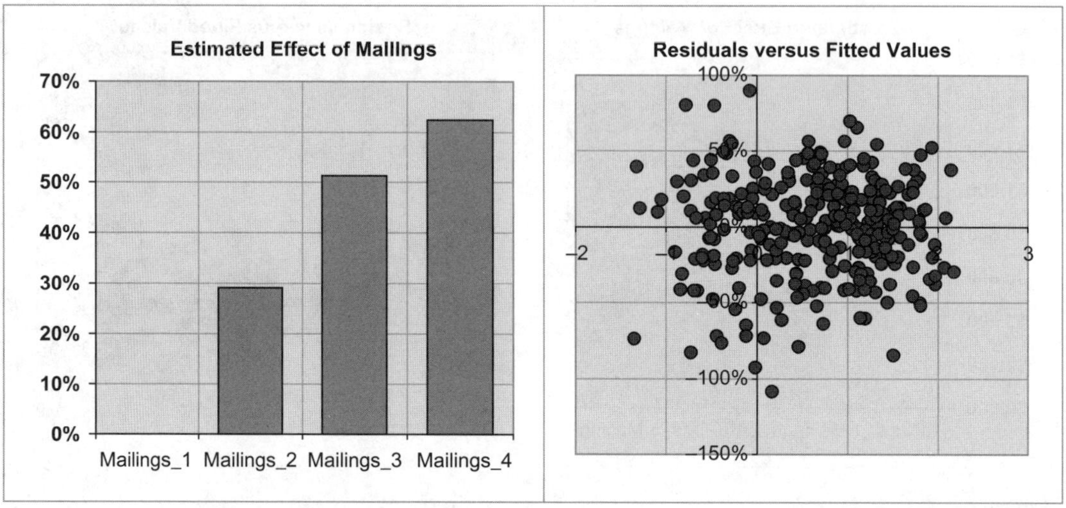

Adding Interactions

The other new technique from this chapter is the use of **interactions**. This allows us to check whether the effect of the main variable of interest—here mailings—might depend on known factors, such as gender, whether you are a previous customer or close to a competing store. To create interaction variables, we just multiply mailings by these three variables.

If you run the backward procedure with these three extra variables added to the previous pool, then you obtain the models listed on worksheet *best models*. These models have sequentially removed age, age2, and gender because they do not seem to have a significant effect on Spend. Both reveal a clear interaction of mailings and being a previous customer. The coefficients for Mail*Prev both say that mailings sent to previous customers induce an extra 10.3% in customer spend compared with new customers.

Model Assessment and Consequences

What would these results mean for the company? How many mailings should they send and to whom? Not surprisingly, the customer spend is highest for unmarried, childless customers who own their own homes. The salary effect is huge (look at the *T*-values!) and means that those on higher salaries spend more. Does this mean we should send more catalogs to these customers?

The model we are fitting assumes that the effect of mailings is *proportional*. If those on higher salaries spend more, and if an extra mailing means a 38.4% higher spend, then it certainly does make sense to focus mailings on those with higher salary. So a key question is whether the assumptions that the effects are all proportional is correct.

That is why we have residual plots. Above right is a plot of the residuals against the fitted values—the analog of the chart that was so terrible before we took the log transform. This plot looks very random and indicates that the model assumptions are satisfied—or at least that there is nothing in the data to suggest that the assumptions are wrong.

Pushing a Bit Further: The Salary Effect

Worksheet *best models* has a plot of the quadratic effect of salary on Spend. There is a point at which the effect reverses, somewhere around $200K per annum. This is an artifact of the quadratic model. We do not really believe that people on salaries higher than $200K would actually spend less, more than their spend would plateau. There are other ways of describing the effect of salary that do not imply that the curve has to eventually turn down (when we know it does not).

One way is to use LN(salary) as an x variable. You can apply the log transformation to x variables as well as the y variable. There is also no reason why we cannot include all three of salary, salary^2, and LN(salary) in the model, and then use a selection algorithm to decide which terms are required and which can be dropped. In the present example, you will find that salary and salary^2 both get dropped, leaving only LN(salary). The model output is on worksheet *pushing further* and has the highest adjusted r^2 of any model we have tried (85.7%).

The coefficient for LN(salary) is 1.004. What does this mean? It means that a unit change in LN(salary) causes almost the same unit change in LN(spend). For instance, a 0.01 increase in LN(salary) means a 0.01004 increase in LN(spend). But wait. A change of 0.01 in LN(value) means a 1% change in the value. So the model says that a 1% increase in salary implies almost exactly a 1% increase in spend. This is not so surprising! And it is a lot simpler to understand and convey than the quadratic model.

Whenever you have a model that predicts LN(y) from LN(x), the coefficient can be interpreted in this simple way. If the coefficient is say 1.7, then it means that a 1% change in x is associated with a 1.7% change in y. One advantage of this way of modeling is that the coefficient does not depend on the units used for x or y. You can change currencies or units of area, and the slope does not change. Coefficients on this log-log scale are called **elasticity** by economists.

Finally, the model says that the number of mailings should stop at 4 or 5, depending on whether a customer is an existing customer or not. This is obtained from the formula for the "top of a quadratic hill," which we have used several times now. Again though, the quadratic model implies that spend would go *down* after this number of mailings, and we probably do not believe this. But the model does give us an indication of the point where mailing becomes ineffective.

20.4. More on Time Series

In the previous chapter, we saw how to use regression to estimate the underlying trend and seasonality in a time series. The seasonal dummy coefficient could be used to produce a seasonally adjusted version of the data that better revealed the performance level and growth.

The key assumption of the model is that the performance (such as monthly sales) is driven by an underlying trend *plus* a seasonal index. Let us look at an example where there is obviously something going wrong with the trend and seasonal regression model, identify the problem, and then see how to fix it.

EXAMPLE 5 *Quarterly shoe sales*

The file ex5 shoe sales.xls has quarterly data on shoe sales across a large chain of shoe stores. There is a very clear seasonal pattern (with the peak being in the last quarter of the year), and there is also a large amount of growth in sales over such a long period, the data having not been corrected for inflation.

The worksheet *ordinary scale* has the results of a trend and seasonal regression analysis of these data. There is a strong quadratic trend in the data, as evidenced by the small p-value for the time^2 term. We can use the dummy coefficients to create centered seasonal indices, and then subtract these from the original data to produce seasonally adjusted sales. The result is in the left plot below.

The regular seasonal pattern is clear in the original series. The idea of seasonal adjustment is to remove this pattern but something seems to have gone wrong. From 1995 to 1997, the seasonally adjusted series is smooth, but at the beginning and end, there still seems to be some repeating pattern. This is revealed even more clearly if we look at the residual plot. In the beginning of the plot, the residuals peak in Q1 and are negative in Q4. At the end of the series, the residuals peak in Q4 and are negative in Q1. The residual plot, which is supposed to be random, has a seasonal component in it!

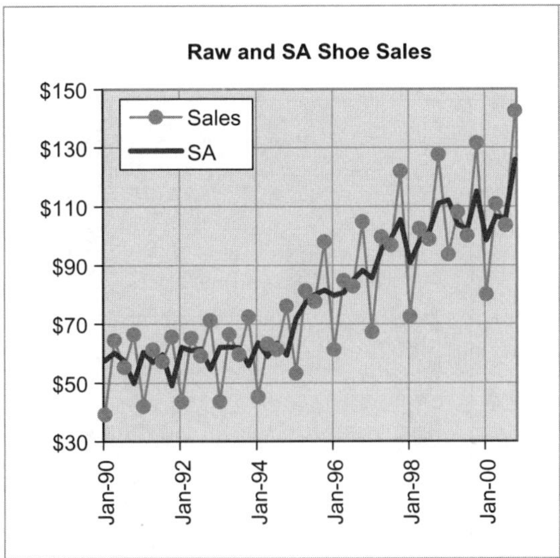

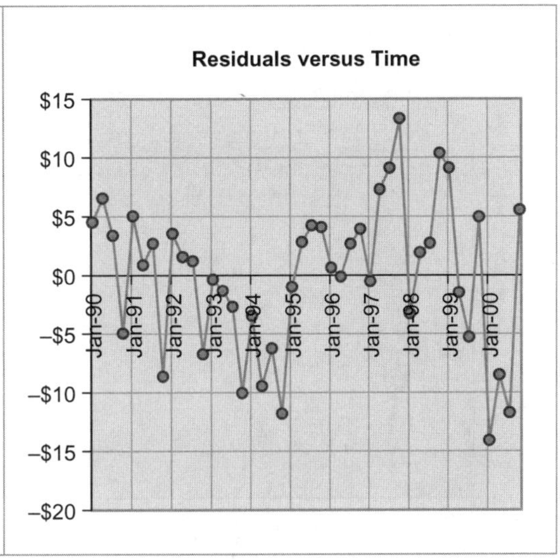

How might this be explained? Let us suppose that season has a *proportional* effect on sales rather than an absolute effect (which is actually the case), and trace through how this would affect our trend and seasonal model. Since there was such strong growth over the 10 years, the seasonal effect would be small at the start of the series when sales were small and large at the end of the series when sales were large. If we subtract off a *fixed* seasonal effect (which is what the model imposes), then we will overcorrect for seasonality at the beginning, undercorrect at the end, and get it about right in the middle—which is exactly what we saw.

Log-Scale Trend and Seasonal Model

If seasons have a proportional effect on sales, then they have a fixed effect on LN(sales). This suggests that we apply our existing trend and seasonality methodology to LN(sales) rather than sales. The results are on the worksheet *log-scale seasonality*.

The adjusted r^2 is slightly better, but the main reason this model is preferred is that the seasonally adjusted series now looks like the seasonality has really been removed, as displayed in the left plot below. The four seasonal dummy coefficients (including the zero coefficient for the baseline quarter) can be centered in the usual way by subtracting off their average. These are then interpreted as *proportional* seasonal indices relative to the year as a whole. Quarter 4 is associated with sales around 22% higher than average, and the following Quarter 1 is around 23% below average.

The residual plot, which you will find on the worksheet, does not have the seasonal component that we saw for the additive model. So we have successfully estimated the seasonal pattern. But neither does it look random. The most simple explanation of this pattern is dependence from quarter to quarter, perhaps driven by some underlying variable such as economic confidence. If the primary aim was to predict sales in future quarters, then the most useful approach would be some kind of autoregression model that uses lags of LN(sales), as described in the previous chapter.

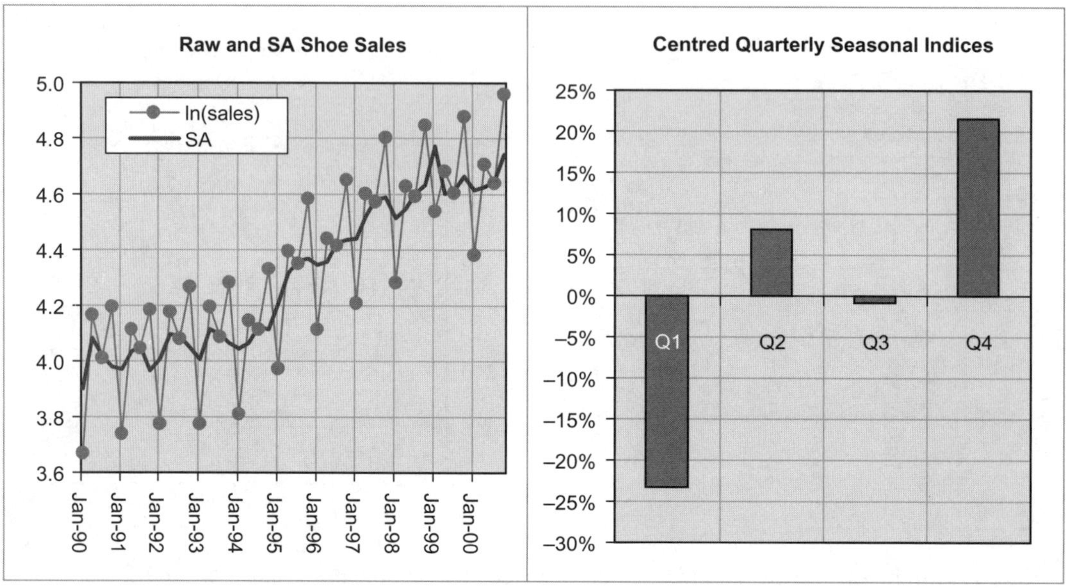

CHECK YOUR UNDERSTANDING

Q5. The file Q5.xls contains data on retails sales across a Californian retailer. The spreadsheet contains the results of a trend and seasonal model, the estimated seasonal indices (centered), and the seasonally adjusted series. Fit a trend and seasonal model that allows for compound growth and proportional seasonal effects.

20.5. SUMMARY

Regression is used to describe the effect of inputs X on an output Y. Sometimes the effect of X on Y itself depends on other input variables. This can be accounted for by multiplying the two input variables together and using this as a new input variable, called an **interaction** variable.

The coefficient for the interaction variable measures how the effect of one variable on Y changes as the other variable changes. To be specific, if you have an equation of the form

$$Y = \boldsymbol{b} + \boldsymbol{m}_1 X_1 + \boldsymbol{m}_2 X_2 + \boldsymbol{\alpha} X_1 X_2 + \text{other terms},$$

then the effect of variable X_1 on the output Y is $\boldsymbol{m}_1 + \alpha X_2$, and the effect of variable X_2 on the output Y is $\boldsymbol{m}_2 + \alpha X_1$.

Sometimes, the effect of an input X is to increase or decrease Y, not by a fixed amount, but by a fixed *proportion* or *percentage*. This can be accounted for by finding an equation that relates LN(y) to the inputs rather than y. The coefficient of X then measures (roughly) the percentage change in Y per unit change in X. If the coefficient is much bigger than around 0.1, it is better to use

$$\text{Exact proportional change} = \text{EXP(coefficient)} - 1.$$

Regression can be used to produce a formula for LN(Y). It also produces predictions for LN(Y), which can be converted into predictions for Y using the function EXP( ).

Applying the log transformation to Y has two other advantages. First, the predicted value of Y can never be negative, which is an attractive feature, since many business outputs such as sales or demand can never be negative. Second, residual plots for real business data open have a "trumpet shape," meaning that variation is larger when the output is larger. This pattern often disappears when you model LN(y) instead of y.

The log transformation can also be applied to x variables. For example, if you have an equation of the form

$$\text{LN}(Y) = 3.45 + 1.25 \times \text{LN}(X) + \text{other terms},$$

then a 1% increase in X is associated with a 1.25% increase in Y. Slope coefficients on the log-log scale are called **elasticity** by economist.

EXERCISES

E1. Car price is measured in units of \$1000, mileage in units of 1000 mi, and age in years. I want to allow for the possibility that the depreciation per mile may depend on the age of the car in years.

(a) What extra term should I add to a regression model?

(b) What term in the model would tell you the depreciation of the first 1000 mi?

(c) What would the coefficient of –0.3 for the interaction term in (a) mean?

E2. Car price is still measured in units of \$1000, mileage in units of 1000 mi, and age in years. You fit a regression model and obtain a prediction equation of the form

$$\text{Price} = 52.5 - 0.35 \times \text{MILES} - 0.02 \times \text{AGE} \times \text{MILES} + \text{other terms}.$$

(a) In simple language, what does the existence of the AGE*MILES term in the model allow for? There is no need to mention the coefficient of –0.02 in this answer.

(b) Describe how the value of a new car depends on mileage.

(c) Describe how the value of a 5-year-old car depends on mileage.

(d) Give a formula for how the deprecation rate per 1000 mi depends on age.

(e) What would happen to the formula if we instead measures price in units of dollars and mileage in units of miles?

E3. We want to explain per annum salary at entry to a company in terms of gender and educational level. Gender differences for no other reason than gender are illegal in most countries of course. We may still wish to measure it though. Salary is measured in units of $1000 and education in units of "effective years compared with year 12." This is obtained by counting the number of years of formal education and then subtracting 12, so education = 0 means year 12. You are told that

- baseline salary for females with year 12 education is $40,000 per annum,
- males with year 12 education receive $5000 more than females,
- females receive $2000 more for each level of education, and
- males receive $2500 more for each level of education.

(a) Give the formula for salary in terms of the education variable and a dummy variable for males.

(b) What is the salary of a male with 15 years of education?

(c) How much more does a males with year 10 education receive than females?

(d) Give a formula for the difference between male and female salary that takes account of the level of education.

E4. You have time series data on weekly revenue (variable REV) and are trying to explain it in terms of previous advertising expenditure (variable ADVERT). All monetary amounts are expressed in units of $1000. You know there are some delayed effects, so you also include a lag of advertising (variable ADVERT1). You arrive at the following regression formula

$$\text{REV} = 50 + 1.2 \times \text{Advert} + 0.3 \times \text{Advert1} - 0.1 \times \text{Advert} \times \text{Advert1}.$$

(a) What is the effect of spending $1000 this week on this week's revenue?

(b) What is the effect of spending $1000 last week on this week's revenue?

(c) What does the interaction term suggest about advertising strategy?

E5. In a gender discrimination case, you have data on the salaries of 273 employees, as well as their gender and educational level. The variable Male is a dummy variable for males, and the variable Education measures the education level on a scale of 10–17. You decide to use a regression model for LN(salary) and obtain the equation

$$\text{LN(salary)} = 3.87 + 0.065\ \text{Male} + 0.011 \times \text{Educ}.$$

(a) What is the salary of a female with education level 10?

(b) What is the salary of a male with educational level 14?

(c) What does 0.065 mean in simple words?

(d) What does the 0.011 mean in simple words?

(e) Express the answer to (d) and (e) as an exact rather than approximate percentage (if you did not already do so).

E6. The demand for a product (variable DEMAND) depends on the price you charge (variable PRICE). You decide to look at the relationship between LN(DEMAND) and LN(PRICE). The equation you obtain is

$$\text{LN(DEMAND)} = 12.23 - 1.27 \times \text{LN(PRICE)}.$$

(a) Explain in simple words the effect of price in demand.

(b) How many will you sell at a price of $8.95? (12,665.03)

(c) What would be the formula for revenue (remembering that revenue equals demand times price so that ln9revenue) equals LN(demand) plus LN(price)?

E7. In each case below, explain in simple words how the inputs affect the output.

(a) We want to explain demand for our product in terms of the recommended retail price and the advertising spend. We use the equation

$$\text{LN(demand)} = 4.53 - 0.95 \times \text{LN(RRP)} + 1.53 \times \text{LN(Advert)}.$$

(b) We want to explain daily sales in terms of a dummy variable that says if the day of week is on the weekend and calendar time measured in days. We use the equation

$$\text{LN(sales)} = 2.65 + 0.35 \times \text{Weekend} + 0.00024 \times \text{Time}.$$

(c) We want to explain employee salary in terms of a dummy variable for being male and the level of experience. We use the equation

$$\text{LN(salary)} = 3.40 + 0.21 \times \text{Male} + 0.055 \times \text{LN(exp)} - 0.008 \times \text{Male} \times \text{LN(exp)}.$$

E8. The worksheet *basic data* in file Q8.xls has data from the NTC Pay equity case on the salary of 273 employees, their gender, age, experience, and educational level. The worksheet regression data have replaced the salary variable with LN(salary), have created a dummy variable for Males, and have also created three interaction variables.

(a) Fit a regression model that predicts ln9salary in terms of the seven variables excluding employee ID.

(b) Predict the salary of a 40-year-old male with 12 years of experience and education level 14.

(c) The coefficient for Gender is negative. Why does this not mean that males are paid less? You might illustrate your answer by calculating the salary of two 35-year-olds with 12 years of experience and level 13 education, one male and one female.

(d) Looking at a residual plot, what obvious issue does the model miss?

(e) The worksheet *extended data* contain quadratics as well as two new variables, namely job grade and an assessment of the employees' aptitude called GPA rating. What do these data say about gender and age discrimination?

(f) One key variable dropped out in part (e). Why do you think it did, and does this mean that it has no relevance to salary?

E9. The data in Q9.xls have data on employment in the food sector in Wisconsin from 1995 to 2000. These data were analyzed in Chapter 19.

(a) Fit a quadratic trend and seasonality model, summarize the seasonal effect, and produce a seasonally adjusted series. Predict employment numbers 3 months after the end of the series.

(b) Fit a quadratic trend and seasonality model to the log of the numbers. Remove any insignificant terms. Summarize the seasonal effect and produce a seasonally adjusted series. Predict employment numbers 3 months after the end of the series.

(c) Are there any obvious weaknesses in this model? Where would you go from here?

E10. The data in Q10.xls have data on maximum daily electricity load in the state of Victoria from 2006 to 2010. The main drivers of electricity usage are seasonal (which is driven by temperature and air-conditioning usage) and day of week. There is also some reason to think that general economic conditions will drive long-term usage.

The basic variables are in *basic data*. Take a moment to read the comments at the top of Columns E–H.

Worksheet *regression data* have created a large number of regression variables. There are 12 monthly dummy variables. There are also seven daily dummy variables to describe the "seasonality" during the week. There are time and time2 term for trend. There is also an indicator of whether or not the day is a public holiday. There are two variables describing economic conditions. These two variables, as well as the performance measure Maxload, have all been "logged." Finally, I have also created lags of low and high temperature to describe the delayed effects of temperature, as well as squares of low and high temperature, since the effect of temperature on electricity usage should be "valley shaped."

(a) Why should temperature have a "valley-shaped" effect on electricity usage?

(b) Fit a regression model that predicts Maxload in terms of these variables. Which terms are not significant, and what does this indicate in simple words?

(c) Fit a regression model that predict LN(MaxLoad) in terms of these variables. Produce charts that describe the daily and monthly seasonal effects.

(d) What is the effect of a public holiday on maximum load?

(e) Keeping in mind that temperature today will not be available, there is some alternative data in predictive data that does not use today's high or low. Fit a regression model that predicts LN(Maxload). How good is this model? What variable does this suggest you should add to the analysis?

Index

Data-Driven Business Decisions, First Edition. Chris J. Lloyd.

STATISTICS IN PRACTICE

Human and Biological Sciences

Brown and Prescott · Applied Mixed Models in Medicine

Ellenberg, Fleming and DeMets · Data Monitoring Committees in Clinical Trials: A Practical Perspective

Lawson, Browne and Vidal Rodeiro · Disease Mapping With WinBUGS and MLwiN

Lui · Statistical Estimation of Epidemiological Risk

*Marubini and Valsecchi · Analysing Survival Data from Clinical Trials and Observation Studies

Parmigiani · Modeling in Medical Decision Making: A Bayesian Approach

Senn · Cross-over Trials in Clinical Research, *Second Edition*

Senn · Statistical Issues in Drug Development

Spiegelhalter, Abrams and Myles · Bayesian Approaches to Clinical Trials and Health-Care Evaluation

Turner · New Drug Development: Design, Methodology, and Analysis

Whitehead · Design and Analysis of Sequential Clinical Trials, *Revised Second Edition*

Whitehead · Meta-Analysis of Controlled Clinical Trials

Earth and Environmental Sciences

Buck, Cavanagh and Litton · Bayesian Approach to Interpreting Archaeological Data

Glasbey and Horgan · Image Analysis in the Biological Sciences

Helsel · Nondetects and Data Analysis: Statistics for Censored Environmental Data

McBride · Using Statistical Methods for Water Quality Management: Issues, Problems and Solutions

Webster and Oliver · Geostatistics for Environmental Scientists

Industry, Commerce and Finance

Aitken and Taroni · Statistics and the Evaluation of Evidence for Forensic Scientists, *Second Edition*

---

* Now available in paperback.

Brandimarte · Numerical Methods in Finance and Economics: A MATLAB-Based Introduction, *Second Edition*

Brandimarte and Zotteri · Introduction to Distribution Logistics

Chan and Wong · Simulation Techniques in Financial Risk Management

Jank · Statistical Methods in eCommerce Research

Lehtonen and Pahkinen · Practical Methods for Design and Analysis of Complex Surveys, *Second Edition*

Ohser and Mücklich · Statistical Analysis of Microstructures in Materials Science

WILEY

CUSTOMER NOTE: IF THIS BOOK IS ACCOMPANIED BY SOFTWARE, PLEASE READ THE FOLLOWING BEFORE OPENING THE PACKAGE.

This software contains files to help you utilize the models described in the accompanying book. By opening the package, you are agreeing to be bound by the following agreement:

This software product is protected by copyright and all rights are reserved by the author and John Wiley & Sons, Inc. You are licensed to use this software on a single computer. Copying this software to another medium or format for use on a single computer does not violate U.S. Copyright Law. Copying the software for any other purpose is a violation of the U.S. Copyright Law.

This software product is sold as is without warranty of any kind, either expressed or implied, including but not limited to the implied warranty of merchantability and fitness for a particular purpose. Neither Wiley nor its dealers or distributors assumes any liability of any alleged or actual damages arising from the use or the inability to use this software. (Some states do not allow the exclusion of implied warranties, so this exclusion may not apply to you.)